THE PASSION OF MAX VON OPPENHEIM

Lionel Gossman is M. Taylor Pyne Professor of Romance Languages (Emeritus) at Princeton University. Most of his work has been on seventeenth and eighteenth-century French literature, nineteenth-century European cultural history, and the theory and practice of historiography. His publications include *Men and Masks: A Study of Molière*; *Medievalism and the Ideologies of the Enlightenment: The World and Work of La Curne de Sainte-Palaye*; *French Society and Culture: Background for 18th Century Literature*; *Augustin Thierry and Liberal Historiography*; *The Empire Unpossess'd: An Essay on Gibbon's "Decline and Fall"*; *Between History and Literature*; *Basel in the Age of Burckhardt: A Study in Unseasonable Ideas*; *The Making of a Romantic Icon: The Religious Context of Friedrich Overbeck's "Italia und Germania"*; *Figuring History*; and several edited volumes: *The Charles Sanders Peirce Symposium on Semiotics and the Arts*; *Building a Profession: Autobiographical Perspectives on the Beginnings of Comparative Literature in the United States* (with Mihai Spariosu); *Geneva-Zurich-Basel: History, Culture, and National Identity*, and *Begegnungen mit Jacob Burckhardt* (with Andreas Cesana). He is also the author of *Brownshirt Princess: A Study of the 'Nazi Conscience'* and the editor and translator of *The End and the Beginning: The Book of My Life* by Hermynia Zur Mühlen and (with Flora Kimmich and Edward K. Kaplan) of *On History* by Jules Michelet, all published by OBP.

The Passion of Max von Oppenheim

Archaeology and Intrigue in the Middle East from Wilhelm II to Hitler

Lionel Gossman

Unless otherwise stated, all contents of this book are licensed under a
Creative Commons Attribution 4.0 unported license available at
http://creativecommons.org/licenses/by/4.0/

© 2014 Lionel Gossman. This work is licensed under a Creative Commons Attribution 4.0 International license (CC BY 4.0). This license allows you to share, copy, distribute and transmit the work; to adapt the work and to make commercial use of the work providing attribution is made to the author (but not in any way that suggests that she endorses you or your use of the work). Attribution should include the following information:

Gossman, Lionel. *The Passion of Max von Oppenheim: Archaeology and Intrigue in the Middle East from Wilhelm II to Hitler.* Cambridge, UK: Open Book Publishers, 2014, http://dx.doi.org/10.11647/OBP.0030

Further details about CC BY licenses are available at:

http://creativecommons.org/licenses/by/4.0/

Digital material and resources associated with this volume are available on our website at: http://www.openbookpublishers.com/9781909254206

ISBN Paperback: 978-1-909254-20-6
ISBN Hardback: 978-1-909254-21-3
ISBN Digital (PDF): 978-1-909254-22-0
ISBN Digital ebook (epub version): 978-1-909254-23-7
ISBN Digital ebook (mobi version): 978-1-909254-24-4
DOI: 10.11647/OBP.0030

Cover image: *A new Haroun Al Raschid. A Dream of Baghdad, Made in Germany*, cartoon by Leonard Raven-Hill, *Punch* (25 January, 1911). Princeton University Library.

Every effort has been made to identify and contact copyright holders; any omissions or errors will be corrected if notification is made to the publisher.

All paper used by Open Book Publishers is SFI (Sustainable Forestry Initiative), and PEFC (Programme for the Endorsement of Forest Certification Schemes) Certified.

Printed in the United Kingdom and United States by
Lightning Source for Open Book Publishers

In fond and grateful memory of my teachers, Miss McCallum (Pollokshields Primary School, Glasgow), Miss Ross (Largs Higher Grade School, Ayrshire), Miss Gibson and Miss Forsyth (Eastwood Secondary School, Renfrewshire), Alan M. Boase and Norman Cohn (Glasgow University), Jean Frappier (Paris) and Jean Seznec (Oxford).

Table of Contents

Dedication — v
Illustrations — ix
Acknowledgments — xiii
Note on Translations — xiii
Foreword — xvii

INTRODUCTION — xxiii

I. FAMILY BACKGROUND, DIPLOMATIC CAREER, ROLE IN WORLD WAR I — 1

   1. The Oppenheims — 3
   2. The Charm of the Orient — 13
   3. Attaché in Cairo. "The Kaiser's Spy" — 33
   4. The Spectre of Pan-Islamism and *Jihad*. The Background of Oppenheim's 1914 *Denkschrift betreffend die Revolutionierung der islamischen Gebiete Unserer Feinde* — 47
   5. Oppenheim's 1914 *Denkschrift* — 81
   6. Promoter of German Economic Expansion and the Berlin-Baghdad Railway — 107

II. THE ARCHAEOLOGIST: TELL HALAF — 117

   7. Discovery and Excavation, Publications and Critical Reception — 119
   8. Financial Difficulties. The Fate of the Tell Halaf Finds — 147

III. "THE KAISER'S SPY" UNDER NATIONAL SOCIALISM. "LEBEN IM NS-STAAT"   159

  9. Questions   161

 10. The Oppenheims and their Bank under National Socialism   163

 11. Waldemar and Friedrich Carl von Oppenheim, so-called "Quarter-Jews," during the National Socialist Regime: Work for the *Abwehr* (German Counter-Intelligence) and Association with the Conservative *"Widerstand"* (German Resistance)   171

 12. Max von Oppenheim, "Half-Jew," during the National Socialist Regime   205

    Oppenheim and the Race Question   205

    Support of the Regime   222

 13. Plotting for Nazi Germany. Oppenheim's Role in the Middle East Policy of the Third Reich   231

 14. Max von Oppenheim's Last Years   277

IV. MAX VON OPPENHEIM'S RELATION TO NATIONAL SOCIALISM IN CONTEXT. SOME RESPONSES OF "NON-ARYAN" GERMANS TO NATIONAL SOCIALISM   283

 15. Two Jewish Organizations: the *Verband nationaldeutscher Juden* (*Association of German National Jews*) and the *Reichsbund jüdischer Frontsoldaten* (*Jewish War Veterans Association*)   285

 16. Some Individuals: Schoeps, Pevsner, Kantorowicz, Landmann   293

 17. By Way of Conclusion   325

APPENDIX of originals and translations of passages quoted   337

INDEX OF NAMES   379

Illustrations

Frontispiece. "Mein Zelt" (My Tent). Dr. Max Freiherr von Oppenheim, *Vom Mittelmeer zum Persischen Golf durch den Haurān, die Syrische Wüste und Mesopotamien* (Berlin: Dietrich Reimer, 1899), vol. 1, frontispiece. — xvi

1.1 Portrait of Salomon Oppenheim jr., founder of the Oppenheim bank. Artist unknown (before 1828). Wikimedia Commons. Original in colour. — 4

1.2 Synagogue in the Glockengasse, funded by the Oppenheim family, 1861. Lithograph by J. Hoegg from a water colour by Carl Emanuel Conrad (1810–1873). Wikimedia Commons. — 5

1.3 Alexander Duncker, *Die ländlichen Wohnsitze, Schlösser und Residenzen der Ritterschaftlichen Grundbesitzer in der Preussischen Monarchie, in naturgetreuen künstlerisch ausgeführten, farbigen Darstellungen nebst begleitendem Text* (Berlin: Alexander Duncker, 1857–1883), vol. 9 (1866–1867), Plate 530. Original in colour. — 8

2.1 "Bedouin Women." Dr. Max Freiherr von Oppenheim, *Vom Mittelmeer zum Persischen Golf durch den Haurān, die Syrische Wüste und Mesopotamien* (Berlin: Dietrich Reimer, 1899), vol. 2, facing p. 124. — 24

2.2 "Bedouin Minstrels." Dr. Max Freiherr von Oppenheim, *Vom Mittelmeer zum Persischen Golf durch den Haurān, die Syrische Wüste und Mesopotamien* (Berlin: Dietrich Reimer, 1899), vol. 2, p. 127. — 24

2.3 "Syrian Villagers." Dr. Max Freiherr von Oppenheim, Vom Mittelmeer zum Persischen Golf, vol. 1, facing p. 254. *Mittelmeer zum Persischen Golf.* Ibid., vol. 1, facing p. 254. — 24

5.1	Al-Ǧihād—El Dschihad, Zeitung für die muhammedanischen Kriegsgefangenen (a fortnightly newspaper published in Arabic and other languages by the Nachrichtenstelle für den Orient for Muslim prisoners-of-war, beginning on 1 March, 1915), Arabic issue, no. 21, 4 November, 1915, front page. Courtesy of Staatsbibliothek, Munich (2 H. un.app. 42t). All rights reserved.	88
7.1	Tell Halaf. "The Pole Goddess," excavated in 1899. Dr. Max Freiherr von Oppenheim, "Bericht über eine im Jahr 1899 ausgeführte Forschungsreise in der asiatischen Türkei," Zeitschrift der Gesellschaft für Erdkunde zu Berlin, 36, 2 (1901): 69–99. Plate 16.	137
7.2	Tell Halaf. "The Goddess with the Veil." Dr. Max Freiherr von Oppenheim, "Der Tell Halaf und die verschleierte Göttin," Der Alte Orient, 10, 1 (1908): 43. Plate 12.	138
7.3	Tell Halaf. "Sphinx." Berlin, Pergamon Museum. Wikimedia Commons. Photograph by Z. Thomas. CC-BY-SA.	143
7.4	Tell Halaf. "Enthroned Goddess." Illustrated London News, October 25, 1930, p. 707.	145
8.1	Façade of Aleppo National Museum, showing plaster casts of caryatids shipped to Berlin by Max von Oppenheim. Wikimedia Commons.	148
8.2	Illustrated London News, October 25, 1930, front page, showing caryatids from Tell Halaf in newly opened Tell Halaf Museum.	149
8.3	Tell Halaf. Orthostat. "Seated Figure holding a lotus flower." New York, The Metropolitan Museum of Art, Rogers Fund, 1943 (43.135.1) © The Metropolitan Museum of Art. All Rights Reserved.	154
8.4	Tell Halaf. Orthostat. "Lion-hunt scene." New York, The Metropolitan Museum of Art, Rogers Fund, 1943 (43.135.2) © The Metropolitan Museum of Art. All Rights Reserved.	155
8.5	Tell Halaf. Orthostat. "Two heroes." Baltimore, MD, The Walters Art Museum, accession no. 21.18. © The Walters Art Museum. All Rights Reserved.	155

8.6	Tell Halaf. Orthostat. "Winged goddess." Baltimore, MD, The Walters Art Museum, accession no. 21.16. © The Walters Art Museum. All Rights Reserved.	155
14.1	Max von Oppenheim (left) and his faithful manservant Sommer. Photograph sent at end of World War II by Oppenheim to his former collaborator Ernst Herzfeld at the Institute for Advanced Study, Princeton, N.J. Ernst Herzfeld Papers, Freer Gallery of Art and Arthur M. Sackler Gallery Archives, Smithsonian Institution, Washington, D.C. © Smithsonian Institution. All Rights Reserved.	279

Acknowledgments

My thanks to David Hogge, Head of Archives, Freer Gallery of Art and Arthur M. Sackler Gallery at the Smithsonian Institution in Washington, D.C., for seeking out and scanning material relevant to Oppenheim in the Myron Bement Smith and Ernst Herzfeld papers. Thanks also to the staff of the Walters Art Museum in Baltimore and the Metropolitan Museum in New York for their assistance in unravelling the fate of the orthostats Oppenheim brought to New York in the 1930s. To my friends and colleagues in Princeton—Walter Hinderer, Christoph and Flora Kimmich, and Peter Paret—and to Professor Susannah Heschel of Dartmouth College, one of the referees of the manuscript, I am indebted for their interest in the project as well as for practical suggestions and advice. As on previous occasions, I have benefited greatly from the sagacity and good counsel of Alessandra Tosi and Corin Throsby at Open Book Publishers.

A note on translations

All translations from German and French are by the author, unless otherwise indicated. In the case of very short passages, the original and a translation are often given side by side in the text. Longer passages are cited most commonly in translation, but occasionally in the original language. In the first case, the original is reproduced, in the second an English translation is provided in an appendix arranged by page number and located at the end of the volume.

I have done the state some service, and they know't;
No more of that. I pray you, in your letters,
When you shall these unlucky deeds relate,
Speak of me as I am; nothing extenuate…

> Shakespeare, *Othello,* Act V, scene 2

You never know what will start off a Jehad!

> John Buchan, *Greenmantle* (1916)

Frontispiece. "My Tent" (Max von Oppenheim in the desert). *"Mein Zelt" (My Tent)*. Dr. Max Freiherr von Oppenheim, *Vom Mittelmeer zum Persischen Golf durch den Haurān, die Syrische Wüste und Mesopotamien* (Berlin: Dietrich Reimer, 1899), vol. 1, frontispiece.

Foreword

I am neither an archaeologist nor a scholar of the Middle East. I came across the figure of Baron Max von Oppenheim while preparing a new translation and edition of an autobiographical memoir by Hermynia Zur Mühlen, the daughter of an Austrian aristocrat and minor diplomat, who had accompanied her father to Cairo in 1906 and who tells of hearing much talk there of the mysterious Baron. I included him among the figures of whom I prepared thumbnail sketches for my edition of Zur Mühlen's memoir (*The End and the Beginning* [Cambridge, England: Open Book Publishers, 2010] pp. 214–20). The sketch of Oppenheim turned out to be rather longer than most, because of the enigmatic and intriguing character of the individual and because I had become sufficiently curious about him to have already begun some quite serious research on him. I found that, besides references to him in works on the archaeology and ethnology of the Middle East, Oppenheim figures quite prominently in the considerable literature on German-Turkish relations just before and during the First World War and on German war strategies in 1914. In addition, Princeton's Firestone Library is one of the few libraries in the United States that holds a copy, on microfilm, of the important "Denkschrift betreffend die Revolutionierung der islamischen Gebiete unserer Feinde" ("Memorandum concerning the Fomenting of Revolutions in the Islamic Territories of our Enemies"), which Oppenheim prepared for the *Auswärtiges Amt*, the German Foreign Office, immediately after the outbreak of war in 1914. The microfilm was made from a version of this memo preserved among the papers, now in the Beinecke Library at Yale, of Ernst Jäckh, a journalist, author of an important book on Turkey, founder in 1912 of a German-Turkish society, and associate of Oppenheim's in promoting Turkish-German collaboration

http://dx.doi.org/10.11647/OBP.0030.19

in the First World War.¹ The memo lays out in detail a strategy for inciting a religious *jihad* among the Muslim subjects of Germany's enemies—the British, the French, and the Russians—against their colonial masters.

At the end of January 2011, I was alerted by an English colleague who teaches in Germany that Oppenheim had become the topic of many articles in the German press in connection with an exhibition, just opened at the Pergamon Museum in Berlin, of the 3,000 year-old artefacts and sculptures Oppenheim brought back from his important excavations at Tell Halaf in northern Syria. Subsequently I found that the English and American media had also picked up on the exhibition.² The Tell Halaf artefacts had been housed in a makeshift museum that Oppenheim himself had created in the 1920s out of a disused factory in the Charlottenburg district of Berlin, after the Pergamon Museum, to which he had offered them, declined to purchase them, allegedly for lack of funds. When the Tell Halaf Museum was hit by an incendiary bomb during one of the allied air-raids on the German capital in late 1943, the combination of the extreme heat from the

---

1   Ernst Jäckh papers, Yale. Princeton University Library, Microfilm 11747, folder 47. Jäckh took a somewhat different view from Oppenheim of Turkey's eventual role in the War. He was convinced that Turkey would enter the War on the side of the Central Powers and he agreed with Oppenheim that this would create a "bloc separating the Allies in the West and in the East, and thus preventing any joint action," and would "draw off Russian, French, and British strength from Germany's fronts—to the Caucasus front, the Dardanelles and the Mesopotamian and Egyptian fronts." The total number of enemy troops thus affected, he thought, might amount to about one million. In a memorandum to the German Foreign Office, written on 6 August 1914, he made no mention, however, of fomenting a Muslim *jihad* against the Allies. A supporter of the modernizing movement in Turkey, he almost certainly had reservations about stirring up old religious passions, even while recognizing the value to Germany of such a strategy. (The memorandum is quoted in Ernst Jäckh, *The Rising Crescent. Turkey Yesterday, Today, and Tomorrow* [New York: Farrar and Reinhart, 1944], pp. 122–23; see also Malte Fuhrmann, "Germany's Adventures in the Orient," in Volker Langbehn and Mohammed Salama, eds., *German Colonialism. Race, the Holocaust and Postwar Germany* [New York: Columbia University Press, 2011], pp. 123–45 [p. 136]). Jäckh moved in a different direction from Oppenheim after the War. He became a supporter of the Weimar republic, helped to found the *Deutsche Hochschule für Politik* in Berlin, and left Germany for Britain after Hitler's seizure of power in 1933. In 1940 he took up a teaching position at Columbia University, where he was one of the founders of the University's Middle East Institute. He died in New York City in 1959. Oppenheim, in contrast, as we shall see, remained in Germany throughout the years of National Socialism and contributed to the formulation and execution of the regime's Middle Eastern policy.
2   See, for instance: http://www.spiegel.de/international/zeitgeist/0,1518,741928,00.html. See also: http://www.gerettete-goetter.de/index.php?node_id=1;http://www.telegraph.co.uk/culture/culturepicturegalleries/8316294/Ancient-Syrian-sculptures-destroyed-in-World-War-II-reconstructed-from-fragments.html; http://www.bbc.co.uk/news/world-europe-12308854; [All links in footnotes active on 30 September, 2012].

fire and the cold water used to extinguish it resulted in the shattering of the sculptures into 27,000 pieces of basalt, many no larger than a human thumb. Oppenheim arranged for the rubble to be salvaged in the hope that one day the sculptures might be recreated. Thirty of them have now been reconstituted—a stunning achievement of restoration by the team of conservators who worked on the project for about a decade. The Pergamon Museum exhibition brought Oppenheim's discoveries at Tell Halaf back again into public view, more prominently than ever.

As a result, Oppenheim himself has also come back into public view—in a new guise: no longer the "Kaiser's Spy," as he was referred to by his British contemporaries in Cairo at the time of Zur Mühlen's visit, at the Foreign Office in London, and by most British writers on the First World War ever since, but rather as a hero of German archaeology, comparable with two other great amateurs, Heinrich Schliemann, the discoverer of Troy, and Carl Humann, the excavator of Pergamon. In April 2011, I came upon a lively TV docudrama about Oppenheim, based on a text written by Gisela Graichen, the author of *Schliemanns Erben* (Bergisch Gladbach: Lübbe, 2001). Oppenheim is seen here again, above all, as a passionate explorer of ancient civilizations, though his political activities are not entirely overlooked and he is also presented as a kind of German Lawrence of Arabia—amateur political intriguer and amateur archaeologist combined. In fact, his one encounter with T.E. Lawrence, which is described in Lawrence's correspondence, is the occasion of a re-enacted scene in the film.[3] On the other hand, a reviewer in the *Journal of the American Oriental Society* of a recently published, short, illustrated book about Oppenheim with the upbeat title *Der Tell Halaf und sein Ausgräber Max Freiherr von Oppenheim: Kopf hoch! Mut hoch! und Humor hoch!* [*Tell Halaf and its Excavator, Baron Max von Oppenheim: Head high! Chin up! Keep smiling!*] describes the book's hero as "the last of the great amateur archaeological explorers of the Near East" and makes no mention of his career as a government agent or as the instigator of a policy of deliberately inciting religious passion and exploiting it for secular geopolitical and military ends.[4] The luxury Geneva Mont Blanc company even produced an

---

3 http://www.youtube.com/watch?v=uthdw5EPTWA&feature=related; http://www.youtube.com/watch?v=ZazXd8mKmNM&feature=related; http://www.youtube.com/watch?v=WybwzYa1SN4&feature=related.

4 Gary Beckman in *Journal of the American Oriental Society*, 123 (2003): 253. Cf. the very different view of Oppenheim as having "initiated the creation of global political Islam" in its modern form ("made in Europe by non-Muslims, exported to, adapted in, and globalized beyond the Muslim lands") presented by Wolfgang Schwanitz, "Euro-Islam by '*Jihad Made in Germany*'," in Nathalie Clayer and Eric Germain, eds., *Islam in Interwar Europe* (London: Hurst, 2008), pp. 271–301 (p. 301). See also Schwanitz, "Die

expensive fountain pen dedicated to the "mécène d'art," Max von Oppenheim.

The picture I had begun to trace of Oppenheim was more complicated and more sombre than those that appeared in connection with the exhibition. My reading of his books on Tell Halaf and on the Bedouins had convinced me that as an archaeologist and ethnologist he was not at all the fraud that some of his contemporaries among the British in Cairo and London believed him to be. Subsequent investigation demonstrated that, though an amateur, he was both talented and dedicated and was taken seriously by the most respected professionals (British and American as well as German) in the two fields. His political activities and projects, however, both before and during the First World War and then again, under the National Socialists during the Second, were troubling. Above all, the attitude of this half-Jewish (according to the Nuremberg Laws) scion of a prominent Cologne Jewish banking family to National Socialism, Jews, and the anti-Semitism from which it was impossible for him not to have known that his career had suffered during the *Kaiserreich* and from which he had even more to fear under the Nazis, was puzzling, unsettling, and raised many question not only about him but also about the affluent, conservative, highly assimilated, and strongly nationalist German-Jewish milieu from which he came.

Reflecting the diversity of Oppenheim's interests and activities, this study of him is something of a mosaic. It derives its unity in turn from the unity Oppenheim sought to give to his own persona. Descended from a family of Jewish bankers, the son of a Catholic mother and a Jewish father who had converted at the time of his marriage, Oppenheim seems to have found his heterogeneous identity burdensome and to have sought escape from it by reinventing himself as a one hundred percent German patriot—whence perhaps his propensity to place himself, both as a diplomat and as an explorer, in situations where he dealt with non-Germans. As a diplomat, the half Jewish banker's son represented Germany to

---

Berliner Djihadisierung des Islam: wie Max von Oppenheim die islamische Revolution schürte," Konrad Adenauer Stiftung. Publikationen, 10 November 2004 (http://www.kas.de/wf/de/33.5678). In his many articles on Oppenheim, Schwanitz regularly refers to him as "Abu Jihad"—father of the modern political *jihad*—and, as the historian Martin Kröger acknowledged with regret in 2010, this catchy tag has stuck, as have the tags attached to other European archaeologists and government agents in the Middle East, such as T.E. Lawrence ("Lawrence of Arabia") and Gertrude Bell ("Queen of the Desert"). ("Max von Oppenheim im Auswärtigen Dienst," lecture to the *Historische Gesellschaft* of the Deutsche Bank, http://www.bankgeschichte.de/de/docs/Vortrag_Kroeger.pdf).

non-Germans and defended Germany's interests against the agents of other nations; as an explorer and ethnologist, he stood out as a German among the exotic peoples he studied and at the same time sought their friendship and trust not only for the sake of his—and German—scholarship but in order to enhance German influence among them. There seems never to have been the slightest crack in Max von Oppenheim's absolute identification with and dedication to Germany. He always insisted that he won the confidence of the Bedouins not, as many other explorers had done, by adopting the disguise of a Muslim Arab but by presenting himself as nothing but the German aristocrat he was (or strove to be).

Cultural historians and literary scholars have shown that many well-established and assimilated German Jews, whether practising or not, converted or still nominally Jewish, were uncomfortable with their mixed identity and sought mightily to reconceive themselves, and have others acknowledge them, as fully German—"plus allemands que les Allemands," an unsympathetic observer might have said. Doubly divided, of part Jewish, part Catholic descent, Oppenheim may well have desired, no less than any full Jew, to redefine himself as wholly and undividedly German. There is in fact no indication that he ever showed interest in either Jewish or Catholic religious practices or institutions. Diplomat, scholar, intrepid explorer, Baron Max von Oppenheim was never anything but a thoroughgoing German patriot. In all likelihood he did his best to suppress even his own awareness of other components of his identity, since that awareness would in itself have represented a threat to the unity and stability of the persona he presented not only to the world but to himself.

Throughout the essay, I have quoted at considerable length from my sources. Even though some of them are still surprisingly pertinent to the current situation in the Middle East, a great deal of this material has fallen into oblivion or become unfamiliar except to specialists. Much of it, moreover, is not easily accessible. Finally, notwithstanding the fact that the texts quoted have obviously been selected by me, I hoped by this means to let the reader hear history speak, as far as this is possible, out of its own mouth.

Introduction

The name of Max, Freiherr von Oppenheim (1860–1946) still rings a bell in two fields of scholarly specialization. Among archaeologists and ethnographers working on ancient Near and Middle Eastern civilizations,[1] he is well known as the discoverer of Tell Halaf, a rich treasure trove of artefacts, some dating from prehistoric times, some from around 1,000 B.C., in Northern Syria, and as an attentive and sympathetic observer and analyst of the customs and social structure of the Bedouins. In the work of historians of the First World War and of German-Turkish relations around that time, he is often evoked as a German agent active in the Middle East in the two decades leading up to the War—"the Kaiser's spy," as he was then known to the British and is still referred to by British historians—and, after the outbreak of war in 1914, as the chief instigator and organizer of a projected Muslim *jihad* against the Entente powers (Britain, France, and Russia), the aim of which was to drastically weaken their military effectiveness in the European theatre by forcing them to divert resources to crucial parts of their empires threatened by Muslim uprisings—in the case of the British to Egypt and India, in the case of

---

1 The terms "Near East" and "Middle East" have become interchangeable. The first official use of the term "Middle East" by the United States government was in the 1957 Eisenhower Doctrine, which pertained to the Suez Crisis. Secretary of State John Foster Dulles defined the Middle East as "the area lying between and including Libya on the west and Pakistan on the east, Syria and Iraq on the North and the Arabian Peninsula to the south, plus the Sudan and Ethiopia." In 1958, the State Department explained that the terms "Near East" and "Middle East" were interchangeable, and defined the region as including Egypt, Syria, Israel, Lebanon, Jordan, Iraq, Saudi Arabia, Kuwait, Bahrain, and Qatar. According to the article "Near East'" in the Associated Press Stylebook (New York, 2000), "there is no longer a substantial distinction between this term [Near East] and Middle East." Likewise, the article "Middle East" states that "Popular usage once distinguished between the Near East (the westerly nations in the listing) and the Middle East (the easterly nations), but the two terms now overlap, with current practice favoring Middle East for both areas." The recommendation is to "use Middle East unless Near East is used by a source in a story." That is the practice that I shall follow here.

http://dx.doi.org/10.11647/OBP.0030.20

the French to their North African possessions, and in the case of the Russians to their territories in the Caucasus. What is less well known and not so often discussed is that the same Oppenheim, who according to the Nuremberg laws was half-Jewish, not only was not persecuted by the National Socialist regime in Germany but actively co-operated with it by submitting to the Nazi *Auswärtiges Amt*, or Ministry of Foreign Affairs, in July 1940, a new plan for German action in the Middle East—suitably revised in light of the defeat of France, the Italian alliance, and the still unbroken non-aggression pact with Russia, to concentrate on Syria and British India. Oppenheim was apparently still committed in 1940 to the goal he had formulated in 1914 in his substantial and detailed *Denkschrift betreffend die Revolutionierung der islamischen Gebiete unserer Feinde* [Memorandum concerning the fomenting of revolutions in the Islamic territories of our enemies]. The last lines of that memorandum run: "Das Eingreifen des Islam in den gegenwärtigen Krieg ist besonders für England ein furchtbarer Schlag. Tun wir alles, arbeiten wir vereint mit allen Mitteln, damit derselbe ein tödlicher werde!"[2] ["For England especially, the intervention of Islam in the present war is a fearful blow. Let us do everything in our power, let us use all possible means to make it a fatal one!"] As one scholar has noted: "What [Oppenheim] had in mind in the 1914 memorandum was not simply a shattering military blow to knock out the enemy's fighting capabilities but a larger political strategy"[3]—ultimately, the destruction of the British Empire and the replacement of Britain as a world power by Germany.

I have divided my study into four main parts: Part I: Family background, diplomatic career, and role in World War I. The "Kaiser's Spy."

---

2 Ernst Jäckh Papers, Yale, MS. group 467, Princeton University Library, Microfilm 11747, folder 47, p. 92. A full reprint of Oppenheim's *Denkschrift*, carefully prepared by Tim Epkenhans and with the original pagination noted, appeared recently in *Archivum Ottomanicum*, 19 (2001): 120–63. The passage cited appears on p. 135 of the original. Page references to the *Denkschrift* in the present text will be to the original pagination in Epkenhans's relatively accessible edition. Epkenhans's introduction to the *Denkschrift* is in the same journal (published by Harrassowitz, the company which in 1939 and 1943 put out the first two volumes of Oppenheim's multi-volume study of the Bedouins), 18 (2000): 247–50, under the title, taken from the *Denkschrift*, "Geld soll keine Rolle spielen." A much abbreviated version of Oppenheim's memorandum, copied into his memoirs by Karl Emil Schabinger, Oppenheim's colleague at the Orient Intelligence Bureau in Constantinople during the First World War, was published by Wolfgang G. Schwanitz in "Max von Oppenheim und der Heilige Krieg. Zwei Denkschriften zur Revolutionierung islamischer Gebiete 1914 und 1940," *Sozial.Geschichte*, 19, Heft 3 (2004): 28–59 (pp. 45–55).
3 Hans-Ulrich Seidt, *Berlin Kabul Moskau. Oskar Ritter von Niedermayer und Deutschlands Geopolitik* (Munich: Universitas, 2000), p. 47.

Part II: Tell Halaf. The Archaeologist. Part III: *"Leben im NS-Staat."* The "Kaiser's Spy" under National Socialism. Part IV: Oppenheim's relation to the NS Regime in context. Responses of some non-Aryan Germans to National Socialism.

The central placement of Part II between the parts devoted to Oppenheim's role in Middle East politics in World War I and in World War II was determined not only by chronology—excavation at Tell Halaf was resumed in the period between the two world wars and Oppenheim's popular writings about Tell Halaf and his worldwide recognition as a scholar also date from that time—but by a desire to acknowledge the place his archaeological and ethnological investigations occupied in the career of a resolute and even ruthless patriot.

In Parts III and IV especially I have tried to find answers to the questions Oppenheim's strange career has suggested to me—questions about the consistency of National Socialist policies, questions above all, about the sense of identity and the attitudes toward National Socialism of highly assimilated, politically conservative, and nationalist German Jews—*Kaiserjuden*, as Chaim Weizmann dubbed them—and so-called *Mischlinge* ("half-Jews," "quarter-Jews," etc.), a large class of people who found themselves in an extremely awkward position during the Nazi period but have been surprisingly little studied. Did Oppenheim feel or want to feel so intensely German that he actually sympathized with National Socialist aims and policies, or at least with some of them? Should his behaviour be understood as an unusually striking case of what has come to be referred to as "Jewish self-hatred"? Or was he chiefly motivated by the unwavering nationalism, dating from the Second Reich, that marked his entire career and that may have allowed him to overlook, for a time at least, the persecution of non-Aryans under the Third Reich, or to think that it would be a passing phase? Though he himself had been baptised and raised as a Catholic, the diplomatic career he had hoped to pursue had been stunted because of his father's Jewish origins. He might have directed his resentment at those whose anti-Semitism was the cause of his having been held back. Did he choose instead to direct it at those whom he associated with an inconvenient heritage and an identity he did not want or recognize? According to one "half-Jew" in the medical corps of the Wehrmacht, "Generally, *Mischlinge* are very anti-Semitic." In the words of another, "I had a feeling that most of the *Mischlinge* felt more German than Jewish and venture to say some, not me, would gladly have joined the SS had they not been tainted by Jewish blood."[4] Or was everyone—the Nazis and Oppenheim alike—chiefly motivated by opportunistic considerations? Were the Jewish organizations mentioned below[5] (the Association of Jewish War Veterans, for example) which expressed support for key aspects of National Socialism only trying to protect themselves and ward off persecution? Was the orthodox rabbi who "openly announced" his "allegiance to National Socialism," and who promised that, were it not for its "anti-Semitic component, National Socialism would find in observant and faithful Jews its most loyal supporters" simply looking out for his coreligionists' security? Was Oppenheim's overriding motive self-preservation and the preservation of his legacy as a scholar of the Middle East?

That latter concern must assuredly have played a role in the adjustment Oppenheim made, after the end of the Second World War, to the persona of the German patriot that he had carefully cultivated and maintained throughout his life. In a letter of several pages sent in June 1946 to Ernst Herzfeld, a former friend and collaborator who had been forced by the Nazi racial laws to resign his chair at the Technische Hochschule in Berlin in 1935 and seek refuge in the United States, he contrived to write exclusively about his scholarly work, to allude only in passing to the War and the Nazi regime, and to keep out of his letter anything that might cast a shadow on the persona he now wanted to project to his Jewish former associate: that of the committed scholar, indifferent to and uncontaminated by the political events that had turned his correspondent's life upside down. There is virtually no reference in the letter to Germany, either to the people or to the culture. Nevertheless, it seems unlikely that Oppenheim had ceased to be the German patriot that he had always been. No less than his activity as a Middle East expert on Germany's behalf in two world wars, his severely damaged treasures and now barely surviving *Max Freiherr von Oppenheim Stiftung* (Baron Max von Oppenheim Foundation) were in his eyes his gifts to Germany, the expression of his dedication to his country. In trying to secure Herzfeld's help for the restoration of the treasures and the rebuilding of the Stiftung, there is no reason to believe that he was in any way turning his back on the patriotism by which he had chosen to define himself over the entire course of his life.

---

4 Both quotations in Bryan Mark Rigg, *Hitler's Jewish Soldiers. The Untold Story of Nazi Racial Laws and Men of Jewish Descent in the German Military* (Lawrence: University Press of Kansas, 2002), pp. 24–25.
5 See Part IV of this study.

I
FAMILY BACKGROUND, DIPLOMATIC CAREER, ROLE IN WORLD WAR I

1. The Oppenheims

Max Freiherr von Oppenheim (1860–1946), was born into an extremely wealthy Jewish banking family in Cologne. The private bank known as "Sal. [i.e. Salomon] Oppenheim jr. & Cie," founded in 1789, had a continuous, unbroken existence until 2010, when, having survived even its *Arisierung* (Aryanization) under the Nazis, it finally succumbed to the world financial crisis and was taken over by the Deutsche Bank. Only a few years earlier, with some 3,100 employees, it had still ranked as one of the largest private banks in Europe, if not the largest.

The Oppenheims are first mentioned as silk merchants in Frankfurt in the sixteenth century. In 1740 a Salomon Oppenheim moved to Bonn, where the Oppenheims became court factors of the Elector Clement August. The founder of the modern bank of Sal. Oppenheim jr. & Cie was a younger Salomon (1772–1828) who transferred his business in 1798 to Cologne.

His sons, Simon (1803–1880) and Abraham (1804–1878), together with their mother Therese, who had taken over the management of the firm on her husband's death, transformed it into "one of the earliest and most important examples of modern commercial and industrial capitalism in Germany." Linked by marriage to other Jewish banking families—the Rothschilds, the Habers, the Foulds—the Oppenheims were involved in the financing of Germany's first industrial firms: they promoted railroad construction, river transportation, and insurance companies, and they helped to finance the up-and-coming heavy industry of the Ruhr.[1] By the 1870s they were

---

[1] For a short summary of Oppenheim activities, see Richard Tilly, "Sal. Oppenheim jr. & Cie," in Manfred Pohl, ed., *Handbook on the History of the European Banks* (Aldershot: Edward Elgar, 1994), pp. 451–57; on Oppenheim participation in railway construction, see Kurt Grunwald, "Europe's Railways and Jewish Enterprise: German Jews as Pioneers of Railway Promotion," *Leo Baeck Institute Yearbook*, 12 (1967): 163–209. The main source of information remains the outstanding work of Michael Stürmer, Gabriele Teichmann and Wilhelm Treue, *Wägen und Wagen. Sal. Oppenheim jr. & Cie. Geschichte einer Bank und einer Familie* (Munich and Zurich: Piper, 1989).

http://dx.doi.org/10.11647/OBP.0030.01

the wealthiest family in Cologne and both Simon and Abraham had been ennobled in recognition of their contribution to the development of the national economies of Germany and Austria. When the German Empress happened to be in Cologne, she dined at the Oppenheims'; Abraham and his wife Charlotte were in turn guests of the royal couple when the latter stayed at the *Residenzschloss* in Koblenz.[2]

Fig. 1.1 Portrait of Salomon Oppenheim jr., founder of the Oppenheim bank. Artist unknown (before 1828). Wikimedia Commons (original in colour).

During most of the nineteenth century, members of the family identified themselves without hesitation as Jews, even if Benedict Fould on a visit to Cologne in 1813 wrote home to his father in Paris that Salomon Oppenheim jr. "n'est pas plus ami que toi des cérémonies juives."[3] Thus in 1841 Simon and

---

2 Michael Stürmer, Gabriele Teichmann and Wilhelm Treue, *Wägen und Wagen*, p. 214.
3 "Is no fonder of Jewish rituals than you" Cit. François Barbier, "Banque, famille et société en Allemagne au XIXe siècle," *Revue de Synthèse*, 114 (1993): 127–37 (p. 131).

Abraham submitted "a humble petition" for a more complete emancipation of the Jews to the King of Prussia. Their youngest brother David (1809–1889), a liberal who in 1842 launched the *Rheinische Zeitung* and brought Karl Marx in to edit it, also embraced the cause of Jewish emancipation and continued to support it even after he himself had converted to Catholicism in 1839 and taken the name Dagobert.[4] In the mid-1850s Abraham donated 600,000 thalers (over a million and a half dollars in today's money by some estimates) for the building of a new synagogue in Cologne, the land for which had been purchased by his father in the 1820s, while in his will (1880) Simon made provision for a home for old, infirm or indigent Jews.

Fig. 1.2 Synagogue in the Glockengasse, funded by the Oppenheim family, 1861. Lithograph by J. Hoegg from a water colour by Carl Emanuel Conrad (1810–1873). Wikimedia Commons (original in colour).

At the same time, however, the family also supported general philanthropic and cultural ventures in Cologne. They clearly wanted to be seen as good

---

4 David Oppenheim's conversion, the first in the family, is noted by Wilhelm Treue in his article "Dagobert Oppenheim: Zeitungsherausgeber, Bankier und Unternehmer in der Zeit des Liberalismus und Neumerkantilismus," *Tradition: Zeitschrift für Firmengeschichte*, 9 (1964): 145–75, and by Shulamit S. Magnus, *Jewish Emancipation in a German City: Cologne 1798–1871* (Stanford: Stanford University Press, 1997), p. 275.

citizens whose Judaism did not prevent them from pursuing the wellbeing of all, Christians and Jews alike, in their community. Almost all the family's numerous charitable bequests, beginning with one from Therese in 1829, stipulate that they are for the "needy of all faiths" or "without regard to religion." The beneficiaries of this Oppenheim generosity ranged from the poor in general to victims of flooding and industrial accidents, starving workers, veterans of the War of Liberation (1812–1813), and officers wounded in the wars of 1866, 1870, and 1914–1918. Substantial sums were contributed to support scholarships at the University of Bonn for gifted boys from poor families, as well as to the Institute for the Deaf and Dumb and the city orphanage. On Abraham's death in 1878, his widow Charlotte (1811–1887)—a granddaughter on her mother's side of the great Mayer Amschel Rothschild—donated 600,000 marks (between two and a half and three million dollars in today's money) to establish the *Freiherr Abraham von Oppenheim'scher Kinderhospital*, the first children's hospital in Cologne (1880) and a few years later (1885) another 400,000 (100,000 for the building, plus an endowment of 300,000) for a new general hospital in nearby Bassenheim, where the family had acquired an estate. In the early twentieth century, Flossy (Florence Mathews Hutchins), the American wife of Simon Alfred von Oppenheim (1864–1932)—Simon's grandson, who headed the bank in the first three decades of the twentieth century—continued the tradition by setting up a convalescent home in Schlenderhan, where the family had also acquired a handsome country house and built up a celebrated stud farm.

Cultural institutions were not neglected. Therese and her two sons Simon and Abraham were among the founding members of the Cologne *Kunstverein* [Art Association] in 1839 and members of the family were subsequently strong supporters of the city's Wallraf-Richartz Museum, which opened its doors in 1861, donating funds for new acquisitions as well as pictures from their own collections. Dagobert was a particularly generous donor and benefactor, as well as a strong supporter of young artists of the Düsseldorf School. The Oppenheims were also among the first to support the *Central-Dombau-Verein*, set up in 1842 to finance and oversee the national project of completing Cologne's great cathedral, and they contributed generously and consistently to it over the next thirty years. In recognition of their munificence, Abraham and Simon were made honorary committee members of the *Verein* in 1860. In 1864 Dagobert, along with some of his business associates, commissioned a stained glass window for the Cathedral representing—not an insignificant choice of subject—the conversion of St. Paul; while after Abraham's death in 1878 his widow Charlotte donated another window in memory of her deceased husband. In 1859 Simon and his son Eduard (1831–1909) played a major role in the establishment of the Cologne Zoo and the "Flora" Horticultural Society. In 1863 a major gift from Abraham, providing a suitable endowment for the annual salary of an outstanding music director for the city, together with further gifts made directly to the institution itself, helped to turn the Cologne *Conservatorium der Musik*, originally founded in 1845 as *Rheinische Musikschule*,[5] into one of the leading music schools in Germany. Further substantial donations from Oppenheim family members followed and in 1910 and 1912 a major expansion of the conservatory, presently the largest in Germany, was made possible thanks to significant gifts from Albert von Oppenheim (1834–1912) and his estate. The second son of Simon and the father of Max von Oppenheim, Albert von Oppenheim, served on the Cologne Conservatory's governing board for fifty years, from 1860 until 1910, and as its president from 1898 until 1910.

Nor were the Oppenheims slow to demonstrate their loyalty through gifts to members of the royal and imperial households—on the silver anniversary of the "Kaiserpaar," Prince William (the future Wilhelm I) and Princess Augusta (1854); on the wedding of Friedrich Wilhelm (the future Friedrich III, felled by cancer after a 99-day reign) and Princess Victoria of England (1855); on the golden wedding anniversary of the *Kaiserpaar* (1870)—and by contributing to monuments honouring the royal family, national heroes, and great moments in Germany's history. In 1871 Simon's son Eduard (1831–1909) contributed toward the construction of the Niederwald monument celebrating the re-establishment of German unity and the German Empire; in 1889 Dagobert gave 3,000 thalers for a monument to Kaiser Wilhelm I in Cologne; in 1897 the Bank contributed 6,000 thalers for a monument to the short-lived Kaiser Friedrich Wilhelm III; and in 1914 Simon Alfred made a large contribution to the proposed— never built—Bismarck National Monument on the Elisenhöhe at Bingerbrück.

In 1867, "for services in railway financing," Simon was ennobled by Emperor Franz Josef of Austria with the hereditary title of baron (*Freiherr*); Abraham received the same honour from the Prussian monarch a year later. The family marked its entry into the higher ranks of German society by the

---

5   It was renamed Conservatorium der Musik in 1858.

purchase of notable landed properties. Schloss Bassenheim was acquired in 1873 (for over 540,000 thalers). At the Schlenderhan estate, purchased a year or two before, Simon's son Eduard founded what soon became the leading horse stud farm (*Gestüt*) in Germany.

Fig. 1.3 Schloss Schlenderhan. Acquired by the Oppenheims in 1867. Lithograph by Thomas Hartmann, after an original by H. Deiters. Alexander Duncker, *Die ländlichen Wohnsitze, Schlösser und Residenzen der Ritterschaftlichen Grundbesitzer in der Preussischen Monarchie, in naturgetreuen künstlerisch ausgeführten, farbigen Darstellungen nebst begleitendem Text* (Berlin: Alexander Duncker, 1857–1883), vol. 9 (1866–1867), Plate 530 (original in colour).

Eduard and *his* son, Simon Alfred (1864–1932), were keen and accomplished horsemen and the Oppenheims were soon prominent in the elite Union-Klub, Berlin's equivalent of the Paris Jockey Club, membership of which was drawn from the Prussian aristocracy, the landed gentry, and wealthy industrialists. The Klub seems to have been a significant entry point for extremely wealthy Jewish or part-Jewish families into the highest ranks of society.[6] For many years Simon Alfred, head of the Oppenheim bank in the early decades of the twentieth century, was its President. "The turf was his world," according to one history of the family and the bank, "Schlenderhan and horse-breeding a noble passion. [...] He liked to be seen and to have his photograph taken, along with his regimental comrades, in his colourful uniform as captain in the elite cavalry regiment of the Zieten Hussars. Congratulatory messages were customarily exchanged with the family of the Crown Prince. Simon Alfred and his family felt at home in the uppermost ranks of German society, in the aristocracy, and on the racecourses of Europe." Meantime at their home, the villa known as "Thürmchen" on Cologne's Riehlerwall, in the years leading up to World War I, Simon Alfred's American-born wife Flossy entertained prominent figures from the commercial, financial, and industrial worlds and aristocrats, high and low, from the ranks of the military, the diplomatic service, and the civil administration, along with family members from near and far.[7]

Max von Oppenheim himself grew up in a magnificent Louis XV-style town *palais* in the Glockengasse which his father, Albert, had acquired from his father-in-law, the Cologne patrician Philipp Engels, and next to which he had built an addition to house his outstanding collection of paintings. This collection, the core of which had been acquired in 1823 by Salomon Oppenheim jr.,[8] included works by van Dyck, Frans Hals, Hobbema, Hans

---

6 According to Philipp, Fürst von Eulenburg, the influential favorite of Kaiser Wilhelm II, "jeder Mensch, der Rennpferde hält, ist nach dem Standpunkt des Unionklubs ein 'hervorragender Gentleman.' Ausserdem sind sehr reiche Juden (wie die Oppenheims) in der Lage, Geld zu 'pumpen.' Das ist ungefähr die moralische Basis des Klubs, der in 'gesellschaftlichen' Fragen und Fragen der 'Ehre'—in dem 'was sich schickt und nicht schickt,'—massgebend ist." (From the typescript of a text by Eulenburg, cited in *Philipp Eulenburgs Politische Korrespondenz*, ed. John C.G. Röhl, 3 vols. [Boppard am Rhein: Harald Boldt, 1976–1983], vol. 3, p. 1916, note 7.) According to Friedrich von Holstein, head of the Political Department at the German Foreign Office in the 1890s, the "Fürstlichkeiten" ("princely types") of the Union-Klub supported the efforts of the club's Jewish members (Max von Oppenheim is explicitly named) to enter areas of government and administration hitherto virtually closed to Jews, such as the Diplomatic Service. (See letter from Holstein to Eulenburg 21 July 1896, in *Philipp Eulenburgs Politische Korrespondenz*, letter 1382, vol. 3, pp. 1916–17.)

7 Michael Stürmer, Gabriele Teichmann and Wilhelm Treue, *Wägen und Wagen*, pp. 315–16.

8 The Sammlung Siebel was acquired by Salomon Oppenheim jr. from Johann Gerhard Siebel (1784–1831), a well-to-do Elberfeld textile merchant, diplomat, writer, art-lover, and keen freemason, who had fallen into financial difficulties. The collection was widely known, having been publicly exhibited in the Düsseldorf gallery.

Holbein the Younger, Memling, Rembrandt, Rubens, Ruisdael, Jan Steen, David Teniers, and Velasquez.[9]

How the Oppenheims viewed their Jewish background or how their view of it may have evolved in the course of their rapid rise to prominence in the nineteenth century is hard to determine. On the window that Charlotte Oppenheim, Abraham's widow, donated to Cologne Cathedral in memory of her deceased husband, the two lowest panes represent, on the left, the Oppenheim coat of arms and the family motto (*Integrita, Concordia, Industria*), and on the right, the family's contributions to the civic life of Cologne. On this pane are represented not only the hospitals, the Horticultural Society, and the Cathedral, but also the new synagogue. Likewise in a frieze decorating a wall in the Cologne City Hall by the then well-known artist and lithographer Tony Avenarius (1836–1912) and depicting various benefactors of the city, Charlotte is shown with a model of the children's hospital in front of her, while at her side Abraham is seen holding the deed of gift of the synagogue. The message of Charlotte's stained glass window seems to be the family's commitment to the entire community and of course, by the placement of a window bearing the family name and coat of arms in the Cathedral, its prominent place in that community.[10] The Avenarius frieze is similarly ecumenical in spirit. Neither Abraham nor Simon followed the example of their younger brother David (or Dagobert) in embracing Christianity. Of Salomon Oppenheim jr.'s six daughters, five in fact still married Jews, mostly the sons of other bankers; only one, Eva, married a Christian, the Prussian Lieutenant-General Ferdinand von Kusserow. (Their son Heinrich was later to head the colonial affairs section of the *Auswärtiges Amt*, the German Foreign Office, and was to have a considerable influence, in this capacity, on Max von Oppenheim, who referred to him as his "uncle.") Simon, however, the only one of Salomon's three sons to have children, appears to have decided that in the interests of the family and the bank, his children, especially his two sons Eduard (1831–1909) and Albert (1834–1912), who were set to take over the business, should consolidate the integration of the family into German

---

9 For information on the charitable and philanthropic activities of the Oppenheims in the nineteenth and early twentieth centuries and on Albert von Oppenheim's remarkable art collection, I am indebted to Viola Effmert's richly documented *Sal. Oppenheim jr. & Cie. Kulturförderung im 19. Jahrhundert* (Cologne, Weimar and Vienna: Böhlau Verlag, 2006). See especially the tables at the end of the volume.

10 For a brief (but not particularly sympathetic) overview of the Oppenheim family's engagement in all aspects of the life of the city of Cologne, from the early nineteenth century to the present day, see Ulrich Viehöver, *Die EinflussReichen* (Frankfurt and New York: Campus Verlag, 2006), pp. 240–43.

and Cologne society by taking Christian wives and themselves converting to Christianity.[11] In 1856, Albert married Pauline Engels, the daughter of a prominent Cologne Catholic family and himself embraced the faith of his wife. The following year his brother Eduard also married a Cologne Christian heiress and converted to Protestantism. As Eduard and Albert were the only male heirs, the family's and the firm's Jewish connection was thereby ended, in principle at least. Max von Oppenheim was the son of Albert. He was baptised at birth and raised as a Roman Catholic. He himself tells that there was a private chapel in the handsome town house of his parents, where mass was regularly celebrated.[12]

---

11 For a somewhat different view of the conversions of Eduard and Albert, largely based on speculations in Michael Stürmer, Gabriele Teichmann, Wilhelm Treue, *Wägen und Wagen*, pp. 206–12, see Morten Reitmayer, *Bankiers im Kaiserreich. Sozialprofil und Habitus der deutschen Hochfinanz* (Göttingen: Vandenhoek und Ruprecht, 1999). According to Reitmayer, the subordinate role in the Oppenheim bank business to which Simon and Abraham had been restricted as long as their mother Therese was still alive (they had held only a 10% share of the firm) led them in their turn to retain control and keep their own sons in a subordinate position. The marriages and conversions of Eduard and Albert are thus construed as acts of revolt resulting from the younger men's resentment at their "crown prince" status (p. 245).
12 It is also noteworthy that Oppenheim's sisters Klara and Wanda both married into Catholic families.

2. The Charm of the Orient

It was intended that, as the oldest of the male children of Eduard and Albert, Max (1860–1946) should enter the family firm and be trained to take it over when the time came. Max, however, was not at all interested in running the bank. He had developed a keen curiosity about the Islamic world and dreamed of devoting his life to the study of the peoples and cultures of the Middle East and North Africa.

Interest in the "Orient" was by no means uncommon at the time, as several excellent studies of Western fascination with the Middle East have amply demonstrated.[1] For a time, as Ottoman expansion brought Islamic rule to the gates of Vienna and the Barbary Corsairs disrupted shipping and raided towns on the Mediterranean, the Muslim Middle East and North Africa were regarded with fear. Travellers did not go there freely and most Western reports of the area and its peoples came from men who had been captured by the Barbary pirates and then escaped. With the Enlightenment and the weakening of Ottoman power and influence came a growing fascination with Turkey and other "Oriental" lands, manifested in the paintings of Antoine de Favray and Jean-Etienne Liotard, for instance. On the one hand, in texts such as Montesquieu's *Lettres persanes* and the anonymous, immensely popular *L'Espion turc*, the perspective of the "Oriental" was used as a device for carrying out an Enlightenment critique of Western customs and institutions. On the other hand, Turkey, Egypt,

---

1 E.g. Sari J. Nasir, *The Arabs and the English* (London: Longman, 1976); Peter Brent, *Far Arabia. Explorers of the Myth* (London: Weidenfeld and Nicolson, 1977); James C. Simmons, *Passionate Pilgrims. English Travellers in the World of the Desert Arabs* (New York: William Morrow, 1987); the magnificently illustrated book of Alberto Siliotti, *Egypt Lost and Found. Explorers and Travellers on the Nile* (London: Thames and Hudson, 1998), and, of course, the (for good reason) controversial study of the late Edward Said, *Orientalism* (New York: Pantheon, 1978). One of the earliest such studies was the aptly titled and still richly informative *The Penetration of Arabia* by the Oxford scholar and teacher of "Lawrence of Arabia," David George Hogarth (London: Lawrence and Bullen, 1904).

http://dx.doi.org/10.11647/OBP.0030.02

North Africa, and Arabia became an exotic destination for the curious and for adventurers of various sorts—personal, political, and commercial (Domingo Badia y Leblich a.k.a. Ali Bey al Abassi, Richard Pococke, James Silk Buckingham, and later, in the nineteenth century, Richard Burton and William Gifford Palgrave, to mention only a few). They also became the objects of a "scientific" interest in exploring and mapping a *terra incognita*. The Enlightenment project of "unveiling" and shedding the light of reason and understanding on everything obscure or mysterious inspired the celebrated journeys of exploration of the Dane Carsten Niebuhr, of the North German doctor Ulrich Jasper Seetzen, of the modest young man from Basel, Jean-Louis Burckhardt, of the Italian Giovanni Battista Belzoni, of the Finn Georg August Wallin, and of the Frenchmen Louis Linant de Bellefonds and Léon de Laborde, who had been preceded, of course, by the pioneering contributors to the celebrated *Description de l'Egypte* (1808–1829). The ambivalence of the relation of these travellers and explorers of the "Orient" toward the objects of their inquiry—at once sympathetic curiosity and condescending conviction of their own superiority, with more than a dash, in some cases, of imperialist acquisitiveness—is amply, if one-sidedly laid bare, at least as far as the English and the French are concerned, in Edward Said's now virtually classic *Orientalism*.[2] By the early nineteenth century the secrecy of the harem had been penetrated and "Oriental" women were being exhibited in full view, in various states of undress (so-called "odalisques"), in the canvasses of artists from colonising lands, such as France (Ingres, Delacroix, Gerôme and Chassériau). It would be hard to imagine a more direct demonstration of the triumph of the West. Naturally enough, Mecca, the holiest site of Islam, became a particularly enticing mystery to be unravelled and exposed to the inquiring Western eye.

By the close of the nineteenth century, interest in the Orient had become inseparable from the colonial ambitions and rivalries of the European powers. At the same time, the coming of the machine age and the high

---

2 Though he attempts to explain it, Said's decision to exclude Germans, Danes, and Italians from consideration is a serious flaw in his book. It may also have led him to mistake Jean-Louis Burckhardt for his relative, the great historian Jacob Burckhardt (p. 160). Both were members of the same prominent, super-rich Basel family, but belonged to different branches and generations. Jean-Louis's family and its business had suffered severely as a result of the Napoleonic wars and the young Jean-Louis was forced to try to make a living in England. His travels in the Middle East were undertaken on behalf of the Society for the Exploration of the Interior Parts of Africa, which hoped to discover the source of the river Niger by having its agent Burckhardt join a party of Africans returning from the Hajd.

degree of self-discipline and self-consciousness, the constraints and artifices required and promoted by modern Western civilization, together with a sense of individual alienation amid the fraying of traditional communal bonds, led to a growing fascination with cultures which were seemingly unaffected by modernity and in which certain human qualities (whose disappearance from modern societies had already been noted with regret by Adam Smith's compatriot Adam Ferguson in his *Essay on the History of Civil Society* [1767]) continued to shape people's lives: heroism; honour; loyalty; the absolute law of hospitality to the stranger; proximity to the world of nature; being simultaneously a proudly independent agent and an inseparable part of a community, rather than an isolated individual in competition with other individuals in a liberal society that, in theory at least, recognized no distinctions among the units composing it. Above all, perhaps, the supposed stability of an unshaken and unquestioned traditional way of life appealed strongly to many in the West who observed with dismay the accelerating mutations of their own culture and society. "We live in an age of visible transition," Bulwer-Lytton observed gloomily in 1833, "an age of disquietude and doubt—of the removal of time-worn landmarks, and the breaking up of the hereditary elements of society. Old opinions, feelings, ancestral customs and institutions are crumbling away, and both the spiritual and temporal worlds are darkened by the shadow of change." In this context the unchanged and seemingly unchanging world of the East held a special attraction.

To Alexandre Dumas, writing four years later, the "strange and primitive world" of the desert, "the counterpart of which is found only in the Bible, […] seemed to have just come from the hand of God."[3] Oppenheim's contemporary and occasional correspondent, Alois Musil, the learned cousin of the great Austrian writer, relates in 1908 that he was drawn to study the tribes of Arabia Petraea because the conditions of

---

3   Lytton and Dumas quoted in James C. Simmons, *Passionate Pilgrims. English Travellers in the World of the Desert Arabs*, pp. 94–99. The Austrian writer Hermynia Zur Mühlen (1883–1951), who spent much time in her youth in North Africa and the Middle East with her diplomat father before she renounced her aristocratic background and became a Communist, had a more ambivalent response: on the one hand the Orient represented, for her too, sunlight, clarity, spontaneity and exuberance, in contrast to the darkness, meanness, and hypocrisy of the European world; on the other hand it was also marked by violence and age-old superstitions and fanaticisms; see her memoir, *Ende und Anfang* (Berlin: S. Fischer, 1929), pp. 94–95 *et passim* (Engl. trans. *The End and the Beginning* [Cambridge: Open Book Publishers, 2010], available at: http://www.openbookpublishers.com/product/65).

life there closely resembled those of Biblical times.⁴ Oppenheim himself noted with admiration that "das Leben der Beduiner ist im wesentlichen heute nicht anders als es uns von den Dichtern und Geschichtsschreibern der altarabischen Zeit vorgeführt wird. Wie die Wüstensteppe seit Jahrtausenden dieselbe geblieben ist, so auch der Beduine [...] von Europas Kultur noch unbeleckt" ["the life of the Bedouins is essentially no different today from what is presented to us in the works of the classical Arabic poets and historians. Just as the desert steppe has remained the same for thousands of years, so has the Bedouin remained unaffected by the culture of Europe"].⁵ The hero of John Buchan's 1916 novel *Greenmantle* was expressing a common view when he told the mysterious and dangerous German agent Hilda von Einem that, in the decades before the outbreak of war in 1914,

> the world, as I see it, had become too easy and cushioned. Men had forgotten their manhood in soft speech, and imagined that the rules of their smug civilisation were the laws of the universe. But that is not the teaching [...] of life. We had forgotten the greater virtues, and we were becoming emasculated humbugs whose gods were our own weaknesses. Then came war, and the air was cleared. Germany, in spite of her blunders and her grossness, stood forth as the scourge of cant. She had the courage to cut through the bonds of humbug and to laugh at the fetishes of the herd.

---

4   Alois Musil, *Arabia Petraea* (Vienna: Alfred Hölder, 1908), vol. 3 ("Ethnologische Reisebericht"), Vorwort, p. v. Musil later published an important 700-page scholarly study of the Bedouins, *The Manners and Customs of the Rwala Bedouins* (New York: American Geographical Society and Czech Academy of Sciences and Arts, 1928).

5   Max Freiherr von Oppenheim, with the collaboration of Erich Bräunlich and Werner Caskel, *Die Beduinen* (Leipzig: Otto Harrassowitz, 1939), vol. 1, p. 26. See also Gabriele Teichmann, "Grenzgänger zwischen Orient und Okzident. Max von Oppenheim 1860–1946," in Gabriele Teichmann and Gisela Völger, eds., *Faszination Orient. Max von Oppenheim—Forscher, Sammler, Diplomat* (Cologne: DuMont, 2001), p. 52: "Was Max von Oppenheim seeking—assuredly not only that—a bright world of harmony and beauty? In his homeland, at any rate, society had been thrust into a historically unprecedented transformation by the industrial revolution which had brought mass migrations of labour, the disappearance of traditions, technical progress that provoked both wonder and anxiety, a fraying of the bonds of religion, and challenges to the old elites from political parties and trades unions—in short a spirit of fundamental change and unrest. In the Orient, in contrast, Oppenheim could imagine himself in a world in which age-old models were still being followed and history seemed, as it were, to have stood still." At least on this point, Oppenheim and Johann Heinrich Count Bernstorff, who was German Consul-General in Cairo during part of Oppenheim's appointment as special attaché there and who did not appreciate Oppenheim's provocations of the British or the memos sent over his head to Berlin, were in agreement. "The Orient seems eternally unchanged," Bernstorff wrote in his memoirs, "in spite of the efforts and activities of native and foreign governments. [...] All innovations do but touch the surface." (*Memoirs of Count Bernstorff*, trans. Eric Sutton [New York: Random House, 1936], p. 34.)

> Therefore I am on Germany's side. But I came here for another reason. I know nothing of the East, but as I read history it is from the desert that the purification comes. When mankind is smothered with shams and phrases and painted idols a wind blows out of the wild to cleanse and simplify life. The world needs space and fresh air. The civilisation we have boasted of is a toy-shop and a blind alley, and I hanker for the open country.

The hero characterizes his own words as "confounded nonsense" invented to trick his interlocutor. But only a few pages later, another of the novel's heroes makes a very similar and—the reader is meant to believe—authentic claim to explain why he is deeply attracted to Islam. He rejects, as a decadent version of the true Orient, the voluptuous, feminized image of the "Orient" propagated by the art of Ingres, Delacroix, Gérôme, Chassériau, and a host of less well known painters, as well, in some measure, as by the writings of some widely read historians. In the work of Edgar Quinet and his friend Jules Michelet, for instance, the "Orient" was represented as the origin, the body, the female, the secret of whose infinite fecundity it is the task of the male to penetrate, transform into knowledge, and make subservient to "higher" intellectual and spiritual ends. The true Orient, however, Buchan's character maintains, is, on the contrary, austere and masculine—not the fetid swamp of Michelet or of the Swiss scholar and investigator of "oriental" matriarchy, J.J. Bachofen, but the arid, bone-dry desert, the home of the fearless and restless Bedouin:

> The West knows nothing of the true Oriental. It pictures him as lapped in colour and idleness and luxury and gorgeous dreams. But it is all wrong. The *Kâf* he yearns for is an austere thing. It is the austerity of the East that is its beauty and its terror ... It always wants the same things at the back of its head. The Turk and the Arab came out of big spaces, and they have the desire of them in their bones. They settle down and stagnate, and by the by they degenerate into that appalling subtlety which is their ruling passion gone crooked. And then comes a new revelation and a great simplifying. They want to live face to face with God without a screen of ritual and images and priestcraft. They want to prune life of its foolish fringes and get back to the noble bareness of the desert. Remember, it is always the empty desert and the empty sky that cast their spell over them—these, and the hot, strong, antiseptic sunlight which burns up all rot and decay ... it isn't inhuman. It's the humanity of one part of the human race. [...] There are times when it grips me so hard that I'm inclined to forswear the gods of my fathers![6]

---

6 John Buchan, *Greenmantle*, ed. Kate Macdonald (Oxford and New York: Oxford University Press, 1993; 1st edn 1916), pp. 179, 182–83.

As is well known, a good number of Westerners did forswear the gods of their fathers, and openly or secretly converted to Islam. Others—Jean-Louis Burckhardt, even Kaiser Wilhelm II—were rumoured to have converted.

Fascination with a society seemingly still free of the constraints of "civilization" and still governed by a shared traditional code of behaviour underlies the admiration for the Bedouins that Max von Oppenheim shared with many of his predecessors and contemporaries—albeit not, to be sure, with all travellers to the Near and Middle East.[7] Even the sober Dane, Carsten Niebuhr, noted with admiration that the Bedouins are "passionately fond of liberty."[8] Jean-Louis Burckhardt, not given to exaggeration of any kind, but still susceptible to Enlightenment and early Romantic ideals, found the Bedouins, in comparison with the European peoples, "with all their faults, one of the noblest nations with which I ever had an opportunity of becoming acquainted." Jean-Louis seems to have viewed them as a kind of Swiss (or Scottish Highlanders) of the desert, free of the corrupting influence of courts and cities. Compared to "their neighbours the Turks, [...] the Bedouins appear to still greater advantage," the young Swiss wrote in his plain and lucid English.

---

7   The half-Jewish Jesuit, William Gifford Palgrave, broke early on with the prevailing admiration for the Bedouins. Relatively rare among the travellers of his day, he far preferred "the Arabs of inhabited lands and organized governments" to the "nomades of this desert." Though "these populations are identical in blood and tongue," the difference between them is comparable to that "between a barbarous Highlander and an English gentleman." (*Personal Narrative of a Year's Journey through Central and Eastern Arabia (1862–63)*, 5th edn [London: Macmillan, 1869; 1st edn 1865], p. 17.) Half a century later, similar views were expressed by Oppenheim's contemporary, the Oriental scholar Martin Hartmann, a champion of progress, modernisation, and free thought and of the efforts of some Muslims to embrace these. In a letter to his friend, the eminent Hungarian Orientalist Ignaz Goldziher, Hartmann poured scorn on the University of Groningen Professor Tjitze de Boer's *History of Philosophy in Islam* (London: Luzac and Co., 1903), now something of a classic: "The opening is shockingly naïve: 'In older time (how old? 1000 years ago? 3000 years ago?), the Arabian desert (unknown to me, except for the Nefud...!) was the roaming-ground of independent (really? mostly this 'independence' looked pretty wretched) Bedouin tribes. With <u>free</u> and <u>healthy minds</u>,' etc.!!! These dirty disease-ridden scoundrels were of free and sound mind!!—i.e. they would sell themselves to anyone for a few pennies and were so 'healthy' that they devoured each other, when they could, over any stranger who came their way. This kind of naivety, nurtured by our drawing-room Arabists, who know nothing of the real world, should no longer be found today in the work of a serious writer." (Martin Hartmann to I. Goldziher, 12 April 1904, in "*Machen Sie doch unseren Islam nicht gar zu schlecht." Der Briefwechsel der Islamwissenschaftler Ignaz Goldziher und Martin Hartmann 1894–1914*, ed. Ludmila Hanisch [Wiesbaden: Harrassowitz, 2000], pp. 210–11.)

8   *Travels through Arabia and other Countries in the East*, trans. Robert Heron, 2 vols. (Edinburgh: G. Mudie, 1792), vol. 2, p. 172.

The influence of slavery and of freedom upon manners cannot any where be more strongly exemplified than in the characters of these two nations. The Bedouin, certainly, is accused of rapacity and avarice, but his virtues are such as to make ample amends for his failings; while the Turk, with the same bad qualities as the Bedouin, (although he sometimes wants the courage to give them vent,) scarcely possesses any one good quality. Whoever prefers the disorderly state of Bedouin freedom to the apathy of Turkish despotism, must allow that it is better to be an uncivilised Arab of the Desert, endowed with rude virtues, than a comparatively polished slave like the Turk, with less fierce vices, but few, if any, virtues. The complete independence that the Bedouins enjoy has enabled them to sustain a national character. Whenever that independence was lost by them, or at least endangered by their connexion with towns and cultivated districts, the Bedouin character has suffered a considerable diminution of energy, and the national laws are no longer strictly observed.[9]

To later nineteenth- and early twentieth-century travellers also, such as Lady Jane Digby, Richard Burton, Lady Anne Blunt, and finally T.E. Lawrence ("Lawrence of Arabia") the people of the desert, unlike the urban Arabs, seemed unspoiled by civilization—though these admirers appear to have thought of them less in terms of the "noble savage" of the Enlightenment or Burckhardt's free and democratic Swiss mountain people, than, in more conservative vein, as aristocrats of the spirit, a kind of "natural gentlemen," the polar opposite of the undifferentiated masses created in Europe by urbanization, industry, and democratic politics.[10] Oppenheim himself used the English term when he noted that "Angeboren ist dem Beduinen eine gewisse Vornehmheit des Benehmens. [...] Jeder Einzelne benimmt sich wie ein Gentleman, wenn er, der altarabischen Verpflichtung zur Gastfreundlichkeit folgend, in seinem Zelt einen Gast empfängt"[11] ["A certain aristocratic demeanor is natural to the Bedouin. [...] Every individual behaves like a gentleman when,

---

9 John Lewis Burckhardt, *Notes on the Bedouins and Wahabys*, published by authority of the Association for Discovering the Interior of Africa, 2 vols. (London: Henry Colburn and Richard Bentley, 1831), vol. 1, p. 358.
10 See Lady Ann Blunt, *Bedouin Tribes of the Euphrates*, ed. W[ilfrid]. S[cawen]. B[lunt], (New York: Harper and Brothers, 1879) and *A Pilgrimage to Najd, the Cradle of the Arab Race*, 2 vols. (London: John Murray, 1881), esp. vol. 1, pp. 408-17. See also, in note 21 below, Benjamin Disraeli on the desert Arabs and the original desert Jews as "an aristocracy of Nature." William Gifford Palgrave appears to have been exceptional in far preferring the urban Arabs to those of the desert.
11 Dr. Max Freiherr von Oppenheim, "Bericht über seine Reise durch die Syrische Wüste nach Mosul." Offprint from *Verhandlungen der Gesellschaft für Erdkunde zu Berlin*, 1894, no. 4 (Berlin: Druck von W. Pormetter, 1894), 18 pp. (p. 15).

in accordance with the age-old Arab obligation to offer hospitality, he receives a guest in his tent."]

It could be that, in Oppenheim's case, admiration of the Bedouins, along perhaps with interest in the Middle East in general, was not unconnected with insecurity about his own place in a society that both admitted him to its ruling elite and, as we shall see, excluded him from it on account of his part-Jewish background. As a traveller in the Middle East and in Africa, and subsequently as an agent of the *Auswärtiges Amt*, he unflaggingly promoted Germany's political and economic interests in the Islamic world. "Wenn ich auf irgend eine Weise deutsch-patriotischen Interessen förderlich sein könnte," he wrote to his early mentor, the Africa explorer Gerhard Rohlfs, "so würde dies zu erreichen mein heissestes Bestreben sein"[12] ["If I could promote Germany's national interests in any way, it would be my most fervent wish to do so."] His enthusiasm for the Bedouins may well have been in some measure at least, another expression of his determination to be and be seen as undivided in his identification with and loyalty to Germany, for his Bedouins are portrayed in the first volume of his monumental four-volume study of them (1939–1946) — the volume to which his contribution, as distinct from that of his collaborators Erich Bräunlich and Werner Caskel, was greatest — with traits that recall both the ideal German of extreme conservative circles in the Wilhelminian era and, in 1939, the ideal German of the National Socialists. They are, we are told, pure, fearless, unspoiled by "civilization": "ein Herrenvolk, urwüchsig, primitiv, wild und kriegerisch" ["a master race, unspoiled, rooted, fierce, and warlike"]. In addition, the Bedouin is described in terms all too familiar to the German reader of 1939 as "unendlich stolz auf die Reinheit seiner Abstammung, die er hütet und pflegt. Nur die Beduinen

---

12 Cit. Wilhelm Treue, "Max Freiherr von Oppenheim. Der Archäologe und die Politik," *Historische Zeitschrift*, 209 (1969): 37–74 (p. 45). Cf. Gabriele Teichmann, "Fremder wider Willen — Max von Oppenheim in der wilhelminischen Epoche," in Eckart Conze, Ulrich Schlie, Harald Seubert, eds., *Geschichte zwischen Wissenschaft und Politik: Festschrift für Michael Stürmer zum 65. Geburtstag* (Baden-Baden: Nomos, 2003), pp. 231–48: "Dem aus jenem Krieg [against France, 1870–1971] hervorgegangenen Kaiserreich zu dienen, dessen Macht zu mehren, war eines der bestimmenden Lebensthemen Max von Oppenheims, das er in verschiedenen Variationen spielte — als Orientforscher und Archäologe, als Diplomat und Propagandist" (p. 231). On changes in German interest in the Near and Far East in the new circumstances of the Second German Empire, see Suzanne Marchand, *German Orientalism in the Age of Empire* (Washington, D.C.: German Historical Institute and Cambridge: Cambridge University Press, 2009), pp. 212–27, 333–67 *et passim*.

sind für ihn *aṣīl* (reinblütig). Tief eingewurzelt ist ihm der Glaube an die verbindende und verpflichtende Macht des Blutes" ["infinitely proud of the purity of his descent, which he watches over and is careful to preserve. Only Bedouins are *aṣīl* [of pure blood] in his eyes. Belief in the binding and commanding power of blood is deeply rooted in him"]. Not perhaps without some bearing on the author's own situation as the son of an "Aryan" and patrician German mother, emphasis is also placed on the important role in their racial make-up that the Bedouins attribute to the mother: "High value is placed on purity of descent not only on the father's side but on that of the mother too. Moreover, it is not only racial purity that counts. Attention is also paid to nobility of descent. Even the greatest warriors of ancient Arabia [...] suffered on account of a mother's descent from a tribe held in low esteem, or even a black woman. To this very day the pure-blooded Bedouin (*aṣīl*) does not take a wife from any tribe deemed not of pure blood or not of noble blood."[13] In the eyes of one of Oppenheim's younger friends and associates, the Breslau Professor of Oriental Philology and translator of the *Gilgamesh* (1911) Arthur Ungnad, there was indeed such a remarkable similarity of the pure Semite to the pure German that he was prepared, in 1923, to entertain the hypothesis of their having been originally one *Volk*:[14]

---

13   *Die Beduinen*, vol. 1, pp. 26, 27. Oppenheim probably knew of the determining role Jewish tradition attributes to the mother in the definition of a Jew. By Jewish standards, he was not Jewish at all, not simply because he had been baptised, but because his mother was a Catholic.

14   The modern reader may be surprised to learn that this was by no means an outlandish position at the time. A lively debate pitted scholars who argued that the Indo-Germanic and Semitic language families were related and had a common origin against those, like Ernest Renan, who rejected that view. Renan, however, argued in favor of the "unité primitive" of the Indo-Germanic and Semitic "races," notwithstanding that the two languages were, in his opinion, completely distinct. "La race sémitique et la race indo-européenne, examinées au point de vue de la physiologie, ne montrent aucune différence essentielle; elles possèdent en commun et à elles seules le souverain caractère de la beauté. [...] Il n'y a donc aucune raison pour établir, au point de vue de la physiologie, entre les Sémites et les Indo-Européens une distinction de l'ordre de celle qu'on établit entre les Caucasiens, les Mongols et les Nègres. [...] L'étude des langues, des littératures et des religions devait seule amener à reconnaitre ici une distinction que l'étude du corps ne révélait pas. Sous le rapport des aptitudes intellectuelles et des instincts moraux, la différence des deux races est sans doute beaucoup plus tranchée que sous le rapport de la ressemblance physique. Cependant, même à cet égard, on ne peut s'empêcher de ranger les Sémites et les Ariens dans une même catégorie. Quand les peuples sémitiques sont arrivés à se constituer en société régulière, ils se sont rapprochés des peuples indo-européens. Tour à tour les Juifs, les Syriens, les Arabes sont entrés dans l'oeuvre de la civilisation générale, [...] ce qu'on ne peut dire

Racially pure Semites, such as may still be found among the Bedouins of the Arabian Desert differ physically only very slightly from people of the Indo-Germanic race, to which we ourselves belong and to which, these days, the misleading name Aryan is given. Stick one of those sons of the desert into the oilskin of a gaunt weather-tanned Nordic fisherman and cover the latter with the picturesque mantle of the Bedouin; the most knowledgeable person will not be able to tell easily which of the two is the Semite and which the European. There are likewise striking linguistic connections between the Semitic and Indo-Germanic races. Everything suggests that the hypotheses, according to which the original homeland of the Semites was Arabia or even Africa, do not hold up. It is far more likely that in distant times, long before any historical records, both peoples formed part of a single people with a single language, probably located in South-Eastern or Central Europe.[15]

In this heroic, aristocratic, and racially pure society of the Bedouins, Oppenheim relates with satisfaction, he was recognized as a German baron and accepted as an equal and a friend. In his writings Oppenheim constantly emphasized the affection, respect, candor, and trust that characterized his relationships with the Bedouins. Unlike many previous travellers, he noted for instance, he did not attempt, by donning a disguise and assuming a Muslim identity, to pass himself off as a Muslim and win acceptance under

---

ni de la race nègre, ni de la race tartare, ni même de la race chinoise, qui s'est créé une civilisation à part. Envisagés par le côté physique, les Sémites et les Ariens ne font qu'une seule race [...]; envisagés par le côté intellectuel, ils ne font qu'une seule famille" (*Histoire générale et système comparé des langues sémitiques*, 3rd edn (Paris: Michel Levy frères, 1863 [1st edn 1855], pp. 490–91). For a good summary of the varying positions in the debate, see Friedrich Delitzsch, *Studien über Indogermanisch-Semitische Wurzelverwandtschaft* (Leipzig: J.C. Hinrichs, 1873), pp. 3–29. Delitzsch, who believed there is a case for a common origin of the two languages and was severely criticized on that account by Renan, criticises in turn Renan's position (a single original race but two original languages) as contradictory (pp. 17–20). Ungnad was clearly on the side of Delitzsch in the debate.

15 Arthur Ungnad, *Die ältesten Völkerwanderungen Vorderasiens: Ein Beitrag zur Geschichte und Kultur der Semiten, Arier, Hethiter und Subaräer* (Breslau: Im Selbstverlag des Verfassers, 1923), pp. 4–5. Under the influence of the race theories of Hans F.K. Günther who announced that "There is no such thing as a 'Semitic race,' there are only Semitic language-speaking peoples, constituted by varying racial combinations" (*Rassekunde Europas* [Munich: J. F. Lehmann, 1929], p. 100), Ungnad subsequently rejected the idea that there was such a thing as a "pure Semite" or a Semitic "race." "Language is one thing, race another, and 'Semitic' describes a language family, not a race," he declared in *Subartu: Beiträge zur Kulturgeschichte und Völkerkunde Vorderasiens* (Berlin and Leipzig: Walter de Gruyter, 1936): "*Semitisch ist eine Sprache und keine Rasse*" (p. 3).

a false pretense.¹⁶ Deceit and concealment had no place in his relations with the peoples of the region, he insisted; he was known to and respected by his Arab friends as a German aristocrat. Hence the pride and pleasure with which he described, in 1900, how, before witnesses, he was ceremoniously made a "brother" of Faris Pasha, the chief of the Shammari Bedouins, the tribe he most admired.¹⁷ "In Northern Arabia, Syria, and Mesopotamia I often lived with the Bedouins, those free sons of the desert, sharing their tents with them," he recounted later, recalling his sojourns in the Middle East both before and during his years of service as attaché at the German Consulate-General in Cairo. "I had a very good understanding of their soul, their language, and their mores. I had grown fond of these people and they welcomed me everywhere with open arms."¹⁸

Was there somewhere in Oppeneim's account of his relations with the Bedouins a discreet or even unconscious reproach to his own society for treating him as not quite one of theirs? Though in his eagerness not to raise the issue of his Jewish ancestry, he avoided referring to anti-Semitism even in private documents, Oppenheim had to have known it was anti-Semitism that was preventing him from being considered fit for the higher levels of the Imperial diplomatic service and from being fully part of the social group to which he did not doubt that he belonged. Could it be that in presenting a Semitic people in a noble, dignified, even heroic light, not only in his writing but in the many photographs he took of groups and individuals, and in showing how he, as a German, was fully accepted into the select ranks of a tribe highly conscious of its members' genealogies, Oppenheim was creating an inverted mirror-image of his own situation in Wilhelminian Germany?

For him, as for others, the tribal communities of the "free sons of the desert" offered a striking contrast to the modern West—and not only, perhaps, to the fraying of traditional social bonds often attributed to the influence of the Jews, but to a vulgar and undiscriminating modern anti-Semitism that failed to distinguish between noble and base.

---

16 Oppenheim, *Die Beduinen*, vol. 1, pp. 3–4.
17 Max Freiherr von Oppenheim, *Vom Mittelmeer zum Persischen Golf durch den Haurān, die Syrische Wüste und Mesopotamien*, 2 vols. (Berlin: Dietrich Reimer, 1899–1900), vol. 2, pp. 65–66.
18 Max von Oppenheim, "Reisen zum Tell Halaf," (1931) in Gabriele Teichmann and Gisela Völger, eds., *Faszination Orient*, pp. 176–203 (p. 177).

Fig. 2.1 "Bedouin Women." Photograph from Oppenheim's *Vom Mittelmeer zum Persischen Golf* (1899). Dr. Max Freiherr von Oppenheim, *Vom Mittelmeer zum Persischen Golf durch den Haurān, die Syrische Wüste und Mesopotamien* (Berlin: Dietrich Reimer, 1899), vol. 2, facing p. 124.

Fig. 2.2 "Bedouin Minstrels." Photograph from Oppenheim's *Vom Mittelmeer zum Persischen Golf.* Ibid., vol. 2, p. 127.

Fig. 2.3 "Syrian Villagers." Photograph from Oppenheim's *Vom Mittelmeer zum Persischen Golf.* Ibid., vol. 1, facing p. 254.

It has in fact been noted that a disproportionate number of full Jews were drawn to "Oriental" studies in the late nineteenth and early twentieth centuries, some even converting to Islam; and it has been speculated that this interest in Islam, while facilitated in many cases by the scholars' knowledge of a Semitic language and familiarity with non-Christian religious ideas and practices, may well have been a response to Christian anti-Semitism.[19] At the same time it seems also to have been motivated both by rejection of the Talmudic spirit of modern Orthodox Judaism, especially as it had evolved among the Jews of Eastern Europe, and by revulsion at the materialist, commercial culture that, in the eyes of some Jewish orientalists no less than in those of Christian anti-Semites, had come to characterize their contemporary Western fellow-Jews.[20] Disraeli's popular novel *Tancred*—published in German translation in the same year (1847) as it appeared in English—turns modern anti-Semitism on its head by claiming that "It is Arabia alone that can regenerate the world" and that between the early Jews and the Arabs there is no essential difference. The former are Mosaic Arabs and the latter Mohammedan Arabs." "The Arabs are only Jews upon horseback," as Disraeli neatly put it. Jew and Arab alike belong to the same Bedouin race, which, moreover, in contrast to the modern European peoples,

---

19 See Martin Kramer, "Introduction," in *The Jewish Discovery of Islam: Studies in Honor of Bernard Lewis*, ed. Martin Kramer (Tel Aviv: Moshe Dayan Center for Middle Eastern and African Studies, 1999), pp. 1–48; also Bernard Lewis, "The Pro-Islamic Jews," in his *Islam in History: Ideas, Men, and Events in the Middle East* (New York: Library Press, 1973), pp. 123–37. Lewis points to the popularity of a simplified story according to which "the Jews had flourished in Muslim Spain, had been driven from Christian Spain, and had found a refuge in Moslem Turkey," and argues that the Romantic "cult of Spain," the contrast between a persecuting society in medieval Europe and a peaceable kingdom in Islamic Iberia, was a "myth" that had been "invented by Jews in nineteenth-century Europe as a reproach to Christians." See also Susannah Heschel, *Abraham Geiger and the Jewish Jesus* (Chicago: University of Chicago Press, 1998), p. 61.

20 On rejection of Orthodoxy by Jewish scholars of Islam such as Abraham Geiger (1810–1874), Heinrich Graetz (1817–1891), and Ignaz Goldziher (1850–1921), the Hungarian Jew who was one of the founders of the modern historical study of Islam, see John M. Efron, "Orientalism and the Jewish Historical Gaze," in Ivan Davidson Kalmar and Derek J. Penslar, eds., *Orientalism and the Jews* (Hanover and London: University Press of New England, 2005), pp. 80–93. Goldziher Islam was purer and less burdened by remnants of idolatry and superstition than Judaism and Christianity, he sympathized with its struggle against "the dominant European plague," and considered working with the nouveaux-riches Jews on the executive board of the Israelite Congregation of Pest, of which he had been appointed Secretary after failing to obtain a university appointment, an "enslavement" (Raphael Patai, *Ignaz Goldziher and his Oriental Diary: A Translation and Psychological Portrait* [Detroit: Wayne State University Press, 1987], pp. 27–29). On Aby Warburg's association of the wealthy Hamburg Jews with an ostentatious and materialist culture, see Ron Chernow, *The Warburgs* (New York: Random House, 1993), pp. 121–22.

is pure and unmixed.[21] One of the early successes of a contemporary of Oppenheim's, the poet Börries, Freiherr von Münchhausen (a descendant of the celebrated eighteenth-century Baron of the same name), who was subsequently a thoroughly anti-Semitic supporter of the National Socialists, was a volume of poems in praise of the heroic Jews of yore. Münchhausen's *Juda. Gesänge* (Goslar, 1900) was praised by Herzl as a call to modern Jews to return to the heroic virtues of their ancestors and, as such, comparable with Byron's appeal to the modern Greeks.[22] But it is by no means unlikely that Münchhausen himself intended his work to be understood by his readers as a call to modern Germans to return to the heroic way of life of their pure Nordic ancestors. Enthusiasm for the "free sons of the desert," in sum, could function as a critique of anti-Semitism that was itself not incompatible with certain strains in contemporary anti-Semitism.

It remains true that in many accounts of travels in modern Muslim lands, Muslims and Jews are presented as mutually opposed and hostile. Thus in *The Travels of Ali Bey in Morocco, Tripoli, Cyprus, Egypt, Arabia, Syria, and Turkey* (London, 1816), Domingo Badia y Leblich described—not, in his case, without compassion and indignation—the contempt in which the Jews of Morocco were held by the Muslim population and the exclusions and humiliations to which they were subject.[23] And in general, Westerners who were drawn to the Arabs and to Islam because of their primitive virtues tended to see Jews from the angle of nineteenth-century anti-Semitism, that is, as rootless and devious harbingers of a destabilizing modernity.

---

21 Benjamin Disraeli, *Tancred* (London and Edinburgh: R. Brimley Johnson, 1904), p. 299. In *Coningsby* (1844) Disraeli had traced the ancestry of the character of Sidonia, whom many readers associated with a member of the Rothschild banking family, to the reconverted "New Christians" of Spain and behind them to the Jews of Arabia. "Sidonia and his brethren could claim a distinction which the Saxon and the Greek and most of the Caucasian nations have forfeited. The Hebrew is an unmixed race. Doubtless among the tribes who inhabit the bosom of the Desert, progenitors alike of the Mosaic and the Mohammedan Arabs, blood may be found as pure as that of the descendants of the Scheik Abraham. But the Mosaic Arabs are the most ancient, if not the only, unmixed blood that dwells in cities" and "an ummixed race [...] are the aristocracy of Nature." (*Coningsby* [Teddington, Middlesex: The Echo Library, 2007], p. 159; see Minna Rozen's essay on Disraeli in Martin Kramer, ed., *The Jewish Discovery of Islam*, pp. 49–75; and Georg Brandes, *Lord Beaconsfield: a study* [New York: Charles Scribner's, 1880], pp. 42–43.)

22 See L. Gossman, "Jugendstil in Firestone: The Jewish Illustrator E.M. Lilien (1874–1925)," *Princeton University Library Chronicle*, 66 (2004): 11–78 (pp. 33–40).

23 *The Travels of Ali Bey in Morocco, Tripoli, Cyprus, Egypt, Arabia, Syria, and Turkey*, 2 vols. (London: Longman, Hurst, Orme and Brown, 1816), vol. 1, pp. 33–35; see also the extensive documentation in Bat Ye'Or, *The Dhimmi: Jews and Christians under Islam* (Rutherford, Madison, Teaneck: Fairleigh Dickinson University Press, 1985; [orig. French edn, Paris: Editions Anthropos, 1980]), especially pp. 291–385.

Richard Burton, for instance, the author of the hugely popular *Personal Narrative of a Pilgrimage to Al-Medinah and Meccah* (1855–1856), refrained from publishing *The Jew, The Gypsy and El Islam*—in which his account of the Jews is said to be partly based on his experiences as British Consul in Damascus (1869–1871)—after "an influential friend who was highly placed in the official world advised against it" for as long as Burton remained in government service, "owing to the anti-Semitic tendency of the book" and thus the risk of giving offence to the "powerful Jews of England." The editor of the posthumously published 1898 edition, W.H. Wilkins, omitted an Appendix on alleged "Human Sacrifice among the Sephardim"—a rehash by Burton of the so-called "Damascus Affair" of 1840 in which, in a revival of ancient blood libel charges, several distinguished members of the Jewish community of Damascus had been accused and convicted of having abducted and murdered a Catholic priest. Wilkins conceded, however, that even without the defamatory appendix the tone of the book was "anti-Semitic," as indeed the section on the Jews assuredly is, in comparison with the favourable presentation of the Gypsies and, especially, of "El Islam."[24]

Following a suggestion of Arthur Ungnad, who had come under the influence of the race researcher Hans F. K. Günther (known as "race-Günther"),[25] Oppenheim himself came to consider the Jews a mixed race, composed partly of invading Semites and partly of the Subaraean people among whom they allegedly settled. The Bedouins, whom he so admired, he considered, in contrast, "pure Semites."[26] The Bedouins thus represented for him what the ancient Jews had represented for Münchhausen, and there could thus no longer be any question of praise of the Bedouins' serving as a disguised critique of popular anti-Semitism.

---

24 Richard F. Burton, *The Jew, The Gypsy and El Islam*, ed. W. H. Wilkins (Chicago and New York: Herbert S. Stone & Co., 1898), pp. vii–x.

25 According to Günther, "a series of false ideas has been spread about the Jews. Thus they are supposed to belong to a Semitic race. But there is no such race. There are only peoples of varying racial composition speaking Semitic languages. The Jews themselves are supposed to constitute a 'Jewish race.' That is also false. The most superficial observation discovers people looking quite different from each other among the Jews. The Jews are supposed to constitute a single religious community. That is equally a most superficial error. For there are Jews of all the major European faiths and even among those most committed to a *völkisch* idea of the Jew, i.e. the Zionists, there are many who do not subscribe to Mosaic doctrines. [...] The Jews are a people, and, like other peoples, they belong to different confessions, and, like other peoples, they are an amalgam of different races..." (*Rassenkunde Europas*, 3rd edn [Munich: J. F. Lehmann, 1929; 1st edn 1926], pp. 100–04).

26 M. von Oppenheim, *Tell Halaf: Eine neue Kultur im ältesten Mesopotamien* (Leipzig: Brockhaus, 1931), pp. 44–45.

Oppenheim's attitude to the Jewish element in his background is a topic to which we shall have to return in the section of our study devoted to his situation, as a *"Mischling"* (i.e. not a pure "Aryan") under National Socialism. For the moment, we can at least safely affirm that, at a time when Germany was vigorously pursuing a close political, military, economic, and cultural association with the Ottoman Empire—to such an extent that both the official and unofficial German responses to the massacres of Armenian Christians in the mid-1890s, in contrast to the outraged popular and official responses in most European countries, were strikingly restrained[27]— Oppenheim's warm relations with the Muslim Near East were in themselves fully consonant with his German patriotism. An emergent new Turkey was widely seen as the creation of German advisers in economics and finance, in the military, in engineering, and even in culture, prompting a close associate of Oppenheim's in his later wartime activities to exclaim, after ushering a group of Ottoman dignitaries around Germany: *"That*'s what the Turks are like? So cultivated and clever, so imposing and simpatico, so European, *ja* – so German!"[28] At one of the high points of German-Turkish relations, Sultan Abdul Hamid II himself noted "une certaine analogie de caractère entre nous et les Allemands"—in contrast to the French, who, he claims, are closer to the Greeks—"et c'est là sans doute," he added, "une des raisons qui nous attirent vers eux."[29] On his side, as is well known, Kaiser Wilhelm II professed profound sympathy with the world's Muslims and in a famous speech at the tomb of Saladin in 1898 declared himself their protector.

---

27 See especially Vahakn N. Dadrian, *German Responsibiity in the Armenian Genocide: A Review of the Historical Evidence of German Complicity* (Watertown, MA: Blue Crain Books, 1996), pp. 8–15, and Margaret Lavinia Anderson, "'Down in Turkey, far away': Human Rights, the Armenian Massacres, and Orientalism in Wilhelmine Germany," *Journal of Modern History*, 79 (2007): 80–111.

28 Ernst Jäckh, "Der Gentleman des Orients," *Reclams Universum*, 29, no. 7 (1912), cit. Margaret Lavinia Anderson, "'Down in Turkey, far away," *Journal of Modern History*, 79 (2007), pp. 97, 108. On an alleged "affinity between the Germanic and Islamic mind," see Hichem Djaït, *Europe and Islam*, trans. Peter Heinegg (Berkeley/Los Angeles/London: University of California Press, 1985), pp. 78–79 et passim.

29 Ali Merad, ed., *L'Empire Ottoman et l'Europe, d'après les "Pensées et souvenirs" du Sultan Abdul-Hamid II* (Paris: Editions Publisud, 2007). This volume consists of 143 pp. of introduction and notes and a reprint (222 pp. separately numbered) of the original text of Abdul Hamid's memoirs—*Avant la Débâcle de la Turquie. Pensées et souvenirs de l'ex-Sultan Abdul-Hamid, recueillis par Ali Yahbi Bey* (Paris and Neuchâtel: Attinger Frères, 1914). These "reflections and recollections," dating from different periods of his reign, were supposedly communicated by the Sultan to his close friends around 1909, during the time of his banishment by the Young Turks to Salonika. The passage cited is on pp. 207–08 of the 2007 reprint of the 1914 text. The text was later translated into Turkish as *Siyasi Hatiratim* (Istanbul, 1974) and Arabic (Beirut, 1977).

In 1883, after Max had obtained a law degree, Albert von Oppenheim permitted his son to undertake a journey to the "Orient," having apparently reconciled himself to the fact that his brother Eduard's son, Simon Alfred (1864–1932), would most probably take over the direction of the bank instead of Max. Thus in the winter of 1883–1884 Max von Oppenheim, aged 23, got to accompany his "uncle," Heinrich von Kusserow (the son of Salomon Oppenheim jr.'s daughter Eva and the Prussian Lieutenant-General Ferdinand von Kusserow), a strong advocate in German government circles of an aggressive colonial policy, to Athens, Smyrna, and Constantinople. In 1886 he spent six months in Morocco on what he describes as a *Forschungsreise* [research trip], and he learned Arabic. He himself outlines the subsequent development of his career until 1909 in the first volume (1939) of his book on the Bedouins. It is obvious even from this brief narrative—on which we shall expand somewhat in the following chapters—that Oppenheim's activity as a scholar and his activity as an agent of the German government were always closely conjoined:

> In 1892 I was able to begin pursuing my scholarly activities in the Orient on a larger scale. With the ethnographer Wilhelm Joest, a fellow-citizen of Cologne, I travelled from Morocco right across North Africa. At the end of the trip I stopped for seven months in Cairo, where I lodged in an Arab house in the native quarter. Here I lived exactly as the local Muslims did in order to develop my fluency in the Arabic language and to study thoroughly the spirit of Islam and the customs and manners of the native inhabitants. My plan was to prepare myself in this way for further expeditions that would lead me into the Eastern part of the Arab world.
>
> In the spring of 1893, my path led me to Damascus. From here I set out on my first truly major research trip in the Near East. It is narrated in my two-volume book *Vom Mittelmeer zum Persischen Golf durch den Haurān und die Syrische Wüste* [1899–1900].
>
> On matters concerning the Bedouins, I could count, throughout the expedition, on a very good adviser, namely Manṣūr Naṣr, a nephew of Sheikh Midjwel el Meṣrab [...] the husband of Lady Digby, the beautiful Englishwoman, who has become celebrated because of her unusual career. After an adventurous life at various European courts, she was on a journey from Damascus to Palmyra in the year 1853, when she fell in love with and married Sheikh Midjwel. To him, in contrast to her earlier European husbands and lovers, she remained faithful. She spent six months out of every year sharing the life of the desert with him, until she died, in August 1881, in her house in Damascus.
>
> As early as this 1893 trip I was able to collect much material on the Bedouins. [...] In the course of this expedition I came to love the wild, unconstrained life of the sons of the desert. [...] In Cairo I had already

become accustomed to eating with my fingers (one may use only those of the right hand), as was still then the practice in the Cairene middle classes, instead of with a knife and fork. On the 1892 expedition, that had naturally been how I ate with the Bedouins, both when I was their guest and when they were my guests. By sharing their way of life in the saddle and in the tent, I acquired ever greater knowledge of their ways. They felt that I was well disposed toward them and that I understood their customs and peculiarities. Hence, they were also well disposed toward me and readily answered any question I put to them. [...]

The return journey from Mesopotamia took me by way of the Persian Gulf and India to our then young and beautiful colony of East Africa. I made an expedition into the interior, in the course of which I acquired an extensive piece of land in Usambara. This was later turned into plantations [*in footnote*: "by the *Rheinische Handel-Plantagen-Gesellschaft*,[30] which here successfully cultivated first the coffee bean, and then, after the coffee worm made its appearance, sisal—until this flourishing plantation was lost to Germany as a consequence of the World War."] [...]

From there I returned to Cairo, where in early 1894 I met Zuber Pasha who, by hunting for men to sell as slaves, had succeeded in establishing a large principality. As he began to become too strong, however, Khedive Ismail [the ruler of Egypt, nominally subject to the Ottoman Sultan in Constantinople] enticed him to Cairo where he detained him in a beautiful palace, which was like a gilded cage. From Zuber Pasha, I obtained extraordinarily interesting information about one of his former generals named Rabeh, who had refused to capitulate to the Egyptians and had moved westwards from the Nile valley with a large number of his former soldiers and their families.

Back in Germany, I wrote up a report on this, as well as on other things I had learned in Cairo about the area around Lake Chad and about the Muslim order of the Senussi, which was of great importance not only from a religious but also from a political standpoint. This report led the *Auswärtiges Amt* to ask me, in the context of our rivalry with France and England, to lead a German expedition into the hinterland of the Cameroons in order to acquire the area up to Lake Chad for Germany. [...]

---

30 Immediately on his return from Africa, Oppenheim had contacted his cousin Simon Alfred and some other Cologne entrepreneurs about exploiting the East Africa territory commercially. This led in 1895, in line with earlier colonial investments by the Oppenheim Bank, to the founding of the *Rheinische Handel-Plantagen-Gesellschaft*. For Oppenheim, patriotism and business, like patriotism and scholarship, went hand in hand (see below, Pt. 1, Ch. 6). The property, which made Oppenheim "Herr eines Fürstentums [...], das grösser war als Reuss ältere und jüngere Linie zusammengenommen" ["lord of a principality (...) larger than Reuss—that of the older and that of the younger line together"], was acquired from the native tribal chief Kipanga for a bottle of schnapps and some 700 marks (Gabriele Teichmann, "Fremder wider Willen," in Eckart Conze, Ulrich Schlie, Harald Seubert, eds., *Geschichte zwischen Wissenschaft und Politik*, p. 233; also *idem*, "Grenzgänger zwischen Orient und Okzident," in *Faszination Orient*, p. 24).

> Our expedition plans had to be abandoned, however. In the competition involving France, England, and Germany the aforementioned Rabeh had moved faster than the European powers. Starting out from the Egyptian Sudan he had led his army from victory to victory, like a black Napoleon, and had seized all the lands south of Wadai [a former kingdom situated between Lake Chad and Darfur] together with the large kingdoms of Bagirmi and Bornu. Nevertheless, his reign was of short duration. He fell in a battle with the French and the empire he founded collapsed. When his lands were divided up by the European colonial powers, my expedition, which was all set to go, became part of the bargaining process. Germany received the so-called "Caprivi-strip" of our Cameroons colony, namely large parts of Bagirmi and Bornu and thereby access to Lake Chad.
>
> From then on I was employed by the *Auswärtiges Amt* and attached to our diplomatic legation in Cairo. From there I was in a position to observe closely all the affairs of the Islamic world. No place was better for this than Cairo. The Egyptian Press, published in the Arabic of the Koran,[31] was of decisive importance for the entire Islamic world from the Atlantic to China. Whereas in Turkey Sultan Abdul Hamid wielded absolute power and did not tolerate the free expression of opinion in the newspapers, Cairo was the resort of all Muslim political refugees, especially those from the Ottoman Empire itself.
>
> But I also managed to establish excellent relations with Sultan Abdul Hamid [... who] asked me to call on him whenever I was in Constantinople, which I regularly did.[32]

By his own characteristically self-promoting account, in short, Oppenheim succeeded in building connections with many different factions and interests in the Muslim world, including both the Sultan and those in the Ottoman Empire who opposed him. He was thus, the reader was to infer, in an excellent position to gather intelligence on behalf of the *Auswärtiges Amt*. He goes on in this retrospective on his career to tell of the "excellent relations" he established through the Sultan with the family of Emir Faisal, who was to become King of Iraq; with Abdul Huda, the Sultan's close adviser and the head of the "widespread Muslim brotherhood of Rifa'ija"; and with many other personalities of the Muslim world, such as one Mohammed Ibn Bessam, from whom he learned a great deal about "the development of power relations in central Arabia in the last [i.e. nineteenth] century and down to the First World War." Perhaps Oppenheim hoped to emulate Emin Pasha—the Jewish-born

---

31 In contrast to the Turkish press in Constantinople, which was not only printed in Turkish but more subject to censorship by the Ottoman authorities.
32 Oppenheim, *Die Beduinen*, vol. 1, pp. 3–6.

convert Eduard Schnitzer, who had become a national hero in Germany on account of his efforts to develop and promote German power and influence in Africa.

With a few interruptions for short missions to Washington and Paris, Oppenheim spent the years from 1896 until 1909, he relates, in Cairo, where his house "was on the border between the native and the European quarters." The lavish style in which he entertained his guests here, it may be added, was soon the talk of Cairo. Crown Prince Wilhelm of Germany, Duke Carl-Eduard of Saxe-Coburg-Gotha (a cousin of George V of England and subsequently an *Obergruppenführer* in the Nazi SA), Princess Radziwill, John Jacob Astor, and Mrs. Cornelius Vanderbilt were among the prominent figures in European and American society, along with many leading Egyptians and other Muslim notables, who enjoyed his hospitality.[33] Even the British, who, as we shall see, distrusted him deeply, conceded shortly before he left Cairo in 1909 that he was "one of the most popular of Cairo's hosts." In the words of the English-language *Egyptian Gazette*, "It is impossible to describe the charm of the baron's house by comparison, since no comparison exists."[34] Oppenheim's glamorous reputation may well have been enhanced by his habit of taking "temporary wives," of whom apparently there were many. One, to whom he was particularly attached, came to a sad end. In a Cairo bazaar in 1908, it is said, he had the audacity to approach a married Arab woman. As he described her in the memoir he wrote toward the end of his life, she was "very pretty, very young" and made her way to the steam baths with a "swinging, elastic gait," hidden behind a veil and guarded by a muscular eunuch. Oppenheim's relationship with her ended in catastrophe when her husband discovered their affair and killed her.[35]

---

33 Gabriele Teichmann, "Grenzgänger zwischen Orient und Okzident. Max von Oppenheim 1860–1946," in *Faszination Orient*, p. 45.
34 *Egyptian Gazette*, 13 April 1909, cit. ibid., endnote 86, p. 102. On his leaving Cairo in 1910, the *Gazette* again wrote (18 October 1910): "His departure from Egypt will be a great loss to the German Agency. [...] His beautiful house was a byword for hospitality and its doors were always open to every savant that passed through Cairo."
35 See http://www.spiegel.de/international/zeitgeist/0,1518,741928,00.html.

3. Attaché in Cairo: "The Kaiser's Spy"

Oppenheim had been thinking of a career in the German diplomatic service at least since the mid-1880s. In 1887 he submitted a formal application only to have it rejected by Herbert von Bismarck, the son of the great statesman and the current State Secretary for Foreign Affairs. The reasons given to Oppenheim were suitably vague. In a private internal communication, however, von Bismarck was more forthcoming: "I am against it, in the first place because Jews, even when they are gifted, always become tactless and pushy as soon as they get into positions of privilege. Then there is the name. It is far too widely known as Semitic and provokes laughter and mockery. In addition, the other members of our diplomatic corps, the quite exceptional character of which I am constantly working to maintain, would not be happy to have a Jewboy added to their ranks just because his father had been crafty enough to make a lot of money."[1]

A second attempt to enter the diplomatic service in 1891 met with a similar rebuff. Despite strong support from Count Paul von Hatzfeld, then German Ambassador to England and the father of a close friend of Oppenheim's, Hermann von Hatzfeld (who started on his own diplomatic career in 1893), the application was rejected on the grounds that, in the view of Friedrich von Holstein, the powerful head of the political department at the *Auswärtiges Amt*, admitting Oppenheim to the diplomatic service, would open the floodgates to other applicants of similar background. Oppenheim, Holstein wrote to Hatzfeld "has two distinguishing features that up until now have been taken to be disqualifying ['disqualifying' in English in the text]. He is a full Jew (we have plenty of half-Jews) and he is a member of a banker's family. We get many applications from people in this category; they

---

1 Quoted by Gabriele Teichmann, "Grenzgänger zwischen Orient und Okzident. Max von Oppenheim 1860–1946," in *Faszination Orient*, p. 28; also quoted by Martin Kröger, "Mit Eifer ein Fremder—Im Auswärtigen Dienst," ibid., p. 111.

can be rejected only if the decision is made on principle. If an exception is allowed, there is trouble."² The following year Hatzfeld—who, as a Catholic, may have been more inclined than the Protestants Bismarck and Holstein to see the young Oppenheim as a fellow-Catholic rather than a *"Semit"* or a "full Jew," who in any case considered the prevailing anti-Semitism "einen verderblichen Wahnsinn" ["a pernicious insanity"],³ and who very much wanted to give a positive response to his son—came back with a more modest proposal. His "protégé" was planning a "wissenschaftliche Forschungsexpedition" ["a scholarly research trip"] for which his father had provided the funds, and wanted to be able to run it from Cairo. He would be content to be attached in some way to the Consulate-General in Cairo. Surely the most "rabid anti-Semite" ["couragiertester Antisemit"] could not object to that and he, Hatzfeld, would take it as a great "personal favour" if something of the kind could be arranged.⁴ Apparently it could not, for in 1895 Hatzfeld again tried to help his son's friend. In a letter to the newly appointed Chancellor, Prince von Hohenlohe, he emphasized Oppenheim's years of study and impressive knowledge of the Islamic world. In view of the objections that had arisen in some quarters to the Jewish family background of his "protégé," however, he suggested that he be given an appointment "not in the diplomatic service itself but as an attaché assigned on a temporary basis to one of our missions in the Near East." As ambassador in London at the time, Hatzfeld was particularly aware of Anglo-French rivalry in the Muslim Middle East and North

---

2 Letter from Holstein to Hatzfeld, 18 August 1891, in *Botschafter Paul Graf von Hatzfeld: Nachgelassene Papiere 1838–1891*, ed. Gerhard Ebel, 2 vols. (Boppard am Rhein: Harald Boldt, 1976), letter 525, vol. 2, p. 854. The fear expressed by Holstein is, of course, the characteristic fear of anti-Semites: that the Jews will "take over." Years later, Oppen heim's appointment as attaché in Cairo led Holstein to make the same dire prediction: "I am firmly convinced that this case does not concern only one Semite and that more of his ilk will push their way through the breach he has made. At present their community is resigned to the way things are, since it is known that, in general Semites are not accepted—I mean no full Jews. The moment a single one gets in, they will scream bloody murder when others are rejected" (Letter to Eulenburg, 21 July 1898, in *Philipp Eulenburgs Politische Korrespondenz*, ed. John C.G. Röhl, letter 1382, vol. 3, p. 1917). It is interesting to note, in view of Oppenheim's later career under National Socialism and his own sedulous avoidance of any recognition of his Jewish background, that Holstein considered him a "Vollblut-Semit"—a full Jew, not even a "half" or "quarter" one.
3 Letter from Hatzfeld to Holstein 1 July 1892, in *Botschafter Paul Graf von Hatzfeld: Nachgelassene Papiere 1838–1891*, letter 545, pp. 891–93. This letter and the accompanying footnotes clearly demonstrate the sincerity and persistence of Hatzfeld's efforts on behalf of Oppenheim.
4 Ibid.

Africa, especially in Egypt, and may well have been genuinely persuaded that Oppenheim, with his knowledge of Arabic and of Middle Eastern cultures and his many Muslim contacts, could render the *Auswärtiges Amt* valuable service by keeping it well informed and so increasing its leverage in thestruggle for power in the region.[5]

Though anti-Semitism was ingrained in the German Diplomatic Service at the time,[6] the anti-Semites were unable in the end to prevent Oppenheim

---

5 "I have known Baron Oppenheim for a number of years now and have always followed with interest his activity and success in the field of Islamic studies—for which he seems to have a special talent. Unfortunately, reservations appear to have been expressed now—so I have heard—concerning the nature of his position in the Foreign Service. […] As far as I can judge the state of affairs, these reservations have to do with Baron Oppenheim's family background, against which certain prejudices are entertained in some of our circles, and for that reason it is deemed desirable to offer him a position not in the diplomatic service proper, but as an attaché assigned on a temporary basis to one of our missions in the Near East." (Cit. Teichmann, *Faszination Orient*, p. 28) Salvador Oberhaus identifies the addressee of this letter, dated 30 December 1895, as Chancellor Hohenlohe, not Bismarck, as in Teichmann. (S. Oberhaus, *"Zum wilden Aufstand entflammen." Die deutsche Propagandastrategie für den Orient im Ersten Weltkrieg am Beispiel Ägypten* [Saarbrücken: Verlag Dr. Müller, 2007], p. 53, no. 30)

6 See Lamar Cecil, *The German Diplomatic Service, 1871–1914* (Princeton: Princeton University Press, 1976), pp. 95–102; Hans-Jürgen Döscher, *Das Auswärtige Amt im Dritten Reich* (Berlin: Wolf Jobst Siedler, 1987). In Döscher's words: "The majority of German diplomats came from aristocratic families, were Protestants, were well-to-do, held a law degree and had done some service in the military. Toward the end of the Wilhelminian era, representatives of the wealthy bourgeoisie—most with acquired titles of nobility—gained access to the diplomatic service, but the doors remained closed to Jewish or Social Democratic applicants until November 1918. The basic outlook of most diplomats was conservative, with strong strains of anti-liberalism, anti-parliamentarism, and anti-Semitism" (p. 306). It is only fair to note, however, that other European countries were probably not very different from Germany, as the following entry in the diaries (11 July 1930) of Harold Nicolson, in no way an ideological anti-Semite, suggests: "We go on afterwards to the Woolfs [Virginia and Leonard]. Hugh Dalton [a Labour M.P., who was Foreign Office Parliamentary Under-Secretary at the time] is there. I attack the nomination board at the Foreign Office, not on the grounds that it rejects good men, but on the grounds that its very existence prevents good men from coming up for fear they may be ploughed [i.e. failed] for social reasons. The awkward question of the Jews arises. I admit that is the snag. Jews are far more interested in international life than are Englishmen, and if we opened the service it might be flooded by clever Jews. It was a little difficult to argue this point frankly with Leonard there." (Harold Nicolson, *Diaries and Letters 1930–1939* [London: Collins, 1966], p. 53.) Nicolson was more frank in a diary entry fifteen years later (13 June 1945): "Though I loathe anti-Semitism, I do dislike Jews." (*Diaries and Letters: The War Years 1939–1945* [London: Collins, 1967], p.469) For an instructive comparison of anti-Semitism in England and Germany, see Geoffrey G. Field, "Anti-Semitism with the Boots Off," in Herbert A. Strauss, ed., *Hostages of Modernization: Studies of Modern Anti-Semitism 1870–1933/39. Germany, Great Britain, France* (Berlin and New York: Walter de Gruyter, 1993), pp. 294–325. In Field's view, the English elites reject public or political anti-Semitism while retaining considerable tolerance for private anti-Semitism.

from being assigned, in 1896, to a position in the Middle East. They did succeed, however, in preventing him from ever becoming a career diplomat. He was never more than a temporary agent or employee of the *Auswärtiges Amt* and he never held a position with full diplomatic rank.[7] His salary, at 8,000 marks, moreover, was insufficient to maintain adequate diplomatic standing and in fact Oppenheim financed not only his luxurious life-style in Cairo but much of his work for the *Auswärtiges Amt* out of the 30,000 marks he received annually from his father.[8] A later attempt to obtain an appointment to a position at the German Embassy in the United States, which he visited twice, in 1902 and 1904, and where he seems to have had a very good time, met with a similar rebuff. The ambassador would have none of him, referring to his "pushiness," "talkativeness," servility, lavish expenditures, and general reputation for deviousness.[9] These repeated

---

7 His appointment was never seen as anything more than provisional. An *Auswärtiges Amt* note in 1898 conceded that he might be permitted to remain one more year in Cairo, at the Consul-General's specific request, but no longer—"länger aber nicht." (Cit. Martin Kröger, "Mit Eifer ein Fremder. Im Auswärtigen Dienst," in *Faszination Orient*, pp. 106–39 [p. 118]). One of his supporters, the Catholic Count von Metternich, who, as Consul-General in Cairo, considered Oppenheim's services "unentbehrlich" ["indispensable"] tried to have his position in the *Auswärtiges Amt* made permanent, with the title of *Legationsrat* [embassy counsellor] in a memo to the *Auswärtiges Amt* in 1900. The title was conceded, but not the permanent appointment (Kröger, *Faszination Orient*, p. 117; Oberhaus, "Zum wilden Aufstand entflammen," p. 56, notes 40, 41), not even on the condition proposed by Metternich, that it would be "subject to his continuing to perform his duties satisfactorily." (Oberhaus, p. 63) After a short-term posting to the Embassy in Washington, where he investigated how the American experience of using railway construction to open up the West might be applied to the Berlin-Baghdad railway project—this resulted in *Die Entwicklung des Bagdadbahngebietes und insbesondere Syriens und Mesopotamiens unter Nutzanwendung amerikanischer Erfahrungen* (Berlin, 1904)—and where he also informed himself on American scholarship and excavation in the Middle East, Oppenheim expressed interest in 1904 in a more extended two-year appointment as attaché in Washington. Though the Consul-General in Cairo supported this request, while regretting the concomitant loss of his services, it was rejected by the German ambassador in Washington on the grounds that Oppenheim was pushy, servile, sneaky, talked too much, spent too lavishly, and was in general not to be trusted (Kröger, *Faszination Orient*, p. 119). Ambassador Speck von Sternburg's misgivings echo Secretary Herbert von Bismarck's objections to the appointment of Jews of a few years earlier and anticipate later judgments (see note 9 below).

8 Oberhaus, "Zum wilden Aufstand entflammen," p. 56, no. 39. Martin Kröger puts some flesh on these bare bones figures when he contrasts them with the 700 marks a Hamburg dock worker at the time earned in a year ("Max von Oppenheim im Auswartigen Dienst," Lecture. *Historische Gesellschaft* of the Deutsche Bank [June, 2010], available at: http://www.bankgeschichte.de/de/docs/Vortrag_Kroeger.pdf).

9 Kröger, *Faszination Orient*, p. 119. Though apparently not universally shared at the *Auswärtiges Amt*— Oppenheim did have some loyal supporters and friends there—this was the general judgment of his enemies. Even the Young Turks, whose policies he was eagerly promoting, urged the German foreign office to prevent him from returning to

humiliations assuredly did not pass unnoticed in a society as rank-conscious as the Second Reich and Oppenheim could not have been insensitive to them. His vanity or his concern for his image was such, however, that he never alluded to them at any point in his life, not even in the manuscript memoir he left after his death (preserved in the Hausarchiv des Bankhauses Sal. Oppenheim jr. & Cie in Cologne). On the contrary, he tended to transform wish into reality in his own mind by repeatedly referring to "diplomatic" missions in which he was engaged and exaggerating his influence on the Kaiser and in official circles in Berlin. Max von Oppenheim was evidently determined not to acknowledge any crack in the upper-class German identity he claimed for himself. Thus when he undertook a lecture tour of the United States in 1931, in order to present the results of his archaeological digs to American audiences, he asked that he be described in the printed announcement of his lecture as "Dr. Baron Max von Oppenheim, former German Minister Plenipotentiary"[10] — a rather inflated title for a man who had never obtained a permanent position in the *Auswärtiges Amt* or a rank higher than temporary *Legationsrat*.

Though his appointment as an attaché directly answerable to the *Auswärtiges Amt*, rather than as an official member of the German Consulate-General in Cairo, was always temporary (it was humiliatingly subject to renewal each year and carried no specific responsibilities), it did in fact allow Oppenheim greater leeway in cultivating certain contacts — with Egyptian nationalists and nationalists from other Muslim countries, for instance — than would have been possible for a ranking diplomat without seriously straining German relations with Great Britain, the power effectively in control of Egypt at the time.[11] Thus in the first decade of the

---

Constantinople in 1916. The Turkish Foreign Minister complained that he had become "impossible." Wilhelm von Radowitz, a career diplomat who was Embassy Counsellor in Constantinople in 1916, received complaints that he was impetuous and intrusive and trying to ingratiate himself with "awkward flatteries," and in December 1916 Richard von Kühlmann, the new German ambassador to Turkey, told his chiefs in Berlin that "in view of the anti-Oppenheim mood in the ruling Turkish circles, I consider Oppenheim's return to Istanbul inappropriate." (Vahakn N. Dadrian, *German Responsibility in the Armenian Genocide*, p. 65)

10   Enclosure containing announcement and summary description of the lecture, in a letter to Myron Bement Smith, 20 November 1931, Myron Bement Smith papers, the Freer Gallery of Art and Arthur M. Sackler Gallery Archives, Smithsonian Institution, Washington, D.C.

11   This was not always viewed favorably by traditional diplomats. Thus Holstein in a letter to Eulenburg of 21 July 1898 saw Oppenheim's activity as a way of getting around the obstacles his Jewish ancestry placed in the way of his diplomatic career: "Do you know anything about a Freiherr von Oppenheim, a member of the Union-Klub who,

twentieth century, Foreign Secretary Baron von Schoen could respond to British and French complaints about Oppenheim's consorting with Arab nationalists that "Oppenheim is not a member of the diplomatic service and he is only very loosely associated with our Foreign Office."[12] Oppenheim was thus able to report to Berlin on aspects of the situation in the Near East of which the official German delegation could not easily have obtained direct knowledge. As he himself noted in his manuscript memoir of his life, "my reports to the *Auswärtiges Amt* [...] were extraordinarily wide-ranging. My assignment was to keep an eye on movements throughout the entire Islamic world from my base in Cairo. First and foremost, I had to pay close attention to the situation among the natives in Egypt itself and then make the most strenuous efforts to obtain news of all the trends and of all events concerning Muslims in every part of the world."[13]

Oppenheim's house in Cairo was frequented by figures from all areas of Egyptian and Muslim culture and politics. He also travelled a great deal throughout the Middle East and managed to maintain good relations with leaders whose interests were often at variance or even opposed: Sultan Abdul Hamid II in Constantinople, the young Austrian-educated Egyptian Khedive Abbas Hilmi II, the Ottoman High Commissioner in Egypt Ahmed Mukhtar Pasha, the sharif of Mecca Hussein ibn Ali (the father of Faisal), various anti-British Egyptian nationalists such as Shaykh Ali Yusuf (editor of an important Cairo newspaper) and Mustafa Kamil (the founder of the nationalist party), and a circle of Arabs, Syrians,

---

two years ago, was attached to the Consulate-General in Cairo as an 'Oriental specialist' without any more clearly defined official rank? He was to keep an eye on the supposedly powerful ferment in the Islamic world in order to warn Europe in good time of any imminent outbreak. To this end, he was to develop good relations with the native-born people and even join their caravans in order to get a sense, in the great markets of the interior, of the prevailing mood in the Islamic world. That at least was the plan. In fact, p. Oppenheim made about as many caravan trips as I have; in contrast he sent in reports, whenever he had an opportnity, of his conversations with the locals, devoted himself to serving disinguished German travellers as a guide, kept, in addition, an open house for guests, in short did everything needed to make his acceptance into the diplomatic service possible. Of half-Jews we have already had and still have a pretty large number. But so far we have not yet had any full-blooded Semites, such as Mendelssohn, Warschauer, Bleichröder, or Oppenheim." Now, however, he has learned that Oppenheim "will be coming to Berlin, to work, first, at getting himself finally accepted into the diplomatic corps, and, second, at advertising the value of his local knowledge for the journey of his Majesty to Egypt; in short, Oppenheim wants to go along on the trip." (*Philipp Eulenburgs Politische Korrespondenz*, letter 1382, vol. 3, p. 1916).

12 Cit. Kröger, *Faszination Orient*, p. 121.
13 Cit. Oberhaus, "Zum wilden Aufstand entflammen," p. 58.

and Turks who had been enemies of Abdul Hamid and had fled from Turkey to Cairo, not to mention the restless Bedouin chieftains with whom he had established bonds of friendship on earlier journeys to the Middle East. As Oppenheim put it himself in his memoir—picking up on the theme, emphasized in much late nineteenth- and early twentieth-century official German writing on German-Muslim relations, of Germany's distinction as the only European great power that had not attacked or sought to dominate Muslims or occupied Muslim lands—he never regarded his Middle Eastern contacts with the condescension characteristic, according to him, of the British and other Europeans. His Muslim friends, he wrote, in a tone of all too characteristic vanity, "saw in me a man who, despite his elevated position in European society and the respect in which he was held by European diplomats, enjoyed being among them, who did not look down on them as the English and most other Europeans did, who dealt directly with them, as the others could not, and who instead took pleasure in the life they then still lived and was happy to share in it with them. The natural consequence of this was that they opened their hearts to me more and more, as the waves of Cromer's policies toward native Egyptians rose higher and higher, and as ever harsher measures, justified by this or that event, were introduced by the occupying power, but also whenever conversation turned to the attitude of the native-born toward the Khedive, the Turks or any other factor. They knew that I would never betray them."[14] Not without humour, Count Paul von Metternich claimed in 1900 that "with the exception of Lord Cromer [Evelyn Baring, Lord Cromer, British Consul-General in Egypt and effective ruler of the country from 1883 until 1907[15]], because of Oppenheim's special knowledge, I was by far the best

---

14 Cit. Oberhaus, *"Zum wilden Aufstand entflammen,"* p. 59. On Oppenheim's contacts in Egypt, see Tilman Lüdke, *Jihad Made in Germany: Ottoman and German Propaganda and Intelligence Operations in the First World War* (D.Phil. dissertation, University of Oxford, 2001; Münster: LIT, 2005), pp. 70–72.

15 After the United States resumed exports of cotton at the end of the Civil War, the price of cotton, Egypt's staple export, collapsed, and the Khedive was forced to borrow heavily from the European powers. Various international committees set up to oversee the financial situation were replaced in 1879 by an Anglo-French commission that effectively controlled the country's finances and its government. Cromer was British Controller-General from 1879 until Britain took over complete control in 1883. He was ruthless in suppressing every threat to British domination. According to the historian Sayyid-Marsot, "Baring believed that 'subject races' were totally incapable of self-government, that they did not really need or want self-government, and that what they really needed was a 'full belly' policy which kept [the country] quiescent and allowed the élite to make money and so cooperate with the occupying power." (Afaf Lutfi Sayyid-Marsot, *A Short History of Modern Egypt*

informed of my colleagues in Cairo about what was going on in native Egyptian circles."[16]

In a period of growing Anglo-German tension, as Germany sought more and more insistently to secure its "place in the sun," the British were well aware of Oppenheim's activities and contacts, distrusted him, had his movements watched, and soon dubbed him "the Kaiser's spy." Though most of his wide-ranging, unsolicited reports to the *Auswärtiges Amt*—no fewer than 467 between 1896 and 1909, a few running to 100 pages or more—seem to have been simply filed away, some were copied or abstracted and transmitted to the German embassies in Constantinople, London, and Paris, as well as to smaller delegations in places with significant Muslim populations, such as Baghdad, Teheran, Bombay, and Calcutta.[17] Several of them emphasized the allegedly growing influence of Pan-Islamism—a movement intended to unite all Muslims under a single banner in order to defend Islam against the encroachments of the West. These reports, it has been claimed, were seen and much appreciated by Kaiser Wilhelm II.[18]

[Cambridge: Cambridge University Press, 1985], p. 76). Cromer was forced to resign in 1907 as a result of outrage provoked in both Egypt and England by his brutal punishment of those accused of having participated in the Denshawai incident (1906), when a number of British officers out pigeon-shooting accidentally killed an Egyptian woman and were set upon by a crowd. Sir Eldon Gorst was appointed to replace him by the new Liberal Government in London in 1907. He tried to soften the British administration, give more power and influence to the Egyptians, and repair relations with the Khedive Abbas Hilmi II.

16 Cit. Oberhaus, *"Zum wilden Aufstand entflammen,"*, p. 62. Subsequently, as German ambassador in London (1903–1912), Paul Graf Wolff-Metternich zur Gracht won the respect and affection of British policy-makers for his efforts to defuse tensions between London and Berlin. His views did not sit well with Wilhelm II and he was recalled in 1912. In 1915, however, he replaced Wangenheim as Ambassador to Turkey. A year later he was again recalled, largely because of his criticism of Turkish policy toward the Armenians.

17 Kröger, *Faszination Orient*, p. 117. On Oppenheim's reports to the German Foreign Office, see Jacob M. Landau, *The Politics of Pan-Islam: Ideology and Organisation* (Oxford: Clarendon Press, 1990), pp. 96–97 and Ch. 2, notes 136–37.

18 Kröger, *Faszination Orient*, pp. 116, 118; see also Landau, *The Politics of Pan-Islam*, p. 98, and Sean McMeekin, *The Berlin-Baghdad Express: The Ottoman Empire and Germany's Bid for World Power* (Cambridge, MA: Harvard University Press, 2010), pp. 22–23. According to McMeekin, the Kaiser was so taken with Oppenheim that he regularly invited him to dinner whenever Oppenheim was back in Berlin, but this seems hardly likely and may reflect either an exaggerated account, in Oppenheim's memoir, of his relations with the Kaiser or exaggerated British views of Oppenheim's importance. In a report dated "Cairo, December 19" [1914] and entitled "German Intrigue in Egypt. Attempts to Weaken British Power. The Activities of Baron von Oppenheim," the London *Times* special correspondent in Cairo claimed that "the Jewish Baron Max von Oppenheim […] from 1905 to 1908 […] corresponded with the Kaiser over the indignant heads of his official chiefs. From the Kaiser he certainly received signal marks of favour, culminating in an invitation to a 'lunch intime' at Potsdam, to which his chief, Count Bernstorff [the German Consul-General in Cairo 1906–1908], was not invited." (*The Times*, 6 January 1915, p. 7).

One, in particular, dated 5 July 1898, is said to have attracted the Kaiser's special attention. Entitled "Die panislamische Bewegung," it pointed to growing Islamic solidarity in the face of ever expanding encroachments by Western Christian powers on traditionally Muslim lands. In addition, Oppenheim reported, anti-European Sufi brotherhoods were at work in North Africa and Arabia, and messianic movements, such as that of the Mahdi in the Sudan, were inflaming many tribes with "a fanaticism bordering on madness." If Muslims could actually be prepared for holy war, *jihad* would be a mighty weapon with unforeseeable consequences and its proclamation would draw volunteers and money from all over the Muslim world, as had happened in the Sultan's war against Russia in 1877–1878. More than ever, Oppenheim claimed, the Sultan was seen by Muslims the world over as the greatest Islamic ruler. As an ally, he would be invaluable inasmuch as, in the event of a European war, his influence could be used against powers with large numbers of Muslim colonial subjects— such as Britain, France, and Russia. In the words of one modern scholar, "[the] message to the Kaiser was clear: prepare the field and use the Sultan for *jihad* in the colonial territories of potential enemies. Berlin might very well need pan-Islamic fanaticism and the anti-European brotherhoods."[19] It has even been claimed, though most scholars dispute it, that Oppenheim's memorandum inspired Wilhelm II's visits to Istanbul, Damascus, and Jerusalem in the autumn and winter of 1898 and, in particular, the Kaiser's famous speech at the tomb of Saladin in Damascus on 8 December, in

---

19   Wolfgang G. Schwanitz, "Euro-Islam by '*Jihad* Made in Germany'," in Nathalie Clayer and Eric Germain, eds., *Islam in Interwar Europe*, p. 277. See also R.L. Melka, "Max Freiherr von Oppenheim: Sixty Years of Scholarship and Political Intrigue in the Middle East," *Middle Eastern Studies*, 9 (1973): 81–93 (p. 81); Jacob Landau, *The Politics of Panislamism*, pp. 96–98; Gottfried Hagen, "German Heralds of Holy War: Orientalists and applied oriental studies," *Comparative Studies of South Asia, Africa and the Middle East*, 24 (2002): 145–62 (p. 149). Landau (*Politics of Pan-Islam*, p. 97) quotes in similar vein from a memorandum of 26 May, 1908 sent by Oppenheim to Bernhard Heinrich von Bülow, the German State Secretary for Foreign Affairs: "In a great European War, especially if Turkey participates in it against England, one may certainly expect an overall revolt of the Muslims in the British colonies. […] In such a war, […] England would need a large part of its navy and almost its entire army [just] in order to keep its colonies." This appears not to have been an unusual idea in German nationalist circles. Thus the left-leaning nationalist politician and journalist Friedrich Naumann observed in 1899: "It is possible that the world war will break out before the disintegration of the Ottoman Empire. Then the Caliph of Constantinople will once more uplift the standard of the Holy War. The Sick Man [Turkey] will raise himself for the last time to shout to Egypt, the Sudan, East Africa, Persia, Afghanistan and India, 'War against England.' It is not unimportant to know who will support him on his bed when he utters this cry." (Cit. Stephen Casewit, "Background to the Holy War of 1914. Toward an Understanding," *Islamic Quarterly*, 29 [1985]: 220–33 [p. 220], and Gottfried Hagen, "German Heralds of Holy War: Orientalists and Applied Oriental Studies," [p. 149]).

which he declared himself the eternal friend of the 300 million Muslims in the world[20] — a pronouncement that, understandably, did not go down well with the British, given the substantial, often restive Muslim population in India, the jewel in the British Imperial Crown, or with the French and the Russians, given the overwhelmingly Muslim populations in the Russian Caucasus and in French North Africa. Other reports stem from the many side-trips Oppenheim undertook during his twelve-year stint as attaché in Cairo — to Turkey, Lebanon, Syria, Mesopotamia, and Algeria. In 1906, for instance, at a time of acute tension among the European powers over Morocco, he reported on the border area between Algeria and Morocco and on the disposition of French troops in it.[21] The report was mostly devoted

---

20 Fritz Fischer, *Griff nach der Weltmacht. Die Kriegzielpolitik des kaiserlichen Deutschland 1914/18* (Düsseldorf: Droste, 1967; 1st edn 1961), p. 111. Fischer's claim seems to have been accepted by Jacob Landau in *The Politics of Pan-Islam*, p. 98, as well as by Donald McKale in his study of Oppenheim's longtime associate Curt Prüfer, *Curt Prüfer: German Diplomat from the Kaiser to Hitler* (Kent, OH: Kent State University Press, 1987), p. 14, and by Gottfried Hagen, *Die Türkei im Ersten Weltkrieg* (Frankfurt, Bern, New York and Paris: Peter Lang, 1990), p. 31. However, it was disputed by Wilhelm Treue ("Max Freiherr von Oppenheim. Der Archäologe und die Politik," *Historische Zeitschrift*, 209 [1969]: 37–74 [pp. 52–53]) and rejected by Herbert Landolin Müller in his *Islam, ğihād ("Heileger Krieg") und Deutsches Reich* (Frankfurt, Bern, New York and Paris: Peter Lang, 1991) p. 196, note 17, as well as by Hagen in an article published twelve years after his 1990 book (see note 19 above). Similarly, it was noted but no longer endorsed by Donald McKale in work published after his book on Prüfer: "The Kaiser's Spy: Max von Oppenheim and the Anglo-German Rivalry Before and During the First World War," *European History Quarterly*, 27 (1997): 199–219 (p. 201), and *War by Revolution: Germany and Great Britain in the Middle East at the End of World War I* (Kent, Ohio: Kent State University Press, 1998), p. 13. Oppenheim is not even mentioned in Jan Stefan Richter's, *Die Orientreise Kaiser Wilhelms II 1898* (Dissertation, Kiel University, 1996; Hamburg: Kovač, 1997). The disagreement on this particular issue reflects a wider disagreement among scholars about the extent of Oppenheim's influence.
21 Kröger, *Faszination Orient*, p. 120. In a letter to the editor of the *New York Times*, dated 23 May 1917 (*New York Times*, 26 May 1917), soon after the U.S. entered World War I, the Columbia University Oriental scholar Richard Gottheil, acknowledging that he had been a friend of "the charming Freiherr von Oppenheim" whose "learned talk" he had much enjoyed in Cairo and again in the United States, claimed that Oppenheim's "scientific work, however, has always been merely the cover for his work in the secret service of the Kaiser." In Gottheil's view, Oppenheim, was a "man of real scholarship" who had early on become "a common spy." As early as 1886, for instance, "he was in Morocco making the attempt to detach the Moroccans from their connection with France, and at the same time he made his first attempt to gain for Germany the aid of the powerful Sanussi Fraternity"; in 1893 a "long journey from Beirut through the Syrian desert to Bagdad and the Persian Gulf" was "not unconnected with the Bagdad railroad scheme"; "in 1894 [...] he made a journey down to the Tchad Sea in anti-English interests and for the purpose of gaining the assistance of Mohammedan tribes for his work in Egypt against the English occupation"; more recently, during his stint in Cairo, he went to considerable lengths, seducing the Khedive's European mistress either personally himself or through

to providing basic information, Oppenheim's defenders at the *Auswärtiges Amt* insisted, and was in no way designed to influence German foreign policy. "A certain animosity toward him developed in France and England," Baron von Schoen, the German Foreign Secretary at the time, acknowledged later, "when, at a time of sharp German opposition to France over Morocco, he did what he could to provide German policy-makers with information on Morocco gathered by him on his travels or by other professional means. That cannot be held against him. Understandably, it did not please the French and the English."[22]

French and English suspicions did run high. The *Journal des Débats* accused Oppenheim of using Pan-Islamist propaganda against France and England and of encouraging the Senussi, one of the most fervently anti-Western Muslim brotherhoods, to spread it. He himself, another paper alleged, had collaborated with an Algerian agitator in the distribution of a Pan-Islamist pamphlet. Reuters reported that Oppenheim planned to take advantage of an upcoming archaeological expedition into Syria in order to stir up trouble for the British in the Sinai. An article on him in *The Times* of London a year into the First World War identified "the Jewish Baron Max von Oppenheim" as the chief intriguer on behalf of German interests in Egypt in the decade preceding the war.[23] (The anti-Semitic note, as we shall see again later, was by no means exclusive to the Germans.) According to the British military attaché in Washington, government circles in the Egyptian protectorate viewed Oppenheim as an "intriguer and plotter"—a reputation that has stuck to him, not altogether undeservedly, in much British writing on the Middle East down to the present day. At one point the British demanded that he be removed or obliged to conduct himself in a manner appropriate to a diplomat. Thanks to the vague character of Oppenheim's appointment, the Germans, as we saw, were able to respond that he was not a member of the diplomatic service. Still, in November 1906, he was warned by the *Auswärtiges Amt*, more concerned with not provoking the British than the Kaiser and the rabidly nationalist Pan-German clique around him (with which Oppenheim himself had connections), that he

---

a third party, in order to obtain and have photographs made of important papers in the Khedive's possession. Gottheil closes the letter on a dark note: "There is much more that I could say about the learned Freiherr von Oppenheim."

22 Cit. in Kröger, *Faszination Orient*, p. 121.
23 "German Intrigue in Egypt. Attempts to Weaken British Power. The Activities of Baron von Oppenheim," *The Times*, 6 January 1915, p. 7, col. A, report from the newspaper's special correspondent, dated Cairo, 19 December.

should "exercise restraint in his contacts with Panislamic and Turkophile elements"—i.e. with groups, whether nationalist or pro-Ottoman, that were working to get the British out of Egypt. He was reminded that his role was that of an observer and intelligence gatherer only: his duties extended no further.[24]

Though, as was to be expected, Oppenheim himself denied that he had ever incited anybody and protested that in his relations with the Egyptians and the Arabs he had always been "receptive," not "aggressive," an observer and listener, not a *provocateur*, his considerable vanity was probably flattered by the role the British attributed to him. As was to happen often in his career, however, his practical influence and effectiveness were much disputed (especially no doubt by those among his compatriots who opposed his having any place in the German foreign service at all) and not everyone, it seems, took him seriously. Sir Ronald Storrs, the sophisticated British Oriental Secretary in the decade leading up to the outbreak of the First World War, while acknowledging that "no power was represented [in Egypt] with more charm and distinction than Germany," insisted that this façade concealed a great deal of anti-British intrigue. "As early as 1905," Storrs wrote in his Memoirs, "Ghazi [Ahmed] Mukhtar Pasha, the gallant old Turkish High Commissioner"—with whom, as noted, Oppenheim entertained good relations—"had declared that 'with twelve Army Corps in Syria and the Germans at our back, it should not be difficult to turn the English out of Egypt.'" The semi-official activities of the German engineer Heinrich August Meissner (Meissner Pasha [1862–1940]) and his assistants in the survey and construction of the Hejaz railway line linking Damascus with Medina, a pet project of Abdul Hamid II, were also viewed with suspicion by the British authorities in Egypt, according to Storrs. "In 1909," Storrs continued, "Baron Oppenheim, known to us all as 'the Kaiser's spy', organized a large reception for the Nationalist leader Mustafa Pasha Kämel [Kamil] in Berlin. He was also in close touch with Mukhtar Pasha, and was known to lose no opportunity of reminding the Extremist Press of the syllogism that Islam was threatened with extinction by Europe, that England and France were at the head of the anti-Islamic movement, that the Sultan was the last hope of the Faithful and that Germany was the friend of the Sultan and therefore the only Muslim-minded European Power."[25] Nevertheless, Storrs discounted the

---

24 Kröger, *Faszination Orient*, pp. 121–23.
25 *The Memoirs of Sir Ronald Storrs* (New York: G.P. Putnam's Sons, 1937), p. 133. See also, McKale, *Curt Prüfer*, pp. 16–20.

significance of Oppenheim's anti-British propaganda activities. "It is true," he added,

> that 'the Kaiser's spy', who was attached as Oriental Secretary to the German Agency but described as 'unofficial' though enjoying diplomatic privileges, was not, save as a genial host and an enterprising rather than a profound archaeologist, taken very seriously by the British, or indeed by the Germans either. When Gorst [Sir Eldon Gorst] succeeded Cromer, a German diplomat in Berlin stated that Baron Oppenheim was not at all happy, as he seemed no longer to be given by the British the importance which he had previously enjoyed. In former days, whenever he had an interview with Mustafa Pasha Kämel, Lord Cromer used to get 'much excited,' post men to watch his house, etc.; whereas now Sir Eldon Gorst simply laughed at him.[26]

Perhaps Gorst could afford to take a different view of Oppenheim, in part because he had had some success in detaching the Khedive, Abbas Hilmi, from both the Egyptian nationalists and the Ottoman "High Commissioner," Mukhtar Pasha, and because, with the death of Mustafa Kamil in 1908, Oppenheim had lost his most important link to the nationalist movement.[27]

---

26 *The Memoirs of Sir Ronald Storrs*, p. 134.
27 See Donald M. McKale, "'The Kaiser's Spy': Max von Oppenheim and the Anglo-German Rivalry Before and During the First World War," *European History Quarterly*, 27 (1997): 199–219 (p. 203). In addition, Cromer's judgment of Disraeli might suggest that he was not particularly partial to Jews and other "Orientals"; see his 1912 *Spectator* essay on Disraeli, reprinted in his *Political and Literary Essays* (London: Macmillan, 1913), pp. 177–203. On his side, Gorst may have been less suspicious of German motives; his niece was married to André von Dumreicher, a Swabian in the Egyptian border patrol.

4. The Spectre of Pan-Islamism and *Jihad*

The contradictory views among contemporaries, German as well as British, of the significance and value of Oppenheim's activity probably reflect not only a gap between the relatively cautious policies preferred by most of the professional diplomats at the *Auswärtiges Amt* and the more ambitious and adventurous aims of the Kaiser and his immediate entourage, but divergent assessments of the significance of Pan-Islamism among Western scholars, Western diplomats and politicians, and Muslims themselves. Was Pan-Islamism truly, as Oppenheim argued in his earlier reports and in the influential memorandum *"betreffend die Revolutionierung der islamischen Gebiete unserer Feinde"* ["concerning the fomenting of revolutions in the Muslim territories of our enemies"] that he submitted to the *Auswärtiges Amt* soon after the outbreak of war in 1914, a force that could be of critical importance in the event of a European war? Or did he (along with a good many others) vastly exaggerate the potential of Pan-Islamism? In an article entitled "Pan-Islamism" which he published in 1904 Carl Becker, a highly regarded German Orientalist, observed that "in the writing on modern Islam in recent years there has been much discussion of Pan-Islamism and the most divergent opinions have been expressed about the extent and the importance of this movement." According to one scholar, quoted by Becker in English, "Pan-Islamism is a mare's nest discovered by the *Times'* correspondent in Vienna"; according to another, however, "it is one of the leading tendencies of modern Islam."[1]

In addition, Oppenheim is often credited with or denounced in recent scholarship for having revived the age-old idea of *jihad* and adapted it for use as a strategy designed to provide political and military support

---

1 C.H. Becker, "Panislamismus," *Archiv für Religionswissenschaft*, 7 (1904): 168–92 (p. 168). Becker attributes the divergence of views, to some extent, to the distinction within Islam of Shi'a and Sunni and to the greater or lesser familiarity of Western commentators with one or the other.

for Germany in its pursuit of its proper "place in the sun" and, in particular, in its rivalry with Great Britain, and for thus cynically stirring up and attempting to exploit the religious commitments and passions of Muslims—Muslim "fanaticism," as many put it—for the purely secular ends of German nationalism. Once again, however, it is by no means obvious that this was an original idea of Oppenheim's. One scholar has even argued plausibly that there was a great deal of loose talk in Germany, both at the *Auswärtiges Amt* and in the political section of the General Staff, about exploiting Muslim resentment and fomenting Holy War as a ready means of promoting Germany's national interests, and that Oppenheim's aim in the 1914 memorandum was to conduct a sober review of what was really possible and in what conditions.[2] As we shall see, the memorandum does contain many cautionary notes. It will be useful to examine the two issues—the importance of Pan-Islamism and of the idea of *jihad*, and Oppenheim's specific role in exploiting them—in turn.

Pan-Islamism was already a hot topic in the last decade of the nineteenth century and the first two decades of the twentieth when Oppenheim became interested in its potential value to Germany. As an Indian writer, a former honorary secretary of the Pan-Islamic Society of London (founded in 1903 by Sir Abdullah al-Ma'mūn al-Suhrawardy [1882–1935], a Muslim legal scholar from Bengal[3]), noted with some irritation in 1908, a "recent epidemic of articles on *Pan-Islamism, Khilafat,* and so-called '*Fanaticism*' has been wilder and more virulent than that which raged three years ago when Abdullah al-Ma'mūn Suhrawardy attached the modern word 'Pan,' which denotes expansion and union, to the old word 'Islam.' A heated controversy has been going on in all the leading European papers and especially those of England and France as to the meaning and the future of the movement."[4] "The British public," the same writer had earlier complained in *The Morning Post* (20 August 1906), "which is already prejudiced against Islam, is led to understand that the whole of the Islamic world is like a ferment which will burst any moment if Great Britain does not use her mighty strength to suppress the spirit of Pan-Islam or so-called fanaticism […]; and

---

2   Herbert Landolin Müller, *Islam, ğihād ("Heiliger Krieg") und Deutsches Reich* (Frankfurt a. M., Bern, NewYork and Paris: Peter Lang, 1991) p. 203.
3   Suhrawardy, M.A. Ph.D. LLD, and D.Litt., was the author of several works on Muslim jurisprudence. His first book, *The Sayings of Muhammad,* published by Constable in London in 1905, enjoyed considerable success and led the author into a correspondence with Tolstoy. See http://www.twf.org/bio/Suhrawardy.html.
4   Mushir Hosain Kidwai. *Pan-Islamism* (London: Lusac & Co., 1908; printed in India), p. 4.

so-called authorities and experts have warned other nations to be ready for a Muslim fanatical movement all over the world if they do not back and support the measures which Great Britain has adopted to suppress it."[5] An article in the monthly magazine *The Nineteenth Century* for September 1907, entitled "The Moslem Menace: One Aspect of Pan-Islam," warned in particular of the threat from the Senussi Brotherhood. Even in Germany, despite Wilhelm II's flamboyant gestures of friendship toward the Muslim world, there was fear and suspicion. A German naval attaché in Rome at the time of the Italian occupation of Tripolitania (present-day Libya) clearly sympathized with the Italians' efforts to quell the uprisings against them by a native population "unwilling to adjust to the new order." In Italy's combat with a "totally uncultured people, to whom the murder of whites is a religious commandment and war against those of other faiths a holy duty, with no holds barred," he noted in a memo entitled "Italy Justified," it will be necessary to proceed "in the English manner," that is to say "without sentimentality or mawkish emotion."[6] As early as 1898, the *Vossische Zeitung*, the long established Berlin newspaper of record, had published an article on "Der Panislamismus" in which the defeat and killing of General Gordon in the Sudan and the unpunished massacres of Christian Armenians in the Ottoman Empire (1894–1896) were said to have alarmingly reinforced the "Mohammedans' sense of their superiority."[7]

The term "Pan-Islamism" itself is relatively modern, having come into use among Westerners around the mid-1870s. Nevertheless, as the modern Turkish scholar Azmi Özcan has pointed out, "much before the term came into use in the West, its closest Ottoman equivalent, *Ittihad-i Islam* or the terms *Ittihad-i Din* and *Uhuvvet-i Din* which carry similar connotations, had long been used in the correspondence between the Ottomans and the Muslim rulers of India, Central Asia, and Indonesia. [...] Thus from the late seventeenth to the mid-nineteenth century, Muslim rulers approached the Ottoman Caliphs asking them to fulfil their Caliphal responsibilities; that is, to give aid and protection."[8] As more and more Muslim lands

---

5 Cit. Herbert Landolin Müller, *Islam, ğihād ("Heiliger Krieg") und Deutsches Reich*. p. 181.
6 Memo of naval attaché Fuchs from Rome, dated 1 December 1911, cit. ibid., p. 184.
7 Cit. ibid., p. 180.
8 Azmi Özcan, *Pan-Islamism: Indian Muslims, the Ottomans and Britain (1877–1924)* (Leiden: Brill, 1997), p. 24. Nearly a century earlier, Carl H. Becker had already argued in his article on "Panislamismus" (*Archiv für Religionswissenschaft*, 7 [1904]: 169–92) that "In theory, the Pan-Islamist idea is already fully present in the primitive community" (p. 172). "The aim of Pan-Islamism is the realization of Islamic ideals and the unity of the entire world in Islam, under the guidance of a single leader" (p. 181). But "there

fell under the sway of Western, Christian powers in the age of European imperial expansion, such appeals became more frequent and more urgent. Muslim leaders in British India and Dutch Indonesia "not only informed the Ottoman public of the plight of their peoples, but also highlighted the hopes and aspirations which the Muslim world entertained from the Ottomans. [...] As a result there was growing discontent and resentment directed against Europeans. Anti-Christian feelings were on the increase along with a new wave of strong religious feelings. Muslims were urged to return to traditional Islam under the leadership of the Sultan as the Caliph of all Muslims. It was against this background," Özcan concludes, "that Ottoman intellectuals began formulating ideas and programmes of a Pan-Islamic nature. [...] But it must be stated that this ideology was not a new discovery, but the practical formulation of already existent political tendencies and feelings in the Muslim world developed through centuries."[9]

In seeking a solution to the calamities befalling the Muslim world from South-Eastern Europe to North Africa, Central Asia, and Indonesia, the Young Ottomans of the 1860s—the predecessors of the Young Turks of a few decades later—were, in their own eyes, simply retrieving and developing the longstanding political and ideological potential of Islam, which, they claimed, had inspired the Sultans, during the great days of the Empire, to try to bring about a union of all the Muslim peoples, of the entire *ummah*. In their programs the Young Ottomans attempted to combine modernity and tradition, the institutions of political liberalism and the Sharia, in which they continued to see the soul of the Empire as an Islamic state, and they were strongly critical of the passivity with which the Porte had responded to appeals for help from brother Muslims in Asia. In one of their newspapers, the *Basiret*, an article appeared on 12 April 1872, which explicitly proposed, for the first time, that a policy of *Itihad-i Islam* [union of Islam] should be adopted to counter the expansionist European ideologies of Pan-Slavism and Pan-Germanism. A year later, the Dutch invasion of the sultanate of Atjeh (sometimes written Aceh) on Sumatra in the East Indies—still a restless region of modern Indonesia today—provoked great anger and indignation in the Ottoman public. Wishful thinking on the part

---

has always been a rift between the political and the religious element. Political unity was an ideal, religious unity a fact. In consequence, political propaganda was carried out using religion as an instrument," (p. 184). "What is happening at present is that the old Panislamic idea is stirring and, as efforts are made to put it into practice, it is being transformed into the Panislamic movement" (p. 192).

9 Özcan, *Pan-Islamism: Indian Muslims, the Ottomans and Britain (1877–1924)*, pp. 33–34.

of the editors of *Basiret* led the paper to announce that Ottoman warships would be sent to Atjeh to defend the native Muslims against the Dutch. Though the Porte officially denied the report, Reuters had already spread it around the world, giving encouragement to the Atjehnese Muslims and causing the Dutch government to take the matter seriously, present it as part of a world-wide Pan-Islamic war against Christians, and seek help from the British to check it. Interestingly, although the British were inclined to discount such a Pan-Islamic movement as too beset by internal contradictions (between modernizers and religious conservatives, for instance) to be effective, the Foreign office was sufficiently impressed by the views of the Dutch to instruct all British consuls in Asia to conduct an investigation of religious and political developments among Muslims in their area.[10] The British had reason to be concerned. While many leading Muslims in British India accepted British rule on the grounds that it did not interfere with the practice of their religion and urged their coreligionaries to do likewise, constant undercurrents of opposition led the Viceroy, Lord Lytton, to sound a note of warning in a dispatch to Disraeli dated 18 September 1876:

> The simple truth is this: if 30,000 Russians crossed the frontier tomorrow, and attacked us […] we could rely on all our Muhammedans to rally round us and oppose them. But if three Turks were to land at Bombay with a message from the Sultan commanding the faithful in India to proclaim a *jehad* against the British Government, our whole Muhammedan population would, (however reluctant), obey the mandate.

In a letter to Queen Victoria a year later (4 October 1877), Lytton reiterated his concern:

> If either by pressure of public opinion at home, or political difficulty abroad, Your Majesty's Government should be forced into a policy of prominent aggression upon Turkey, I am inclined to think that a Mohammmedan rising in India is among the contingencies we may have to face.[11]

The Russo-Turkish War of 1877–1878 did indeed create a great outpouring of support for Turkey among Indian Muslims. Prayers for the success of the Ottoman army were offered in every mosque, articles supporting the Ottoman cause filled the developing Muslim press, a great amount of money and jewelry was donated to relief organizations, and some *fatwas*

---

10   Ibid., p. 40, note 63.
11   Both letters from Lord Lytton cited ibid., p. 90.

were issued reminding Muslims that the war between Russia and the Ottomans was a *jihad*, and that all Muslims were therefore obligated to help the Ottomans in every way they could.¹²

In 1880, a year before the French annexation of Tunis and two years before the British occupation of Egypt provoked further outrage among many Indian Muslims,¹³ the British Ambassador to Constantinople sent a note to the Foreign Secretary at the time, Lord Granville, in which he anticipated Oppenheim's later plan to engage the Sultan on the side of Germany in the event of a European war and get him to incite Britain's Muslim subjects in India to rise in rebellion:

> The danger [...] is that if in the course of events, England is compelled to enter upon a policy hostile to Turkey or which in the Sultan's opinion may threaten his independence or his sovereign rights, [...] he may have recourse to every means in his power to cause trouble and embarrassment. With this object in view, he may endeavour to excite the Muhammedans of India against British rule and so bring about another rebellion in that country. To this effect he will make use of all the power and influence he possesses as head of the Muhammedan faith.¹⁴

The Ottoman victory over Greece in 1897 was the occasion of great rejoicing among Indian Muslims. It thus reinforced the sense of Muslim solidarity that had been created earlier by the less happy outcome of the war between the Ottomans and Russia. One congratulatory message sent to the Sultan by the Muslims of Karachi went quite far in proclaiming the unity of all Muslims:

> We, thy faithful servants, [...] although we seem to be in the enjoyment of the fullest tranquillity [under British rule], consider it our duty to declare that we regard ourselves morally and actually under the benevolent protection of the sovereign of all Muhammedans. Consequently all that we possess, our whole fortunes, our houses and our estates, our bodies and our souls, are exclusively at the disposal of the great Muhammedan Government. We are proud to be members of this sacred community, and we experience an immutable joy in the wisdom, greatness and goodness of Your Majesty.¹⁵

By the end of the century, and most probably well before that, Abdul Hamid II himself was able to envisage how he could exploit the feelings of

---

12   Ibid., pp. 64–69.
13   Ibid., p. 98.
14   Note from Austen Henry Layard to Lord Granville 25 May 1880, cit. ibid., p. 92.
15   Cit. ibid., p. 102.

Muslims around the world and, if it should suit him, use his authority as Caliph to unleash a *jihad* against the European colonial powers.

> The bonds of religion that unite us all must be tightened every year: therein lies our hope for the future! Are not England, France, Russia and Holland all in my power? One word from the Caliph would be all it takes to unleash *Jihad*. And then, woe betide the Christian powers! The hour has not yet struck, but it will come, when all the Muslim faithful will rise up as one man to break the yoke of the Giaour [infidel] — the 85 million in the English possessions, the 30 million in the Dutch colonies, the 10 million in Russia, etc.[16]

And in another place, the Turkish Sultan zeroes in on enemy number one — "les Anglais, plus à craindre que toute autre nation" ["the English, more to be feared than any other nation"], as he put it as early as 1882:[17]

> All England's enemies — and in fact all the world's powers ought to count themselves among these, but especially Russia, France, and Germany — all England's enemies ought to place a very high value on our friendship. One does not have to be very intelligent to understand that I, the Caliph, the Commander of all the Faithful, could with a single word seriously endanger English dominance in India. England's enemies let the propitious moment slip by [i.e. the time of the Boer War]. With my help Russia and Germany could easily have overturned England's house of cards in India. The German Emperor was too chivalrous and no doubt in the depths of his heart he has a soft spot for his fair-haired cousins; and then, in addition, he felt obliged to act with moderation because of family ties. It is a great pity that no advantage was taken of the favourable circumstances, for that was the moment when it would have been possible to settle accounts with England for all its brutal actions against other nations, for all the violence perpetrated against the poor Hindus. The time for vengeance will come all the same! The Hindus will rise up and break the yoke of England.[18]

Not surprisingly, Abdul Hamid did what he could — and apparently spent considerable sums of money — to encourage Pan-Islamist sentiments among his subjects, since he saw in Pan-Islamism a means of shoring up his loosely bound and disintegrating Empire and in particular of holding together the Turks and the Arabs, who were not always on the best of terms. The emphasis in Abdul Hamid's propaganda was not only on the Ottoman Empire as the last vestige of the temporal power of the *ummah* or worldwide community of Islam, but on the caliphate as a necessity of faith

---

16   *L'Empire Ottoman et l'Europe, d'après les "Pensées et souvenirs" du Sultan Abdul-Hamid II* (see ch. 2, note 29 above), p. 170.
17   Ibid., p. 96.
18   Ibid., pp. 136–37, passage dated 1902.

transmitted legitimately from Abu Bakr, the father-in-law of the Prophet and after the latter's death the first Caliph, down to the Ottomans. "The caliph," in this framework, as Albert Hourani put it in his classic *Arabic Thought in the Liberal Age 1798–1939*, "is the shadow of God on earth, the executant of his decrees; all Muslims should obey him, being thankful if he does right, patient if he does wrong."[19] Abdul Hamid, in short, laid claim to both secular authority as Sultan of the Empire and religious authority over all Muslims world-wide as Caliph.

There was, in addition, another, politically less conservative line of Pan-Islamist sentiment. Those who followed this line, according to Hourani, did not consider the personal rule of a Muslim autocrat a necessary focus of Muslim unity. In fact, the spread of the notion that all Muslims must join together to defend themselves against the increasingly dominant West and ultimately revive the glory days of the early Umayyad (7th–8th centuries) and Abassid (8th–13th centuries) Caliphates is usually attributed to the oratory, writing, and personal charisma of Jamāl al-Din al-Afghānī (1837–1897), who travelled through all the countries of the Middle East, as well as India and Egypt, propagating a Pan-Islamic idea that was not dependent on the leadership of a Muslim Emperor. Al-Afghānī's aim appears to have been to arouse Muslims to resist both European aggression from without and corrupt, tyrannical regimes within. He was willing to work with Abdul Hamid, however, or any other ruler who could be brought to serve his purposes. On his side, Abdul Hamid was similarly ready to engage in a tactical alliance with al-Afghānī and to subsidize his activities financially. Al-Afghānī was thus invited to the Sultan's court in 1892 for the purpose of working on a resolution of the conflict between Shi'a and Sunni Muslims and bringing the two groups together. Al-Afghānī devised a plan whereby the Ottoman Sultan, the Shah of Persia, and the Sultan of Morocco were to set up an organization in Constantinople, with Abdul Hamid at its head, consisting of two representatives from every Muslim country, one representing the state and one (chosen from among the country's *ulama* or experts in Islamic law) representing the people. If any European power interfered in the affairs of any Muslim country, the organization would declare *jihad* and prohibit trade relations with that power. Al-Afghānī sent out letters to the Shi'a *ulama* of Iran, Iraq, India, the Arab countries, and Turkestan and supposedly received 200 positive

---

19 Albert Hourani, *Arabic Thought in the Liberal Age 1798–1939* (Cambridge: Cambridge University Press, 1983), p. 107.

responses within six months. The project fell through, however, due to the mutual distrust of Abdul Hamid and his advisers and al-Afghānī—a distrust which reflected a fundamental difference between the Pan-Islamic conceptions of the two. "Afghani aimed at the wider and deeper religious and intellectual renaissance of the Muslims through the removal of the main obstacle to political unity," according to the Indian Muslim scholar Anwar Moazzam. "On the other hand, the Sultan had supported the Islamic unity project for no other reason than to strengthen his political authority in Asia as the spiritual head of the Muslims." Al-Afghānī's advocacy of constitutional reform in politics and his defence of a more open intellectual engagement with religious dogma and tradition in matters spiritual were further inevitable sources of disagreement and conflict.[20]

It may well have been the case that "the concept of a united Muslim community with a spiritual and political leader at its head was essential to late nineteenth-century Pan-Islam," as Jacob Landau has put it.[21] Achieving that unity, however, was not easy, due to tensions both within the Pan-Islamic movement—between religious conservatives and modernizers, Ottomans and Arabs, Shi'a and Sunni—and without, between Pan-Islamism and the Pan-Turkism espoused by many of the Ottoman modernizers. It is true that even the largely secular Committee of Union and Progress, the so-called "Young Turks" who deposed Abdul Hamid in 1909, finally also came around to throwing their weight behind Pan-Islamism as a means of promoting their own vision of a modern empire firmly under the control of Constantinople.[22] This shift in policy took place after significant territorial losses in Europe in the Balkan Wars drastically reduced the non-Muslim population of the Empire, making the Young Turks' earlier idea of a multi-ethnic secular state less opportune, and after the Italian invasion of Tripoli demonstrated that the threat from Western imperialism had by no

---

20 Anwar Moazzam, *Jamal al Dīn al-Afghānī: A Muslim Intellectual* (New Delhi: Nauran Rai Concept Publishing Co., 1983), pp. 28–29. See also Bassam Tibi, *Arab Nationalism. Between Islam and the Nation-State*, 3rd edn (New York: St. Martin's Press, 1996), pp. 91–92.
21 Jacob M. Landau, *The Politics of Pan-Islam*, p. 18.
22 On the exploitation of Pan-Islamism by Abdul Hamid and then by the Young Turks, see Landau, *The Politics of Pan-Islam*, Chs. 1, 2. The tension between the modernizing and Pan-Turkish ambitions of the Young Turks, on the one hand, and Pan-Islamism, on the other, was noted by the German Oriental scholar Carl Becker in his 1904 article, "Panislamismus" (see note 1 above). According to Becker, the Panislamist idea was contrary to the real interests of Turkey as conceived by the Young Turks. (See also C. Snouck Hurgronje, *The Holy War "Made in Germany"* [New York and London: G.P. Putnam's Sons, 1915], pp. 66–68).

means abated. Still, doubt remained about the unity and effectiveness of the Pan-Islamist movement, resulting in a correspondingly divided European response to it: fear on the one hand, scepticism on the other.

As early as the 1880s, the British government had been receiving reports of suspected Ottoman intrigues not only through their own channels, but also from other European sources, notably France and the Netherlands. Like the British, the French and the Dutch were becoming increasingly concerned about a perceived growing Muslim revival in the world and at times they sought to collaborate in countering what they identified as the "Pan-Islamic movement." In December 1880, for instance, the Dutch Foreign Minister communicated with the British about a rumoured plan to incite the Muslim populations of India and Indonesia to revolt and suggested that the two countries collaborate in setting up some sort of surveillance of the pilgrims going from their respective colonial possessions to Mecca, since these pilgrims, it was alleged, were to be the principal agents of the plan. As it happens, the Indian government believed the fears were exaggerated, even though, as we have seen, certain Viceroys of India and ambassadors to Constantinople did not.[23] With the passage of time, however, the fears gathered strength. In 1906 the German ambassador in Paris reported a conversation with his counterpart, Salih Munir Pasha, the ambassador of the Porte. Munir Pasha, the German ambassador wrote, observed a more serious Pan-Islamic movement developing in Algeria and Morocco, which he believed was closely connected with "rising fanaticism" in Egypt. "By raising the level of wellbeing in Egypt and spreading education among the *fellahin* [peasants], the English had at the same time, awakened their religious and national spirit," Munir Pasha had said. "The reward of the English for the benefits they had demonstrably brought about was a deep-rooted hatred of them, which sooner or later was bound to lead to the outbreak of a general uprising. [...] Concerning the fanaticism fermenting in Morocco and the Algerian border districts, it was highly characteristic that the Muslims in these parts, who hitherto had refused to recognize the Ottoman Sultan in Constantinople as Caliph and were ill-disposed to the Turks because they considered their own Sultan of Morocco to be the rightful Caliph, were now recognizing the Sultan of the Holy Places and thereby the Ottoman Sultan in the hope of making common cause with all other Muslims against the hated foreigner—i.e. the French and the English. [...] Munir Pasha believes," the German ambassador's report concluded, "that at some point, and perhaps in

---

23 Özcan, *Pan-Islamism: Indian Muslims, the Ottomans and Britain (1877–1924)*, pp. 94–95.

the not too distant future, a gigantic struggle of Muslims in Africa and Asia against the tyranny of the Europeans is inevitable."[24]

In a similar vein, a few years later the Permanent Under-Secretary of State at the Foreign Office Sir Arthur Nicolson, who had seen service in Berlin and Morocco and who was always distrustful of Germany, warned both his chief, the Foreign Secretary Sir Edward Grey, and Britain's ambassador in Constantinople, Sir Gerard Lowther, of the threat posed by Pan-Islamism: "I think that this Pan-Islamic movement is one of our greatest dangers in the future, and is indeed far more of a menace than the 'Yellow Peril.' [...] Germany is fortunate in being able to view with comparative indifference the growth of the great Mussulman military power, she having no Mussulman subjects herself, and a union between her and Turkey would be one of the gravest dangers to the equilibrium of Europe and Asia."[25] Sir Arthur could have found support for his apprehension in the ideas of Dr. Karl Peters, an energetic German explorer, official of the Imperial Colonial Office, and Reichskommissar for the Kilimanjaro region of German East Africa, known for his ruthless treatment of native Africans. According to Dr. Peters, writing presciently in 1906, "There is one factor that might fall on our [i.e. the German] side of the balance and in the

---

24 Cit. Herbert Landolin Müller, *Islam, ǧihād ("Heiliger Krieg") und Deutsches Reich*, pp. 182–83. Munir Pasha's view was also that of Edward Dicey, a British journalist specializing in foreign affairs, who had worked for *The Daily Telegraph* and served as editor of *The Daily News* and the weekly *Observer*. In *The Egypt of the Future* (London: William Heinemann, 1907), he warned that the defeat of Russia by a non-European nation (i.e. Japan) had had enormous resonance in the colonial territories of the Europeans (pp. 140–42) and that the British were deluding themselves in thinking that the Egyptians would be loyal out of gratitude for the "justice of our sway and the success of our administrative policy," which had resulted in the raising of living standards (p. 146). Muslims were far more closely bound together by their religion than by any national sentiment, he maintained: "A Moor or a Malay, a Soudanese, a Tunisian, or an Algerian, are to all intents and purposes more fully brethren than a couple of fellaheen who live and work side by side in the same village, supposing one to be a Moslem and the other a Copt" (p. 144). He had long argued that "the mere rumour of Turkish intervention would unite the whole Egyptian nation into partisans of the Sultan" (p. 146). Recent events—such as "the riot of Alexandria, the attempt to blow up the arsenal of Khartoum, the raid by Soudanese who had served under the Khalifa upon a village occupied by Anglo-Egyptian soldiers, a raid which was only possible on the hypothesis that the sympathies of the Soudanese were with the insurgents, not with the Anglo-Egyptian soldiery, the sudden occupation of Akaba by Turkish troops, the revival of the Sultan's shadowy Suzerainty over Egypt"—bore out his contention that "in the event of a collision between Turkish and Egyptian troops the latter would refuse to fight against the former and their refusal would enlist the sympathies of the whole Moslem community" (pp. 147–48).
25 Dated 23 January 1911, cit. Joseph Heller, *British Policy toward the Ottoman Empire 1908–1914* (London: Frank Cass, 1983), p. 39.

case of a world-war might be made useful to us: that factor is Islam. As Pan-Islamism it could be played against Great Britain as well as against the French Republic; and if German policy is bold enough, it can fashion the dynamite to blow into the air the rule of the Western powers from Cape Nun in Morocco to Calcutta."[26]

The Italian invasion of nominally Ottoman controlled Tripolitania at the end of 1911 and "the response of Muslims far and near to the invasion of Muslim territory" raised the level of anxiety about Pan-Islamism. "Right from the inception of this war," Jacob Landau writes, "Pan-Islam served as a bond for disparate tribes in Libya, as well as between them and the Ottomans, and between both of these and other Muslims within and without the empire. Pan-Islam was a dominant factor in uniting these diverse elements. [...] Numerous cables of identification with the [Ottoman] Government arrived from Muslim dignitaries and communities both within and without the empire. The war was widely considered a *jihad*. Enver Pasha [one of the leaders of the Committee of Union and Progress—the so-called "Young Turks"—then in control in Constantinople] issued a proclamation to the warriors, urging them to fight the enemies of Islam and assuring them of the support of the world's Muslims." Enver himself went off to take part in the defence of Tripoli.[27] "The entire Muslim press in the Ottoman Empire and many Muslim newspapers abroad (including Shiite ones in Iran)," Landau continues, "supported the Ottoman Government and its military forces on Pan-Islamic grounds, emphasizing the need for unity and union. [...] There are indications that the Benevolent Islamic Society—the main channel for the Pan-Islamic activities of the Committee of Union and Progress—organized a sizeable share of the non-state Muslim assistance to Libya. In this manner, the war contributed to the institutionalization of Pan-Islam as a force to be employed [...] in

---

26 Cit. Samuel M. Zemer, *The Disintegration of Islam* (New York, Chicago, Toronto, London and Edinburgh: Fleming H. Revell Company, 1916), p. 127 (Students' Lectures on Missions, Princeton Theological Seminary, 1915).
27 Having led Turkey into the First World War, having fled the country on the collapse of the Empire in 1918, having been convicted in his absence by the new Turkish Republic of needlessly plunging the country into a disastrous war, Enver allied himself in the years immediately following the war with Communists in Germany and Soviet Russia. This enabled him to claim in 1922: "I am pursuing today the same purpose that I pursued before and during the Revolution of 1908, during the Tripolitanian War, the Balkan Wars, and the World War. And this purpose is very simple: to organize and bring to action the Islamic world of four hundred million people [...] and to save it from the European and American oppression which enslaves it." (Cit. Mustafa Aksakal, *The Ottoman Road to War in 1914* [Cambridge: Cambridge University Press, 2008], pp. 15–16).

order to assist Muslims militarily, politically, and economically. [...] On the whole, manifestations of Islamic solidarity were so impressive that they created a backlash of accusations of Pan-Islamic fanaticism, not merely in the Italian Press but in that of other European states as well."[28]

While holding that it would be unwise for Britain and France to "side against Italy now," the British Foreign Secretary Sir Edward Grey admitted that the Italian seizure of Tripolitania (described by a former Under-Secretary at the Foreign Office and—significantly—current Viceroy and Governor General of India, Sir Charles Hardinge, as the worst "case of brigandage" he had ever heard of) might cause "great embarrassment" to Britain as an imperial power with numerous Muslim subjects. A few days later Hardinge referred in fact to "considerable effervescence" among the Indian Muslims and warned that "it is most important for us to be able to show to the Muhammadans of India that we have been doing what we can to put an end to the war with Italy which they resent very much and regard as the beginning of the end of Islam in Europe."[29] An article entitled "Indian Muslims and Pan-Islamism" that was published three months later in English translation in the New Delhi newspaper *Comrade*, gives credence to Hardinge's concern:

> To the man in the street Pan-Islamism was synonymous with a gigantic union of the Moslems of the world, having for its cherished object the extermination of Christianity as a living political force. [...] The bombardment of Meshed [in Persia] by the Russians, the descent of Italy on Tripoli, the onslaught of the Balkan Allies on Turkey, with all their attendant horrors, have made the Moslems of India a changed people. They are not what they were two years ago... The brotherhood of Islam, or Pan-Islamism if you will, transcends all considerations of race and colour and is of an extra-territorial type in which all the Moslem populations of the world merge their geographical identity and become one nation.[30]

Equally characteristic, however, despite the alarmist tone of some of his own reports, was Ambassador Lowther's suggestion—in response to Nicolson's warning of January 1911—that the Pan-Islamic movement was in all probability less dangerous than Nicolson believed: the Shi'a Persian abhorred the Sunni and was unlikely to collaborate with the Ottomans; the

---

28 Landau, *The Politics of Pan-Islam*, pp. 134–37.
29 Heller, *British Policy toward the Ottoman Empire 1908–1914*, pp. 53, 55–56.
30 Cit. Landau, *The Politics of Pan-Islam* p. 191. On Panislamic ideas and Ottoman sympathies among Indian Muslims in the period leading up to the Great War, see also Özcan, *Pan-Islamism: Indian Muslims, the Ottomans and Britain (1877–1924)*, Chs. 4, 5.

Arab had no respect for the Turk as a Muslim and felt, moreover, that the Caliphate should be in Arab hands; in India, Sunni Muslims regarded the Young Turks, now in control in Constantinople, as "sacrilegious revolutionaries," who had deposed God's elect from the Caliphate and replaced him with a puppet.[31] Likewise, on 27 November 1911, in his maiden speech in Parliament as Conservative M.P. for Hull Central, Sir Mark Sykes—the future co-signer of the Sykes-Picot agreement by which Britain and France defined their respective spheres of influence in the Middle East after the expected collapse of the Ottoman Empire at the end of World War I—gave expression to an ambivalent judgment. Muslim anger and resentment were real and to be feared, but they were unlikely to be controlled and directed by Pan-Islamism. On the one hand, in Egypt and North Africa "there is the fuel of fanaticism;" if the spark should fall, "it may blaze up," and "that spark may come from Tripoli." On the other, "I do not believe Pan-Islamism is a force."[32]

Scepticism about the strength of Pan-Islamism was in fact as common as fear of it. From the start, as has several times been suggested, there were divergent and competing strains in Pan-Islamism: an arch-traditionalist, orthodox religious strain; a secularizing and modernizing strain; a Turkish-dominated Imperial strain that claimed the title of Caliph for the Ottoman emperor; and a nationalist, predominantly Arab strain that rejected that claim and sought freedom for the various subject peoples from the yoke of Ottoman imperialism. Modern scholars have explored these tensions within the movement in great depth, but they were already becoming familiar to readers both of scholarly writings and of the popular press by the first decade of the twentieth century. While some—like Oppenheim and Lord Cromer, the British Consul-General in Egypt—took Pan-Islamism seriously, the former in order to exploit it to Germany's advantage, the latter because he saw it as

---

31 Cit. Landau, *The Politics of Pan-Islam*, p. 191.
32 Hansard, vol. 32, 27 November 1911 http://hansard.millbanksystems.com/commons/1911/nov/27/sir-edward-greys-statement#S5CV0032P0_19111127_HOC_302. See also a letter dated 9 November 1911 to Professor E.G. Browne, an Oriental scholar at Cambridge with whom Sykes had studied: "I am terrified at Grey's policy. It is getting us into the very devil of a mess. Italy's action unless repudiated must set the whole of the Moslem world against us, and if the Moslem world is against us we are done. We only rule by favour of Moslems because we play the game nine times out of ten." (Shane Leslie, *Mark Sykes: His Life and Letters* [London: Cassell and Company, 1923], p. 201). After spending time in Egypt, Sykes took the threat of Pan-Islamism very seriously; see Donald M. McKale, "The Kaiser's Spy': Max von Oppenheim and the Anglo-German Rivalry Before and During the First World War," *European History Quarterly*, 27 (1997): 199–219 (pp. 208–09).

a threat to British dominion in India and to the imperial lifeline connecting London with Bombay and Calcutta, many others held that, because of the radically divergent aims and ideologies of the parties supporting it, it did not constitute a real threat to Western interests.

A leading figure among the sceptics was the internationally respected Dutch scholar of Islamic culture, Christiaan Snouck Hurgronje. In 1901, in an article published in French in the *Revue de l'Histoire des Religions*, he poured scorn on what two French scholars had called "la concentration de l'action panislamique à Constantinople, sous la direction du Sultan" ["the concentration of Pan-Islamic activity in Constantinople under the aegis of the Sultan"]. The religious Islamists around the Sultan, he claimed, were too busy conducting "every possible intrigue, employing every slander or other poisonous weapon in order to discredit each other in the mind of the Sultan and strike a mortal blow against their rivals" to constitute a real power. "There is certainly a strong Pan-Islamist tendency in Turkey," he conceded, "and in a sense the Sultan can be seen as the supreme head of this movement." Moreover, "religion, especially in the Islamic world, is the most powerful of political motivations." In the decadence of the Ottoman Empire, "it provides the Turkish state with a grand principle to inscribe on its banner as it confronts the European world, a principle by which it can call for support on the millions of Muslims living outside its jurisdiction. But this movement of Pan-Islamism is anything but well organized. In fact it is eloquent demonstration of the weakness of Turkey's present institutions that they are incapable of making better use of such a redoubtable force."[33]

Snouck Hurgronje maintained this position into the early years of the First World War, when he lashed out at cynical German exploitation of Pan-Islamism and *jihad* as instruments in a purely European struggle and at the willingness of German scholars of Islam to rally behind a policy that they knew was ill-advised, dangerous to European civilization, and, not least, damaging to progressive, modernizing elements in the Islamic world itself. Most Europeans, he noted, are easily misled into imagining that the Caliphate is "a sort of Mohammedan papacy" with absolute spiritual authority over the Faithful. In fact, he objected, "such a thing there never was, and Islâm, which knows neither priests nor sacraments, could not have had occasion for it." He acknowledges that "the multitude preferred legend to fact; they imagined the successor of the Prophet as still watching

---

33 C. Snouck Hurgronje, "Les Confréries religieuses, La Mecque, et le Panislamisme," *Revue de l'Histoire des Religions*, 44 (1901): 262–81 (pp. 268–71).

over the whole of the Muslim community." Nevertheless, the Ottoman attempt to resuscitate the Caliphate did not and could not produce the powerful instrument the German war strategists thought they could use for their own ends. "The re-born Caliphate lacked important traditional characteristics; and in other respects also it could not be considered as the regular continuation of its predecessor. Several of the oldest Mohammedan countries remained entirely outside the Turkish sphere of influence; and those were not only such where, as in Persia, a dynasty opposed to the Turks raised the banner of heresy, but also perfectly orthodox countries in Central Asia, in India, in North-Western Africa, where the Turkish sword found no occasion to assert itself. In Morocco, the Turkish Caliphate was even directly ignored, as the local princes, descendants of the Prophet, themselves assumed the highest title."

Elsewhere, new Mohammedan dominions arose which "never came into contact with any real or supposed political centre of Islâm, such as those in the Far East of Asia and in Central Africa." It is only "in this last century that the Turks, through a concourse of circumstances, have sometimes succeeded in coining some small advantage out of this doubtfully legal, now meaningless title." Despite all those caveats, however, the Dutch scholar, writing a century ago, noted in words that have lost none of their force today (2012) that "means of communication, increased a thousandfold, have now brought into contact Mohammedan nations which formerly knew nothing, or hardly anything, about each other's existence." In particular, writing from the perspective of a former adviser (1889–1906) to the Governor-General of the Dutch East Indies during the final phase of the Atjeh War, Snouck Hurgronje deplored what he described as the lack of "sufficient historical remembrance" in the "approximately 230,000,000 of Mohammedans living under non-Moslim rule" and their consequent failure "to understand that the change in administration [i.e. to colonial rule] has been an improvement for them. They see the political past of Islâm only through the veil of legend and when the present gives occasion for grievances and objections—and where are these lacking?—they are rather prone to believe that all their complaints would be cured, if only the Commander of the Faithful could take their interests in hand." Of "the maladministration under which the real subjects of the Sultan of Turkey are laboring" they, of course, know nothing.

After reviewing all the elements of the situation, Snouck Hurgronje concluded that talk of "an organization of Panislâm under the direction of Abdulhamîd" was "without foundation," as he claimed he himself had already sought to demonstrate as early as 1898 in an article describing the atmosphere of intrigue and rivalry "around the despot." At the time of the revolution in Constantinople in 1908, part of which he witnessed, he had found that earlier view completely justified. "That gang of shallow intriguers was little qualified to lead a serious international movement." The arrival of the Young Turks in 1908 should have led to complete elimination of "the medieval mixture of religion and politics" and establishment of a secular modern state. "The upholding of Islâm as a state-religion was on their part a concession to the old tradition without prejudice to the complete equality of the adherents of all religions as citizens of the Turkish Empire." Unfortunately, "the greed of the European powers did not grant Young Turkey the rest necessary for internal reform [...] The Committee of Unity and Progress [...] found itself constrained on one side to resort again to the hateful governing method of despotism, on the other side to grant many concessions to the detriment of its own program, even to Moslim orthodoxy and to the beliefs and superstitions of the multitude. The fetish of the Caliphate had to be exhumed again from the museum of antiquities where it had temporarily been stored. As to the idea of *jihâd*, which was so closely connected with it, the European powers took care that it was not forgotten. Turkey was continually forced to a *jihâd*."

Snouck Hurgonje thus made clear that, in his view, it was European interference, the persistent European exploitation of the weakness of the Ottoman Empire, that had made Pan-Islamism and the revival of the idea of *jihad* possible and thus allowed Germany to exploit both in its own interests. The bottom line remains, however, that Pan-Islamism is a blunt and ineffectual instrument. "It is a fact that Panislâm cannot work with any program except with the worn-out, flagrantly unpracticable, program of world-conquest by Islâm; and this has lost its hold on all sensible adherents of Islâm; whereas, among the stupid multitude, which may still be tempted by the idea of war against all *kâfirs*, it can stir up only confusion and unrest. At most it may cause local disturbances; but it can never, in any sense, have a constructive influence."[34]

---

34 C. Snouck Hurgronje, *The Holy War "Made in Germany"*, pp. 17–18, 25–27, 29–32. The bulk of this work is a denunciation of the endorsement by German scholars, notably Carl Becker, a friend and colleague, of German efforts to exploit Pan-Islamism (in which Oppenheim played a major role). It first appeared in Dutch in the journal *De Gids* early in 1915 and was immediately translated into English. (On the Snouck Hurgronje-Becker debate, see Peter Heine, "C. Snouck Hurgronje versus C.H. Becker. Ein Beitrag zur Geschichte der angewandten Orientalistik," *Die Welt des Islams*, new series 23/34 [1984]: 378–87).

Among German Oriental scholars themselves, prior to the outbreak of war in 1914, many expressed no less scepticism than Snouck Hurgronje about the power and effectiveness of Pan-Islamism. One of the most outspoken was the controversial, maverick Berlin Orientalist, Martin Hartmann, in whom sympathy with the aspirations of the contemporary Arab peoples was combined with advocacy of modernization, criticism of "outdated" religious and ethnic "fanaticism," and fierce opposition to Ottoman imperialism.[35] In an article entitled "Das Ultimatum des Panislamismus," written in 1912 — hence at the time of the Italian invasion of Ottoman-ruled Tripolitania and calls by many Muslims, notably the Senussi, for a *jihad* to resist the infidels — Hartmann wrote that, while the outrage of the Muslim world at the "Banditenstreich" of the Italians was understandable, the Muslim reaction was neither reasonable nor unified:

> The storm provoked by the actions of the Italians in the Muslim world has brought forth strange blooms. It is understandable that outrage at this "act of brigandage" has overwhelmed even the children of those who have themselves been land robbers throughout all the centuries since the emergence of Islam, as well, indeed, as the descendants of those tribesmen whose race trampled the soil of Hungary and laid siege to Vienna. Memories easily prove short, alas, in such circumstances. But let us consider the forms taken by this indignation. The mildest is the threat of a general Muslim boycott of all Italians. Rather more shrill is the threat of Holy War, that is, of a war against all Infidels, except for those expressly designated by the leaders of the Muslim community as friends of Islam. This idea is pure madness. It was recently formulated, however, with great care by some respected Muslims and widely broadcast. Unless a timely warning is issued, it could well cause considerable damage.

Hartmann cites a report in the *Vossische Zeitung* about a meeting, in a house in a fashionable section of Berlin, of "massgebenden Vertretern des Panislamismus" ["influential representatives of Pan-Islamism"], the outcome of which was a resolution sent out to all parts of the Muslim world, calling on Turkey to fight to the last to keep Tripolitania out of the hands of the Italians, on pain of the Ottoman Emperor's losing his title to be the modern Caliph and finding himself replaced by an Arab Caliph. According to the newspaper report, Hartmann writes, what this Pan-Islamist organization demands of Turkey, and what it proposes to bring about, if

---

35 On this original and unusual figure, see the excellent article by Martin Kramer, "Arabistik and Arabism: The Passions of Martin Hartmann," *Middle Eastern Studies*, 25 (1989): 283–300.

necessary over the heads of the Ottomans, is a boycott of Italians not only in Turkey, but in all the lands that are home to Muslims—hence, in Egypt, India, Algeria, Tunisia, the Crimea, the Caucasus, etc. The Caliphate must, in short, make use of its right to call upon *all* Muslims, wherever they may be, for help in the form of fighting men and money. Indeed, should the European powers, which have repeatedly guaranteed Turkey's integrity, fail to rein in the Italians, all international commitments should be considered void, including the commitment not to invoke "Holy War." In the event that Turkey fails to assume its responsibilities, the world should take note, anything might happen when, in a couple of months' time, the pilgrimages to Mecca begin.

The manifesto, Hartmann writes, refers to a powerful "Pan-Islamist organization, led by persons educated in Europe" and capable of carrying out measures "even over the heads of the rulers of the Ottoman Empire." But no such organization, Hartmann asserts mockingly, exists. What does exist is a number of small groups, consisting of a few individuals who imagine that they have an influence on the entire Islamic community and that they can move it to act as a unity. In fact, according to Hartmann, the notion of a union of all the Muslims in the world is a completely Utopian one that has been pursued in vain ever since the collapse of the Abasside Caliphate in the year 750 and that even Abdul Hamid II, despite spending enormous sums of money on it and being restrained by no scruples whatsoever, did not come close to realizing. As soon as the representatives of the various Islamic groups try to reach agreement on a common line of action, the vast differences—ethnic, economic, even religious—among the world's millions of Muslims immediately become evident. The gathering of countless Muslims from all parts of the world in Mecca on Holy Days will not erase these differences, Hartmann insisted. Any momentary enthusiasm aroused there and encouraged by skilful agitators will subside as soon as the pilgrims return home and have to deal with their own individual concerns and personal situations. According to Hartmann,

> Europe can only laugh at the bloodthirsty speeches the Pan-Islamists believe will bring the poor devils gathered together [in Mecca] from all parts of the Muslim world, ninety percent of whom are utterly ignorant, to the boiling point. Europe can only laugh at the threat of Holy War. While that threat has been heard often in recent times, nothing has ever come of it. "Holy War"! Do these people still not understand that making war costs money, a tremendous amount of money? Who is going to provision the huge war chest? Who is going to administer it? Who will lead the Pan-Islamist armies? Are the intellectuals sitting in Berlin really so

simple-minded that they believe it is still possible in our time to get the entire Islamic world to rise up and wage war against the Infidels? It is curious that it is they who are calling for Holy War. This pose does not suit them. In fact, it could prove to be fatal to them. The Islamic champions with Holy War in their backpacks are those strict dogmatists who hold to the most far-out prescriptions of Sharia or sacred law: stoning of those who have engaged in forbidden sex, eighty strokes of the lash for drinking wine, cutting off the hands of those who have engaged in theft. *That* is the spirit of Pan-Islamism. The flirting of a thin layer of Islamic intellectuals in various European capitals with this spirit, their seizing every opportunity to point to the supposedly great power of Pan-Islamism, is nothing but a comedy performed for political ends. It is also a double game, inasmuch as those very people otherwise constantly wave the flag of nationalism, and, as Young Turks, Young Egyptians, Young Persians, preach modernization to their countrymen and disdain the religious element. They had better beware; if they do inflame the fanaticism of the Islamic masses, the latter will take a closer look at them and play them a nasty trick by denouncing them as Unbelievers, pork-eaters, and wine-drinkers.[36]

Moreover, they would be treated with particular severity once the consequences of their agitation became evident. For any attempt to stir up a Pan-Islamist movement in Mecca, Hartmann warns, would have significant consequences. For example, if an organization to combat the Western nations [*"die Kulturvölker"*], or even only the Italians, were to be set up on a religious basis, the area in which the two holy cities are situated would immediately be occupied by an Infidel power; an orderly Infidel administration would result in the improvement of the entire country; corrupt and incompetent Ottoman bureaucrats would be eliminated, and an end would be put to the unremitting violence of the Bedouin riff-raff; construction of the important railway line linking Damascus to Medina and Mecca, presently at risk of being abandoned, would be resumed and completed, etc. "Turkey," Hartmann concludes, can only say "'Heaven preserve me from friends such as these [Pan-Islamists].'"

In general, Hartmann argues, it is dangerous for a country to try to save itself by appealing to religious prejudice: "As long as a part of humanity clings to the idea of the superiority of a particular religious community, there will always be attempts to embody that superiority in a lasting organization under a strong leader, who will almost always be the creature

---

36 M. Hartmann, "Das Ultimatum des Panislamismus," *Das freie Wort. Frankfurter Monatschrift für Fortschritt auf allen Gebieten des geistigen Lebens*, 11 (April 1911-April 1912): 605–10.

of a small group of people with particular interests of their own." The attempt to fuse the Roman Church and the State in Europe and its ultimate failure is cited as a warning example, and Hartmann concludes on the need in the Islamic world also, for the sake of its own survival, of greater realism and a separation of religion and politics.

Another article about Muslim unrest had already appeared, slightly earlier, in the same liberal journal in which Hartmann's article was published—in itself a sign of increased anxiety in Europe, in the wake of the Italian invasion of Tripolitania. Entitled simply "Über den Panislamismus," it offered a judgment of the movement not unlike that of Hartmann. Promoted by Abdul Hamid, the author argued, Pan-Islamism had been taken over by the seemingly modern and secular "Young Turks," by whom the Sultan was deposed, as a "political idea" that "constituted, and had to constitute a pivotal point also of the new course on which the country has embarked." For it offered the only means of creating "a common bond among the non-coherent Iranian-Aryan, Semitic, and Turkish races which had been squeezed together to form a purely external union, […] a living bond that could take the place of the seemingly arbitrary historical unification of such heterogeneous elements. It retained an essentially religious character, for in the absence of the "driving force of a shared national spirit and culture" ["*gemeinsame nationale und kulturelle treibende Kraft*"] that sustained the European states—a defect seemingly aggravated or perhaps caused by diversity of race—the only bond that could provide the Ottoman Empire with a truly "felt and living unity" ["*gefühlte Lebenseinheit*"] was one that, since the beginning of modern times had more and more receded into the background in Europe, namely religion. As the Middle East was placed more and more on the defensive against the ever increasing strength of the West, it was understandable psychologically that, since its peoples (Arabs, Turks, Indians) lacked any strong sense of nationality, the last and strongest line of defence would be felt to be their shared religion. It was not at all certain, however, in the author's view, that religious affiliation would outweigh feelings of ethnic community, that Muslims of Slavic origin would not be more drawn to their ethnic fellow-Slavs or that the Arabs, despite the emphatic Pan-Islamist tendencies of the press in Cairo, might not be less well disposed to Pan-Islamism than their northern co-religionists, the Turks. If England were to encourage the Arabs, or at least the Eastern Arabs in their desire for independence from Ottoman rule, Arab aspirations would inevitably come into conflict with the Caliphate of the Padishah. Finally, though the Muslim populations of China and

India are considerable, they still constitute a minority in their respective countries, so that a really dangerous movement there would more likely take the form of Pan-Asianism than Pan-Islamism. The author concludes on a prudent note:

> Nonetheless, the power of Islam should not be underestimated. However primitive its ideas may seem, as though emerging out of a bygone world into our present, however alien its theocratic politics, its view of woman as a piece of property and its denial of both the internal and the external freedom of the individual, these ideas have struck such deep roots in a millennium and a half that uprooting them by force would seem ill-advised and dangerous, if not impossible.

Equally, however, it would be foolish, in the author's view, for the Turks to play the Pan-Islamist card:

> As a sense of national and cultural identity enters the popular consciousness and sensibility of the East, and as the influence of modern economics and ways of life makes itself felt, the dominant role of religious doctrine is bound to diminish. [...] Pan-Islamism, in sum, is only even *conceivable* to the extent that it is strongly supported by the Ottomans; it is not impossible as a counterweight to Pan-Slavism; but it can never be based purely on religion as long as the Turkish Empire remains a European power in terms of its military technology, finances, and diplomacy, and does not, overlooking its true interests for the sake of chimerical ideas, withdraw from the "concert of nations" into a position of isolation. However much it may be the spoken or unspoken wish of Turkish politicians and patriots, therefore, Pan-Islamism cannot for the foreseeable future offer a firm enough basis to justify risking, for its sake, the loss of what has already been gained.[37]

More surprisingly, an article in the form of a letter to the editor appeared in the venerable London magazine *The Spectator* several years before the Italian invasion of Tripolitania, expressing—in somewhat halting English—doubts about Pan-Islamism on the part of the letter-writer, whom the magazine identifies as "a member of the sect of the Senoussi"—i.e. of the fundamentalist brotherhood that was particularly strong in Cyrenaica and Tripolitania and that subsequently led the campaign against the Italians and called for the support of all Muslims in a Holy War to defend Islam against the Infidel. "The term 'Pan-Islamism'," the letter-writer declared in his opening paragraph, "is a broad designation expressing a number of ideas more or

---

37 A. Tavilet, "Über den Panislamismus," *Das freie Wort. Frankfurter Monatschrift für Fortschritt auf allen Gebieten des geistigen Lebens*, 11 (April 1911–April 1912): 218–21. This author's home base is identified as Constantinople.

less identified with its actual significance, which is that of a tentative desire to regenerate Islam on an 'Islamistic' plan. Now this, it must be understood, means of necessity a hatred of the alien races, and, above all, of the alien religion." Recent disturbances in Asia and Africa have drawn attention to the world of Islam. Even a power that had hitherto remained in the background "has of a sudden stepped forward into the light and proclaimed herself the protector of Islam,—I allude to Germany." Nevertheless,

> although myself a Moslem, travelling for the past eight years in all the Mohammedan countries, and having held familiar intercourse with other Moslems, both of the religious and political order, having, in short, followed the course of Pan-Islamism according to the ideas of the Khaliph of Islam—or at least of him who proclaims himself such, and who is also thus regarded in Europe—I humbly own that I have never yet been able to get to the bottom of what may be the precise *état d'âme* of my co-religionists, or understand what may be their true aspirations. So inconsequent are they as to all their points of view in general, that the most penetrating mind, it would seem, would never be able to arrive at any positive fact. I must indeed hasten to say that my dear co-religionists themselves do not know what they want. [...] It is painful and humiliating for a Mohammedan to have to own to such a state of things. It is, however, the painful truth.

"Under these conditions," the writer, who names himself Saleb el Khalidi, concludes, "'Pan-Islamism,' as understood by the politicians of Europe, is a mere chimera." The "unity and solidarity" that make for the strength of the European states, "are unknown to the Moslem people." Consequently, "the sole results which could accrue from Pan-Islamism in the present day would be *isolated* explosions of fanaticism in divers Mohammedan countries, but never—I repeat and affirm it—never a general explosion of the followers of the Prophet the world over." This situation is further aggravated from the Muslim point of view by the fact that the "Pan-Islamistic movements, which have arisen in certain Mohammedan countries, and to which Europe—still so ignorant in Oriental matters—has attributed so great an importance" are in general primarily instruments in the hands of ambitious and self-seeking leaders, even if a few are inspired by "patriotic motives." These individuals "speculate on the simplicity of their co-religionists. [...] The people are ignorant, [...] easily caught by florid speeches and [...] incapable of seeing that they are being duped and betrayed." The "two greatest champions of Pan-Islamism," in the writer's view, "are his Majesty the Sultan Abd-ul-Hamid and the Sheikh Senoussi, chief of that flourishing confraternity of Muslims to which the latter gave his name." Shortly after his accession to the throne, Abdul Hamid, the author of the letter goes on, "upon the advice of his councilor [sic], the Sheikh Said Abd-ul-Houda, thought of reviving the ancient Khaliphat, and thus grouping about his throne the entire Muslim population of the world. It was formidable, this weapon he wished to forge in order to serve him against Europe. I am not exaggerating when I say that half his revenues are annually spent on matters closely touching Pan-Islamism."

Unfortunately for the Sultan, however, "up to the present, the Pan-Islamic policy of Abd-ul-Hamid has succeeded nowhere but in Egypt, and there only in part." On the contrary, "today, the whole Ottoman Empire is stirring. By reason of his pernicious mode of government, by his cruelty, and by the dishonesty of his officials, the Sultan has alienated all, and the temporal, as well as the spiritual power of Abd-ul-Hamid wanes day by day. The Arabs of Yemen, of Hidjaz, and of Hauran are in open revolt against Turkey," while "the Bedouin chiefs are determined to make the Ottoman troops evacuate the whole of the Yemen territory, as well as that of Hidjaz, and to proclaim as Khaliph of Islam the Imam Mahmoud Yabia, having his residence at Mecca." In short, "the rising of all Arabia has almost annihilated the Pan-Islamic projects of Abd-ul-Hamid" and "as a consequence the sole qualified representative of Pan-Islamism is the Sheikh Senoussi."

The writer goes on to describe "this chief, whose fame rests on a solid basis." Shekh Sidi Mohammed Ben Ali Senoussi, born at Tlemcen (Algeria) presented himself "not as a reformer, nor as an innovator, but simply as a regenerator." His aim was "to revive and stereotype the religious principles in such fashion as obtained in the days of the Prophet, whose descendent [sic] he was." Persecuted by other imams jealous of his growing popularity, he had to seek refuge in Mecca and among the Bedouins "who received him with great respect" as a holy man. He then moved to Tripoli, "which he traversed from end to end […] preach[ing] to the people who flocked to him from all sides," and "bidding them unite as well as observe rigorously the principles enjoined by the Koran." All over Tripoli, Egypt and Hidjaz, he founded monasteries, whose Superiors were in effect "at the same time Judges and Governors of the surrounding districts." His son and successor Sidi El Mahdi continued his father's policies and came to be regarded as the "'Moslem Messiah' who was one day to rid Islam of the Christian yoke, rendering the Moslem faith master over the entire world." For this reason, news of his death was received with disbelief by his many followers, and indeed was soon declared erroneous. He had been seen "garbed as a dervish and living amid a flock of gazelles." In fact, a widely read public letter signed by the present chief of the sect, El Mahdi's nephew, proclaimed that he had not died but had gone on a secret journey.

This "strange missive ended with the announcement of the approaching joyful time—that the hour for ridding themselves of the Christian yoke was at hand." "Moslems," the author of the *Spectator* letter declares, "are actually convinced that Sidi El Mahdi will shortly appear at the head of a great army to wage the Holy War." In a final summing up, the readers of the *Spectator* are warned that, "bizarre" as it may appear, this situation

> merits the attention of all the Powers who have interests in the East and in Africa. A general coalition of Moslems comprising the inhabitants of Tripoli, of Egypt, and of Hidjaz, Utopian as it may appear, is yet possible. It must not be forgotten that the Senoussi possess an actual political organization, that they are well posted as to all movements, that they have a very considerable supply of magazine rifles, and that they are aided in their crusade by the heads of the Moslem States, and even by a great European Power [i.e. Germany], of whose assistance the Senoussi avail themselves, but with whom, like all their co-religionists, they nevertheless have no sympathy whatever.

In a word, "every hope of the Pan-Islamist lies with the Senoussi, who, I repeat, are far from being a foe to be despised." In sum, only a fully and authentically religious Pan-Islamism has any chance of succeeding.

It turns out, however, that the author of the letter is not too happy about this situation: "In my humble opinion, the Pan-Islamists do more harm than good to their co-religionists. What Islam should do is to range itself frankly on the side of modern ideas, putting aside religious ones. One may be a true believer without nourishing hatred for all others and refusing to be associated with their works. The emancipation of the people can only be won by science and progress." In the end, the author of the *Spectator* letter (about whose alleged identity as a "member of the sect of the Senoussi" it is permissible to entertain some doubt) comes down on the side of those European scholars, like Hartmann and Hurgronje, who soon afterwards expressed scepticism about the effectiveness of the Panislamist movement and the chances of reconciling the divergent interests of Turks and Arabs, fundamentalist religious leaders and nationalist or Ottoman politicians. Instead, he advocates Islam's full embrace of modernity: "Barbarism and a clinging to ancient ideas will but hasten the end and bring complete disaster. Islam has but to make her choice between her emancipation and her ruin."[38]

---

38 *The Spectator*, 24 August 1907, Correspondence columns. It is, of course, possible that the author of this letter was either a European agent interested in dissuading influential Muslims from buying into Pan-Islamism or a Muslim interested in reassuring Europeans that Pan-Islamism did not constitute a serious threat. The Senussi Sidi al-Mahdi referred to in the article should not be confused with the self-proclaimed "Mahdi" (Muhammed Ahmad of Dongola), who led the revolt in the Sudan (1881–1885) and whom the Senussi

The appearance of Saleb el Khalidi's lengthy letter in a general interest magazine such as *The Spectator*—with echoes of it reaching the New York magazine *Current Literature* for July-December 1907 and as far away as New Zealand, where it was summarized in the *Nelson Evening Mail* for 8 November 1907 in an article entitled "The Menace in North Africa: The Spread of Islamism"—is a sign that concern with the issues of Pan-Islamism and "Holy War" was not confined to scholarly or diplomatic circles but extended outward to a broad general public. Western writers reporting on the movement in such magazines and newspapers shared the uncertainty of the scholars about the importance to be attached to Pan-Islamism. A quite detailed and well-informed article, which appeared in the Boston-based *North American Review* soon after the Italian invasion of Tripolitania had unleashed calls for a *jihad*, reflects both the considerable anxiety provoked in the West by Pan-Islamism and the disagreement about its significance: "Hardly a day passes that the newspapers of Europe do not contain much information on the subject [of Pan-Islamism]," the author of the *North American Review* article observes. "In one issue of a London daily I found half a column on the Mohammedan unrest in India, the report of a Pan-Islamic conference in Egypt, a despatch from Russian Turkestan about a fanatic who had been arrested for preaching the Holy War, and an official French telegram from Lake Tchad about a new 'general order' intended by the military authorities to discourage some agitators of the Order of Derkawa who were stirring up trouble among the blacks of that district. [...] The Italian raid in the Tripolitaine and the recent overwhelming defeat of the Turks have revived the subject. [...] Broadly speaking," the author explains, "Pan-Islamism is the idea of uniting all the followers of Mohammed. But for what purpose? By what means? Before these questions the dream of unity at once breaks down."

The author then proceeds to identify and describe "three distinct and mutually hostile elements in the Pan-Islamic movement"—essentially extreme traditionalists, modernizers, and a hard to define group of religious zealots willing to use modern methods to achieve their ends:

First there is the Mohammedan 'Old Guard.' They are intellectual

---

al-Mahdi denounced as an impostor. The Senussi al-Mahdi focussed on religious and spiritual issues and avoided political engagement. The brotherhood became "a political and military force capable of organizing around resistance against the French colonial drive from the south and, after 1911, the Italian occupation of Libya" only after his death and under the leadership of his successor, Ahmed al-Sharif al-Senussi (Claudia Anna Gazzini, *Jihad in Exile: Ahmed al-Sharif al-Sanussi 1918–1933* [Unpublished M.A. thesis, Princeton University, 2004]).

reactionaries who have learned nothing and have forgotten all that knowledge which once made them powerful, all the science and art which was the glory of the Great Caliphs. The 'black' ecclesiastical coterie at Rome is wildly progressive compared to them. They are true to the old traditions which destroyed the library at Alexandria twelve centuries ago. All the truth of the world is in the Koran; everything not in that sacred book is false. Like all fanatics, they are visionary. They take no thought of practical ways and means. They attribute the decline of Islam to the sins of the people. If they would only return to the primitive purity of their religion, Allah would draw his sword and the career of conquest which marked the early days of Mohammedanism would return.

The "apostles of this revival," begging their way to China, Siberia, India, the Sudan, Central Africa, and Morocco, are received everywhere as holy men and "the people listen to their preaching with awe." The extent of their influence is hard to judge, according to the author of the article. "It is easy to dismiss them as ignorant fanatics," he concludes prudently. "But the world has seen many momentous things done in the name of Ignorance and Fanaticism."

The second faction of the Pan-Islamists is as far removed as possible from the first: "Its inspiration comes from the 'Europeanized' Mohammedans" who "have studied in the Sorbonne, at Oxford, or at least in one of the many European schools which have been established in the Levant. Most of them are—although they might not admit it—Free Thinkers [...] but they consider that some religion is necessary for the masses." Encouraged by the victory of an Eastern people over a great Western power in the Russo-Japanese war, "they dream of rejuvenating the lands of Islam after the manner of the Japanese. [...] The best of the Egyptian and Indian 'Nationalist' movements, the cream of the Young Turks and of the Persian 'Constitutionalists' belong to this faction." They hope to achieve their aims "by reason" and "have no hostility toward Christian nations." This strand of Pan-Islamism enjoys the sympathy of "disinterested observers—that is practically every one but colonial administrators," the author of the article claims. Unfortunately, however, the inability of the followers of the Young Turks to "govern wisely has discredited them everywhere" and "given a new argument to European colonialists in their contention that the Mohammedans are unfit to manage their own affairs."

The third group identified by the author is "less clear-cut in outline. It is marked by a bewildering mixture of crude fanaticism, mysticism, and European culture." Its partisans differ from the second group "in the sincerity of their religious life and in their belief in the arbitrament of war."

The "order of the Snoussia" is the standard-bearer of this rapidly expanding group. But "while the book of its founder resembles nothing in the literature of Christendom except some of the writings of the medieval Anabaptists and the more frenzied of the Russian Mystics," the "Snoussia" differs from the first group in its "keen interest in such practical things as rifles and military training." Unlike other brotherhoods that embrace poverty, its leaders are excellent fund-raisers and organizers, and the order "encourages its members to enlist in the native regiments [of the colonial powers] and get training in the ways of European warfare." There is, in addition, "a constant pilfering of arms and ammunition [...] in almost every native regiment." Few police officers in Egypt or Tunisia would question the claim "that the Snoussia could put into the field 'several' thousand troops, drilled by European officers, abundantly supplied with arms and ammunition, and supported by some artillery." They are believed to have a major depot of arms at an oasis along the Egyptian-Tripolitanian border, where no European has yet penetrated. Some people believe they even have the capacity to manufacture arms. Stories circulate about "high-power, modern, repeating rifles which do not bear the trade-mark of any European manufacturer" and "native rumor says that there is a great arsenal in this mysterious oasis where Mohammedan graduates of Western technical schools are manufacturing arms and ammunitions against the great day"—i.e. the day of the *jihad*. Indeed the rapidly growing popularity of the "Snoussia" is due "unquestionably to the widespread belief that it is making practical preparation for the Holy War."

"So far at least," the writer concludes, "the differences in ideals of these factions have prevented any united action. And there can be no real Pan-Islamism until these differences are dissolved or until one faction swallows up the other two." Colonial administrators are most concerned about the third faction, since it is "not only talking about a militant rebirth of Mohammedanism" but "actively preparing for it." Nonetheless, it is hard to obtain any solid information. Hence the French in North Africa, for instance, "are divided into two camps: those who believe that a Holy War is a serious and imminent menace and those who scoff at the idea." The author's personal experience leads him "to believe that the majority of the French who have lived long enough in the country to know the language do not scoff." Among the English officers and administrators in Egypt there is a similar difference of opinion, though in general they appear to worry less since they finally succeeded in putting down the Mahdi uprising in the Sudan. Still, there is uncertainty about the trustworthiness of the native troops. "Would the Egyptian troops march against the new Mahdi?" for instance. All in all, however, "the overwhelming majority of European residents of North Africa do not fear the Holy War." There is too much rivalry among the various Muslim orders for them to unite their efforts. "The Dominicans and the Jesuits never hated one another the way these rival Mohammedan sects do," one man told the author of the article. Moreover most of their leaders, he claimed, can in the end be bought. "If a new Mahdi sprang up, he would attract attention at once. If he could not be bribed, he would be suppressed and it would be one of the big Sheiks whose prestige was threatened by the upstart who would hand him over to the Europeans. But there will never be a new Mahdi. It is cheaper and simpler to buy them before they gather enough followers to fight." Then there is the absence of a single language: not only do Turks, Arabs, and Persians not speak the same language, Arabic speakers themselves are separated by their countless dialects. "Here in North Africa," the author's informant explains, "a Moor cannot understand an Algerian." Anyway, "the only really warlike people," in his view, "are the Berbers of the mountains" and "their language is not even remotely related to Arabic. Besides, the Mohammedans as a people are unarmed. The rifles they buy from gun-runners are low grade and inside of a year are too rusty to work. They are split up into little tribes, with all the jealousy of tribal organization, different dialects and customs, rival Caïds. There is no more political or racial unity than there is of religious unity. Pan-Islamism is a story to frighten children. The Mussulmans are corrupt to the core. [...] Every leader—Cadis, Ulema, Caïds, and Marabouts—all are for sale."

In sum, the optimism of many Europeans about the inefficacy of Pan-Islamism is based, according to the author of the *North American Review* article, on "contempt for the native and great faith in the military power of Europe." He himself, however, is not one hundred percent convinced: "There is always the other side to be remembered; the earnest, serious men who are not optimistic about it." Consequently, "a serious and vehement difference of opinion exists about the danger of a Pan-Islamic revolt. The crux of the matter is whether or not the varied tribes of the Mohammedan world, speaking different dialects and languages, and the varied religious sects, with their rival leaders, can unite." While "it certainly does not seem probable," not so long ago "an authority on the Near East told me that national jealousy between Servia and Bulgaria was so great that there was not the remotest chance of a Balkan federation!"

In the closing page of this 1913 article the author speculates on the effect on European politics and the balance of power in Europe in the event of a "Pan-Islamic revolt." His reflections suggest that the view of Pan-Islamism and its potential that was being fervently promoted at the *Auswärtiges Amt* and in the Kaiser's circle by Max Freiherr von Oppenheim was by no means unusual or unique to Oppenheim and was probably not invented by him. The American journalist considers first the effect of a Panislamist revolt on the countries of the Triple Entente: England would no longer be able to withdraw troops from India for deployment in Europe and could count only on her "minute home army"; Russia would be kept busy with her own very large Mohammedan population; "France, with her great North African empire, would be denuded of troops" and her efforts to put down the revolt "would bankrupt her." In contrast, Germany and Austria—that is, the Central Powers—"alone of the great nations would be unaffected by a Mohammedan revolt. With the military power of her chief rivals strained to the utmost, would Germany be expected not to attempt to gain her coveted 'place in the sun'?"[39]

If Oppenheim's idea that Pan-Islamism was a force to be reckoned with (and eventually exploited as an instrument in European power politics) was not especially original in the first decade of the twentieth century, neither was his related interest in *jihad* and its potential. The notion of *jihad* or "Holy War" is closely connected with Pan-Islamism, inasmuch as the Pan-Islamists stress the duty of all Muslims to come to the defence of the world community of Muslims, wherever and whenever any part of it is attacked or wronged by an Infidel power. The term *jihad*, however, has many meanings, which modern scholars have explored at length. "The word *djihād* in modern Arabic stands for rather a vague concept," according to the Dutch scholar Rudolf Peters:

> In accordance with its original meaning, it can denote any effort toward a subjectively praiseworthy aim, which need not necessarily have anything to do with religion. Hence it has been used to mean class struggle, the struggle between the old and the new and even the efforts of Christian missionaries. But even when it is used in an Islamic context, it does not always denote armed struggle. It may also mean a spiritual struggle for the good of Islamic society or an inner struggle

---

39 Albert Edwards, "The Menace of Pan-Islamism," *North American Review*, 197 (May 1913): 645–57.

against one's evil inclinations. This wide semantic spectrum of the word *djihād* has confused many a foreign visitor with a defective knowledge of the Arabic language. Hearing the word *djihād* being used in sermons, in mosques or on the radio, they were led to think that a massacre of non-Moslems was at hand.[40]

In the West, indeed, Peters argues, the term has had a more specific meaning than in Arabic:

> The Islamic doctrine of *jihād* has always appealed to the Western imagination. The image of the dreadful Turk, clad in a long robe and brandishing his scimitar, ready to slaughter any infidel that might come his way and would refuse to be converted to the religion of Mahomet, has been a stereotype in Western literature for a long time. Nowadays this image has been replaced by that of the Arab "terrorist" in battledress, armed with a Kalashnikov gun and prepared to murder in cold blood innocent Jewish and Christian women and children. The assumption underlying these stereotypes is that Moslems, often loosely called Arabs, are innately bloodthirsty and inimical toward persons of a different persuasion, and that [...] their religion [...] preaches intolerance, fanaticism and continuous warfare against unbelievers. This view of Islam and Moslems, which developed in the Middle Ages, acquired new life and vigour in the era of European imperialism. Moslems were depicted as backward, fanatic and bellicose, in order to justify colonial expansion with the argument that it served the spread of civilization, what the French called *mission civilisatrice*. At the same time, this offered a convenient pretext for the use of force against the indigenous population, for behind the outward appearance of submissiveness of the colonized Moslems, the colonizers saw the continuous danger of rebelliousness lurking, nourished by the idea of *jihād* and waiting for an opportunity to manifest itself. The French orientalist Louis Mercier expressed these fears in the following words: "Cependant, tous ceux d'entre nous, qui ont vécu de longues années au contact étroit d'une population musulmane, d'orient ou d'occident, ont eu de multiples occasions de sentir, j'en suis persuadé, que l'idée du jihâd

---

40   Rudolf Peters, *Islam and Colonialism: The Doctrine of Jihad in Modern History* (The Hague and New York: Mouton, 1979), p. 3. An even more far-reaching caveat had been issued by the German travel writer, Otto C. Artbauer, almost seven decades earlier, at the turn of the century, in his popular *Die Rifpiraten und ihre Heimat* [The Bandits of the Rif and their Homeland]. "The meaning of the word *jihad* as understood by Mohammed and as it appears in the Koran is not properly struggle against infidels in general, but rather struggle against the evil inclinations in one's own self. The word and its meaning are constantly misused by both Europeans and Orientals. Whenever foreigners are beaten up somewhere in the Orient, they immediately imagine that they have been the victims of *jihad*. If one tribe steals some camels from another in the East, there will be a call for *jihad*. Spanish and French newspapers especially are constantly discovering some hermit wandering around in the Atlas mountains and preaching *jihad* against all foreigners. All that is utter nonsense" (O.C. Artbauer, *Die Rifpiraten und ihre Heimat. Erste Kunde aus verschlossener Welt* [Stuttgart: Stecker & Schröder, 1911], pp. 214–15, under "Dschihad" in the list of terms following the index).

persiste à travers le temps au point de dominer, fût-ce d'une façon latente, toute la vie de cette population, d'imprégner ses aspirations profondes et d'influer sur son attitude, dans ses relations avec les *infidèles*."[41]

Peters emphasizes that in the Muslim world *jihad* has always had multiple meanings, ranging, in one classification, from "the '*Jihad* of the Heart', i.e. struggling against one's sinful inclinations, the '*Jihad* of the Tongue', i.e. ordering what is good and forbidding what is evil (*al-amr bi-l-mdruf wa-l-nah an al-munkar*) and the '*Jihad* of the Hand', i.e. the administering of disciplinary measures such as beating, by rulers and men of authority in order to prevent people from committing abominable acts," to "the '*Jihad* of the Sword', i.e. fighting the unbelievers for religion's sake." At the same time, however, he also holds that "this last meaning [...] is always meant when the word *jihad* is used without qualification." In all its forms, "the direct purpose of *jihad* is the strengthening of Islam, the protection of believers and voiding the earth of unbelief. The ultimate aim is the complete supremacy of Islam, as one can learn from K 2:193 and 8:39 ('*Fight them until there is no dissension [or persecution] and the religion is entirely Allah's*')."[42] Understandably, Muslim scholars and holy men have pored over the meanings of this crucial term, argued about them, and sought to lay down rules and conditions that would take account of the changing historical situations in which Muslims have found themselves: in what circumstances and for what ends, for instance, is raising *jihad* legitimate? In order to conquer the world for Islam? In order to resist any infidel invader of a Muslim territory? Or to resist only those infidel rulers who interfere with the Muslim's practice of his religion? Who may be killed in a *jihad* and who may not? What special arrangements can be made with particular infidels to avoid war?

The invasion and occupation of Muslim lands by European powers in the age of imperialism—the British in India and then also in Egypt; the French, followed later by the Italians, in North Africa; the Dutch in the East Indies; the Russians in the Caucasus—led both to the development of Pan-Islamism as a political program, as we have seen, and, concomitantly, to an upsurge in calls for *jihad. Jihad* was invoked in the revolt of Dipanegara against Dutch rule in

---

41 Peters, *Islam and Colonialism*, pp. 4–5.
42 Ibid., p. 10. See also the entry on "*Jihad*" in Avraham Sela, ed., *Political Encyclopaedia of the Middle East* (Jerusalem: Jerusalem Publishing House, 1999), pp. 425–26. This excellent short article outlines clearly both the complex meanings of *jihad* (and the absence of any single, set doctrine) and its invocation in modern history since the Mahdi in the Sudan in the 1880s.

Java (1825–1830) and again, half a century later, in the Atjeh War between the Sultanate of Atjeh and the Dutch in Sumatra (1873–1904); it was invoked in India in the first half of the nineteenth century by Muslims in Northern India and Bengal who urged rebellion against the British, albeit such violence was later declared illegitimate, chiefly by Muslim scholars from the upper classes, many of whose members had been recruited for employment in the British administration and therefore advocated an accommodation with it. Since the British guaranteed freedom of religion, according to those authorities, India was neither *Dar al-Islam* (the territory of Islam) nor *Dar al-harb* (the territory of war against the enemies of Islam) but a neutral area in which Muslims enjoyed security, *Dar al-aman*.[43]

The Russo-Turkish War of 1877–1878 was widely viewed by Muslims as a *jihad* in defence of Islam. In pamphlets distributed in India, those who did not participate in it, at least by contributing financially, were threatened with punishment and disgrace both now and in the hereafter.[44] The British bombardment of Alexandria on 11 July 1882, the prelude to what amounted to a take-over of Egypt, provoked an immediate call for *jihad*. A *jihad* proclamation was published in *al-Waqa'ial-Misriyyah*, the Official Gazette of Egypt and all over the country, *ulama* preached *jihad* and exhorted the Egyptians to support the army in its struggle against the unbelievers.[45] The invasion of Tripolitania by an Italian army of 60,000 men three decades later provoked, as we have seen, a similar response. A call to *jihad*, spelling out in detail the duties of "all Moslems, especially in such countries as have been occupied by the enemies of the Religion" and the rewards that may be expected by the warrior and martyr, was published by Sayyid Ahmad al-Sharif, the leader of the Senussi brotherhood, in the Cairo newspaper *al-Mu'aijad* on 29 January 1912. Characteristically, this was interpreted by the correspondent of *The Times* of London as a call for war against Christians, whereas the newspaper insisted that *jihad* was being urged on all Muslims only against the Italians as invaders of a Muslim land.[46] Soon afterwards, in 1913–1914, a treatise on *jihad*, by Sayyid Ahmad al-Sharif,

---

43 Peters, *Islam and Colonialism*, pp. 46–49.
44 Özcan, *Pan-Islamism: Indian Muslims, the Ottomans and Britain (1877–1924)*, p. 75.
45 Peters, *Islam and Colonialism*, p. 79.
46 See Erich Graefe, "Der Aufruf des Scheichs der Senusija zum Heiligen Kriege," *Islam* 3 (1912): 141–50 (p. 142). It is also worth noting that, for whatever reason, the *Times* correspondent downplayed the likely effect of the Senussi call: "Until the actual text is known, it is difficult to gauge the probable effect of the exhortation, but in view of the general terms in which it appears to be couched, and emanating as it does only from the brother of El Senousi, it is not thought that very great importance need be attached to the proclamation" (*The Times*, 19 January 1912, report from Cairo dated 18 January).

was published in Cairo. It addressed the Libyan Muslims in particular: "How can you live with vipers and scorpions and with those who openly profess polytheism and the Trinity and who destroy the *mihrabs*? [prayer niches oriented toward Mecca in the wall of mosques]. How can the light of the sun of Islam shine over you when the Banner of the Cross and Darkness flutters amongst you?"[47]

This extensive review of perceptions of Pan-Islamism and *jihad* in the decades leading up to the outbreak of war in 1914 suggests that there was nothing truly surprising or particularly original about Oppenheim's recommendation, in his memorandum of that year, that as soon as Turkey had been persuaded to enter the War on the side of the Central Powers the Sultan-Caliph should proclaim *jihad* against the enemies of Islam. Fomenting revolution as a war strategy was in itself by no means new in 1914: at war with Austria in 1859, Napoleon III had threatened to stir up the various national groups in the Habsburg Empire; Bismarck and Moltke adopted the same strategy on the eve of the Austro-Prussian War; in 1870–1871 Molkte dispatched agents—among them Gerhard Rohlfs, a mentor of the young Oppenheim—to Tunisia to stir up the Arabs against France; and years later, anticipating a possible two-front war (in the East against Russia and in the West against France), his nephew, usually known as Moltke the Younger, considered how Germany could benefit from Russian weakness on its "vulnerable borders" (Russian-occupied Poland, Finland, and the Caucasus).[48] There was also nothing novel or unfamiliar in 1914 about a call for *jihad*. What was different from previous such calls was the exploiting of *jihad* and the exciting of Muslims to rebellion by a European power as part of its war strategy in a struggle with other European powers.[49] To the German leadership, encouraging *jihad* among Muslims and promoting Communist revolution in Russia were equivalent strategies designed to benefit Imperial Germany. As is well known, it was German officials who facilitated Lenin's return to Russia through Germany from neutral Switzerland in 1917.

---

47 Cit. Peters, *Islam and Colonialism*, p. 87; also p. 186, note 125.
48 See, *inter alia*, Hans-Ulrich Seidt, *Berlin Kabul Moskau. Oskar Ritter von Niedermayer und Deutschlands Geopolitik* (Munich: Universitas, 2000), p. 44.
49 See Gabriele Teichmann "Fremder wider Willen—Max von Oppenheim in der wilhelminischen Epoche" in *Geschichte zwischen Wissenschaft und Politik. Festschrift für Michael Stürmer zum 65. Geburtstag* (Baden-Baden: Nomos, 2003), pp. 231–48 (p. 239): "Zwar gehörte das Kampfmittel der nationalrevolutionären Aufhebung seit Beginn des 19. Jahrhunderts zum Arsenal europäischer Machtpolitik. Oppenheim war jedoch der erste, der eine Weltreligion politisch zu instrumentalisieren versuchte."

5. Oppenheim's 1914 *Denkschrift*

The full text of Oppenheim's *Denkschrift betreffend die Revolutionierung der islamischen Gebiete unserer Feinde* [Memorandum concerning the fomenting of revolutions in the Islamic territories of our enemies], carefully prepared by the Freiburg scholar Tim Epkenhans, was published and thus made generally accessible in 2001 in the academic journal *Archivum Ottomanicum* (vol. 19, pp. 120–63). It will be presented here, therefore, only in its broad outlines. Our attention will focus on its reception, on the means employed to execute its proposals, including the *fatwa* issued in the name of the Sultan-Caliph, and on its effectiveness.

The memorandum is dated "Berlin, im Oktober, 1914." At that time Turkey had not yet officially entered World War I. A brief reminder of the succession of events leading up to Turkey's entry into the war will not be out of place:

On 28 July 1914 Emperor Franz Josef declared war on Serbia after rejecting a relatively accommodating Serbian response to Austria's demand that the Serbian conspirators responsible for the assassination of the Austrian Crown Prince and his wife in Sarajevo be delivered to Vienna to stand trial there.

On 31 July Russia, as an ally of Serbia, mobilized; in response, on 1 August, Germany mobilized and declared war on Russia.

On 3 August Germany declared war on France, which was allied to Russia, and poured troops into neutral Belgium; Britain sent Germany an ultimatum demanding the withdrawal of German troops from Belgium.

On 4 August Britain declared war on Germany.

On 2 August, in view of the seeming inevitability of a major war in Europe, a secret treaty of alliance was signed by the Ottoman Empire, which feared for its future in the event of a victory of the Entente powers, and Germany, which was eager to block a crucial line of communication, through the Bosphorus, between the Western powers and their Russian ally, as well as to use the Ottomans in order to extend their influence in the Muslim world. It was not until almost three months later, however, on 25 October, that the strongly pro-German Ottoman War Minister, Enver Pasha, with the support of Navy Minister Djemal Pasha and Interior Minister Talat Pasha, instructed Rear-Admiral Wilhelm Souchon—a German naval officer who had sought refuge in Turkish waters for his warships, the *Goeben* and the *Breslau*, after they had shelled ports in French Algeria, and who had been appointed Commander-in-Chief of the Ottoman Navy—to enter the Black Sea with his warships, now reflagged as Turkish ships, renamed the *Yavuz Selim* and the *Medilli*, and manned by their original German crews wearing fezzes. Their mission was to attack Russian harbors and naval vessels. As had certainly been anticipated, this action (29 October), provoked a Russian declaration of war on Turkey (2 November). On 5 November, Russia's allies, Britain and France, in turn declared war on Turkey.[1]

It was thus early November before Turkey was drawn openly into the conflict. There were significant elements in Turkey that opposed entry into the war. According to the celebrated Turkish woman writer and activist Halide Edib Adivar, "in 1914 not only the masses but most of the intellectuals and leading forces of the Unionists [i.e. the Young Turks] were against the war. Only Enver Pasha and a certain convinced military group, along with the profiteers, were in favor of war." She herself opposed Turkish entry into the war.[2] Arnold Toynbee, then a 26-year old Fellow of Balliol in the service of British Intelligence, claims to have seen a privately circulated German memo of 1916, in which it was stated that "Turkey's entry into the War was unwelcome to Turkish society in Constantinople, whose sympathies were with France, as well as to the mass of the people, but the Panislamic propaganda and the military dictatorship were able to stifle all opposition."[3] The Ottoman cabinet itself was divided. A small but powerful war party, led by Enver, favoured immediate entry into the war; another, far less powerful group of ministers was completely committed

---

1 On the hesitations, orders, counter-orders, and secret counter-counter-orders culminating in the shelling of the Russian ports, see the detailed study of Carl Mühlmann, *Deutschland und die Türkei 1913–1914* (Berlin-Grünewald: Dr. Walther Rothschild, 1929), pp. 71–74 (Politische Wissenschaft, Heft 7).
2 *Memoirs of Halide Edib* (New York and London: The Century Co., n.d., c. 1926), p. 381.
3 A. J. Toynbee, *Turkey: A Past and a Future* (London: Hodder and Stoughton; New York: George H. Doran Company, 1917), p. 21. Toynbee may have been citing Harry Stuermer, the Constantinople correspondent of the *Kölnische Zeitung* from Spring 1915 to Christmas 1916, who left Germany for Switzerland in 1917, and who likewise claimed that Turkish opinion was opposed to war (*Two War Years in Constantinople: Sketches of German and Young Turkish Ethics and Politics*, trans. E. Allen and the author [New York: George H. Doran Company, 1917], pp. 209–11). On anti-war sentiment in Turkey see, in addition, Rafael de Nogales, *Four Years Beneath the Crescent* (New York: Charles Scribner's Sons, 1926), p. 13.

to maintaining Turkey's neutrality as a fundamental policy; while a third group, the largest, without opposing entry into the war in principle, held that for tactical reasons it was in Turkey's best interest to remain neutral for as long as possible. The treaty of alliance with Germany had been negotiated by the war party without the knowledge of the other members of the cabinet. The Grand Vizier, Said Halim Pasha, who as Foreign Minister had been involved in the negotiations for the treaty and had appended his signature to it, but was—in the words of Djemal Pasha, the Navy Minister and future commander of the Fourth Turkish Army in the Sinai—"utterly opposed to our participation in the war," insisted that the treaty be kept secret. When knowledge of it finally reached the other members of the cabinet, it was met with vehement protest on the part of the majority. The deliberate provocation constituted by the bombardment of the Russian ports by the "Turkish" fleet, similarly decided by the pro-German war party without consulting their cabinet colleagues, resulted in the Grand Vizier's threatening to resign and in the actual resignation of several other ministers.[4] Oppenheim's memorandum was thus composed at a time when there was still some uncertainty about Turkey's eventual role in the war, despite the pressure from Berlin and the considerable power wielded by the "Three Pashas"—War Minister Enver, Navy Minister Djemal, and Interior Minister Talat.[5]

Hence the emphasis, at the beginning of the memorandum, on the necessity of active Turkish co-operation, military as well as propagandistic: "The most important precondition for fomenting revolution in the Islamic territories of our enemies is the energetic co-operation of the Turks under the banner of the Sultan-Caliph." Oppenheim goes on to observe, generally, that half-measures in support of his proposals will get nowhere: "We have to supply the Turks with men, money, and matériel, for only by deploying considerable resources can we obtain a satisfactory result." The end,

---

4 Djemal Pasha, *Memories of a Turkish Statesman 1913–1919* (New York: George H. Doran, 1922), pp. 130–33; Mühlmann, *Deutschland und die Türkei 1913–1914*, pp. 39–43, 51–56, 71–77; Sina Akşin, *Turkey: from Empire to Revolutionary Republic*, trans. Dexter Mursaloğlu (London: Hurst & Company, 2007), pp. 95–96.

5 In a letter to Ernst Jäckh, dated Therapia (the elegant waterside district to the north of Constantinople where many embassies were located) 13 October 1914, the writer (possibly a naval officer, named Janson) complained that "we found things here very different from the way we imagined them to be in Berlin. To pick out the thing that most affects the military man: we were sent out here on the explicit understanding that we would be used in a military offensive. For the moment, there is no question of that and there is still constant discussion as to whether and when Turkey will take an active part in the war." (Ernst Jäckh Papers, Yale. MS group 467, Princeton University Library, Microfilm 11747, box 1)

however, will be worth every effort expended to achieve it, for "only when the Turks invade Egypt and revolts break out in India will England be made to yield. Public opinion in 'greater England' will force the government in London either to send as much as half the fleet to India in order to protect the many Englishmen living there, as well as the billions invested in the country, and to sustain Britain's place in the world, or—since it can be expected that England on its own [i.e. without its empire] will be unable to achieve that last goal—to make peace on terms favorable to us."[6]

The memorandum makes detailed practical suggestions for creating an efficient, well-organized propaganda machine, to be run by the Turks and the Germans, with the latter in full control, but in such a way that the Turks are unaware of this.[7] The aim of the propaganda is to persuade all Muslims, but especially the Muslim subjects of the British, the French, and the Russians, that the Germans are winning the war and will emerge victorious from it, and thus to encourage Muslims under British, French, and Russian rule to rise up against their foreign masters. To this end, Oppenheim proposes establishing a *Nachrichtenstelle* [intelligence bureau] in Berlin, to be directed by himself and staffed by German Orientalists and foreign-born lecturers, for the purpose of preparing leaflets in all the relevant languages; making use of all the German consulates in the Middle East (which should expect an appropriate increase in their monthly budgets) as well as of private German citizens in foreign service and German businessmen abroad, in order to ensure the widest possible distribution of the propaganda material; and not least, setting up information agencies or reading rooms (*Nachrichtensäle*) in all major population centres.[8]

On the question of action to be taken against the enemy, the memorandum describes in great detail the situation in the main British, French, and Russian territories inhabited by Muslims (population of the area, proportion of Muslims, whether predominantly Shi'a or Sunni, attitudes of the leaders and of the various classes of the population to rule by Christian Europeans, strength and morale of native and European armed

---

6 *Denkschrift* in *Archivum Ottomanicum*, 19 (2001): 120–63 (see Introduction, note 7 above), p. 2. (All page numbers of the *Denkschrift* refer to the original pagination.) Oppenheim's prediction that Britain on its own, without the Empire, would be unable to sustain its place in the world has turned out to be entirely accurate.
7 Ibidem, p. 8.
8 Oppenheim had been pressing from the beginning for systematic conduct of a propaganda war in the Islamic lands. (Memo from Oppenheim to Bethmann Hollweg 18 August 1914; see Wolfgang G. Schwanitz, "Djihad 'Made in Germany': der Streit um den Heiligen Krieg 1914–1915," *Sozial.Geschichte*, 18 [2003]: 7–34 [p. 11]).

forces, conditions that would need to be created in order to incite the people to rise up, etc.). Sections are devoted to Egypt and Arabia; Kyrgyzstan and Turkestan; Morocco, Algeria and Tunisia; and India. The first and last of these sections—on Egypt and India—are by far the most substantial and detailed, the chief enemy, in Oppenheim's eyes, being without doubt Britain, and the potential effect of uprisings in India and Egypt on the the military capabilities of the Triple Entente, in his view, greatest.[9] A successful Turkish attack on Egypt, for which the assistance of the Bedouins should be sought, would be likely to set off massive revolts in Egypt and mutinies in the Anglo-Egyptian army, resulting in closure of the Suez Canal to British ships and disruption of the crucial British connection with India. Without such action by the Turks, however, nothing can be expected of the Egyptians. (In general, Oppenheim expressed a stereotypical view of "Orientals" in this memorandum intended for German officialdom. Thus the Turks were poor organizers and would achieve nothing without German guidance; the Armenians and the Christian Georgians "probably deserve their reputation as cowards, plotters, and schemers"; the great mass of "Orientals" was in general "apathetic.")

Further sections of the memorandum deal with the role to be played by Persia and Afghanistan and with ways of persuading their rulers to co-operate, both militarily and through propaganda, with the Central Powers.[10] Again the social and political situation of both countries is described, their military potential analyzed in some detail, and the best means envisaged of overcoming the mutual distrust that Oppenheim sees as preventing a highly desirable triple alliance of the three Muslim powers: Turkey, Persia, and Afghanistan. Such an alliance, in Oppenheim's view, would be directed chiefly toward promoting uprisings in India, both by appealing to Muslim solidarity and by means of a military push toward the Persian Gulf and the North-West Territories.[11] Useful by-products of

---

9 Thus Morocco, for example, though ripe for revolt, is too divided tribally to be of more than secondary significance as far as the war itself is concerned. Moreover, the Moroccans consider their own Sultan to be the legitimate Caliph and do not recognize the Turkish Sultan as the supreme religious authority (*Denkschrift*, pp. 95–96).

10 *Denkschrift*, pp. 59–78.

11 Subsequently the Turks, fearful that German plans for the region would lead to its exploding in revolution, pursued a policy intended to "restrict the revolutionary activities of the Germans." Instead of bringing the Persians into the German-Turkish alliance, as the Germans wished, "so as to provide the necessary backing for the progress of German operations with regard to Afghanistan and against India," the Turks envisaged a far more conservative Holy Alliance of the three Islamic nations—Turkey, Persia, and Afghanistan—by which Persian neutrality would be reaffirmed and guaranteed.

such military action are also considered, such as gaining control of the Anglo-Persian Oil Company's wells, storage depots, and refineries and thus cutting off supplies of oil to the British fleet—as well as laying the groundwork for a German take-over of the facilities after the war. (As noted earlier, Oppenheim was always attentive to the economic and commercial possibilities inherent in the various projects, political and scholarly, that he supported.) Finally, Oppenheim suggests methods of exploiting anger and resentment among the Muslim colonial troops in the British and French armies: by dropping propaganda leaflets from the air encouraging them to desert and go over to the Germans, and by separating Muslim POWs from their French and English comrades and placing them in separate camps where they would receive favourable treatment, where all their religious needs would be catered to, and where an effort could be made with the assistance of specially brought in imams to "fanaticize" as many as possible. Those who responded best to this treatment would then be persuaded to participate in anti-Entente propaganda, and, in some cases, to return to the front to work in Germany's interest—either by fighting on the German side or by infiltrating their former British or French units and sowing dissent and disaffection among fellow-Muslims.

The indispensable condition of Oppenheim's proposals was that, as most Muslims, according to him, accepted the Turkish Sultan's claim to be the Caliph or religious leader of the *Ummah,* all propaganda directed toward Muslims be carried out in the name of the Caliph and thus be invested with the "nimbus," as Oppenheim put it, of the successor of the Prophet.[12] "As soon as Turkey strikes, the call to Holy War and emancipation from foreign rule must immediately be sounded."[13] Oppenheim was taken at his word. On 11 November, nine days after Russia responded to the Turkish naval attacks of late October by declaring war on the Ottoman Empire, and

---

Ambassador von Wangenheim, who was sceptical of the grandiose projects developed by Oppenheim and some others at the *Auswärtiges Amt*, urged the Kaiser to support this move and to underwrite the neutrality of Persia, but his advice was rejected (see Jon Kimche, *The Second Arab Awakening* [London: Thames and Hudson, 1970], pp. 34–35).

12 *Denkschrift*, p. 7. Oppenheim conceded that the Moroccans claimed that their own Sultan was the true Caliph but noted that even they acknowledged the Turkish Sultan as head of the most powerful Islamic state.

13 *Denkschrift*, p. 7. In August 1914, the importance of the Sultan-Caliph's proclaiming *jihad* to all Muslims in Asia, India, Egypt, and Africa had already been emphasized by Kaiser Wilhelm II himself when in August 1914 he pressed Enver Pasha, the Turkish War minister, to bring Turkey into the war (see Wolfgang G. Schwanitz, "Djihad 'Made in Germany'," *Sozial.Geschichte*, 18 [2003], p. 11).

six days after Britain and France followed suit, Turkey belatedly declared war on Britain and France and their allies. Five *fatwas* were drawn up and signed by Sheikh ul-Islam Khairi, the Grand Mufti of Constantinople. Couched in the form of a series of questions to and answers from the learned Sheikh, the *fatwas* proclaimed that the pursuit of *jihad* against the Entente powers was a holy obligation of every individual Muslim, including Muslims living under the rule of any one of those powers and thus subject to the harshest reprisals from their rulers, such as "death for themselves and the destruction of their families." Any Muslim failing in this duty, it was stated, will incur the wrath of God; any Muslim who engages in combat against the soldiers of Islam (hence any Muslims fighting in the British, French, and Russian armies) will merit the fires of hell.[14]

On 11 November, at a solemn ceremony in the great mosque of Mehmet II the Conqueror in Constantinople, the banner of the Prophet was unfurled and Sheikh ul-Islam Khairi girded the Sultan with the sword of the Prophet. The Sultan and the War Minister, Enver Pasha, delivered fiery speeches calling upon the people to join in the struggle against the enemies of Islam. On 14 November the formal promulgation of the *fatwas* calling for *jihad* was marked by a spectacle carefully planned and directed by the German authorities, of which the Dutch Orientalist Snouck Hurgronje wrote contemptuously that it had to have reminded any Westerner "of a musical comedy of Offenbach."[15] A crowd of demonstrators, accompanied by a band, gathered in front of the German Embassy, where they were greeted from the balcony by Ambassador von Wangenheim and fourteen Moroccan, Tunisian, and Algerian POWs, specially brought in from camps in Germany to create a vivid image of the solidarity of all Muslims. Interpreter Karl Emil Schabinger, who had travelled with the group—and who later succeeded Oppenheim as head of the latter's intelligence bureau or *Nachrichtenstelle für den Orient*—stood behind the POWs, prompting them to cries of "Long Live the Sultan and Caliph." After the crowd had been harangued by the leader of the Young Turks' Progress and Union Party and a Turkish-speaking member of Ambassdor Wangenheim's staff, to which it responded

---

14 The texts of the *fatwas* and of the proclamation that followed, translated into English, can be found in Geoffrey Lewis, "The Ottoman Proclamation of Jihād in 1914," *Islamic Quarterly*, 19 (1975): 157–63. Lewis gives the date on which the *fatwas* were signed as 11 November; the date of their promulgation as 14 November, and the date of their publication in the newspaper *Iqdām* as 15 November. Gottfried Hagen (*Die Türkei im Ersten Weltkrieg*, pp. 3–4) gives the date of signing as 7 November.

15 C. Snouck Hurgronje, *The Holy War "Made in Germany"*, p. 50.

Fig. 5.1 El Dschihad or Al Ǧihād, newspaper published in Arabic and other languages by the Nachrichtenstelle für den Orient for Muslim prisoners-of-war who had served in the armies of the Entente powers. First number appeared in Arabic on March 1, 1915, thereafter fortnightly, then irregularly until 1918. Reproduced in Gerhard Höpp, Arabische und Islamische Periodika in Berlin und Brandenburg 1915–1945 (Berlin: Das Arabische Buch [Forschungsschwerpunkt Mittlerer Orient], 1994), p. 61.

with cheers for the Kaiser and Germany, Islam's ally, the demonstration moved on to the Embassy of Austria-Hungary and then to the inner city, where Schabinger recounts that one of the accompanying policemen, fired up by patriotic enthusiasm, entered a hotel, took out his revolver and fired point blank at a handsome English grandfather-clock in the entrance hall.[16] The next day, 15 November, the five *fatwas* appeared in print in the newspaper *Iqdām* and in French translation in the Constantinople French newspaper *La Turquie*. Finally, on 25 November, the official proclamation of *jihad* was published in Turkish in the newspaper *Sabah*, along with the names of the signatories, led by Sheikh ul-Islam Khairi. A French translation came out the following day in *La Turquie*.

In *Ambassador Morgenthau's Story*, published at the end of the war (1918), the American ambassador to Constantinople gives a vivid account of the proclamation and of one of the pamphlets preaching *jihad* that followed it. Soon after the Sultan's declaration of war, Morgenthau writes,

> the Sheik-ul-Islam published his proclamation, summoning the whole Moslem world to arise and massacre their Christian oppressors. "Oh, Moslems," concluded this document, "Ye who are smitten with happiness and are on the verge of sacrificing your life and your goods for the cause of right, [...] gather now around the Imperial throne, obey the commands of the Almighty, who, in the Koran, promises us bliss in this and in the next world; embrace ye the foot of the Caliph's throne and know ye that the state is at war with Russia, England, France, and their Allies, and that these are the enemies of Islam. The Chief of the believers, the Caliph, invites you all as Moslems to join in the Holy War!"
>
> The religious leaders read this proclamation to their assembled congregations in the mosques; all the newspapers printed it conspicuously; it was broadcast in all the countries which had a large Mohammedan population— India, China, Persia, Egypt, Algiers, Tripoli, Morocco, and the like; in all these places it was read to the assembled multitudes and the populace was exhorted to obey the mandate. The Ikdam [*Iqdām*], the Turkish newspaper which had passed into German ownership, was constantly inciting the masses. "The deeds of our enemies," wrote this Turco-German editor, "have brought down the wrath of God. A gleam of hope has appeared. All Mohammedans, young and old, men, women and children, must fulfil their duty so that the gleam may not fade away, but give light to us for ever. How many great things can be accomplished by the arms of vigorous men, by

---

16　Ulrich Trumpener, *Germany and the Ottoman Empire 1914–1918* (Princeton: Princeton University Press, 1968), pp. 117–18; Wolfgang G. Schwanitz, "*Djihad* 'Made in Germany'," *Sozial.Geschichte*, 18 (2003), pp. 11–12.

the aid of others, of women and children! [...] The time for action has come. We shall all have to fight with all our strength, with all our soul, with teeth and nails, with all the sinews of our bodies and of our spirits. If we do it, the deliverance of the subjected Mohammedan kingdoms is assured. [...] Allah is our aid and the Prophet is our support."

The Sultan's proclamation was an official public document, and dealt with the proposed Holy War only in a general way, but about this time a secret pamphlet appeared which gave instructions to the faithful in more specific terms. [...] It was printed in Arabic, the language of the Koran. It was a lengthy document [...] full of quotations from the Koran, and its style was frenzied in its appeal to racial and religious hatred. It described a detailed plan of operations for the assassination and extermination of all Christians—except those of German nationality. A few extracts will portray its spirit:

O people of the faith and O beloved Moslems, consider even though but for a brief moment, the present condition of the Islamic world. For if you consider this but a little, you will weep long. You will behold a bewildering state of affairs which will cause the tear to fall and the fire of grief to blaze. You see the great country of India, which contains hundreds of millions of Moslems, fallen, because of religious divisions and weaknesses into the grasp of the enemies of God, the infidel English. You see forty millions of Moslems in Java shackled by the chains of captivity and of affliction under the rule of the Dutch. [...] You see Egypt, Morocco, Tunis, Algeria, and the Sudan [...] groaning in the grasp of the enemies of God and his apostle. [...] Wherever you look you see that the enemies of the true religion, particularly the English, the Russians, and the French, have oppressed Islam and invaded its rights in every possible way. We cannot enumerate the insults we have received at the hands of these nations who desire totally to destroy Islam and drive all Mohammedans off the face of the earth. This tyranny has passed all endurable limits; the cup of our oppression is full to overflowing. [...] In brief, the Moslems work and infidels eat; the Moslems are hungry and suffer and infidels gorge themselves and live in luxury. The world of Islam sinks down and goes backward, and the Christian world goes forward and is more and more exalted. The Moslems are enslaved and the infidels are the great rulers. This is all because the Moslems have abandoned the plan set forth in the Koran and ignored the Holy War which it commands. [...] But the time has now come for the Holy War, and by this the land of Islam shall be for ever freed from the power of the infidels who oppress it. This holy war has now become a sacred duty. Know ye that the blood of infidels in the Islamic lands may be shed with impunity—except those to whom the Moslem power has promised security and who are allied with it. (Herein we find that Germans and Austrians are excepted from massacre.) The killing of infidels who rule over Islam has become a sacred duty, whether you do it secretly or openly, as the Koran has decreed: 'Take them and kill them whenever you find them. Behold we have delivered them unto your hands and given you supreme power over them.' He who kills even one unbeliever of those who rule over us, whether he does it secretly or openly, shall be rewarded by God. And let every Moslem, in whatever part of the world he may be, swear a solemn oath to kill at least three or four of the infidels who rule over him, for they are the enemies of God and of the faith. Let every Moslem know that his reward for doing so shall be doubled by the God who created heaven and earth. A Moslem who does this shall be saved from the terrors of the Day of Judgment, of the resurrection of the dead. [...] The time has come that we should rise up as the rising of one man, in one hand a sword, in the other a gun, in his pockets balls of fire and death-dealing missiles, and in his heart the light of the faith [...]."

Specific instructions for carrying out this holy purpose follow. There shall be a "heart war"—every follower of the Prophet, that is, shall constantly nourish in his spirit a hatred of the infidel; a "speech war"— with tongue and pen every Moslem shall spread this same hatred wherever Mohammedans live; and a war of deed— fighting and killing the infidel wherever he shows his head. [...] "The Holy War," says the pamphlet, "will be of three forms. First, the individual war, which consists of the individual personal deed. This may be carried on with cutting, killing instruments, [...] like the slaying of the English chief of police in India, and like the killing of one of the officials arriving in Mecca by Abi Busir (may God be pleased with him)." The document gives several other instances of assassination which the faithful are enjoined to imitate. Second, the believers are told to organize "bands," and to go forth and slay Christians. The most useful are those organized and operating in secret. "It is to be hoped that the Islamic world of to-day will profit very greatly from such secret bands." The third method is by "organized campaigns," that is, by trained armies.[17]

With the proclamation of *jihad*, the primary condition of Oppenheim's project had been satisfied and the way was clear for implementing the other proposals in his memorandum. The Ottoman Fourth Army in Damascus was placed under the command of Djemal and the German Chief of Staff Kress von Kressenstein and prepared for what was to have been a surprise attack on Egypt and the Suez Canal in early 1915. A special agent was sent to the consulate at Tripoli with orders to subvert French rule in Morocco, Algeria, and Tunisia.[18] Missions to Afghanistan and Persia were organized, with the aim of persuading the rulers of those countries to engage in military actions directed against India and British interests in the Persian Gulf. Oppenheim recommended key members for both missions: Oskar

---

17 *Ambassador Morgenthau's Story* (New York: Doubleday, Page & Company, 1919), pp. 161–66.
18 Donald McKale, *War by Revolution: Germany and Great Britain in the Middle East at the end of World War I*, pp. 50–51.

Niedermayer for the mission to Afghanistan and Wilhelm Wassmuss to stir up trouble for the British in Persia.[19] Convinced, as the 1914 memorandum shows him to be, of the power of propaganda, Oppenheim himself set up the so-called *Nachrichtenstelle für den Orient* [Orient Intelligence Bureau] under the roof of the *Auswärtiges Amt* in Berlin and then in offices of its own in the Tauntzienstrasse in Berlin's West End. Its function was to gather intelligence and to spread Pan-Islamist ideas among Muslims everywhere, including those serving in the armies of the Entente, encourage participation in the *jihad* against the British, French, and Russian enemies of Islam, convince Muslim opinion that Germany was the friend of Islam, and, not least, counter the propaganda of the British and French by reporting on German military successes.[20] For Oppenheim was realistic enough to have understood that the Muslim leaders and populations were not sufficiently "fanatical" to join in the "Holy War" if they were not convinced that by doing so they would be on the winning side.

With sections devoted to Arabia, Persia, Turkey, India, and Russia, the *Nachrichtenstelle* employed many German academics specializing in various branches of "Oriental studies" and a fair number of Muslim associates, chiefly from Egypt and North Africa. It was drastically underfunded, not well organized, and beset by rivalries.[21] Nevertheless, in addition to placing pro-German articles in newspapers in Constantinople and elsewhere and producing a twice-monthly Arabic language news-sheet, *El-Dschihad*, for

---

19 See Hans-Ulrich Seidt, *Berlin Kabul Moskau. Oskar Ritter von Niedermayer und Deutschlands Geopolitik*; Donald McKale, *War by Revolution: Germany and Great Britain in the Middle East at the end of World War I*, pp. 79–85.
20 On the *Nachrichtenstelle für den Orient* and the related *Nachrichtensäle* or reading rooms, see Gottfried Hagen, "German Heralds of Holy War: Orientalists and Applied Oriental Studies," *Comparative Studies of South Asia, Africa and the Middle East*, 24 (2004): 145–62; idem, *Die Türkei im Ersten Weltkrieg: Flugblätter und Flugschriften in arabischer, persischer und osmanisch-türkischer Sprache* (Frankfurt a. M., Bern, New York and Paris: Peter Lang, 1990; Heidelberger Orientalistische Studien, no. 15); Herbert Landolin Müller, *Islam, ğihād ("Heileger Krieg") und Deutsches Reich*, pp. 203–07; Gabriele Teichmann, "Fremder wider Willen—Max von Oppenheim in der wilhelminischen Epoche" in *Geschichte zwischen Wissenschaft und Politik. Festschrift für Michael Stürmer zum 65. Geburtstag*, p. 239.
21 See Tilman Lüdke, *Jihad Made in Germany*, pp. 117–22. Schabinger von Schowingen, who became director in March 1915 after Oppenheim had been posted to Constantinople, complained that "the Odol-Toothpaste and Mouthwash Company invests more in its advertising than Imperial Germany for its war propaganda" (cit. p. 118, note 11). Under Schabinger, who considered an annual budget of 2,000,000 marks barely adequate, the monthly allowance of the *Nachrichtenstelle* was 5,000 marks (Müller, *Islam, ğihād und Deutsches Reich*, p. 207). Schabinger's successor in 1916, the Jewish scholar of Semitic studies Eugen Mittwoch—who was later removed by the National Socialists from his chair at the University of Berlin—put in a request to the Imperial treasury for 100,000 marks (under $2,000,000 in 2012 currency) for the year 1917–1918.

dissemination among Muslim POWs,[22] the Bureau did turn out and arrange for distribution of a considerable quantity of leaflets and pamphlets, thanks largely to substantial contributions by Oppenheim out of his own pocket.[23]

The *fatwas* were widely distributed, on the Western front as well as in the Muslim lands, in Arabic, Persian, and other languages, as well as Turkish. It was obvious, however, that the Entente powers could easily obtain *fatwas* from local legal experts declaring obedience to the colonial powers lawful and binding on Muslims in their jurisdiction. In addition, Sharif Hussein of Mecca, encouraged by the British, was campaigning to have himself recognized as the legitimate Caliph, rather than the Ottoman Sultan whose right to the title of Caliph was not universally recognized by Muslims—as some German Oriental scholars and German diplomats well informed about Islam had not failed to point out, in at least one case to the Kaiser himself.[24]

The effectiveness of the *fatwas* issued by Sheikh ul-Islam Khairi was thus uncertain. Leaflets were therefore produced in which the emphasis fell on the anti-colonialist argument: atrocities committed by the colonial powers, discrimination against Muslims in the French army; British exploitation of India. Combatting British and French propaganda was a special concern of Oppenheim's and there was a considerable output of brochures boasting of the numbers of British, French and Russian soldiers captured, ships destroyed, pieces of artillery seized, and so on. Illustrated albums designed to enliven these dry statistical accounts were provided with captions in Turkish, Arabic, Persian, and Urdu. Sometimes literary forms were put to use, as in a poem in Arabic, composed in 1915 by a member of the Young Egypt National Committee in Berlin and calling for Islamic unity and *jihad*. Three poems in Persian sang the praises of the German army in the form and language of Persian epics.[25] A project dear to Oppenheim was the

---

22 On this paper, see Peter Heine, "Al-Ǧihād: eine deutsche Propagandazeitung im 1. Weltkrieg," Die Welt des Islams, new series, 20 (1980): 197–99. It was published in other languages besides Arabic: Russian, Turkish, Hindi-Urdu.
23 1,012 publications in nine European and fifteen Asian languages over the four years of the war, amounting to a total of 3 million copies, according to Teichmann, "Fremder wider Willen" (as in ch. 2, note 12 above).
24 E.g. the Oriental scholar Bernhard Moritz and the diplomat Friedrich Rosen; see Friedrich Rosen, *Aus einem diplomatischen Wanderleben* (Berlin: Transmare Verlag, 1931), vol. 2, pp. 197, 318–19.
25 See Gottfried Hagen, "German Heralds of Holy War: Orientalists and Applied Oriental Studies," Comparative Studies of South Asia, Africa and the Middle East, 24 (2004): 145–62 (p. 153). For samples, see Gottfried Hagen, *Die Türkei im Ersten Weltkrieg: Flugblätter und Flugschriften in arabischer, persischer und osmanisch-türkischer Sprache* (as in ch. 2, note 12 above).

establishing of reading rooms (*Nachtrichtensäle*) throughout the Ottoman Empire, at which the local population could have access to the most recent news of the war and also find out about Germany, its war effort, and its industrial and commercial prowess. Oppenheim himself travelled widely to implement this project and boasted of having set up more than seventy-five such *Nachrichtensäle*.[26] In addition, Oppenheim understood the potential of film as a medium of communication and opinion-forming and set about producing propaganda films for showing in Muslim countries. How effective all this activity was, however, is uncertain, to say the least. Oppenheim's claim that "up to 10,000 people" a day visited some of the provincial reading rooms and 20,000 a day the reading room in Pera (the commercial centre of Constantinople) is not credible.[27]

As we have seen, ideas close to Oppenheim's had been bandied about well before the war and they continued to enjoy the support of influential figures in the *Auswärtiges Amt* and the German army and navy. General Helmuth von Moltke, for instance, the Chief of the General Staff, was convinced, once war had broken out, that "the fanaticism of Islam" should be deployed against the British and the Russians through the fomenting of violent uprisings in India and the Caucasus.[28] At the *Auswärtiges Amt*,

---

26 According to a memorandum printed by the Reichsdruckerei, dated "Berlin 1916," and entitled *Die Nachrichtenstelle der Kaiserlich Deutschen Botschaft in Konstantinopel und die deutsche wirtschaftliche Propaganda in der Türkei, von Max Freiherrn von Oppenheim, Kaiserlichen Minister-Residenten* [*The Intelligence Bureau of the Imperial German Embassy in Constantinople and German economic propaganda in Turkey, by Baron Max von Oppenheim, Imperial Minister Resident*], p. 13. The memo was probably printed for distribution to a large number of embassies and *Auswärtiges Amt* personnel. On one of the rare copies of this text, in the University Library in Cologne, the indication "Streng vertraulich" ["Strictly Confidential"] has been crossed out.

27 Gottfried Hagen, "German Heralds of Holy War," p. 13. Wilhelm Treue, "Max Freiherr von Oppenheim: Der Archäologe und die Politik," *Historische Zeitschrift*, 209 (1999): 37–74 (pp. 70–71). As Treue notes, "Oppenheim omits to explain how 20,000 or even 10,000 people could be accommodated in a 12-hour period in a room filled with reading material." On Oppenheim's production of propaganda films, see Gotttfried Hagen, *Die Türkei im ersten Weltkrieg*, p. 41 and Gabriele Teichmann, "Fremder wider Willen—Max von Oppenheim in der wilhelminischen Epoche," p. 243.

28 "It is of the greatest importance [...] to start insurrections in India and Egypt, also in the Caucasus. By means of the treaty with Turkey, the Foreign Office will be in a position to bring this idea to realization and to excite the fanaticism of Islam" (Von Moltke to the German Foreign Office, Berlin, 5 August 1914, in Max Montgelas and Walther Schücking, eds. *Outbreak of the World War: German Documents collected by Karl Kautsky*, trans. Carnegie Endowment for International Peace [New York: Oxford University Press, 1924], document 876, pp. 598–99). On the strong support in German military circles for the *jihad* idea, see also Tilman Lüdke, *Jihad Made in Germany*, pp. 72–74. In his 5 August memo to the Foreign Office Moltke has a suggestion that anticipates in its impercipience

Arthur Zimmermann, then Under-Secretary for Foreign Affairs—he was to gain notoriety later for the so-called "Zimmermann telegram" which, as Foreign Secretary, he sent to the German Ambassador to Mexico in January 1917 and which helped to bring the United States into the War on the side of the Entente[29]—strongly supported exploiting Muslim resentment as an effective strategy for Germany. On 27 August, over a month before Oppenheim submitted his memorandum, the *Auswärtiges Amt* instructed the German Embassy in Constantinople to "ruthlessly and unsparingly (*rücksichtslos und schonunglos*) carry out the plan for arousing Panislamic sentiment against England and its colonial possessions."[30] In a secret World War II U.S. State Department communication Franz von Papen, who was active in Turkish affairs in both World Wars, is said to have "during World War I [...] prepared several reports which he presented to the German General Staff and in which he suggested a plan for a '*Jihad*', a Moslem Holy War and general revolt in the British Empire to be called for by the Caliph (the Sultan of Turkey) and organized by German agents."

According to this document, however, "Von Papen was not himself the originator of the '*Jihad*', as this had previously been taken up by several German politicians and members of the German diplomatic service, among whom particular mention may be made of Professor Max von Oppenheim, archaeologist and [...] Oriental Secretary to the German Consulate-General in Cairo. Von Papen's ideas," the report continues, "were of special interest to German Headquarters and by order of Falkenhayn, then Chief of the German General Staff, von Papen was transferred on the entry of Turkey into the war, to the Eastern Front."[31] A comment by Ambassador Morgenthau appears to

---

Zimmerman's notorious telegram of 1917 (see note 29 below). He urges that public opinion in America, which "is friendly to Germany," be mobilized with the help of German-Americans; "perhaps the United States can be persuaded to undertake a naval war against England, in return for which Canada beckons to them as the prize of victory."

29 In 1916, Zimmermann became Foreign Secretary and in that capacity *was* responsible for a coded telegram to the German Ambassador in Mexico, proposing that the Mexicans be promised German support for an attack on the U.S. to regain their lost territories. Unfortunately for Zimmermann, the British got hold of the telegram, succeeded in decoding it and communicated it to President Wilson. Intended no doubt to distract the Americans and keep them out of the European war, the Zimmermann telegram thus in fact helped to bring them into it.

30 Peter Hopkirk, *On Secret Service East of Constantinople: The Plot to Bring Down the British Empire* (London: John Murray, 1994), pp. 54–55; Vahakn N. Dadrian, *German Responsibility in the Armenian Genocide*, p. 51; see also Mustafa Aksakal, *The Ottoman Road to War in 1914*, pp. 16–17.

31 U.S. National Archives II, College Park, Md. Record Group 165, Box 3053, reports on diplomatic and consular representatives accredited to foreign countries, report by the

confirm the broad currency of the *jihad* plan. He had been informed, he relates, rather nonchalantly by his German counterpart Hans von Wangenheim of a plan to "arouse the whole fanatical Moslem world against the Christians," as though there was nothing startling or unusual about it.[32]

As it happens, Wangenheim appears to have been one of a number of people who were sceptical of both the wisdom and the effectiveness of the strategies outlined by Oppenheim in his memorandum. The German Consul-General in Cairo (1906–1908), Count Bernstorff, who favoured a conciliatory policy toward Great Britain and over whose head Oppenheim had sent his memos from Cairo directly to the *Auswärtiges Amt* in Berlin, was another.[33] Strong misgivings about his country's Near Eastern policy in general were also voiced—directly to the Kaiser—by a German diplomat who not only had broad experience of the Orient (having served as interpreter to the German representatives in Beirut and Teheran, as consul in Baghdad and

---

U.S. Naval Attaché, Istanbul, 14 January 1942, quoted by Wolfgang G. Schwanitz, *Gold, Bankiers und Diplomate: Zur Geschichte der Deutschen Orientbank 1906–1946* (Berlin: Trafo Verlag Wolfgang Weist, 2002), p. 321.

32 "In the early days Wangenheim had explained to me one of Germany's main purposes in forcing Turkey into the conflict. He made this explanation quietly and nonchalantly, as though it had been quite the most ordinary matter in the world. Sitting in his office, puffing away at his big black German cigar, he unfolded Germany's scheme to arouse the whole fanatical Moslem world against the Christians. Germany had planned a real 'holy war' as one means of destroying English and French influence in the world. 'Turkey herself is not the really important matter,' said Wangenheim. Her army is a small one, and we do not expect it to do very much. [...] But the big thing is the Moslem world. If we can stir the Mohammedans up against the English and the Russians, we can force them to make peace'." (*Ambassador Morgenthau's Story*, pp. 160–61). See also Peter Peter Hopkirk, *On Secret Service East of Constantinople*, p. 55.

33 Johann Heinrich von Bernstorff, born in London, the son of a Prussian ambassador to Great Britain, was appointed German ambassador to the United States in 1908 and held the post until the outbreak of war between Germany and the U.S. in 1917. After WWI he was a founding member of the German Democratic Party, a strong supporter of the movement to establish a Jewish state in Palestine, and a President of the German Association for the League of Nations. Explicitly denounced by Hitler as one of those who bore responsibility for the collapse of Germany, he emigrated to Switzerland in 1933 and died in Geneva in 1939; see Gerhard L. Weinberg, *Germany, Hitler and World War II* (Cambridge: Cambridge University Press, 1995), p. 38. On his "sharp disagreement" with Oppenheim's estimate of the Panislamic movement and of Egypt's likely response in the event of war, see Donald McKale, *Curt Prüfer: German Diplomat from the Kaiser to Hitler,*, p. 17. In his memoirs, Bernstorff refers to his consistent "desire that Germany should live in amity with England" and to his policy as Consul-General in Cairo as "an attempt to allay the English suspicion of Germany." He even expresses high regard for Lord Cromer, the British Consul-General in Egypt and the *bête noire* of Islamists, Egyptian Nationalists, and Oppenheim, and sympathizes with Cromer's bitterness, at the end of his tenure there, at Egyptian ingratitude for the benefits and reforms he had brought to the country and at their siding against him with the Turks "who had brought nothing but disaster" (*Memoirs of Count Bernstorff*, trans. Eric Sutton [New York: Random House, 1936], pp. 17, 94).

Jerusalem, as German ambassador to Morocco in Tangiers, and as a specialist in oriental affairs at the *Auswärtiges Amt*) but was, in addition, a respected Islamic scholar (the author of a Persian grammar and of the still standard German translation of the *Rubaiyat of Omar Khayyam*). Friedrich Rosen, like Oppenheim, was of part-Jewish ancestry (his British-born mother Serena Anna Moscheles, though baptised at birth, was a daughter of the Czech-Jewish composer and musician Ignaz Moscheles, who had enjoyed brilliant success in London), and his career, like Oppenheim's had suffered on that account. However, unlike the nationalist and anglophobic Oppenheim, Rosen believed good Anglo-German relations should be a cornerstone of German foreign policy and did what he could to dissuade his superiors at the *Auswärtiges Amt*—and on a couple of occasions, in 1907 and again in 1913, the Kaiser himself—from a policy of close co-operation with the Ottomans. Such a policy was bound, he argued, to arouse British suspicion and hostility and reinforce the British-French-Russian coalition.[34] There was also scepticism among German officers and advisers attached to the Turkish army. According to one historian, "many considered [trying to unleash a Holy War against the allies] a waste of valuable manpower and resources, and very likely to backfire on them."[35]

The sceptics and critics were outweighed, however, by the advocates, prominent among them Chancellor Bethmann-Hollweg (who also supported Oppenheim's intriguing with the revolutionary Indian Ghader Party to encourage terrorist action in India and mutinies among Hindu troops in the British army[36]) and, not least, the Kaiser himself. True, there were dissenting voices and strong misgivings about the promotion of *jihad* not only in sections of the general population in Germany, as word of renewed massacres of Armenians (1915–1916) spread, but among German consular officers and other Germans who witnessed atrocities committed in the name of *jihad* against the Armenians in their jurisdictions. Even the reaction to the massacres was relatively muted in Germany, however, compared with the outcry in other European countries.[37] And a considerable pamphlet literature, some

---

34 Friedrich Rosen, *Aus einem diplomatischen Wanderleben*, vol. 2, pp. 176–80, 197–98.
35 Peter Hopkirk, *On Secret Service East of Constantinople*, p. 132.
36 Oppenheim was apparently highly gratified that the network of Indian science students in Germany and Switzerland that he had secretly organized included chemistry students who were ready to undertake suicide bombings: "Sie haben sich dem Tode geweiht und unter Eid verpflichtet, den Verräter zu töten" ["They are committed to die for their cause and have sworn on oath to kill any traitor"]. Cit. Seidt, *Berlin Kabul Moskau*, p. 47.
37 See Margaret Lavinia Anderson, "'Down in Turkey, far away': Human Rights, the Armenian Massacres, and Orientalism in Wilhelmine Germany," *Journal of Modern History*, 79 (2007): 80–111; on protests by some German officials, military men, and residents, see Dickran H. Boyajian, *Armenia: The Case for a Forgotten Genocide* (Westwood, N.J.: Educational Book Crafters, 1972), pp. 337–44; Jean-Marie Carzou, *Un Génocide*

of it no doubt officially inspired, attempted to reassure ordinary Germans about their country's alliance with a Muslim nation against other Christian, European nations.[38] The author of one 80-page pamphlet, rousingly titled *Hie Allah! Das Erwachen des Islam* [Lo, Allah! The Awakening of Islam], recalled the profound effect upon the "entire Islamic world" of the "famous speech in which the Kaiser announced that three hundred million Mohammedans had no better friend than him." (The allusion is to the Kaiser's proclaiming himself the friend of Islam in a speech at the tomb of Saladin in Damascus in 1898.) Pan-Islamism, the writer wrote reassuringly, did not represent a threat to all Christian nations, and especially not to Germany, which had never attempted to subject any Muslim people to its rule, and the Sultan-Caliph's *jihad* was not directed against Christians in general, but only against the enemies and oppressors of Islam. Given that Islam prefers no particular form of state, makes no ethnic or racial distinctions among the faithful, and permits each community to pursue its own interests and ideals and to adopt its own administrative forms, "it is not possible to gather all these different interests under a single umbrella and direct them toward a specific goal." Only when Islam is threatened "can the Caliph, by proclaiming Holy War, call upon all Muslims to unite under him and serve him with all their might and main." The outbreak of war has now "roused the feeling of community among all the Islamic peoples, irrespective of origin and race, to fever pitch, so that we can now observe the emergence of a powerful movement directed against those nations that in the course of time have overrun Muslim lands and subjected their populations to unrestrained domination and arbitrary rule"—i.e. Britain, France, and Russia, but not Germany or Austria-Hungary.[39] This reassuring view of the *jihad* proclaimed by the Sultan-Caliph was supported by a Muslim scholar writing in a Berlin-based journal in 1916. Many non-Muslims interpret *jihad* "mistakenly," he asserted, as a movement to impose the Muslim religion on the entire world.[40]

---

exemplaire: Arménie 1915 (Paris: Flammarion, 1975), pp. 168–94; Vahakn N. Dadrian, *German Responsibility in the Armenian Genocide*, 16, 73, 119, *et passim*.

38 On the series of *Politische Flugschriften*, edited by Ernst Jäckh, Oppenheim's colleague at the *Nachrictenstelle für den Orient*, and on numerous pamphlets and articles by Carl Becker and Martin Hartmann, two of Germany's leading Oriental scholars, see Snouck Hurgronje, *The Holy War "Made in Germany,"* pp. 51–52, 62–64.

39 Gustav Diercks, *Hie Allah! Das Erwachen des Islam* (Berlin: Karl Curtius, 1914), passages cited on pp. 12, 60–61.

40 Abdul Malik Hansa Bey, "Der Panislamismus: Seine Bedeutung und seine Grenzen," *Die islamische Welt: Illustrierte Monatschrift für Politik, Wirtschaft und Kultur*, 1 (1916): 18–20.

Another, somewhat shorter pamphlet of thirty-eight pages (*Dschihad. Der Heilige Krieg des Islams und seine Bedeutung im Weltkriege* [Jihad: Islam's Holy War and its Significance in the World War], by a Dr. Gottfried Galli), which appeared in 1915, acknowledged the seeming anomaly of the Crescent fighting with the Cross against other great Christian nations and the anxieties raised in German Christian and especially missionary circles by the Armenian massacres. Nevertheless, it justified Germany's alliance with an Islamic nation on the grounds of a common struggle against the *Weltherrschaft* [dominion over the whole world] that certain other nations sought to impose. With his appearance at Tangiers, his journey to Jerusalem, and his announcement at Saladin's tomb that he was the friend of all the world's Muslims, the Kaiser himself had taken the lead in promoting this alliance between Germany and Islam. Germany's "Holy War" against England and the Ottoman-proclaimed *jihad* against the Entente powers were both inspired by the same popular resentment of foreign interference: "The Holy German War, shoulder to shoulder with the *jihad,* is the first fruit of [the Kaiser's] policy and the most portentous for the entire future." Its success, the reader was advised in the Foreword, depended on a correct understanding of *jihad* by the German people.

The main text proceeded, first, to emphasize that Germany herself was engaged in a Holy War "arising from the depths of popular feeling and the consciousness that what is at stake is the protection of the nations's holiest heritage"; and, second, to reassure readers about the nature of *jihad*. To the question whether "such an alliance [with an Islamic nation] does not constitute a desacralizing of our own Holy War" the author answered: "A quick look at the history and doctrine of Islam demonstrates without any ambiguity that all the earlier hostility to Christians and all the horrors of earlier *jihads* have as little to do with the essence of Islam as the Inquisition, burning at the stake, witch-hunts, and so forth have to do with the essence of Christianity." But what about the Armenian massacres? "Do they not demonstrate the opposite—the true nature of Islam?" The answer to that was easy: "No, no, and again no!" The massacres, the author maintained, were the product of intrigues by the English and the Armenians themselves.[41]

---

41 That was the official German-Turkish line. In 1915, after consultation with ambassador Wangenheim the Sublime Porte issued an official denial of complicity in the massacres: "Far from having condoned or organized mass murders, the Porte declared, it has merely exercised its sovereign right of self-defense against a revolutionary movement, and the responsibility for everything that had happened in the Armenian districts had to be

The pamphlet continued with an attack on two severe critics of Germany's *jihad* strategy: Johannes Lepsius, a Protestant German Orientalist and missionary (he was the son of the founding father of German Egyptology Carl Richard Lepsius and himself a founder of the German *Orient Mission*), and the eminent Dutch Oriental Scholar, Christiaan Snouck Hurgronje. Lepsius had been presenting the *jihad* strategy as having played into the hands of the chauvinistic and irreligious Young Turks, while his *Bericht über die Lage des armenischen Volkes in der Türkei* (1916) was a meticulously documented denunciation of the massacres as coldly and cynically planned and executed by the Committee of Union and Progress—i.e. Enver, Talat and Djemal—in order to create, for political reasons, a uniform and homogeneous population in the Ottoman Empire.[42] In his just published

---

borne exclusively by the Entente Powers themselves, because they had organized and directed the revolutionary movements in the first place." (Trumpener, *Germany and the Ottoman Empire*, p. 210; see also Taner Akçam, *A Shameful Act: The Armenian Genocide and Turkish Responsibility* [New York: Metropolitan Books and Henry Holt and Company, 2006], p. 214; Vahakn N. Dadrian, *German Complicity in the Armenian Genocide*, pp. 81–83; Suzanne L. Marchand, *German Orientalism in the Age of Empire*, pp. 454–57).

42 Lepsius claimed that the deportations and massacres were organized by the Committee of Union and Progress, did not have the support of the Turkish people as a whole and especially not that of truly religious Muslims, and were in no way motivated by national security concerns. In addition, the efforts of von Wangenheim and, more forcefully, of his successor Count Wolff-Metternich to get the Committee to call a halt to the massacres—which, quite apart from moral and humanitarian considerations, the ambassadors realised were damaging to Germany's cause in the war—had been ignored. Lepsius ended his introduction to the documents by quoting from a report by Wolff-Metternich dated 10 July 1916, which does implicate Islam itself to some extent in the policy being pursued by the Committee of Union and Progress: "The Turkish government has not allowed itself to be dissuaded from carrying out its policy of eliminating the Armenian Question by exterminating the Armenian race either by our remonstrances or by those of the American Embassy and the Papal Nuntio or by the threats of the Entente powers, still less by fear of public opinion in Western countries. [...] The forced Islamisation of the Armenians should not be seen as a measure inspired by religious fanaticism, not at least in the first instance. Such sentiments were probably quite foreign to the potentates of the Young Turk movement. It remains no less the case that every true Ottoman patriot must above all profess adherence to Islam. In the East, religion and nationality are one. The history of the Turkish Empire, from its beginnings to the present time is there to demonstrate it and every Ottoman is convinced of it in the depths of his heart. Official and semi-official statements claiming the contrary, along with the entire battery of quotations from the Koran and from Islamic tradition belong to the fine phrases that are served up to Europeans since the promulgation of the firmans instituting reforms to convince them of the tolerant spirit of Islam and of the Ottomans. In the same way, if government ministers deny the stories that keep circulating about instances of religious persecution, this is above all for the sake of good form; yet their protestations do contain a grain of truth in as much as the dominant motive is not religious fanaticism, but the determination to amalgamate the Armenians with the Muslim element of the Empire." (*Archives du génocide des Arméniens, recueillies et présentées par Johannes Lepsius*

Deutschland und der Heilige Krieg (Leipzig, 1915; Engl. trans. *The Holy War "Made in Germany,"* New York, 1915) Snouck Hurgronje, for his part, as we saw earlier, denounced German scholars for publicly rallying behind an atavistic, religion-inspired form of war that they themselves had condemned in their pre-War writings.[43] In contrast, the author of *Dschihad: Der Heilige Krieg des Islams* insisted that *jihad* was "a struggle for existence. The dross of bygone days has been cleaned out of it and it has been freed from fanatical hostility to those of other faiths." Indeed, he argued, only good could come of the collaboration of Germany and Islam. Adapting two well known lines by the mid-nineteenth-century poet Emanuel Geibel, *Denn es soll am Deutschen Wesen/Einstmal noch die Welt genesen* ["For in days to come the world will be cured through the German spirit"], the author of the pamphlet claimed that, far from pursuing atavistic goals, Islam "is consciously seeking to cure itself through its contact with German culture."[44]

Oppenheim's project did not achieve the results its author and advocates expected. The British were not surprised by what was to have been a surprise Turkish attack on the Suez canal that would set Egypt afire, and the Turks were beaten back.[45] Oppenheim had hoped through his personal contacts with Faisal, one of the sons of Hussein, the sharif of Mecca and guardian of the Muslim holy places, to win the support of the Arabs for his *jihad*, but

---

[Paris: Fayard, 1986], pp. 39, 58. The German text was unavailable to me; this modern French edition presents a translation of a later [1919], expanded and altered version of the *Bericht*, in which, having been subjected to pressure to refrain from making public statements for the duration of the war and not to "offend the sensibilities of our Turkish ally," Lepsius undertook the task of "sanitizing to a certain degree official German records, whereby Germany could be purged of any guilt or complicity regarding the fate of the Armenians" and Turkey alone made to appear responsible for it [Vahakn N. Dadrian, *German Responsibility in the Armenian Genocide*, p. 155]).

43 Carl Becker, the scholar at whom Snouck Hurgronje's attack was primarily directed, himself admitted that he had changed his tune only after the outbreak of war: "In times of peace, I was always strongly opposed to the so-called Islam policy in foreign affairs; it seemed to me that it was playing with fire," he wrote on 31 August 1914 to Ernst Jäckh, one of Oppenheim's close collaborators (cit. Ludmila Hanisch, *Die Nachfolger der Exegeten: Deutschsprachige Erforschung des Vorderen Orients in der ersten Hälfte des 20. Jahrhunderts* [Wiesbaden: Harrassowitz, 2003], p. 80).

44 Gottfried Galli, *Dschihad. Der Heilige Krieg des Islams und seine Bedeutung im Weltkriege unter besonderer Berücksichtigung der Interessen Deutschlands* (Freiburg i.B.: C. Troemer's Universitätsbuchhandlung, 1915); passages cited are in the Foreword and on pp. 5, 6, 8–9, 14, 16.

45 It is often noted that the objectives of this military campaign were not clearly established and that the resources mobilized for it were inadequate. It was disruptive, but did not achieve the goal some had set for it of destroying the lifeline of the British Empire. See Jehuda L. Wallach, *Anatomie einer Militärhilfe. Die preussisch-deutschen Militärmissionen in der Türkei 1835–1919* (Düsseldorf: Droste, 1976), pp. 191–96.

he was outmanoeuvered by his British counterpart T.E. Lawrence. After playing a double game for a while, Hussein threw in his lot with the British and led the Arabs in an uprising against the Ottomans.[46] The legitimacy, in Muslim eyes, of Oppenheim's *jihad*, which had always been precarious, was now fatally compromised. A *jihad* initiated by the government of the notoriously irreligious Committee of Union and Progress and directed against only specified infidel nations, while being supported and largely directed by another infidel nation, had not been overwhelmingly convincing to begin with and it had not succeeded in arousing the "fanaticism of Islam." Oppenheim himself seems to have acknowledged as much since, after he returned from a tour of Syria and Northern Arabia in 1915, the *jihad* theme played a diminished role in his propaganda literature. When, in addition, with the Arab uprising against the Ottomans, a large part of the Muslim world openly rejected his *jihad*, Oppenheim's grandiose project of widespread revolt by the Muslim subjects of the Entente powers was doomed. A thoughtful analysis of the failure of the project, offered by Hans-Ulrich Seidt in two chapters (appropriately entitled "Krieg der Amateure" [War of the Amateurs] and "Gefährliche Träume" [Dangerous Dreams]), of his *Berlin Kabul Moskau* (2002) identifies three main causes of the failure of the project: insufficient preparation, inadequate resources, and poor organization.

> Anyone looking through the series of documents entitled "Measures and incitements against our enemies" ["*Unternehmungen und Aufwiegelungen gegen unsere Feinde*"] in the archives of the *Auswärtiges Amt* and expecting to find a cool, calculated, meticulously planned "Grab for World Power" ["*Griff nach der Weltmacht*"[47]] will be disappointed. There is no doubt that Max von Oppenheim was thinking boldly in terms of Germany's bid for world power and that he conceived and proposed to the Imperial government a comprehensive and complete plan for the Orient, based on the inciting of revolution. But his plan lacked both careful preparation and sound material groundwork. The personnel and material needed for its realization were not there. [...] It was inevitable that Max von Oppenheim's dream of a "Holy War" would be followed by a painful awakening. [...] The German Orientalist Ernst Jäckh who had been in Constantinople from December 12th

---

46 On Hussein's complicated and drawn out double game, see the account in Djemal Pasha's *Memories of a Turkish Statesman 1913–1919*, pp. 209–37. The proclamation outlining Hussein's reasons for raising the standard against Constantinople (weak government; anti-religious legislation; arbitrary rule by Enver, Djemal, and Talat; unjust punishment, including hanging, of "people of rank") is given in English translation on pp. 226–27.

47 Seidt is citing the title of F. Fischer's groundbreaking study of 1961 (see ch. 3, note 20 above).

to 22nd sounding out the chances of provoking a revolutionary upheaval of the East drew up a sobering report on January 3, after his return. In his *Bericht über die Organisation in Konstantinopel zur Revolutionierung feindlicher Gebiete* ["Report on the Organization in Constantinople for Fomenting Revolutions in Enemy Territories"] Jäckh painted a grim picture: "The general impression can be summed up thus: all our undertakings have been set up belatedly and in an improvised manner, for no preparations had been made in peacetime." Jäckh's report and the documents in the *Auswärtiges Amt* give evidence of a shattering discrepancy between political will and operational capacity, between ambitious goals and unavailable means. Improvisation and wishful thinking took the place of careful planning and prudent information-gathering.[48]

A more emotional, but no less negative assessment of the "Holy War" strategy and of Oppenheim's part in it was given by the Constantinople correspondent of the *Kölnische Zeitung*, Harry Stuermer. Stuermer, who appears to have shared Lepsius's outrage at the Armenian deportations and massacres and at Germany's complicity, because of her alliance with the Ottomans, in what he characterized as crimes against humanity, expressed strong misgivings in reports to his newspaper and to the *Auswärtiges Amt*, but gave free rein to his indignation only after he left Germany in 1917. His *Zwei Kriegsjahre in Konstantinopel: Skizzen deutsch-jungtürkischer Moral und Politik* appeared in that same year in neutral Switzerland, where he had settled, as well as in English translation, despite efforts by the Germans to prevent its publication. Stuermer had nothing good to say of the government of the Young Turks. It was, he claimed, xenophobic, chauvinist, racist, and hypocritical:

---

48 Seidt, *Berlin Kabul Moskau*, pp. 56–57. On reasons for the failure of the *jihad*, see also Landau, *Politics of Pan-Islam*, pp. 100–03; Tilman Lüdke, *Jihad Made in Germany*, pp. 122–24, 131–32, 152–54, 189–90; and Marchand, *German Orientalism in the Age of Empire*, pp. 446–63. Marchand quotes Ernst Herzfeld, a future collaborator of Oppenheim's in evaluating the latter's finds at Tel Halaf, as having considered "the *jihad* a farce and the war itself a crime" (p. 462). In a letter to Carl Becker, dated January 1915, Herzfeld asked "why would the [Ottoman] Empire's subjects fight for a hated, corrupt, and deceitful regime" (p. 454). Landau argues, however, that Oppenheim's *jihad* project was not quite the complete failure that "Entente sources and later historians would have us believe" and that it did win the support of some notable Muslim leaders and scholars. A similarly nuanced view of the Suez operation is offered by Jehuda L. Wallach, *Anatomie einer Militärhilfe. Die preussisch-deutschen Militärmissionen in der Türkei 1835–1919*, pp. 191–96. Wallach quotes a high-ranking German officer's view that the operation was successful in tying up significant British military units, but that for the grandiose goal some people had had in mind — the destruction of the British Empire by cutting off its lifeline to India and the East — not nearly enough resources had been committed.

> Pan-Turkism, which seems to be the governing passion of all the leading men of the day, finds expression in two directions. Outwardly it is a constant striving for a "Greater Turkey," a movement that for a large part in its essence, and certainly in its territorial aims, runs parallel with the "Holy War"; inwardly it is a fanatical desire for a general Turkification which finds outlet in political nationalistic measures, some of criminal barbarity, others partaking of the nature of modern reforms, beginning with the language regulations and "internal colonisation" and ending in the Armenian persecutions. [...] In little-informed circles in Europe people are still under the false impression that the Young Turks of to-day, the intellectual and political leaders of Turkey in this war, are authentic, zealous, and even fanatical Mohammedans, and superficial observers explain all unpleasant occurrences and outbreaks of Young Turkish jingoism on Pan-Islamic grounds, especially as Turkey has not been slow in proclaiming her "Holy War." But this conception is entirely wrong. The artificial character of the "*Djihad*," which was only set in motion against a portion of the "unbelievers," while the others became more and more the ruling body in Turkey, is the best proof of the untenability of this theory. The truth is that the present political regime is the complete denial of the Pan-Islamic idea and the substitution of the Pan-Turkish idea of race.[49]

The reality, according to Stuermer, is that the Young Turks are themselves exploiting Pan-Islamist sympathies and Muslim religious feeling as cynically, for their own political ends, as the Germans are.

The strategy, however, has not worked:

> It is a very painful task for a German [...] to deal with the many intrigues and machinations of our Government in [its] relation to the so-called "Holy War" (Arab. *Djihad*), where in [its] quest of a vain illusion [it] stooped to the very lowest means. Practically all [its] hopes in that direction have been sadly shattered. [Its] costly, unscrupulous, thoroughly unmoral efforts against European civilization in Mohammedan countries have resulted in the terrific counter-stroke of the defection of the Arabs and the foundation of a purely Arabian Caliphate under English protection. [...] The so-called "Holy War," if it had succeeded, would have been one of the greatest crimes against human civilization that even Germany has on her conscience. [...] But the attempt against colonial civilization did not succeed. The "*Djihad*," proclaimed as it was by the Turanian pseudo-Caliph and violently anti-Entente, was doomed to failure from the very start from its obvious artificiality. It was a miserable farce, or rather a tragicomedy, the present ending of which, namely the defection of the Arabian Caliphate, is the direct

---

49 Harry Stuermer, *Zwei Kriegsjahre in Konstantinopel: Skizzen deutsch-jungtürkischer Moral und Politik* (Lausanne: Payot, 1917). Quoted from the English translation: *Two War Years in Constantinople: Sketches of German and Young Turkish Ethics and Politics* (New York: George H. Doran, 1917), pp. 152–53, 176–77.

contrary of what had been aimed at with such fanatical urgency and the use of such immoral propaganda. [...] The attempt to "unloose" the Holy War was due primarily to the most absurd illusions. It would seem that in Germany, the land of science, the home of so many eminent doctors of research, even the scholars have been attacked by the disease of being dazzled by wild political illusions, or surely, knowing the countries of Islam as they must, they would long ago have raised their voices against such arrant folly.[50]

Stuermer then zooms in on the shady characters employed by Oppenheim's *Nachrichtenstelle* to spread propaganda in support of the *jihad*. Many of the individuals who, claiming to be devout Muslims, offered their services and received funding from the *Nachrichtenstelle*, were simply crooks who milked the German government—and Oppenheim himself, since he was helping to finance the program with his own money—for all they were worth:

Numerous examples [...] might be cited [...] of the German Embassy being made the dupe of greedy adventurers who treated them as an inexhaustible source of gold. First one would appear on the scene who announced himself as the one man to cope with Afghanistan, then another would come along on his way to Persia and play the great man "on a special mission" for a time in Pera while money belonging to the German Empire would find its way into all sorts of low haunts [...] Even a *bona fide* connoisseur of the East like Baron von Oppenheim, who had already made tours of considerable value for research purposes right across the Arabian Peninsula, and so should have known better than to share these false illusions, doled out thousands of marks from his own pocket—and millions from the Treasury!—to stir up the tribes to take part in the *Djihad*.[51]

In the end, Oppenheim himself, looking back on the *jihad* plan and his propaganda efforts, admitted that they had been a washout, "ein Schlag ins Wasser"[52]

---

50   Ibid., pp. 126–29.
51   Ibid., pp. 134–35.
52   Tilman Lüdke, *Jihad Made in Germany*, p. 186, quoting Oppenheim's manuscript autobiography in the *Hausarchiv* of the Oppenheim Bank.

6. Promoter of German Economic Expansion and the Berlin-Baghdad Railway

The fervent German nationalism sustaining Oppenheim's activities as the "Kaiser's spy" and adviser to the *Auswärtiges Amt* in Oriental matters was not confined to the sphere of politics. Even his work as explorer, archaeologist and ethnographer was aimed not only at advancing knowledge and satisfying his own genuine curiosity, but also at enhancing Germany's standing in the world and winning for her, through extraordinary achievement in scholarship and culture, the "place in the sun" to which, like all devoted supporters of the Wilhelminian *Kaiserreich*, he believed she was entitled. Thus it was his intention that his discovery of Tell Halaf should bring honour and glory to Germany, as the engineer Carl Humann's excavations at Pergamon had done several decades earlier. Though he was unable to undertake a thorough excavation of the site when he first discovered it in 1899 but had to replace the stone figures he had found and cover them over again with earth, Oppenheim wrote, it was his earnest hope that "it would be vouchsafed to German scholars to bring them back out again from their graves and deliver them to our German museums."[1] Likewise, while the baron may have defected from the family business and sought instead to align himself with the aristocratic ideals and way of life of the conservative German ruling class rather than with the bourgeois values of industriousness, entrepreneurial speculativeness, and intelligent pursuit of financial gain that had presided over the Oppenheims'

---

1 Max Freiherr von Oppenheim, "Bericht über eine im Jahre 1899 ausgeführte Forschungsreise in der Asiatischen Türkei," *Zeitschrift der Gesellschaft für Erdkunde zu Berlin*, 36, 2 (1901): 69–99 (p. 91).

http://dx.doi.org/10.11647/OBP.0030.06

rise to wealth and social distinction, the banker's son was by no means oblivious of the role economics played in increasing a country's power and prestige. The example of England, which he seems to have had constantly in mind, left little doubt about the connection between industrial and commercial might and world dominance and, as we shall see, he quickly perceived the coming preponderance of the United States.

By the time the First World War broke out, it was not unusual for German scholars of the "Orient" to emphasize their country's economic interest in the region. In 1914 Carl Becker, for instance, wrote that "we have the greatest interest in supporting Turkey for a double reason: because of our geographical location and because our industries need to be able to expand. The more pieces of the Ottoman Empire are broken off and fall under the sway of our economic competitors, the narrower the field of activity available to us. Who will protect the railways we are building and the agricultural developments we are financing from Kurdish hordes or marauding Arab Bedouins? We can never penetrate with our armies deep into the interior of a sovereign Turkey. Our economic and cultural investment there can be protected only by the Turks themselves."[2] Oppenheim, for his part, had been attentive to economic matters from the very beginning of his career. He had shown keen interest, as noted earlier, in the commercial exploitation of the German East African colony when he visited it on one of his *"Forschungsreisen"* [journeys of research and exploration] in the early 1890s[3] and in the narrative of that journey through Syria and Mesopotamia to the Persian Gulf, published in 1899, along with meticulous geographical descriptions and sympathetic accounts of the peoples and the artistic treasures of the region, he included several pages on railway construction and railway projects in the area of Haifa, Beirut and Damascus, information on their financing, and thoughts on their chances of profitability.[4] According to one scholar, he at one time supported proposals by the extreme right-wing *Alldeutscher Verband* [Pan-German League] to settle German colonists on land in the Middle East.[5] He was an early and

---

2 C. Becker, *Deutsch-türkische Interessengemeinschaft* (Bonn, 1914), p. 17, cit. in Lothar Rathmann, *Stossrichtung Nahost 1914–1918. Zur Expansionspolitik des deutschen Imperialismus im ersten Weltkrieg* (Berlin: Rütten & Loenig, 1963), pp. 29–30.
3 See ch. 2, note 30 above.
4 Dr. Max Freiherr von Oppenheim, *Vom Mittelmeer zum Persischen Golf durch den Haurān und die Syrische Wüste* (Berlin: Dietrich Reimer, 1899), vol. 1, pp. 21–23.
5 Lothar Rathmann, *Stossrichtung Nahost 1914–1918*, p. 29, note 25. Even in his relations with the Bedouins, a key contact and an indispensable source of information about them, according to Oppenheim himself, was Mohammed Ibn Bessam, "one of the

enthusiastic advocate of a German-devised project, for which the Kaiser had obtained authorization from the Sultan in 1898 and which was viewed with disquiet by the other great European powers, especially the British, to extend the railway line linking Haydarpaşa on the Eastern side of the Bosphorus, directly across from Constantinople, with Angora (present-day Ankara) and Konya in central Anatolia, to Baghdad (and eventually, it was hoped, to Basra on the Persian Gulf). To Oppenheim, as to many others at the time, the construction of a railway line running continuously from Berlin to Baghdad, from Germany to the East, would be a major step both in expanding German power and influence and in undercutting British dominance of the trade with Asia through the Suez canal, while also, at the same time, improving the lot of the local population.

In fact, the journey north from Damascus in 1899, in the course of which Oppenheim made his truly momentous discovery of Tell Halaf — the basis of his reputation as an archaeologist — was undertaken in response, as he later explained, to a request "by Georg von Siemens, one of the founders of the Deutsche Bank, to determine the best route for the stretch of the proposed Baghdad railway between Aleppo and Mosul."[6] The Deutsche Bank, of which Siemens was then a director, was heading the consortium behind the Berlin-to-Baghdad railway project, and it was entirely natural that it should seek the advice of an experienced traveller in the Middle East who also happened to be a member of one of Germany's most prominent banking families. The *Auswärtiges Amt* would not allow Oppenheim to accept this commission openly, however, for fear that the participation of its Cairo agent in the controversial project would be viewed with displeasure and suspicion by the British. Deeply unhappy about being blocked from

---

    most important wholesale merchants in the Arab world, whose family was close to the all-powerful Rashidis [the longtime rivals of the Saudis as rulers of Arabia], and had branches of their business in Mecca and Jiddah, Damascus and Baghdad, Bombay, where they supplied horses to the British army [...], as well as Cairo and Tripoli." (*Die Beduinen* [Leipzig: Otto Harrassowitz, 1939], vol. 1, p. 7). It seems fair to assume that the interest in economic matters of the banker's son from Cologne facilitated the formation of the close relationship he came to enjoy with the wealthy Arab trader.

6 Dr. Baron Max von Oppenheim, *Tell Halaf. A New Culture in Oldest Mesopotamia*, trans. Gerald Wheeler (London and New York: G.P. Putnam's Sons, n.d. [1933]), p. 1. This is the authorised English translation of *Der Tell Halaf. Eine neue Kultur im ältesten Mesopotamien* (Leipzig: Brockhaus, 1931). Wherever possible, references will be to this translation. Reviewing the English text in the *TLS* in 1933 (8 June, p. 395), the British archaeologist Campbell Thompson observed that "Baron von Oppenheim, who was originally in the service of the German diplomatic mission in Egypt in 1896, was sent to prospect for the line of the Baghdad railway" and that it was while on this mission that he came upon Tell Halaf, which "fired the Baron's desire to become an archaeologist."

taking part in a project in which he was keenly interested ("eines, wie Sie wissen, längst von mir gehegten Lieblingsplanes," as he wrote to Bernhard Moritz, a friend and fellow-Orientalist), Oppenheim undertook to travel through the area in a private capacity and to carry out the commission simultaneously with and under cover of an extension into Northeastern Syria of his ongoing ethnographic study of the Bedouins.[7] It is easy to understand how the discoverer of Tell Halaf came to be (mis)identified in a recent (1992) English-language guide to the ancient monuments of Syria, as "Baron Max von Oppenheim, a Prussian engineer involved in surveying the route of the Berlin-Baghdad railway."[8]

The 30-page *Bericht über eine im Jahr 1899 ausgeführte Forschungsreise in der asiatischen Türkei* [Report on a journey of exploration in the Asiatic territories of Turkey undertaken in 1899], which Oppenheim chose to publish in 1901 in the journal of the Berlin Geographical Society, rather than in a journal devoted to archaeology or the ancient cultures of the Middle East, reflected the conditions that had presided over the journey. It offered a description of the places visited on the trip prior to the discovery of Tell Halaf, a brief account of the Tell Halaf site with some speculations as to its origin and character, and a short survey, with some illustrations, of the first striking finds at the site. It also included, however, a comparative account of the various possible routes for the construction of the Eastern sections of the Berlin-to-Baghdad railway, along with an analysis of the economic advantages and disadvantages of each route and the likely economic impact its selection would have. Indeed, just as only a day and

---

7 Letter to Moritz, cit. Teichmann, "Grenzgänger zwischen Orient und Okzident," *Faszination Orient*, p. 40. See also Oppenheim's own account of this venture in *Die Beduinen* (Leipzig: Otto Harrassowitz, 1939), vol. 1, p. 8: "Georg von Siemens, the Director of the Deutsche Bank, had approached me with the request that I lead an expedition that was to advise the bank about the best route for the proposed Baghdad railway. At the request of the *Auswärtiges Amt*, however, I had to refrain from accepting this invitation as well as from further publication on the topic of the Orient. My superiors judged it unacceptable for an agent of the Political Section of the *Auswärtiges Amt* to treat matters in which the interests of England and France were far greater than ours. As a result, the expedition to seek out the best route for the Baghdad railway was led by the German Consul-General in Constantinople, Dr. Stemmrich, who was responsible for our commercial interests in Turkey." Nonetheless, "I was at least able to respond to a further request from Herr Siemens—to inform him in a private capacity of what I judged to be the best route for the line on the especially difficult stretch between Aleppo and Mosul. To my great delight, my suggestions were adopted."
8 Ross Burns, *Monuments of Syria: An Historical Guide* (London: I.B. Tauris, 1992, rev. edn 2009), p. 295.

a half⁹ could be devoted to exploration of the Tell Halaf site because the travellers had to "keep moving on" [*wir mussten weiter marschieren*], more space was allotted in the *Bericht* to discussion of the railway project (the last seven pages or so of the published report) than to Tell Halaf (three pages). Oppenheim conceded that "it would be inappropriate here," i.e. in an article in a scholarly geographical journal, "to consider in detail the question of the profitability of this project in relation to world trade, mail connections with India and East Asia, and other factors unconnected with the land itself." But he justified devoting so much space to the projected rail line on the grounds that "carefully observing the economic conditions and prospects of a land and its people is as much part of the task of a scientific exploration of unknown regions, with due consideration of the history of each, as studying them from a purely geographical, archaeological, or other similar point of view."[10] The reader of Oppenheim's report learned which of the routes currently under consideration for the various sections of the Eastern part of the line was likely to be easiest and least expensive to build,[11] what mineral deposits (copper, coal, oil) along the proposed routes were or might be expected to become available for commercial exploitation once the railway had been constructed, what the possibilities were for more intensive agricultural cultivation (cotton, tropical products) in particular areas, and how likely the various populations were to discern the value to them of the access provided by the railway and to use it to their advantage. "We Germans," he wrote, "are to be congratulated on being called upon

---

9   Or was it three days? In the "Bericht" (*Zeitschrift der Gesellschaft für Erdkunde zu Berlin*, 36, 2 [1901]: 69–99) Oppenheim writes of working on the site for "leider nur anderthalb Tage" [unfortunately only a day and a half], but in his 1931 book *Der Tell Halaf. Eine neue Kultur im ältesten Mesopotamien* (Leipzig: Brockhaus, 1931), p. 16 (*Tell Halaf. A New Culture in Oldest Mesopotamia*, p. 8), he refers to the preliminary excavation as having lasted "nur drei Tage lang" [three days only].

10 Max Freiherr von Oppenheim, "Bericht über eine im Jahre 1899 ausgeführte Forschungsreise in der Asiatischen Türkei," *Zeitschrift der Gesellschaft für Erdkunde zu Berlin*, 36, 2 (1901): 69–99 (p. 91).

11 Thus Oppenheim advised against attempting to extend the line eastwards from Ankara because of the mountainous terrain and advised instead building outwards from Konya to Aleppo and Mosul and creating an extension to the Mediterranean, so that inner Mesopotamia could have access to a port. In a recent popular study by Wolfgang Korn, *Schienen für den Sultan. Die Bagdadbahn, Wilhelm II, Abenteuerer und Spione* (Berlin: Fackelträger, 2009), it is claimed, in contrast, that "Oppenheim had hardly carried out the task assigned to him, which was to look into whether and how the topography might be suitable for laying a railway line. As he did not deliver on that, the Baghdad Railway Company had to send out its surveyors and engineers to determine an appropriate route without the benefit of prior information" (pp. 141–42).

to lend a hand in this great work of civilization, which will at the same time open up new markets for our German industries and in turn give us access to indispensable subtropical products."[12] Oppenheim subsequently expressed his "great joy that my proposal to take [the line] through the middle of the desert by way of Jerablus and Ras el Ain was accepted."[13]

Three years after the 1899 journey through northern Syria Oppenheim's interest in the Berlin-to-Baghdad railway project was still very much alive. He made two trips to the United States, in 1902 and 1904, to study how a combination of private enterprise and federal policy had encouraged the vast railway expansion westward and to ascertain how "areas hitherto unopened or only slightly opened were brought to the highest pitch of prosperity through new railways."[14] He appears not to have been acting for his own personal benefit or for that of the family bank. The latter, though it had been heavily involved in railway construction in Germany, was not involved in the financing of the Baghdad railway. At the same time, there is no evidence that he was attached to the German Embassy and on an official mission, as he claimed in his 1931 book *Der Tell Halaf*. The outcome of those two trips, which were widely discussed in the American press and during which he was fêted and entertained by leading families in New York and Newport,[15] was a 350 page volume entitled *Zur Entwickelung des Bagdadbahngebietes und insbesondere Syriens und Mesopotamiens unter Nutzanwendung amerikanischer Erfahrungen* [On the Development of the Areas through which the Baghdad Railway will Pass and, in particular, of Syria and Mesopotamia in the Light of American Experiences], published in Berlin in 1904 at the expense of the Deutsche Bank. The book, doubtless intended to stimulate investor interest, consisted first, "of an investigation of the American situation, of the support given to private initiatives by public agencies," which was likely to be of great interest to the German bankers involved in the Berlin-to-Baghdad project, inasmuch as they had

---

12 Oppenheim, "Bericht über eine im Jahre 1899 ausgeführte Forschungsreise in der Asiatischen Türkei," p. 99.
13 *Tell Halaf. A New Culture in Oldest Mesopotamia*, pp. 1–2.
14 Ibid., p. 1. "Um für den Bau der Bagdadbahn die dortigen Erfahrungen bei der Erschliessung noch unbebauter Landstrecken für die grossen Eisenbahnsysteme zu studieren." (Cit. Wilhelm Treue, "Max Freiherr von Oppenheim: Der Archäologe und die Politik," *Historische Zeitschrift*, 209 [1969]: 37–74 [p. 55]).
15 "I have delightful memories," he wrote later, "of the important lessons learned, and of the friendly welcome and the great hospitality I met with on this occasion all over the United States" (*Tell Halaf: A New Culture in Oldest Mesopotamia*, p. 2).

to work out an appropriate collaboration of private enterprise and the Turkish State; second, detailed reports on the areas through which the line to Baghdad was expected to be built and which would thus be more firmly connected with Constantinople and thereby with Germany; and third, the labour situation and the relevant agencies and authorities the builders of the railway might have to deal with. Overall, the book proposed a vision of a revived Middle East closely connected with Europe and above all with Germany. In this vision Oppenheim's passionate devotion to Germany and his attraction to and interest in the Islamic world were seamlessly woven together.

"At present the Orient is learning from Europe," Oppenheim noted. In turn, "Europe is learning from America." Railways in America had been the most efficient means of spreading civilization to the West; from that experience Europe in turn could learn how the Baghdad Railway could be made to play a similar role for Europe. America, he wrote with some apprehension, "constituted a growing economic threat to Europe," both because of its vast wealth and because of the efficient way in which private enterprise and public policy worked together there in the national interest. At the same time, however, much as he admired the country's openness, optimism, and energy, he warned of coming crises in America. Europe, in his view, would be well advised to "make herself independent of America," and the Baghdad Railway, by opening up vast new areas of the Middle East, would offer an alternative to America both as a market and as a supplier of natural resources. On her own, Germany could not stand up to the growing power of the United States. For that reason it was necessary to reorganize Europe as an economic power and to develop the Middle East as a complementary region. Thus what was needed was a transfer of knowledge and civilization: from America by way of Europe to the Middle East. Germany, he judged, was "best suited to take the lead in this process" since, having no territorial designs on the Ottoman Empire, she enjoyed the trust and friendship of the Sultan and the Muslim populations of the Empire. The greatest potential for development of the region, in Oppenheim's view, lay in the development of agriculture in the once "fertile crescent" and in the exploitation of the petroleum resources of the region. The principal agent of this process would be the privately financed Baghdad railway in "tactful" collaboration with the government of Turkey. Oppenheim recommended that the sources of financing (the German banks) remain discreetly in the background: "The Sultan and the populations of the areas affected should have no doubt that the development of their land was for the benefit of Muslims and as far as possible the work of Muslims." If he did at one time subscribe, as has been claimed, to the *Alldeutsch* plan for setting up colonies of Germans to develop the Middle East, he had left that idea behind him. There should be no question of colonists and missionaries: "The area to be opened up by the Baghdad Railway belongs to Islam."

As it turned out, the visionary aspect of Oppenheim's book did not appeal to Siemens' successor at the Deutsche Bank, Arthur von Gwinner: "No one who bears responsibility for large sums of other people's savings can invest several hundred million marks of German capital without adequate guarantees," he commented dryly. Oppenheim's predictions about the development of the region were no more than muddled "drivel" that ought to have stayed in the inkpot; the explorer himself had been mainly interested in "drawing attention to himself and making himself seem important."[16] Years later, however, in his book on the Bedouins, Oppenheim again insisted that "the whole area was covered with 'Tells' (hillocks concealing ruins), bearing witness to an earlier time when it had supported a large population. Besides," he added, "it was by no means, as many people think, a barren desert. It was neither a sandy wasteland nor a marshland. It was part of that territory which Professor J.H. Breasted — the late Director of the University of Chicago's Oriental Institute — defined as 'the fertile crescent,' and in which in ancient times great kingdoms and princedoms had flourished."[17]

That Oppenheim took economic matters very seriously and was keenly interested in them is further confirmed by a memorandum printed by the Imperial Printing Office in 1916, apparently for distribution to various embassies and *Auswärtiges Amt* personnel. Entitled *Die Nachrichtenstelle der Kaiserlich Deutschen Botschaft in Konstantinopel und die deutsche wirtschaftliche Propaganda in der Türkei, von Max Freiherrn von Oppenheim, Kaiserlichen Minister-Residenten* [*The Intelligence Bureau of the Imperial German Embassy in*

---

16 See Gabriele Teichmann, "Fremder wider Willen," pp. 239–40; idem, "Grenzgänger zwischen Orient und Okzident. Max von Oppenheim 1860–1946," in *Faszination Orient*, pp. 40–45; Wilhelm Treue, "Max Freiherr von Oppenheim: Der Archäologe und die Politik," p. 56; and Wolfgang Korn, *Schienen für den Sultan. Die Bagdadbahn, Wilhelm II, Abenteuerer und Spione*, pp. 141–42. The Library of Congress has one of the extremely rare copies of Oppenheim's *Zur Entwickelung des Bagdadbahngebietes und insbesondere Syriens und Mesopotamiens unter Nutzanwendung amerikanischer Erfahrungen* (Berlin: Printed by Liebheit & Thiesen, 1904); call number 4DS.905.
17 *Die Beduinen*, vol. 1, pp. 8–9.

Constantinople and German Economic Propaganda in Turkey, by Baron Max von Oppenheim, Imperial Minister Resident], the 30-page booklet emphasized the economic importance to Germany of Turkey and the Ottoman lands as a trading partner in which Germany already had invested heavily and which had great potential as a market for the exports of German industry. Eleven pages of carefully designed tables provided comparative statistics of the total value of Turkey's trade in 1913–1914 with twenty of its foreign trading partners (in which Germany occupied third place after England and Austria-Hungary), a break-down of imports and exports to each of those countries according to product categories, and a further break-down of these twenty-eight categories into sub-categories.[18] Apart from justifying his own activity as organizer of the *Nachrichtenstelle*, the intelligence and propaganda bureau in Berlin and Constantinople, Oppenheim's chief objective in the pamphlet was to persuade his countrymen and their government that it is in Germany's interest to take advantage of the wartime political alliance with the Ottomans and the goodwill enjoyed by Germany, according to him, in the Muslim population, in order to secure a prominent place for Germany, after the war, both as an investor in the Ottoman economy and as a major trading partner. According to Oppenheim, this required a concerted effort to replace the hitherto dominant French culture by distributing German magazines, brochures, and films, especially those that concern the German economy and German achievements in industry, to schools, clubs, local cinemas, and the *Nachrichtensäle* (the reading-rooms he had set up in various locations in Turkey), and by showing how German products—agricultural machines, for instance—and German know-how could benefit the local populations and help them develop economically.

---

18 There is a copy of this pamphlet in the Archives of the *Auswärtiges Amt* (see *A Catalog of Files and Microfilms of the German Foreign Ministry Archives 1920–1945*, ed. George O. Kent, 4 vols. [Stanford: The Hoover Institution, 1962–1972], vol. 3, p. 375). I gratefully acknowledge the kindness of the Universitäts- und Staatsbibliothek Köln in making a copy available to me by Interlibrary Loan.

II
THE ARCHAEOLOGIST: TELL HALAF

7. Discovery and Excavation, Publications and Critical Reception

Oppenheim's excavations at Tell Halaf and the scholarly articles and books to which they gave rise—along with the massive and influential study he initiated of the numerous Bedouin tribes, their individual histories, their laws and customs, their internal social organization, and their interconnections—while not unrelated to his demonstrated patriotism, do show him in a somewhat different light from his activity as the "Kaiser's spy." It is only fair, therefore, to devote a section of this study to what was, after all, a significant aspect of the persona he saw himself as and wanted others to see him as. Our main focus in this study is on history and politics, and on the situation and outlook of a German with a part-Jewish family background who was dedicated to the aggrandizement of Germany, even under National Socialism; however, it is not possible to do justice to the complexity of the man or take the measure of his motivations without considering his no less enduring commitment to the archaeology and ethnography of the Middle East and in particular to his excavations at Tell Halaf.

That many archaeologists working in the Middle East at the time also served intermittently as agents of their governments is a well established fact. One need think only of T.E. Lawrence ("Lawrence of Arabia") and his teacher, the Oxford archaeologist D.G. Hogarth. As it happens, both men were working at Carchemish in Northern Syria at the same time that Oppenheim was excavating at Tell Halaf, less than 200 kilometres away. In fact Oppenheim and Lawrence, who came to play similar roles in their country's politics—Oppenheim by trying to foment Muslim uprisings against the British, French and Russians, and Lawrence by successfully fomenting Arab revolts against the Ottoman ally of the Germans—did meet and spend several hours together two years before the outbreak of war.¹ Nevertheless, the archaeologists were not simply political agents in disguise. They were scholars keenly and genuinely interested in the objects of their investigations and most of them also had an interest in the present-day inhabitants of the ancient sites. Though he had had no formal training, Oppenheim, the amateur archaeologist and ethnographer, was clearly moved by indefatigable and respectful curiosity about the ancient cultures and peoples of the Middle East, by sensitivity to the forms and meanings of the artefacts uncovered by his excavations, and by a desire to share his discoveries with others by means of patient, detailed descriptions, excellent photographic images, and informed and serious, if sometimes controversial, scholarly analyses and speculations. There was also no doubt here, as in the other areas of his activity, a strong interest in making himself known and establishing a reputation for himself, in this instance as "the discoverer of Tell Halaf."

As with other similarly dedicated explorers of earlier cultures, interest in the past was often accompanied in Oppenheim by an admiring or, at times, patronizing attitude toward the present-day inhabitants of the ancient sites. His respect for and empathy with the peoples of the Middle East and North Africa is manifested in the numerous beautiful photographs of individuals and groups with which he illustrated his books, beginning with the impressively informative, straightforwardly narrated *Vom Mittelmeer zum Persischen Golf durch den Haurān, die Syrische Wüste und Mesopotamien* of 1899–1900 and culminating forty years later in *Die Beduinen*.² Though a

---

1 *The Home Letters of T.E. Lawrence and his Brothers* (Oxford: Basil Blackwell, 1954), p. 225.
2 2 vols. (Leipzig: Otto Harrassowitz, 1939, 1943) and 2 posthumous volumes (Wiesbaden: Otto Harrassowitz, 1952, 1967–1968). These four volumes constitute a substantial work of scholarship, each one running to nearly 500 pages with very large, well designed fold-out maps in a pocket of the binding. The first two volumes, devoted to the Bedouin tribes of Mesopotamia and Syria and to those of Palestine, Transjordan, the Sinai and the Hijaz respectively, carried on the title page the notice "Unter Mitbearbeitung von Erich Bräunlich and Werner Caskel" [with the collaboration of Erich Bräunlich and Werner Caskel]. Volume 3, published posthumously in 1952, and dealing with the Bedouins of the northern and central parts of the Arabian peninsula still carried Oppenheim's name as author and, on the title-page, "Bearbeitet und herausgegeben von Werner Caskel" [prepared and edited by Werner Caskel]. (Bräunlich had died in 1945 in a prisoner of war camp in Yugoslavia.) Oppenheim also figured as the author of a fourth volume (1952), which was divided into two parts, the first devoted to Iran and the second containing an index and bibliography for all four volumes. Caskel's name again appeared alone as the editor. Oppenheim's collaborators, Bräunlich and Caskel, were in fact responsible for much of the work even on the volumes published during Oppenheim's lifetime, but Oppenheim was the instigator and guiding spirit behind the entire project, and he provided much of the data.

relatively early work, the two-volume *Vom Mittelmeer zum Persischen Golf* already demonstrates not only the author's considerable literary talent, both narrative and descriptive, but his ability to combine a highly personal account of the territories he has travelled through and of their inhabitants with an impressively comprehensive picture of them embracing geography, history, customs and mores, current politics and administration, economy and commerce, art and architecture, as well as biographical portraits of individuals.[3]

Empathy, however, did not exclude from time to time, as was to be expected of a conservative upper-class German and loyal subject of the Kaiser, recommending stringent measures to deal with disorderly situations. In an earlier account, for instance, of part of the 1893 journey through the Syrian desert and Mesopotamia, Oppenheim deplores the "Räuberunwesen der Beduiner" [monstrous plundering way of life of the Bedouins] and proposes, if only as a last resort, the forceful removal of the entire Bedouin population from Mesopotamia into the Arabian desert.[4] Likewise, in his dealings not with statesmen and powerful chiefs but with ordinary "natives" [*"Eingeborene"*], empathy does not erase a

---

3 In the Foreword to volume 1, dated Cairo, March, 1899, Oppenheim writes that it was not his intention to provide a simple travel account but "to portray land and people in their historical development and in their ethnographic and religious particularity. In doing so," he goes on, "I considered myself obligated to quote, in each case, from the rich literature that deals with the history and geography of Syria and Mesopotamia and that includes, along with the works of classical Graeco-Roman and Arabic writers and modern Arab chroniclers, a whole series of older European travel accounts and numerous new scholarly works—these last scattered in not easily accessible journals." (p. v) The names of individuals and places were given in Arabic script as well as in German. This added a touch of *couleur locale*—while also serving as a signal of the writer's authority.

4 Describing the efforts of the Ottoman administration to pacify the Bedouins and get them to settle, he notes that those who do are soon preyed upon by their former friends and relatives until they resume their old ways and resort again to plunder as a way of life. "In my opinion, only one thing will work in dealing with the Bedouins," he writes, "and that is the deployment of force—strong garrisons manned by good regiments of men mounted on mules, camels, or horses to hold the Bedouins in check, pursue them relentlessly and punish them energetically when they exact tribute from the peasants or plunder them; and if all else fails, driving the entire Bedouin population out of Mesopotamia into the desert lands of Arabia" (Dr. Max Freiherr von Oppenheim, "Bericht über seine Reise durch die Syrische Wüste nach Mosul," Offprint from *Verhandlungen der Gesellschaft für Erdkunde zu Berlin*, 1894, no. 4 [Berlin: Druck von W. Pormetter, 1894], 18 pp. [p. 12]). A version of this well written text was also published soon afterwards, in the oldest German geographical journal, *Petermanns Geographische Mitteilungen*. Five years later, material from it was incorporated—but without the suggestions for reining in the Bedouins—into the two-volume *Vom Mittelmeer zum Persischen Golf durch den Haurān und die Syrische Wüste*.

certain condescension, even toward people for whose services he was genuinely grateful and of whom he seems to have been truly fond. In the monograph on Tell Halaf that he published in 1931, for instance, he pays generous tribute to his two devoted Lebanese servants, the cousins Tannus and Elias Maluf. The former, a strong, powerfully built man, was illiterate but took care of the Baron's personal security, as well as that of the caravans and the camp, served as an invaluable intermediary and negotiator with the Bedouins, and tended his master loyally whenever the latter fell sick. Elias, a village teacher, spoke French, had a scholar's knowledge of the Arabic language, and served as Oppenheim's secretary in all matters concerning Arabic, providing him with meticulous records in Arabic script of place names and proper names, along with accurate European transcriptions. Yet even in Oppenheim's touchingly affectionate portraits of the two men it is impossible not to detect a patronizing tone.[5] As for the Bedouin workers he employed at the Tell Halaf site, he declared: "So far as I possibly could, I helped the workmen and their families, and they looked on me as a father. [...] They were like children and were treated as such."[6]

* * *

In 1899 Oppenheim had spent "three days only" (or perhaps even only a day and a half)[7] at the Tell Halaf site, partly, as he explained later, because "we had neither the proper outfit, the time, nor any permit to carry out more detailed investigations"[8] and partly also, no doubt, because he felt impelled to continue his covert prospecting for the Baghdad railway. He was greatly excited by what he had discovered, however. It marked, in his own words, "a turning-point in my life"[9] and, passing through Constantinople on his return from Syria, he sought official permission to excavate the site. The discovery and excavation of Tell Halaf was indeed to be the crowning achievement of Oppenheim's career and one of the great achievements of modern archaeology. Two relatively short accounts of the preliminary 1899 excavations were published: the already mentioned "Bericht über eine im Jahre 1899 ausgeführte Forschungsreise

---

5 *Tell Halaf. A New Culture in Oldest Mesopotamia* (see above, ch. 6, note 6), pp. 9–10.
6 Ibid., p. 17.
7 See ch. 6, note 9 above.
8 *Tell Halaf. A New Culture in Oldest Mesopotamia*, p. 8.
9 Ibid., p. 7.

in der Asiatischen Türkei" ["Report on a journey of exploration in Asiatic Turkey in 1899"], which appeared in the *Zeitschrift der Gesellschaft für Erdkunde zu Berlin* [Journal of the Berlin Geographical Society] in 1901,[10] and a 43-page essay *Der Tell Halaf und die verschleierte Göttin* [*Tell Halaf and the Veiled Goddess*], which appeared in 1908 in a series put out by the Berlin *Vorderasiatische Gesellschaft* [Near Eastern Society].[11]

Nevertheless, ten years elapsed after the initial discovery before Oppenheim took advantage of the authorization he had obtained from the head of the Ottoman Imperial Museums. No doubt he was fully taken up by his activities as *Legationsrat* [legation counsellor] in Cairo. In 1909, however, he was advised by the Turkish government that he must act immediately on his right to excavate or forfeit it, since English and American scholars were now soliciting permission to explore the neglected site. In addition, he had received a letter, signed by eleven German colleagues in the field of Oriental studies, urging him to begin serious work at the site: "None of us can forget your lecture at the Congress of Orientalists in Copenhagen and your study of 'Der Tell Halaf' in the Publications of the *Vorderasiatische Gesellschaft*," the letter ran. "The whole scholarly world very much hopes that you will crown the work you began a decade ago with a full-scale excavation of the site." Oppenheim, the letter continued, was clearly the man for the job, being one of the few scholars with the means to undertake it. "The resources of the State in Germany are entirely devoted to the Babylonian excavations. The study of Hittite and Islamic culture has thus been left entirely to the initiative of private individuals. At the same time, what an honourable opportunity there is here for a person who can undertake such a project at his own expense. And the time to do so is now, for your publications have long drawn the attention of others to the riches of this site."[12] In other words,

---

10 Vol. 36, no. 2 (1901): 69–99.
11 *Der Alte Orient*, vol. 10, no. 1 (Leipzig: J.C. Hinrichs'sche Buchhandlung, 1908).
12 Cit. G. Teichmann, "Grenzgänger zwischen Orient und Okzident. Max von Oppenheim 1860–1946," p. 53. The signatories included several of the most eminent scholars of the Middle East in Germany and Central Europe, e.g. C. H. Becker, Ignaz Goldziher, and Ernst Herzfeld. The letter is dated 1919 by Ludmila Hanisch (*Die Nachfolger der Exegeten. Deutschsprachige Erforschung des Vorderen Orients in der ersten Hälfte des 20. Jahrhunderts*, p. 129). However, it is unlikely that "the work begun a decade ago" refers to the extensive excavations of 1911–1913 (less than a decade before 1919), rather than the preliminary excavation of 1899, and the study referred to is clearly that of 1908. The International Congress of Orientalists also met in Copenhagen in 1908 and would thus in 1909 have been fresh in the memory of the letter-signers.

if Oppenheim does not act immediately, the glory of developing the site will almost certainly be lost to German scholarship.

Disappointment at his failure to make headway at the *Auswärtiges Amt* may well have combined with the pressure from the Turkish authorities and from his Orientalist colleagues to persuade Oppenheim that he should return to the work of research and exploration that had always engaged him. He himself later claimed that he did so at some sacrifice to his career, since he had been appointed to an ambassadorial position, but it is not at all clear what this position might have been. It is also possible that he was still, officially or unofficially, serving German national interests. A report in the *New York Times* from the paper's special correspondent in Cairo refers to Oppenheim's passing through Constantinople in 1910 on an "enigmatical journey to the Khabur River and the Urfa region," ostensibly "to exhume the statue of a Hittite goddess on the banks of the Khabur." The report goes on to claim that "according to Syrian advices, the real object of the Baron's visit was to purchase the support of Arab and Kurdish tribal chiefs in the Khabur region for the Baghdad Railway Company."[13] It is equally possible, however, that this report, written after the start of the First World War and several years after the event referred to in it, simply reflects the general suspicion with which Oppenheim was regarded by the British and the French and those sympathetic to their cause.

What is certain is that on 1 November 1910, Oppenheim resigned his position at the *Auswärtiges Amt* and prepared to begin a thorough excavation of the site he had discovered a decade earlier. It was a very expensive operation. Oppenheim wanted his expedition to be on a par with that of Robert Koldewey at Babylon and to use the methods elaborated by Koldewey. That meant hiring architects experienced in archaeological work, transporting all the required supplies and every piece of equipment to Tell Halaf, and staying on site for an extended period of time.

"Tell Halaf is many days' journey from the nearest towns, Der es Zor, Mardin, and Ourfa," he related later in the substantial, well illustrated book on Tell Halaf, which Brockhaus of Leipzig brought out in 1931, and in which he gave an account of the 1911 excavation. Moreover, even these

---

13 *New York Times*, "German Intrigue in Egypt. Attempts to Weaken British Power. The Activities of Baron von Oppenheim," 6 January 1915; report dated Cairo, 19 December 1914, p. 7.

7. Discovery and Excavation, Publications and Critical Reception 125

places were capable at that time of meeting only the needs of the local Arabs:

> I had to bring nearly everything needed for the excavating and for life on Tell Halaf on camel-back from Aleppo: the heavy expeditionary baggage brought with me from Europe, the scientific apparatus, the tools for digging, a field railway with twelve tip-waggons, and nearly all the materials for building the house for the expedition. [...] Taken altogether, nearly 1000 camels were used for our transport from Aleppo to Tell Halaf, and for safety's sake a road was used that needed almost twenty days for the journey.[14]

Finding workers was also not easy. The excavation was begun on 5 August 1911 with "a gang of ten men made up of my own servants and of Arabs." As the local Bedouins, intimidated by the Chechens in the region and by other more powerful Bedouin tribes, were afraid to work for Oppenheim, two hundred Christian Armenians had to be hired from a nearby community, and "supplies and flour for their bread [had to be brought in] at our own cost from the villages." They turned out to be difficult workers, especially after, "in spite of every precaution taken, the dried up walls in one of our deep trial trenches fell in, with the result that several workmen were buried and one young man was killed." Fortunately for Oppenheim, it was possible to replace the restive Armenians with Bedouins from a nomadic tribe "not dependent on the Chechens." "In the end we had an average of 550 Bedouins working for us." The pay was not great and care was taken to ensure that there was no slacking off. Still, the total wages bill must have been substantial.

> To each twenty workmen or so there were two foremen with pickaxes, either kinsmen of the Sheikh or especially good workers; also four or five men using mattocks, who put the earth into baskets, when it was taken away by the rest of the gang—youths, boys or girls. The workers with iron tools earned about 80 pfennig [approx. $4.00–$6.00 in 2011 currency], the other men about 60, and the boys and girls 40 pfennig a day, and had to find their own food. For these wages they had to work ten hours daily. The payment of wages for work done regularly every ten days without any deduction and in good coin had never before happened in those parts. [...] In the work of excavation the men with the pickaxes first loosen up the ground, whether the object is to dig trial trenches or to lay bare a definite layer. Then come the mattock men and take it into the baskets of the women and older boys, who carry them away under the arm, on the shoulder, or on the head, and empty

---

14 *Tell Halaf. A New Culture in Oldest Mesopotamia*, p. 11.

them where they are told. [...] It is then the overseer's duty to see that the bearers do not get too little soil put in their baskets through politeness being shown to the ladies or for some like reason.[15]

Besides the workers, Oppenheim had engaged a team of highly skilled German professionals to accompany him on the mission. These included, for the 1911–1913 excavation, two architects who had worked with Koldewey, as well as engineers, photographers, physicians, and secretaries. In addition, a specialist was brought in from the Royal Museums of Berlin to make plaster casts of most of the sculptures, since the Ottoman antiquities law of 1874 had been changed in 1884 and no longer permitted sharing of the finds. In the unhealthy climate several staff members fell seriously ill (as, at one point, did Oppenheim himself) and had to be sent back to Germany and replaced. Oppenheim does not say how this highly specialized team was remunerated, what the cost of its day-to-day upkeep was or how much he spent on the building he had constructed to house it over what was expected to be a long period. A drawing made of the house confirms his own verbal description: "With its high walls and great courtyards it looked like a castle. [...] Here I lived with my staff and servants like a desert prince."[16] Oppenheim was obviously dedicated to his task and spared no expense in executing it. It has been estimated that it cost him the equivalent of 7–8 million Euros in today's money (2011).[17]

The first stage of the excavation of Tell Halaf was completed in August 1913. Work was supposed to resume in the winter of 1914 to 1915, but World War I intervened. It was not until 1927, after Germany joined the League of Nations, that Oppenheim was able to obtain permission from the authorities of what was now the French mandate of Syria to return to Tell Halaf and continue his investigation of the site.

By the time Oppenheim and his team went back to Germany in 1913, however, much had been accomplished. The physical characteristics of the site had been determined, a serious attempt had been made to reconstruct

---

15 Ibid., pp. 16, 20.
16 Ibid., p. 21. The illustration (not in the original German text of 1931) is on the following page.
17 http://www.tell-halaf-projekt.de/de/max_von_oppenheim/oppenheim.htm *sub* "Tell Halaf Museum." See also Nadja Cholidis and Lutz Martin, *Der Tell Halaf und sein Ausgräber Max Freiherr von Oppenheim* (Berlin: Vorderasiatisches Museum/Staatliche Museen zu Berlin, 2002), p. 35, where the cost of the 1911–1913 excavations is estimated at around 750,000 Reichsmarks of the time (approx. $200,000 of the time, the equivalent of approx. $4.5 million today). Whatever the correct figure, the sum was clearly in the millions.

its history, and the excavations had yielded significant finds in the form of sculptures, reliefs, and pottery. The excavations discovered several stages in the settlement of Tell Halaf. Handsomely decorated and painted pottery found at the lowest level of the excavations bore witness to a chalcholithic culture (i.e. one in which stone tools are beginning to be replaced by metal tools) in the 5th or 6th millennium B.C. The relief sculptures and some sculptures in the round that had been dug up in 1899 had been identified in the 1901 *Bericht* and then again in the 1908 essay *Der Tell Halaf und die verschleierte Göttin* as Hittite and had been attributed, on the basis of inscriptions on some of them, to the reign of a ruler named Kapara, whom Oppenheim took to be a princeling of the Mitannian age or of a somewhat later period—i.e. to some time between 1450 and 900 B.C.[18]

After the excavations of 1911–1913 and 1929 and under the influence of the established academic archaeologist Ernst Herzfeld,[19] Oppenheim revised this judgment, and dated the sculptures to a far earlier period from around 3000 to 2000 B.C. Superimposed on the two earlier cultures (one of the 5th millennium B.C. and one of the 3rd), he now argued, were the palaces and temples of an Aramaean kingdom that dated from the end of the second and the beginning of the first millennium B.C. Oppenheim and his team identified two major structures in the Aramaean city, which they described as the Northeastern Palace or Citadel and the Western or Temple Palace. Various inscriptions indicated that the Temple Palace, with its monumental entrance façade of towering caryatids in the form of the three principal deities mounted on huge fabulous beasts—the weather god Teshub flanked by his wife, the mother goddess Hebat, and their son, the mountain god Sarruma—and its walls decorated with relief sculptures,

---

18 "Both as a whole and in its details," according to the 1901 *Bericht* (p. 90), "the form of some of our finds bears a great resemblance to Hittite artifacts. But other elements, especially the mystical fertility goddess, are completely unrelated to anything as yet discovered among the artifacts of ancient civilizations. It is not impossible that in Tell Halaf we have come upon the palace of one of the kings of the still unknown Mittani people, which must have lived here in Mesopotamia. Ras el 'Ain, which is part of Tell Halaf, was virtually made to be the capital of a small principality. Countless tumuli in the neighborhood […] testify to the existence here, in the Babylonian-Assyrian period, of a rich and vibrant culture."

19 Herzfeld (1879–1948) had a distinguished career. He participated in the excavation of Assur (1903–1905), was appointed Professor of "Landes- und Altertumskunde des Orients" at the Technical University of Berlin in 1920, conducted extensive archaeological work in Iran (1925–1934), and, obliged to vacate his position in Berlin on racial grounds in 1935, was appointed to the Institute for Advanced Study in Princeton (1936–1944). His papers are preserved in the Archives of the Freer and Sackler Galleries in Washington, D.C.

had been built by a ruler whose name was Kapara, and who was now defined as Aramaean. Following Herzfeld, however, Oppenheim now held that many of the relief orthostats and some of the sculptures, including the caryatids of the Temple Palace and the sphinxes guarding the entrance, as well as two female figures that held a special attraction for him, dated from the third millennium B.C. These, it was conjectured, had been part of an earlier palace that had been destroyed; Kapara had come upon them as the site was being cleared for the construction of his palace; and he had reused them for his own building:

> From the circumstances of the finds and on archaeological and stylistic grounds it would seem to be an impossibility that the statues were made under Kapara and belong to the end of the second millennium. Rather they were [...] used over again by Kapara and belong to the third millennium. As often happened in ancient times, Kapara simply put his own name on the old sculptures.[20]

This was the account that Oppenheim presented to the public, after further excavation of the site in 1927, in *Der Tell Halaf. Eine neue Kultur im ältesten Mesopotamien*, a handsomely illustrated volume, published in 1931 by Brockhaus, the well established Leipzig firm known for its widely used encyclopedias and reference works, and clearly intended for a broad rather than a specialized readership. The account was unchanged in the English translation of the book that appeared two years later in London and New York, in a brief, richly illustrated article by Oppenheim in the scholarly journal *Syria*, the organ of the Institut Français du Proche-Orient,[21] and then again in the full French translation of the book, brought out by Payot in Paris in 1939 and said to be a revised and updated version of the 1931 text.

From the beginning, however, this chronology was regarded with great scepticism by most scholars. Although the book was very well received on the whole, most reviewers questioned Oppenheim's (i.e. Herzfeld's) "sensationally early datings" of the sculptures and large relief orthostats.[22] One eminent English archaeologist, the Australian-

---

20 *Tell Halaf. A New Culture in Oldest Mesopotamia*, p. 37. See also, at the end of the volume, Appendix 1 ("Stilkritische Untersuchung und Datierung der Steinbilder") by Ernest Herzfeld.
21 "Tell Halaf, la plus ancienne capitale soubaréenne de Mésopotamie," *Syria*, 13 (1932): 243–56.
22 Edith Porada, review of Max Freiherr von Oppenheim, *Tell Halaf*, vol. 3: *Die Bildwerke* (part of the multi-volume scholarly work devoted to Tell Halaf, of which only the first volume appeared during Oppenheim's lifetime and which, though it carried Oppenheim's name, was largely produced by his younger friends and associates): "None

born V. Gordon Childe, reviewing the 1933 English translation in the journal *Man*, noted that "the sculptures are well illustrated and clearly described." On the other hand, "Professor Herzfeld's attribution of them on 'stylistic grounds' to the fourth and third millennia [...] is, to say the least, highly speculative and controversial," so that "one is inclined to regret that the author of a book directed to the general public should have accepted such a chronology without reserve."[23] In the *Times Literary Supplement*, the anonymous reviewer—in fact, Reginald Campbell Thompson, who was a teacher of both T.E. Lawrence and Max Mallowan and had excavated at Nineveh, Ur, and Carchemish—"congratulated [the Oppenheim team] on its finds." "The stone statues," he declared, "must be seen to be believed" and "throw a new light on the civilization of the Upper Euphrates." The painted pottery he judged "of immense interest." The book, moreover, was "beautifully illustrated." But, while acknowledging the possibility that the slabs on which Kapara's name is incised might well, as Oppenheim claimed, "be an instance of a later king absorbing his predecessor's work," Thompson objected strongly to Oppenheim's chronology: "We cannot accept his extraordinarily high date for these slabs, which are here assigned to a period not later than 2900 B.C., long before the end of the painted pottery; in other words that they are prehistoric, although not one of them appears to have been found in a true prehistoric layer." Anticipating a criticism made by several of his colleagues, Thompson thus questioned Oppenheim's and Herzfeld's reliance on stylistic grounds alone to justify their chronology, without any support from stratigraphy or inscriptions: "Crudity of workmanship is no criterion necessarily for assessing a high date to sculptures."[24]

Leonard Woolley, who had directed the excavations at Carchemish in 1912–1914, at the same time as Oppenheim was excavating Tell Halaf (and who was also, during World War I, engaged in intelligence work on the side), also saluted Oppenheim on his achievement and generally

---

of the scholars who had to express an opinion about these works followed Herzfeld. [...] Instead, the controversy centred on the classification of the sculptures as either Hurro-Mitannian or Aramaic and on their dating between 1400 and 800 B.C" (*Artibus Asiae*, 20 [1957]: 86–88 [p. 86]). For an overview of the enduring debate about the chronology of the Tell Halaf finds, see W.F. Albright, "The Date of the Kapara Period at Gozan (Tell Halaf)," *Anatolian Studies*, 6 (1956): 75–85.

23 *Man*, May 1934, p. 78.
24 *Times Literary Supplement*, 8 June 1933, p. 395.

accepted, with only a few reservations, the latter's assessment of the oldest stratum:

> The appearance of Baron von Oppenheim's book giving for the first time an account, popular but reasonably full, of his discoveries at Tell Halaf is very welcome. The volume is well illustrated. It contains photographic reproductions of some seventy of the stone sculptures and eight plates of pottery as well as some of the gold, ivory, and other objects; the text gives an account of the site, of its excavations, and of its history and a description of the sculpture and small objects by von Oppenheim himself, while appendices by Herzfeld, Langenegger, Karl Müller, Hubert Schmidt, Meissner, and Jensen deal with the more technical aspects of the work and of the material.
>
> Tell Halaf, a group of mounds on the banks of the Khabur River in northern Mesopotamia, proved to be a most remarkable and a most productive site. In the lower strata of the mound there were found no buildings but great quantities of pottery. At the bottom came a monochrome ware associated with stone weapons and implements which was unquestionably Neolithic; above this came an elaborately painted ware with designs sometimes geometrical, sometimes naturalistic, in a paint which at its best is as lustrous as that of Mycenaean pottery. Hubert Schmidt contributes a short but valuable study of this material, which he distinguishes into four periods. Similar wares have been found at Carchemish, Sakjegeuzi, and, more recently, at Arpachia, near Nineveh, and there is no doubt that it is extremely early; at Tell Halaf Schmidt records the finding of a few copper implements associated apparently with the " first painted period," so that we may even from the outset be dealing with a chalcolithic rather than a truly neolithic culture; but in bringing the later phases of the ware down so late as 2000 B.C. von Oppenheim is surely minimizing its antiquity.

On the buildings and statuary, however, Woolley expressed serious doubts about the chronology proposed by Oppenheim:

> In the upper levels, below scanty remains of Hellenistic date, the excavators traced the town wall with its gates and a few adjacent buildings; one of the mounds inside the rampart yielded a large temple of the Assyrian period, resting upon walls of an earlier date; but the greater part of the work was concerned with the Citadel which lay at the north side of the town close to the river; here there was a very large complex of palace and other buildings erected by Kapara, an Aramaic ruler whom Bruno Meissner would date to the twelfth century B.C.— other authorities would certainly consider this date some hundreds of years too early. The palace produced an astonishing array of stone sculptures, statues in the round, carved bases, and, above all, reliefs on

basalt or limestone slabs which decorated the façade of the building; the study of these, from an artistic and a chronological point of view, occupies a large part of the volume. Further, at Jebelet el Beda, 70 kilometres south of Tell Halaf, Baron von Oppenheim discovered a burial-place surmounted by basalt statues of a remarkable sort.

The mounds of Tell Halaf yielded no remains whatever dating between the close of the Painted Pottery period and the time when Kapara (or more probably his father, for the palace shows traces of rebuilding) re-occupied the deserted site. Baron von Oppenheim and Professor Herzfeld are convinced that the sculptures, many of which are inscribed with the name of Kapara, are of a much older date and were simply re-used by him, and since there is no building earlier than the twelfth century to which they can be assigned, it follows that Kapara must have found them in the Painted Pottery level and that they rightly belong to the third millennium B.C.; Professor Herzfeld on stylistic and technical grounds distinguishes the bulk of the sculptures into groups which he dates to *c.* 3000, *c.* 2800, and *c.* 2600–2550 B.C. respectively. It is a theory which few scholars will be inclined to accept.

There is too close a parallel between the sculptures of Tell Halaf on the one hand and of Carchemish, Senjirli, and Sakjegeuzi on the other for them to be very far removed from one another in point of time; recognizing this, Professor Herzfeld attributes the monuments of these sites also to various dates in the third millennium. Now, the buildings in which the monuments occur belong definitely to the first millennium; therefore the Tell Halaf theory must apply equally to them and in each of the four cases a late builder must have delved in the prehistoric strata, discovered prehistoric sculptures, all intact, and incorporated them in his own work. This is carrying coincidence too far. At Carchemish there are, indeed, instances of older sculptures being re-used, but such are generally re-used merely as building material and not for decoration.

The fact that a number of the Tell Halaf slabs bear the name of Kapara, which to many people would seem conclusive, is dismissed on the assumption that the inscription was cut on the ancient stones discovered by him. Other difficulties are as lightly met; thus that the domestication of the horse and the use of Assyrian horse trappings and harness would by this theory be carried back into the third millennium is held not to weaken the argument but only to enhance the interest of the carvings; on the basis of a purely subjective criticism which in some instances can be proved misleading we are asked to jettison all that we have yet learned about the chronology of north Syrian art. It is generally agreed that the earlier Carchemish sculptures are of about the twelfth century B.C. and others two or three centuries later; both the Senjirli and the Sakjegeuzi sculptures fall well within the first millennium and some of the latter are approximately dated by inscriptions. The Tell Halaf reliefs resemble those, for instance, of Carchemish in their use—alternate slabs of limestone and basalt forming a façade—often in their subjects and sometimes in their style; and in so far as the style differs, the Tell Halaf orthostats seem to be not so much primitive as provincial. Similar basalt carvings are not uncommon in north Syria, [...] and it is probable that they decorated the buildings of local magnates who could not command the services of the better artists employed in the royal cities.

The case of the Jebelet el Beda statues is quite different. Here we have figures which are either very ancient or preserve remarkably well the ancient tradition; their dependence upon Sumerian art is obvious, but to bring them into close relation with the Tell Halaf orthostats is wholly unjustified.

"They are of great importance," however, Woolley readily conceded, "and so are the sculptures of Kapara's palace and the prehistoric pottery." Woolley's ultimate judgment of Oppenheim's work was thus mixed: "Baron von Oppenheim is to be congratulated on his discoveries, and everything that throws light on their character and on the conditions in which they were found is a welcome addition to knowledge. It is the more to be regretted that the chronological theories put forward in the present volume should rob it of so much of its value as a contribution to history."[25]

Most other reviewers agreed with Woolley on the issue of chronology. For example, the University of Pennsylvania Assyriologist Ephraim A. Speiser (1902–1965)[26] in the *American Journal of Archaeology*:

> Even more disturbing, though no less fascinating, is the chronology of the several sculptural stages represented by the carvings from Tell Halaf and Jebelet-el-Beda. The author would place his earliest specimens in the fourth millennium and the rest of his sculptures not later than the third. In this view he is supported by the expert, if apodictical, opinion of Herzfeld. But nearly all critics would relegate the bulk of the Tell Halaf carvings to the end of the second millennium! On both sides the arguments employed have been chiefly of a stylistic nature, inasmuch as the circumstances of discovery admit of no definite stratigraphic interpretation. Throughout this discussion the author has remained unshaken by the opinion of the majority.

Nevertheless, Speiser kept the door slightly ajar on the chronology question. Oppenheim, he wrote, should "derive much joy from a very recent discovery

---

25 C. L. Woolley, review of *Tell Halaf: a new culture in oldest Mesopotamia*, in *Journal of the Royal Asiatic Society*, July 1934, part 3: 593–97. Woolley (1880–1960) subsequently headed up the joint British Museum-University of Pennsylvania team that in 1922–1934 conducted one of the most spectacular excavations of the twentieth century, at Ur.

26 A native of Austrian Galicia, Speiser immigrated to the United States at the age of eighteen and became a Professor at the University of Pennsylvania.

at Warka, where a stele has been unearthed in one of the Jemdet Nasr deposits (end of the fourth millennium) which bears a remarkable resemblance to the older sculptures from Tell Halaf." Above all, Speiser responded warmly to Oppenheim's passionate engagement with his material and zoomed in on an aspect of it to which Oppenheim himself drew attention and to which we shall turn shortly: "One is awed by the mysterious power of the veiled goddess who, in addition to guiding the excavation, appears to have inspired the correct solution of one of the most knotty problems resulting therefrom. The baron is to be congratulated on more counts than one."[27]

On the other hand, Speiser did question the claim, which Oppenheim took over from his friend, the Assyriologist Arthur Ungnad,[28] that an autonomous "Subaraean" culture, extending over much of Northern Mesopotamia under the domination of various invading ethnic groups, was of equal significance to the ancient Babylonian and ancient Egyptian cultures. Oppenheim had adopted Ungnad's thesis that, albeit not unified politically into a single empire, Subartu constituted an influential grouping of several political centres, of which the earlier Tell Halaf of the third millennium B.C. had allegedly been one of the most important.[29] Speiser disputed this claim:

> Baron von Oppenheim regards the Khabur region as the center of a third great and independent culture by the side of those of Egypt and Babylon. To the new civilization he would apply the name "Subaraic," following the lead of Arthur Ungnad. In a very broad sense this view may pass as correct: the cultural background of Tell Halaf is certainly neither Egyptian nor Sumerian, and there is some excuse for calling it Subaraean. But the implied assumption that this third cultural group (which used to be called "Syro-Hittite") was necessarily homogeneous will not stand closer scrutiny. As a matter of fact, the unity of the so-called Babylonian civilization is now known to be also a myth. Many disparate elements entered into the make-up of the Sumerian culture, and matters are even more complicated in Central Mesopotamia, Syria, and Anatolia.

---

27 E.A. Speiser, review of *Tell Halaf: a new culture in oldest Mesopotamia*, in *American Journal of Archaeology*, 38 (1934): 610–12.
28 Ungnad (1879–1945) was professor successively at Jena, Greifswald and Breslau with a stint as visiting professor at the University of Pennsylvania (1919).
29 *Tell Halaf: a new culture in oldest Mesopotamia*, p. 54: "The Subaraic culture is undoubtedly just as important as the Old Babylonian and the Old Egyptian. Through the discovery of Tell Halaf and of the statues of Jebelet-el-Beda the proof is given for Upper Mesopotamia also of the existence of this third culture in Hither Asia, independent and rooted in the land, and stretching back into the earliest prehistoric times."

On the whole, despite serious misgivings about both chronology and the so-called Subaraean culture, reviews of Oppenheim's book were extremely favourable. It is clear that British and American professional and academic scholars held Oppenheim, though an amateur, in high esteem. Many were especially responsive to the author's talent for lively description and narrative. In the *Journal of the Royal Central Asian Society*, the reviewer underlined the vividness of Oppenheim's narratives and descriptions and his sensitivity to the aesthetic qualities of the reliefs and three-dimensional sculptures his team had excavated at Tell Halaf. "The career of an archaeologist is one of the most interesting and romantic that it is possible to choose in these law-abiding days of easy travel," this reviewer wrote. "Yet it is seldom that an archaeologist is found who is able at the same time both to produce his results in a scientific and reliable manner and to convey to the general reader the delight and excitement of his work. This is not the case with Baron von Oppenheim. His book, *Tell Halaf,* is enthralling from beginning to end. It is admirably balanced; the various chapters deal in the most interesting manner possible with what their titles say that they deal with; [...] and they tell us of discoveries which must prove of considerable importance in the history of the Near East. The book is at the same time a thrilling tale of adventure."[30] In the same vein,

---

30 D.T.R. in *Journal of the Royal Central Asian* Society, 20 (1933): 451–54. This reviewer, however, also took up the issue on which Speiser had criticized Oppenheim, i.e. the latter's claim that there was an autonomous "Subaraean" culture, as well as the racial "hypothesis of a large Nordic element in Western Asia," which the reviewer sees as popular among German anthropologists: "Chapter II deals with the history of Northern Mesopotamia, the ancient Subartuland, home, according to von Oppenheim, of an homogeneous culture in early times, with its own particular racial type and its own particular art. This culture von Oppenheim calls the Subaraic; to its art are to be assigned the works which we know as Hittite and which have hitherto been dated too late, since they have been attributed to the culture established in Asia Minor by conquering Indo-European tribes early in the second millennium. The author suggests that these works must be assigned to the old Subaraic civilization [...] established in the north-western part of Mesopotamia. The 'Hittite' remains—Karkemish, Senjirli, etc.—have, thinks von Oppenheim, little to do with the purely Hittite culture, which was intrusive above them (p. 56). The Hittite picture writing he also regards as much older than is generally supposed. It must have been older than cuneiform; have been more or less forgotten, and then revived, perhaps somewhat fictitiously, at a comparatively late date.This suggestion seems perhaps somewhat too elaborate. The Hittites as we know them—von Oppenheim calls them Nasians—he regards as of Nordic race, who were linguistically members of the Kentum group. But here we are on very insecure ground, and the hypothesis of a large Nordic element in Western Asia, though upheld by certain German anthropologists (especially Günther), is not one which can be generally accepted. The Mitanni, of whom we hear so much in the history of Egypt's foreign relations, von Oppenheim also regards as Indo-Europeans, but they were members of the Satem group, and had little to do with the

The Geographical Journal praised Oppenheim for having written a book that was both an important contribution to scholarship and a lively evocation of an earlier culture. "Imagination," this reviewer wrote, "is an essential quality for the archaeologist."

> His problem is to reconstruct history, which is a thing of motion, out of material which is in its nature stationary. His actual finds are clues; what interests him are not the pieces of pottery, statues, bronzes, in themselves, but the life and continual change which they represent, by which they were once cast casually on buried shelves of Time, where the archaeologist laboriously digging finds and uses them to reconstruct the living picture. This work of imaginative reconstruction has been going on very rapidly of late in near and central Asia, and every discovery, while it throws light on its own immediate age and locality, opens up new and unexplored problems for future investigation. Baron von Oppenheim's book is important in both these aspects, for not only are the statues and reliefs found at Tell Halaf unique as artistic objects of the very greatest interest, but the theories which the author bases on their discovery open up the very obscure question of the pre-Sumerian and pre-Semitic inhabitants of the Euphrates and Tigris valleys.

Not least, according to *The Geographical Journal*'s reviewer, Oppenheim's book "introduces us, in a lively, simple style to a most engaging, adventurous, and enthusiastic personality." The dramatic narrative of Oppenheim's discovery of the site is singled out for special mention.[31]

Oppenheim had in fact followed a tradition set by earlier archaeologists, such as the remarkable Austen Henry Layard, who had been commissioned by the British Museum in the mid-nineteenth century to conduct excavations at ancient Nineveh and Babylon (*Discoveries in the ruins of Nineveh and Babylon* [London: John Murray, 1853]), in providing not only vivid descriptions of the finds but lively personal narratives of the journey to the site (almost always eventful and often dangerous), of individuals and peoples encountered along the way, of life at the site, and of the actual excavation of the site. Thus *Tell Halaf. A New Culture in Oldest Mesopotamia* opens on the exciting little narrative mentioned by the *Geographical Journal* reviewer. At a Bedouin camp, Oppenheim relates, where he was being entertained in 1899 by the tribal leader, Ibrahim Pasha, with whom he had become friendly, he learned of "remarkable statues said to have been found on a hill by the small village of Ras el Ain."

> The village was inhabited by Chechens, Mohammedans coming from the Caucasus and akin to the Cherkesses (Circassians), who after the Russian

Hittites."
31 F.S. in *The Geographical Journal*, 82 (1933): 364–65.

conquest of their home had fled as religious refugees to an Islamic land, that is, Turkey. The Chechens, I was told, had wanted some years before to bury one of their dead on the hill, and, while doing this, they had come upon stone statues of animals with human heads. Filled with superstitious dread, they filled in the hole again and buried the body at another place. In that same year the neighbourhood was visited by drought, locust swarms and cholera. This was attributed by the Chechens to the evil spirits that they believed to have been in the statues, and now set free. As a result they most carefully avoided speaking of the statues, fearing that others might dig out the fabulous beings and thereby bring ill-hap on them once more.

Oppenheim and his team immediately set off for Ras el Ain. After various adventures along the way, they "dismounted at the house of the Mukhtar, the village headman of the Chechens."

It was not until we had partaken of the feast that I started to speak with great care of the remarkable statues. As I had foreseen, they denied everything. However, I did not give up; I described the stones and promised the Chechens a good reward if I could get guides to the place of the finds. It was all in vain. Then I appealed to the laws of hospitality, and demanded, as the guest, not to be told what was untrue, but to have my request granted. Thereupon the Mukhtar and the village elders swore on the Koran that they had not lied. I now played my last trump. I hurled a curse at my hosts for having sworn falsely on the Koran. [...] There was then a dramatic scene. All the Chechens stood up. Some drew their long narrow daggers; such a thing as this had not yet befallen the hot-tempered, proud Caucasians. My soldiers ran to my side; the situation grew threatening. I shouted to the Chechens to cap their false oath with the murder of their guest in their own house. At the last moment three old Chechens and the guides sent with me by Ibrahim Pasha came between us. [...] A sudden silence fell on them. [...] The Mukhtar acknowledged his wrong, and asked me to stay; and on this the Chechens most solemnly promised to take me up the hill on which the statues were said to have been found.[32]

* * *

The 1901 *Bericht* already contained several careful descriptions of sculptures and reliefs which, though cursory compared with the later writings, testify to Oppenheim's propensity to engage personally with the ancient culture he was investigating, as well as to the strong attraction its art held for him. He was especially taken, Oppenheim acknowledged in this short text, with "a bust of a beardless human figure, certainly that of a woman, whose head was most expressive, despite the lack of any musculature."

---

32 *Tell Halaf. A New Culture in Oldest Mesopotamia*, pp. 6–7.

7. Discovery and Excavation, Publications and Critical Reception 137

Fig. 7.1 Tell Halaf. "The Pole Goddess," excavated in 1899. Dr. Max Freiherr von Oppenheim, "Bericht über eine im Jahr 1899 ausgeführte Forschungsreise in der asiatischen Türkei," *Zeitschrift der Gesellschaft für Erdkunde zu Berlin*, 36, 2 (1901): 69–99, plate 16.

A photographic illustration in the article showed how "the bust, more than three times life-size, atop a cubic base, formed a whole hewn out of a single block of stone." It "thus appeared to provide a uniquely simple solution to a problem still facing many artists today":

> How to present a bust on a socle. Only the head of the human figure was represented here; even the shoulders and upper arms found in Greek hermae were missing. Instead, two cubic stone strips ran down the front of the column; on one of them there was a cuneiform inscription. But on the two lateral surfaces wing-like traces were to be seen, as if the figure had been represented with folded wings. The lower part of the stone column was not found. The lips were thin, the nose, of which only a part remained, must have been prominent; the eyes—one of them was found—were of smoothly polished black basalt and were framed in white plaster. Like other sculptures at Tell Halaf, the statue was made of dark volcanic stone. The hair was not worn in long, hanging locks, as in the other figures at Tell Halaf; but it had been carefully arranged and there was a band over the forehead, from which hung a remarkable headgear. [...] The whole style of this ornament, along with a mystical element in the expression of the countenance, inevitably led

one to imagine that the sculptor wanted to represent the face, between the two thick bands at the temples, as covered with a veil, from the lower part of which little bands hung down around the neck. Very similar veils are still found today in certain Bedouin tribes in Lower Egypt and, above all, among Arab women of the Persian Gulf area. We can certainly conjecture that the veiled woman of Tell Halaf is the oldest example yet found of a veiled stone image. Perhaps we are dealing here with Ishtar, the Babylonian Earth Goddess, who is already mentioned in the Old Testament, and from whom the Syrian Astarte and then Venus derive.

Oppenheim's fascination with this figure emerges again in the 1908 essay in which it once more occupies a prominent place and is the object of a more detailed description. It is now identified as the figure of a goddess. Stone no. 14, found in prospection hole D, he writes,

> was the most remarkable of our finds. It was the torso of a human figure. The moment I saw it, I had the impression that the artist's aim had been to represent a veiled woman, a goddess. The head emerged directly from a stone block that was barely broader than the neck. There were no shoulders or arms. From the area of the breast down, the stone had been

Fig. 7.2 Tell Halaf. "The Goddess with the Veil". Dr. Max Freiherr von Oppenheim, "Der Tell Halaf und die verschleierte Göttin," *Der Alte Orient*, 10, 1 (1908): 43. Plate 12.

I picked it up and took it back to the house. The other eye socket was empty. On the head there was a cap-like head covering that clung close to the form of the head. Its outer edge, over the forehead, was marked by a broad band. The small head-covering bore flat, curl-like decorative marks. (Quite possibly the artist wanted to represent only a headband around the head, and on the head itself hair arranged in flat curls.) Two substantial bands came down from the headband in front of the ears to the shoulders. At their ends they curled spiral-like outwards and upwards. Between these two bands, below the chin, this unusual headgear ended with another set of smaller bands descending almost to the breast area. The ends of these were also decorated in most cases (two out of every three) and curled outwards. Shorter bands alternated with longer ones and with still shorter ones that did not curl at the end. [...] The entire form of this headgear, together with the mystical element in the expression, inevitably leads one to think that what we are confronted with is the head of a woman and that the sculptor wanted to represent the face between the two broad bands descending from the temples as covered with a veil, from the lower part of which the smaller bands hung down around the neck. Very similar veils are still worn today by Arab women in the area of the Persian Gulf and by Egyptian Bedouin women in the neighbourhood of the Suez Canal. [...] Is the veiled goddess of Tell Halaf to be seen as a herma-like bust sculpture, or is the column-like stone I dug up only part of a massive stone slab, an orthostat with the body of a Sphinx? In favour of the first hypothesis is the way the head is held straight, together with the treatment of the breast area. But the lines of the back of the head and the lower neck in stone fragment no. 15 support the hypothesis that the head of our goddess too was of a piece with the back of a quadruped animal figure. [...] Further excavations will solve this question.[33]

The excavations of 1911–1913 allowed the figure to be identified as a Sphinx. A long description in the 1931 monograph on Tell Halaf picks up on the earlier accounts and carries them forward. I quote at length because of Oppenheim's preoccupation with this figure:

> Among the most important sculptures of Tell Halaf are the two great statues that stand in the archway of the passage to the first room in the temple-palace, that is to say, at the section of the mud-brick wall with the façade reliefs. They are veiled winged sphinxes, parts of which I found as early as 1899. They were so set into the arch of the gateway passage that their fore-part projected out about 0.90 metres in front of the façade into the open, while their flanks made a continuous surface with the

---

33 *Der Tell Halaf und die verschleierte Göttin* (Leipzig: J.C. Hinrichs'sche Buchhandlung, 1908), pp. 24–27. (This is a separate publication of 43 pp. by the Vorderasiatische Gesellschaft of the article in *Der Alte Orient*, vol. 10, no. 1.)

mud wall in the gateway arch. [...] In front, the statues are treated in the round; at the sides, as reliefs. [...]

A lot of small bits from the upper surface of the relief at the side, especially from the wing, had been splintered off the basalt block when the temple was burned down; but we found them nearly all again. The front part of the sphinx is worked out in a different way to any of the other statues on Tell Halaf. Over the well-chiselled lion's paws—which here again are like bear's paws—the legs rise up like square pillars, and end above directly in the disproportionately large woman's head, which stands up from the almost flat line of the back between the pillar-like legs. Here nothing can be seen of any muscles. The look of the whole reminds us of the later hermae or of pillar-gods. On the front of the left leg-pillar Kapara's inscription is chiselled running downwards.

The head is a masterpiece of the old sculptor's art. The flat chin is strongly retreating. The nose, long and pointed in profile, forms, when looked at from one side, an unbroken, lightly curved line with the retreating forehead and the upper part of the head. Involuntarily we are reminded of the beak-faces of the seal-cylinders and tablets from the oldest south Mesopotamia, but, above all, of the huge stele of Jebelet-el-Beda. The hair on the head is set in curls. Round the forehead clings a band which seems to be tied behind the head and ends in two hanging tassels. On this band there hang alternatively [sic] longer and shorter strips, whose lower ends turn backwards in a spiral, and which beyond the ears cover all the back of the head. [...] Round the neck, a hand's breadth under the chin, strips hang down here. Under the band on the forehead tufts of hair are chiselled from ear to ear.

The mouth is marked only by a narrow line; the lips are barely shown. What is different from all the other Tell Halaf statues is the eyes. Instead of a big white inset, in which a small flat round polished centre of black stone is inlaid as the pupil, we have here an oval black stone centre, markedly standing out, filling almost the whole eye socket, and with a narrow white ring round it. One of these eyes I found *in situ* when I made the discovery in 1899, and I was able to save it.

The face has something decidedly mystical about it. The eyes look far darker than any other inset eyes at Tell Halaf. From the very first moment I was convinced that I had a veiled goddess before me. She does not see so well through the veil, and so her eye is darker, blacker, more piercing. That the artist meant to represent a veil is furthermore shown beyond any questioning by the band on the forehead with the two ends hanging down at the back of the head and emphasized by tassels. The veil makes the effect of a headdress. Today veils quite like this are worn on the upper Tigris, in Mosul, for instance. [...] The Mosul veil is the same as the sphinx's, down to the smallest details. Only wanting are the small hanging strips on the forehead band and below. Veils like this with all kinds of ornaments

7. Discovery and Excavation, Publications and Critical Reception 141

hanging down in front are found in many other parts of Islam.

That the mouth, nose and eyes, as well as the hair under the forehead band, are represented in the veiled goddess is quite in agreement with how the veil is depicted in antiquity. In Egypt, under the garments of veiling, the breast, navel and limbs were drawn so as to be fully visible. But we have only to think of modern sculptures of veiled persons in Italian graveyards; here also in spite of the veiling we can see the forms and even the details of the faces.

In this sphinx we have the oldest veiled statue in the world. There is no other of its kind. [...] I will not here go [...] into a discussion of the ancient myths of the veil. I have briefly discussed the subject in [...] *Tell Halaf and the Veiled Goddess*. [...] Professor Alfred Jeremias, however, has given a more detailed account of the subject under the title *The Veil: from Sumer up to the Present Time* (Old Orient Series, 1931).[34] [...]

The relief on the side surface of the veiled sphinx shows a winged lion. The artist looks at his statue half sideways from the front, and accordingly gives it both the hind-legs, but from the side view he makes only the side of the left fore-leg appear. This is in contrast to later Assyrian embossed colossi—bull-men and lion-men: they are copied from ours but on them there are represented on the side-surface four legs in motion, although the front which is carved as a statue in the round, shows both the beast's fore-feet. In the Tell Halaf statues everything is more realistic. The beast has only four legs, and so, in spite of the combination of sculpture in the round and relief only four are depicted. This is old Subaraic.[35]

Oppenheim's extremely personal, almost obsessive, and distinctly proprietary relation to the sphinx figure anticipates his even more intense investment in another goddess figure from Tell Halaf, discovered in the course of the excavations of 1911–1913 and usually referred to as "thronende Götttin" [enthroned goddess]. I shall again quote at some length from the text of the 1931 book (in the English translation of 1933) in order to convey a sense of the combination of objective description and lively subjective response that is characteristic of Oppenheim's archaeological writing:

> Perhaps the most impressive statue on Tell Halaf is the great throned goddess (1.80 metres high, 0.82 metres broad, 0.95 deep) which we found walled in a huge mass of mud bricks, and over a grave shaft driven into the living rock not far east of the south citadel gate.
>
> The statue, weighing almost four tons, is of basalt, like all the large pieces of Tell Halaf sculpture in the round. It represents a woman seated upright

---

34 *Der Schleier von Sumer bis Heute. Mit 8 Abbildungen im Text und 15 auf Tafeln* (Leipzig: F. C. Hinrichs, 1931).
35 *Tell Halaf. A New Culture in Oldest Mesopotamia*, pp. 108–12.

on a high chair without back or arms. The stiff, calm and stately bearing at once marks her out as a goddess on a throne. Her feet are resting on a low stool. Seen from the side, the chair shows cross-pieces below and has a net-like ornamentation on the edge of the seat.

The statue is, as it were, put together from three cubes or rectangles climbing like a pyramid. From the footstool rises the lower part of the woman's body which is shaped like a cube. Its rigid lines show hardly any bodily form, and it almost gives the impression as if the goddess were holding a broad board on her knees and the clothing were hanging down from it. On the upper surface of the squared block rests the outstretched forearm with the hand laid flat on it, while the right hand is holding a beaker well forward on the lap. Perpendicular to this cube, set far back, a fresh cubic block then rises to the woman's shoulder. From this the head stands up on a high neck. In spite of its highly primitive lines the expression on the face is remarkably impressive. The chin is retreating and runs downwards to a point; the cheek-bones and cheeks are strongly marked. The eyes (they are not inlaid) are on the small side. [...] From the forehead there falls on each side of the face and in front of the ears a heavy lock on to the breast; it is independently carved and grooved in a slant. The lower part of the face is flat; the lips of the small mouth are delicately and beautifully curved. [...] The line of the nose runs up over the forehead and head in a single bold curve. Particularly striking is the retreating forehead, like that which we find on the oldest Hither Asiatic statues. Seen in profile the head reminds us of the beak-nosed faces on the early Sumerian cylinders and the double stela of Jebelet-el-Beda. [...] The stunting of the arms too is shared by this figure with the god on the double stela of Jebelet-el-Beda.

The woman is wearing a gown. Its sleeves reach just short of the elbow and have a broad edging. This edging bears a zigzag motive and runs on at right angles down to the lap; another strip made up of ribbons or bands with an angular motive follows the lines of the upper arms and shoulders up to the neck. [...]

The upper part of the body leans slightly backwards.

The throned figure in its great calm has something majestic about it. The countenance shows in a very high degree the mystical archaic smile. In spite of the over-great head and the cubical shape, of the wholly lacking indication of the breast and the too broad shoulders and equally broad lap, the effect is extraordinarily impressive. The goddess's smile has a fascination that grows on the onlooker. It is a work of the greatest artistic perfection. Anything like this so to speak 'Cubist' goddess is not to be found anywhere else in the world. In some ways, the well-known beautiful old Greek seated goddess in white marble of the Berlin Museum might be compared with her; this, too, has the mysterious smile. But in strength, originality and dignified character the goddess of Tell Halaf stands above the Greek goddess, who is a descendant of ours, coming two thousand years later.

Fig. 7.3 Tell Halaf. "Sphinx". Berlin, Pergamon Museum. Wikipedia. Photograph by Z. Thomas. CC-BY-SA.

It was one of the great events of my excavations and one of my greatest joys as a discoverer, to see this statue literally rising out of the ground. After the greatly denuded mass of mud bricks had been laid bare [...], its surface was cleared. In doing this we first of all came upon the top of the head. It looked like a great dark iron pan, but soon the outlines of the head showed themselves. Now one layer of mud bricks after the other was carefully lifted away. [...] The work had to be carried on most carefully, so that the pickaxes should not do any hurt to the statue. It was hours and, indeed, days before the great throned goddess at last stood before us in all her greatness. What was our joy when we found that the statue was wholly unhurt! Our Beduin workmen came to call this goddess my bride, because I kept on going to her and could not be out of sight of her. [...]

Beyond all question what we have here is the great Subaraic goddess – Hepet.[36]

Oppenheim sometimes referred to this much loved statue as a "Venus." In her memoirs, the popular detective story writer Agatha Christie describes a visit she and her husband, the distinguished archaeologist Max Mallowan,

---

36 Ibid., pp. 189–91. I have quoted the text of the English translation of 1933, since it is widely accessible, resisting the temptation to revise and correct it. It is, unfortunately, a poor translation.

paid to the special museum in Berlin in which, in the 1930s, Oppenheim exhibited some of his finds from Tell Halaf: "I recall a visit we paid to Baron von Oppenheim in Berlin where he took us to the Museum of his finds. Max and he talked excitedly for (I think) five solid hours." Now and again, "Baron von Oppenheim stopped in his eager dissertation to say lovingly: 'Ah, my beautiful Venus,' and stroke the figure."[37] Later still, in 1943, when the Tell Halaf Museum received a direct hit during an allied air raid on Berlin and the sculptures were blown to pieces, Oppenheim's greatest concern was for his "Venus." In a letter to the Director of the Near Eastern section of the Pergamon Museum, he expressed the hope that "the pieces into which the individual stone sculptures have been shattered might be gathered up and brought to the State Museums, so that at some later stage the sculptures can be reconstituted from them." His greatest concern, he declared, was "naturally, to save the enthroned goddess." "Do you think that she can reasonably be put together again," he asked, "from the fragments that have been salvaged?"[38] With all his male bonding to his fearless and warlike Bedouin tribesmen, Max von Oppenheim may well have shared a view of the Orient, common among Western men of the time, as the origin of everything, essentially female, and shrouded in the mystery of Woman. He might not have been too happy to see his "enthroned Goddess" cautiously described in the posthumously published volume III (1955) of the great Tell Halaf catalogue as "Grabfigur einer thronenden Frau" [tomb-sculpture of a woman seated on a throne].[39]

---

37 Agatha Christie Mallowan, Come, Tell Me How You Live (London: Collins, 1946), pp. 51-52. It was Mallowan who gave the generic name "Tell Halaf pottery" to all pottery in the style of the coloured, geometrically designed pottery found by Oppenheim at Tell Halaf.
38 Cit. Teichmann, *Faszination Orient*, p. 93.
39 Max Freiherr von Oppenheim, *Tell Halaf* (Berlin: De Gruyter, 1943–2010), vol. 3 (1955), ed. Anton Moortgat, Tafel I (image) and pp. 35–36 (description). The physical description is detailed, but the figure is always referred to simply as "die Frau."

7. Discovery and Excavation, Publications and Critical Reception   145

ALMOST "CUBIST" IN STYLE, AND SMILING THE STIFF, ARCHAIC SMILE FREQUENTLY SEEN IN ANCIENT STATUARY: A HUGE GODDESS ENTHRONED.

Fig. 7.4 Tell Halaf. "Enthroned Goddess". *Illustrated London News*, October 25, 1930, p. 707.

8. Financial Difficulties. The Fate of the Tell Halaf Finds

On his return from Syria in the late fall of 1913, Oppenheim approached the Royal Museums in Berlin about donating the share of the finds at Tell Halaf that, with great difficulty, he had persuaded the Ottoman authorities to permit him to ship back to Germany—43 boxes containing the smaller orthostats and some fragments, along with plaster casts of those items that could not be removed. In return, he asked that the Royal Museums contribute 275,000 marks (around one and a half million dollars in today's money) toward the expenses of packing, shipping, insurance, and restoration; that he have some say in how the items were displayed; and that space be made available for ongoing work associated with the finds. No agreement was reached, however. The Near Eastern collection, then housed in cramped quarters in the basement of the Kaiser Friedrich Museum, could not accommodate more artefacts; in addition, the Royal Museums were, or claimed to be, strapped financially. Then, in 1914, war broke out.

In 1926, with the opening of the new Pergamon Museum, in which the Near Eastern collection was assigned the main floor of the south wing, another opportunity presented itself. But again only a selection of the smaller orthostats and fragments actually found a place in the museum. In 1927, after Germany had joined the League of Nations, and again in 1929, Oppenheim was able to return to Syria, now a French mandate, to resume work at Tell Halaf and at the same time negotiate a distribution of the sculptures and other finds from the 1911–1913 excavations with the new authorities there. For what was to remain in Syria he helped to set up a special museum in Aleppo (the National Museum, founded in 1931), for which he provided plaster casts of the sculptures he had now been authorized to ship back to Germany.

http://dx.doi.org/10.11647/OBP.0030.08

Fig. 8.1 Façade of Aleppo National Museum, showing plaster casts of statuary shipped to Berlin by Max von Oppenheim. Wikimedia Commons.

For these latter items, the Near Eastern section of the State Museums no longer being an option, he accepted an offer by the Technical University of Berlin to place at his disposal, at no cost to him, a disused machine factory in the Charlottenburg district of the city. Despite inflation and economic depression, which ate into his fortune, Oppenheim succeeded in turning the old factory into a makeshift museum, the central feature of which was a reconstruction, from both original parts and plaster casts, of the grand entrance to the Temple Palace with its monumental statues. The opening ceremony took place on Oppenheim's 70th birthday, 15 July 1930, in the presence of the original excavation team and a large number of scholars. A couple of weeks later it was opened to the general public from 10 am until 3 pm daily and from 10 am until 2 pm on Sundays, with no admission charge.

The Tell Halaf Museum immediately drew worldwide attention and was visited by archaeologists from every corner of the globe. The veteran Australian-born archaeologist V. Gordon Childe hailed it as "one of the most original and instructive museums in Europe."[1] The Baedeker Guide to Berlin soon awarded it a star. On 25 October 1930 the mass circulation weekly *Illustrated London News* carried a long article on it, based on a text by Oppenheim himself.

---

1 *Man*, 34 (May 1934), p. 78.

8. Financial Difficulties. The Fate of the Tell Halaf Finds   149

Fig. 8.2 *Illustrated London News*, October 25, 1930, front page, showing caryatids from Tell Halaf in newly opened Tell Halaf Museum.

The striking front cover of this issue was entirely taken up by the towering caryatids forming the entrance to the so-called Temple Palace as reconstituted at the Museum; the inside pages were also profusely illustrated. On 1 November 1930, there was a follow-up article, while a further article on 16 May 1931, also largely by Oppenheim himself, was devoted to the monumental figures he had discovered at Jebelet el-Beda, about forty-five miles from Tell Halaf. Harry Graf Kessler tells of attending a lecture Oppenheim gave on his finds in the Berlin Singakademie in October 1930. The hall, he notes, was "full to overflowing."[2] Well timed to coincide with the opening of the Museum, Brockhaus of Leipzig brought out the substantial, handsomely illustrated monograph *Der Tell Halaf. Eine neue Kultur im ältesten Mesopotamien* in 1931. This in turn was quickly translated into English, published in London and New York, and, as we saw, widely and, on the whole favourably reviewed.[3] A beautifully illustrated article by Oppenheim himself summarizing the finds at Tell Halaf appeared in French in the scholarly journal *Syria* in 1932 and was published separately as a pamphlet a year later.[4] A full French translation of the 1931 German text, revised, updated, and even more beautifully illustrated, was brought out by Payot in Paris in 1939.

The publication of the 1931 book and of its 1933 English translation elicited three substantial review-articles, embellished by illustrations, in the *New York Times*. These were not scholarly pieces (their authors were Gabriele Reuter, a successful German novelist who had begun to write reviews for the *New York Times* in the late 1920s, Louise Maunsell Field, a popular American novelist and critic, and Raymond R. Camp, who mostly wrote about hunting). Unlike the specialists, they did not question Oppenheim's chronology or even indicate, except for Field, that it had been subject to serious question. On the contrary, the reviewers highlighted Oppenheim's dramatic account of the discovery of the site, the sensational conclusions to be drawn from his dating of the statuary and reliefs, and his claims for a Subaraean civilization older than and on a par with the Sumerian and Egyptian civilizations. The development of the sphinx sculptures at Tell Halaf, in particular, elicited comment. Thus, according to Camp, Oppenheim had shown that "the great

---

2   Harry Graf Kessler, *Das Tagebuch*, ed. Günther Riederer and Jörg Schuster, 9 vols. (Stuttgart: Cotta, 2004–2010), vol. 9 (13 October 1930), p. 385.
3   Decades later, however, one notable scholar, the highly regarded Egyptologist Henri Frankfort, who was head of the Warburg Institute in London in the late 1940s and early 1950s, was to refer to it as "that boastful account, full of misleading statements and comparisons" (*Journal of Near Eastern Studies*, 11 [1952], p. 225).
4   "Tell Halaf, la plus ancienne capitale soubaréenne de Mésopotamie," *Syria*, 13 (1932): 243–56; published separately by P. Geuthner, Paris, 1933.

Sphinx of Egypt [...] is probably the ultimate result of the motif established by the fourth stage of the sphinx at Tell Halaf," while Field drew special attention to "Oppenheim's interesting theory concerning this puzzling conception. It is his belief that the sphinx originated not in Egypt but in Subartu and was developed from the characteristic figure of a goddess standing on a lioness."[5]

Finally—and surprisingly, in view of Oppenheim's part-Jewish background and distinctly Jewish-sounding name—the first, sumptuously produced quarto volume of a scholarly inventory and study of the Tell Halaf finds, to which many specialists contributed, was published with countless high quality illustrations in wartime Berlin (1943) with Oppenheim named as the principal author. Three further volumes appeared after the War (and after Oppenheim's death), between 1950 and 1962. In 2010 a short additional volume was devoted to the painstaking restoration of the sculptures, which had been shattered when the museum created to display them was hit by an incendiary bomb during an allied raid on Berlin in late Sepember 1943. At the Tell Halaf site itself excavation continues to this day resulting in an ongoing production of scholarly studies. A website is now devoted to this continuing work of research: www.grabung-halaf.de.

Oppenheim's fortune had been depleted both by the enormous expense of the Tell Halaf excavations[6] and by the economic situation in Germany in the aftermath of World War I. His financial situation was further eroded by the banking crisis of 1931, which affected the Oppenheims as well as virtually all German banks. Nevertheless, concurrently with the Museum, he set up a library and a foundation, the *Max Freiherr von Oppenheim Stiftung* or *Orient-Forschungs-Institut*, for promoting the study of the ancient and modern Middle East and continuing research—after the death of Oppenheim himself—in the area of Tell Halaf in particular.[7]

---

5 Raymond R. Camp, "Origins of Mysterious Sphinx now Traced by Archaeology," *New York Times*, 31 January 1932; Louise Mansell Field, "Kings who Ruled in Mesopotamia. Baron Max von Oppenheim's 'Tell Halaf' is a Story of Adventure and Discovery in the Ruins of Subaraic Culture,"*New York Times*, 27 August 1933. Gabriele Reuter's review, "A German Record of Ancient Life" appeared in the *New York Times*, 13 March 1932.

6 Recently estimated at the equivalent of 7–8 million euros (see http://www.tell-halaf-projekt.de/de/max_von_oppenheim/oppenheim.htm).

7 "The Tell Halaf Museum is administered by the 'Max von Oppenheim Foundation (Middle East Research Institute)' established by Baron von Oppenheim at 6 Savigny Platz, Berlin. The Foundation's field of research is the ancient and modern Middle East. Baron von Oppenheim has had the permits to carry out excavations at the sites of Tell Halaf, Fakhariya-Washukani und Djebelet el Beda, which were awarded him by the French Mandate authorities in Syria, registered in the name of his foundation. In this way he has ensured that the work of excavation, which will take many more years, can

Among other things, the Stiftung turned out a short, well designed, and well illustrated guide to the new museum, with a 23-page introduction in which Oppenheim's interpretation of the finds and of the "Subaraean culture" they allegedly represented was clearly and succinctly outlined. In order to finance these projects, however, Oppenheim not only had to cut back somewhat on his lavish living style, he had to take out substantial loans. Thus, on the strength of his limited partnership in the Oppenheim bank, he borrowed 250,000 Reichsmarks from the Otto Wolff trading company in Cologne, which, since 1923, he had been advising on its business with Turkey.[8] But that sum was evidently not enough to ensure funding for the Museum and the Foundation, for he now began to think of selling some of his finds from Tell Halaf.

It appears to have been with that possibility in mind that he travelled to the United States in the late spring of 1931. On 9 May 1931, a little more than a week after his arrival, the *New York Times* interviewed him at his hotel in New York, the elegant Ambassador on Park Avenue at 51st Street (torn down in 1966), and carried a report headlined "German to Study Ancient Finds Here. Baron von Oppenheim, Berlin Archaeologist Wants to See Treasures from Ur. He Excavated Tell Halaf. Tells of Huge Stone Carvings 5,000 years old and of Civilization in 4,000 B.C." It is clear from the *Times* article that Oppenheim still held to his chronology of the finds at Tell Halaf: "Although the excavations at [...] Ur have been rich in treasures of gold and small objects of art, Baron von Oppenheim said, the finds at Tell Halaf have been richer in stone carvings, some of great size, 5,000 years old or more." Oppenheim told the *Times* that he "intended to study the Near Eastern exhibits at the Metropolitan Museum of Art and at museums in Chicago, Philadelphia, Boston and other cities." He appears also to have been in contact with the University Museums of Yale, Columbia, Princeton, and Harvard and to have given talks at those institutions. By his own account, "I came to the United States to study the remains of Babylonian art in American museums, especially the results of the excavations made in Ur, Bismaja, and Kish. I came also to discuss my discoveries with American authorities before putting the final touches on my Tell Halaf publication, which has just been issued (in German) by F.A. Brockhaus, Leipzig." He returned to the U.S. in the fall of 1931 "in response to several invitations extended to me last summer to lecture on my findings at the Tell Halaf

---

continue after his death." (*Führer durch das Tell Halaf-Museum, Berlin, Franklinstr. 6* [Max Freiherr von Oppenheim Stiftung, 1934], p. 26).

8   Teichmann, *Faszination Orient*, pp. 79–80.

8. Financial Difficulties. The Fate of the Tell Halaf Finds 153

at some of your museums." This time, he told Myron Bement Smith (1897–1970), an archaeologist, architect, and art historian who had been appointed Secretary of the newly created American Institute for Persian Art and Archaeology (later known as the Asia Institute) in New York City, that his "stay in the United States will extend to May 1932." He was therefore "most willing," as he put it to Smith, to respond to additional lecture invitations and promised that "the address would naturally be in English" (which his correspondence demonstrates he knew quite well) and would be "enlivened by beautiful lantern slides and a short moving picture illustrating the Tell Halaf Museum in Berlin."[9]

It seems likely, however, that in addition to drumming up interest in Tell Halaf and in the forthcoming English translation of his book Oppenheim was also, perhaps mainly, interested in the sale of selected items from his collection—or even, it has been suggested, of the collection as a whole[10]—for he had brought samples to show to potential purchasers. Unfortunately, his timing was not good, for the U.S. was sinking ever deeper into the Great Depression. It does not appear that any deals were made. Nevertheless, Oppenheim did not give up the idea of selling off some of his finds to raise money for the support of the Museum and the

---

9 Letter to Myron Bement Smith, dated "The Ambassador, New York, November 20th 1931."Myron Bement Smith papers, the Freer Gallery of Art and the Arthur M. Sackler Gallery Archives, Smithsonian Institution, Washington, D.C. Myron Bement Smith helped Oppenheim prepare a hand-out folder describing the lecture, which was entitled "The Wonders of Tell Halaf—A Hitherto Unknown Near-Eastern Culture of 5,000 Years Ago, described by its excavator, Dr. Baron Max von Oppenheim, Former German Minister Plenipotentiary." In an earlier letter, sent from the Ambassador hotel on 11 November, Oppenheim had explicitly sought Smith's "assistance in arranging a number of lectures that I intend to hold on my Tell Halaf." He also submitted the texts of the hand-out and of his lecture to Smith so that the latter could check the English for him (letters of 24 November and 10 December). Smith and Oppenheim remained in contact for several years after that and Smith and his wife were entertained by Oppenheim in Berlin and given a tour of the Tell Halaf Museum in May 1933. In a letter to Ernst Herzfeld, written after the War, Oppenheim recalls having been invited to Princeton and having given a lecture there on Tell Halaf (letter dated 21 June 1946, Herzfeld papers, the Freer Gallery of Art and the Arthur M. Sackler Gallery, Smithsonian Institution. B-16; see Appendix for text of this letter).
10 Nadja Cholidis and Lutz Martin, *Der Tell Halaf und sein Ausgräber Max Freiherr von Oppenheim*, p. 50. In support of this claim, the authors cite a letter of 31 December 1930 from Oppenheim to Jacob Gould Schurman, a former President of Cornell and former U.S. Ambassador to Germany (1925–1929), and a few days later, a note to an agent of the German Consulate-General in Chicago, in which Oppenheim imagines a completely new presentation of his finds: "It would be easy to reconstruct the interesting old Temple Palace of Tell Halaf, with its façade statues, as the building in which the treasures would be housed! That would be something fantastic, grandiose, completely original."

Stiftung. In anticipation of better times to come, he left his samples in the Hahn Brothers' fireproof warehouse on East 55th Street in New York: "I did not let myself be downcast by my failure to make sales," he noted later in an autobiographical sketch.[11] The eight orthostats ultimately found a new home, after 1945, at the Metropolitan Museum in New York and at the Walters Art Gallery in Baltimore.

Fig. 8.3. Tell Halaf. Orthostat. "Seated Figure holding a lotus flower." New York, The Metropolitan Museum of Art, Rogers Fund, 1943 (43.135.1) Image © The Metropolitan Museum of Art. All Rights Reserved.

---

11 Ibid. Also Teichmann, *Faszination Orient*, pp. 82–83. By vesting order 1330 (27 April 1943), the orthostats came into the hands of the Alien Property Custodian, an agency of the U.S. government, and were put up for sale in October 1943. As the Metropolitan Museum in New York and the Walters Art Gallery in Baltimore were the highest bidders, the orthostats went to them. The Metropolitan paid $4,000 for its four orthostats. My thanks to Dr. Yelena Rakic of the Near Eastern Department at the Metropolitan Museum in New York for tracking down the fate of the orthostats left in the Hahn Brothers' warehouse. See http://www.archives.gov/iwg/declassified-records/rgs-60–131–204-justice/rg-131-case-files.html#335

8. Financial Difficulties. The Fate of the Tell Halaf Finds   155

Fig. 8.4 Tell Halaf. Orthostat. "Lion-hunt scene." New York, The Metropolitan Museum of Art, Rogers Fund, 1943 (43.135.4) Image © The Metropolitan Museum of Art. All Rights Reserved.

Fig. 8.5 Tell Halaf. Orthostat. "Two heroes pinning down a bearded foe." The Walters Art Museum, Baltimore. Accession no. 21.18. Photo © The Walters Art Museum. All Rights Reserved.

Fig. 8.6 Tell Halaf. Orthostat. "Winged goddess." The Walters Art Museum, Baltimore. Accession no. 21.16. Photo © The Walters Art Museum. All Rights Reserved.

In the meantime, Oppenheim's only recourse was to borrow more money using his Tell Halaf finds as security. A list drawn up in 1943 identified forty objects that had served as collateral for such loans. This led on one occasion to a dramatic confrontation. One of Oppenheim's creditors was a Dutch branch of the private, Berlin-based von der Heydt bank. Eduard von der Heydt, whose business associates included the Ruhr industrialists Stinnes and Thyssen and who was also the financial trustee and friend of the exiled Hohenzollerns, had written into the loan contract dawn up with Oppenheim in 1931 that, should Oppenheim not pay off his debt by 1934, the bank had the right to immediate seizure of the collateral. When this situation materialized, Eduard von der Heydt demanded that the items in question in the Tell Halaf Museum be immediately surrendered to him. He apparently intended to have them shipped to Ascona in Switzerland, where, in 1926, he had purchased the celebrated Monte Verità property, and where he intended that they should enhance his already world-renowned collection of Asian art. Oppenheim refused to yield his treasures and this led to an altercation of which we shall have more to say at a later point. Fortunately, Oppenheim was bailed out financially by a consortium of family members and friends. (Among the latter was his boyhood friend and old Cairo associate Hermann von Hatzfeld, whose father, Count Paul von Hatzfeld, had done what he could, many years before, to combat the prejudice against Oppenheim in the *Auswärtiges Amt*.)[12]

Oppenheim's struggle to ensure the preservation and protection of his finds continued throughout the decade and into the War years. In 1935 he again entered into negotiations with the Near Eastern Section of the State Museums. But no agreement could be reached on price. Oppenheim based his estimate of the value of his finds on figures—in the millions—obtained at the end of the 1920s. The Museum authorities, citing among other things the allegedly uncertain legal status of the finds, claimed that these figures were now obsolete and proposed instead sums ranging between 460,000 and 475,000 Reichsmarks—sums that Oppenheim indignantly rejected. (His debts at this time ran to over a million, owed to several banks, among them his family's bank, as well as to the consortium that had bailed him out in 1934 and to his cousin Simon Alfred von Oppenheim personally.) The authorities were in no hurry to compromise. It was in their interest to play a waiting game. As there were no competing offers, they figured,

---

12 Teichmann, *Faszination Orient*, p. 84.

"the other side will gradually be worn down... The collection cannot escape us. If we only wait, the price will necessarily come down." Realistically and cynically it was noted that Oppenheim, who was making the negotiations over price difficult, was almost eighty years old. In the end, Oppenheim failed to persuade the Museum to take over and house the finds from Tell Halaf. It took air raids on Berlin, as a result of which he was bombed out of his residence on the Savigny-Platz, with serious damage to some of the artefacts stored there as well as to the research library, to get the authorities to intervene and help him arrange for the most valuable books and Orientalia to be removed and stored in various castles and country houses around Berlin. And it was not until September 1943, when the Tell Halaf Museum itself received a devastating direct hit from an incendiary bomb, that its invaluable treasures, now in smithereens, were gathered up and finally removed to the relative safety of the bombproof vaults of the Pergamon Museum.[13]

---

13 See Teichmann, *Faszination Orient*, pp. 85–93.

III
"THE KAISER'S SPY" UNDER NATIONAL SOCIALISM. "LEBEN IM NS-STAAT, 1933–1945"*

---

* "Life in the National Socialist State. 1933–1945," the title of the final section (dated 28 June 1946) of Oppenheim's memoir of his life, deposited in the Max Freiherr von Oppenheim Stiftung in Cologne.

9. Questions

By all accounts this period of Oppenheim's life and activity is marked by unanswered, perhaps unanswerable, yet unavoidable questions. "How was Max von Oppenheim able to protect himself and his work so successfully from discrimination and persecution?" asks his biographer Dr. Gabriele Teichmann—the Director of the Oppenheim Family Archive—towards the close of her richly informed contribution to the outstanding collective volume put out by the Max-Freiherr-von-Oppenheim-Stiftung and entitled *Faszination Orient: Max von Oppenheim, Forscher, Sammler, Diplomat*.[1] Having considered the explanations Oppenheim himself provided in the manuscript of an unpublished autobiographical memoir on which he worked in his last years, Teichmann concludes that these "are not completely convincing."[2] In similar vein, Nadja Cholidis and Lutz Martin, who participated in the restoration of the Tell Halaf finds and who view Oppenheim's career almost heroically, in the light of his motto "Kopf hoch! Mut hoch! Und Humor hoch!" ["Head high! Chin up! Keep smiling!"], acknowledge in their 2002 book *Der Tell Halaf und sein Ausgräber Max Freiherr von Oppenheim*—albeit in an endnote—that "it has to come as a surprise that Max von Oppenheim lived through the Nazi period, despite many annoyances, without serious threat either to his person or to his work. He himself suggests that this was thanks to influential friends, his international reputation, and his knowledge of the Orient. But it is well enough established that these factors alone would not have sufficed to provide protection. The present state of research into this part of his biography does not permit us to offer a convincing explanation."[3]

---

1 Cologne: DuMont, 2001.
2 Ibid., pp. 90–92.
3 *Der Tell Halaf und sein Ausgräber Max freiherr von Oppenheim* (Berlin: Vorderasiatisches Museum; Mainz: Philipp von Zabern, 2002), note 25, pp. 68, 70.

In the absence of reliable information, some have opted simply to avoid any mention of his situation as a non-Aryan during the years of National Socialism. In her otherwise informative article on Oppenheim in the *Neue Deutsche Biographie*[4] Ursula Moortgat-Correns is silent on the topic. Similarly, Werner Caskel, who was Oppenheim's long-term assistant and collaborator, and who, moreover, was half Jewish himself, contrives to say virtually nothing about this period in his obituary tribute to Oppenheim in the venerable *Zeitschrift der deutschen Morgenländischen Gesellschaft*[5] and does not even mention that Oppenheim was of part-Jewish descent.[6] This is obviously not a course we can follow here. Our effort to gain some insight into the matter will involve us in many seemingly digressive discussions as we approach if from a variety of perspectives.

Let us look first at the situation of the family as a whole and of the Bank from which the family cannot be dissociated.

---

4   Vol. 19, pp. 562–63.
5   Vol. 101 [1955], pp. 3–8.
6   In the handsome *Festschrift* offered to Caskel himself to mark his 70th birthday (ed. Erwin Gräf [Leiden: E.J. Brill, 1968]) there is likewise no mention of the part-Jewish background that led to Caskel's having to give up his professorship at Greifswald. We are told only that "On July 1, 1938, Caskel left Greifswald and moved with his family to Danzig" (p. 20).

10. The Oppenheims and their Bank under National Socialism

In general, the Oppenheims, both the bank itself and the members of the family, got through a time of acute difficulty for "non-Aryan" enterprises and of extreme danger for "non-Aryans" themselves better than most. Private banks, of which there were an unusually large number in Germany—1,406, of widely varying size and importance, in 1925[1]—were in fact viewed positively by some supporters of National Socialism inasmuch as it was possible to argue that they were rooted in local communities and contributed to the welfare of those communities.[2] This was not how they were viewed, however, if they happened to be Jewish owned, which many (notably the larger ones) were.[3] The process of "Entjudung" [elimination of all Jewish influence] of German banks and businesses has been described in a number of meticulously researched scholarly studies.[4] As a result of various anti-Jewish measures affecting both businesses and the individuals running them, hundreds of smaller Jewish-owned private banks went

---

1 Wilhelm Treue, *Das Schicksal des Bankhauses Sal. Oppenheim jr. & Cie. und seiner Inhaber im Dritten Reich* (Wiesbaden: Franz Steiner Verlag, 1983; *Zeitschrift für Unternehmensgeschichte*, Beiheft 27), p. 1. This number was reduced by half, as a result of the financial crisis of 1931, to 709 at the end of 1932.
2 Ibid., p. 10.
3 Ingo Köhler, *Die 'Arisierung' der Privatbanken im Dritten Reich* (Munich: C.H. Beck, 2005), pp. 92–93.
4 E.g. W. E. Mosse, *Jews in the German Economy: The German-Jewish Economic Elite 1820–1935* (Oxford: Clarendon Press, 1987); Keith Ulrich, *Aufstieg und Fall der Privatbankiers* (Frankfurt a.M.: Fritz Knapp, 1998); Ingo Köhler, *Die 'Arisierung' der Privatbanken* (2005). For useful summary accounts see Klaus-Dieter Henke, *Die Dresdner Bank 1933–1945: Ökonomische Rationalität, Regimenähe, Mittäterschaft* (Munich: R. Oldenbourg, 2006), pp. 49–51 and Gerald D. Feldman, review of Köhler's *Die 'Arisierung' der Privatbanken*, in *Business History Review*, 80 (2006): 404–06.

http://dx.doi.org/10.11647/OBP.0030.10

under or were bought up at bargain basement prices by "Aryan" firms and institutions between 1934 and 1938.[5]

As has often been noted, however, for several years after Hitler seized power in 1933, and for as long as the pragmatically minded Hjalmar Schacht was in charge of the Reich's finances (so until 1937–1938) the great Jewish-owned private banks—such as the Warburgs, the Mendelssohns, and the Oppenheims—were considered essential to the national economy because of their importance to the German export trade, their international reputation and connections, their access to much needed foreign capital and foreign currency, and in some cases their role in the financing of German industry.[6] Schacht saw to it, therefore, for purely practical reasons—but often in the teeth of opposition from fanatical, ideologically committed members of the Nazi Party—that they were allowed to continue operating.[7]

---

5 See Köhler, *Die 'Arisierung' der Privatbanken*, pp. 94–104, especially Table 8 on p. 103; Michael Stürmer, Gabriele Teichmann, Wilhelm Treue, *Wägen und Wagen*, p. 368; Wilhelm Treue, *Das Schicksal des Bankhauses Sal. Oppenheim jr. & Cie.*, p. 13; Keith Ulrich, *Aufstieg und Fall der Privatbankiers*, pp. 309–53.

6 In June 1933, for instance, nine "Jewish" private banks were still participating in a consortium of twenty banks led by the Dresdner Bank, the object of which was to finance works projects to relieve unemployment (Köhler, *Die 'Arisierung' der Privatbanken*, p. 140, note 153).

7 On Hjalmar Schacht and Jews in the German economy, see Max M. Warburg, *Aus meinen Aufzeichnungen* (New York: Eric M. Warburg, 1952), pp. 153–54; Edward N. Peterson, *Hjalmar Schacht: For and against Hitler* (Boston: Christopher Publishing House, 1954), pp. 245–50; Schacht's own account in his autobiography, *My First Seventy-Six Years*, trans. Diana Pyke (London: Allan Wingate, 1955), pp. 353–57; Helmut Genschel, *Die Verdrängung der Juden aus der Wirtschaft im Dritten Reich* (Göttingen: Musterschmidt, 1966), pp. 105–08, 136–37; Uwe Dietrich Adam, *Judenpolitik im Dritten Reich* (Düsseldorf: Droste, 1971), pp. 122–24, 133–36; E. Rosenbaum and A.J. Sherman, *Das Bankhaus M.M. Warburg & Co. 1798–1938* (Hamburg: Hans Christians, 1976), pp. 207–08; W.E. Mosse, *Jews in the German Economy: The German-Jewish Economic Elite 1820–1935*, pp. 374–76; Reinhard Rürup, "Das Ende der Emanzipation," in Arnold Paucker, ed., *Die Juden im Nationalsozialistischen Deutschland 1933–1943* (Tübingen: J.C.B. Mohr [Paul Siebeck] 1986), pp. 97–114 (pp. 102, 104–05); A.J. Sherman, "A Jewish Bank during the Schacht Era: M.M. Warburg & Co. 1933–1938," in Arnold Paucker, ed., *Die Juden im Nationalsozialistischen Deutschland 1933–1943*, pp. 167–72; Christopher Kopper, *Hjalmar Schacht. Aufstieg und Fall von Hitlers mächtigstem Bankier* (Munich and Vienna: Carl Hanser, 2006), pp. 219–30, 240–41, 274–93, 317–18; Gabriele Hoffmann, *Max M. Warburg* (Hamburg: Ellert & Richter, 2009), pp. 144–45. A memo of 3 May 1935 from Schacht to Hitler ("Imponderabilia des Exports"), cited by Rürup, appears to convey Schacht's position well: "Let the Jews be stamped by means of appropriate legislation, in whatever degree is desired, as residents with fewer rights, but for whatever rights are left to them, let them be granted the protection of the state against fanatics and ruffians." Genschel's work indicates that the elimination of Jews from the German economy accelerated rapidly after Schacht was replaced at the Economics Ministry in November 1937 and dismissed from his position as President of the Reichsbank in January 1938: of 39,532 firms still in Jewish hands in Germany in April 1938, 14,803 had been liquidated and 5,976 "entjudet" [dejudaized]

"Aryanizing" them, moreover, was not as easy as Aryanizing small or medium-sized commercial or industrial concerns. While many of the smaller private banks had sold out or been liquidated by 1935–1936, as one scholar has put it, "it was frequently difficult to find qualified purchasers for businesses that produced nothing but relied on personal contacts and business judgments." Thus Mendelssohn "remained a successful bank for the first five years of the Nazi regime and continued to be a member of the consortium issuing government debt."[8]

This does not mean, however, that the anti-Semitic propaganda of the National Socialist Party, even before it came to power, the boycotts it organized after it came to power, and the many methods it used, both legal and informal, to harass, humiliate, and ostracize Jews,[9] did not have negative consequences for businesses that depended greatly on trust, longstanding relations, and personal contacts. As one scholar wrote recently, "the withdrawal of community respect and social status narrowed the sphere of activity of the bankers and thereby prepared the way for their exclusion from economic life. Any investigation of the repressive preliminaries and basic conditions of the 'Aryanisation' of private banks cannot therefore be limited to the effects on the banks' balances of boycotts and formal measures of economic exclusion but must necessarily also take extra-economic processes of exclusion into account."[10] As any dealings with Jews, whether commercial or purely social, were frowned upon and taken note of by the Gestapo, Aryan clients gradually withdrew their business from Jewish-owned banks, and this loss was only partly compensated, for the surviving Jewish banks, by the transfer to them of the accounts of Jews shut out of "Aryan" or "Aryanized" institutions. In general, the volume of business at Jewish banks shrank drastically.[11]

---

    by April 1939, after the *Reichskristallnacht* (9–10 November 1938), while 4,136 were in process of "Entjudung" and the remaining 7,127 were being investigated for likely "Entjudung" (p. 206). The intensification, in 1938, of regulations intended to achieve the "Entjudung der Wirtschaft" ["dejudaizing of the economy"] emerges clearly from Peter Deeg's depressing compendium, *Die Judengesetze Grossdeutschlands*, published by Julius Streicher's Verlag Der Stürmer in 1939.

8 Harold James, *The Deutsche Bank and the Nazi Economic War against the Jews* (Cambridge: Cambridge University Press, 2001), p. 68.

9 See Max Warburg, *Aus meinen Aufzeichnungen*, pp. 148–49; Treue, *Das Schicksal des Bankhauses Sal. Oppenheim jr. & Cie.*, p. 15; On the boycotts, see especially Helmut Genschel, *Die Verdrängung der Juden aus der Wirtschaft im Dritten Reich*, pp. 43–56, 108–11.

10 Köhler, *Die 'Arisierung' der Privatbanken*, p. 104.

11 Keith Ulrich, "Das Privatbankhaus Simon Hirschland im Nationalsozialismus," in Manfred Köhler and Keith Ulrich, eds., *Banken, Konjunktur und Politik* (Essen: Klartext, 1995), pp. 129–42 (pp. 134–35); idem, *Aufstieg und Fall der Privatbankiers*, pp. 277–78. On the

Pressure was also put on firms to remove Jewish members from their supervisory boards. While a few resisted as best they could, all, in the end, had to yield. Even businesses which had long associations with Jewish bankers, as the great HAPAG-Lloyd shipping company of Hamburg had, for instance, with the Warburgs, urged their Jewish board members to retire or forced them out.[12] Relatively slow at first, this process gathered momentum in 1935 with the publication of the Nuremberg "Laws" and then again at the end of 1937, when the Economics Ministry, the *Reichswirtschaftsministerium* (at the helm of which, in November of that year, Schacht had been replaced, thanks to the machinations of Göring, by Walther Funk), announced that any business with even a single Jew on its board would be defined as "non-Aryan" and thus subject to "Aryanization."[13] Of 108 board seats occupied by partners of M.M. Warburg & Co. at the beginning of 1933, eighteen had to be vacated during the course of the year. Between 1936 and 1937, however, the Warburgs were removed from eighty more.[14] Holding positions on multiple boards obviously provided access to a great deal of information about companies and about economic conditions. The individuals holding such positions, often the partners of the largest private banks, were thus in a position to offer valuable advice on mergers and similar policy decisions and were, aptly enough, referred to in German by the English-language term "big linkers." It has been shown that, while the number of "Aryan" "big linkers" (where a "big linker" is defined as an individual sitting on at least ten boards) and the number of board positions they occupied remained fairly steady in the range of twenty-two to twenty-six individuals and 318–373 positions for the years 1932–1938, the number of non-Aryan "big linkers" dropped precipitously from thirty-four in 1932 to sixteen in 1934, eight the following year, and only

---

massive loss of business sustained even by the larger Jewish private banks between 1935 and 1938, see Köhler, *Die 'Arisierung' der Privatbanken*, p. 103, table 8.

12 As early as May 1933, Jewish directors Theodor Frank and Oscar Wassermann resigned from the managing board of the Deutsche Bank in an arrangement brokered by Reichsbank president Schacht "as part of the political concessions made by the bank to National Socialism." Though Wassermann had agreed to leave by the end of 1933, his departure was announced by his colleagues in advance of the annual general meeting scheduled for 1 June. Wassermann, who had been the spokesman of the board and had been in charge of the bank's overall policy in the late 1920s, "was thus pushed out prematurely" (Harold James, *The Deutsche Bank*, p. 25).

13 Köhler, *Die 'Arisierung' der Privatbanken*, p. 140; Kopper, *Hjalmar Schacht. Aufstieg und Fall von Hitlers mächtigstem Bankier*, pp. 317–18.

14 W.E. Mosse, *Jews in the German Economy*, pp. 377–78; see also Stürmer, Teichmann and Treue, *Wägen und Wagen*, p. 377.

one in 1938; correspondingly, the number of board positions held by non-Aryan "big linkers" declined from 496 to 246 between 1932 and 1934, to 126 in 1935, and to fifteen in 1938.[15]

It may not be fortuitous that of the thirty-four Jewish or part-Jewish "big linkers" counted in 1932 the only one remaining in 1938 was Waldemar von Oppenheim or that, of the total of twenty-five board seats still occupied by any of the thirty-four "big linkers," Waldemar held fifteen (ten of them in companies heavily involved in German rearmament)[16], his younger brother Friedrich eight, and the Breslau banker Ernst-Heinrich Heimann two. All three men were classified, according to the Nuremberg laws, as "Mischlinge zweiten Grades"—that is, "three-quarters" Aryan and only "one-quarter" Jewish. The Oppenheims' business activities, in short, were by no means unaffected by the new political regime; they did lose seats on company boards. But they were considerably less drastically affected than those who, however acculturated and assimilated, still remained and identified themselves as Jews, like the Warburgs. Likewise, both the overall balance sheet and the net assets of the bank shrank between 1932—when they had already been diminished as a result of the bank crisis of 1931—and 1935. But by 1936 the balance sheet had begun to pick up quite sharply and it maintained itself throughout the years of the Second World War.[17] It is true that the company encountered hostility from some local competitors and was subjected to various more or less petty inconveniences. In addition, in 1936 two of its Jewish partners (Wilhelm Chan and Otto Kaufmann) had to withdraw from the firm. Above all, despite its having obtained an attestation from the local branch of the Nazi Party in June 1933, certifying that "the capital of your bank is overwhelmingly in the hands of the Christian families von Oppenheim

---

15 Köhler, *Die 'Arisierung' der Privatbanken*, p. 139, table 11. In absolute terms, the total number of positions on company boards still held in 1938 by the thirty-four non-Aryan "big linkers" of 1932 had dropped to twenty-five; of these, fifteen were held by Waldemar von Oppenheim, making him the only remaining "big linker" in the group, eight were held by Friedrich von Oppenheim, who in 1935 had still held fifteen, and two were held by Ernst Heinrich Heimann of the Breslau bank of that name, who by the end of 1933 had already lost five of the fourteen he held in 1932 and thus fallen below the level required to count as a "big linker" (see p. 141, table 12).

16 Treue, *Das Schicksal des Bankhauses Sal. Oppenheim jr. & Cie.*, p. 24. Citing a police document, Treue gives the number of board seats still held by Waldemar von Oppenheim in 1938 as eighteen.

17 Ibid., pp. 14, 21; Stürmer, Teichmann and Treue, *Wägen und Wagen*, pp. 377–79; see also chart, p. 489.

and Pferdmenges,"[18] Sal. Oppenheim jr. & Cie. had to undergo a change of name, Oppenheim being generally perceived as a Jewish name. (That, it will be recalled, had been one of Herbert von Bismarck's reasons for closing the door of the *Auswärtiges Amt* on Max von Oppenheim.)

On 1 January 1931 Simon Alfred von Oppenheim, Max von Oppenheim's cousin,[19] then head of the firm and nearing the age of seventy, had brought in the highly respected and experienced banker Robert Pferdmenges as a partner, perhaps with the intention of providing support and guidance to his still relatively young and inexperienced sons, Waldemar, then thirty-seven years old and a partner since 1922, and Friedrich Carl, then thirty-one years old and a partner only since 1929. Fortunately, Pferdmenges — who was later to be a close financial adviser of Chancellor Konrad Adenauer — was not only impeccably Aryan, but no friend of the NSDAP. He also appears to have been a fundamentally decent person. Thanks to him a "friendly" Aryanization of the bank took place and in May 1938 its name was changed to Bankhaus Robert Pferdmenges & Co. No doubt the disappearance of the name Oppenheim from their venerable firm caused the family pain. "I was always proud to have been an Oppenheim," Max von Oppenheim had written to Waldemar, the son of his cousin Simon Alfred, at the end of 1935, "and I was always proud of our bank in Cologne, which has grown and prospered with such distinction from the very beginning, and which has contributed so much to the economic and indeed to the cultural development of the western provinces of Prussia."[20]

The Oppenheims had to endure other humiliations aimed at eroding their reputation as one of the most prominent and respected families in the city of Cologne. A street in Cologne named in their honour had its name changed. At the Wallraf-Richartz-Museum, though pictures from the bequests of Dagobert and Albert von Oppenheim were still, in 1937, identified as such, the source of new acquisitions purchased with Oppenheim Foundation money was not acknowledged. On the fiftieth anniversary, in 1938, of the children's hospital founded by Abraham von Oppenheim's

---

18 Facsimile of document in Treue, *Das Schicksal des Bankhauses Sal. Oppenheim jr. & Cie.*, Appendix 1.
19 It will be recalled that Simon Alfred took over the running of the bank after Max, who was first in line for the job, decided that he did not want it.
20 Quoted in Stürmer, Teichmann and Treue, *Wägen und Wagen*, p. 372. On the Warburgs' similar attachment to their banking business and acceptance of a "friendly" Aryanization in order to preserve it, see Ron Chernow, *The Warburgs* (New York: Random House, 1993), p. 469.

widow Charlotte, the original endowment of which had been regularly supplemented by further gifts from the family, the name Oppenheim was not mentioned either in newspaper reports of the celebrations or in the speech given by the man who had chaired the hospital board for 25 years. Likewise, the Freifrau von Oppenheim Hospital in Bassenheim, which Charlotte had founded in 1885, was officially renamed. At St. Mary's Hospital, which had enjoyed generous support from Abraham, Charlotte and Dagobert, the marble plaques bearing their names were removed.[21] Max von Warburg has described in his memoirs what happened on a personal level to people perceived to be Jewish or of Jewish extraction. Social relations withered, as acquaintances and even friends sought to avoid associations that might get them into trouble. Even though, unlike the Warburgs, who had remained Jewish, the Oppenheims were Christian, the Oppenheim children were made to feel uncomfortable at school and their education had to be entrusted to private tutors. Still, the two Oppenheim brothers, officially classified according to the Nuremberg Laws as "Mischlinge zweiten Grades" [mixed-breeds of the second degree, i.e. with only one Jewish grandparent] stayed on as partners, albeit now keeping discreetly in the background.

That the "Aryanization" of Sal. Oppenheim jr & Cie. had made little substantive change to the bank did not escape the attention of the most rabid National Socialist ideologues. An article entitled "Aryanizing Cologne" in *Das Schwarze Korps*, the organ of the SS, for 14 July 1938, asked the pointed question: "Why suddenly Pferdmenges, when the firm carries on unchanged?"[22] In fact, with Pferdmenges and the two Oppenheim brothers as partners, the bank continued to operate throughout the Second World War—in marked contrast to all the other major Jewish private banks, which had either been taken over by non-Jews or absorbed by big public banks such as the Deutsche Bank—and inevitably, like other major German banks, it helped to finance the German war effort. Had it not prepared a press announcement in May 1938, on the 150th anniversary of its founding, which emphasized that "the bank now going under the name of Pferdmenges & Co. stands today fully engaged in the struggle to carry out the enormous tasks required by the new Germany"?[23] It has also

---

21 Treue, *Das Schicksal des Bankhauses Sal. Oppenheim jr. & Cie.*, p. 15.
22 Ibid., p. 20.
23 Quoted in Stürmer, Teichmann and Treue, *Wägen und Wagen*, pp. 381–82. Significantly, no newspaper, it appears, dared to print the announcement. The implicit allusion to Sal. Oppenheim & Cie. was doubtless deemed too dangerous.

been claimed that it was involved in and benefited from the Aryanization of Jewish businesses in German-occupied countries. At the end of the War Pferdmenges was even accused of being a "Nazi banker" and between 1946 and 1947 was banned by the British from engaging in any financial or commercial activity.[24] The issue of its wartime record and of the conduct of the partners themselves is evidently a sensitive one for the bank and since the end of the War the Oppenheims have financed a number of scholarly studies in an effort to show that the bank and its partners have nothing to hide. Quite recently, in 2007, the bank took the extreme step of going to court over a book by a popular journalist that was critical not only of its postwar behaviour but of its wartime record. Though they failed to have the book banned altogether, the bank's lawyers succeeded in obtaining a court order requiring the publisher to black out passages in the book that the bank deemed defamatory.[25]

---

24 Ulrich Viehöver, *Die EinflussReichen* (Frankfurt and New York: Campus Verlag, 2006), pp. 254–55. "Waldemar von Oppenheim, Mitinhaber von Pferdmenges & Co. sowie des Bankhauses Salomon Oppenheim" and "Dr. Robert Pferdmenges, Mitinhaber von Pferdmenges & Co., Vorsitzender des Vorstandes der Kabelwerke Rheydt AG, Vorstandsmitglied der AEG, von Harpener Bergbau, usw" were both named in the report of the Kilgore Committee of the U.S. Senate on the responsibility of German monopolies for Nazi war crimes, as cited in the U.S. Army's publication *Allgemeine Zeitung* (Berlin) for 12 October 1945 (Cit. In Dietrich Eichholtz and Wolfgang Schumann, eds., *Anatomie des Krieges: Neue Dokumente über die Rolle des deutschen Monopolkapitals bei der Vorbereitung und Durchführung des zweiten Weltkrieges* [Berlin: VEB Deutscher Verlag der Wissenschaften, 1969], pp. 493–94).

25 The text—by the prolific popular writer Werner Rügemer—was originally accepted as an article for publication in a collective volume, edited by Carl Amery, the spiritual father of the German Greens and the author himself of many books critical of establishment politics and policies. As Alfred von Oppenheim, the heir to the bank and its highly successful CEO, died in 2005, just as the volume was going to press, the publisher, Luchterhand, decided out of a sense of propriety to drop Rügemer's highly critical article. Rügemer expanded it into a book, which was put out in 2006 by the Nomen-Verlag of Frankfurt a.M. under the title *Der Bankier—Ungebetener Nachruf auf Alfred Freiherr von Oppenheim* [The Banker: An Unsolicited Obituary of Alfred Freiherr von Oppenheim]. The censoring and blacking out of passages in the book provoked strong protest at a meeting of the German PEN club. On the whole episode see *Marxistische Blätter*, 46, Heft 1 (2007): 108–10; http://www.zeit.de/2006/30/l-Oppenheim/seite-1; http://de.wikipedia.org/wiki/Werner_R%C3%BCgemer; http://www.attac-koeln.de/index.php?option=com_content&task=view&id=602&Itemid=149.

11. Waldemar and Friedrich Carl von Oppenheim during the National Socialist Regime

The Oppenheims themselves, all of whom, like the vast majority of so-called *Mischlinge* [persons of mixed race], survived the Nazi regime,[1] have come under scrutiny and the well-documented studies produced under Oppenheim auspices have not held back from confronting obvious questions about their decision not to emigrate and about the character of their lives during the years of National Socialism.[2] For one thing, it hardly needs to be emphasized, emigration was not something undertaken lightly, especially by families who, like the Oppenheims or the Warburgs, had a massive economic, social, and psychological investment in Germany. In addition to the huge financial sacrifice involved because of the taxes levied on émigrés and the virtual impossibility for them of expatriating their assets, there was the uncertainty of life in a foreign land[3] and the wrenching separation from one's entire world. There was also the hope — as it turned out, the illusion — that the Nazi regime would change its ways; or, as many believed, would not last or would be replaced by a rightwing government

---

1 See James F. Tent, *In the Shadow of the Holocaust: Nazi persecution of Jewish-Christian Germans* (Lawrence: University Press of Kansas, 2003), pp. 2, 14, 16 *et passim*. Tent shows that while harassment of *Mischlinge* increased constantly and the threat of total extermination became more acute as the war raged on, it was almost exclusively *Mischlinge* who had chosen to identify as Jews that were murdered, whereas the 90% who identified as Christians survived.
2 On the emigration question, see, for instance, Stürmer, Teichmann and Treue, *Wägen und Wagen*, pp. 371, 394, 403.
3 It is not perhaps as widely known as it might be that a fair number of Jews who had emigrated immediately after the Nazi takeover failed to establish themselves in their country of refuge and returned to Germany. This appears to have been especially the case in 1934, when persecution seemed to have abated somewhat.

dominated by traditional conservative nationalists;[4] or, at very worst, that "Mischlinge," especially "Mischlinge zweiten Grades" or "three-quarters Aryan," as Waldemar and Friedrich von Oppenheim both were, would be seen as German and escape the fate of full Jews.

Such considerations were not altogether unreasonable at the time. Many writers have noted both the deliberately unsystematic manner in which anti-Jewish measures were introduced and applied by the Nazis—even as the process as a whole proceeded relentlessly—and the relative slowness of most German Jews to respond to them and grasp their full significance. A change in civil status was at first not perceived as simply the first step toward a "reinliche Scheidung zwischen den Juden und allem, was deutsch ist" ["a clearcut removal of the Jews from everything German"], as the Party's aim was defined in some notes for a speech by the Interior Minister in late 1938,[5] much less as the first step toward the total extermination of the Jews.[6] One scholar has argued plausibly that it was the very endemic nature of anti-Semitism in Germany, even after emancipation in 1869, that led German Jews—especially the large number of highly assimilated and well established Jews, many of whom had little or no contact with either their religion or any organized Jewish community, and felt far more German than Jewish, or indeed not Jewish at all—to underestimate the significance of Hitler's coming to power and to imagine, at least up until

---

4 See, for instance, George Grosz, *An Autobiography*, trans. Nora Hodges (Berkeley and Los Angeles: University of California Press, 1998), pp. 287–89: "Thomas Mann was of the opinion that Hitler could not possibly last more than six months, an opinion shared at that time by many well-informed people. […] Not only [the shrewd Dorothy Thompson] but other experts on Germany, many influential industrialists, bankers, economists, journalists, many unusually skeptical diplomats and professional politicians the world over predicted only a short rule for him."

5 Quoted by Reinhard Rürup, "Das Ende der Emanzipation," in Arnold Paucker, ed., *Die Juden im Nationalsozialistischen Deutschland 1933–1943*, p. 100. On the "unsystematic and fitful" process of "disemancipation," see Peter Pulzer, "The Beginning of the End" in Arnold Paucker, ed., *Die Juden im Nationalsozialistischen Deutschland 1933–1943*, pp. 17–27 (pp. 24–26).

6 For an example of how slow (and perhaps loth) well-established and highly assimilated German Jews were to acknowledge the dangers of National Socialism, not only before the *Machtergreifung* in January 1933, but after it and even after the March 1933 election, see Avraham Barkai, *Oscar Wassermann und die Deutsche Bank* (Munich: C.H. Beck, 2005), pp. 3–64. In 1931, Kurt Blumenfeld, a longtime friend, warned Wassermann, who was then director of the important Bamberg-based Bankhaus A.E. Wassermann and a member of the board of the Deutsche Bank, of the danger posed to Jews by the rise of National Socialism. Wassermann retorted angrily that Blumenfeld was one of those people who smelled anti-Semitism everywhere and reacted immediately to every story of a ritual murder (p. 63).

the state-sponsored *Kristallnacht* made nonsense of any such illusions, that some sort of more or less tolerable life would still be possible for them in Germany.[7] Outbursts of popular anti-Semitism were, after all, not unknown and the Jews had survived them. It was not completely nonsensical to associate the hooliganism of the Nazi street gangs with the Hep Hep riots of 1819—or with similar events in the late 1870s and early 1890s or with the Scheunenviertel riot in Berlin as recently as 1923—all of which, after all, had passed.[8] Then there was the idea that, having used

---

7   In *Last Waltz in Vienna: The Destruction of a Family 1842–1942* (London: Mamillan, 1981), the Viennese George Clare (Klaar) describes his surprise, as an adolescent, on reaching Berlin from newly annexed Vienna, where there had been an explosion of popular anti-Semitism, to discover that Jews there, just prior to *Kristallnacht*, were leading, superficially at least, a "normal" life. "What would you like to do this evening," his slightly older German cousin asks him. "D'you want to go to a cinema, the theatre or just for a drive round Berlin?" "But how can we?" Clare asks. "We're Jews." "Yes and don't I know it," his cousin replies. "But what's that got to do with it?" "It seemed incredible to me," the mature George Clare continues in his memoir, "but it was perfectly true—in Berlin, in the capital of the Third Reich, in the very lion's den, Jews were still allowed in September 1938 to visit places of entertainment, coffee houses; some even still owned patisseries, they could own cars and shop where they pleased. On the whole of the Kurfürstendamm, one of the city's most elegant streets, I saw only one shop with the sign 'No Jewish customers,' so universally displayed in Vienna. Indeed, many Kurfürstendamm shops were still run by their Jewish proprietors. [...] Nor, as I could see for myself, did the 'Aryan' German customers keep away from those shops. [...] Later that evening, when we drove back to our hotel, through crowded, busy streets, brighly lit by many-coloured neon lights, [...] I sensed the invigorating pace and intensity of Berlin. [...] I was overwhelmed by that city and also breathed more freely there than I had in Vienna during the previous six months. With every additional day my impression grew stronger, and it was shared by my parents, that after Nazi Vienna, one felt in Berlin almost as if one had emigrated and escaped from Hitler's rule" (p. 209). These are, of course, an adult's memories of his experiences as a youth. In addition, Berlin should probably not be taken as characteristic of Germany as a whole. Nonetheless, the testimony is worth noting.
8   On the German Jews' familiarity with anti-Semitism as an impediment to their grasping the significance of National Socialist anti-Semitism, see the stimulating essay by Peter Pulzer, "The Beginning of the End," in Arnold Paucker, ed., *Die Juden im Nationalsozialistischen Deutschland 1933–1943*, pp. 17–27. Pulzer cites (pp. 23–24) from George Clare's memoir (see note 7 above): "We knew about anti-Semitic tirades, of course; we knew about the 1933 anti-Jewish boycott, but [...] having used anti-Semitism to help him achieve power, like so many demagogues before him, did Hitler have any choice but to allow his storm-troopers their field-day? Had we not been there before? What about Lueger's anti-Semitic speeches? They had sounded just like Hitler's. [...] Had one Jew ever been physically harmed under Lueger? Hitler was a rabble-rouser, just like the young Lueger. Would he, now that he had achieved his ambition, behave any differently? In any case, Germany's powerful and traditional conservatives were bound to make him toe the line. [...] The sound and fury of the early days could not last for ever. Even Hitler would have to mellow in the end. Political realities [...] would see to it."

demagogic means to gain power, Hitler would abandon them once firmly settled in power. The poet Stefan George, for instance, expressed the view that "right now there is total confusion and we feel helpless; but if these people [the Nazis] were to come to power, they would immediately speak a different language and drop their marketplace yelling and screaming."[9] In order to govern, many believed, the NSDAP would have to yield to the usual social, political, and economic pressures. "Auch Hitler wird mit Wasser kochen" ["Like anybody else, Hitler will use water to cook with"], the Austrian writer Hermynia Zur Mühlen later recalled, was a common reaction.[10] For *Mischlinge* especially, the thought that the situation would stabilize and that they would not be subject to whatever restrictions might be imposed on full Jews must have been hard to resist.

Estimates of the numbers of *Mischlinge* in Germany, of both first and second degree, vary widely between 750,000, according to the Reich Ministry

---

9 Words reported by his longtime Jewish disciple Ernst Morwitz; see Ulrich Raulff, *Kreis ohne Meister: Stefan Georges Nachleben* (Munich: C.H. Beck, 2009), p. 282.

10 *The End and the Beginning: The Book of My Life*, trans. and ed. L. Gossman (Cambridge: Open Book Publishers, 2010), p. 160. Carl Goerdeler, for instance, considered it not unlikely that "under pressure from the practical domestic and foreign problems that had to be resolved, the National Socialists would be ready to follow a constructive policy. He was guided in this view by his own experiences in November 1918. [...] The assumption that in confronting the practical problems of government, the new men and groups would sober up and be led to call in experienced advisers was not mistaken at the time. Even in January 1933, it was not aberrant to work for such an outcome." (Ines Reich, *Carl-Friedrich Goerdeler. Ein Oberbürgermeister gegen den SS-Staat* [Cologne, Weimar, Vienna: Böhlau, 1997], p. 161). Similarly, the diplomat Hans von Herwarth, whose grandmother was Jewish, was urged by his superior, Rudolf Nadolny, the German ambassador to the Soviet Union in 1933, not to give up his job in the German Embassy in Moscow. "He did this, I believe," Herwarth wrote later, "out of the optimistic conviction that the National Socialist regime would either have to change or that it would collapse. [...] I had shared Nadolny's view that Hitler's party must somehow evolve and thus avert disaster. This hope was fed by our readings in the works of historians and scholars, who pointed out that no movement is able to maintain its ideological zeal for long" (Hans von Herwarth, *Against Two Evils* [London: William Collins, 1981], p. 101). See also Karl A. Schleunes, *The Twisted Road to Auschwitz: Nazi Policy toward German Jews 1933–1939* (Urbana: University of Illinois Press, 1970), p. 187: "The most basic impediment to emigration was the deep attachment most German Jews felt for their country. Germany was their fatherland. The Jewish emancipation in Germany had coincided with the developing nationalism of the nineteenth century. Jews had shared in Germany's growth and died in her defense in World War I. Their deepest political allegiance was to Germany. [...] In their own image they were German and all of Hitler's fulminations could not shake the foundations of that image. Hitler's attacks were vicious but they were also patent nonsense. Given a choice between staying in Germany or accepting the insecurities of emigration, most of them preferred to stay in Germany. [...] The hope that 'all this Hitler business' would end the way of a bad dream undoubtedly shaped much of their thinking. In the meantime they would have to ride out the storm, as Jews had ridden out other storms in their history. Indeed, after the initial shock of 1933, there were those who thought the storm was past."

of the Interior on 3 April 1935, and 80,679 (52,005 of the first degree, i.e. with two Jewish grandparents, and 32,669 of the second degree, i.e. with only one Jewish grandparent), according to the census of 17 May 1939.[11] Policy toward them was uneven, but became increasingly harsh around the time of the Wannsee Conference (January 1942) and dangerously so after the attempt on Hitler's life in 1944—as both Oppenheim brothers were to find out. A significant faction at the Interior Ministry aimed to exclude *Mischlinge* from the strictures applied to Jews by distinguishing them carefully from individuals defined as Jews. In a memorandum of 30 October 1933 to Interior Minister Wilhelm Frick, Bernhard Loesener, the official placed in charge of Jewish affairs, while agreeing that "special rigor is called for to cleanse the German professional civil service of all foreign influence," argued against any general application of a Supplementary Decree (11 April 1933) to Paragraph 3 of the Law for the Restoration of the Professional Civil Service, passed four days earlier, which required that "all civil servants who are not of Aryan extraction are to be retired." The Supplementary Decree defined "a non-Aryan […] as any person who descends from non-Aryan, and especially Jewish parents or grandparents. It suffices if one of the four grandparents is non-Aryan." Loesener pointed out in his memo that while the legislation affected full Jews economically and emotionally by depriving them of their livelihood and their social position, "the children […] and particularly the grandchildren of mixed marriages face both these difficulties *and* the emotional burden of being placed in the same category as Jews. In other words, they feel defamed and forcibly deprived of their German national identity [*deutsches Volkstum*], even though they feel they belong exclusively to the German nation." Moreover, the provisions of the Decree were being applied far beyond the civil service, resulting in the exclusion of people who had only one Jewish grandparent from "professions demanding a university degree, […]

---

11 Jeremy Noakes, "The Development of Nazi Policy toward the German-Jewish 'Mischlinge' 1933–1945," *Leo Baeck Institute Yearbook*, 34 (1989), pp. 291–354; Beate Meyer, *"Jüdische Mischlinge." Rassenpolitik und Verfolgungserfahrung 1933–1945* (Hamburg: Dölling und Galitz, 1999), pp. 96–107, 162–64. However, Maria von der Heydt gives the figures for the 17 May 1939 census as 72,738 "half-Jews" and 42,811 "quarter-Jews" ("Möglichkeiten und Grenzen der Auswanderung von jüdischen *Mischlingen*, 1938–1941," in *"Wer bleibt opfert seine Jahre, vielleicht sein Leben." Deutsche Juden 1938–1941*, ed. Susanne Heim, Beate Meyer, Francis R. Nicosia [Göttingen: Wallstein, 2010], pp. 77–95); those are also the figures given by James F. Tent, *In the Shadow of the Holocaust: Nazi Persecution of Jewish-Christian Germans* (Lawrence: University Press of Kansas, 2003), pp. 2, 103. Some estimates were far higher than even the Interior Ministry's; see Richard Lawrence Miller, *Nazi Justiz: Law of the Holocaust* (Westport, CT and London, 1995), p. 18. The sharp decline from 1935 to 1939 is hard to explain by emigration.

even athletics and all kinds of physical activity (labour service, military associations, civil air defence, even tennis clubs, rowing clubs, etc.)." Thus "German-Jewish *Mischlinge* and their children become social outcasts. This affects them emotionally more than full Jews, especially since most *Mischlinge* are, unfortunately, found in families whose members are in the military officer corps or have a high number of university degrees. Given their current scope, the Aryan provisions will also remove from the national community [*Volksgemeinschaft*] descendants of men who have rendered great service to German science or to the renewal of Germany."[12]

Summarising his view that "it is harmful for the principles of paragraph 3 of the Law for the Restoration of the Professional Civil Service, the so-called 'Aryan Paragaph' [...] to be extended to areas for which they were never intended," Loesener noted that "the provisions regarding *Mischlinge* primarily affect those who *otherwise stand firmly on the side of the government* [italics added], and whose upbringing and intelligence make them valuable to the German nation" and that "the enormous pressure on the persons in question, which for now is expressed only in petitions [for exemption from the provisions of the law], must gradually lead to more forceful reactions [that] would present an additional burden if not danger [to the state]." As Loesener noted elsewhere "the completely loyal attitude of half-Jews [...] would come to an end" and result in the "creation of a large number of new opponents [...] of half-Germanic heredity"; in addition, "as each half-Jew has one Aryan parent, thus Aryan relatives and friends," all of those Aryan relatives and friends "would inevitably turn into enemies of the state"; the equivalent of two divisions of soldiers would be lost; the German economy would be weakened; families would be torn apart; and an "unfavorable new impression" would be created abroad.[13] Loesener's later claim that the Nuremberg Laws, which he helped to draft, were not the point at which Nazi persecution of the Jews really took off, the cause of "all the misery, all the murders and other atrocities committed against the Jews," but were in fact intended to introduced some stability into a volatile situation

---

12 Karl A. Schleunes ed., Carol Scherer trans., *Legislating the Holocaust: The Berhard Loesener Memoirs and Supporting Documents* (Boulder, CO and Oxford: Westview Press, 2001), pp. 40–43, 154. For the purposes of "dejudaizing the state bureaucracy," "it is enough," in order to be classified as non-Aryan, according to a 1939 compilation put out by the notorious Julius Streicher, "for one parent or one grandparent to be non-Aryan"; "A grandparent is non-Aryan when his or her parents were not Aryan" (Peter Deeg, *Die Judengesetze Grossdeutschlands* [Nuremberg: Verlag Der Stürmer, 1939], pp. 71–72, 83).

13 *Legislating the Holocaust: The Bernhard Loesener Memoirs*, pp. 57–58.

and, in particular, establish the status and rights of *Mischlinge*, seems not entirely self-serving.¹⁴ "Half-Jews" and even more so, "quarter-Jews" like the Oppenheim brothers, could well have found a degree of reassurance in the new laws, even if, as one scholar rightly insists, survival in Nazi Germany could not be ensured by insisting on one's rights and "in reality, the regulations only guaranteed that certain persons would be targeted as victims, not that the remainder were safe."¹⁵

The historian Bryan Rigg's study of non-Aryans in the military throws some light on the situation of the *Mischlinge*. Rigg calculates that "at least 150,000" *Mischlinge* served in Hitler's armies; he notes that many were

---

14 "In broad circles at that time, these laws were not viewed as something unprecedented and new, or the beginning of a more severe anti-Semitic harassment, but rather as the *conclusion of an epoch of particularly vile harassment* [italics in text]. This conclusion, moreover, had turned out to be much milder than had been feared. Evil Party demands had been kept out of the law, including the demand for the classification of one-eighth Jewish *Mischlinge* as Jews, the sterilization or the death penalty for 'violators of German blood' (*Blutschänder*), the sterilization of all Jews and half Jews, and the compulsory dissolution of racially mixed marriages. Here, after all, was a law, announced and signed by Hitler himself [...]; as vile as it was, it at least provided something to hold on to, a solid foundation for the future." It was not so viewed outside Germany, Loesener acknowledges, but that was because "there was less awareness there of developments prior to the promulgation of the laws." "[I]t is a misjudgement of historical truth," he concludes, "to see all the misery, all the murders and other atrocities committed against the Jews, as simply the result of the Nuremberg Laws—as though they had, in a manner of speaking, unleashed everything Hitler's Germany has on its conscience, or that without them none of this would have happened. [...] For me, given my knowledge of the facts, [...] it is a simple statement of fact to point out the following: the completely hellish form of the persecution of the Jews in later years became horrible reality *not as a result of, but rather despite the Nuremberg Laws* [italics in text]. [...] The prohibition of marriage between Jews and those of 'German blood'; the prohibition of extramarital sexual relations between them, the prohibition upon Jews to employ female domestic servants of German blood under the age of 45, and the prohibition [...] for Jews to fly the German flag [...] were meant to bring order into what had become a chaotic situation and to mark the end of the persecution of the Jews" (*Legislating the Holocaust: The Bernhard Loesener Memoirs*, pp. 54–56). On Hitler's intention, through the Nuremberg Laws, of ensuring control of anti-Jewish measures, cracking down on undisciplined individual acts of violence, and neutralizing the extreme radicals in the Party, see Ian Kershaw, *Hitler 1888–1936. Hubris* (London: Allen Lane, 1998), pp. 562–71: "The Nuremberg Laws served their purpose in dampening the wild attacks on the Jews which had punctuated the summer. Most ordinary Germans not among the ranks of the party fanatics had disapproved of the violence, but not of the aims of anti-Jewish policy—the exclusion of Jews from German society, and ultimately their removal from Germany itself. They mainly approved now of the legal framework to separate Jews and Germans as offering a permanent basis for discrimination without the unseemly violence. Hitler had associated himself with the search for a 'legal' solution" (p. 571). See also Saul Friedländer, *Nazi Germany and the Jews*, vol. 1, *The Years of Persecution* 1933–1939 (New York: Harper Collins, 1997), p. 147.

15 Richard L. Miller, *Nazi Justiz*, p. 19. See also Karl A. Schleunes, *The Twisted Road to Auschwitz*, pp. 130–31.

decorated for bravery and that a fair number were committed Nazis.[16] *Mischlinge* were to be found at the very highest levels of the armed forces. Erhard Milch, who was appointed state secretary of the Aviation Ministry in 1933, directly answerable to Göring, and in that capacity was chiefly responsible for establishing and building up the Luftwaffe, was at least a *Mischling* of the first degree, possibly even a full Jew.[17] It was with reference to him that Göring, his friend, protector, and at times rival, is said to have made his notorious statement: "Wer Jude ist, bestimme ich" ["I decide who is a Jew"].[18] Equally, by lying low and accommodating as much as possible to the situation, it was possible for a *Mischling* to get through the entire period of the war unscathed, as the example of the "half-Jew" Rudolf Petersen, the director of a major Hamburg import-export business, demonstrates. (His mother, from the Jewish banking family of

---

16 Bryan Rigg, *Hitler's Jewish Soldiers: The Untold Story of Nazi Racial Laws and Men of Jewish Descent in the German Military* (Lawrence, KS: University Press of Kansas, 2002), p. 51. According to Peter Deeg, "it suffices to have one non-Aryan grandparent" to be excluded from service in the Wehrmacht. However "by the law of 25 July 1935 exception can be made for non-Aryans who have no more than two fully non-Aryan grandparents" (Deeg, *Die Judengesetze Grossdeutschlands*, pp. 82, 83). Rigg claims that those *Mischlinge* who were admitted or drafted into the Wehrmacht could not rise even to the rank of NCO (Rigg, *Hitler's Jewish Soldiers*, p. 23), though here too exceptions were made.

17 See Rigg, *Hitler's Jewish Soldiers*, pp. 29–30; Samuel W. Mitcham Jr., *Men of the Luftwaffe* (Novato, CA: Presidio Press, 1988), pp. 4–14; Bernt Engelmann, *Deutschland ohne Juden: eine Bilanz* (Munich: Schneekluth, 1970), pp. 212, 238; for a brief summary, http://en.wikipedia.org/wiki/Erhard_Milch. In his admiring biography of Milch, David Irving accepts the story invented by Göring that Milch was actually the son of his mother's lover and not the son of the "racially" Jewish Navy pharmacist Anton Milch, who in fact appears to have been a patriotic subject of the Kaiser far more than he was a Jew (*The Rise and Fall of the Luftwaffe: The Life of Erhard Milch* [London: Weidenfeld and Nicolson, 1973], pp. 327–29). It was not uncommon at the time for *Mischlinge* to try to escape their classificiation by claiming that an Aryan lover, rather than the father of record, the Jewish husband of their mother, was their real father. A bureaucracy was instituted (the *Reichssippenamt*) to deal with such appeals, said to have numbered more than 52,000, of which only about 4,000 were successful (Jürgen Matthäus, "Evading Persecution," in *Jewish Life in Nazi Germany, Dilemmas and Responses*, ed. Francis R. Nicosia and David Scrase [New York and Oxford: Berghahn Books, 2010], pp. 47–70 [p. 52]).

18 At a secret meeting (6 July 1942) attended by Speer and Rosenberg among others, Göring complained that bureaucratic application of the racial laws was hampering the war effort. He gave an example: "Yes, this is a very useful product, extremely useful; it could do us a power of good. We cannot adopt it, however, because it happens that the fellow is married to a Jewess or is a half-Jew." In response to such mindless judgments, Göring noted that "at this moment we have hired a Jew in Vienna and another who is an expert in photography because they have know-how that we need. It would be madness to say: 'He has to go! He did great research work, has a fantastic brain, but his wife is a Jewess and so he can't work at a university. In such cases the Führer has allowed exceptions, even in the field of operetta." (Quoted in Englemann, *Deutschland ohne Juden*, p. 238).

Behrens, converted only at the time of her marriage to his father.) Though he had to give up some highly visible positions and, in general, live a prudently secluded life, Petersen, despite being classified a *Mischling* of the first degree, kept his company running under Nazi rule and in 1945, as a notable local businessman untainted by Nazi associations, was appointed the first post-war mayor of Hamburg by the British occupation authorities. In his own words: "Even though I was much disturbed from the beginning by the conduct of the Nazis, they won favour in my eyes because of their opposition to the communists. I did not discern the danger lurking in Nazidom or foresee how it would subsequently develop. In particular, I did not take the Jewish question too seriously. I understood it when my brother had to resign as mayor in 1933. [...] Naturally, I lived through many hard times during the war. Being deprived of my civil rights was extremely painful to me. Yet I did not suffer any interference in the firm and, even during the Nazi period, we were able to carry on the business. When I reflect that leading citizens always behaved in a friendly manner toward me, and that I never said 'Heil Hitler,' I cannot reasonably say that I had to bear a special burden of misfortune."[19] As *Mischlinge* of the second degee, the Oppenheims could well have felt that they could get by.

Nonetheless, it appears that Waldemar von Oppenheim's wife, Gabriele Goldschmidt-Hergenhahn, a distant descendant of another Jewish banking family, and probably "half-Jewish" herself, repeatedly urged her husband to emigrate, for the sake of their children. He, however, refused, citing his commitment both to the bank, as the elder of the two Oppenheim partners (Eberhard von Oppenheim and Harold von Oppenheim, the two oldest of Simon Alfred's four sons, had shown little interest in banking and were no longer partners in the firm), and to the family's celebrated stud farm at Schlenderhan. Waldemar's younger brother Friedrich Carl appears also to have reached the conclusion that he should not leave Germany. When war with Britain and France broke out, he and his wife Ruth, Freiin von Zedlitz, who was descended from a very old German noble family, were in the United States visiting relatives. Ruth immediately returned to Cologne,

---

19 Testimony cited in Beate Meyer, *Jüdische Mischlinge*, pp. 215–26, Chapter entitled "Der 'Halbarier' Rudolf Petersen (1878–1962) — Durch Anpassung und kaufmännische Tüchtigkeit unbehelligt" ["The half-Aryan Rudolf Petersen (1878–1962) — Unmolested, thanks to accommodation and business skills"]. Petersen may have exaggerated somewhat the "friendly manner of the leading citizens toward me." His aim in the post-war period was to promote reconciliation and forgiveness and get the city of Hamburg back on its feet again.

crossing the Atlantic on a Dutch liner, in order to be with their three young children. Friedrich Carl, who was thirty-nine at the time and hoping to avoid being called up to serve in a war judged inopportune and foolhardy in the conservative nationalist circles to which he belonged (and perhaps also fearing an intensification of anti-Semitic regulations in Germany) stayed on in America. Soon, however, he was receiving urgent calls from Ruth to return to Germany, as the Party had threatened her with retaliatory action and confiscation of the couple's assets if he stayed away. To get back, he had to travel to the U.S. West Coast, take ship for Japan, and cross Russia by the trans-Siberian railway, returning to Germany only in February 1940.[20]

Of the lives of the four Oppenheim brothers, the sons of Max von Oppenheim's cousin Simon Alfred, during the years of National Socialism it is hard to form an accurate idea. Only a few pieces of information, of varying degrees of certainty, are available.

About Eberhard, the oldest, born in 1890, we know very little. An entry in the diary of U.S. Ambassador William Dodd for 19 January 1934 records that the ambassador's wife and family "attended a party of Eberhard von Oppenheim who is a Jew still living in style near us. Many Nazi Germans were present. It is reported that Oppenheim has given the Nazi Party 200,000 marks and has been given a special Party dispensation which declared him an Aryan." By 1934 Eberhard was no longer a partner in the bank. He had ceased to be one in 1931 when Pferdmenges was brought in and appears to have been something of a playboy, more interested in raising and riding racehorses than in running a bank. In the late 1920s he had been President of the Cologne Riding and Hunting Association. If Dodd's report is true, was Eberhard trying to buy his way out of trouble, or did he actually sympathize with at least certain aspects of the new regime? Like his "uncle" Max, he remained unmolested throughout the entire period of National Socialism and died sixteen years after the end of the Second World War, aged over 70. The rest of the family appears to have had little to do with him.[21]

---

20 See Stürmer, Teichmann and Treue, *Wägen und Wagen*, pp. 394, 403–04; Treue, *Das Schicksal des Bankhauses Sal. Oppenheim jr. & Cie.*, pp. 24–25, 29.
21 *Ambassador Dodd's Diary 1933–1938*, ed. William E. Dodd and Martha Dodd (New York: Harcourt Brace, 1941), p. 73. Eberhard was, of course, not "a Jew." According to the Nuremberg Laws, he would have been a quarter-Jew or "Mischling" of the second degree. Did Dodd's referring to him as a Jew reflect a general public perception of Eberhard von Oppenheim, indeed of *all* Oppenheims, or does it tell something about Dodd's way of thinking—once a Jew, always a Jew, especially if you are from the world of finance? As for the "special dispensation" declaring him an Aryan, this was never more than a rumour. Such rumours were not infrequent (Max von Oppenheim was the

Not much is known either about Simon Alfred's second son Harold (born 1892), except that he had a career as a singer and entertainer. There is a recording by him of a Schubert song ("Ständchen," no. 4 of the "Schwanengesang" cycle) on the pre-War German Clangor label (record no. M9628) and he also recorded one of Tamino's arias from *The Magic Flute*. In fact, he appears to have enjoyed some success as an opera and operetta singer and in February 1933 sang the leading male role in the premiere of Erich Korngold's adaptation of Leo Fall's 1908 operetta *Die geschiedene Frau* at the Theater am Nollendorfplatz in Berlin, under the baton of Korngold himself.[22] A few years earlier The *New York Times* (28 April 1928) had reported favourably on his debut recital of German Lieder, French and English songs, and some Italian opera arias at Steinway Hall in New York, declaring that he had "a true, ringing tenor voice." Unlike his younger brothers, Harold von Oppenheim does seem to have made the decision to emigrate, first to New York and then, soon afterwards, to Mexico City, where he appears to have been part-operator of a club known as "7–11." A report in the entertainment news magazine *The Billboard* (8 April 1942) tells of his being held for questioning by the Mexican authorities regarding spy activities. It seems that the activities in question were not, however, on behalf of Nazi Germany, but on behalf of—probably rightwing—opponents of then current Mexican President Manuel Avila Camecho. "The Baron," according to the report, "was reputed to be an ex-patriated Austrian [sic] nobleman who found it better to flee the Hitler regime than to remain in his homeland. […] He is being held so that more information can be learned of the activities of Mrs. Elizabeth Pitt De Almazan, a German-born suspect

---

subject of a similar rumour) and probably reflect the popular anti-Semitic cliché that rich Jews always find a way to pull strings in their favour. It does appear, however, that Eberhard was well disposed toward the National Socialists. According to another story about him, he tried to join the Party but was turned down because of his part-Jewish ancestry.

22 See Brendan G. Carroll, *The Last Prodigy: A Biography of Erich Wolfgang Korngold* (Portland, OR: Amadeus Press, 1997), p. 222. According to Carroll, the production of the operetta ran into financial difficulty and was made possible only by an advance of 30,000 marks by Harold's banker father, Simon Alfred von Oppenheim; it was, moreover, "the unknown" Harold von Oppenheim's "one and only leading role" and "his only stage appearance"; allegedly, "he ended his days in South America singing in cheap bars. A tragic figure, he died from drug addiction" (note 12 to Chapter 15, p. 387; no evidence is provided for this assertion). One witness of the 1933 production wrote that "der füllige Herr von Oppenheim tenorisiert seine Rolle recht sympathisch; er gefiel auch mit einer Solo-Nummer, ist aber für das Genre doch viel zu schwer: er opert" ["the ample Herr von Oppenheim sings his tenor role most engagingly; he was also a success in a solo number, but he is too heavy for the genre of operetta: he performs as if it were an opera"]. (Edwin Neruda, cit. In Arne Stollberg, ed., *Erich Wolfgang Korngold. Wunderkind der Moderne oder letzter Romantiker* [Munich: edition text+ kritik, 2008], p. 254).

arrested early this week. Von Oppenheim landed here [i.e. in New York] from Le Havre with Mrs. Almazan in 1939 and shortly afterwards they appeared in Mexico City. They are said to have moved in circles whose loyalty to the government is considered doubtful." Harold von Oppenheim was married briefly (1923–1926) to a Spanish woman, Manuela de Rivera, by whom he had a son and a daughter, who in turn produced several children. Perhaps "Mrs. Almazan" was his mistress at the time of their leaving Germany, and, though Almazan is not an uncommon name, she may have been related to General Juan Andreu Almazan (1891–1965), a one-time Mexican revolutionary and supporter of Zapata. In the 1930s Almazan turned to the right. In 1940 he ran for President of Mexico and lost, whereupon he left Mexico crying fraud and planning to build support for an insurrection against President Manuel Avila Camecho. He soon returned to Mexico, however, and attended Camecho's inauguration. In all probability he and those near to him were under constant surveillance by the authorities thereafter. Harold von Oppenheim appears to have led a very different life from his brothers in the bank and there is not much evidence that he was in close touch with them. Max von Oppenheim does, however, seem to have maintained some contact with his cousin's most wayward son, as we shall see.

Friedrich Carl, the youngest of the four brothers, who at age fifteen had volunteered as a cadet in World War I and at age seventeen had seen two months' service on the Eastern Front, joined the Stahlhelm, the notorious paramilitary association of right-wing, nationalist veterans, in January 1932. He was followed in July 1932 by his brother Waldemar, who, being a few years older, had served as an officer in the Prussian Zieten Hussar regiment in France during the War and been decorated with the Iron Cross First and Second Class, as well as the Cross of the Order of the House of Hohenzollern. What could have induced the two brothers to join such an organization—at a relatively late date besides?

It is worth recalling that, though on several occasions it collaborated with the Nazis, the *Stahlhelm* was also fiercely attached to its independence and that this in the end led to some serious run-ins with the Nazis and ultimately to a take-over of the entire organization by the SA.[23] In addition, the membership, rightwing and nationalistic as it was, may have been less monolithically anti-Semitic than it is usually reputed to have been. The founders of the organization, it is said, had wanted it to mirror the situation at the front: membership was to be open to all, irrespective of social class

---

23 Hermann Beck, *The Fateful Alliance: German Conservatives and Nazis in 1933 — The 'Machtergreifung' in a New Light* (New York and Oxford: Berghahn Books, 2008), pp. 270–74.

or religious affiliation. An early proposal by anti-Semitic elements to impose restrictions on membership was rejected in 1922, the leadership having argued strongly that members were "neither Jews nor non-Jews, but Stahlhelm men." There is thus some very modest support for the claim made—after 1945—by one of the movement's two leaders that "the majority of the former frontline soldiers rejected the sickly hatred of Jews preached by Hitler."[24] In 1924, however, the proposal was renewed, this time with the support of Theodor Duesterberg, one of the leaders, and this time it passed. Jews were excluded from membership.[25] Those Jews who had joined before that date gradually left the movement and the anti-Semitic element gained ground. The anti-Semitism of the movement at this point may still have been of the old-fashioned variety common among conservatives, however, and not yet radically racist, so that *Mischlinge* like the Oppenheims (and perhaps converted Jews too) could still be admitted. When Duesterberg himself, having agreed to be the candidate of the German National People's Party (DNVP) and to run against Hitler for the Presidency of Germany in the fall of 1932, was denounced in the Nazi press as racially contaminated on account of a Jewish grandfather that the Nazis had unearthed and as a result felt constrained to step down from his leadership position, "countless old comrades stayed loyal to [him]," he claimed. "My case forced all the members of the great Stahlhelm movement to take a clear, unambiguous, personal stand on the race issue. The overwhelming majority stood up for a Christian, humane, and just worldview, to which they remained faithful even during the Hitler years."[26]

---

24 Theodor Duesterberg, *Der Stahlhelm und Hitler* (Wolfenbüttel and Hannover: Wolfenbüttler Verlagsanstalt, 1949), p. 13. This text, however, is unreliable. Written after the War, it aimed to exculpate not only the Stahlhelm organization but, above all, the book's author, Duesterberg. The founder and co-leader of the organization, Franz Seldte, emerges from the book as the villain who pushed for collaboration with the Nazis, while Duesterberg constantly tried to prevent it. It is true that Duesterberg agreed to run against Hitler in 1932 and that Seldte, in contrast, joined the NSDAP in 1933 and served as Minister of Labour under Hitler. Nevertheless, in the 1920's it appears to have been Seldte who, extreme conservative as he was, gave formal support to the republic and resisted pressure from anti-Semitic elements to exclude Jews from the organization, whereas Duesterberg represented an "openly anti-republican, völkish, and anti-Semitic tendency" (Irmgard Götz von Olenhusen, "Vom Jungstahlhelm zur SA," in Wolfgang R. Krabbe, ed., *Politische Jugend in der Weimarer Republik* [Bochum: Universitätsverlag Dr. N. Brockmeyer, 1993], pp. 146–82 [p. 156]).

25 Volker R. Berghahn, *Der Stahlhelm. Bund der Frontsoldaten 1918–1935* (Düsseldorf: Droste, 1966), pp. 65–67.

26 Duesterberg, *Der Stahlhelm und Hitler*, p. 35. Of the movement in general, Duesterberg declared that in the 1920s it stood against the "Hitlerwahn" which resulted, in his view, from the harsh provisions of the Versailles treaty, the high rate of unemployment and general spiritual and material impoverishment: "The Stahlhelm stood like a rock against this mass delusion" (p. 13).

Most important perhaps, the Stahlhelm was closely tied to the German National People's Party (DNVP)—itself a coalition of the German Conservative Party, the Free Conservative Party and a segment of the pre-War National Liberals. In October 1931, just before the Oppenheim brothers joined it, the Stahlhelm allied itself with the DNVP and the NSDAP (the National Socialists), to form the so-called Harzburger Front under the leadership of the far-right press magnate Alfred Hugenberg, a co-founder in 1891 of the Pan-German League and sometime financial adviser to the Krupp company. Hugenberg favoured an authoritarian state—at first through a return to the monarchy, later in the form of a fascist republic. Encouraged by a close associate and confidant, Reinhold Quaatz (who advocated tactical collaboration of the DNVP with the Nazi Party and pursuit of a populist, *völkisch*, and—albeit his own mother was Jewish—anti-Semitic line) Hugenberg supported the NSDAP in the many newspapers he controlled, even though his extreme right-wing conservatism remained distinct from National Socialism.[27] The Harzburger Front collapsed at the time of the February 1932 elections. Nevertheless, Hugenberg continued to believe, along with many right-wing conservatives, that Hitler could be used as a tool and that, when the time was ripe, it would be easy to "push him so far into a corner that he'll squeak," as Franz von Papen put it. As we know, the reverse happened: it was Hitler who successfully exploited the rightwing conservatives to give his movement respectability.[28]

The Oppenheim brothers, like some others, may well have believed that joining the Stahlhelm and throwing their weight behind the extreme right, nationalist conservatives was not only a way of confirming their German national credentials but the best way of dealing with Hitler and National Socialism, inasmuch as the DNVP—despite having a strong anti-Semitic strain itself (full Jews were not admitted to party membership

---

27 In his own speeches, for instance, Hugenberg appears not to have sought to exploit anti-Semitic feelings in his audiences. (Hermann Beck, *The Fateful Alliance: German Conservatives and Nazis in 1933*, p. 180). On Quaatz's anti-Semitism and advocacy of co-operation with the National Socialists, see *Die Deutschnationalen und die Zerstörung der Weimarer Republik: Aus dem Tagebuch von Reihnold Quaatz 1928–1933*, ed. Hermann Weiss and Paul Hoser (Munich: R. Oldenbourg, 1989), Introduction, pp. 19–21.

28 On Hitler's outmanoeuvering of Hugenberg, see Ian Kershaw, *Hitler 1889–1936: Hubris*, pp. 419–23, 477–78; see also Joachim Fest, *The Face of the Third Reich*, trans. Michael Bullock (London: Weidenfeld and Nicolson; New York: Pantheon Books, 1970), pp. 33, 156–58; Karl Dietrich Bracher, *The German Dictatorship*, trans. Jean Steinberg (New York: Praeger, 1970), pp. 86, 190, 194–96, 202; Hermann Beck, *The Fateful Alliance: German Conservatives and Nazis in 1933*, pp. 83–113 *et passim*.

and there was disagreement about admitting baptized Jews and "half-Jews") — remained in principle committed to the *Rechtsstaat*, the rule of law and due process, and was strongly opposed to populist disorders and violence. It was indeed the only party left to represent a "law and order" position.[29] It is also highly likely that the brothers sympathized with the politics of the national conservatives, especially the strong anti-Bolshevism that inspired both the National Socialists and those conservatives who were later to plot the overthrow and, finally, the assassination of Hitler. It was not without reason that, as one historian observed, "the British mistakenly believed that the national-conservatives scarcely differed from Hitler and the Nazis."[30] In November 1935, however, both Oppenheim brothers withdrew from the Stahlhelm. They had to. As Hitler was not about to permit the existence of a powerful, independent paramilitary organization, no matter how supportive of Nazi policies and objectives it had shown itself to be, the Stahlhelm was integrated in that month into the SA.[31]

---

29 Treue, *Das Schicksal des Bankhauses Sal. Oppenheim jr. & Cie.*, pp. 24–25, 29. On the DNVP, see the excellent pages in Hermann Beck, *The Fateful Alliance*, Ch. 5. Beck demonstrates convincingly that, in the matter of anti-Semitism at least, the DNVP did not live up to hopes that might have been placed in it by conservative and nationalist Jews and part-Jews. While local Party organizations tended to consider each individual application for membership by baptized Jews or part-Jews on its merits, the Party headquarters in Berlin was anxious to fend off the charge of being "judenfreundlich" [Jew-friendly] made by the Nazis, who claimed, for instance, that the DNVP had only reluctantly supported the boycott of Jewish businesses. In Beck's words, "the party that, more than any other, had been the standard-bearer of the conservative German establishment, the embodiment of the values of the Empire, the bureaucracy, and the traditions of the old Prussian Rechtsstaat, had failed abysmally when put to the text" (p. 216).
30 Leonidas E. Hill, "The Pre-War National Conservative Opposition," in Francis R. Nicosia and Lawrence D. Stokes, *Germans against Nazism: Nonconformity, Opposition and Resistance in the Third Reich* (Oxford and New York: Berg, 1990), pp. 221–52 (p. 241). Hill notes that while the National Conservatives later "objected to the arbitrary use of police power and the incarceration of opponents in concentration camps, [...] few of them criticised this practice in the early years of the [National Socialist] regime, when their special enemies, the Communists and the Social Democrats, were persecuted" (p. 231). See also the short essay by Hans Mommsen, "Bourgeois (National Conservative) Resistance," in Wolfgang Benz and Walter H. Pehle, *Encyclopedia of German Resistance to the Nazi Movement* (New York: Continuum, 1997), pp. 35–44. Mommsen emphasizes the anti-democratic character of the National Conservative resistance to the Nazi regime, the unwillingness of its leaders to form a covert organization within the country, and their focus on "revolution from above."
31 In an essay dated March 1933 the Jewish rightwinger Hans-Joachim Schoeps, who, like other champions of a "conservative revolution," had been generally supportive of a "national renewal" of Germany and for that reason by no means unsympathetically disposed toward National Socialism, expressed alarm at the introduction, as a result of the events of 30 January and the vote of 5 March, of a totalitarian (as distinct from an authoritarian) political order and the suppression of all independent opinions and

In consequence, the Oppenheim brothers were now, even though only quarter-Jews, excluded from membership.

During the Second World War, the two younger brothers continued to be associated with right-wing conservative circles and interests, this time in the form of the ambiguous national conservative "resistance" to Hitler. In October 1941 Waldemar was recruited for service in the *Abwehr*, the counter-intelligence service of the German armed forces High Command under Admiral Wilhelm Canaris, who had been appointed to head the agency on 1 January 1935.[32] Canaris seems to have been a convinced supporter of National Socialism around the time of his appointment, but the Fritsch and Blomberg affairs, experienced by senior military officers as a deliberately planned effort on the part of the Nazi Party to humiliate the professional armed forces and put them in their place, began a process of partial disaffection, which was aggravated by what many in the top ranks of the military felt were Hitler's reckless foreign policy provocations.[33] Canaris was involved in several of the military's poorly organized and

---

positions. Schoeps warned that "the fact that a magical spell comes today only from the S.A., whereas the the Stahlhelm and the image of man behind it now have far less power to impress, at least as far as the urban masses are concerned, throws a shadow over the prospects of conservatism" ("Die Gegenwart," in *"Bereit für Deutschland": Der Patriotismus deutscher Juden und der Nationalsozialismus. Frühe Schriften 1930 bis 1939* [Berlin: Haude & Spenersche Verlagsbuchhandlung, 1970], pp. 91–92).

32 For a detailed account of the recruitment of Waldemar von Oppeneim to the Bremen branch of the *Abwehr*, see the well-documented study of Winfried Meyer, *Unternehmen Sieben: Eine Rettungsaktion für vom Holocaust Bedrohte aus dem Amt Ausland/Abwehr im Oberkommando der Wehrmacht* (Frankfurt a. M.: Anton Haim, 1993), pp. 173–77. Oppenheim was approached in June 1941. Doubtless hoping to achieve maximum protection for his family, however, he had at first made acceptance of the invitation to serve as an agent of the *Abwehr* conditional on his reinstatement as an officer in the Wehrmacht, the higher ranks of which were officially closed to non-Aryans, *Mischlinge* as well as full Jews. When Bremen would not or could not meet this condition, Oppenheim offered his services to the Hamburg branch of the *Abwehr* and accepted the offer from Bremen only when Hamburg also failed to deliver on his demand.

33 On 4 February 1938, Hitler dismissed War Minister Generaloberst Werner von Blomberg, on the grounds that his newly wed wife had been a prostitute, and Army C-in-C Generaloberst Werner von Fritsch on a trumped up charge of homosexuality, prepared by Himmler and the Gestapo. This provoked great resentment in the army and drove a wedge between the army and the Party that encouraged various moves on the part of the military top brass to undermine Hitler's foreign policy designs and ultimately his very authority. On the Fritsch and Blomberg affairs and moves by army leaders to counter Hitler's plans, see Michael Mueller, *Canaris: The Life and Death of Hitler's Spymaster*, trans. Geoffrey Brooks (London: Chatham Publishing, Lionel Leventhal; Annapolis, MD: Naval Institute Press, 2007; orig. German 2006), pp. 113–58. On Canaris's employment of Jews, *ibid.*, p. 214. On the ineffectiveness of plans to thwart Hitler and even arrest him, see also Bracher, *The German Dictatorship*, pp. 391–99, 433–44.

uncoordinated attempts to obstruct the Führer's plans, which were deemed premature and ill-conceived, and even to displace him altogether. His chief of staff at the *Abwehr*, Colonel (as of December 1941, Major-General) Hans Oster, was one of the most consistent and courageous leaders of the secret resistance to Hitler.[34] Even though Canaris may well have shared to some extent the endemic anti-Semitism of German (as of many European) conservative circles, he was not a racial anti-Semite and was in no way supportive of either the street violence of Nazi fanatics or the severe anti-Jewish measures imposed by the Party.[35] In fact, he employed a number of Jews in the *Abwehr*, including some "full Jews," and resisted pressure from Himmler and others to dismiss them, insisting that they had proved useful, productive, and reliable. In this way he and Oster deliberately arranged for some Jews to get out of Germany and provided a degree of protection for others, such as Waldemar von Oppenheim, who, as *Mischlinge*, might otherwise have been subject to harassment and intimidation.[36]

---

34   On Oster, see Joachim Fest, *Plotting Hitler's Death: The Story of the German Resistance* (New York: Henry Holt, 1996; orig. German 1994); Klemens von Klemperer, *German Resistance against Hitler: The Search for Allies Abroad* (Oxford Clarendon Press, 1992); Winfried Meyer, *Unternehmen Sieben*; Roger Moorhouse, *Killing Hitler* (New York: Bantam Dell [Random House], 2006]; Romedio Graf von Thun-Hohenstein, "Widerstand und Landesverrat am Beispiel des Generalmajors Hans Oster," in Jürgen Schmädcke and Peter Steinbach, eds., *Der Widerstand gegen den Nationalsozialismus* (Munich and Zurich: Piper, 1985), pp. 751–62.
35   When he heard of Heydrich's efforts to speed up mass killings of Polish Jews, along with the Polish nobility and Catholic clergy, Canaris expressed his horror: "For these methods the world will hold the Wehrmacht responsible," he warned General Keitel, head of the armed forces high command (Mark Mazower, *Hitler's Empire: Nazi Rule in Occupied Europe* [London: Allen Lane, 2008], p. 70). See also the remarks on the "traditional anti-Semitism" of Carl Goerdeler, another key figure of the so-called *Widerstand* or German resistance to Hitler, in Ines Reich, *Carl-Friedrich Goerdeler: Ein Oberbürgermeister gegen den SS-Staat*, pp. 155–60, 203–07.
36   See especially Winfried Meyer, *Unternehmen Sieben*, pp. 230–41. In the competition among the various Nazi secret services, the *Abwehr* and its chief, Admiral Canaris, were often accused by the Gestapo of "Jew-friendly actions" ["judenfreundiche Praxis"]. According to one report, at a meeting with Hitler in February 1942, Himmler denounced Canaris: "It was well known," Himmler claimed, "that, on account of his positive attitude to Jews, the head of the *Abwehr* used the services of countless Jewish contact men and intermediaries both in Germany itself and abroad" (cit. pp. 239–40). Hitler is said to have flown into a rage and ordered General Wilhelm Keitel, the Commander-in-Chief of the Wehrmacht, to suspend Canaris immediately. It was a full week before the Admiral was able to arrange a meeting with Hitler and get himself reinstated (Michael Mueller, *Canaris*, p. 214). In his memoirs, written after the War, Ernst von Weizsäcker, appointed Secretary of State at the *Auswärtiges Amt* in 1938, paints a fine, short portrait of Canaris, confirming that the *Abwehr* "knew not a little of what Himmler was up to, and was able to help many who would otherwise have fallen into the hands of the Gestapo" (*Memoirs of Ernst von Weizsäcker*, trans. John Andres [London: Victor Gollancz, 1951], pp. 143–44).

Waldemar was charged with collecting intelligence for the *Abwehr* about the armaments industries in Britain and the U.S, and, in particular, intelligence of interest to the German navy about the two countries' shipbuilding industries. In a memorandum from Admiral Gottlieb Bürkner, representing Canaris, he is said to have produced "very useful information."[37] Thirty-one of his reports on "U.S. oil tanker production, U.S. aircraft production, U.S. merchant shipbuilding capacity, the training of convoy crews, flying schools in Canada, the tonnage of British ships transporting supplies across the Atlantic, the tonnage of Norwegian ships in enemy service, and U.S. aid to Russia" had been judged of sufficient interest to be passed along to other government agencies. In addition, he had travelled to Stockholm and been instrumental in negotiating an order for forty-five "fishing boats" that the Hugo Stinnes company had placed with Swedish shipbuilders on behalf of the OKM (*Oberkommando der Kriegsmarine*, i.e. Navy High Command). This Waldemar had managed to do in the autumn of 1942 in the face of vehement objections from the British and American governments to the government of Sweden. The latter conceded that the vessels could indeed be used for purposes other than fishing, but refused to prohibit the deal unless it could be demonstrated that they could *not* be used for fishing. In fact, the "fishing boats" were used by the Germans as escort vessels in convoys between Stavanger and Bergen in Norway and then as flakships in the anti-aircraft defence of German harbours.[38] For his part, Canaris himself told Himmler that his agent 2048 (pseudonym: "Baron")—i.e. Waldemar—who was being kept under surveillance by the Gestapo because he was one quarter Jewish, had also provided invaluable information about long-term Allied war plans: in a report to the *Abwehr* he had provided information about a conference held in Washington between December 22, 1941 and January 14, 1942 and code-named "Arcadia," at which Churchill and Roosevelt agreed to adopt a "Europe first" strategy, that is, to concentrate their efforts on the war in Europe before turning to the Far East.[39]

---

37 According to Canaris's biogapher, Michael Mueller, Oppenheim "between the autumns of 1941 and 1942 was one of the most important informers on the American armaments industry" (Michael Mueller, *Canaris*, p. 214).

38 Treue, *Das Schicksal des Bankhauses Sal. Oppenheim jr. & Cie.*, Appendix 8 and p. 24. See also on the "fishing boats," Gerard Aalders and Cees Wiebes, *The Art of Cloaking Ownership. The Secret Collaboration and Protection of the German War Industry by the Neutrals. The Case of Sweden* (Amsterdam University Press/Netherlands State Institute for War Documentation, 1996), pp. 128–31.

39 Winfried Meyer, *Unternehmen Sieben*, pp. 249–50. Plans for the invasion of North Africa were also discussed at the "Acadia" conference.

Waldemar von Oppenheim made several trips to neutral countries in the service of the *Abwehr* in the years 1939–1944, most frequently to Stockholm, where he was a personal friend of the Wallenberg brothers Jacob (1892–1980) and Marcus (1899–1982), who headed the Wallenberg family bank, Stockholms Enskilda Bank. (He was also related to the Wallenbergs through the marriage of Count Ferdinand Arco-Valley [1893–1968], a son of his cousin Emmy von Oppenheim, to Gertrud Wallenberg, a sister of Jacob and Marcus.) Marcus Wallenberg had for many years been connected with his banking counterparts and with politicians in London, while Jacob, the Managing Director of the bank since 1927, maintained close relations with German financial and government circles. During the banking crisis of 1931, for instance, Jacob had been brought in as an adviser to the German government on the reconstruction of the German banks and had been in correspondence at that time with many leading bankers in Germany—including, in all probability, the Oppenheims. Jacob Wallenberg has been described as Sweden's main negotiator on trade with Germany and in that capacity made frequent trips to Berlin, both before the War and during the War, between December 1939 and December 1943. The Americans even considered him a German sympathizer.[40] In fact, he was in close contact with the so-called German Resistance and in particular with one of its leaders, Carl Goerdeler, a former Mayor of Leipzig, with whom he met eleven times, either in Berlin or in Stockholm, between the outbreak of war and November 1943.[41] In September 1939 Goerdeler, who was then employed by the Robert Bosch engineering company of Stuttgart, travelled to Stockholm to seek Jacob Wallenberg's help in finding a Swedish buyer for the Bosch company's foreign subsidiaries. Bosch, though a longtime advocate of Franco-German reconciliation and peace among the European powers and not a Nazi supporter—in fact he did what he could to assist persecuted German Jews—was nonetheless anxious to prevent the seizure

---

40 This was probably due not only to his frequent trips to Berlin and his activity as a facilitator of trade relations between Sweden and Germany during the War years but to his role in the complicated Bosch affair. The U.S. government considered the ownership of the Bosch subsidiary in the U.S. unclear and seized it as enemy property in May 1942. The discovery of the secret provision in the Bosch archives after the War confirmed American suspicions that a dummy ownership had been set up during the War. The issue was ultimately settled out of court, but the Enskilda bank suffered a considerable loss of reputation as a result. See Gerard Aalders and Cees Wiebes, *The Art of Cloaking Ownership*, pp. 37–53, 127–52.
41 Klemens von Klemperer, *German Resistance against Hitler* (Oxford: Clarendon Press, 1992), pp. 343–49.

of his company's foreign subsidiaries by Germany's enemies in the event that war did break out. Wallenberg arranged for the Enskilda Bank to purchase the subsidiaries; but a secret clause committed the bank to sell them back to Bosch once the war was over. The Wallenbergs' bank thus served as a safe haven for Bosch's foreign assets. Waldemar von Oppenheim assisted Goerdeler in the negotiations with Wallenberg.[42]

Goerdeler subsequently tried to get Wallenberg, who had come to know many of the members of the conservative "resistance" in the course of his visits to Berlin, to act as an intermediary between the conservative opposition to Hitler and the British. Long convinced that Britain and Germany had a common interest in combating Russian Bolshevism and should never have gone to war with each other, Goerdeler visited Stockholm several times, notably in the summer and fall of 1943, with secret peace proposals that he asked Wallenberg to communicate to the representatives of the British government. Mostly these involved the replacement of Hitler as German Chancellor, a return to the 1939 status quo in Europe and British support for an all-out German offensive against Bolshevist Russia. (Later, in November 1944, after he had been arrested by the Gestapo and imprisoned, Goerdeler drafted a letter to Jacob Wallenberg, in which he begged him to persuade the Allies that it was in their interest to accept and make peace with National Socialist Germany in order to defend Europe against Russian domination, and to make pardoning him and a few others, who he claimed would be indispensable intermediaries in the negotiations, a condition of entering into such negotiations.)[43]

---

42 See note 40 above. See also Winfried Meyer, *Unternehmen Sieben*, p. 177, and a report (dated 17 August 1944) to Ernst Kaltenbrunner, chief of the *Reichssicherheitshauptamt*, outlining some of the results of an investigation into the failed attempt to assassinate Hitler (Hans-Adolf Jacobsen, *"Spiegelbild einer Verschwörung." Die Opposition gegen Hitler und der Staatsstreich vom 20 Juli 1944 in der SD-Berichterstattung. Geheime Dokumente aus dem ehemaligen Reichssicherheitshauptamt* [Stuttgart: Seewald Verlag, 1984], 2 vols., vol. 1, p. 246). The first part of this document, which deals mostly with Goerdeler and his relations with the Wallenbergs, refers to the 1939 negotiations between Jacob Wallenberg and Goerdeler concerning the Bosch foreign subsidiaries, "wobei zeitweise auch der Kölner Bankier Waldemar von Oppenheim (Bankhaus Pferdmenges) als entfernter Verwandter Wallenbergs eingeschaltet war" [in the course of which at times the Cologne banker Waldemar von Oppenheim (Pferdmenges Bank), as a distant relative of Wallenberg, was brought in]. On Robert Bosch's assistance to persecuted Jews, see Peter Hoffmann, *Carl Goerdeler and the Jewish Question 1933–1942* (New York: Cambridge University Press, 2011), p. 56 *et passim*; also Gerhard Ritter, trans. R.J. Clark, *The German Resistance: Carl Goerdeler's Struggle against Tyranny* (London: George Allen and Unwin, 1958), pp. 80–81.
43 On Goerdeler's negotiations, through Jacob and Markus Wallenberg, with representatives of the British government, see the full text of the 17 August 1944 report to Kaltenbrunner,

Stockholm was inevitably a hotbed of intrigue during the war, with peace feelers being put out to both the Russians and the Western powers from the secret German opposition and, as Germany's situation grew increasingly dire, from some high-placed Nazi officials.[44] Waldemar von Oppenheim was at the centre of one of those intrigues. On 13 April 1942 under the heading "Renewed Peace Proposals from Hitler?" various international news agencies, citing reports current in Washington, claimed that a "German banker presently in Stockholm is trying to make contact with representatives of Great Britain in order to communicate to the Allies Hitler's definitive conditions for peace. These include giving Germany a free hand to achieve the destruction of Russia, making concessions to the occupied countries, and restraining Japanese imperialism, the successes of which are said to have much troubled Hitler." A Reuter's report to this effect, entitled "Hitler's 'Final Terms' — Agent sent to Stockholm?", appeared, for instance, in the *Manchester Guardian*. The reports were seemingly taken with some seriousness for Sumner Welles, the U.S. Foreign Minister at the time, was asked about them — and replied that they were of no interest to the U.S. Government.[45] Not surprisingly, they caused considerable irritation at Ribbentrop's *Auswärtiges Amt*.

A further news agency report on 16 April aggravated the situation. According to a note in the political section of the *Auswärtiges Amt*, "the Stockholm correspondent of the *Daily News*, Ralph Hewins, reports that Hitler has sent a peace negotiator to Sweden and that the latter is seeking to establish contact with British circles. Hewins adds that the representative is a banker from Cologne who has contributed a great deal of money to the

---

in Hans-Adolf Jacobsen, *"Spiegelbild einer Verschwörung,"* vol. 1, pp. 246–49; also Klemperer, *German Resistance against Hitler*, pp. 342–44, 394–95. On Goerdeler's peace proposals, see the "position paper" for the British Government drawn up by Goerdeler and dated 19/20 May 1943 in Sabine Gillmann and Hans Mommsen, eds., *Politische Schriften und Briefe Carl Friedrich Goerdelers* (Munich: K.G. Saur, 2003), vol. 2, pp. 944–49; also Appendix 2 of the 17 August 1944 report to Kaltenbrunner in *"Spiegelbild einer Verschwörung,"* vol. 1, p. 249. Goerdeler's letter of 8 November 1944 to Wallenberg is in *Politische Schriften und Briefe Carl Friedrich Goerdelers*, vol. 2, pp. 1192–95.

44 In the considerable literature on this topic, see, for example, Ingeborg Fleischhauer, *Die Chance des Sonderfriedens: Deutsch-sowjetische Geheimgespräche 1941–1945* (Berlin: Siedler Verlag, 1986), especially pp. 81–85; Klemperer, *German Resistance against Hitler*, pp. 370–73; Reinhard R. Doerries, *Hitler's Intelligence Chief Walter Schellenberg* (New York: Enigma Books, 2009), pp. 105–09, 148–51, 193–95; L. Bezymensky, "Himmler's Secret Plan," *International Affairs*, 3 (March 1961): 72–77.

45 See Winfied Meyer, *Unternehmen Sieben*, p. 519, endnote 12, citing documents at the Press Section of the *Auswärtiges Amt* and the U.K. Public Record Office (now National Archives).

Nazi Party and is a friend of von Papen."[46] On the basis of this information, the agent was identified in American radio broadcasts as the Cologne banker Kurt von Schröder, who had indeed been an active supporter of Hitler from an early date and who on 4 January 1933 had hosted at his villa in Cologne-Lindenthal the momentous meeting between Hitler and von Papen that facilitated Hitler's assumption of power. (As it happens, as head of the J.H. Stein bank in Cologne and President of the *Industrie und Handelskammer* [Chamber of Industry and Trade], Schröder had done what he could after 1933 to create difficulties for the Oppenheims.) In the meantime the *Auswärtiges Amt* and the *Reichssicherheitshauptamt*—the umbrella security organization under Himmler, of which the Gestapo constituted section IV—had been apprised that the Cologne banker Waldemar von Oppenheim, active since 1941 in the Bremen branch of the *Abwehr* under the code name "Baron," might well be the alleged agent, not Schröder. The German Embassy in Stockholm sent a secret message to Berlin confirming, after careful inquiries, that Schröder's name had not in fact figured for some time in Sweden's register of incoming travellers, but that "Baron Waldemar von Oppenheim had indeed been present in Stockholm" and, according to the banker Jacob Wallenberg, had "been in negotiations with Swedish companies about the financing of a German order for 80 [sic] motorized fishing boats to be built by Swedish yards." It had not been possible, however, to confirm the rumours circulating in the international press. These had not, moreover, been picked up by the Swedish press, which had reported only that Oppenheim had booked into the Grand Hotel.

A secret Russian communication, dated 13 April, however, contained the information that "the banker Baron Waldemar von Oppenheim arrived in Stockholm on 8 April" and that

> he had with him about 20 kilograms of diplomatic mail for two addresses: the German Legation in Stockholm and secondly the Swedish Ministry of

---

46 Ibid., endnote 13. It is not clear in which *Daily News* Hewins' report appeared—the Chicago *Daily News* or the New York *Daily News*. It is also possible that the newspaper in question was actually the London *Daily Mail*, as suggested by Ladislas Farago, *The Game of the Foxes: The Untold Story of German Espionage in the United States and Great Britain During World War II* (New York: David McKay, 1971), p. 534. In the 1930s Hewins had been a reporter for the British paper, which at the time, under Rothermere, was favorably inclined toward Hitler and Mussolini and, in its early stages, toward Moseley's British Union of Fascists. After the war Hewins wrote biographies of Count Folke Bernadotte (1950) and Quisling (1965). The former had an anti-Jewish slant; the latter was greeted with dismay in Norway because of its relatively sympathetic portrayal of Quisling, the Norwegian collaborator with the Nazis.

Foreign Affairs. The correspondent of the English "Daily Telegraph" reported that he had two meetings with the Swedish banker Wallenberg, whom he asked to get into touch with English financiers on the question of concluding an Anglo-German peace based on a return to the position up to 1939 and on the question of launching a joint attack on the USSR with the aim of destroying it totally. Wallenberg, according to our information, declined this proposal and recommended applying directly to the British Legation. It is characteristic that other British and American correspondents who know about this do not want to say anything, but in conversation among themselves point out that this information should go straight to the Prime Minister and secondly that Swedish censorship did not permit them to write anything about his arrival in Stockholm. Oppenheim on 12 April flew by special plane to Berlin.[47]

The British and American intelligence agents who subsequently got hold of and decoded this Russian communication identified the individuals involved as best they could. The recipient was "possibly Captain 1st Rank Mikhail Aleksandrovich Vorontsov," the sender was probably Aleksandr A. Pavlov, the Soviet news agency TASS's correspondent in Stockholm; Wallenberg "probably" referred to "Jacob Wallenberg and his brother Marcus Wallenberg Jr. bank directors," of whom it was noted that they were "both involved in peace talks at different times." At first, Baron Waldemar von Oppenheim was marked "not traced," but a later addendum to the British and American agents' decipherment and translation of the Russian communication provided the following information about Waldemar: "It was later stated that his purpose was to make unofficial contact with the British Commercial Attaché on behalf of the German Government and through the agency of Swedish business connections; and rumoured that he was to present Hitler's peace offer to the British." It was further noted that he was "again in Stockholm in August 1943, also in March 1944, when he visited Jacob Wallenberg."[48]

---

47 http://www.nsa.gov/public_info/_files/venona/1942/13apr_waldemar_von_oppenheim.pdf.
48 http://www.nsa.gov/public_info/_files/venona/1942/13apr_waldmer_von_oppenheim_correction.pdf. The documents are from the Venona Project, a collaboration of the British and American intelligence services initiated in 1943, under orders from the deputy Chief of Military Intelligence Carter W. Clarke, who distrusted Stalin and feared that the Soviet Union would sign a separate peace with the Third Reich and thus allow Germany to focus its military forces against Great Britain and the United States. The task of Venona was to intercept and decode secret Russian communications. It is striking that the Soviets, on their side, feared that Germany would conclude a separate peace with the British and Americans.

The proposals Oppenheim is alleged to have planned to present to the British are strikingly similar to those usually attributed to Goerdeler. At the same time, rumour apparently had it that he was the bearer of "Hitler's" final peace offer. While it is difficult determine on whose behalf he might have been acting, the most likely candidates are Goerdeler or elements in the *Abwehr* that were party to the schemes of the national conservative "resistance" —not excluding Canaris himself, adept as he may have been at not exposing himself.

What apparently provoked the flurry of reports, rumours, and speculations were some casual, unguarded dinner table comments allegedly made by Waldemar von Oppenheim about the insanity of Britain and Germany being at war with each other when both were under threat from Bolshevism. Referring to his pre-War contacts with the British banker Charles Jocelyn Hambro (1893–1967) (who in 1942 was in charge of the Scandinavian operations of the Special Operations Executive [SOE] set up by Churchill to conduct guerrilla warfare against the Axis powers and aid local resistance movements), Oppenheim is supposed to have said that it would be easy to negotiate a peace agreement "if only he and Sir Charles could sit down at a table together and talk things over."[49] Oppenheim's comments were taken by diplomatic observers and journalists in Stockholm as indicating an interest in meeting with official representatives of the British Government, and in the international press it was assumed that Oppenheim was the bearer of a new peace initiative from Hitler.[50] The rumours, together with information that he had met people "with Anglo-American connections" at Marcus Wallenberg's estate in Malmvik and at an auction of racehorses at Ulriksdal, led to his being summoned to Berlin immediately on his return to Cologne and accused of having abused the Führer's name and engaged in unauthorized manoeuvres detrimental to German interests. He was placed under house arrest and on 17 April was interrogated by the Gestapo about his recent trip to Stockholm.

Oppenheim insisted that he had spent time only with the Wallenbergs, with whom, having been partly trained at the Enskilda Bank many years before, he was on friendly terms; that his business had been of a purely

---

49 Note (dated 14 April 1942) by Frank Kenyon Roberts, Central Department, British Foreign Office, cit. Winfied Meyer, *Unternehmen Sieben*, endnote 17.
50 Precisely for that reason, the Foreign Office advised its representatives in the U.S., the Soviet Union, Sweden, and Switzerland that rumours of a German peace initiative in Stockholm had not been followed up and were of no interest to the government in London (ibid., endnote 19, coded Foreign Office message, dated 19 April 1942).

economic nature; and that it concerned the interests of the German Navy, which had forbidden him to speak of it with anybody. The rumours about his bearing peace proposals might have arisen, he explained, as a result of his having visited a night club where a celebrated Chilean singer was performing. She was signing autographs and must have noticed his name when he gave her his card to sign. He could only assume that she was the source of the rumours. He himself had in no way contributed to them and was fully aware that, as a quarter Jew, he had to exercise particular caution.[51] Oppenheim was kept under arrest for a while and his passport was withdrawn. Various representations by Canaris and the Bremen branch of the *Abwehr* convinced Himmler—to whose Waffen-SS Oppenheim had agreed, under a good deal of pressure, to sell the family's valuable horse-breeding stables at Schlenderhan and who had responded in September 1942 with a letter to the effect that this "co-operation" had earned him the gratitude and regard of the Reichsführer-SS[52]—that the baron's services were genuinely useful, but Ribbentrop and the Foreign Office remained suspicious, refused to return his passport and relented only several months later. In the last week of July, however, it has been claimed, Waldemar was permitted to make a trip to Paris to negotiate the transfer to the Wallenbergs of foreign stocks and bonds sequestered by the Germans. He thus allegedly acted as an intermediary between the German government and the Wallenbergs in the sale to the latter of looted stocks.[53]

Waldemar von Oppenheim's connection with the *Abwehr* appears to have ceased, however, by the end of 1942,[54] and in 1944, following Stauffenberg's failed attempt to assassinate Hitler on 20 July, he was among the thousands of people arrested, along with many leaders of the conservative "resistance," including Canaris, Oster, and Goerdeler. He was taken to the Gestapo prison in Cologne, where for three weeks he was detained incommunicado and subjected to intense daily interrogation, from

---

51 Winfried Meyer, *Unternehmen Sieben*, pp. 248–49; documentation on p. 520, endnote 20.
52 See the relevant documents in Treue, *Das Schicksal des Bankhauses Sal. Oppenheim jr. & Cie.*, Appendix 13.
53 Ladislas Farago, *The Game of the Foxes*, pp. 535–36.
54 Wilhelm Treue speculates on the reasons for the *Abwehr*'s no longer using his services. "Had he come under suspicion? Had the military people also decided to steer clear of him?" (*Das Schicksal des Bankhauses Sal. Oppenheim jr. & Cie.*, p. 28). It may not be irrelevant that by 1942 official policy toward *Mischlinge* was becoming more and more oppressive; see James F. Tent, *In the Shadow of the Holocaust*, pp. 138–50; Konrad Kwiet, "Without Neighbors: Daily Living in *Judenhäuser*," in *Jewish Life in Nazi Germany, Dilemmas and Responses*, ed. Francis R. Nicosia and David Scrase, pp. 117–48 (pp. 133–34).

which he returned, according to his wife, "broken in spirit." In addition, though an official Nazi Party document issued by the local Cologne authorities in 1940 had certified the Oppenheim brothers as "*Mischlinge* of the second degree [*zweiten Grades*], according to the Nuremberg Laws" and thus "not subject to any economic disadvantage," a secret Gestapo report from the end of July 1944, declared that they should be reclassified as *Mischlinge* of the first degree, since it had been reported that their mother, née Florence Hutchins, had been baptised shortly before her marriage and could therefore be presumed to have been Jewish. Indeed, the document continued threateningly if no less implausibly, it is not impossible that the brothers had in fact three Jewish grandparents—one on their father's side and now possibly two on their mother's side—and were therefore to be considered as Jews.[55] The document also accused them of having met with other Jews abroad (the author of the document includes the Wallenbergs among these!) while Friedrich is said to have helped several German Jews who had left for Holland to get out of Holland in 1940 when that country was invaded. Though Waldemar had been instructed to report back to the Gestapo two days after his release, he was advised by longtime friends—wisely, as it turned out—to go into hiding. By 1944 it had become impossible not to observe that the status of *Mischlinge*, which had always been uncertain and subject to review, had deteriorated significantly and that more and more were being rounded up and sent off to work camps.[56] With his wife and children, Waldemar moved from one hiding place to another until the Allies entered Cologne in March 1945. One writer claims, however, that Himmler and Walter Schellenberg, Himmler's personal aide and head of foreign intelligence following the abolition of the *Abwehr* in 1944, looked up his file in February 1945 (when he had already gone underground) with a view to employing him to present Himmler's peace proposals to Count Folke Bernadotte of Sweden.[57]

Though he stayed in Germany throughout the war and did significant intelligence work for the German armed forces, Waldemar von Oppenheim was clearly no Nazi. An anecdote about him in the memoirs of one of

---

55 Treue, *Das Schicksal des Bankhauses Sal. Oppenheim jr. & Cie.*, p. 38 and appendices 6b and 7.
56 James F. Tent, *In the Shadow of the Holocaust*, pp. 138–50.
57 On the experiences of Waldemar von Oppenheim and his family in hiding, see Treue, *Das Schicksal des Bankhauses Sal. Oppenheim jr. & Cie.*, pp. 35–36; on the alleged plans of Himmler and Schellenberg, see Ladislas Farago, *The Game of the Foxes*, p. 536. Some egregious errors in Farago's book and the complete lack of documentation in it have led professional historians to question its general reliability.

Hitler's would-be assassins, Rudolf Christoph von Gersdorff, leaves little doubt about that. Gersdorff describes how, having miscalculated the timing of an encounter he was to have with Hitler, he had to go quickly to the toilet to defuse the bomb that he had intended for the Führer:

> Without waiting for the march past of the honour battalions I went to the Union-Klub in Schadowstrasse, hoping that I would find myself alone there around that time. However, I ran into another member of the club, Baron Waldemar von Oppenheim, the Cologne banker and owner of Schlenderhan, the best pure breed stud farm in Germany. To my surprise he said to me shortly after we had greeted each other: 'I could have done Adolf in today. He was in an open car being driven very slowly past my ground floor room at the Bristol Hotel. It would have been the easiest thing in the world to throw a hand grenade over the sidewalk at him.' But he had not known exactly when Hitler was to drive by and he did not have an appropriate explosive device with him. Though Oppenheim knew me and could easily guess my political position, his speaking out was an act of great courage. I said nothing of what I myself had just been up to, in good part so as not to burden him with the knowledge of it.[58]

Like Canaris and Goerdeler, or for that matter Gersdorff himself, who continued to serve in the Wehrmacht after his aborted assassination attempt and received multiple decorations for bravery and a promotion near the very end of the War to the rank of Major-General, Waldemar von Oppenheim appears to have been a German nationalist of the old school—"vor der Machtübernahme [...] deutsch-national eingestellt," ["a supporter of the DNVP before our take-over"] as a Gestapo document of 4 August 1944 put it—in short, the kind of conservative from the aristocracy, the top echelons of finance and industry, and the higher ranks of the military, with whom he mixed at Berlin's elite Union-Klub. It is not surprising that he felt sufficiently confident in Gersdorff to say what he reportedly said to him. The membership of the Union-Klub was on the whole repelled by the populist violence of the Nazis and was in turn regarded with distrust by the latter. Not surprisingly, all the members fell under suspicion in the wake of the 20 July conspiracy.[59]

Most of what is known about the activities of Waldemar's brother,

---

58 Rudolf-Christoph Freiherr von Gersdorff, *Soldat im Untergang* (Frankfurt, Berlin and Vienna: Ullstein, 1977), pp. 132–33. On Gersdorff's planned assassination attempt, see Michael C. Thomsett, *The German Opposition to Hitler* (Jefferson, N.C. and London: McFarland, 1997), pp. 176-79.
59 See Treue, *Das Schicksal des Bankhauses Sal. Oppenheim jr. & Cie.*, pp. 37, 38, and appendix 6b, p. 68.

Friedrich Carl von Oppenheim, during the years of National Socialism concerns the efforts to save Jews that earned him a place, in 1996, among the Righteous Among the Nations at Yad Vashem, the Holocaust Museum and Memorial in Israel. According to his story on the Yad Vashem website, he too was "inducted, after the outbreak of war, into Canaris' *Abwehr*," which entitled him to "a special pass and virtually unrestricted travel abroad."[60] If Friedrich Carl did perform services for the *Abwehr*, however, he appears to have contributed far less to its work than his brother. The literature and the documents concerning him deal almost exclusively with his actions on behalf of Jewish employees of the Oppenheim bank, on behalf of the Jewish families Lissauer and Griessmann, owners of a firm—Lissauer & Co. of Cologne, one of the largest metal traders in Germany—with which the Oppenheims and their bank were closely connected, and on behalf of the predominantly Jewish employees of the Lissauer company. When pressure was put on the Oppenheims to fire their own key non-Aryan employees, including an old school friend of Friedrich's who worked in the securities department of the bank, Oppenheim at first resisted, claiming that the entire department would then have to be closed down and that that would result not only in losses to the bank but in laying off many Aryan employees. Forced in the end to yield, he succeeded in finding a job for his friend, even though the latter had no expertise in the Lissauer's primary business, at a branch of the Lissauer firm in Antwerp. Likewise, he was able to find employment with Lissauer for another Jewish friend, an assistant judge in Cologne, who had lost his position in March 1933. Though he himself, as already noted, returned to Germany from the United States after the outbreak of World War II, he urged the Lissauer and Griessmann families to move to Holland in 1937 and helped them transfer their business, along with most of their employees (over one hundred), to their Dutch subsidiary Oxyde N.V. in Amsterdam. With the invasion of Holland in May 1940 the families were again in danger. Friedrich von Oppenheim travelled to Holland and seems to have won support from Helmut Wohlthat—a protégé of Schacht who in 1939 had negotiated the Rublee-Wohlthat agreement establishing financial conditions for the emigration of Jews from Germany and who had been named commissioner for the Dutch Central Bank—for

---

60 http://www1.yadvashem.org/yv/en/righteous/stories/oppenheim.asp. Other sources, such as Treue, *Das Schicksal des Bankhauses Sal. Oppenheim jr. & Cie.* and Gabrielle Teichmann, "Friedrich Carl von Oppenheim: A Case Study of a Gentile Rescuer," *Journal of Holocaust Education*, 7 (1998): 67–88, make no reference to his having been inducted into the *Abwehr*.

his argument that it was in Germany's interest to allow the Lissauers to emigrate to the U.S. As an American law had been passed prohibiting any resident of Germany or German-occupied territory from disposing of funds in the U.S. and as a good part of the Lissauer company's assets were in the U.S., the company could meet its obligations to the Oppenheim bank, to which it owed a great deal of money, only if the Lissauers were located in the U.S. This would benefit Germany inasmuch as payments would be made in much needed foreign currency. Despite fierce opposition from the SS, the necessary visas were finally issued for eleven members of the Lissauer and Griessmann families, and in September 1940 the two families left the Netherlands for Hendaye on the Franco-Spanish border in a bus accompanied by a Wehrmacht escort. From there they reached Lisbon and sailed to South America.[61]

Friedrich von Oppenheim intervened again in 1942–1943 in an effort to protect the Jewish workers at Oxyde N.V. At the start of the deportation of the Jews of Holland in June 1942, a proviso in the deportation policy allowed for deferring the deportation of Jewish metal traders in view of their importance to the German war effort. As usual, there was a different response to this proviso from the SS *Reichssicherheitshauptamt*, which was relentless in its anti-Jewish policy, and *Wehrmacht*-run institutions like the *Reichsbüro für Nichteisenmetalle* (Reich Agency for Non-ferrous metals), which took a more pragmatic view. 2,300 metal workers obtained deferments. In November 1942, however, Hitler himself ordered that all Jews should be removed from Holland by May 1943, so that by early 1943 the number of employees with deferments had been reduced by 500. There was a danger that the company would simply be liquidated. Realizing that it served as a life raft for most of its employees, Oppenheim moved to take it over and put it under the control of the Pferdmenges (formerly Oppenheim) Bank, but the "Aryanisation" office in The Hague rejected his plan on the grounds that the bank lacked the necessary expertise. Oppenheim then approached the German metal trading company Possehl and a new company, Possehl-Oxyde, was formed in which the bank had a 25% interest. The new company could now be classified as 'Aryanized' and a clause in the founding document stated that Oxyde had to place a number of its Jewish experts at the disposal of the new company for the initial period of

---

61 Gabriele Teichmann, "Friedrich Carl von Oppenheim: A Case Study of a Gentile Rescuer," pp. 71–73. Teichmann points out that, in fact, "the foreign currency benefits that had served as justification for their emigration never materialised."

transition "as they are essential to wind up the business and to train Aryan personnel." Oppenheim made many visits to Holland, the purpose of which appears to have been to do whatever he could to save the former Oxyde employees from deportation. In the end, very few survived the Holocaust. Nevertheless, "working for Oxyde, for those who did not go underground, provided temporary respite from deportation and helped increase the chance of survival in the camps."[62] Oppenheim's frequent trips to Holland, however, had not gone unnoticed by the Gestapo. In April 1944 the local Gestapo, which issued his exit visas, banned any further foreign travel and in the summer of 1944 he was summoned to Berlin to be interrogated.

As we have seen, Friedrich was included in the secret Gestapo report of July 1944 proposing a change in status for the two brothers from *Mischlinge* of the second to *Mischlinge* of the first degree. It was also stated that there was "a strong suspicion that Waldemar and Friedrich Carl von Oppenheim had used their journeys abroad to conduct murky affairs." Friedrich in particular, it was noted, had helped several Jews to emigrate to Holland and then to escape from there to other places. Soon after Waldemar had been arrested, imprisoned, and, on his release, gone into hiding, Friedrich and his family left Cologne for Ast, the country estate he had been allowed to purchase near Landshut in Bavaria at the time of the sale of Schlenderhan to the SS. A month later he was denounced by the estate manager and his wife for having made "defeatist" comments about the way the war was going and for having declared openly that if he had been Stauffenberg he would not have chosen to use a bomb but would have shot at close range. On 4 September he was arrested by the Regensburg branch of the Gestapo and imprisoned. A few days later, his wife Ruth was also imprisoned for making negative comments about the state, but was released on 8 December for lack of evidence. Fortunately for Friedrich, the prosecutor was apparently willing and able to delay the case's coming to court—long enough for Friedrich von Oppenheim to be liberated by the advancing Americans on 1 May 1945.[63]

Friedrich's relation to the Nazi regime seems in sum to have been less compromised by the—perhaps, in the circumstances, unavoidable—complicity and collaboration that characterize Waldemar's relation to it, as well as that of many other members of the conservative "resistance." Perhaps this is

---

62 Gabriele Teichmann, "Friedrich Carl von Oppenheim: A Case Study of a Gentile Rescuer," p. 84.
63 See Treue, *Das Schicksal des Bankhauses Sal. Oppenheim jr. & Cie.*, pp. 38–43.

accounted for by his being the junior of the two, and reputedly less "serious" than his brother. He, however, had been the first to join the Stahlhelm and there is no reason to think that his basic political views were in any significant way different from those of his brother.

Compared to Eberhard, Waldemar, and probably Friedrich, one other member of the Oppenheim clan has even more impeccable rightwing credentials. This is Anton Graf von Arco auf Valley (1897–1945), the son of Simon Alfred von Oppenheim's sister Emmy (1869–1957) and her husband Maximilian Graf von Arco auf Valley, a descendant of a long line of Catholic noblemen. Anton von Arco auf Valley was thus a first cousin of Waldemar and Friedrich von Oppenheim and the son of Max von Oppenheim's cousin Emmy.[64] He has gone down in history as the fanatically rightwing student who assassinated Kurt Eisner, the first president of the revolutionary Bavarian Republic in February 1919. Eisner was a socialist and a Jew, albeit a non-practising one. Anton von Arco auf Valley had served in a Bavarian regiment in the last year of the First World War, and as an aristocrat, monarchist, German nationalist and professed anti-Semite (despite—or because of—his own part-Jewish ancestry), detested Eisner and all he stood for. He came up behind Eisner, as the latter was walking from the Foreign Ministry in Munich to the opening session of the newly elected *Landtag*, and fired two shots point blank at him, hitting him in the head and the back and killing him instantly. Arco himself was then shot several times by one of Eisner's bodyguards and gravely wounded, but he survived. The night before, he had left a note explaining and justifying the action he was about to carry out:

> I. Eisner. 1: His hidden objective is anarchy. 2: He is a Bolshevist. 3: He is a Jew. 4: He is no German. 5: He does not feel as a German does. 6: He undermines every patriotic thought and feeling. 7: He has betrayed the country. The entire Bavarian people cries out: Away with him. But he does not leave. Hence!!!
>
> II. My motives! I hate Bolshevism! I am and I think as a German! I hate Jews! I love the real people of Bavaria! I am a true monarchist unto death! I am a true Catholic![65]

---

64 Emmy's other son, Ferdinand von Arco auf Valley, married Gertrud Wallenberg, thus reinforcing the business connections of the Cologne Oppenheims and the Stockholm Wallenbergs.

65 Quoted in Friedrich Hitzer, *Anton Graf Arco. Das Attentat auf Kurt Eisner und die Schüsse im Landtag* (Munich: Knesebeck & Schuler, 1988), pp. 391–92. A facsimile of the note is provided on the front and back endpapers of the book.

In his moving book on the German Revolution of 1918–1919 Sebastian Haffner describes Arco as a "half-Jewish Nazi."[66] In fact, he was by Nazi standards a quarter Jew, since Emmy von Oppenheim's father had married into an old Cologne Christian family and had himself converted and Emmy's husband was a Catholic. But that quarter had been enough to get him excluded from the extreme rightwing occultist and racist *Thule Gesellschaft*, one of the seedbeds from which the National Socialist German Worker's Party (NSDAP) grew. In the words of Rudolf von Sebottendorf, a founder of the *Thule Gesellschaft*, Arco "had Jewish blood in his veins from his mother (born Oppenheim), he is a *Jüdling* [a *Yid*] and was thus admitted to neither the Thule Society nor the *Kampfbund* [a league of rightwing German "patriotic" societies]. He wanted to show that a half-Jew could also perform a heroic act"[67] — i.e. an act of which, in the circles Arco frequented, only authentic Germans were considered capable. Finally brought to trial in 1920, Arco was sentenced to death, but was widely hailed in reactionary post-Revolutionary Munich as a hero and in court was praised for having committed a noble rather than an ignoble act. The day after the trial closed, his sentence was commuted to life imprisonment. In fact, he was released on 13 April 1924 (his cell being immediately occupied by Adolf Hitler after the failure of the Beer Hall Putsch) and in 1927 he was pardoned. Testimony to Arco's good standing with the National Socialist regime was an order bearing the seal of the Chief Prosecutor of the High Court of Berlin that was sent to the office of the Public Prosecutor in Munich on 3 May 1941, with instructions from the State Minister of Justice that Arco's death sentence of 16 January 1920 should be stricken from the court records.[68]

It is instructive that on 30 November 1918, a few months before Arco's assassination of Eisner, his uncle Simon Alfred von Oppenheim, the head of the bank and the patriarch of the family at the time, had written to him from Cologne that "it is unheard of that a land like Bavaria should let itself be led by an idiot like Kurt Eisner and in general that the Bavarian people should let itself be led, or more accurately terrorized, by the Munich workers. In the long run this situation is obviously unsustainable." Monarchist and

---

66 *Die verratene Revolution. Deutschland 1918/19* (Bern, Munich and Vienna: Scherz, 1969), p. 184.
67 Rudolf von Sebottendorf, *Bevor Hitler kam* (Munich, 1934), p. 82, cit. Hitzer, *Anton Graf Arco*, p. 391. See also Sterling Fishman, "The Assassination of Kurt Eisner," in Klaus L. Berghahn, ed., *The German Jewish Dialogue Reconsidered: A Symposium in Honor of George L. Mosse* (New York: Peter Lang, 1996), pp. 141–54.
68 Hitzer, *Anton Graf Arco*, pp. 397–98; Fishman, "The Assassination of Kurt Eisner," p. 151.

conservative like his nephew—"Alles für König und Vaterland!" the latter had exclaimed in his note—but no less a defender of law and order, Simon Alfred did not approve of his nephew's subsequent action. Nevertheless, he saw Arco as a "Heldensohn" ["young hero"], expressed much compassion for him, and in a letter to a friend dated 18 March 1919 implicitly compared his killing of Eisner to the murder of Marat at the time of the Jacobin Terror: "About poor Tony we have only scraps of news, the latest not encouraging at all. The way things look now, the best one can wish for him is a quick end, for there is almost no hope of extricating him from the clutches of the Spartacus supporters. They will place him under the guillotine if possible as the murderer of their 'Saint' Eisner. Should he, against all expectations, survive and be rescued, he would spend the rest of his life, I am told, as a pathetic cripple. In addition to a bullet in the head and two in the chest, he was also hit, after all, in the marrow of his spine, and that has left him at this time completely disabled."[69]

Arco was likewise the relative evoked by Max von Oppenheim in the letter of 4 December 1935 to Waldemar von Oppenheim, referred to earlier in this chapter, in which the older Oppenheim declared that he had always been "proud to have been an Oppenheim" and considered with satisfaction the contribution the Oppenheims had made to "the economic and cultural development of the western provinces of Prussia." "Oppenheim family members have also done much for Germany," he went on. "I need point only to Toni Arco who is rightly celebrated as the saviour of Bavaria."[70]

---

69 Michael Stürmer, Gabriele Teichmann, Wilhelm Treue, *Wägen und Wagen. Sal. Oppenheim jr. & Cie. Geschichte einer Bank und einer Familie*, pp. 332–33.
70 Ibid., p. 372.

12. Max von Oppenheim, "Half-Jew," during the National Socialist Regime

Oppenheim and the race question

Having outlined what is known of the relation of some younger members of the Oppenheim family to the Nazi regime in the years 1933–1945, we can now turn back to their senior, Max von Oppenheim. Politically and socially conservative, a fervent nationalist committed to achieving world power status for Germany, the "Kaiser's spy" probably supported Hugenberg's Harzburger Front, just as Waldemar and Friedrich von Oppenheim appear to have done, and may well have expected, as they are likely to have done, that the populist anti-Semitism of the NSDAP would moderate once the Party came to power, or at least would not affect those who were only partly Jewish by birth and not at all by affiliation. By the time the 150th anniversary of the founding of the Oppenheim bank comes around in 1939, Max von Oppenheim wrote optimistically to Waldemar in December 1935, "the current unfriendliness with regard to the Jewish origins of the Oppenheims will certainly have faded."[1]

Of that unfriendliness, he had had some experience. In 1935 there had been a move to expel him, as a *Mischling ersten Grades* ("half-Jew") from the Union-Klub. Though he had been able to gather enough influential support to prevent this, he had been deeply offended at being treated in such a dishonourable manner, as he saw it, by people he had always thought of as belonging to his own world. Also in 1935, as noted earlier, Eduard von der Heydt, head of the Heydt Bank, from whom he had borrowed money, using some of his finds from Tell Halaf as collateral, cited non-payment of

---

[1] Michael Stürmer, Gabriele Teichmann, Wilhelm Treue, *Wägen und Wagen*, p. 373.

the debt as justification for his intention to seize some of the sculptures and remove them to his private estate in Ancona, Switzerland. Oppenheim got wind of his plans, however, and von der Heydt was barred from entering the Museum. Enraged, he wrote a letter to the Deutsche Bank containing extremely offensive comments about Oppenheim. Given Oppenheim's outlook and view of himself as a German aristocrat, there was only one possible line of action. Max Freiherr von Oppenheim challenged his offender to a duel using pistols. Von der Heydt, however, refused on the grounds that as an Aryan and a member of the NSDAP he could not engage in a duel with a non-Aryan. Oppenheim took the matter to a court of honour, won his case, and obtained an apology from von der Heydt.[2] But the experience of being told that he was not *satisfaktionsfähig* [duel-worthy] cannot have been anything but deeply troubling and humiliating for a Herr Baron who was used to mixing with the aristocracy and had always considered himself and presented himself as belonging to the German élite.

In matters concerning the Tell Halaf finds, the research foundation that he had set up and that bore his name (the *Max Freiherr von Oppenheim Stiftung*), as well as his own scholarship, Oppenheim also might have sensed a change of attitude toward him. A Festschrift in his honour, with contributions from 26 leading scholars of the arts, languages, religions, and mythologies of the ancient Near East, had appeared in 1933.[3] Nevertheless, his attempts to put his foundation on a secure financial basis by having it transformed into an institution financed by the state met with no success. As he sought a proper permanent home for the finds by having them acquired by and transferred to the Vorderasiatisches Museum, the museum authorities were similarly unco-operative. They wanted the objects but believed that, in view of Oppenheim's age, they could only gain by playing a waiting game. In addition, Oppenheim's

---

2 Gabriele Teichmann, "Grenzgänger zwischen Orient und Okzident" in *Faszination Orient*, pp. 84, 86–87.
3 *Aus fünf Jahrtausenden morgenländischer Kultur. Festschrift Max Freiherrn von Oppenheim zum 70. Geburtstage gewidmet von Freunden und Mitarbeitern*. The dedication read: "Max Freiherrn von Oppenheim, dem hochherzigen Freund und Förderer der Wissenschaft, dem hochverdienten Erforscher des Alten Orients, der mit glücklicher Hand die Schätze des Tell Halaf ans Tageslicht förderte und zu neuem Leben erweckte, dem hervorragenden Kenner von Land und Leuten, Wissenschaften und Künsten der islamischen Welt, dem uneigennützigen Stifter des Orient-Forschungs-Instituts." Contributors included Erich Bräunlich, Theodor Dombart, Adolf Grohmann, Enno Littmann, Bruno Meissner, Dietrich Opitz, Friedrich Sarre, Eckhard Unger and Arthur Ungnad, as well as a number of scholars who had to emigrate, and Curt Prüfer, an old associate from Cairo days who was to join the NSDAP in December 1937.

scholarly competence was questioned and the excavation techniques he had used at Tell Halaf were faulted. Above all, his acceptance of Ernst Herzfeld's dating of the Temple Palace sculptures to the 3rd millennium B.C. drew criticism. Though this criticism was largely justified—Oppenheim had held obstinately to Herzfeld's chronology despite its rejection by a wide range of scholars in many countries—the tone of the criticism was new. It now reflected an eagerness in some scholarly circles to discredit and marginalize an interloper from a wealthy Jewish banking family who had been able to buy his way, as it were, into domains where he did not properly belong.[4] In addition, as Herzfeld had had to give up his chair at Berlin University on racial grounds in 1935 and had emigrated to the United States (where he became a permanent member of the Institute for Advanced Study in Princeton), there was now merit in attacking his dating of the Tell Halaf sculptures. According to the editor of the posthumously published third volume (1955) of the great scholarly study and catalogue of Tell Halaf, Oppenheim did come to reject Herzfeld's chronology "at the end of his life."[5] One may well wonder whether he did so freely or in order to distance himself prudently from his former collaborator.

Publication of the massive scholarly study and catalogue of Tell Halaf that Oppenheim and his collaborators had been working on for several years and of his extensive research on the Bedouins, which likewise relied on significant input from collaborators, had also become problematical, and since he was now in his seventies, the issue was pressing. As he and his team of co-workers began getting the first volume of his study of the Bedouins ready for the press, he was informed by the foundation supporting the publication of the work that special permission would be required from

---

4   Gabriele Teichmann, "Grenzgänger zwischen Orient und Okzident" in *Faszination Orient*, pp. 85–86.
5   Max Freiherr von Oppenheim, *Tell Halaf* (Berlin: De Gruyter, 1943–2010), vol. 3 (1955), ed. Anton Moortgat, Introduction by Moortgat, p. 3. Moortgat discusses the chronology issue in detail and gives his own reasons for rejecting Herzfeld's assessment (pp. 16–17). If Oppenheim did change his mind about the chronology, it was probably some time in the very late 1930s or early 1940s, for the Herzfeld chronology was retained in the "revised" edition of the 1931 book on Tell Halaf that appeared in French in 1939. Moreover, there is some question as to whether Oppenheim did change his mind. In a letter to Herzfeld, written not long before he died, he asks his former collaborator about publications in the U.S. on problems related to the age of the Tell Halaf statues, "which are of such great interest to me." As he was seeking Herzfeld's assistance at that time, he may, of course, have been aiming to win his former collaborator's goodwill by implying that the question was still open (Letter from Oppenheim to Herzfeld 21 June 1946, Landshut, Ernst Herzfeld Papers, the Freer Gallery of Art and Arthur M. Sackler Gallery Archives. B-16).

the *Reichsschriftumskammer*, the recently founded state writers' association set up by Goebbels, to which anyone publishing in Germany had to belong and from which non-Aryans were excluded. Oppenheim called on his old friends at the *Auswärtiges Amt* to intervene on his behalf. He wrote to Foreign Minister von Neurath, a diplomat of the old school, seeking support for his publication plans and at the same time inquiring politely, out of concern for one of his main collaborators, Erich Bräunlich—and also perhaps in order to draw attention to the fact that the authorship of the book in question was not exclusively non-Aryan—whether having worked with him could constitute a problem for his Aryan co-writers. To the *Reichsschriftumskammer* he wrote requesting that "an exception be made in his case" on account of his many and varied contributions. The exception was granted—it is not known to whose influence this was due—and in 1937 the Leipzig company of Harrassowitz was informed that "as a publisher and member of the *Reichsschriftumskammer*," the firm "would not encounter difficulties if, on this one exceptional occasion, a contract was signed for publication of a scholarly work with an author who could not provide proof of Aryan descent."[6]

The following year the first volume of *Die Beduinen* appeared, with the author's clearly Jewish-sounding name, Max Freiherr von Oppenheim, prominently featured on the binding and the title page. The second volume followed six years later in 1943, with Oppenheim's name still similarly displayed, while the names of his collaborators, who were in fact responsible for much of the work, were listed only in fairly small print on the title page, after the volume number. They were Erich Bräunlich, Dean of the Faculty of Philology and History at the University of Leipzig, and Werner Caskel, a loyal, longtime assistant of Oppenheim's, who, being by Nazi standards half-Jewish, like Oppenheim, had lost his teaching position at Greifswald University but, again like Oppenheim—thanks perhaps to his association with the latter—was never molested by the regime. In fact, Caskel was suggested as a suitable translator of *Mein Kampf* into Arabic.[7]

---

6 Cit. Gabriele Teichmann, "Grenzgänger zwischen Orient und Okzident" in *Faszination Orient*, pp. 87–88.
7 See Stefan Wild, "National Socialism in the Arab near East between 1933 and 1939," *Die Welt des Islams*, new series, 25 (1985): 126–73. In 1934–1936 a proposal for the publication in book form of a translation of *Mein Kampf* into Arabic that had appeared in serialized form in a Baghdad newspaper was being discussed by various *Auswärtiges Amt* officials and Hitler himself. The venerable Arabic Scholar Bernhard Moritz was consulted on the matter and opposed the project on the grounds that the translation had been made from the English translation and not from the original German and was moreover a selection of passages rather than a complete translation (Wild, pp. 155–57). In 1938 Moritz

In the same year, 1943, at the height of the Second World War, the first volume of the massive, profusely illustrated, and richly informed scholarly study and catalogue of Tell Halaf appeared with the distinguished Berlin publisher de Gruyter. Once again, Oppenheim's name was prominently displayed on the cover and on the title-page. In 1933, moreover, Oppenheim had been granted a monthly stipend of 1000 Reichsmarks by Hitler's then Vice-Chancellor Franz von Papen, an old associate of Oppenheim's from World War I days, to enable him to work on this publication. With the promulgation of the Nuremberg Laws in 1935, this subsidy had been withdrawn. Nevertheless, thanks to the support of Professor Helmuth Scheel—Director of the Prussian Academy of Sciences, editor of the *Zeitschrift der deutschen morgenländischen Gesellschaft* [Journal of the German Oriental Society], and a specialist in Ottoman history—Oppenheim had again been in receipt, since 1941, of a stipend of 1300 Reichsmarks per month from the *Deutsche Forschungsgemeinschaft* [German Research Foundation] to help him bring the project to completion. At a conference of German scholars of the Middle and Far East in Berlin in 1942, at which the opening address was given by the fanatical Nazi Paul Ritterbusch, head of a section of the *Reichswissenschaftsministerium* responsible for harnessing the humanities and social sciences to the war effort, Oppenheim was not among the twenty-two university scholars invited to deliver papers. But that was probably because he did not hold and never had held an academic position. His name, unlike that of Jewish scholars such as Ernst Herzfeld or Eugen Mittwoch, was not simply erased from the records. On the contrary, his

---

proposed that the work be done from scratch by the pro-Axis Syrian leader Shakib Arslan with the collaboration of Werner Caskel, then still in Greifswald, though he acknowledged that Arslan might be considered unsuitable because of his age and Caskel might be considered unsuitable because of his "Abstammung" [non-Aryan descent] (p. 165). A further proposal circulating after the outbreak of war was to make a translation with a Koranic ring to it that would suggest Hitler's coming was the fulfilment of various prophetic passages in the Koran. This time Arslan and Moritz himself were the suggested translators and Caskel was the authority consulted by the *Auswärtiges Amt*. Caskel's opinion is worth citing: "I have given your idea much thought," he wrote in reply: "The difficulty of the translation lies not so much in finding the correct equivalent for particular phrases and expressions as in conveying the tone of the work as a whole. For that, what is needed is élan and the ability to be carried away by enthusiasm and I fear that the two gentlemen you have in mind, Emir S.A. and Prof. M., do not possess those qualities in adequate measure. I would think one ought to be looking out for someone close to one of the 'authoritarian' political parties, such as the Syrian People's Party." He added, for good measure, that Hitler's book "supposes a knowledge of the historical situation of Germany in the last thirty years," which the Islamic reader cannot be assumed to possess, so that the reader will need the help of footnotes (p. 167).

accomplishment at Tell Halaf was described, praised, and even illustrated in an article on the achievements and future tasks of German archaeologists in the Middle East by a Professor at the University of Berlin.[8]

On his side, Oppenheim appears to have done what he could to reassure the new masters of Germany of his readiness to toe the line ideologically. At the centre of a speech drafted in late 1935 for delivery at the opening of an extension to his Tell Halaf Museum (15 July 1936) — an event attended, along with members of the press, scholars and friends, by high-ranking officials, including Foreign Minister von Neurath and future Foreign Minister Joachim von Ribbentrop — he made the claim that the finds at Tell Halaf and at another excavation site at nearby Tell Fakhariyah were the products of an Aryan culture.[9] It is characteristic of the problems Oppenheim still faced that this embrace of prevailing racial preoccupations was viewed by some of those it was intended to impress as a ploy. (Indeed, his extraordinarily well-informed modern biographer, Gabriele Teichmann, also describes it as a "Strategie.") Thus Otto Kümmel, Director-General of the State Museums, wrote to the Minister of Science, Education and National Culture that "Fakhariyah has not yet been explored; we do not know what it contains. Declaring it similar to Washukanni is equally ungrounded, though doing so has an obvious purpose, as has the elevation of the Mitanni to the status of Aryans — a view that Oppenheim, hardly an Aryan himself, has not tired of propagating since 1933, for obvious reasons." The context of Kümmel's letter was a request from Oppenheim for money and foreign currency — in extremely short supply in the Third Reich — to finance a new journey into Syria. Kümmel used Oppenheim's Jewish ancestry to argue against granting his request: "Quite apart from other reservations one might have,

---

8   Julius Jordan, "Leistungen und Aufgaben der deutschen Ausgrabungen im Vorderen Orient," *Der Orient in deutscher Forschung: Vorträge der Berliner Orientalistentagung, Herbst 1942*, ed. Hans Heinrich Schaeder (Leipzig: Otto Harrassowitz, 1944), pp. 228–38 (p. 234). Jordan's Nazi credentials were impeccable. An archaeologist employed by the Baghdad Museum, he also lectured on archaeology and Nazism and was expelled from Iraq by Nuri al-Said in 1939 for inciting students to anti-British activity. (Reeva S. Simon, *Iraq Between the Two World Wars* [New York: Columbia University Press, 1986], p. 38).

9   After 1933, according to one scholar, "it was the new dogma to search for 'Indo-Germanic,' that is, Aryan contributions to Near Eastern civilization. Hittites and Hurrians gained new popularity and research into their Indo-European languages and their material artifacts [...] was encouraged. [...] Ancient Near Eastern Studies was put to use in support of claims to Aryan, 'Indo-European' pre-eminence throughout history" (Stefan R. Hauser, "German Research on the Ancient Near East and its Relation to Political and Economic Interests from Kaiserreich to World War II," in Wolfgang G. Schwanitz, ed., *Germany and the Middle East 1871–1945* [Madrid: Iberoamericana and Frankfurt a.M.: Vervuert, 2004], pp. 155–19 [pp. 168, 170]).

this son of a full Jew and a possibly Aryan mother, this member of the one Jewish family whose female offspring have contaminated with their Jewish blood more old aristocratic families than any other, would be a very peculiar representative of National Socialist Germany. Even people with whose work he associates his own, such as Günther [Hans F.K. Günther], the scholar of race, and Reinerth [Hans Reinerth], the scholar of prehistory, while they will be in favor of the excavations, will assuredly not be in favor of the excavator."[10]

Equally characteristic of Oppenheim's situation during the Third Reich, however, is the fact that his request was in the end granted. Many officials wanted the honour of the excavations at the Syrian sites to accrue to Germany and Oppenheim held the rights to carry them out. In fact, he had submitted his request chiefly because he had been presented by the French mandate authorities in Syria, who were under pressure from scholars of the Oriental Institute at the University of Chicago to cede the excavation rights to them, with the stark choice of either exercising his rights or forfeiting them. It was therefore essential, if German archaeology was to retain its place at the sites, that the excavations be resumed without

---

10 Letter dated 9 August 1937, cit. Teichmann,"Grenzgänger zwischen Orient und Okzident" in *Faszination Orient*, p. 89. Hans F. K. Günther (1891–1968), often referred to as "Rassengünther," was the leading proponent in Germany (along with Ferdinand Clauss) of race theories, of the superiority of the "Nordic race" in particular, and of a policy of *Aufnordung* (using the methods of eugenics to restore, as far as possible, the purity of the Nordic race). He was the editor of the journal *Rasse. Monatsschrift der nordischen Bewegung*, and the author of numerous "ethnographic studies" classifying and describing the physical and moral characteristics of the various races of mankind. These works of *Rassenkunde* became virtually official doctrine in Nazi Germany. In 1931 he was appointed to a chair at the university of Jena by Wilhelm Frick, the Education Minister of the state of Thuringia—the first National Socialist Minister in the government of any German state—over the protests of the faculty. Günther joined the NSDAP in 1932. He was present, as an "honoured guest," at a three day conference in 1941 marking the opening of Rosenberg's *Institut zur Erforschung der Judenfrage*, in the course of which the goal of the destruction of the Jews as a people was formulated. He himself, in the 1920s, had favored their removal from Germany, possibly to Palestine, as an "honourable" solution to the "Judenfrage" (Hans F. K. Günther, *Rassenkunde des deutschen Volkes* [Munich: J. F. Lehmann's Verlag, 1922], Appendix on "Rassenkunde des jüdischen Volkes," pp. 367–434 [pp. 430–34], and *Rassenkunde Europas*, 3rd edn [Munich: J.F. Lehmann's Verlag, 1929; 1st edn 1926], p. 105). His services to the cause of National Socialism were recognized in 1941 when Rosenberg presented him with the Goethe Medal. Hans Reinerth (1900–1990), a specialist in the pre-history of Germany, was also a member of Rosenberg's *Kampfbund für deutsche Kultur*, joined the NSDAP in 1931, held a chair at the University of Berlin, and headed the *Reichsbund für deutsche Vorgeschichte* from 1933 until 1945. He was closely associated with the *Amt* or *Dienststelle Rosenberg*, the organization through which Rosenberg translated his cultural politics into action.

delay. In March 1939, therefore, Oppenheim was able to set out, at the age of 79, on a planned four-month trip to Syria. As it turned out, however, the French had by then become acutely apprehensive of Nazi Germany and suspicious of the many Germans visiting Syria. They were doubtless also not oblivious of Oppenheim's activities prior to and during the First World War. In Beirut Oppenheim learned that he had been barred by the Mandate authorities from further travel in Syria. He obtained permission to visit Aleppo but access to the excavation sites in the Northeastern part of the country was adamantly refused. Oppenheim defied the ban, but was turned back as he approached the sites and had to return home to Germany without accomplishing his mission, even if he was able to claim later that he had not forfeited his rights.[11] In the end C. W. McEwan of the Oriental Institute of Chicago did get to excavate the site at Tell Fakhariyah in 1940. Nonetheless, after the fall of France, the German government again demanded that the right to excavate at Tell Halaf and Fakhariya be restored to Max von Oppenheim and his Foundation. The prestige of German scholarship was not neglected by the National Socialists and was in fact regarded as a significant part of German wartime propaganda.[12]

In fact, Oppenheim's reference to race and to the Mitanni culture as Aryan in his speech of 15 July 1936 may not have been simply a ploy, as his detractors claimed, even if it was obviously opportune. Like many scholars of the ancient Middle East, Oppenheim had an interest in

---

11 For a detailed account of the complex political and scholarly wrangling over the sites, in which the French authorities, the Vichy authorities, the Germans, the Americans, and—after Syria was occupied by the British and the Free French—the Gaullists were all involved, see R.L. Melka, "Max Freiherr von Oppenheim: Sixty Years of Scholarship and Political Intrigue in the Middle East," *Middle Eastern Studies*, 9 (1973): 81–93 (pp. 83–85). The French may, in addition, have had reason to suspect that Oppenheim's mission was not entirely scholarly. According to the author of an article in *Spiegelonline* (28 January 2011), "there are some questions about whether there was more to it than that. The trip was paid for by a special fund administered by Hermann Göring, the head of Germany's air force."

12 The German demand was communicated to the French at the end of July 1940. The French stalled until the project was overtaken by events when the British and Gaullist French succeeded in occupying Syria; see Chantal Metzger, *L'Empire colonial français dans la stratégie du Troisième Reich (1936–1945)*, 2 vols. (Paris: Ministère des Affaires étrangères; Brussels: Peter Lang, 2002), vol. 1, p. 343. On the mobilization of *Wissenschaft* (science and scholarship) under the Third Reich for propaganda and other war-related purposes, see Frank-Rutger Hausmann, *"Deutsche Geisteswissenschaft" im Zweiten Weltkrieg: Die "Aktion Ritterbusch" 1940–1945* (Dresden and Munich: Dresden University Press, 1998) and, in connection with Middle and Far Eastern studies in particular, Paul Ritterbusch, "Eröffnungsansprache" [Opening Address] in *Der Orient in deutscher Forschung: Vorträge der Berliner Orientalistentagung, Herbst 1942*, ed. Hans Heinrich Schaeder (Leipzig: Otto Harrassowitz, 1944), pp. 1–5.

questions of race. His guide in the matter had for many years been one of his principal professional associates, Arthur Ungnad, an orientalist twenty years his junior. Ungnad had led the way in claiming that the Mitanni were an Aryan people and Oppenheim had followed suit. Ungnad's interest in questions of race was itself, at first anyway, part of a long tradition among nineteenth-century linguists and philologists.[13] Unlike Gobineau and Vacher de Lapouge, who were focused on establishing a hierarchy of races, the interest in race among scholars in the philological tradition, such as Ernest Renan and Max Müller, was rooted in Biblical and theological studies. Most often it concerned the relation between the two language families generally considered the most ancient—the Semitic, long unrivalled in that position, and the Indo-European, as identified by Franz Bopp in articles in the *Transactions* of the Berlin Academy of Sciences (between 1824 and 1831) and in the volumes of his *Comparative Grammar* (1833–1852). Did the Semitic and Indo-European languages emerge from a single origin, as some scholars argued? And if so, were the "races" that spoke them—the Indo-Europeans or Aryans and the Semites—also originally one race? Can their original unity be demonstrated? What is the nature of the differences between them? How did these differences arise? How profound and significant are they and what do they portend for the future? While the category of "race" figured frequently in the debates and discussions of the scholars, it was still an amorphous concept, as Maurice Olender has demonstrated in the case of Renan, whom he shows shifting back and forth between something close to a biological understanding of race and a linguistic or cultural understanding:

> What did Renan's "portraits of races" look like? Humanity, he tells us, was long ago divided into families, each different from the others, each with its virtues and faults. "The fact of race was then paramount and governed all

---

13 Succinctly described recently in Maurice Olender's *The Languages of Paradise: Race, Religion and Philology in the Nineteenth Century*, trans. Arthur Goldhammer (Cambridge, MA: Harvard University Press, 1992; orig. French, *Les Langues du paradis: Aryens et Sémites, un couple providentiel* [Paris: Seuil, 1989]). This tradition should probably be distinguished, despite many disturbing connections and overlappings, from that represented by race theorists such as Gobineau (*Essai sur l'Inégalité des races humaines*, 1856), Vacher de Lapouge (*L'Aryen et son role*, 1899), William Ripley (*The Races of Europe*, 1899), Joseph Deniker (*Races et peuples de la terre*, 1900), or Madison Grant (*The Passing of the Great Race or the Racial Basis of European History*, 1916), even though Olender himself believes that in the work of the scholars "we cannot fail today to see looming in the background the dark silhouette of the death camps and the rising smoke of the ovens" (*The Languages of Paradise: Race, Religion and Philology in the Nineteenth Century*, p. xi).

aspects of human relations" (1859, p. 445). This very remote time in ancient history cannot be understood without a concept of racial distinctions, "the secret of all the events in the history of humanity" (p. 446). Originally, then, races were "physiological facts," but gradually their importance waned. Owing to great conquests and to the spread of religions such as Buddhism, Christianity, and Islam, the era of racial determination gave way to an age of "historical facts." "Language thus virtually supplanted race in distinguishing between human groups, or, to put it another way, the meaning of the word 'race' changed. Race became a matter of language, religion, laws, and customs more than of blood" (vol. 6, p. 32).

Renan immediately tempers this assertion by insisting that the "hereditary qualities" of blood help to perpetuate institutions and "habits of education." Although, for Renan, "races are durable frameworks" (1859, pp. 447–48), things have reached the stage where they are "no longer anything more than intellectual and moral molds" on which physical kinship has "almost" no influence. Renan even goes so far as to propose that the term "linguistic races" be substituted for "anthropological races" (vol. 8, p. 1224) [...] Aryans and Semites might exhibit "no essential difference" in physical type and yet belong to "two [distinct] races" by virtue of their "intellectual attitudes and moral instincts" (p. 577). [...] Race, once of paramount importance, has since lost its decisiveness. Humans [...] "have no right to go around the world probing into craniums and then grabbing people by the throat and telling them, "You are our blood; you belong to us" (p. 898).[14]

Renan's analysis of the relation of Semitic and Indo-European races and languages was witheringly criticized in a work closely studied by Ungnad, the Hebraist Friedrich Delitzsch's *Studien über Indogermanisch-Semitische Wurzelverwandtschaft* [Studies on the Relations of Indogermanic and Semitic Roots]. According to Delitzsch, Renan makes two incompatible claims: that the Semitic and Indo-European languages are radically different and that the Semitic and Indo-European peoples were originally one. Delitzsch cites Renan: "il faut reconnaître que, pour les mythes comme pour la langue, un abîme sépare les deux races" ["It has to be acknowledged that as far as myths and language are concerned, the two races are separated by an abyss"]. One would imagine, he goes on, that the two peoples must therefore have been quite distinct. But no. Renan holds that both belong to a

---

14 Maurice Olender, *The Languages of Paradise: Race, Religion and Philology in the Nineteenth Century*, pp. 58–60. The references are to Renan's article, "Nouvelles Considérations sur le caractère général des peoples sémitiques," *Journal Asiatique*, série 5, 13 (1859): 214–82, 417–50; and to volumes 6 (*Histoire du people d'Israel*, 1887) and 8 (*Histoire des langues sémitiques*, 1855, and "Des Services rendus aux sciences historiques par la philologie," in *Mélanges religieux et historiques*, 1878) of Renan's *Oeuvres complètes*, ed. Henriette Psichari, 10 vols. (Paris: Calmann Lévy, 1947–1961).

single "Caucasian race": "il est difficile d'admettre que des peuples offrant les mêmes caractères physiologiques et psychologiques ne soient pas frères" ["It is hard to conceive that peoples with the same physiological and psychological characteristics are not fraternally related"]. Delitzsch cites Renan's summary articulation of his position: "I imagine the emergence of the Semitic and the Aryan languages as two distinct, though parallel phenomena, in the sense that two fractions of a single race, separated immediately after their birth, [here Delitzsch interjects impatiently 'What in all the world can have been the cause of this portentous separation? And how is one to conceive a process of separation immediately after birth?'] produced them under the influence of analogous causes and in accordance with almost identical psychological elements in their make-up." Delitzsch went on to present a case, based, he claimed, on "empirical" linguistic evidence, for the historical *"Urverwandtschaft"* ["original relatedness"] of the Indo-Germanic and Semitic languages and peoples.[15]

Ungnad, it will be recalled (see pt. I, ch. 2 above), had held in his essay on *Die ältesten Völkerwanderungen Vorderasiens* [The Earliest Migrations of Peoples in the Near East] of 1923 that there was very little to distinguish physically the pure "Semitic" type (as represented, for instance, by the modern Bedouin) from the pure "Indo-Germanic" type; that the hypothesis of Arabia or Africa as the original home of the Semites was "untenable"; and that there were "striking linguistic connections between the Semitic race and the Indo-Germanic race." It was thus "quite likely," he had concluded, in the same vein as Delitzsch, "that in South-Eastern or Central Europe in times long before our earliest historical records both peoples had formed a single people with a single language. The Semites separated at an early date [from the common source] and followed routes that we can only guess at, and can no longer identify in any detail, but that most probably took them by way of Asia Minor into Western Syria, the area between the Mediterranean and the Euphrates."[16] By the time he published *Subartu* (1936), however, Ungnad had changed his tune. Not only had the earlier, traditional focus on the relation of "Semitic" and "Indo-Germanic" shifted to a more general interest in biologically defined race and in race

---

15 Friedrich Delitzsch, *Studien über Indogermanisch-Semitische Wurzelverwandtschaft* (Leipzig: J.C. Hinrichs'shce Buchhandlung, 1873), pp. 18–19, 113.
16 Arthur Ungnad, *Die ältesten Völkerwanderungen Vorderasiens: Ein Beitrag zur Geschichte und Kultur der Semiten, Arier, Hethiter und Subaräer* (Breslau: Im Selbstverlag des Verfassers, 1923), p. 5.

migrations, there was no longer any question in this work of a "Semitic race": "Semitisch ist eine Sprache und keine Rasse" ["the term Semitic designates a language, not a race"]; it is essential to separate completely questions of race and questions of language. Ungnad's terminology and categories of race were now taken over from Hans F.K. Günther's "Rassenkunde" or Science of Race, which was to be more or less official doctrine during the National Socialist years[17] and from the work of Eugen Fischer, Director of the Kaiser Wilhelm Institute of Anthropology, Human Heredity, and Eugenics (1927–1942), Rector of the University of Berlin (to which post he was appointed by Hitler in 1933) and author, in 1933, of a pamphlet entitled *Der völkische Staat, biologisch gesehen*.[18] According to Günther, instead of a "Semitic" race, two races dominate in the Middle East—the *vorderasiatische Rasse* [Middle Eastern race] and the *orientalische Rasse* [Oriental race]. The former, Günther claims, is related to the *dinarische Rasse*, which predominates in South-Eastern Europe but stretches northwards into the Alpine lands and Bavaria;[19]

---

17 Arthur Ungnad, *Subartu: Beiträge zur Kulturgeschichte und Völkerkunde Vorderasiens* (Berlin and Leipzig: Walter de Gruyter, 1936), pp. 2–3. In a note (p. 2, note 1), Ungnad refers explicitly to Günther's *Rassenkunde des deutschen Volkes* (Munich: J.F. Lehmann's Verlag, 1922), *Rassenkunde Europas* (Munich: J.F. Lehmann's Verlag, 1926) and *Rassenkunde des jüdischen Volkes* (Munich: J. F. Lehmann's Verlag, 1930) as "the best source of information" on questions of race.

18 (Berlin: Junker und Dünnhaupt, 1933). Fischer distinguishes here between the nineteenth-century idea of the nation state, which rests on a cultural and spiritual foundation and on the concept of the free, autonomous individual, and the new *völkisch* state, which is the political form of a community of race, resting essentially on "Blut und Boden" (blood and soil). Ungnad refers to Fischer in his review of Oppenheim's 1931 Tell Halaf book as being at the origin of the "now familiar" racial category of "vorderasiatisch," which "for over a decade I have used to describe the Subaraean people." Fischer, we are told, fully approved of this usage (*Zeitschrift der deutschen morgenländischen Gesellschaft*, Neue Folge, 10 [1931]: 372–81 [p. 375]).

19 *Rassenkunde Europas*, 3rd edn (Munich: J. F. Lehmann's Verlag, 1929), pp. 92, 152. "There is still not much that can be said today about the first appearance of the Dinaric race. It must originally have formed a single human group along with the Middle Eastern race. Its original home is likely to have been in the area of the Caucasus. Then after the migration of a part of this human group, a change in the selection process resulting from the different environment must have made of the original single human group two groups, which are distinguishable from each other by several characteristics, but not so that their original belonging together is not still discernible"(p. 152). Unlike Ungnad, however, Günther holds that the moral and psychological differences between the *vorderasiatisch* race and the *dinarisch* race are considerable. Among the images Günther provides of individuals of predominantly "Dinaric" race, one finds those of Jacob Burckhardt, the great Swiss historian, and Alphonse Daudet, the well-known French writer; among those of individuals of predominantly "Middle Eastern" race, those of Paul Wallott, the architect of the Reichstag (a descendant of Huguenot refugees from Southern France), the painter Gauguin, Joseph Stalin, and a Governor-General of Canada.

the latter is related to the *westische* or Mediterranean race.[20] There is no such thing as a Semitic "race." "There are only peoples, made up of various racial strains, who speak Semitic languages."[21] V*orderasiatisch, orientalisch, dinarisch, westisch*, these were now the categories referred to by Ungnad. The pages of *Subartu* likewise show the influence of Günther in numerous references to physical characteristics, especially facial features and the shape and dimensions of the cranium, as markers of race.

As for the Jews, they are an overwhelmingly mongrel people. This had already been affirmed by Ungnad as early as 1923 in *Die ältesten Völkerwanderungen Vorderasiens*, where he made a point of distinguishing the *Habiräer* or *Hebräer*—the Hebrews—from those he at that time still described as "pure Semites." The *Hebräer*, originally nomads, had already mingled freely with other peoples by the time they invaded Palestine, where, once again, they mixed with the people they had conquered. "Were the Hebrews racially pure Semites?" he asked; "Our answer must be an unequivocal 'No.' Even if the earliest nomads of Mesopotamia were relatively pure racially, the Hebrews had mixed so extensively with the local populations in the countless foreign states in which they had been employed, such as Babylonia, Subartu-Mitanni, the Hittite kingdom, Egypt, perhaps also Elam, that by the time of their move to Palestine there was already absolutely no question of racial purity with them. Moreover, they now mixed further here with the Canaanites, who were themselves a mixed race formed by Semites, Aryans, and Hurritic Subaraeans. For that reason there is probably less Semitic blood flowing in the veins of the descendants of those Hebrews, namely the Jews, than the total amount constituted by the admixture of blood from numerous other races."[22] On the topic of the Jews at least, Ungnad's views were already in line with those put forward at great length by Günther the previous year in a 70-page appendix to his *Rassenkunde des deutschen Volkes* of 1922, entitled *Rassenkunde des jüdischen Volkes*. By 1936, Ungnad has followed Günther not only in abandoning the notions of a "Semitic" race and "Semitic blood" but in attributing explicitly a high value to

---

20 Ibid., pp. 96, 152–53. "Because of characteristics they have in common, we shall also have to assume a common origin in an old stone age human group of the Nordic and Mediterranean races, along with the Oriental race" (p. 152).
21 Ibid., p. 100.
22 Arthur Ungnad, *Die ältesten Völkerwanderungen Vorderasiens*, p. 16.

racial "purity," already implicitly judged desirable in 1923, even if he also gave a fairly compassionate account of the conditions in which a people loses its racial purity and in the process acquires undesirable characteristics:

> Those characteristics of the Middle Eastern racial type [*der vorderasiatischen Steilköpfe*] that we find so unattractive retreat more and more into the background as we move away from those regions where there was a great deal of intermingling with other races. The average height too seems to increase as we move in this direction, so that, for example, the Circassians of Ciscaucasia [the Northern Caucasus region], who also speak a Caucasian language, already approximate very closely both physically and morally to the Dinaric racial type. Their pride, their daring, their code of hospitality, on the one hand, the hot-tempered anger that is expressed in blood feuds, on the other, are character traits that we also encounter among European peoples in whom the Dinaric racial element predominates. Even in descriptions of peoples of this same race settled on Russian soil in the Caucasus, we do not come across any mention of characteristics that we would find repugnant, if we disregard their habit of violently taking the law into their own hands. This runs counter to our modern notions of justice, but it is a trait that is also commonly found among peoples of Dinaric race. As peoples remain purest also in their morals and customs wherever they have not mingled with elements foreign to their own kind and have also been able to retain their own native language, it would therefore be premature to condemn the Middle Eastern racial type [*vorderasiatischer Steilkopf*] wholesale as inferior. The situation is rather this: bad characteristics develop first in those areas that have suffered for thousands of years under the yoke of an alien race. Here the vanquished succeeded in surviving to the extent that they did what they could to adapt to their new masters. But as such an adaptation of moral and psychological characteristics is possible only up to a certain point, dissimulation, hypocrisy, avariciousness, and dishonesty inevitably took the place of those characteristics of the masters that were racially alien to the vanquished. In the course of time, through a natural process of selection, those sections of the vanquished people that had been successful at adapting became more and more dominant, while those that were less successful at adapting were eliminated. This demonstrates the danger of subjecting a racially distinct people—not only for the vanquished but also in the long run for the victorious ruling stratum, for it too degenerates and declines in a racially alien territory.[23]

Given that the purest members of the *vorderasiatische Rasse* are, according to Günther himself, so close physically to the *dinarische Rasse* that they may

---

23 Ungnad, *Subartu*, pp. 16–17.

be considered a branch of the latter and that, again according to Günther, the closeness of the *orientalische Rasse*, of which he views the Bedouins as the purest specimens, to the *westische* (or Mediterranean) *Rasse* requires one to consider whether these two races also might not have a common origin, Ungnad's earlier assertion, in the 1923 essay, that the German and the Bedouin, the pure Indo-Germanic and the pure "Semitic" (the term he still used then as a racial category) are virtually indistinguishable physically thus retained, *mutatis mutandis*, a certain validity in the context of the prevailing theories of Günther.[24] The Jews, in contrast, are a mongrel people. And while no race has maintained its purity absolutely and all peoples are made up, in greater or lesser degree, of a combination of races, the Jews are the least "pure" racially of any. According to Günther, their racial make-up is primarily *vorderasiatisch* and *orientalisch*, with admixtures in varying degrees of *hamitisch* (East African), *nordisch*, *innerasiatisch*, *westisch* and *negerisch*, and, most of all, in the case of the majority Ashkenazim or Eastern Jews, who make up nine-tenths of the entire Jewish population, *ostbaltisch* (essentially Slavic, one of Günther's least favourite races) as well as *mongolisch* (thanks to the alleged mass conversion of the Chasars between the 8th and 11th centuries).[25]

It was this extreme racial impurity, Günther holds, that produced in the Jews a strong feeling of guilt and the idea of "original sin"—an idea utterly alien, in his view, to peoples who have remained more racially pure, such as the Germans—and that led the Jews later, in an effort to halt the process of racial disintegration, to impose severe strictures against marriage with non-Jews and thus to create a "second order race." This "second order race" regards all other races and peoples as alien and is in turn regarded as alien by all other races and peoples. The characteristics associated with Jews, moreover, are the inevitable consequence of their excessive racial mixing and their history of having to adapt to ever changing masters. To Oppenheim's colleague Ungnad, as we saw, the development of unattractive characteristics—"dissimulation, hypocrisy, avariciousness, and dishonesty"—is the unavoidable result of frequent mixing with peoples of different race and of having to adapt to life under masters of different race. To Günther,

---

24 Though of somewhat mixed race, like all peoples, according to Günther, the German people was predominantly *nordisch*, not *westisch*. The Bedouin would thus be racially related to those European peoples in whom the *westisch* (or Mediterranean) race dominates, rather than to the Germans.

25 *Rassenkunde des deutschen Volkes* (1922), Appendix on "Rassenkunde des jüdischen Volkes," p. 400; *Rassenkunde Europas*, 3rd edn (1929), p. 104.

this race-based incompatibility of the Jews with the peoples they live among is at the core of the "Jewish problem," and the only solution of that problem lies in a radical separation of the Jews from the ambient population. What underlies the "Jewish problem," in sum, is not that the Jews are a distinct and inferior race, but that they are so mixed racially as to constitute an alien, disturbing element in any community.

Max von Oppenheim did not wait until 1935–1936 to use the language of race in ways that were generally compatible with National Socialist practice. He had already asserted in the Tell Halaf book of 1931 not only that the Mitanni were an "Indo-Germanic" people, but following Ungnad—and Günther—that the Jews are a "*Mischvolk*" and he had contrasted them with the pure-race Bedouins.[26] That was already far less a way of defending the Jews—by making hostility to the "Semitic race" irrelevant as a basis for hostility toward Jews—than a way of degrading the Jews and justifying suspicion and dislike of them[27] while at the same time releasing the Bedouins, and by extension the other peoples of the Middle East, in whom Oppenheim goes to some pains to emphasize the "Indo-Germanic" component, from the obloquy of being placed in the same category (i.e. "Semites") as the Jews. Oppenheim's stance on race issues thus fits well with the role that he was to play, during the Second World War, in German

---

26 Max Freiherr von Oppenheim, *Der Tell Halaf: eine neue Kultur im ältesten Mesopotamien* (Leipzig: F.A. Brockhaus, 1931), p. 45 (on the Jews as a *Mischvolk*), p. 59 (on the Mitanni as *Indogermanen*). Likewise in the *Führer durch das Tell Halaf-Museum* [Guide to the Tell Halaf Museum], put out by the Max Freiherr von Oppenheim Stiftung in 1934, we learn that the Mitanni kings "stayed with their old Aryan divinities, Mitra, Varuna, Indra and Nasatya" (p. 19) and that "Fecherija-Waschkukani" was the capital of the "Aryan Mitanni" (p. 23).

27 In his celebrated 1927 biography, *Kaiser Friedrich der Zweite*, the Jewish scholar Ernst Kantorowicz had already popularized the notion of the inferiority of a *Mischvolk* when he contrasted the Sicilians—an "unzuverlässiges Mischvolk" (unreliable people of mixed race)—and the "verrasste Volk von Palermo" ("racially degenerate population of Palermo") with the "Gemeinschaft des Stammesblutes" (community of tribal blood) of the thirteenth-century Germans. (See Martin Ruehl, "'In this Time without Emperors': The Politics of Ernst Kantorowicz's *Kaiser Friedrich der Zweite* reconsidered," *Journal of the Warburg and Courtauld Institutes*, 63 [2002]: 187–242 [p. 203]). Placing a high value on racial purity was certainly not new in the 1920s and 1930s. In 1904 David George Hogarth, the teacher of "Lawrence of Arabia," had expressed admiration for the racial purity of the Arabs of the Arabian Peninsula: "The blood and the social life of this race, which all travellers who have seen it at its best assert to be physically the finest of the Caucasian type, owes to the natural barriers set about the 'Island of the Arabs' an immunity from alien contamination which those of no other race above the savage state have enjoyed" (*The Penetration of Arabia* [London: Lawrence and Bullen, 1904], pp. 7–8). Earlier still, none other than Benjamin Disraeli had declared that "an ummixed race [...] [is]the aristocracy of Nature" (see ch. 2, note 21 above).

negotiations with al-Husseini, the Mufti of Jerusalem, and other anti-Jewish Arab leaders, with the aim of engaging the Arabs on the side of National Socialist Germany and against "the British and the Jews." To these negotiations we shall address ourselves shortly. Our aim here has simply been to suggest that Oppenheim's interest in and stance on questions of race—above all his dismissive reference to the Jews as a *Mischvolk* and his emphasis on "Aryan" components in the racial make-up of the peoples of the Middle East—while certainly opportune, need not be considered a calculated "ploy," as his anti-Semitic colleagues charged, but rather reflects positions on the question of race that he had come to hold before the Nazis came to power in 1933 and that he had arrived at in the same way as many other German scholars.

It is also worth recalling that in his writings of the 1920s, when Ungnad and Oppenheim were reading him, even "Rassengünther," now rightly viewed as representing the nadir of Nazi racial pseudo-science, took what, in the light of the "final solution," might be regarded as the "moderate" Nazi position with respect to the "Jewish problem," a position many ordinary Germans who voted for the National Socialists appear to have found acceptable. That is, he advocated not the destruction of the Jewish people but its separation from its host people. He even saw a possibility of co-operation with Zionism in solving the "Jewish problem"[28] and expressed sympathy for those German Jews who had so identified with German culture and the interests of the German people [*"die sogar ausgesprochen vaterländisch-deutsch fühlen"*] that for them separation would cause great inner personal pain [*"eine seelische Qual"*]. He also proclaimed, in a seeming echo of Herder, that "every people living its own independent life has a unique, incomparable, and indestructible value," that "the habit of measuring peoples in order to determine which has the higher value is utterly senseless," and that, in short, "every people has its own particular value." Günther even claimed to see a valuable lesson for all races in the Jews' determined efforts to preserve their distinct identity, albeit now only as a "second order race"—the lesson, namely, that "the perfection of every breed lies in maintaining its isolation from other breeds" [*"in der Reinheit der Absonderung liegt die Vollkommenheit jeder Artung beschlossen"*].[29] Whether he was writing in good faith or not,

---

28 Otto Hauser, a popular writer of novels and poems as well as books on early history and race, had taken a similar position in his *Rasse und Rassefragen in Deutschland* (Weimar: Alexander Duncker, 1915), pp. 105–07.

29 *Rassenkunde des deutschen Volkes* [Munich: J.F. Lehmann's Verlag, 1922]; 3rd edn (1929), Appendix (pp. 367–434) on "Rassenkunde des jüdischen Volkes," pp. 433–34.

Günther clearly wished to convey an impression of reasonableness and to make it easy for others to embrace his views.

In sum, like many Germans (and by no means Germans only), Oppenheim was thinking in the racial categories that became essential to the program of the National Socialists *before* the latter came to power and he had already presented the Jews in an unfavourable light as a *Mischvolk*. That, it is surely unnecessary to emphasize, does not imply that he in any way advocated discrimination against Jews, much less persecution of them.

Support of the Regime

Of Max von Oppenheim's response to the rise of National Socialism and to Hitler's *Machtergreifung* in 1933 we have only a few indications. The letter of 1935 to Waldemar, in which he expresses the hope that by the time the 150th anniversary of the Oppenheim bank comes around in 1939 the "current unfriendliness with regard to the Jewish origins of the Oppenheims" will have subsided, has already been mentioned. Oppenheim's biographer Gabriele Teichmann relates an episode that occurred shortly after the *Machtergreifung*:

> While the new regime was celebrating its triumph with torchlight parades and songs at the Brandenburg Tor, Max von Oppenheim was sitting with two guests, Cornelius Vanderbilt Jr. of New York and his nephew Harold von Oppenheim, at a night spot not far off, when "some half-drunk men stormed into the place yelling 'Jews out!' The owner and the waiters calmed them down by assuring them that there were no Jews in the place. A little later they returned, whereupon one of the guests got up and went determinedly toward them. It almost came to a brawl. But then these people withdrew and did not come back."[30]

Teichmann is relying here on the *Lebenserinnerungen* or recollections written by Max von Oppenheim years later, after the fall of the Nazi regime. The brief quotation is likewise taken from this manuscript text in the Oppenheim archives. Cornelius Vanderbilt Jr., in contrast, gave a rather different

---

30 *Faszination Orient*, pp. 83–84. Harold von Oppenheim, the second of Simon Alfred von Oppenheim's four sons, was not exactly Max von Oppenheim's nephew, but rather the son of his cousin. However, in English too, the term "nephew" is sometimes used to describe the latter relationship. Max von Oppenheim had been well received by the upper crust of New York society on his visits (1902–1904, 1931–1932) to the United States, and his association with the Vanderbilts, including the much younger, somewhat rebellious and progressively minded Cornelius Vanderbilt Jr. (1898–1974), probably dates from the time of those visits. Cornelius Vanderbilt Jr. was a gifted newspaperman and a champion of F.D. Roosevelt.

account of this episode in a book published in English in the United States only two years after it took place. I quote the entire passage:

> I was tired of Nazi parades. In less than three days I had beheld twelve of them, each one "the biggest," "the most stupendous," "overwhelmingly inspiring," each one "symbolizing the revolt of Youth, the glory of a bloodless revolution, the proud awakening of the creative Nordic race." So, pleading a headache, I fought my way through the brown columns of roaring youngsters and rushed back to my hotel, just in time to receive messages, one from the Crown Prince, another from his son Prince Louis Ferdinand. The former was willing to grant me an interview in his Berlin palace at Number Thirty-Six Unter den Linden; the latter promised if I were in Holland to try to let me see his grandfather the Kaiser. I felt elated. No other journalist had succeeded in talking to the Hohenzollerns since the victory of Hitler brought them out of their retirement to the forefront of the European drama. I decided to celebrate.
>
> "Let's go and get a peek at the night life of this crazy city," I proposed to my friends; and off we went to a well-known cafe. We were five, four Americans and one German, an elderly Baron who used to occupy a high position at the Imperial Court in Potsdam. Outspoken in his praise of the Nazi regime, the Baron insisted on our drinking a toast to its chief.
>
> "Here is to the greatest of all living Europeans!" he began, rising to his feet and standing at attention.
>
> We stood up too. We expected to listen to a lengthy speech, the eloquence of the elegant Baron being favourably known to all his friends. Just then we heard a crash. It sounded like the detonation of a bomb, as if this garishly decorated cafe had been dynamited and wrecked. Turning toward the windows, we saw raised chairs, waving rifles, whirling nightsticks. A score of young Nazis – the eldest of them could not have been more than twenty–were jumping in through the smashed windows, firing at the ceiling, knocking down the tables, the bottles and the pinkish lamps.
>
> "Verfluchte Ausländer–"
>
> "Verfluchte Juden–"
>
> "Verfluchte Schieber–"
>
> "They are looking for foreigners, Jews and profiteers," obligingly translated the Baron, trying to force a smile. "Youth will be youth, don't you know____Look here, my friends–"
>
> His last four words were addressed (in German) to the advance guard of the youngsters who had by that time reached our table.
>
> "Get out of here, you dirty swine," was the curt answer.
>
> "But you don't quite understand, my friends–"
>
> They did not wish to understand, and they made this clear. When I saw the Baron next, the front of his shirt was red and his coat was tail-less. We were standing on the sidewalk, pleading with the Nazis to let us have our hats and overcoats.

"Outrageous–revolting–scandalous!" muttered the champion of Awakening Germany, wiping the Burgundy off his shirtfront. "I shall take it up immediately with Captain Goering and Admiral von Levetzov!"

Captain Goering—the all-powerful Minister without portfolio in Hitler's cabinet—was not available at the moment. He was riding at the head of the parade and was not expected back in his palace until dawn. We had to be satisfied with seeing Admiral von Levetzov, the then Chief of the Berlin police, at one time the leading naval hero of Germany. A very tall, bald-headed, handsome man, he received us with all the courtesy possible under the circumstances: he was sitting at his massive desk at headquarters, going over twenty-five hundred complaints registered that night by "foreigners, Jews and profiteers."

"I am awfully sorry, my dear Baron," he said with a sympathetic sigh, "but you really ought to know better than to patronize those contemptible night-clubs in this historical hour of our national existence!"

The Baron opened his mouth wide.

"I insist upon an apology, Admiral. My friends here have been manhandled by these roughnecks. Think of what they will tell their friends and relatives in America!"

"I would advise them"—the Admiral's face became stern and defiant—"to tell their friends and relatives in America that we, the Germans, refuse to forget our two million dead. That no one could blame our youth for reprimanding, perhaps a bit too energetically, the persons who dance and drink while we are fighting for our future."

"And how about our hats and overcoats, Admiral," I interrupted this strange explanation of the Police Commissioner.

"I shall see to it that your personal property is restored to you," he answered dryly.[31]

Twenty-four years later, in a book of recollections, *Man of the World. My Life on Five Continents*, Cornelius Vanderbilt Jr. gave a much briefer but essentially identical account of the episode. Here the "Baron" is identified as Oppenheim:

> Brodix [Vanderbilt's assistant and close friend] and I spent the night with an old friend, Baron Oppenheim, an "Aryan of honor." That evening in a café we were addressed as "foreign swine" by some juvenile delinquents calling themselves Hitler Youth and the baron's appeal to the police got nowhere.[32]

---

31 Cornelius Vanderbilt, Jr., *Farewell to Fifth Avenue* (New York: Simon and Schuster, 1935), pp. 178–81. It is unclear from either Teichmann's version of this episode or Vanderbilt's whether it took place at the time of Hitler's speech of 10 February 1933, at the Sportpalast, immediately after the *Machtergreifung* or somewhat later, at the time of his 8 April speech at the same place.

32 New York: Crown Publishers, 1959, p. 155. Vanderbilt's presenting the rumour that Oppenheim had been made an "honorary Aryan" by Hitler—a common type of

12. Max von Oppenheim, "Half-Jew," during the National Socialist Regime 225

Vanderbilt's immediately recorded account of this episode suggests that Oppenheim was—overtly at least—supportive of the new regime. After all, he was not obliged to praise Hitler and drink a toast to him in the company of Americans. It is quite possible that he intended, for opportunistic reasons, to give a public demonstration of his acceptance of the new regime. At the same time, however, like many other conservative nationalists, he may also have been not unfavourably disposed to National Socialism, being put off primarily, as was common among the old conservatives, by the vulgarity and rowdiness of the mass movement's supporters.[33] He himself admitted in his manuscript *Erinnerungen* that he "at first welcomed much in the actions of the Nazis, such as the combating of unemployment within Germany and the increasing respect won for the German Reich abroad." Though he does not mention it specifically, it is quite likely that he also shared the view, common among conservatives, that Hitler was the best bulwark against Bolshevism. He added, it is true, that he was horrified by "the inner core of Hitlerism, [...] the ever more savage and unrestrained actions taken against those who think differently and for themselves, against the Jews, against the Christian religion and in general against the individual's freedom of thought..."[34] These misgivings too were shared by

---

rumour, explicitly repudiated by Oppenheim in his manuscript *Lebenserinnerungen* (see Teichmann, *Faszination Orient*, p. 91)—as a fact here does not disqualify his earlier account of what he himself directly witnessed.

33   It should not be forgotten that there were many Jews, traditionally fervent supporters of the Italian state, to which they owed their emancipation, among the founders and strongest supporters of Italian fascism in the early years. Until the late introduction of anti-Semitic measures in 1938, "Jews were as likely to be members of the Fascist Party as other conservative-minded Italians" (Alexander Stille, *Benevolence and Betrayal: Five Jewish Families under Fascism* [New York: Farrar, Straus and Giroux, 1991], p. 12). Stille estimates that about a third of Italy's 50,000 Jews were members of the Italian Fascist Party. In England, "the columns of the *Jewish Chronicle* convey beyond doubt that at first established Jewry opposed Fascism not on principle, but only when alarmed by anti-Jewish innuendos." One member of Mosley's British Union of Fascists, who had stood for Parliament as a BUF candidate, resigned from the party in 1937 on the grounds that "anti-Jewish propaganda, as you [Mosley] and Hitler use it, is a gigantic sidetracking stunt, a smoke-screen to cloud thought and divert action with regard to our real problems" (Gisela C. Lebzelter, "Political Anti-Semitism in England 1918–1939," in Herbert A. Straus, ed., *Hostages of Modernization: Studies on Modern Anti-Semitism 1870–1933/39—Germany-Great Britain-France* [Berlin and New York: Walter de Gruyter, 1993], pp. 385–424 [pp. 418, 421–22]). Though this repudiation of anti-Semitism appears to have come from the "leftist" wing of British fascism, it suggests that conservative supporters of the NSDAP in Germany, on their side, might similarly have seen the Party's antiSemitic tirades and violence as not essential to what they understood its fundamental focus and purpose to be, and as likely to be allowed in time to fade into the background.

34   Cit. by Teichmann in *Faszination Orient*, p. 87.

many other traditionally conservative, nationalist, and patriotic Germans, who nevertheless continued to serve the Nazi regime faithfully and energetically even after it had embarked on aggressive military adventures of which, for practical reasons, they often did not approve—military men as well as diplomats like Secretary of State Ernst von Weizsäcker and Oppenheim's friend Werner Otto von Hentig. It may also not be irrelevant that the lines about "the inner core of Hitlerism" were penned not only after the National Socialist regime had grown ever more violent and repressive but after its catastrophic end, when it had become as politic to appear to have been opposed to it or at least to have had reservations about it as it had been politic before to appear to support it.[35]

There is no evidence that Oppenheim ever spoke or acted in a manner that might have been perceived as critical of the regime he later professed to have regarded with horror. As a "half-Jew," it would obviously have been extraordinarily dangerous for him to do so. Even the "internal exile" chosen by some was probably not an option for him. "Lying low" may not have been a possibility for a fairly prominent "Mischling ersten Grades." Perhaps only collaboration and public professions of support, such as the toast to Hitler recorded by Vanderbilt, could offer a shred of hope that a *Mischling* such as he might avoid trouble. Waldemar, as we saw, found some protection through participation in the *Abwehr*. Yet even he, though classified only as a "quarter-Jew," finally fell into the clutches of the Gestapo. In contrast, Max von Oppenheim appears not to have been molested at any time under the Nazis. In 1936 he was still playing elegant host at the Tell Halaf Museum, where the Australian archaeologist Marjorie Seton-Williams tells of being shown around by him, followed by a manservant who poured the pair a glass of wine every time they stopped to discuss one of the items on display.[36] On 29 January 1937, in recognition of his services to the national cause during the First World War, he was awarded the *Ehrenkreuz für Frontkämpfer* [Medal of Honour for frontline soldiers] "in the name of the Führer and Reichskanzler."[37]

---

35 Weizsäcker's Memoirs, written after the War and published in 1950 (English translation, 1951), are an example of such a shift in emphasis.
36 M.V. Seton-Williams, *The Road to El-Aguizein* (London: Kegan Paul International, 1988), pp. 71–72.
37 Sean McMeekin, *The Berlin-Baghdad Express* (Cambridge MA: Harvard University Press, 2010), p. 360, citing Oppenheim's memoir "Leben im N-S Staat. 1933–1945" and referring to a copy of the Ehrenkreuz award in the Oppenheim Stiftung archives in Cologne (p. 411, note 54). It needs to be emphasized, however, that the significance of this award is difficult to assess in Oppenheim's case. Though it was the first decoration issued by

12. Max von Oppenheim, "Half-Jew," during the National Socialist Regime 227

Most telling perhaps are the regular visits he received in 1942 and 1943, before he was bombed out of his elegant Savigny-Platz residence in late August 1943, from the diplomat Curt Prüfer. Oppenheim had mentored Prüfer in pre-World War I days in Cairo, when Prüfer, a student of Arabic and Middle Eastern culture with a fairly recent doctorate (1906) from Erlangen, had been Dragoman or interpreter at the German Agency in the Egyptian capital.[38] Based on their shared interest in the Middle East and their conservative and nationalist politics, a friendship had formed at the time between the older man and the younger, who subsequently went on to enjoy a successful career at the *Auswärtiges Amt* (A.A.) during the Weimar Republic, notwithstanding his contempt for the Republic, and who, having joined the NSDAP in 1937, had risen, under the Nazis, to be Director of the *A.A.*'s Personnel Division—in which capacity, according to a senior colleague at the *A.A.*, he saw to it that "there was an ever decreasing power of resistance to the Party"[39]—and then Ambassador to Brazil. On his return to Berlin from Brazil, after that country declared war on Germany in late 1942, Prüfer took to visiting and having lunch with "Onkel Max," as he referred affectionately to his former mentor, with some regularity—once or twice a month. As was often the case in conservative milieux, Prüfer's apparently deeply ingrained anti-Semitism did not prevent him from making exceptions in individual cases—or, for that matter, from being disturbed by increasingly credible accounts of mass deportations and executions of Jews. Oppenheim, moreover, had the advantage of being only half Jewish.[40]

---

the Third Reich, it was Hindenburg's creation, not Hitler's, and it was awarded to several millions of German World War I veterans.

38 Donald McKale, *Curt Prüfer, German Diplomat from the Kaiser to Hitler* (Kent, OH: Kent State University Press, 1987), pp. 15–16, 197 (Ch. 2, note 10). Prüfer was one of the contributors to the Oppenheim Festschrift in 1933 (see note 3 above).

39 Ulrich von Hassel, *Römische Tagebücher und Briefe 1932–1938*, ed. Ulrich Schlie (Munich: Herbig, 2004), p. 157.

40 On Prüfer's anti-Semitism, see Donald McKale, *Curt Prüfer*, pp. xii, 59–61 *et passim*; the same author's *Rewriting History. The Original and Revised World War II Diaries of Curt Prüfer, Nazi Diplomat*, trans. Judith M. Melton (Kent, OH: Kent State University Press, 1988), pp. xvi-xix; and Sean McMeekin, *The Berlin-Baghdad Express,* pp. 358–59. Prüfer did, however, note in his diary for 12 October 1942 that "yesterday, on the journey through Spain, I heard for the first time, from the mouth of a German, albeit that of an SS-man, about the mass deportation of Jews. He spoke of it quite casually and coldly. To be sure, rumours of these deportations had reached us from Germany along with reports of them from hostile sources, but they seemed so monstrous to us that we took them to be 'horror stories' or at least vastly exaggerated, like so many other items of news spread

Prüfer's diary entries for the period 1942–1943 suggest that "Onkel Max," though showing signs of age, was otherwise living a perfectly normal life. Thus for 21 November 1942, Prüfer wrote in his diary: "Lunch at Uncle Max's; a jocose and very lively skeleton. Extremely interested in all questions regarding the Orient, drinks wine, schnapps, coffee, and smokes despite his 82 years and bladder and prostate irritations." For 12 January 1943: "Had lunch with Uncle Max. The conversation was the same as 30 years ago. But notwithstanding a certain dusty atmosphere, these visits still have a beautiful nostalgic sheen for me." Ten days later: "I visited Max for lunch. *Poor old man! He is, after all, a good soul*" [in English in the text; perhaps a reference to *King Lear* II. iv]. On 2 March 1943: "I had lunch with Uncle Max, who was, as always, serene. In his old age he is becoming calm and cheerful." However, on 7 July 1943, when he and Baron Herbert von Richthofen, another *Auswärtiges Amt* regular, deputy head of its Oriental (i.e. Middle Eastern) Division in the 1920s and subsequently ambassador to Belgium (1936–1939),[41] had lunch together at "Uncle Max"'s, he learned some bad news. The latter's "nephew" [i.e. Waldemar] had "reported terrible tales from Cologne," namely that "the downtown area is almost

---

by enemy propaganda that had turned out to be incorrect. This unfavorable impression was reinforced in the further course of the journey. The gentlemen from the *Auswärtiges Amt* and the NSDAP who had been sent out to meet us spoke among themselves, in completely casual tones, of things that sounded so improbable that we would not have believed them had any traveller recounted them." On 22 November, after many conversations in Berlin with fellow-diplomats and military men, Prüfer again noted in his diary, in French this time: "On m'a raconté ce matin des histoires affreuses sur le traitement des Persans [i.e. the Jews]. Ils ont été massacrés hommes, femmes et enfants en grand nombre par des gaz asphyxiants ou par la mitrailleuse." Prüfer's apparent shock at learning of these acts of barbarism was intensified by the realization that "Dies weiss jedes Kind in allen Details" ["Every child knows about this in full detail"]. It is also tinged with fear of the ultimate consequences: "La haine qui, forcément, doit en surgir ne sera jamais éteinte" ["The hatred that must necessarily be born of this will never be extinguished"]. (Both diary entries cited in Hans-Jürgen Döscher, *Das Auswärtige Amt im Dritten Reich. Diplomatie im Schatten der 'Endlösung'* [Berlin: Siedler Verlag, 1987], p. 253; the 22 November diary entry is also to be found in McKales' *Rewriting History*, p. 11. Oppenheim, it needs to be emphasized, however, was not a "converted Jew," as McKale erroneously states.)

41 Richthofen, from a distinguished aristocratic family, had probably first got to know Oppenheim and Prüfer while employed at the German Consulate-General in Cairo from 1911 until the outbreak of war. He was deputy head of the *Auswärtiges Amt*'s Middle Eastern Division in the 1920s (see William Cleveland, *Islam against the West: Shakib Arslan and the Campaign for Islamic Nationalism* [Austin: University of Texas Press, 1985], Ch. 7, note 11, pp. 199–200), then ambassador to Denmark (1930–1936), to Belgium (1936–1939), and to Bulgaria (1939–1941). In 1945 he was arrested by the Red Army and in 1951 sentenced by a Soviet court to twenty-five years in prison for "preparing and leading a war of aggression." He died in the Lubyanka Prison in Moscow in 1952.

completely destroyed," while "fatalities are pegged at 20,000, those rendered homeless at 100,000." Still, on 14 July, Prüfer helped "Uncle Max" celebrate his upcoming 83rd birthday.

Meantime Prüfer was approaching retirement and had obtained permission to take a leave, for health reasons, with his family in Switzerland. Not, however, before a "parting visit with Uncle Max" on 30 July 1943. This time he found his old companion-in-arms "very depressed" because of the parting, perhaps, but also, it is not unreasonable to surmise, because—with the devastating bombings of German cities and the encirclement and destruction of the 6th Army at Stalingrad—it had became apparent that the tide of the war had turned very unfavourably for Germany. Defeat now seemed by no means improbable, unless a change of leadership could be effected that would make peace negotiations possible. (This bleak prospect may well have been an additional—perhaps the main—reason for Prüfer's having requested permission to go to Switzerland.) As Prüfer himself had noted in his diary a few days before (26 July 1943), "Mussolini has abdicated. Fascism is done for. The King has taken over the high command, Badoglio is head of the government. [...] M's decision to resign, if it was done voluntarily, was a great and noble deed. Can we summon similar courage?"[42]

---

42 Diary entries in McKale, *Rewriting History. The Original and Revised World War II Diaries of Curt Prüfer*, pp. 10, 33, 41, 107, 111, 118, 119.

13. Plotting for Nazi Germany
Oppenheim's Role in the Middle East Policy of the Third Reich

One topic of conversation between Prüfer and his old mentor at these lunches was assuredly familiar to both of them from their years together in Cairo just before World War I; for both were once again engaged in plots, this time involving Arab leaders and Nazi officials, to stir up trouble for the British in the Middle East. Prüfer, hardly back from Brazil, had just replaced another *Auswärtiges Amt* associate of Oppenheim's, Fritz Grobba, as the *Amt*'s man in charge of German relations with the Arabs and his visits to Oppenheim were almost certainly inspired, at least in part, by a desire to benefit from the old man's experience. As for Oppenheim himself, while most of his Jewish Orientalist colleagues—and some non-Jewish ones—had emigrated,[1] he seems to have thought of himself as a patriotic German who, since before World War I, had consistently placed his expertise and his many connections in the Islamic world at the service of his country. Now in his early 80s, he had been retired for many years from the *Auswärtiges Amt*, by which he had once been employed (albeit always, as we saw, in some special capacity, never as a regular career diplomat), but he had apparently not severed his links with it or with colleagues still on active duty in it. Thus from 1926 on he had made a practice of sending the Oriental Section at the *Auswärtiges Amt* copies of all the communications he received from Shakib Arslan, the Geneva-based Lebanese Druze and champion of Islamic unity and independence, with whom he had worked during World War I and who thought of Oppenheim as his "très cher

---

1 See Ludmila Hanisch, *Die Nachfolger der Exegeten. Deutschsprachige Erforschung des Vorderen Orients in der ersten Hälfte des 20. Jahrhunderts*.

http://dx.doi.org/10.11647/OBP.0030.13

ami et frère."[2] Moreover, he appears to have promoted a direct exchange of letters between Arslan and von Richthofen, the deputy head of the Oriental Section, and to have consulted with the latter before himself replying to Arslan.[3]

There is in fact every reason to believe that Oppenheim was later quite actively involved in relations and negotiations between officials of the Third Reich and the leaders of the pro-Axis Arab independence and unity movements. Among the former, he knew the career diplomats von Richthofen (1879–1952), Prüfer (1881–1959), Grobba (1880–1973), and the latter's rival at the *Auswärtiges Amt* Werner Otto von Hentig (1886–1984), from having served like them in the Middle East before and during the First World War. Von Richthofen had been Third Secretary at the German Consulate-General in Cairo from 1911 until 1914; Prüfer, as we saw, had also been posted to Cairo in the years before World War I and then saw service in Constantinople, where he almost certainly met up again with Oppenheim; Grobba had occupied a position similar to Prüfer's in Jerusalem and the two men had come to know each other well;[4] and von

---

2 William L. Cleveland, *Islam against the West: Shakib Arslan and the Campaign for Islamic Nationalism*, pp. 140, 141. See also Chantal Metzger, *L'Empire colonial français dans la stratégie du Troisième Reich (1936–1945)*, vol. 1, p. 582, note 2; p. 598, no. 3. On Arslan, see Martin Kramer's review of Cleveland: www.geocities.com/martinkramerorg/Arslan.htm, and Jakob Kreis, "Shakib Arslan's Libyan Dilemma," in *Rethinking Totalitarianism and its Arab Readings* (Proceedings of the Conference "European Totalitarianism in the Mirrors of Contemporary Arab Thought" [Beirut, 6–8 October 2010]), http://www.perspectivia.net/content/publikationen/orient-institut-studies/1–2012.
3 William L. Cleveland, *Islam against the West*, Ch. 7, note 17, p. 200: "Von Oppenheim began one of his covering notes to his *Auswärtiges Amt* contact of the time, von Richthofen, with the words: 'As agreed, I am sending you Amir Shakib Arslan's latest letter with my request for a response so that I can write to him myself'" (14 December 1928). In her extremely well researched study, *L'Empire colonial français dans la stratégie du Troisième Reich (1936–1945)*, Chantal Metzger goes so far as to describe Oppenheim as the animating spirit of the "Section Proche Orient-Afrique du Nord de *l'Auswärtiges Amt*." After Germany's defeat in World War I, she claims, "the baron set up a network of like-minded people. He was able to surround himself with diplomats of caliber and his team was active on the margins of the *Auswärtiges Amt* and the *Abwehr*. He enjoyed good relations with Admiral Canaris and co-operated with the *Sicherheitsdienst*. Two diplomats in his team stand out: Fritz Grobba and Werner-Otto Hentig" (vol. 1, p. 174). Shakib Arslan continued to communicate with Oppenheim through the Second World War, confiding his views to him in 1942 on the growing rivalry between Amin al-Husseini, the Mufti of Jerusalem, and Rashid-Ali al-Gailani, the former Premier of Iraq, for leadership of the Arab movement in support of Germany and against colonial rule in the Middle East. (See Berndt Philipp Schröder, *Deutschland und der Mittlere Osten im Zweiten Weltkrieg* [Göttingen: Musterschmidt, 1975], pp. 224–28).
4 Rivalry and disagreement with al-Gailani (*Akten der deutschen auswärtigen Politik 1918–1945*, Serie E [Göttingen: Vandenhoeck & Ruprecht, 1969], vol. 1, document 175

Hentig, having already been assigned to the German embassies in Teheran and Constantinople, where for a time he and Prüfer lodged together,[5] had shared with Oskar Niedermayer the leadership of a famous mission to Afghanistan shortly after the outbreak of World War I, the object of which was to bring Afghanistan into the War on the side of the Central Powers and arouse the Indians to rebel against the British. Oppenheim, it will be remembered, had recommended Niedermayer for this mission. If Prüfer referred to Oppenheim as "Onkel Max," Hentig wrote of him no less affectionately as "mein alter Freund 'Maxbaron' Oppenheim."[6]

Among the Arab leaders, Oppenheim, as noted, was a longtime friend of Shakib Arslan, who in turn had been an advocate of co-operation between proponents of Islamic unity and Germany since the turn of the century.[7] Arslan had stood at the Kaiser's side when the latter made his celebrated proclamation in Damascus in 1898,[8] had lived in Berlin in the last years of the First World War and again at various periods in the 1920s during his long years of exile from Syria (mostly spent in Geneva), and had been one of the first to seek direct contact with the Nazis after they came to

---

[27 January 1942] pp. 310–11; vol. 4 [1975], document 166 [12 November 1942], pp. 289–90) led al-Husseini to complain repeatedly to Secretary of State von Weizsäcker that Grobba was unreliable, sided with al-Gailani, and was more interested in the independence of Iraq than in that of the other Arab states (ibid., vol. 2 [1972], document 281 [10 June 1942], note by Weizsäcker, pp. 479–80). These complaints resulted in Grobba's being dismissed from his post as head of the Middle East Section of the *Auswärtiges Amt* and replaced by Prüfer. Nevertheless, even after this the two German Middle East experts remained on seemingly friendly terms. Grobba wrote Prüfer addressing him as "Lieber Prüfer," and accompanying his best wishes for a Happy New Year with "herzlichen Grüssen von Haus zu Haus" [warmest greeting from my family to yours] (ibid., vol. 4, document 321 [28 December 1942], pp. 596–97). Prüfer, however, seems not to have had a high opinion of Grobba. He describes him as an intriguing "fishwife," "absolutely unreasonable," and "incapable of seeing the forest for the trees," because he was so "blinded by vanity and ambition" that "he can no longer see that we are supposed to make German policy as a whole" (McKale, *Rewriting History. The Original and Revised World War II Diaries of Curt Prüfer*, 12 November, 20 November, and 23 November, pp. 5–6, 10, 11–12). On the rivalry of Grobba and von Hentig, which appears to have been based on personal antipathy and social background as well as different views of policy in the Middle East, see Helmut Mejcher, "Hitler's Route to Baghdad?" in Haim Goren, ed., *Germany and the Middle East, Past, Present, and Future* (Jerusalem: Hebrew University Magnes Press, 2003), pp. 71–83 (pp. 77–79).

5 Werner Otto von Hentig, *Mein Leben: Eine Dienstreise* (Göttingen: Vandenhoeck & Ruprecht, 1962), p. 202.
6 Ibid., pp. 193, 329.
7 Cleveland, *Islam against the West: Shakib Arslan and the Campaign for Islamic Nationalism* pp. 139–49.
8 Ibid., p. 141 and Ch. 7, note 18 (p. 200).

power. In late 1934 he had written to Prüfer presenting the advantage to Berlin of a German commitment to the Muslims in what he claimed was the highly likely eventuality of a new war between France and Germany and suggesting that a meeting be arranged for him with officials of the German government in Berlin—a proposal to which Prüfer responded negatively, deeming it, in accordance with Nazi foreign policy at the time, dangerous and impractical.[9] Oppenheim also quickly got to know the two most active advocates of the Arab cause in Rome and Berlin during World War II: Haj Amin al-Husseini, the fiercely anti-British, anti-Zionist (and anti-Jewish) Grand Mufti of Jerusalem, who had fomented both the Arab riots of 1929 in Palestine and the major revolt that broke out in 1936, and Rashid Ali al-Gailani, a no less strongly anti-British former Prime Minister of Iraq and leading figure in the Arab independence movement. To escape imprisonment by the British, al-Husseini had had to flee in October 1937 first to French-held Lebanon, then to Iraq, where he was welcomed as a hero and courted, on account of his enormous prestige, popularity, and influence, even by the ostensibly pro-British Prime Minister Nuri al-Said. Abetted by al-Husseini, encouraged by Grobba, then German ambassador to Iraq, and counting on aid from Germany, al-Gailani led a 1941 coup that overthrew Nuri al-Said and the pro-British Regent Abdul-Ilah. Having once again become Prime Minister, he ordered the Iraqi army to attack the British air base at Habbaniya, only to be almost immediately ousted in turn by an invading British force and obliged to seek refuge, along with al-Husseini, first in Teheran and then (when Iran was in turn occupied soon after by the British and the Russians) in the capitals of the Axis powers. Strongly in sympathy in any case with the ideologies of the Fascists and National Socialists and, in al-Husseini's case especially, with the violent anti-Jewish policies of the latter, the two leaders eagerly threw in their lot with the Axis and tried to tie the Arab and Islamic cause to that of Berlin and, to a lesser extent, Rome.[10]

---

9 Ibid., p. 142. Sensing that his man would not take no for an answer, Prüfer even took the trouble to warn his colleagues at the A.A. "against the reception of Arslan by leading government personalities" (ibid.).

10 Not coincidentally perhaps, the failure of al-Gailani's coup, was immediately followed in Baghdad, in the power vacuum before the arrival of British troops, by an anti-Jewish *farhud* or pogrom in which—according to the report of an official Iraqi investigation commission appointed by the new government of Jamil al-Mifdai—110 Jews were killed, many wounded, and over 900 Jewish homes destroyed (B. Schechtman, *The Mufti and the Fuehrer: The Rise and Fall of Haj Amin el-Husseini* [New York and London: Thomas Yoseloff, 1965], pp. 114–15). The 1941 *farhud* marked the beginning of the end of the large and ancient Jewish community in Iraq.

That was not as easy as one might have thought. There is general agreement among most historians that on the Arab side National Socialist Germany was much admired. (Fascist Italy considerably less so—despite al-Husseini's high regard for Mussolini and the latter's proclaiming himself the Protector of Islam[11]—on account of Italy's conquest and colonial occupation of Libya and brutal suppression of revolts in that country.) But there is equally general agreement that Hitler, for various reasons, dragged his feet in the matter of collaboration with the Arab independence movement, or with any other independence movement of colonial peoples. From his racist perspective, the Arabs were alien and inferior, like the Jews. "In contrast to hopes in Imperial Germany for aid from the Arabs in World War I," one scholar writes, referring to and citing *Mein Kampf*, "Hitler harbored no hopes for 'any mythical uprising in Egypt.' [...] English machine guns and fragmentation bombs would bring such a holy war 'to an infernal end.' It was [...] 'impossible to overwhelm with a coalition of cripples a powerful state that is determined to stake, if necessary, its last drop of blood for its existence. As a *völkish* man, who appraises the value of men on a racial basis, I am prevented by mere knowledge of the racial inferiority of these so-called oppressed nations from linking the destiny of my own people with theirs.'"[12]

Hitler, according to Hans-Ulrich Seidt,

> was not interested in collaborating with the colonial peoples oppressed and exploited by the British. He had a very clear recollection of the years 1920–1921, when his party was beginning to gain a footing politically in Munich. At that time there was talk in nationalist circles in the Bavarian capital of the NSDAP's forming an alliance, as the "freedom movement of the German nation," with all "oppressed nations." Various Egyptians and Indians were introduced to Hitler; they impressed him as "pompous asses full of verbiage but devoid of any solid foundation in reality." He was irritated that even in the nationalist camp there were Germans "who let themselves be taken in by Orientals with such an inflated sense of their own importance." For that reason he took a firm stand early on,

---

11 Schechtman, *The Mufti and the Fuehrer*, pp. 77, 119. In March 1937, Mussolini had opportunistically proclaimed himself "Protector of Islam" after a state visit to Libya (invaded by Italy in 1911–1912 and completely occupied in the course of the 1920s) and the brutal suppression of resistance to Italian rule that culminated in the execution of the Senussi rebel leader, Omar al-Mukhtar. Italy simultaneously began a propaganda campaign designed to pacify Muslim sentiment around the Mediterranean and deflect anti-colonial feelings toward the British and the French.

12 Jeffrey Herf, *Nazi Propaganda for the Arab World* (New Haven and London: Yale University Press, 2009), pp. 15–16.

in Munich, against his party's entering into political relationships with representatives of oppressed colonial peoples. "I have always resisted any such engagements. Not simply because I have better things to do than to waste weeks in such fruitless palavers. Even if one were to be dealing with authentic, authorised representatives of such nations, I considered the whole business unsuitable, indeed quite harmful."[13]

Consistently with this position, Hitler expressed no interest in collaboration with Indians working to free their country from the British and no confidence that a "coloured" people could ever overcome its superior white Northern masters. On the contrary, he often expressed admiration for the achievement of a small "Germanic" people, such as the British, in conquering and establishing its rule over large non-European territories and populations.

A second impediment to Hitler's responding positively to the overtures of Arab leaders, notably al-Husseini and al-Gailani, was in fact his enduring hope of working out an arrangement with the British, whereby in return for his being given a free hand in Europe, he would respect and uphold the integrity of the British Empire.[14] There was, in addition, much doubt about the readiness and capacity of the Arabs to

---

13   Cit. Hans-Ulrich Seidt, *Berlin Kabul Moskau: Oskar Ritter von Niedermayer und Deutschlands Geopolitik*, pp. 220–21. See also Francis R. Nicosia, *The Third Reich and the Palestine Question* (Austin, TX: University of Texas Press, 1985), pp. 82–84.
14   As late as 19 May 1941, after Hess's surprise landing in Scotland, Secretary of State von Weizsäcker noted: "I have always had the impression that the Führer was interested in reaching a compromise agreement with England, one that would leave the British Empire intact while England accepted that it would have no say in matters concerning the Continent. Hess must have been obsessed by this idea" (*Die Weizsäcker-Papiere 1933–1950*, ed. Leonidas E. Hill [Frankfurt, Berlin and Vienna: Propyläen-Ullstein Verlag, 1974], p. 255). Only a few days earlier Ribbentrop had told John C. Cudahy, the U.S. Ambassador to Poland before the war and to Belgium between 1939 and 1940, that the obstinate resistance of the British was "for the Führer a great tragedy, for he, who wanted at heart to be a friend of England, had been chosen by fate to break the great Empire. In his efforts to create a good relationship with England, the Führer had accepted [...] a limitation of the German fleet at thirty-five percent of the English fleet, and had, finally, wanted to make available to England twelve German divisions for all eventualities; i.e. he had been willing to guarantee the British Empire with German blood. In return, England should only have recognized Germany as the dominant power in Europe" (*Documents on German Foreign Policy* [Washington, D.C.: Government Printing Office, 1969], series D, vol. 12, p. 708, document 451, [5 May 1941]). See also on Hitler's interest in an agreement with Great Brtain Lukasz Hirszowicz, *The Third Reich and the Arab East* (London: Routledge & Kegan Paul; Toronto: University of Toronto Press, 1966), pp. 38–39; Francis R. Nicosia, *The Third Reich and the Palestine Question*, pp. 72–76; Stefan Wild, "National Socialism in the Arab Near East between 1933 and 1939," *Die Welt des Islams*, new series 25 (1985): 126–73 (pp. 143–45).

engage in military action. In a memorandum of 29 July 1937, entitled "The Palestine Question," von Hentig had noted that the only strong protests against the partition of Palestine recommended by the Peel Commission had come from the Mufti, al-Husseini, and from the Iraqi government. All the other Arab and Muslim countries, though opposed to "permitting the Jewish state to come into being," were "not in the least inclined to quarrel with England over this question." Two weeks later a document on the same topic, prepared at Secretary of State von Weizsäcker's request, stated that "in view of the development of Anglo-German relations, a decision to support the Arab world with money and arms is out of the question." An additional memorandum instructed German missions abroad, in diplomatic steps connected with Palestine, to take care that the Reich's "relations with England should under no circumstances be placed under unnecessary strain" and to keep in mind "the notorious political unreliability of the Arabs."[15]

A lucid summary of Hitler's position in Middle East politics is provided by the historian Francis Nicosia, who sees it as adapting, but not essentially diverging from, that of Weimar:

> The most comprehensive account of Weimar policy in the region was to be provided by Moritz Sobernheim, head of the Jewish affairs section of the German foreign office. In a lengthy report on a visit to Palestine in the spring of 1925, he set out as Germany's primary goal the restoration of her great power position in Europe and the world, and as her regional goal the restoration of a strong political, economic, and cultural presence. He also outlined as one means to those ends, full German acceptance of the *status quo* in the Middle East. According to Sobernheim, this included first and foremost recognition of Great Britain's pre-eminence in the region, support for the Jewish National Home in Palestine, and rejection of Arab demands for independence.
>
> The National Socialist assumption of power in January 1933 did not alter the foundations of German Middle East policy established during the Weimar period. Although the domestic and foreign policy objectives of the new regime changed radically, it maintained the same approach to the Middle East for the rest of the decade. Great Britain continued to be the most critical factor affecting the formulation of German foreign policy. At least since 1923, Hitler had believed some form of Anglo-German understanding, preferably an alliance, to be an essential preparation for the conquest of *Lebensraum* in Central and Eastern Europe. Such an understanding would include full German support for Great Britain's

---

15 Documents cited in Schechtman, *The Mufti and the Fuehrer*, p. 78.

imperial interests throughout the world, and preclude any support for the independence movements that were becoming more and more troublesome to Great Britain during the 1930s. Hitler's *Englandpolitik* was also fully in keeping with his racial *Weltanschauung* and the tenets of National Socialism, which could only conceive of a world perpetually under white European domination, and which precluded any form of German support for colonial peoples against the racially superior, Germanic, Anglo-Saxons.[16]

The strategic and racial requirements of the Hitler regime in the pursuit of its *Englandpolitik*, in short, precluded support for Arab nationalist movements in the Middle East. Arab efforts to enlist German support against the Anglo-French presence in the Middle East were firmly rebuffed, and German political and economic aims in the Middle East were pursued, as they had been during the Weimar period, without any attempt to undermine Great Britain's position in the area. Finally, the German position on Zionism and the Palestine question after 1933 remained the same as before, albeit for different reasons. With the goal of rapidly removing the Jewish population from Germany, the Hitler regime for a time supported both Zionist emigration to Palestine and the continued development of the Jewish National Home embodied in the Balfour Declaration and incorporated into Great Britain's Palestine Mandate. However, the regime also remained firmly opposed to the establishment of an independent Jewish state in Palestine, as recommended by the Peel Commission in its partition plan of July 1937. In addition to traditional anti-Semitic myths of an international Jewish conspiracy, which would thus allegedly acquire an independent power base in Palestine, the German government also feared an addition to the growing coalition of states hostile to the new Germany.[17] Its position

---

16 Francis R. Nicosia, "Fritz Grobba and the Middle East Policy of the Third Reich," in Edward Ingram, ed., *National and International Politics in the Middle East: Essays in Honour of Elie Kadourie* (London: Frank Cass, 1986), pp. 206–28 (pp. 207–08). On Moritz Sobernheim (a Jewish scholar of Islam), the immediate German response to the Balfour Declaration, and German-Jewish and German-Zionist relations from the end of World War I until 1933, see Francis R. Nicosia, "Jewish Affairs and German Foreign Policy During the Weimar Republic. Moritz Sobernheim and the Referat für jüdische Angelegenheiten," *Leo Baeck Society Yearbook*, 1988, pp. 261–83.

17 In addition to the Nicosia article of 1986 referred to in the previous note, see Lukasz Hirszowicz, *The Third Reich and the Arab East*, pp. 26–42; Andreas Hillgruber, "The Third Reich and the Near and Middle East 1933–1939," in Uriel Dann, ed., *The Great Powers in the Middle East* (New York and London: Holmes & Meier, 1988), pp. 274–82; Bernard Lewis, *Semites and Anti-Semites* (New York and London: W.W. Norton, 1986), Chapter 6: "The Nazis and the Palestine Question" (pp. 140–63). On debates, within the German leadership, about the ha'avara agreement (allowing emigrant German Jews to export capital to Palestine in the form of imports of German goods into the Mandate

was thus not markedly different from that of the British government, which, with the publication of the report of the Woodhead Commission in 1938, had declared partition impractical.

Finally, even after the outbreak of war led to the abandonment of hope for a British-German understanding, a corresponding modification of the Arab policy of the Third Reich, and greater (but always cautious and, in the view of the Arab leaders, insufficient) willingness to embrace the cause of Arab independence, Hitler continued to hold back in deference to the interests of his Italian ally as well as those of Vichy France, of which he hoped to make an ally. There was also good reason to avoid giving offence, as encouragement of Arab unrest might well have done, to Spain and Turkey.[18] To repeated calls by both al-Gailani and the Mufti, Amin al-Husseini, for a strong public declaration of Axis support for the independence of the Arab states and of opposition to the Jewish National Home in Palestine, Hitler responded at a meeting with al-Husseini in Berlin on 28 November 1941 that public declarations were useless when not backed up by armed force and that a declaration of support for Arab independence by Germany was especially inopportune at that particular

---

territory) and on Palestine as an appropriate destination for Jewish emigrants, see Hans Adolf Jacobsen, *Nationalsozialistische Aussenpolitik 1933–1938* (Frankfurt a. M. and Berlin: Alfred Metzner, 1968), pp. 156–57; R. Melka, "Nazi Germany and the Palestine Question," *Middle Eastern Studies*, 5 (1969): 221–33; Lukasz Hirszowicz, *The Third Reich and the Arab East*, pp. 29–33; Francis Nicosia, *The Third Reich and the Palestine Question*, pp. 112–23, 126–44, 151–59 *et passim*. To those most eager to rid Germany of its Jews, such as many in the SS, as well as to others who, for humanitarian reasons, wanted to help Jews to emigrate, Palestine seemed to offer the most convenient and practical solution to the "Jewish problem." Others, however, feared the creation in Palestine of a new anti-German centre of Jewish power and insisted on dispersal of the Jews.

18 Hirszowicz, *The Third Reich and the Arab East*, pp. 86–92; Heinz Tillmann, *Deutschlands Araberpolitik im Zweiten Weltkrieg* (Berlin: VEB Deutscher Verlag der Wissenschaften, 1965), pp. 161, 165–66; Martin Kolinsky, *Britain's War in the Middle East: Strategy and Diplomacy, 1936–42* (Basingstoke and London: Macmillan, 1999), pp. 153–55. On 26 December 1941, Under-Secretary for Foreign Affairs Woermann reiterated that "we have always been extremely careful to distinguish between the Arabs of the Near East and the Arabs of North Africa. Our Arab policy does not apply west of Egypt. And in view of our policy in relation to France, Italy, and Spain, we have no interest in encouraging Arab nationalism in North Africa." For this reason, Woermann did not favor Husseini's proposal, supported by Oppenheim and Grobba, that a special "Arab League" be set up, recruited from volunteers and prisoners of war (i.e. from French North Africa) to fight for Germany (*Akten der deutschen auswärtigen Politik 1918–1945* [Göttingen: Vandenhoek & Ruprecht, 1969], series E, vol. 1, pp. 99–100, document 59). Following Hitler himself in his conversation with the Mufti, Woermann also warned on 28 February 1942, that in view of German-French relations the issuing of any declaration about the independence of Arab lands was inopportune (ibid., p. 100, note 2).

moment, since it would alienate the French, and thus make it necessary to tie up in the West forces needed for the crucial war in the East. According to a memorandum drafted by an official of the *Auswärtiges Amt*, Hitler gave the following explanation to the Mufti at their meeting:

> Germany stood for uncompromising war against the Jews. That naturally included active opposition to the Jewish National Home in Palestine, which was nothing other than a center, in the form of a state, for the exercise of destructive influence by Jewish interests. [...] Germany was at the present time engaged in a life and death struggle with two citadels of Jewish power: Great Britain and the Soviet Union. [...] This was the decisive struggle; on the political plane, it presented itself as a conflict between Germany and England, but ideologically it was a battle between National Socialism and the Jews. It went without saying that Germany would furnish positive and practical aid to the Arabs involved in the same struggle, because platonic promises were useless in a war for survival or destruction, in which the Jews were able to mobilize all of England's power for their own ends.
>
> The aid to the Arabs would have to be material aid. Of how little help sympathies alone were in such a battle had been demonstrated plainly by the operation in Iraq [i.e. al-Gailani's coup d'état and the attack on the British base at Habbaniya in April, 1941], where circumstances had not permitted the rendering of really effective, practical aid. In spite of all the sympathies, German aid had not been sufficient and Iraq was overcome by the power of Britain, that is, the guardian of the Jews. [...]
>
> The Führer therefore had to think and speak coolly and deliberately, as a rational man and primarily as a soldier, as the leader of the German and allied armies. Everything of a nature to help in this titanic battle for the common cause, and thus also for the Arabs, would have to be done. Anything, however, that might contribute to weakening the military situation must be put aside, no matter how unpopular the move might be.
>
> Germany was now engaged in very severe battles to force the gateway to the northern Caucasus region. [...] If, at such a moment, the Führer were to raise the problem of Syria in a declaration, those elements in France which were under de Gaulle's influence would receive new strength. They would interpret the Führer's declaration as an intention to break up France's colonial empire and appeal to their fellow-countrymen that they should rather make common cause with the English to try to save what still could be saved. A German declaration regarding Syria [...] would at the present time create new troubles in Western Europe, which means that a portion of the German armed forces would be immobilized in the west and no longer be available for the campaign in the east.
>
> The Führer then made the following statement to the Mufti, enjoining him to lock it in the uttermost depths of his heart.
>
> 1. He (the Führer) would carry on the battle to the total destruction of the Judeo-Communist empire in Europe.

2. At some moment which was impossible to set exactly today but which was not distant, the German armies would [...] reach the southern exit of Caucasia.

3. As soon as this had happened the Führer would on his own give the Arab world the assurance that its hour of liberation had arrived. Germany's objective would then be solely the destruction of the Jewish element residing in the Arab sphere under the protection of British power. In that hour the Mufti would be the most authoritative spokesman for the Arab world. It would then be his task to set off the Arab operations which he had secretly prepared. When that time had come, Germany would also be indifferent to French reaction to such a declaration.

[...] For the good of the common cause it would thus be better if the Arab proclamation were put off for a few more months than if Germany were to create difficulties for herself without being able thereby to help the Arabs. [...] The moment that Germany's tank divisions and air squadrons had made their appearance south of the Caucasus, the public appeal requested by the Grand Mufti could go out to the Arab world.

The Grand Mufti [...] asked whether it would not be possible, secretly at least, to enter into an agreement with Germany of the kind he had just outlined for the Führer. The Führer replied that he had just now given the Grand Mufti precisely that confidential declaration.[19]

The widely held view, in sum, is that Hitler was not interested in the Middle Eastern countries bordering the Mediterranean—Egypt, Palestine, Lebanon, Syria—and was quite content to oblige his Italian ally by keeping

---

19 "Record of the Conversation Between the Führer and the Grand Mufti of Jerusalem on 28 November 1941, in the presence of Reich Foreign Minister [i.e. Ribbentrop] and Minister Grobba in Berlin," memorandum dated Berlin 30 November 1941, in David G. Dalin and John F. Rothmann, *Icon of Evil: Hitler's Mufti and the Rise of Radical Islam* (New York: Random House, 2008), Appendix of Correspondence and Documents, pp. 159–62. Original German text (see Appendix to the present volume), signed [Paul Otto] Schmidt, in *Akten zur deutschen auswärtigen Politik 1918–1945* (Göttingen: Vandenhoek & Ruprecht, 1970), series D, vol. 13.2, pp. 718–21. An entry in al-Husseini's diary confirms this report of his interview and conversation with Hitler (Rothmann, *Icon of Evil*, pp. 162–65). By June 1942 the theme of the common enemy—the Jews and the English—had been expanded to include the Americans. Grobba reports that on 25 June 1942 the Mufti had a conversation with Erwin Ettel, German Ambassador to Iran from 1939 until the embassy was closed in 1941 and one of al-Husseini's main contacts with the *Auswärtiges Amt*, in which he asserted that Germany and the Arabs were united in their common battle against the Jews. "Germany was the only country in the world that did not limit its fight against the Jews to its own territory but had announced an uncompromising fight against world Jewry. The Arabs felt at one with the Germans in this battle against the Jews. The fight against England was inseparable from the fight against Jewry. The English were now, together with the Americans, the friends and protectors of the Jews" (Fritz Grobba, *Männer und Mächte im Orient. 35 Jahre diplomatischer Tätigkeit im Orient*" [Göttingen: Musterschmidt, 1967], p. 270).

to what had been agreed between them: that the entire Mediterranean region would be an Italian sphere of influence. Likewise, there was no question of encouraging nationalist movements in the North African territories of Italy, Vichy France, and Spain. Everything West of Egypt, it was repeatedly emphasized, was strictly out of bounds.[20] Hitler's interest in parts of the Middle East beyond the Mediterranean—the Arabian Peninsula, Iraq, Iran, the Caucasus—was greater, since these territories were a source of oil. Hence his insistence on putting off the public declaration of support for Arab independence in all the territories occupied by Britain, France, and Russia that al-Gailani and the Mufti kept asking for and at the same time his promise that with military success on the crucial Eastern front he would be in a position to provide practical assistance to the Arabs, by directing the German army to enter Iraq from the North, by way of the oil-rich Russian-held Caucasus.[21]

Most documents at the *Auswärtiges Amt* from the years 1940–1941 do indeed testify to a policy of consistent deference to Germany's Italian ally with only cautious expressions of support for Arab demands.[22] Germany disclaimed any political ambitions in the region (though many memos noted that political *"indifférence"* in no way ruled out playing an important role in the economic and cultural life of the Middle Eastern lands and especially in developing the oil resources of the region).

---

20 "In den arabisch besiedelten Gebieten westlich von Ägypten soll keine nationalarabische oder sonstige politische Propaganda betrieben werden" ["No Arab nationalist or other political propaganda is to be implemented in the the areas settled by Arabs west of Egypt"] ran an instruction issued by Ribbentrop on 12 February 1942. This confirmed a longstanding policy of deference to Italian and then Vichy French interests (*Akten zur deutschen Auswärtigen Politik 1918–1945* [Göttingen: Vandenhoek & Ruprecht, 1969], series E [1941–1945], vol. 1, p. 406, document 231 [text of a telegram from Woermann, head of the A.A.' s Political Section to the German Embassy in Rome]).

21 Ian Kershaw suggests that Hitler's eagerness to reach the oilfields of Baku led him to depart from his original plan of advancing on the Caucasus *after* taking Stalingrad and to adopt instead a strategy that, in Kershaw's words, was "sheer lunacy" and resulted in a catastrophic defeat, namely dividing the German army into two groups, the stronger of which pushed south into the Caucasus, while the weaker was left with the task of taking Stalingrad (*Hitler 1936–45. Nemesis* [New York and London: W.W. Norton and Company, 2000], p. 529).

22 "In my opinion there can be bo doubt that we must give Italy absolute precedence in organizing the Arabian area," Ernst Woermann, the head of the Political Section of the A.A., declared in a memorandum, dated 21 July 1940 (*Documents on German Foreign Policy*, series D, vol. 10, p. 261 [Government Printing Office: Washington, D.C., 1957], document 200). Despite criticisms of this policy by many of the old Middle East hands at the A.A. it was never abandoned in any significant way and was repeatedly confirmed in successive memoranda.

Innumerable drafts of a brief, suitably vague statement to be broadcast in Arabic to the appropriate audiences—the wording of which was constantly scrutinized and slightly revised—asserted Germany's longstanding "sympathy" with the aspirations of the Arab peoples, but stopped short of "recognizing" the independence of the states of the region.[23] Nevertheless, among some Middle East hands at the *Auswärtiges Amt*, there was a constituency that represented the views of the Arabs and argued that it would be in Germany's interest in the struggle against Great Britain to pursue a more aggressively pro-Arab policy and a more energetic exploitation of Arab hostility to the British, the French, and the Jews than had obtained in the years leading up to the 1939 war. Tellingly, one of those Middle East specialists, noting at the end of 1942 that "the news from the Mediterranean sounds increasingly unfavorable," that "Tobruk has fallen," that "the Yanks have all of Algeria and Morocco well in hand," that "Musso has taken steps for a separate peace with the U.S.S.R." and that "the Italian fleet was allegedly not deployed, because it has no oil," attributed these serious setbacks to the shortsightedness of Germany's Middle East policy since the outbreak of war. "I can only ask, why does [the Italian fleet] have no oil?" Curt Prüfer wrote in his diary, and provided the answer to his own question: "Again, as in the first war, the Orient and the Mediterranean are being neglected. *Germania non discet* [Germany does not learn]."[24]

On 25 July 1940, one month after the fall of France, Max Freiherr von Oppenheim submitted a memorandum on policy in the Middle East to Theodor Habicht, a former leader of the Nazi Party in Austria best remembered for having masterminded the murder of Dolfuss and the failed coup attempt in Austria in 1934, and, by the outbreak of war, an Under-Secretary of State at the *Auswärtiges Amt* and head of its Political Section, as well as the "confidant" and "personal adviser" of Ribbentrop.[25]

---

23 See, for instance *Documents on German Foreign Policy*, series D, vol. 11, documents 127, 133, 160, 596; vol. 12, document 83; *Akten zur deutschen Auswärtigen Politik 1918–1945*, series E, vol. 1 (Göttingen: Vandenhoek & Ruprecht, 1969), documents 26, 131.

24 McKale, *Rewriting History. The Original and Revised World War II Diaries of Curt Prüfer*, p. 7 (14 November 1942).

25 Michael Bloch, *Ribbentrop* (London: Bantam Press, 1992), pp. 272, 279. According to Philip Rees, *Biographical Dictionary of the Extreme Right since 1890* (New York: Simon and Schuster, 1990), Habicht was an "Undersecretary in the Foreign Department of the NSDAP" (i.e. the *Aussenpolitisches Amt* of the Nazi Party). However, he is listed as Undersecretary in the *Auswärtiges Amt* and head of both the Political Section and the Information Section in *Biographisches Handbuch des deutschen Auswärtigen Dienstes*, ed. Maria Keipert, vol. 2 (Paderborn: Ferdinand Schöningh, 2005), pp. 153–64 and as

Though its general aims were similar to those of the 1914 memorandum, the 1940 memorandum was much shorter and it took account of the changed situation in 1940. (There was no reference to *jihad* in it, for example, because Germany's ally Italy and potential ally Vichy France had many Muslim subjects in their colonial territories.)[26] Oppenheim outlined the steps to be followed in order to make maximum use, for Germany's ends, of the situation in the Muslim world. That he and Fritz Grobba may have worked on the memorandum together is suggested by the important role Oppenheim assigned in it to Grobba, who as German ambassador to Iraq from 1932 until the outbreak of war in 1939—when Iraq, under pressure from the British to observe the terms of the Anglo-Iraqi Treaty of 1930 and against the wishes of many members of the Iraqi cabinet, severed diplomatic relations with Germany—had energetically sought to promote German influence in the region.

In an accompanying letter, Oppenheim declared that, given "the special knowledge" of the Middle East that he had acquired as a result of having been "active there for decades, partly as a scholar and partly as an agent of the *Auswärtiges Amt*—up to and during the Great War," he was dismayed, as were "many Orientals who had opened their hearts to him," by "Germany's cautious hesitation up to now to become involved in the problems of the Middle East." This caution was especially unwarranted, in his view, as the region was capable of "playing an important role" in Germany's war against England.[27] Oppenheim thus indirectly justified his submitting the memorandum, even though he no longer held any official position in the *Auswärtiges Amt*, on the grounds that, as a patriotic German and as head of the Orient Intelligence Bureau [*Nachrichtenstelle für den Orient*] in the First World War, he was both obligated and singularly qualified to express

---

"Sonderbeauftragter für Propaganda," immediately responsible, like Secretary of State Weizsäcker, to Foreign Minister Ribbentrop, in Bernd Sösemann, *Propaganda: Medien und Öffentlichkeit in der N-S Diktatur*, 2 vols. (Stuttgart, Franz Steiner, 2011), vol. 1, p. 764.

26 Ribbentrop specifically instructed that "es soll keine allgemeine islamische Propaganda auf religiöser Grundlage betrieben werden. Propaganda mit Schlagworten wie 'heiliger Krieg' soll daher unterbleiben" ["No general Islamic propaganda based on religion is to be utilized. Any propaganda using slogans like 'holy war' must cease"] (*Akten zur deutschen Auswärtigen Politik 1918–1945* [Göttingen: Vandenhoek & Ruprecht, 1969], series E [1941–1945], vol. 1, p. 406, document 231 [text of a telegram from Woermann to the German Embassy in Rome]).

27 Quoted in Heinz Tillmann, *Deutschlands Araberpolitik im Zweiten Weltkrieg*, p. 162.

13. Plotting for Nazi Germany Oppenheim's Role in the Middle East Policy

an opinion and offer advice on the matter, the more so as he remained in close contact with and enjoyed the confidence of important leaders of the Arab world.

Here is the text of the memorandum:

> As Head of the Orient Intelligence Bureau at the Foreign Office and later at our embassy in Constantinople during the World War, I am taking the liberty, at a moment when the war against England is entering a decisive phase, to put forward the following suggestions:
>
> The time has come for us to intervene energetically in the Middle East against England.
>
> There are two urgent tasks.
>
> 1) Supplying Berlin with direct and reliable information about the Middle East.
>
> 2) Fomenting revolution, first in Syria, to counteract English plans to occupy that country, then in the neighbouring Arab lands, in Iraq, Transjordan, Palestine, and Saudi-Arabia. The aim would be to tie up British strike power, obstruct the export of oil and thus prevent supplies of oil from reaching the British naval and merchant fleets, cripple traffic through the Suez Canal for the English, and finally completely destroy British domination in the Near East.
>
> In order to carry out this task, our former ambassador in Baghdad, Dr. Grobba, should be sent as soon as possible to Syria. Syria is the only country from which, at the present moment, the fight against England can be carried on. Dr. Grobba must be headquartered in Damascus. Current business, such as the affairs of the citizens of the Reich in Syria, could be dealt with by a consular official working under him and located perhaps in Beirut. Dr. Grobba's assignment, in contrast, would be to devote all his energy to the fomenting of an uprising of the entire Middle East against England. Dr. Grobba has the reputation there of being England's most dangerous enemy. His very name would work like a programme for action, his appearance and activity in Damascus like a call to battle, not only for Syria, but for all the Arab lands. The latter, — Iraq especially, are only waiting for a signal from Germany in order to move against England. In addition, Dr. Grobba is accredited as Ambassador to Ibn Saud, and he is on friendly terms with the Mufti of Jerusalem, who is presently in Baghdad. Naturally, he needs to be supplied with appropriate assistants as well as with the necessary financial and other means, with radio and communications devices, etc. He also needs to be authorized to have a say in how the weapons of the French army are disposed of as that army is demobilized. These weapons should be transferred to the Arabs for the fight against England. Naturally an understanding with Italy needs to be reached concerning not only this matter, but Dr. Grobba's other tasks also.

In Syria the French High Commissioner and Ambassador Puaux,[28] who has been a very great enemy of ours ever since the failure of his fight against National Socialism in Vienna, must be removed and the current pro-French Syrian Directorate replaced by a Syrian regime better disposed toward us.

In Iraq, the pro-English Foreign Minister Nuri as-Sa'id must be got rid of, by force if necessary. The Iraqi army must destroy the English air base at al-Habbaniya and with the help of the tribesmen take up arms against the British troops, shut off the oil pipeline to Haifa, and throw the English out of the whole of Iraq, especially out of Basra.

In Transjordan, Emir Abdallah, who has committed himself completely to the English, needs to be removed.

In Palestine, the struggle against the English and the Jews is to be taken up again as energetically as possible. Ibn Saud must be induced to take part in it also. But he will do so only if he is promised Aqaba and Ma'an, towns in Southern Transjordan to which he has a well-founded claim. It is possible that his demands will extend to the whole of Transjordan. In Palestine, a government should be set up under the Mufti. Jerusalem might be given a special administration in which representatives of the different faiths (Catholic, Protestant, Orthodox) and of the Jews would work together under the Mufti. Only those Jews should be allowed to remain in Palestine who were there before World War I.

As far as Syria is concerned, its future is not easily decided. Iraq would like to incorporate this land, and the Syrian Muslims as well as some of the Syrian Christians, namely the Greek Orthodox, would undoubtedly welcome the union of their homeland with Iraq. But Ibn Saud will combat such a union with all the means at his disposal, since he is a personal enemy of Iraq's current ruling dynasty (the former Grand Sharifs of Mecca) and would fear the rise of a more powerful realm on his northern frontier. The simplest solution would be to place one of the sons of Ibn Saud on a throne to be established in Syria. (A direct incorporation of Syria into Saudi Arabia is out of the question on religious grounds, the fanatical Wahhabi faith that dominates in Saudi Arabia being unacceptable in Syria.) The Saudi prince would have to give up any idea of introducing his form of Islam into Syria. Lebanon would be constituted, as before the First World War, as a region of the Syrian state, with its own administration. Naturally, those areas that the French incorporated into Lebanon—Tripoli, Saida, Sur, the Bekaa Valley with Baalbek and Mount Hermon—must be separated again from the new administrative region.

---

28 Gabriel Puaux, decorated for bravery in World War I, was named French Ambassador to Austria in 1933. In 1938 he did his best to thwart the *Anschluss*. He also, on the outbreak of war in 1939, cancelled Oppenheim's excavation rights at Tell Fakhariya in Northern Syria, a fact of which Oppenheim was no doubt mindful when composing his memorandum. Dismissed by Vichy from his post in Syria, Puaux finally joined the French Resistance.

After the peace, after the victorious end of the struggle against England, a union of the aforementioned Middle Eastern states should be created. This union must also be joined by Yemen and the small states of the Arabian Peninsula, Oman, Bahrein, Kuwait, etc.

Egypt has been left out of consideration so far. In this connection, however, it should be noted briefly that the integration of Egypt into the said union of states would be of the greatest importance. At the present moment, I would deem it very advantageous to treat the Egyptians currently still in Germany as well as possible and they should be made aware of the unfriendliness with which the Germans living in Egypt have been treated, under pressure from the English, by the Egyptian government. In our press we are drawing attention to every sign of the differences separating the Egyptian government, the Egyptian people and its army, and the English, so as to suggest that we view the Egyptians as secret allies. On our side, therefore, we should not treat the Egyptians in Germany as enemy aliens.[29]

Finally, I would like to point out that special, friendly treatment of Moroccan, Algerian, and Tunisian prisoners-of-war would bear useful fruit. In the Great War, all Muslim and also all Indian prisoners-of-war were held in a special camp in Wünsdorf, not far from Berlin. A mosque was built for them there, newspapers were published for them in the appropriate languages, etc.

The main thing is for Ambassador Dr. Grobba to leave for the Middle East as soon as possible. It would be good if, prior to his departure, he could consult with Emir Shakib Arslan in Geneva in order to discuss with him questions concerning the new order to be established in the states of the Arab region, in particular in Syria. Shakib Arslan, who stands wholeheartedly on the side of Germany and, as I know for a certainty, has done for decades, possesses a vast knowledge of both people and situations in the region. If we plan to deal seriously with these problems, his advice would therefore be extraordinarily useful.

As long as it is not possible to execute the plan of sending Ambassador Grobba to Syria, inasmuch as Germany still recognizes the role of the French in Syria, it might be possible to begin to carry out the proposed actions from Ankara, perhaps through the Iraqi embassy there.[30] Should the negotiations

---

29 They were, in fact, being so treated at the time by the Nazi state's officials and were subject to internment. See Wolfgang G. Schwanitz, "Aziz Cotta Bey, deutsche und ägyptische Handelskammern und der Bund Ägypter deutscher Bildung," in Gerhard Höpp, ed., *Fremde Erfahrungen: Asiaten und Afrikaner in Deutschland, Österreich und in der Schweiz bis 1945* (Berlin, 1996), pp. 359–84; Gerhard Höpp, "Der verdrängte Diskurs: Arabische Opfer des Nationalsozialismus," in G. Höpp, ed., *Blind für die Geschichte: Arabische Begegnungen mit dem Nationalsozialismus* (Berlin: Klaus Schwarz, 2004), p. 215–68, especially pp. 220–31.

30 In a memorandum to his superiors at the *Auswärtiges Amt*, dated 27 August 1940, a month after Oppenheim submitted his memorandum, Grobba reported that, in return for a public declaration by the Axis powers recognizing "the right of all Arab countries

lead to Iraq's joining our side, a new Syrian National Government should be called into being and located provisionally on the Syrian-Iraqi border. This government should then be recognized by Germany and Italy. We would then communicate to the French government that we are recognizing it while at the same time notifying the French that Ambassador Grobba is being sent to Damascus to protect German interests in Syria and act as our government's observer there.

I do not underestimate the difficulties the Arab insurgents will encounter in facing up to the still intact British army in Iraq and Palestine. The strength of the English troops' resistance will be considerably diminished, however, as further German successes in the war with England are announced, the more so as the troops in question are largely recruited from the colonies.

Moreover, the English position in Egypt and India would be weakened by an Arab uprising. The flow of oil to the English in Haifa would be cut off and—this is particularly important—the occupation of Syria by the English would be prevented and communication between the English in Iraq and the Turks would be interrupted.

The immediate goal of negotiations to be entered into with Iraqi representatives must be to get Iraq to declare its desire to restore diplomatic relations with Germany.[31] Our response to this declaration would enable Ambassador Dr. Grobba to return to Iraq. From his position there he could establish contact with Syrian nationalists and move to Damascus after calling for an independent Syrian government.[32]

Oppenheim's memo directly reflected the views of the Arab leaders at the time, the Lebanese Druze Shakib Arslan, the Palestinian Amin al-Husseini, and the Iraqi Rashid Ali al-Gailani. The call for a grand union of the Muslim states of the Middle East once the British had been defeated was a goal embraced by all three. The emphasis on Syria would have been especially pleasing to Shakib Arslan. A political activist throughout his life, Arslan, as already noted, had long placed

---

to shape their national unity in accordance with their wishes," the Iraqi government was willing to sign a secret agreement with the governments of Germany and Italy, laying out the details of a "friendly collaboration." The secret negotiations would be carried out in Ankara, at the German Embassy and the Iraqi Legation. (*Documents on German Foreign Policy 1918–1945* [Washington, D.C.: Government Printing Office, 1957], series D, vol. 10, pp. 556, 558, document 403). The German ambassador to Turkey from 1939 until 1944, was Franz von Papen, an old associate of Oppenheim's and a supporter of his *Jihad* plan in 1914.

31 These had been broken off at the beginning of the War.
32 English translation (by Lionel Gossman) of the original German text of Oppenheim's memorandum (see Appendix) reproduced in Wolfgang G. Schwanitz, "Max von Oppenheim und der Heilige Krieg. Zwei Denkschriften zur Revolutionierung islamischer Gebiete 1914 und 1940," *Sozial.Geschichte*, 3 (2004): 55–59.

13. Plotting for Nazi Germany Oppenheim's Role in the Middle East Policy

his hopes for Arab independence on Germany and had spent the last two years of the 1914–1918 war there. Prevented by the French Mandate authorities from returning to Syria after the War, he had continued his struggle for Arab independence and unity from his exile in Geneva. As we saw, he was in regular correspondence with Oppenheim, to whom he communicated his goals, his ideas and his proposals for action. The recommendation that the pro-British Nuri al-Sa'id should be "removed" can only have been welcomed by the fiercely anti-British and pro-German al-Gailani, who, having replaced al-Sa'id as prime minister in March, 1940 had had to keep him on as foreign minister.[33] So too, the suggestion that a "Greater Syria" might eventually be united with Iraq in a grand union of Arab states could not but have been well received by the Mufti, who told Hitler at his meeting with him in November 1941 that "the Arabs were striving for the independence and unity of Palestine, Syria, and Iraq."[34] In fact all the Mufti's demands were met in Oppenheim's memo, down to his suggested appointment as head of the new Palestinian state and the chilling proposal that of the 400,000 Jews in Palestine (a fair number of them, of course, refugees from Nazi Germany), only those who had been resident there before World War I (about 60,000) should be allowed to remain. In Germany, in 1940, Oppenheim, who did not indicate what the fate of those to be "removed" should be, obviously felt less compunction to be evasive on the subject of the Jewish settlers in Palestine than the Mufti had been in his testimony to the Peel Commission on 12 January 1937.[35]

---

33 In fact, in late 1940, al-Sa'id himself began making overtures both to the Italians—even though by the terms of the Anglo-Iraqi Treaty of 1930 Iraq was required to move against them on their entering the war against Britain in June, 1940—and to the Mufti. However, as he was generally considered a "traitor" by the pro-Axis Iraqi nationalists, these belated attempts at collaboration were viewed with suspicion and came to nothing (Majid Khadduri, "General Nūrī's flirtations with the Axis Powers," *Middle East Journal*, 16 [1962]: 328–36).

34 Memorandum by an official of the Foreign Minister's Secretariat consisting of a record of the conversation between the Führer and the Grand Mufti on 28 November 1941, in Dalin and Rothmann, *Icon of Evil*, Appendix, p. 159.

35 Before the Peel Commission on 12 January 1937, according to Dalin and Rothmann, al-Husseini reiterated his longstanding demand for the cessation of all Jewish immigration to Palestine "and called for the removal of 80% of the Jews already in the country (four hundred thousand) to bring their total number back to the level that prevailed prior to World War I (eighty thousand)" (*Icon of Evil*, pp. 33–34). Al-Husseini's actual testimony before the Commission seems rather less specific and considerably more evasive. Nevertheless, his answers to questions from Earl Peel and from the vice-chairman, Sir Horace Rumbold, were so obviously evasive that they aroused the commissioners' fears

Habicht's response, two days later, to Oppenheim's memorandum was curt. "Thank you for sending your memorandum of 25.7.40. The questions raised in it are already the subject of close and thorough study at the Foreign Office."[36] While Habicht's note might well have

---

for the fate of the Jews in Palestine under an Arab government. Here is the relevant exchange as recorded in *Palestine Royal Commission: Minutes of evidence heard at public sessions* (London: H.M. Stationery Office, 1937), 56th Meeting (Public) 12 January 1937, p. 298:

4643. *Chairman* [Earl Peel]: You want completely to stop Jewish immigration. If you are setting up a Government here, what do you want to do with the 400,000 Jews or more in the country at present? — They will live, as they always have lived in Arab countries, with complete freedom and liberty as natives in the country. In fact, Moslem rule in ancient history and the history of the Arabs has always been known for tolerance toward the Jews. As a matter of fact, the Eastern countries under Arab rule were shelters for Jews who used to emigrate there when persecuted in Europe. According to the annals of history the Jews have had their quietest and most peaceful times in Arab countries under Arab rule.

4644. His Eminence was complaining that now there are far too many Jews, that the Arabs including the Christians were now only 70 per cent, of the population whereas 14 years ago they were 93 per cent? — That is his complaint.

4645. At the same time, if the Arabs had this treaty they would be prepared to welcome the Jews already in the country? — That will be left to the discretion of the Government, which will be set up under the treaty and will be decided by that Government on the considerations most equitable and most beneficial to the country. [...]

4648. *Sir Horace Rumbold*: Does His Eminence think that this country can assimilate and digest the 400,000 Jews now in the country? — No.

4649. *Chairman* [Earl Peel]: Some of them would have to be removed by a process kindly or painful as the case may be? — We must leave all this to the future.

36 Quoted by Tillmann, *Deutschlands Araberpolitik*, p. 170, note 211. Tillmann considers this response "ein glatter Affront." Melka agrees and attributes the brusqueness of the reply to the fact that, since Habicht, "unlike Oppenheim's other friends in the Foreign Office, was a Nazi Party member [since 1926] and member of the Nazi group in the Reichstag before 1933, [...] he was hardly likely to have much sympathy for an old Jewish aristocrat and his advice" ("Max Freiherr von Oppenheim," *Middle Eastern Studies*, 9 [1973]: 81–93 [p. 86]). However, several months earlier, in an acrimonious dispute between the *Auswärtiges Amt* and the *Aussenpolitisches Amt* [foreign section] of the Nazi Party over German policy in Afghanistan, reflecting no doubt the standing rivalry between Rosenberg (head of the *Aussenpolitisches Amt*) and Ribbentrop (head, as Foreign Minister, of the *Auswärtiges Amt*) and involving von Hentig and Grobba, Ribbentrop's man Habicht had sided — at a meeting "to which, significantly, Dr. Grobba was not invited" — with von Hentig and against Grobba, who represented the position embraced by the *Aussenpolitisches Amt*. Grobba's view had been that Germany should pursue a policy of co-operation with the current Afghan government, since the country, he claimed, had been deeply penetrated by Germany economically, culturally, and militarily, while von Hentig had argued — somewhat uncharacteristically, since he was not usually inclined to support adventurism — that the current Afghan government was, to the contrary, "subservient to England" and should therefore be removed by fomenting an insurrection and restoring Amanullah Khan, King of Afghanistan from 1919 until 1929 and leader of a surprise attack against British India in 1919, to the throne. The NSDAP's *Aussenpolitisches Amt* was extremely dismissive of Hentig's "sabotaging attitude." ("It is known that he has lacked any understanding of Germany's successful penetration [of Afghanistan] during recent years"; he "had until recently been claiming for years that Afghanistan

been intentionally cold or even—as some scholars have written—discourteous, his impatience with what he seems to have implied was the meddling of an outsider was not wholly unjustified. Some of the matters raised by Oppenheim had in fact been the subject of a secret report to the *Auswärtiges Amt*, dated 6 July 1940, from Von Papen, then German ambassador in Ankara. In this report Von Papen summed up the content of discussions he had had at his private summer residence in Therapia, outside Istanbul, with the Iraqi Justice Minister Naji Bey Shawkat. Shawkat, who had been recommended to him by the Grand Mufti,[37] then an exile in Baghdad, had assured him that the "Anglophile" Nuri al-Sa'id was deeply unpopular, that the Iraqi people so longed to shake off the constraining remnants of the English yoke that the cabinet had refused to break off relations with Italy in spite of pressure from the British ambassador and al-Sa'id. At the same time, the Iraqi gave a clear indication that the Arabs counted more on German than on Italian assistance in their struggle for independence. To von Papen's prudent reiteration of the official German line that "the future development of the political situation in the Near East was a matter of interest primarily to Italy," and that he, "could be regarded only as an intermediary for proposals addressed to Italy via the Reich government," Shawkat replied that, just "as the Arab national movement had fought Anglo-French imperialism, so it would have to oppose Italian imperialism" and that "it was therefore in the interest of the Axis powers for Germany to use her influence with Italy, in order to support a solution that would be compatible with the interests of the Arab movement." "As a first step," von Papen continued, "the Iraqi Minister of Justice recommended the re-establishment of the Arab national government in Damascus" (participation of Arab nationalists in the government of the Syria mandate having been ended by the French in March-July 1939)—a measure "strongly endorsed by the Grand Mufti

---

was of no political interest to Germany"; and in any case the planned insurrection has been so "superficially" prepared that even Afghan supporters of Amanullah residing in Germany "have stated that improvised insurrections would never be successful" and would lead only to civil war. (See *Documents on German Foreign Policy* [Washington, D.C.: United States Government Printing Office, 1954], vol. 8, pp. 527–29, 550–55, documents 449, [12 December 1939] and 470 [18 December 1939].) It is possible that Oppenheim sealed the fate of his memorandum to Habicht by attributing a key role in his proposal to Grobba.

37 *Mufti-Papiere. Briefe, Memoranden, Reden und Aufrufe Amīn al-Husainīs aus dem Exil, 1940–1945*, ed. Gerhard Höpp (Berlin: Klaus Schwarz, 2001), documents 1 and 2 (letters from al-Husseini to von Papen, 21 June 1940 and 22 July 1940), pp. 15–16.

of Jerusalem." The Arab national government would then "resume its struggle in Palestine," which Shawkat considered, according to von Papen, "should be of particular value to us at a moment when the most diverse interests were clashing in Syria. It is assumed that England will shortly attempt to occupy Syria and disarm the French forces. The Arab uprising could successfully intervene in such a moment of weakness."[38]

On 21 July 1940 — hence still prior to Oppenheim's submission of his memorandum — Ernst Woermann, an Under-Secretary at the *Auswärtiges Amt* and then head of the Political Department, responded to both von Papen's memorandum and another related memorandum on "The Situation in the Area of the Mediterranean and the Near East."[39] Woermann noted that an annex to the latter, almost certainly the work of one or more Arab leaders, "contained an endorsement of the establishment of a northern Arab empire under the leadership of Iraq" and under the protection of "Germany or Germany and Italy together." Von Papen, however, Woermann continued, had reminded the Iraqi Justice Minister of Germany's view "that the future development of the political situation in the Near East was of interest primarily to Italy." In the Under-Secretary's own opinion, which was that of the more conservative *Auswärtiges Amt* officials, "there can be no doubt that we must give Italy absolute precedence in organizing the Arabian area. [...] This, consequently, rules out any German claim to leadership in the Arabian area, or a division of that claim with Italy." Woermann's rejection of an activist German role in the politics of the Middle East — combined with a reminder that "this political *désintéressement* should not be taken to signify that we renounce any economic interest in that area," notably as regards "air routes" and "Iraqi oil" — was thus a reiteration of Germany's established policy. Woermann acknowledged that "all views about the Arabian area received here indicate a unanimous anti-Italian attitude among the Arabs" but warned that "we ought not to allow ourselves to become involved in this Arabian game," the aim of which was to "get from us support against Italy." In short "our policy, including our radio propaganda in the Near East or directed toward North Africa [...] must be conducted, as in the past, on the sharpest

---

38 *Documents on German Foreign Policy 1918–1945* (Washington, D.C.: Government Printing Office, 1957), vol. 10, pp. 141–43, document 125, report by von Papen, Therapia, 6 July 1940.
39 This document was not found by the editors of the *Documents on German Foreign Policy 1918–1945*.

anti-British, and a muted anti-French note."[40]

In a circular sent on 20 August 1940 to Embassies and Legations in Afghanistan, Bulgaria, Greece, Hungary, Iran, Romania, Switzerland, and Yugoslavia, as well as to various consulates in Turkey and the Middle East, the *Auswärtiges Amt* issued directives that clearly formulated German policy and warned against responding to Arab overtures:

> Leading Arab personalities have in recent times repeatedly approached our foreign Missions with the request to bring about a policy statement by the Reich Government on the independence movement of the Arab countries and to promote support for their aspirations. This affords occasion to state the following fundamental considerations about the coming reorganization of the Arab region:
>
> Germany pursues no political interests in the Mediterranean area, whose southern and eastern part is formed by the Arab world. Germany will therefore let Italy take the lead in the political reorganization of the Arab area. This consequently rules out any German claim to political leadership, or the sharing of leadership with Italy in the Arab territories, which consist of the Arabian Peninsula, Egypt, Palestine, Transjordan, Syria-Lebanon, and Iraq.
>
> This political *désintéressement*, however, does not at all mean that in those areas Germany renounces the pursuit of interests in matters of economy, transportation, and cultural policy. First and foremost, Germany will assert, and settle in concert with Italy, her claim with respect to participation in the exploitation of oil resources, the securing of her air routes, and the continuation of her archaeological activities.
>
> These directives, however, must be treated confidentially. They are not of a nature to be divulged to representatives of foreign powers. Especially, they must not be made known to [leading] Arab personalities. It is desirable, nevertheless, on every occasion to stress to them the common German and Arab interest in England's defeat, and assure them of Germany's full sympathy in their people's fight for liberation. Please avoid entering into any discussion, however, of the question of the future political organization of the Arab region, and if necessary observe a noncommittal attitude; on no account are you to say anything to Arab representatives about a *désintéressement* on the part of Germany.[41]

It seems clear that, as Habicht had asserted in his reply to Oppenheim, there had indeed been and still was ongoing discussion at the *Auswärtiges Amt* of various courses of action Germany might pursue in the Middle East and that the "energetic intervention" Oppenheim advocated in his memorandum

---

40 *Documents on German Foreign Policy 1918–1945* (Washington, D.C.: Government Printing Office, 1957), vol. 10, p. 261, document 200, memorandum by the Director of the Political Department, Berlin, 21 July 1940.
41 *Documents on German Foreign Policy 1918–1945* (Washington, D.C.: Government Printing Office, 1957), vol. 10, p. 515, document 370, Circular of the Foreign Ministry, 20 August 1940.

had, on the whole, been rejected in favour of continuation of the policy of *désintéressement* (as the ever cautious Woermann put it) and overall deference to Italy as the main Mediterranean power. Oppenheim, in contrast, had conceded only, almost as an afterthought, that "Naturally an understanding with Italy needs to be reached concerning not only [the transfer to the Iraqis of the weapons of the French army in Syria] but Dr. Grobba's other tasks also."

Nonetheless, only a week after Woermann sent out his circular, Grobba, who was also attached to the Political Department of the *Auswärtiges Amt*, submitted a memo directly to Foreign Minister Ribbentrop that diverged quite markedly from the official line, with copies to Habicht, Woermann, and Secretary of State von Weizsäcker. Dated Berlin, 27 August 1940, it gave an account of a meeting Grobba had had in Berlin with the Grand Mufti's private secretary, Osman Kemal Haddad. Haddad had been sent to Berlin by al-Husseini to discuss with members of the *Auswärtiges Amt* the possibility of an agreement on direct Arab-German collaboration. "Under instructions from the Grand Mufti," Haddad explained that Iraq had broken relations with Germany unwillingly and only under threat from the British and from the French Armée d'Orient; that "a committee for collaboration among the Arab countries [had] been formed under the chairmanship of the Grand Mufti," with representatives from Iraq (including the Iraqi army), Syria, Saudi Arabia, and Palestine (the last-named represented by the Grand Mufti himself); and that "this committee had already decided some months ago that it should seek to establish contact with Germany." Since then, "there [had] been a radical change in the situation in Iraq—1) through the defeat of France and the elimination of the Armée d'Orient; 2) through the weakening of England and the withdrawal from Iraq of English troops and aircraft; and 3) through the reinforcement of the Iraqi Army," which now "had a total of five divisions already, with a sixth being currently formed." Iraq had therefore taken an independent attitude toward England and rejected the demand for the transit of Anglo-Indian troops from the Bahrein Islands and India." The committee had then decided to send Naji Shawkat, the Iraqi Minister of Justice, to von Papen in Turkey. From their talks together, "the committee had gained the impression that Germany was sympathetic toward the aspirations of the Arabs, but that she would negotiate on the pertinent questions only in concert with Italy. The committee realised that Italy occupied a predominant position in the Eastern Mediterranean" and so the Iraqi Minister President Rashid Ali al-Gailani had decided to send a special envoy to Rome. In the meantime, however, "the Italian Minister [in Baghdad], on instruction from the Italian Government, had already informed the Minister President in writing that it was the goal of the Italian Government that all Arab countries in the Near East which were under British or French Mandate or protection should become independent." Knowing the official German policy of leaving the Middle East to the Italians, but deeply distrustful of Italy, and extremely eager to involve Germany directly in their struggle, the Arab leaders were clearly trying to suggest, according to Grobba, that there was no obstacle to German involvement in their independence plans, since the Italians had already accepted all their proposals.

Grobba then outlined the wishes of the Arab committee. The first, as formally expressed by the committee itself in a document appended to his memorandum, was for "a joint declaration […] of the German and Italian Governments" consisting of five parts.

> I. The German and Italian Governments recognize the full independence of the Arab countries which are already independent or are under French mandate (Syria and Lebanon) or under British mandate and protectorate (Transjordan, Palestine, the Arab countries on the coast of the Arabian Peninsula—Kuwait, Oman, Masqat, Hadhramaut, South Yemen as part of the state of Yemen, and the other countries recognized as Arab countries on the basis of an Arab majority of the population). Germany and Italy will make no use of any juridical or other means to abridge the independence of these Arab countries, e.g. by establishing mandates, that hypocritical device of the League of Nations and the democracies to disguise their imperialistic greed.
> II. Germany and Italy recognize the right of all Arab countries to shape their national unity in accordance with their wishes. […]
> III. Germany and Italy recognize the right of the Arab countries to solve the question of the Jewish elements in Palestine and the other Arab countries in a manner that conforms to the national and ethnic interests of the Arabs and to the solution of the Jewish question in the countries of Germany and Italy.
> IV. Germany and Italy have no imperialist designs with respect to Egypt and the Sudan, and recognize the independence of these two countries, as set forth under number I of this Declaration.
> V. Germany and Italy have no greater wish than to see each Arab nation enjoying abundant prosperity and taking its historical and natural place in the sun.

The second wish was for "a declaration by the two governments, in writing, that they are in accord with" the resumption of diplomatic relations between Iraq and Germany, with a view to "friendly collaboration between the two Governments in all questions of interest to both countries." On its side, the Government of Iraq agrees "to accord to Germany and Italy a preferred position with respect to the exploitation of Iraqi mineral resources, especially petroleum, and the economic development of the country." In addition, Iraq offers its "good offices to enable Germany and Italy to achieve a like understanding with the other Arab countries, especially Syria, Palestine, Transjordan, and Saudi Arabia."

Once these conditions were agreed to, Grobba went on to explain, the Iraqi government would "dismiss Nuri Sa'id as Foreign Minister and replace him probably with Naji Shawkat," the Justice Minister who had earlier contacted von Papen. It also proposed "the conclusion of a secret agreement between it and the German and Italian Governments" laying out the details of their "friendly collaboration." These negotiations, it was suggested, should take place in Ankara—i.e. under the aegis of Ambassador von Papen. Finally, the Iraqi government and the countries declared independent (Syria, Palestine, and Transjordan) would declare their strict neutrality. But that would not prevent them from starting "a general uprising in Transjordan and Palestine" for which "up to 10,000 men and the required number of officers" would be made available. The preparations would be "organized from Syria" and the uprising could draw on the French Army weapons being surrendered to the Italians in Syria in accordance with the French-Italian armistice agreement. Still, more would be needed, and financing this development would require "30,000 pounds sterling, gold," of which the Arab national committee could raise about 10,000, the remainder to be supplied by Germany and Italy. The Arabs, Grobba reported, believe they can handle the 30,000 to 40,000 British troops still in Palestine. If these troops could be tied down by the projected uprisings and if the Iraqi government prevented the transfer of Anglo-Indian troops from India to Egypt via Iraq, Italy's military situation in the eastern Mediterranean (where the Italian army was not doing at all well in combat with the British) would be considerably relieved. Though he did not explicitly endorse these Arab proposals and arguments, Grobba must have appeared to be implicitly endorsing them, since he did not question them or offer any criticism of them.[42]

In view of official German policy in the Middle East, the written statement of support for the independence of all the Arab countries

---

42 *Documents on German Foreign Policy*, vol. 10, pp. 556–60, document dated Berlin, 27 August 1940, consisting of a letter from Grobba, and an enclosure with the text of the joint German and Italian declaration, as proposed by the Arab committee.

under British and French control allegedly communicated by the Italian Ambassador in Baghdad to the Iraqi Minister President caused a great deal of consternation in German diplomatic circles. Germany had persistently refused to issue such a written statement and continued to resist Arab pressure to do so. In his interview with the Mufti in November 1941, as we saw, Hitler still would not yield on this point. Nevertheless, Woermann sent out a memo on 28 September 1940, explaining that, as "we cannot, without loss of prestige, allow the steps taken by the Arabs at various times to obtain such a statement from us to go completely unanswered, it is therefore proposed that the following oral statement, to be broadcast in Arabic on the radio, be made to the private secretary of the Grand Mufti who has been waiting here for over a month: 'Germany's desire has always been that the Arab countries should rid themselves of English and French rule, enjoy greater autonomy than heretofore, and achieve complete independence. The Arab countries may therefore count on Germany's full sympathy in their efforts to attain this goal.'"[43] The wording of even this cautious oral statement was repeatedly reviewed, revised, and refined, so that it would win Arab support while making no commitment on Germany's part to intervene actively. Thus Weizsäcker suggested in a letter to the German Embassy in Rome two days later, on 30 September, that it be watered down to "Germany has always followed with interest the struggle of the Arab countries to attain their independence. In their striving toward this goal, the Arab countries will be able in the future also to count upon the full sympathy of Germany"—to which might be added, Weizsäcker suggested, if the Italians agreed—"who finds herself in full accord with her Italian ally in this matter."[44]

On the very same day, however, Grobba sent a memo around to his colleagues in the *A.A.*, warning against Germany's associating too closely with Italy in Middle Eastern affairs. The Arabs, he wrote, "had studied the question whether a collaboration with Soviet Russia might be advisable. […] If they saw their independence threatened by Italy, they might possibly

---

43 *Documents on German Foreign Policy* (Washington, D.C.: Government Printing Office, 1960), vol. 11, p. 220, document 127.
44 Ibid., p. 228, document 133, 30 September 1940. Weizsäcker came up a few days later with yet another modification which was intended to adapt the statement "to the oriental mentality […] without conceding anything of substance." The Secretary of State emphasized that "the statement is to be made to the private secretary of the Grand Mufti here orally." It was then to be "broadcast over the German radio in the Arabic language." Clearly, there was to be nothing in writing (ibid., pp. 268–69, document 160, 6 October).

consider alignment with Soviet Russia as the lesser evil."[45] On 3 October, von Papen chipped in with a memo from Turkey to the effect that "the Arabs' abysmal distrust of the plans of Rome" had been heightened by the Italian government's insistence that its minister in Baghdad had acted without official authorization in providing a written statement of support for Arab independence. As a result, Justice Minister Shawkat, representing the Arab National Committee, had told him that "All the hopes of the Arab world were pinned on Germany. If these hopes were disappointed, the Arab countries would eventually do better to come to an understanding with the English regime." Von Papen went on to point out that the Reich's refraining from "participation in the solution of the Arab problem of the Near East had a significance for the postwar settlement in the Near East that should by no means be underestimated." Italy's hegemony in the Mediterranean, he pointed out, would give her "absolute control of the maritime route (through the Suez canal) to our Central African possessions, which are to be regained, as well as to the oil deposits in the Near East." This meant that it was in Germany's national interest that "a safe land route via the Balkans and Turkey to the Persian Gulf [...] be established after the war." Hence there was no way for Germany to avoid "dealing with the Arab problem of the Near East." It was "a question that we have to face." Bridges would have be rebuilt with Turkey, which had "been driven by the Italian threat into the English orbit," and "a secure and friendly relation established with the Arab states of the Near East."[46] Like Grobba, Von Papen was thus challenging the policy of *désintéressement* and complete deference, in Middle East affairs, to Italian ambitions.

There appears to be agreement among historians that there were different factions in the *Auswärtiges Amt*—a more aggressive faction and a more cautious and circumspect one, the latter usually said to have been represented by Secretary of State, Ernst von Weizsäcker.[47] Von Papen

---

45 Ibid, p. 229, document 134, 30 September 1940.
46 Ibid, pp. 241–43, document 146, 3 October 1940.
47 See, for instance, Marion Thielenhaus, *Zwischen Anpassung und Widerstand: Deutsche Diplomaten 1938–1941* (Paderborn: Ferdinand Schöning, 1984); the more nuanced assessment in Hans-Jürgen Döscher, *Das Auswärtige Amt im Dritten Reich. Diplomatie im Schatten der 'Endlösung'* (Berlin: Wolf Jobst Siedler, 1987), pp. 181–91; and the firsthand testimony of Wipert von Blücher, Ambassador to Iran (1931–1935) and to Finland (1935–1944) in his *Gesandter zwischen Diktatur und Demokratie: Erinnerungen aus den Jahren 1935–1944* (Wiesbaden: Limes Verlag, 1951), pp. 117–18. Wolfgang G. Schwanitz ("'Der Geist aus der Lampe': Fritz Grobba und Berlins Politik im Nahen und Mittleren Orient," *Comparativ*, 14 [2004]: 126–50), places Grobba in the first group, Hentig, along with

(who had associations with Foreign Minister Ribbentrop going back to the First World War[48] and was serving, as of 1939, as Ambassador to Turkey) is said to have been at the centre of a group of old Middle East hands that included Hentig, Hentig's rival Grobba, and a couple of Oriental scholars, with Oppenheim—on the strength of his earlier role as an agent of the *A.A.* and an authority on the "Orient"—in an associated and advisory capacity.[49] In general, this group was critical of the policy of deferring to Italy in the Mediterranean and the Middle East and supported a more energetic policy focused on Germany's own national interests. As Hentig noted in his autobiographical memoir (written after 1945), "Hitler had generously delivered the entire Near East into the hands of Mussolini's colonial policy. In doing so he was acceding to the wishes of the Italian Ministry of Colonies, without considering that the Italians were then the most hated Europeans in the Arab world. The Arabs saw the English as taskmasters, the French as exploiters; but the busy Italian settlers had taken their land and thereby the foundation of their livelihood."[50] Hentig claimed that his "well-known negative view" of Germany's policy of deference to Italian ambitions, "which of course no one dared to bring to Hitler's attention," could have got him into serious trouble. If he continued to express it, he was warned, he could find himself "an die Wand gestellt" [before a firing squad].[51]

Prüfer, in the second, more circumspect one (pp. 135–36). According to Schwanitz, the first group favored destroying British power in the Middle East "durch die Inszenierung von *Jihad*-Aufruhen" [by setting-up *Jihad*-uprisings] whereas the opposite side was against making the Middle East a major theatre of war. Still, though there was no love lost between Grobba and Hentig, and Hentig generally followed the more cautious line of the long-established diplomats at the *Auswärtiges Amt*, both were opposed to the policy of deference to Italy and in favour of a more active German presence in the Middle East. Both also had a close connection with Oppenheim, as did Prüfer.

48 See Wolfgang G. Schwanitz, *Gold, Bankiers und Diplomaten. Zur Geschichte der Deutschen Orientbank 1906–1946* (Berlin: Trafo-Verlag, 2002), pp. 321–22.

49 According, at least, to a highly fictionalized and often inaccurate biography of Von Papen by Tibor Koeves (*Satan in Top Hat: The Biography of Franz von Papen* [New York: Alliance Book Corporation, 1941], pp, 333–5). Even if the group did not exist as described by Koeves, there was a good deal of co-operation among its alleged members. On Von Papen's central role in Nazi Middle East policy, see Karl Heinz Roth, "Berlin-Ankara-Baghdad: Franz von Papen and German Middle East Policy during the Second World War," in Wolfgang G. Schwanitz, ed., *Germany and the Middle East 1871–1945* (Madrid: Iberoamericana; Frankfurt a.M.: Vervuert, 2004), pp. 181–214.

50 Werner Otto von Hentig, *Mein Leben. Eine Dienstreise*, p. 335.

51 Ibid., p. 342. Grobba later asserted that Hentig opposed an active, interventionist German policy in the Middle East—a policy Grobba was convinced would bring Britain to its knees by destabilising the whole region and cutting British lines of communication with India—because, as an old school diplomat, he was opposed to Hitler; see Grobba's 82-page review, written in 1957, of a 208-page report by Generals Felmy and Warlimont

Whether independently or under the influence of von Papen, Grobba, and associates, Ribbentrop began in late 1940 to take a greater interest in how the situation in the Middle East might be exploited to Germany's advantage. He had already, in the summer of 1940, agreed that the *Abwehr*, under Canaris, should engage more actively in intelligence-gathering in the Arab lands, and Canaris had in fact dispatched an agent—Alfred Roser—to Damascus in the early fall of 1940 to set up a spy ring and establish contact with anti-British groups in Palestine. Later in the same year—thanks, in all likelihood, to Grobba—Weizsäcker and perhaps also Ribbentrop agreed to meet with Haddad, the Mufti's private secretary, who, as we saw, had been sent to Berlin to negotiate with the *Auswärtiges Amt*.[52] The memo prepared by Wilhelm Melchers, then head of the Middle East section of the *A.A.*, for those participating in that meeting with Haddad suggests that (no doubt in light of the reports being received from *Abwehr* agent Roser) views of the situation in the Middle East and of what German policy should be there had evolved over the summer.

The somewhat pessimistic memo of the conservatively inclined Melchers offered a comprehensive review of all the major countries of the Middle East. Beginning with "Arabia" in general, it recalled that "even before and after the outbreak of the war, Germany saw in Arab nationalism her natural ally," whereas Italy, in contrast, "finds the latter irksome" and has therefore ruled out any "recognition in writing of the independence of the Arab countries and of their right to form a union." Since, however, "the line of German policy has been determined so as to give Italy in principle the absolute lead politically in the Arab area, [...] in conformity with Italy's

---

on Germany's exploitation of Arab nationalist movements in World War II, drawn up in 1955 for the Historical Division of the U.S. Army in Europe (U.S. National Achives 2, RG338, FMS, P-207ArchII, RG 338, FMS, P-207), cit. in Wolfgang Schwanitz, "The Jinnee and the Magic Bottle: Fritz Grobba and the German Middle Eastern Policy 1900–1945," in Wolfgang G. Schwanitz, ed., *Germany and the Middle East 1871–1945*, pp. 87–117. While Hentig might well have been circumspect and no blind devotee of Hitler, however, it is unlikely to have been out of opposition to Hitler that he allegedly did not support the adventurous policy in the Middle East advocated by Grobba, as the latter argued (p. 110). Hitler himself was opposed to deep involvement in Middle Eastern affairs, and and if, as Grobba claims, Hentig was less supportive of an aggressive Middle East policy than Grobba, that is quite likely to have been because he had learned from his experience in Afghanistan in the First World War not to expect too much from intervention in the Middle East.

52 Philip Mattar, *The Mufti of Jerusalem: Al-Hajj Amin al-Husayni and the Palestinian National Movement* (New York: Columbia University Press, 1988), p. 101. Relying on the same sources as Mattar, Hirszowicz notes meetings of Haddad with Grobba, Melchers, and Weizsäcker, but says nothing of a meeting with Ribbentrop (*The Third Reich and the Arab East*, p. 82).

wish, we issued only an *oral* statement to the effect that we *were watching with interest the struggle of the Arabs for independence and would continue to sympathize with their efforts to achieve freedom.*" The upshot has been that "all the statements heretofore made in the press and on the radio were merely propaganda." Meanwhile, reports coming in from a wide range of sources, "show the situation in the Arab area becoming increasingly tense, particularly in Syria and Iraq."

In Syria (where, as a British historian of the Middle East campaigns explains, "Germany obtained no official footing after the collapse of France," since "the terms of the German armistice were mainly concerned with affairs in metropolitan France," and it was thus "left to Italy to determine the amount of demilitarization to be enforced in French overseas territories"[53]) there is great "antipathy of the Arabs toward the Italians," much "disappointment of the Arabs over the reserve of the Germans on the Armistice Commission," and a "feeling of having been sold out by them to Italy." Among the French, support for de Gaulle is on the increase, the British are conducting an active propaganda campaign, and there is a large concentration of Australian troops on the border with Palestine. The Italian armistice commission itself "would like to see us in Syria because they see their situation as untenable."

In Iraq, the memo notes the "untenable position of the [pro-Axis] Gailani government": its army is "presumably unable to defend itself against the English" and it is under threat of an English blockade of its ports and an embargo on petroleum imports. Moreover, "the oral statement [in support of independence] by the Axis is inadequate as a political instrument for the Iraq Minister President" [i.e. Gailani] and there has been a "complete loss of prestige of the Italians and a decline in morale" because of the destructive British attack on the Italian navy at Taranto in November 1940.

In Palestine, Arab-Jewish hostilities have quieted down, the people want peace, and "the achievements of the Italian Air Force are apparently minimal." In Saudi Arabia, the king does not trust German policy. Egypt is firmly in English hands, defended by an army of 175,000 English, Australian, New Zealand, and Indian troops; and the Indians, though Mohammedans, "are to be considered reliable." Older officials and rich families are also pro-English. Only "the younger officials and officers of the

---

53 Major-General I.S.O. Playfair, *The Mediterranean and Middle East*, vol. 2 (London: Her Majesty's Stationary Office, 1956), p. 193.

insignificant Egyptian Army are probably pro-German. The lower classes are not interested in politics."

Melchers concludes his report with a warning and some proposals. The warning: "The activity of the English and de Gaullists, the defeats of the Italians, and disappointment with Germany could result in a defection of the Arabs to the side of the English [...] and may perhaps even create a disastrous situation in the whole of North Africa." In assessing the significance of this for Germany Melchers notes soberly, however, in the sceptical style of the diplomats allegedly closer to Weizsäcker than to Ribbentrop, that "the national, military, cultural, and state-building forces of the Arabs should not be overestimated" and that "we have no reason at all to be sentimental about these people, who are basically anti-European and torn by religious, family, and tribal differences." Nevertheless, he also invokes the argument put forward not long before by von Papen that "the Arabs, as inhabitants of the land-bridge and routes leading to southern and eastern Asia as well as to East Africa [...] are a tremendously important power factor." In addition, as they are the foremost representatives of Islam in the world "Germany must not jeopardize her great prestige here if she does not wish to suffer most severe reverses for a long time to come."

Melchers therefore proposes that "without basically giving up the principle of Italian precedence in the Arabian area," the Germans should demand, "in the interest of [...] an efficient conduct of the war" that their own "military and political authorities establish liaison with those of the Italians," in order to "plan measures whereby the reverses that threaten in the Arab area may be avoided." To this end, thought should be given to providing "a written declaration in which the Arabs as well as the Egyptians are assured political freedom and self-determination"; a German armistice delegation composed of "suitable military and diplomatic personnel" should be sent to Syria to collaborate with the Italian delegation and with Vichy's newly appointed High Commissioner, General Henri Dentz—considered by the British Commander-in-Chief in the Middle East, Sir Archibald Wavell, "completely subservient to Vichy and most unlikely to resist German penetration"[54]—"in paralyzing English and Gaullist activity and in getting

---

54 Cited in Isaac Lipschits, *La Politique de la France au Levant 1939–1941* (Paris: A. Pedone; Amsterdam: Systèmes Keesing, 1963), p. 86. On 6 December 1940, Dentz replaced Puaux, who had been trying to play both sides of the fence, maintaining relations with the British while defending Pétain as "le gardien de l'unité de la patrie" (ibid., pp. 68–76). According to Lipschits, Dentz "was in every respect a supporter of Marshall Pétain. In his view, the Gaullists were dissidents, while the British were the executors

rid of the unreliable officials of the present High Commissioner"; a committee of Arab nationalists should be formed in Syria to take the place of the former Syrian Government and "become the first exponent of the establishment of an independent Greater Syrian state to include Palestine and parts of Transjordan"; Ibn Saud of Saudi Arabia should be wooed by the promise — as Oppenheim had suggested in his memo — of "the territories of 'Aquaba and Ma'an now belonging to Transjordan and always desired by him"; and finally (another suggestion of Oppenheim's) "the Arab world should be promised a solution of the Jewish question that it would find tolerable." Melchers concluded, again in the spirit of Oppenheim's memo, that "the execution of only some of these proposals would profoundly stir up the entire Arab world [...] and probably take the wind out of the sails of England and of de Gaulle."[55] Even if Oppenheim's memo played no part in the development of National Socialist Germany's policy in the Middle East, there is no doubt that it articulated many ideas and suggestions that became part of ongoing discussions at Ribbentrop's *Auswärtiges Amt*.

In late 1940, one of Oppenheim's basic recommendations was acted upon when it was decided to send a respected and experienced German diplomat on a mission to Syria, albeit the mission was entrusted not to Grobba, as Oppenheim had proposed in his memorandum of July 1940, but to Grobba's rival at the *Auswärtiges Amt*, von Hentig. At first it might seem that Oppenheim's memorandum had little to do with the decision. In contrast to what Oppenheim had proposed, it was impressed on Hentig that he was being sent on a "fact-finding" mission and was to avoid any provocative activity.[56] In Hentig's own words, "In consideration of [Hitler's negotiations

---

of 'democratico-Masonic politics' and the representatives of 'judeo-saxon finance'" ["fut sous tous les rapports un partisan du Maréchal Pétain. Pour lui, les gaullistes étaient des dissidents et les Britanniques les exécuteurs de 'la politique démocratico-maçonnique' et les représentants de la 'finance judéo-saxonne'"] (p. 171).

55 *Documents on German Foreign Policy*, (Washington, D.C., 1960), vol. 11, pp. 826–29, document 481, "Brief for the Conference in the Office of the State Secretary on December 9, 1940."),.

56 His instructions, as drawn up by Melchers, communicated to him in Ankara where he had been waiting for several weeks for a travel permit from the French, and signed by Weizsäcker, stipulated "Your trip is purely of an informational nature." Its purpose was, first, "to report on the political and military situation in Syria and, as far as possible, the neighboring areas. Does England constitute a serious threat to Syria by way of Palestine? Are the resources of France adequate for defense? What progress is being made by the de Gaulle movement? What are the methods by which English propaganda is operating and what success does it have?" Second, "to gather relevant data for our policy toward the Arab states," and third, "to observe Germany's own interests of an economic and cultural nature and to report on them." He was instructed, finally, "to avoid anything that might be construed as approval or support of any tendencies directed against the

with Pétain at] Montoire and of the Führer's Italian policy, the Political Section [of the *Auswärtiges Amt*] decided that I should limit myself strictly to a four-week visit for purely information-gathering purposes."[57] Since Hitler hoped at this point to turn Vichy France into an ally, in sum, the aim of the mission was ostensibly not to fan the flames of revolution in the Arab lands, starting with Syria, as Oppenheim and some in the *Auswärtiges Amt* (such as Grobba) had urged. It was simply to report on the situation in the French Mandate territory, where, as Melchers' memorandum had noted and as Hentig himself was to confirm, there was considerable sympathy among high-ranking officials for de Gaulle, German nationals were being harassed, and even the Italian armistice commission was subject to irksome restrictions on its movements. Moreover, as Melchers had also pointed out and as Hentig confirmed subsequently, Arab opinion was deeply hostile to Italy and perplexed that Germany, the truly victorious power in Arab eyes, was not represented on the commission and was doing nothing to stop the humiliations and injuries to which the French authorities were subjecting resident German nationals and their Arab friends.[58] There was certainly matter enough to investigate in the course of a "fact-finding mission."

Nevertheless, the French were extremely wary of Hentig's plans, delayed delivery of his travel permit, kept him under constant surveillance during his visit, and treated him with suspicion bordering on hostility. At one point the hotel where he was staying was surrounded by agents of the "Deuxième Bureau," the French military intelligence, and he was required to show his papers. Hentig later professed to having kept a low profile throughout his four-week mission: "The French and the English have often claimed that I brought unrest to the land," he wrote later. "Perhaps that is what they feared. But even those hostile to my activities, such as the English Consul-General—who significantly, still remained undisturbed at Aley, twenty minutes above Beirut—knew that this was not the case."

It is by no means clear, however, that Hentig's mission was as harmless as he claimed or as his official instructions seem to indicate. The British Consul in Damascus described its purpose in a telegram to the Foreign office as "to report to Berlin on the general situation and on the state of

---

French government" (*Documents on German Foreign Policy*, vol. 11, pp. 1053–54, document 626 [dated Berlin, 8 January 1941]).
57 Hentig, *Mein Leben: Eine Dienstriese*, p. 337.
58 Ibidem, p. 336.

13. Plotting for Nazi Germany Oppenheim's Role in the Middle East Policy   265

Anglo-French relations; to establish contact with Syrian nationalists; and to launch an anti-British propaganda campaign."⁵⁹ On 7 April 1941, several months before America entered the War, the *New York Times* featured a still more alarming report of Hentig's activities in Syria.⁶⁰ Three Germans, the article claimed, had been

> responsible for the Nazi agitation in Syria, accompanying the plotting for a coup d'état in Iraq. They were Herr von Hoentig, a specialist in agitation in the Orient; Dr. Fritz Grobba, the German Minister to Iraq and Saudi Arabia; and Max von Oppenheim, a distinguished archaeologist and acute propagandist. [...] Herr von Hoentig devoted himself exclusively to stirring up unrest. He warned wealthy Syrians that Syria would soon come under German domination and that those who had not lined up with the Germans would go to a concentration camp. To poor Arabs, he pictured Adolf Hitler as the protector of Islam, sent by Allah to aid the devout. To them he said the British intended to divide Syria between a Jewish Palestine and Turkey. This had considerable success among the simpler Arabs, who also were dazzled by promises of a vast German-protected Arab kingdom. Herr von Hoentig also organized sabotage and assassination gangs and introduced a number of German Oriental agents to the country, where they still remain. He brought to Syria the propaganda film "Victory in the West," which had been used to scare European countries. The film was shown day after day in the Hotel Metropol in Beirut to specially selected parties of Arabs, who at the same time were entertained with Nazi propaganda. [...] Herr von Hoentig succeeded, according to his own boasts in Ankara, in penetrating illegally into Iraq [...] and stirring up trouble there. He set the stage for the coup d'état in Iraq.

In his official history (1956) of the war in the Mediterranean and the Middle East, Major-General I.S.O. Playfair recalls that in September 1940 the Mufti, al-Husseini, had suggested that "from a centre in Syria, the Germans should organize large anti-British movements in Palestine and Transjordan." At first "the German government showed little interest," Playfair writes, but "whether on account of the Mufti's promptings or not, in January 1941 the German Foreign Office sent an emissary, von Hentig —a disciple of Wassmuss, the German Lawrence—to Syria."⁶¹ General

---

59 Cit. Lipschits, *La Politique de la France au Levant 1939–1941*, p. 83.
60 "Three Reich Plotters Try to Win Syria. Following Gains in Iraq, Nazis seek support for Hitler as 'Protector of Islam'." The general drift of the report was correct: Oppenheim was actively involved in the preparations of Hentig's mission, while Grobba's activities were centred in Iraq. All three men were indeed behind a broad plan to stir up the Arabs and tie up large numbers of British troops in the Middle East.
61 Major-General I.S.O. Playfair, *The Mediterranean and the Middle East*, vol. 2, pp. 193–94.

de Gaulle himself noted in a telegram of 13 February 1941 to General Larminat in Brazzaville that "German infiltration into the Empire continues. In Syria a German mission led by von Hentig and Roser arrived in Damascus on January 26 and has visited Aleppo, by way of Homs. Ostensibly this mission is about economics but its real purpose is espionage, anti-British propaganda, and contacting the nationalists. They have met with those nationalist leaders who are most hostile to France and with all the Germanophile Syrians, in particular Sadi Kailani." De Gaulle was well aware, moreover, of Hentig's role in the Middle East in the First World War and drew the obvious conclusion. "Von Hentig," he explained in a follow-up telegram two days later, "was the principal collaborator of von Niedermayer in 1916 when the latter's mission was to bring about Afghanistan's entry into the War on the side of Germany." The Nazi government had appointed him director of the Asia section at the Wilhelmstrasse: "His presence in Syria, authorised by Vichy, highlights German plans not only for Syria but for the countries situated between Syria and the Indies."[62]

This view of Hentig's mission was made official in 1942 in a pamphlet put out by the Free French in London in which it was asserted that from the moment he arrived in Beirut, on 11 January 1941, "M. von Hentig began to work on public opinion, addressing himself preferably to milieux hostile to France."

> His propaganda was at first insidiously subtle. At a meeting in the Hotel Metropole on January 25, to which he invited the main political and religious leaders, he seduced his audience by his affability and affected to pass lightly, out of courtesy, over the thorny problems inevitably created by the French administration. But this discreet behavior was not continued for long. Soon, in the same locale, there was a showing of, among others, the film *"Sieg im Westen"* (Victory in the West), in which the defeat of France is portrayed in the most vivid and striking images. At the same time, M. von Hentig asked the Muslims for their opinions on the creation of an Arab empire; he envisaged the convocation of an Islamic congress in Damascus; he encouraged the formation of youth groups on the German model; he fired up the extremists against the English and advised them to get together with the Iraqi Futuwwah movement. All this under the nose of the representatives of Vichy. Then the clandestine propaganda of the outfit communicated the keyword slogans, which did not take long to reappear throughout the country in the form of demands, outcries, and riots. [...]

---

62 Charles de Gaulle, *Lettres, notes et carnets* (Paris: Plon, 1981), vol. 3: June 1940-July 1941, pp. 256–57.

Soon the superiority of the French was being questioned, along with their right to retain their title to the Mandate. Finally they were compared to the chosen race, the German race, which alone deserves to rule. And the populations of Aleppo, Hama, and Damascus began to sing:

Bala Missiou, bala Mister,
Kelloh barra, haïdé sikter,
Bissama Allah, oua alard Hitler.

("*No more Monsieur, no more Mister: all of you, get out, scram. In Heaven Allah, here on earth Hitler!*")

The effect of all this activity was multiplied by a journey through Syria undertaken by Messieurs von Hentig and Roser in the course of which they presented their films and openly proclaimed the coming of the German Era. In Damascus, Tripoli, Lattaquieh, Aleppo, and even beyond the Euphrates, they carried out a round of visits, with an air of officialdom, to all the notables of each place, to religious leaders, to schools. [...] In every place where people thought they had something to complain about, it was explained to them that it was useless to pay any attention to the French since they retained only the shadow of authority, that a very different future was on the way, and that it was with those who held that future in their hands that they should be dealing. It is worth noting that in March of this year a tailor in the el-hoja souk in Damascus began turning out swastika flags for some individuals who expected to be making use of them in the very near future. [63]

The character and thrust of Hentig's mission have been summed up by a modern French historian as follows:

What Hentig undertook was above all a campaign of anti-French propaganda. He did everything he could to undermine the prestige of France in the Levant. To this end he showed the film "Sieg im Westen" in all the territories of the Mandate and exploited to the full the discontent provoked among the Syrians by the bad economic situation and the non-ratification of the 1936 Franco-Syrian Treaty of Independence. Von Hentig directed his propaganda especially toward nationalist circles and had conversations with several leaders of the Nationalist Block. He found very receptive interlocutors. The populations of Syria and Lebanon had become more and more germanophile as the German armies, surrounded by a halo of invincibility moved ever closer to their two countries. As Dentz declared at his treason trial in 1945: "The Reich appeared at that point as a liberator. The Reich was the power that was going to liberate all the Arab lands, unite

---

[63] *Les Allemands en Syrie sous le gouvernement de Vichy* (London: Publications de la France combattante, brochure no. 201, 1942), pp. 5–6. The Futuwwah movement advocated by Hentig was a pan-Arab, fascist youth movement organized on the model of the Hitler Jugend and officially instituted in Iraqi schools in 1939 by Sami Shawkat, the Iraqi Minister of Education and brother of Naji Shawkat (see Reeva S. Simon, *Iraq Between the Two Wold Wars*, pp. 110–14).

them, and create the great Arab Empire. No one expected that liberation and that great Empire to come from France, conquered and shorn of its prestige. England was always perceived as the promoter of the resented Mandate idea and the enemy of Arab emancipation. It was the Reich, victorious, coming ever nearer, especially after the invasion of Greece [in March 1941], that was the future liberator."[64]

In view of this apparently more activist character of Hentig's mission, it comes as no surprise that he was supplied by Oppenheim, before he set out, with thirteen letters of introduction to Syrian notables, all of whom were explicitly identified by Oppenheim in a covering note with tags such as "completely nationalist," or "like all Bedouins, unquestionably an Arab nationalist," or, in the weakest case, "apparently French-oriented but nevertheless nationalist." Among them were three powerful Bedouin chieftains with whom the old scholar had established relations of friendship or "blood-brotherhood" during his own earlier stays in Syria, a former President of the Syrian Republic under the Mandate, the Director of the Syrian Museums, a professor and lawyer in Damascus married to a German woman, and Adel Arslan, the brother of the exiled Pan-Islamist leader Shakib Arslan.[65] Hentig himself recorded later that, as he travelled from place to place around the country establishing contact with local dignitaries and chieftains, he was constantly approached, in his capacity as a representative of the victorious German government, by all manner of politically interested parties: Arabs, Chaldeans, Kurds, Armenians, leaders of the various religions, even Jews willing to collaborate with the

---

64 Lipschits, *La Politique de la France au Levant 1939–1941*, pp. 83–84. See also on Hentig's mission to Syria and Lebanon, Chantal Metzger, *L'Empire colonial français dans la stratégie du Troisième Reich (1936–1945)*, vol. 1, pp. 338–45. According to Metzger, when he stopped off on his way to Syria at Ankara, Hentig already established contact with a disaffected, pro-German, anti-British French official, the Corsican Columbani, who had been chief of police in Syria and whose close contacts with Syrian nationalists had led to his being recalled to Paris. Columbani, who was also a confidant of Al-Husseini, the Grand Mufti of Jerusalem, supplied Hentig with information about French troop numbers and strengths, military supplies, etc. (pp. 339–41).

65 See Oppenheim's letter to Hentig, accompanying the letters and cards of introduction and containing a list of the names, together with "notes on the persons to whom I have given you introductions" in Robert L. Melka, "Max Freiherr von Oppenheim: Sixty Years of Scholarship and Political Intrigue in the Middle East," *Middle Eastern Studies*, 9 (1973): 81–93 (pp. 90–92). See also Hentig, *Mein Leben: Eine Dienstreise*, p. 341. In return for this service, Melka relates, Oppenheim asked Hentig to intervene with the French authorities in order to ensure continuation of his excavation concession at Tell Fakhariya, which the French had transferred to an American team from the Oriental Institute at the University of Chicago.

National Socialists "against their own people, especially the orthodox Zionists, if Hitler would guarantee them an independent Jewish Palestine." Whatever his instructions about avoiding interference in the political situation in Syria may have been, Hentig did not discourage these approaches. On the contrary, he undertook, as he conceded later in his Memoirs, "first, to defend our Arab friends from the most egregious attacks on them by the Mandatory power and to obtain the release of as many of those who had been imprisoned or sent to camps as possible," and second, while avoiding any hard and fast commitments, to leave those who had approached him "in no doubt as to our essential orientation and attitude."

Thus he explained to one Arab leader (who was to be the first Prime Minister of Lebanon after that country gained independence in 1943) that "in response to specific political conditions, a government must often temporarily adopt an attitude that deviates from its permanent national policy. It was, however, the 'policy of the German People' to collaborate in the struggle for the independence of the Arab lands [*die Unabhängigkeit der arabischen Länder mitzuerkämpfen*]." That, he assured his Arab friends "was our permanent position, overriding any opinions and measures that might at a given moment be taken by a German government." The Jewish delegation, in contrast, was advised that "in consideration of the interests of our Arab friends and of our general principles, the conditions it had set forth could never be accepted." Hentig was somewhat more sympathetic in his response, however, than Oppenheim had been in his memorandum of July 1940. The delegation's leader, "a superior-looking young officer type," was assured that "I personally have always been a supporter of a Jewish national state in a territory with a favourable climate and adequate space for settlement."[66] Hentig had in fact been a

---

66 Hentig, *Mein Leben: Eine Dienstreise*, pp. 338–40. The "the superior-looking young officer type" referred to by Hentig was Naftali Lubenchik, representing the Lehi group of Revisionist Zionists led by Avraham Stern (usually referred to as the "Stern Gang"). In December 1940 or January 1941, Lubenchik was sent by Stern (who had already tried to negotiate a deal with the Italian Fascists) to Beirut to meet with Hentig and offer to "actively take part in the war on Germany's side" in return for German support for "the establishment of the historic Jewish state [i.e. on both banks of the Jordan] on a national and totalitarian basis" (Joseph Heller, *The Stern Gang: Ideology, Politics and Terror, 1940–49* [London: Frank Cass Publishers, 1995], pp. 78–79, 85–87; Colin Shindler, *The Land beyond Promise: Israel, Likud and the Zionist Dream* [London and New York: I.B. Tauris, 2002], pp. 22–27). Despite the rebuff received by Lubenchik, Stern renewed his overture to the Germans in December 1941, with even less success (Heller, pp. 90–91).

consistent supporter of the *Zionistische Vereinigung für Deutschland,* the main, twenty thousand member strong German Zionist organization, founded in 1896, and had done everything he could to facilitate the emigration of German Jews to Palestine. After the November 1938 pogrom it was Hentig who was approached by the *ZVfD* for help in preventing a planned parading of arrested Jewish men through the streets of Berlin. By January 1941, however, advocacy of Jewish emigration to Palestine had become completely inopportune. On the other hand, a project to settle European Jews in "a territory with a favourable climate and adequate space," namely Madagascar—a project discussed in various quarters since the 1920s and approved by Hitler, Göring, Ribbentrop, Eichmann, and many others in the National Socialist Party—had again come under active consideration in the *Auswärtiges Amt,* following the armistice with France. Though it was totally unacceptable to the extremist splinter group of Revisionist Zionism that had approached Hentig, such a solution of the "Jewish problem" would probably have been supported by Oppenheim—as well, no doubt, as al-Husseini and the Arabs.[67]

On 26 February 1941, on his return from Syria, Hentig drew up a broad-ranging report on the situation in the Arab lands of the Middle East. Some of its recommendations were included in a "Memorandum on the Arab question" and "how it should be handled with reference to our aim of achieving England's defeat" produced by Woermann (the Head of the Political Department of the *A.A.*) a little over a week later, on 7 March. A key issue was raised and resolved at the outset: "The Islamic idea (Holy War) is impracticable under the present grouping of powers. Arab nationality and Islam are not identical. The Arabs to be brought into our plans are fighting

---

[67] On the Madagascar project, see Christopher R. Browning, *The Final Solution and the German Foreign Office: a study of Referat D III of Abteilung Deutschland, 1940–43* (New York: Holmes and Meier, 1978), pp. 34–45. According to Francis Nicosia, Hentig had been in favor of the ha'avara Agreement (on ha'avara, see note 17 above) and of the emigration of German Jews to Palestine prior to the outbreak of war and had at that time, in order not to alienate the British, opposed supplying arms to Arab insurgents in the Palestine Mandate. "He supported a policy of concentrating Jews in Palestine and their autonomy in a Palestinian state with an Arab majority, as Germany's response to the recommendations of the Peel Commission" (F. Nicosia, *The Third Reich and the Palestine Question,* pp. 132–33, 181). At the same time, however, Hentig had also made various suggestions for countering Zionist efforts to establish an independent Jewish state in Palestine (p. 124). By 1941, he may well have come around to supporting the Madagascar solution of the "Jewish problem." On Hentig's support of the *Zionistische Vereinigung für Deutschland,* see Carsten Teichert, *Chasak! Zionismus im nationalsozialistischen Deutschland 1933–1938* (Cologne: ELEN Verlag, 2000), pp. 215, 248, 383, 472.

not for religious but for political aims." In other words, as Oppenheim's silence on the topic in his memorandum to Habicht of 25 July 1940 had implied, *jihad* should no longer be regarded in 1940–1941 as the key element that it had been in Imperial Germany's plans in 1914–1918. The Woermann memorandum then went on to deal with the importance of the Arab area in general and with the possibilities for action by Germany in the form of propaganda, sabotage, uprisings, and publication of the written statement, insistently demanded by the Arab leaders, of Axis support for the independence and ultimate unity of all the Arab lands.

"In the context of the war with England," it was asserted, "the Arab area holds a position of great strategic significance," since it "forms a land bridge between Africa and India." Over it, "through Iraq, Transjordan and Palestine," and through the Suez canal, "vast numbers of [British] troops and quantities of war material" have been shipped westward to Egypt and war material has also been shipped over it "to Turkey and probably also to Greece." (Greece, it will be remembered, had been attacked by Italy at the end of October 1940 and the campaign had not gone well at all for the Italians, so that by the time Hentig composed his report, Germany was on the verge of coming to the aid of its Italian ally with its own invasion of Greece; as for Turkey, a confidential letter from Ambassador von Papen to Secretary of State von Weizsäcker of 8 April 1941 makes it clear that Turkey was also in constant fear of attack by the Axis.[68]) In addition, it was noted, as if in anticipation of operation

---

68 Von Papen reports to Weizsäcker that, according to the Secretary General at the Turkish Foreign Ministry, Numan Menemencioglu, Turkey is fearful of both warring powers and "has no use for either a total English or a total German victory." While expressing his "excitement" at the "fabulous successes" of the German army in Yugoslavia, von Papen also notes darkly that "the excitement here is even greater because many people believe it will now be Turkey's turn" (*Documents of German Foreign Policy*, series D, vol. 12, pp. 491–93, document 295). That this fear was not unfounded is suggested by a directive of the *Oberkommando der Wehrmacht* of 30 June 1941, announcing "continuation of the struggle against the British position in the Mediterranean and the Near East by means of a concentric attack which is to be launched from Libya through Egypt, from Bulgaria through Turkey, and possibly from Transcaucasia through Iran. [...] For this purpose provision should be made for concentrating in Bulgaria as soon as possible forces strong enough to make Turkey politically compliant or to break her resistance by force of arms" (ibid., document 617, pp. 1012–13, note 3). The British invasion of Syria in June 1941 was undertaken largely to prevent Germany from establishing the power-base there that Oppenheim and von Hentig advocated, since that would have isolated Turkey and brought such pressure to bear on her, that she might have been forced to permit the transit of German war material, thus endangering not only Palestine, but Egypt and Iraq, which had only recently been wrested back from the pro-Axis al-Gailani (see Kolinsky, *Britain's War in the Middle East*, pp. 166–69).

"Barbarossa," "through these areas passes also a main route on which England and the Soviet Union might join hands if the occasion should arise." The Middle East countries are also vital to the British because of the oil fields of Mosul and the pipeline to the Mediterranean at Haifa.

"A decisive blow to the British Empire" could thus be delivered in this area "through operations against Egypt and/or military occupation of the Arabian land bridge." Admittedly, "this area lies beyond the reach of the Axis powers *at the present time* [italics in text]—except with respect to the Luftwaffe," but that situation would change if Turkey could be brought into the war on the side of the Axis. In the meantime, propaganda needs to be vigorously carried out by radio broadcasts in Arabic, by exerting influence on Arab newspapers and magazines, by cultivating relations with Arab personalities and by doing "something conspicuous from time to time, such as the dispatch of Minister von Hentig to Syria." The *Abwehr* should be given "greater latitude" with respect to acts of sabotage and uprisings by the Arabs, a line of action from which, "in compliance with the wishes of the Foreign Minister, it has refrained for the most part, out of consideration for Italy." As for the written declaration of support for Arab independence and unity, "purely from the standpoint of Germany's interest, there could be no objection to such a declaration. Given the Arabs' dislike of the English and of the Italians, it would be easy for us to attain a position of influence in a Greater Arab empire. [...] The difficulties arise from considerations relating to other powers"—i.e. Italy, France, Turkey, and the Soviet Union. At some point the Italian Government needs to be induced to "define its objectives in the Arab area," but the moment may not yet be opportune.

Likewise, "a declaration favouring a Greater Arabia would, because of Syria, be contrary to our general policy of not including the French colonial empire, at the present time, among the subjects under discussion." In Syria, such a declaration might "bring about an open defection to the de Gaulle camp. Even France herself and other parts of her colonial empire might in this way be driven further toward de Gaulle and England." Still, "as regards France, this question is of more than mere tactical significance. Underlying it is the question whether French influence in Syria is to continue at all." But that question is as yet "not ripe for discussion." As for the Soviet Union (relations with which, in February 1941, were still officially governed by the non-aggression treaty of August 1939), German policy in Iraq might have to take Soviet interests into account. All in all, therefore, "it appears to be difficult to issue a declaration in favor of a Greater Arab federation which [...] goes substantially beyond our former declaration. Some kind of reaction to the wishes expressed by the Grand Mufti [...] would, however, be desirable." This part of the memorandum closes on a prudent note: "It will always be safe to repeat in talks with the Arabs that the victory of the Axis powers is certain, that Germany has no territorial ambitions in this area, and that we are linked with the Arabs by being opponents of their English oppressors; that we share their views on the Jewish question; and that the Arabs can always be sure of our support within practical limits whenever they themselves take up the struggle against England."

The rest of the memorandum was mainly about Iraq and how it might be supported militarily and financially if it were to enter the war on the side of the Axis. The presciently cautious position expressed on this matter probably reflected the views of Hentig rather than Grobba. From a military point of view, it was stated, "open resistance by Iraq against England" at the present time, "could have only a brief success, and in the final outcome [...] strengthen British prestige." Hence "it must be our policy to keep Iraq's confidence in us alive" through the delivery of requested weaponry—"once a route for the transport of the material has been settled"—in order that "Iraq will strike when the over-all military and political situation makes such action desirable." However, "Iraq's open rebellion against England should not be actively promoted until the moment is conducive to success." In conclusion, the memorandum advised the "removal of de Gaulle followers in key positions from Syria" and "in accordance with the proposals of Minister von Hentig," the setting up of "a German delegation to the Italian Armistice Commission in Syria, to be headed by Minister von Hentig (formally in his military capacity as Major in the reserves)."[69]

It seems likely that von Hentig made the final report on his mission, and perhaps earlier reports too, available to Oppenheim, for in a second memorandum to the *Auswärtiges Amt* on 22 March 1941, the old scholar essentially backed up Hentig's views.[70] As summarized by the late Robert Melka, this second memorandum of Oppenheim's contained an overview of his ideas on the mandated territories of the Middle East, based, he said, on his long experience there. Oppenheim, according to Melka,

described the peoples of the mandates, with few exceptions, as deeply

---

69 *Documents on German Foreign Policy*, series D, vol. 12, pp. 234–43, document 133.
70 This memorandum, referred to by Melka, *Middle Eastern Studies*, 9 (1973): 81–93, is preserved in the Records of the German Foreign Office Received by the Department of State, Microcopy T-120, Roll 735, "Reise Syrien 1940–41, Allgem. Schriftwechsel, Ausgrabungen Oppenheim, Roser, Lageberichte—W.O von Hentig, frames 351092, 351096–8."

opposed to French and British domination. At the present time Syria was the only country of the Middle East accessible to Germany [all the others—Egypt, Palestine, Transjordan, Iraq, Saudi Arabia—being directly or indirectly, under British control or influence], which should seize this opportunity "in order to establish ourselves there strongly and in wide spheres of action." This, von Oppenheim thought, could best be done through a German armistice commission. The Italian commission was isolated and had no influence with the local population, and therefore the Germans must have their own commission, which, because of the high qualifications of its members, would become "the strong point of German power, and especially the point of support for our Arab friends," not only in Syria, but in neighbouring countries as well. Such a policy, he concluded, would be welcomed by the Arabs and would enable Germany to play a leading role in the future united Arab state, which she should promote.

"Von Oppenheim's memorandum," in Melka's view, "contained such recent information on Syria, which he had not visited since the spring of 1939, and bears such a close resemblance to the report and recommendations which von Hentig submitted on February 26, that it is difficult to escape the conclusion that it was drafted under the latter's inspiration."[71] However, while the Italian government gave its consent to the dispatch of German liaison personnel to the Italian Armistice Commission in Syria, the French in a clear sign of their deep suspicion of this particular German diplomat's aims and activities absolutely refused to have him return to Syria. Woermann, on his side noted that, as "Herr von Hentig is a man especially suited for the task, […] the matter has become a question of prestige to us as a result of the French refusal." He suggested that Hentig and Jacques Benoist-Méchin, the French rightwing writer, Vichy diplomat, and friend of the German ambassador in Paris, Otto Abetz, get together and work things out. Though he noted in the same memorandum that "we must insist on sending Hentig," three weeks later (in a memorandum of 8 May 1941) he climbed down and, in light of Abetz's insistence that he did "not consider sending Minister Hentig to Syria advisable at this time," proposed that Rudolph Rahn, an official at the German Embassy in Paris—who was, on the whole, unsympathetic to Arab nationalism and an advocate of working with Vichy France—be sent instead.[72]

---

71 Robert L. Melka, "Max Freiherr von Oppenheim: Sixty Years of Scholarship and Political Intrigue in the Middle East," p. 88.
72 *Documents on German Foreign Policy*, vol. 12, pp. 561–62, 742–43, documents 352 (15 April

The French authorities' already considerable suspicion of von Hentig and his plans for Syria had clearly been aggravated as a result of his activities in the Mandate during his visit in February. They were convinced that it was von Hentig who was behind the serious unrest in Syria in the months of March and April following his visit.[73] Earlier reluctance to let him into the country was thus turned into adamant refusal. All in all, it seems safe to assume that, even if Hentig's vision of German policy in the Middle East was more cautious and less grandiose than that of his friend "Maxbaron," the two men worked closely together and were totally committed to the goal they had both sought to realise under the Kaiser a quarter of a century earlier: the triumph of Germany and the destruction of the British Empire. Oppenheim was happy to collaborate with all—Grobba, Prüfer, Shakib Arslan and, in all likelihood, the Mufti, al-Husseini—who shared that commitment and who believed, whatever their personal rivalries, that the Middle East held a key to Germany's victory in the war.

1941) and 476 (8 May 1941). On Rahn's activities in Syria and later in the French North African colonies, see Hirszowicz, *The Third Reich and the Arab East*, pp. 161–64, 184–88, 270–71, 288–89.

73   Hirszowicz, *The Third Reich and the Arab East*, p. 162. With the old Directorate still in power in Vichy-ruled Syria and no reform in sight, the nationalists organized a general strike in March 1941. This sparked off many demonstrations and much violence. "Arrests are in their hundreds," the long-time nationalist leader Shukri Al-Quwatli (later President of Syria) wrote in a letter dated 2 April 1941, "and the number of people searched for in their homes, causing them to flee, is over five hundred. [...] There is much oppression, and injustice knows no bounds. Despite all this the nation is standing firm. [...] The Senegalese [French troops] are everywhere. The strike is general. The army and the tanks are in the streets. Yesterday there were casualties. All the Syrian towns are on strike" (cit. Salma Mardam Bey, *Syria's Quest for Independence 1939–1945* [Reading, England: Ithaca Press, 1994], p. 30).

14. Max von Oppenheim's Last Years

Oppenheim's fate until the end of the war was substantially similar to that of most Germans. He suffered material hardship, which he bore stoically, but appears not to have been in any way molested. Though he himself later attributed the relative security he enjoyed to the protection of well-placed old friends from the time of the *Kaiserreich*, he seems not to have suffered, as many of them did, and as Waldemar and Friedrich Carl, the sons of his cousin Simon Alfred, also did, in the wake of Stauffenberg's attempt on Hitler's life in 1944. In the unfinished autobiographical notes he prepared in the last year of his life, he specifically names Canaris, for example, as one of those who looked out for him, but there is no indication that he was in danger after Canaris was arrested and executed as a result of Stauffenberg's failed coup. It is even possible that he himself was able to provide some protection to his loyal assistant and collaborator, Werner Caskel, who, as a "half-Jew" himself, had had to give up his teaching position at the University of Greifswald (though he succeeded in holding on to it until 1938), but was also not otherwise interfered with. Instead, Caskel was consulted, like Oppenheim, on matters in which he was thought to have special expertise.[1] One such matter, as we saw, was the preparation of an adequate Arabic translation of *Mein Kampf* to replace the makeshift versions circulating in the Arabic-speaking world. Concerning Oppenheim's life during the war Caskel observes in the eulogy he read to the *Deutsche Morgenländische Gesellschaft* only

---

1   In a letter from one elderly Orientalist to another, dated 14 March 1940, Caskel is said to be "not in receipt of a government pension" but "presumably getting some money from Oppenheim." Besides that, "he has duties connected with the war. I have not been able to find out anything specific about them (and I did not want to inquire outright), but they do seem to be bringing in some income" (cit. Ludmila Hanich, *Die Nachfolger der Exegeten*, p. 121, no. 427). Caskel went on to have a good career after the war as a professor at the universities of Berlin and Cologne.

that the scholar "accepted all the deprivations of wartime without complaint" and was "satisfied with a very simple room in which to carry on his work."[2]

This he did, preparing his book on the Bedouins with considerable help from Caskel and from Erich Bräunlich, an Oriental scholar who had signed the 1933 *Bekenntnis der Professoren an den deutschen Universitäten und Hochschulen zu Adolf Hitler* [Oath of Allegiance of German University and College Professors to Adolf Hitler], in the offices of the *Max von Oppenheim Stiftung*, which he had set up in his property on the Savigny Platz. On the night of 23–24 August 1943, however, the property was severely damaged in an R.A.F. bombing raid. "A considerable portion of the splendid things stored in the building—porcelain, mirrors, metal objects—has been destroyed, many objects have been smashed to pieces in the vitrines or have tumbled down from the walls," Oppenheim wrote after surveying the scene. "Thank God, the beautiful Arab room from Damascus, next to my study on the Knesebeckstrasse, with its boiseries and its walls and ceilings of wood has been spared.[3] [...] Unfortunately, on the Savigny-Platz side, the part of the library that had been set up in the office, in the co-workers' room, and in my study is a complete mess, the shelves have collapsed and many books have been destroyed or rendered unreadable. [...] To my great dismay, this is also the case with my scholarly papers. And so a great part of my life's work has been wiped out."[4] A couple of weeks later the Tell Halaf Museum

---

2 Werner Caskel, "Max Freiherr von Oppenheim" (Nachruf), *Zeitschrift der deutschen morgenländischen Gesellschaft*, 101 (1951): 3–8 (p. 6).
3 But see below, note 4.
4 Cit. Teichmann, *Faszination Orient*, p. 92. In a letter of June 1946 to his old colleague Ernst Herzfeld, who, having lost his position at the University of Berlin in 1935, had emigrated to the United States and was living in Princeton, N.J., Oppenheim painted an even bleaker picture of his losses: "My entire library of around 42,000 volumes went up in flames," as a result of bombing raids on Berlin in August 1943, "from which I was lucky to escape with my life. I had stored part of it, along with other beautiful things from the Stiftung in a castle in Mark Brandenburg but that too burned down and was looted. I had hidden away other valuable objects from the oriental collection in the cellars of the National Museums and in a different castle in Mecklenburg. That castle met the same fate as the first one. There was also much damage to what had been stored in the Museum. About 800 to 900 volumes in all were saved, along with a few items from the collection. The beautiful Arab room from Damascus was also destroyed by fire. The original sculptures from Tell Halaf were blown to pieces, but not entirely destroyed. The pieces were carefully collected, sorted, and stowed away in the deep cellars beneath the Pergamon Museum, so that, God willing, they can be put together again at some later date. After all, that is what we already did once, around 1930, with many Tell Halaf sculptures that had been blown apart by the wicked Tiglatpilesar I, when he set fire,

14. Max von Oppenheim's Last Years   279

Fig. 14.1 Max von Oppenheim (left) and his faithful manservant Sommer, photograph sent by Oppenheim at end of World War II to his former collaborator Ernst Herzfeld, at the Institute for Advanced Study, Princeton. Ernst Herzfeld Papers, Freer Gallery of Art and Arthur M. Sackler Gallery Archives, Smithsonian Institution, Washington, D.C. Photo © Smithsonian Institution.

3,000 years earlier, to the Temple Palace at Tell Halaf. Most of the small orthostats had already been taken to the National Museums and are still, I hope, safe there. In Dresden in the night of terror of 13–14 February 1945 I was bombed out for a second time and lost everything in the way of books and other things that I had managed to gather together again. But once more I survived along with Sommer." Among the items lost, he specifies, was his carbon copy of a supplement—on the prehistoric finds—to volume 1 of the great study of Tell Halaf, which had appeared with de Gruyter in Berlin in 1943, along with all supporting papers and documents. The original manuscript of this supplement was in the hands of Professor Ernst Weidner in Graz (an expert on Babylonian astronomy, appointed to the chair at Graz in 1943) but he had heard nothing from him for a year and a half and so could only hope that "nothing bad had happened to this excellent man and to my manuscript" (letter dated Landshut, 21 June 1946, Ernst Herzfeld Papers, the Freer Gallery of Art and Arthur M. Sackler Gallery Archives, B-16). E. Weidner lived until 1976.

itself was slightly damaged in another raid. Then in late November 1943 Oppenheim, who in the meantime (having been bombed out of Berlin) had taken refuge in Dresden, along with his manservant Adolf Sommer, received the devastating news that his Museum had been hit by an incendiary bomb and had burned to the ground and that most of the precious sculptures in it, which he had pleaded in vain with the state museum authorities to have stored in a safe place, had been shattered to smithereens. In February 1945, Dresden was the target of a notoriously destructive air attack. Supposedly, the eighty-four year old scholar escaped the burning city in a wheelbarrow pushed by the faithful Sommer.

He lost all his remaining possessions, including manuscripts of the later volumes of the book on the Bedouins and all his personal memorabilia.[5] In March 1945 he was taken in by his youngest sibling, his sister Wanda. Widowed since 1938, Wanda still lived in the handsome late seventeenth-century Schloss Ammerland on the picturesque Starnbergersee about sixteen miles from Munich, which had been the family home of her husband Franz Karl, Graf von Pocci (b. 1870), a son of the prolific mid-nineteenth century artist, cartoonist, writer, and composer Franz Graf von Pocci, and a minor poet and *littérateur* in his own right. Perhaps it was the extraordinary popular reputation of her father-in-law (after whom streets are named in Munich, Landshut, and Ingolstadt) that enabled Wanda von Pocci to live through the Nazi regime, like her brother, without major incident. She died in Munich in 1954.

As Oppenheim was now in need of constant medical attention and had to be in a place with appropriate medical facilities,[6] he settled in the Spring of 1946 in Landshut, the capital of Lower Bavaria, about fifty miles north-east of Munich and only four miles from a property belonging to Friedrich Carl von Oppenheim, the youngest son of his cousin Simon Alfred. Friedrich Carl had taken refuge there with his wife Ruth after the Gestapo arrested his brother Waldemar in Cologne, but he too was soon

---

5   In his Preface to vol. 3 of *Die Beduinen* (1952), Werner Caskel regrets having had to work on the volume without the active assistance of Oppenheim and Bräunlich, both of whom had died. "How a part of the manuscript was pulled out from beneath a flaming rafter and how the material for the fourth volume was saved from the fate of being burned to bits is a story in itself," he writes. "Even so, much was lost" (p. v).

6   Or, as he himself claimed in the letter of 21 June 1946 to Herzfeld, because the all too lovely Schloss Ammerland was under threat of *Beschlagnahme* (of being commandeered or taken over—by the Americans?) and he had therefore once again been forced to move out (Ernst Herzfeld Papers, the Freer Gallery of Art and Arthur M. Sackler Gallery Archives, B-16).

in trouble, as already noted, having been denounced by one of his estate employees for making defeatist comments. Fortunately, a sympathetic or prescient official delayed proceedings against him and he was released from custody by the Americans in late April 1945. Friedrich Carl and Ruth took the old scholar under their wing and also helped him out financially. He was grateful: "Without you two I could not live or go on working, and if I cannot go on working, I do not want to go on living."[7]

And work he did. In the short time remaining to him, he wrote up some parts of an autobiography and left notes for others; tried to reconstitute his shattered library and to secure what was left of his famous collection of artefacts; and worked on the second, as well as on the third and, in his own view, "most important" volume of the monumental scholarly catalogue and study of Tell Halaf[8] — the volume devoted to the sculptures at both Tell Halaf and Jebelet el Beda, some forty-five miles to the South-West, where he had excavated in 1929. He also maintained an active correspondence with Caskel and other collaborators. Helmuth Scheel, whom he had designated as General Director and Curator of the Max Freiherr von Oppenheim Stiftung and who edited the second volume of the catalogue (published four years after Oppenheim's death in 1950), confirms in a Foreword (p. iii) that Oppenheim was working on that volume at the time of his death and that putting it together had been an enormously difficult task due to the loss of many notes and drawings as a result of the War. Only the printer's galleys and the proofs of the illustrations survived, according to Scheel (p. iv). In a letter of June 1946 to his former collaborator Ernst Herzfeld Oppenheim also claims to have "written a fairly large book on the history of the Mitanni, whose capital Wassukani, I believe, lies buried in Tell Fakhariya, next to Tell Halaf, in the area of the springs feeding the river Khabur." "The proofs have already been produced," he went on, "but the work has not yet been published. The original manuscript used by the printer no longer exists, but thank God the proofs do." While this book (which I have been unable to identify) may well have been written before Oppenheim moved to Bavaria, it seems

---

7 Cit. Teichmann, *Faszination Orient*, p. 94.
8 Published between 1943 and 1962 in four sumptuously illustrated quarto volumes (volumes 2, 3, and 4 after Oppenheim's death) by de Gruyter of Berlin with a supplementary fifth volume, in 2010, dedicated chiefly to the reconstruction of the artefacts shattered as a result of the November 1943 air raid on Berlin. Oppenheim describes the planned third volume as "the most important" in his letter to Ernst Herzfeld of 21 June 1946.

that in Landshut he was planning to work back from the surviving proofs to his original manuscript.[9]

On 6 November 1946, a few months after describing his many activities, accomplishments, and travails in his letter to Herzfeld, the veteran scholar and diplomat had to be taken to the hospital in Landshut, where nine days later he died. He was eighty-six years old.

---

9   Letter to Ernst Herzfeld, 21 June 1946 (see note 4 above). A specialist scholar whom I consulted about this work was unable to identify it. There can be no question of its having been volume 2 of the Tell Halaf Catalogue, even though both are described as having suffered the same fate (loss of original notes and manuscripts, with only the galleys surviving). Oppenheim describes the two works quite distinctly in his letter to Herzfeld.

IV
OPPENHEIM'S RELATION TO THE NATIONAL SOCIALIST REGIME IN CONTEXT

15. Jewish Organizations

"Kaiser's Spy," urbane man of the world, self-satisfied member of the German upper class, dedicated archaeologist and scholar of the ancient Middle East, sympathetic student of Muslim peoples and cultures, and in all situations and at all times undeviating German patriot, Max von Oppenheim resists easy characterization. It might be tempting to interpret his disregard of the Jewish element in his family background—to the point of actively collaborating with the National Socialist regime—in terms of the popular concept of "Jewish self-hatred," but that would only be to give a familiar and in itself quite problematical name to a phenomenon that does not lend itself to easy explanation.

Toward the end of her biographical sketch of Oppenheim in *Faszination Orient*, Gabriele Teichmann suggests that "politically and in spirit, he felt at home only in the Wilhelminian era." His social and political conservatism combined with grandiose schemes and openness to new techniques and media—as manifested, for instance, in his promotion of modern methods of propaganda—were typically Wilhelminian, in Teichmann's view. Certainly, there is very little to distinguish him, in outlook, from the many old nationalists from the upper classes of Imperial Germany whom he considered his friends and colleagues. His world, like that of those he associated with both as an archaeologist and as a would-be diplomat, was essentially the world of the Second German Empire. Baptised as a Catholic, with a Christian mother and a Christian convert father, it is quite likely that he did not think of himself as having any significant connection at all with Jews or Judaism and very likely indeed that—like many people of part-Jewish or even full-Jewish background in the Germany of the Second Empire—he did not want to have any.[1] With the Oppenheim bank, yes;

---

1 See Ritchie Robertson, *The 'Jewish Question' in German Literature 1749–1939* (Oxford: Oxford University Press, 1999) for many penetrating analyses of individual cases.

whence his regret that it had to be removed from family control. But the bank was a German institution in his eyes, the very manifestation of his family's devotion to Germany and of its participation in the expansion of German economic and political power in the world. He did not think of it, as he apparently did not think of himself, as Jewish.

Bryan Rigg's two books, *Hitler's Jewish Soldiers* (University of Kansas Press, 2002) and *Lives of Hitler's Jewish Soldiers* (University of Kansas Press, 2009), are among the few readily accessible historical studies that address the question of *Mischlinge* ("half-"and "quarter-" Jews, according to the Nuremberg Laws): who they thought they were, how they felt about their more or less remote Jewish ancestry (if they were even aware of it before Hitler forced the awareness on them), how they felt about National Socialism. Most of them served in the German armed forces during World War II with courage and many were decorated for exceptional bravery. Very often, even when they had misgivings about Hitler, they remained dedicated to Germany, to the project of Germany's renewal, and to achieving German predominance in Europe, if not the world—just as Canaris, Goerdeler and so many other German patriots did. Some occupied important positions and contributed mightily—like Field-Marshal Erhard Milch and Admiral Bernhard Rogge—to the success of German arms. For this, in a few cases, they were rewarded by Hitler with a Certificate of *Deutschblütigkeit*, by which the stain of the Jewish strain in their racial make-up was erased.

It is worth noting that, besides *Mischlinge*, many "hyperacculturated" persons of Jewish ancestry on the national-conservative right of the political spectrum[2]—including even those who, formally at least, remained identifiable as Jews—were susceptible to the appeal of certain aspects of National Socialist ideology. The line between national conservative parties that looked back to the old *Kaiserreich* and the National Socialists who claimed to look forward to a new Germany was sufficiently porous to allow, as we have seen, for various temporary collaborations and alliances, such as the Harzburger Front. Like many of their compatriots, conservative assimilated Jews or people of part-Jewish background were quite likely to see in the National Socialist movement a powerful engine of national

---

The portrait that the (now French) novelist, critic, and translator Georges-Arthur [originally Jürgen-Athur] Goldschmidt draws of his father, a successful German lawyer and judge, in his *La traversée des fleuves—autobiographie* (Paris: Seuil, 1999, pp. 32–44) is exceptionally revealing and persuasive.

2 I have borrowed the term "hyperacculturated" from Ritchie Robertson's *The 'Jewish Question' in German Literature 1749–1939*, p. 345 *et seq.*

regeneration through which the perceived injustices of the Versailles treaty could be corrected and the Weimar republic, widely resented as an alien, un-German product of defeat and subversion or treason, replaced by a strong, close-knit, unified community. Instead of the warring classes and autonomous individual citizens of liberal society (*Gesellschaft*), Germany would rest on a foundation of co-operating orders, individuals who felt themselves parts of an organic whole (*Gemeinschaft*), and strong leadership. In addition, conservatives—Aryan and non-Aryan alike—were often predisposed by their deep fear of Bolshevism to take an indulgent view of National Socialism.[3]

In the hope of coming to a somewhat better understanding of Oppenheim's position, as a "half-Jew," with respect to National Socialism, I propose in the following pages to consider a number of German Jewish organizations and individuals who were in one way or another sympathetic to the movement, at least in the early years of its exercise of power in their homeland. If full Jews, individuals who were willing still to identify as Jewish, could find something positive, even perhaps attractive, in National Socialism, the fact that a "half-Jew" appeared to welcome the new regime and actively collaborated with it, at least until 1942, might be less perplexing. I have very much in mind here a remark by the young author of *The Lives of Hitler's Jewish Soldiers*: "In the end the Third Reich cannot be limited to extremes. Not every soldier was an archetypal Nazi, nor was every soldier a pure Aryan. History does not fit into simple black and white categories. We must struggle to understand the grey middle where real life happens" (p. 277).

* * *

With barely 4,000 members, the extreme rightwing and nationalist *Verband nationaldeutscher Juden* (League of National German Jews), founded in 1921 by Max Naumann, a Berlin lawyer and decorated World War I officer) could

---

3 "We should not ignore or underestimate the fact that this elemental uprising of the Volk has beaten down and overthrown Bolshevism in Germany, perhaps for ever—something no other power could have achieved," Hans-Joachim Schoeps, the fully Jewish founder in 1933 of *Der deutsche Vortrupp, Gefolgschaft deutscher Juden*, wrote at the end of March 1933; and again, in October of the same year: "The epoch-making contribution of National Socialism has been to have overcome Bolshevism in Germany and rendered it incapable of action for as far ahead as one can see" (Hans-Joachim Schoeps, *"Bereit für Deutschland!" Der Patriotismus deutscher Juden und der Nationalsozialismus. Frühe Schriften 1930 bis 1939* [Berlin: Haude & Spener, 1970], pp. 93, 105).

not and cannot be considered representative of mainstream German Jews. It was in fact often in opposition to the *Centralverein deutscher Staatsbürger jüdischen Glaubens* (Central Association of German Citizens of the Jewish Faith, founded in 1893 with the aim of combating anti-Semitism in Germany), which in the mid-1920s had a membership of between 60,000 and 70,000. Nevertheless, its influence may well have been considerably broader than its membership. The *Verband* saw its role as one less of recruiting members than of winning support among German Jews for nationalist programs and movements and encouraging full assimilation to the German people and culture. Its statutes stipulated that

> The aim of the *Verband nationaldeutscher Juden* is to bring together all those Germans of Jewish descent who, while openly acknowledging their descent, feel that they are so integrally bound up with German being and German culture that they cannot feel or think except as Germans. The *Verband* combats every expression and activity, whether by Jews or by non-Jews, that springs from an un-German spirit and obstructs the resurgence of the vitality of the German *Volk*, of Germany's honour, and of Germany's self-respect, and thereby stands in the way of Germany's regaining its high-standing position in the world.[4]

The *Verband* repeatedly denounced *"Ostjuden"* ["Eastern Jews," i.e. recent Jewish immigrants from Poland and Eastern Europe] as alien and uncultured—an old story among established German Jews going back at least to Walther Rathenau's notorious article "Shema Israel" of 6 March 1897, in Maximilian Harden's weekly *Die Zukunft*, and even further to the denunciation of the Eastern European influence on Judaism by some nineteenth-century Jewish scholars of Islam. Some local sections of the *Verband* even supported those who advocated deportation of the *"Ostjuden."* German Jews, or rather Jewish Germans, Naumann insisted, should on no

---

4   Quoted in Klaus J. Herrmann, *Das Dritte Reich und die deutsch-jüdischen Organisationen 1933–1934* (Cologne, Berlin, Bonn and Munich: Carl Heymann, 1969), p. 74, document E611967. Neumann's position was an extreme expression, in post-WWI conditions, of a position that had been shared by "most of the liberal, assimilating German Jewish community" in the period preceding the War. "For most members of the C.V. [*Centralverein deutscher Staatsbürger jüdischen Glaubens*] it was always clear, at least during the period before 1914, that their primary loyalty was to *Deutschtum*, to German *Gesinnung*" (Jehuda Reinharz, *Fatherland or Promised Land: The Dilemma of the German Jew, 1893–1914* [Ann Arbor: University of Michigan Press, 1975], p. 227). Even after 1918 the *Centralverein* remained true to this position, albeit somewhat modified in response to a revived anti-Semitism (Steven E. Aschheim, *Brothers and Strangers: The East German Jew in German and German Jewish Consciousness, 1800–1923* [Madison: University of Wisconsin Press, 1982], pp. 216–25).

account be associated with those foreigners from *"Halb-Asien,"* as their eastern homelands were often described.⁵ Zionism was rejected on similar grounds as un-German. Naumann proposed that those German Jews who embraced it should be treated not as German citizens but as foreigners on German soil, with no more rights than any other foreigners.⁶ In general, loyalty was professed to the new National Socialist regime, with criticism directed only at its policy of racially-based anti-Semitism, its failure to distinguish between deeply loyal, thoroughly assimilated German Jews and Eastern Jews.⁷ In August 1932, several months before Hitler came to power, Naumann was urging the liberal Jewish community in Germany to overlook the "regrettable side-effects" of Nazi anti-Semitism and to join the National Socialists "even if they behave as if they are our enemies."⁸ One is astonished to discover that some religious Jews embraced this position.

---

5   The reference was to Karl-Emil Franzos's *Aus Halb-Asien: Culturbilder aus Galizien, der Bukowina, Südrussland und Rumänien* (1876). See also Ron Chernow's observation that Rudolf and Lola Warburg decided to stay in Germany in part because "they suffered from the upper-class Jewish mythology that they were somehow immune to the abuse being meted out to poorer Jews" (*The Warburgs*, p. 465). The distinction between *Ostjuden* and German Jews was still a feature, in 1976, of a former Stefan George fan's justification of his political "ambivalence" in the 1930s; see Klaus Kyriander, *Von Vater zu Sohn: Eine mehr oder weniger sokratische Apologie* (Ettenheim: F.X. Stückle, n.d. [1976]), pp. 17–18. In contrast, and in reaction to the apparent failure of the project of assimilation, a few German Jews (e.g. Arnold Zweig) came to see their "Oriental" brothers, the *Ostjuden*, as having preserved an authenticity that modern, westernized, assimilated Jews had lost (Noah Isenberg: "To Pray like a Dervish," in Ivan Davidson Kalmar and Derek J. Pensar, *Orientalism and the Jews* [Hanover and London: University Press of New England, 2005], pp. 94–108).
6   Naumann's position recalls that of Carl Friedrich Goerdeler, who had been a Nazi sympathizer in the early 1930's but later became one of the heroes of the conservative "Widerstand" or Resistance. In a document of December 1941 Goerdeler supported the establishment of a Jewish state. (He suggested Canada or South America as suitable sites.) Only those Jews who were war veterans, or whose families had been citizens since before 1871 or who were citizens by 1914 and had converted to Christianity or who were the children of mixed marriages concluded before February 1933 would qualify as German citizens. All others would be treated as "foreigners" on German soil, citizens of the new Jewish state, with only the same rights as other foreign residents (Peter Hoffmann, *Carl Goerdeler and the Jewish Question 1933–1942* [New York: Cambridge University Press, 2011], pp. 115–16).
7   News of Naumann's position reached the U.S. in an article entitled "Jewish Body Backs Reich: Leader Urges Nationalist German Group to Have Faith" in the *New York Times* for 23 June 1933. To the NSDAP, however, the members of *VndJ*, as "Assimilanten," stood in the way of making Germany "Judenrein" (Jew-free) and the *VdnJ* was one of the first Jewish associations to be banned, in 1936 (Ulrich Dunker, *Der Reichsbund jüdischer Frontsoldaten 1918–1938* [Düsseldorf: Droste, 1977], p. 116).
8   Cit. Carl J. Rheins, "The *Verband nationaldeutscher Juden*," *Leo Baeck Institute Yearbook*, 25 (1980): 243–68 (p. 266).

Thus an orthodox rabbi from Ansbach in Bavaria could declare: "From a Jewish point of view I reject the doctrines of Marxism and openly announce my allegiance to National Socialism, with the exception, naturally, of its anti-Semitic component. Absent this anti-Semitic component, National Socialism would find in observant and faithful Jews its most loyal supporters."[9]

The *Reichsbund jüdischer Frontsoldaten*, the strongly nationalist Jewish veterans' association, with a far larger membership than the *Verband* (30,000, according to one of its leaders[10]), while fully engaged in combating anti-Semitism, also expressed strong sympathy with many of the aspirations of the National Socialists. Certain of the association's leaders tried to persuade the NSDAP to drop its anti-Semitic ideology and give up violence against Jews in recognition of the association's commitment to the NSDAP's goals of overturning the provisions of the Versailles treaty, rejuvenating Germany, imposing order on the "chaos" of Weimar, and restoring Germany to a position of power and respect in Europe and the world. On 29 March 1933 a first petition was addressed to the new *Reichskanzler*, Adolf Hitler, expressing dismay at the call for a boycott of Jewish stores and, at the same time, commitment to the essential aims of the Nazi Party: "Wir widerholen in dieser Stunde das Bekenntnis unserer Zugehörigkeit zum deutschen Volke, an dessen Erneuerung und Aufstieg mitzuarbeiten unsere heilige Pflicht, unser Recht und unser sehnlichster Wunsch ist."[11] ["We reiterate in this hour the affirmation of our complete belonging to the German *Volk*. It is our sacred duty, our right, and our innermost desire to collaborate in its rejuvenation and advancement."] This position was confirmed in a lead article at the end of April in the association's magazine by its executive

---

9 *Bayerische Israelitische Gemeindezeitung*, 1933, no. 17, p. 257, cit. Herrmann, *Das Dritte Reich und die deutsch-jüdischen Organisationen 1933–1934*, Introduction, p. 3. As Herrmann notes, such statements were doubtless issued in the hope that they would result in a toning down of the anti-Semitic program of the NSDAP.

10 Dr. Leo Loewenstein, "Die Linie des Reichsbundes jüdischer Frontsoldaten," in *Wille und Weg des deutschen Judentums* (Berlin: Vortrupp Verlag, 1935), p. 7. To this figure he added 14,000 young people in the "uns angegliederten Sportbund" [Sports Association affiliated with us] (ibid., p. 10). According to Paul Yogi Mayer, the founder of the youth group "Schwarzes Fähnlein" (1933), the Sportbund had 216 affliated clubs and a membership of "over 20,000" (Paul Yogi Mayer, "Jews and Sport in Germany," *Leo Baeck Institution Yearbook*, 25 [1980]: 221–41 [p. 230]).

11 Cit. Ulrich Dunker, *Der Reichsbund jüdischer Frontsoldaten 1918–1938*, p. 116.

director Ludwig Freund:

> We have already stated on several occasions that the fundamentals of the National Socialist worldview would have attracted many Jews, just as Fascism did in Italy, had the movement not, in contrast in this respect to its Italian brother, made fighting the Jews in its own land part of its program. Today we ask how long leading and clear-thinking National Socialist men in the present government plan to stick to this part of the programme.[12]

The question raised by Freund concealed a hope nourished by at least some assimilated and conservative German Jews and part-Jews (including Oppenheim in the letter to his cousin's son Waldemar, cited above), as well as by a fair number of conservative right-wing non-Jews who had lent their support to National Socialism, namely that as the regime became established, the violence and rowdiness accompanying its beginnings would subside and its rabble-rousing anti-Semitism sink back into a "normal" and entirely acceptable hostility to "*Ostjuden*" and, at worst, traditional covert anti-Semitism. The sharpest blow to the Jewish Veterans' Association was delivered in the form of the Defence Law of 21 May 1935, by which Jews were excluded from service in the Wehrmacht. The Veterans protested that as loyal Germans they had been struck where they were most German, in their "honour" as soldiers of the Reich. For many, the failure of repeated efforts to have the law rescinded was the point at which they finally gave up on National Socialism.[13]

---

12 Ibid., pp. 146–47.
13 Carl J. Rheins, "*Deutscher Vortrupp, Gefolgschaft deutscher Juden*, 1933–1935," *Leo Baeck Institute Yearbook*, 26 (1981): 207–29 (p. 223).

16. Some Individuals: Schoeps, Pevsner, Kantorowicz, Landmann

Some individual cases reveal a similar pattern of acceptance, even sympathy, despite questions and misgivings. Rabbi Leo Baeck accompanied a protest against the boycott of Jewish stores with the assurance that German Jews longed to "take part in the renewal and resurgence of the German people."[1] Probably Hans-Joachim Schoeps (1909–1980) is the best known of Jewish apologists for the new regime. The son of a patriotic Prussian Jew who had served as an army medical officer in World War I, Schoeps could claim to be descended, on his mother's side, from a Jewish volunteer in the War of Liberation of 1813. In February 1933 Schoeps—then a student of religion, history, and literature with a recently acquired (1932) doctorate in the philosophy of religion from the University of Leipzig and expectations of an academic career (he did go on to become the author of several scholarly books on Judaism, Christianity, and Prussia, some translated into English)—founded a deliberately small and select association, to which he gave the name *Der deutsche Vortrupp: Gefolgschaft deutscher Juden* [The German Advance Guard: A Loyal Following of German Jews].

Schoeps was a complex figure. Brought up, as he himself relates, in a home where religion played almost no role, he was nonetheless unwilling, because of his carefully thought-through conservatism, to ignore or deny his Jewish origins. Indeed, it was because of his Jewishness (so he claimed) that he was naturally and profoundly conservative.[2] On the one hand he remained deeply committed to an idea (or ideal) of Prussia as a state based on the rule of law (*Rechtsstaat*) and on government by an elite dedicated to the good of the state as a whole, yet respectful of particular spheres of

---

1   Cit. Robertson, *The 'Jewish Question' in German Literature 1749–1939*, p. 384.
2   Hans-Joachim Schoeps, *Rückblicke. Die letzten dreissig Jahre (1925–1955) und danach* (Berlin: Haude & Spenersche Verlagsbuchhandlung, 1963), p. 72.

human interest and action, such as religion, the arts, and local communities. On the other hand, he was convinced that the upsurge of popular energies and drives in National Socialism had been necessary to bring about the overthrow of the corrupt and selfish liberal regime that had taken the place of the old Prussian state. "One can think what one likes of Adolf Hitler," he wrote in January 1933, "but there is no belittling what he has succeeded in achieving politically; he has pulled people out of the isolation of their individual fates and bound the masses, through his own person, to the nation again."[3] "National Socialism," he declared unequivocally in a later article entitled "The Jew in the New Germany" (October 1933), "is saving Germany from ruin. Germany is today experiencing the regeneration of the entire *Volk*."[4]

Fully aware, from the perspective of his political conservatism, of inadequacies and dangers in National Socialism, Schoeps was convinced of the need to support the movement in order to secure its victory over both Bolshevism and western-style liberalism. However problematical the "Positiva" of the new force that had broken into the established social and political order might be, they had the merit of challenging the liberal idea of the state as grounded in "Besitz und Bildung" ["property ownership and education"] and having as its primary function the protection of the interests of consumers. As a revolt against the "Sinnlosigkeit unseres allzuvernünftigen Lebens" ["the senselessness of our all too rational way of life"], and the "bedrohlich amerikanisierte Wirklichkeit unseres Daseins," ["the menacingly americanized reality of our existence"],[5] National Socialism was a healthy development—arising from the depths

---

3 "Das neue Gesicht der Politik," one of a selection of articles, originally published in various journals and reproduced in Schoeps, *"Bereit für Deutschland!" Der Patriotismus deutscher Juden und der Nationalsozialismus: Frühe Schriften 1930 bis 1939*, p. 76.

4 "Der Nationalsozialismus rettet Deutschland vor dem Untergang; Deutschland erlebt heute seine völkische Erneuerung" (Schoeps, *"Bereit für Deutschland!"*, p. 106).

5 Schoeps, "Jugend und Nationalsozialismus" (September 1930) in *"Bereit für Deutschland!"*, p. 60. See also "Das neue Gesicht der Politik" (January 1933): "If the state in the Age of Liberalism was considered the agent of society and, at the same time, of culture, new forces have today broken into the depoliticized space of culture and society. The positive aspects of these new forces may well be problematical, but with respect to the ideologies of Liberalism, they are at one in rejecting the view that the role of the state is simply to guarantee satisfaction of the demands of consumers. With the bankruptcy of liberal social thought" the liberal credo that "political commitment and responsibility develop only through the possession of culture and property [*Bildung und Besitz*] has simply been eliminated." Equally, the new forces are opposed to socialist "collectivism": "The situation today has given rise to a new reality, viz. that the principle behind clubs and fraternities [*das 'bündische' Prinzip*] is gradually assuming a political form as the absolute opposite of the socialist collective" (*"Bereit für Deutschland!"*, pp. 71–72).

of the national soul—that might eventually be made to evolve in the direction of an authoritarian rather than a totalitarian state, a state founded on order and history rather than popular impulse and "Blut und Boden" ["blood and soil"].[6]

Schoeps's vision of a reborn Germany is very close to that of traditional German conservatives. It also bears some resemblance to the "New Reich" prophesied by Stefan George and embraced as an ideal by the poet's disciples. While pursuing his doctorate in Leipzig Schoeps had in fact formed a friendship with Wolfgang Frommel, a leading advocate and champion of George's ideas, albeit never a member of the poet's inner circle, and he had been admitted to Frommel's own circle. He also frequented other, more traditional conservative milieux.[7] In 1938, Schoeps—like Hans Rothfels, the Jewish historian who had also been favourably disposed to many features of National Socialism—finally had to flee Germany. (He was able to reach sanctuary in Sweden thanks to the active intervention on his behalf, at some risk to himself, of none other than Werner Otto von Hentig.[8]) Until the last minute, however, he did everything he could to win support for National Socialism among patriotic German Jews. Even when it became impossible not to recognize that racial anti-Semitism would not be eradicated from the Nazi programme, he urged these Jewish patriots to respond to the humiliations they were having to endure at the hands of their fellow-Germans by resolutely insisting on their "German-ness" and refusing to leave their homeland, even while harbouring no illusory hope that their increasingly difficult loyalty would have any practical salutary effect.[9] This he did in the face of the evident displeasure with which such urgings were viewed by the Nazi authorities. The goal of the Nazis, after all, was to make Germany "*judenfrei*" and efforts to achieve this goal had even led to limited co-operation at certain points with the Zionists.[10] On his return to Germany

---

6 Schoeps, "*Bereit für Deutschland!*", pp. 60–62, 68, 71, 74–78, 90–91, 94, 106–07, 225 *et passim*. See also Carl J. Rheins, "Deutscher Vortrupp. Gefolgschaft deutscher Juden 1933–1935," especially p. 217.
7 Hans-Joachim Schoeps, *Rückblicke. Die letzten dreissig Jahre (1925–1955) und danach*, pp. 81–82, 85–87.
8 See Schoeps's own account of this rescue operation, ibid., pp. 108–13.
9 Schoeps, "*Bereit für Deutschland!*", pp. 99–103. A stoical attitude, similar to that recommended by Schoeps, was expressed by the Jewish scholar and member of the George Circle, Ernst Kantorowicz (see below).
10 Karl A. Schleunes, *The Twisted Road to Auschwitz*, pp. 192–200. Schleunes cites an SS order of April 1935: "The attempts of German-Jewish organizations to persuade Jews to remain in Germany is […] in direct contradiction to National Socialist principles and must, therefore, be prevented in any form." See also Francis R. Nicosia, "German Zionism and Jewish Life in Nazi Berlin," in *Jewish Life in Nazi Germany, Dilemmas and Responses*, ed. Francis R. Nicosia and David Scrase, pp. 89–116.

in 1945 Schoeps understandably felt intense remorse at having encouraged "national German" Jews to remain in their homeland and accept their tragic destiny instead of advising them in good time to flee at any price.[11]

* * *

The case of Nikolaus Pevsner, the art historian from Leipzig, who, after emigrating to England, became a pillar of the British art and architecture establishment and was knighted by Queen Elizabeth II in 1969, is no less instructive, despite significant differences. As the present writer knew Pevsner personally, and as recent biographical studies have shed much light on his early life and career, his relation to National Socialism will be examined here in some detail.[12]

Nikolai (familiarly "Nika," later Germanified to Nikolaus) Pevsner was born into a Jewish family of relatively recent immigrants. His father Gilel (i.e. Hillel, the name of the great Jewish sage from Babylon), later changed to Hugo Pewsner was in the fur trade and had come to Leipzig from White Russia (today's Belarus). The family of his mother, Annie Perlmann, had moved to Germany from Poland at a somewhat earlier date and could count some scholars among its members. The home of Hugo and Annie Pevsner at the time of Nikolai's birth was in the Waldstrassenviertel, a heavily Jewish section of Leipzig. Subsequently, as Hugo's business flourished and as the Pevsners became more integrated into German society, they moved to the elegant Konzertviertel where the celebrated Gewandhaus is situated. Though he had a "heart of gold," Hugo Pevsner was "not very cultured," according to his son, and his "bad German," spoken with a Russian accent, together with his general "lack of polish," was an embarrassment. On the other hand, the circle of poets, philosophers, musicians, academics, and artists that his mother, who had artistic interests, intellectual ambitions, and left-liberal political leanings—she was a pacifist during the First

---

11   Schoeps, *Rückblicke. Die letzten dreissig Jahre (1925–1955) und danach*, pp. 100–01.
12   I have been a close friend of Pevsner's son Dieter and the latter's wife Florence, since the mid-1950s when Dieter and I were graduate students at St. Antony's College, Oxford. I also knew Nikolaus Pevsner personally, heard him lecture, and once showed him around Baltimore when he was to give a talk there and I was teaching at the Johns Hopkins University. From my then strongly left-leaning perspective I admired his work and shared many of his views on art and architecture, in particular his concern with the place of art in society. To a considerable degree, I still share that concern, to which a couple of modest recent contributions to the study of the so-called "Nazarene" artists of early 19th century Germany testify, though I had no idea at the time of writing these of Pevsner's interest in and respect for that much neglected school of artists.

World War, held the Kaiser responsible for it, and shared the antipatriotic sentiments of her oldest son Heinz—had gathered around her was "too democratic and unpatriotic" in the eyes of the young Nikolaus. It may well also have included too many Jews for his comfort. According to his exceptionally well-informed biographer, Susie Harries, "the only constant in the thinking" of Nikolaus Pevsner, coming as he did from a family that belonged to neither orthodox Jewish nor German Christian society, was "the kind of patriotism that stems from a desire to belong."[13] Walther Rathenau's characterization of himself probably corresponds quite well— except for the open avowal of "Jewish descent," which Pevsner preferred not to mention or hear mentioned—to the way Pevsner wanted to think of himself: "I am a German of Jewish descent, my people is the German people, my fatherland is Germany, my religion that Germanic faith which is above all religions."[14]

The desire to belong, to be fully German, could conceivably have been one factor—besides the young woman's good looks, charm, and intelligence—in the young Pevsner's choice of Karola ("Lola") Kurlbaum to be his bride. At the same time, his decision to marry into a long-established German Lutheran family was probably made easier by the fact that his father-in-law, Alfred Kurlbaum, was known to be especially friendly to Jews, had taken a Jewish girl as his second wife, and could thus be trusted to be free of anti-Semitic prejudice. The desire to belong certainly underlay Nikolaus Pevsner's decision to convert to Lutheranism, which he himself described as an "act done for me to become a normal German," and not to tell his three children of their Jewish ancestry. It also caused him to regard the *"Ostjuden"* or Eastern European Jews, with their foreign looks and strange ways, as not only many German Christians but many assimilated German Jews did, with dislike and disdain. "Assimilation," according to Hannah Arendt, "is only possible if

---

13 Susie Harries, *Nikolaus Pevsner: The Life* (London: Chatto and Windus, 2011), pp. 36, 38. Nikolaus received lessons in Hebrew from a black-bearded Dr. Kohn, doubtless in anticipation of his *bar mitzvah* ("the Jewish first Communion," as he described it himself) but he did not complete the course and the ceremony never took place (Stephen Games, *Pevsner—The Early Life: Germany and Art* [London and New York: Continuum, 2010], p. 40). In general, the Pevsners were not practising Jews, but Nikolaus acknowledged that his father, though he never said anything about it, was probably upset by his son's not going through the traditional Jewish rite of confirmation.

14 Quoted by Robert G.L. Waite, *The Vanguard of Nazism: The Free Corps Movement in Postwar Germany, 1918–1923* (Cambridge, MA: Harvard University Press, 1952), p. 219.

one assimilates oneself to anti-Semitism."[15]

And Pevsner did. He not only feared anti-Semitism in others, he felt it in himself. "Dostoievsky believes that the destructive elements of Russian and German socialism are peculiarly unwestern," he noted in his diary. "I think this must be right because so many of the leaders are in fact Jews, and the Jews are the most non-western element." "I am [...] a strong anti-Semite and can only get over this by becoming a christened non-Jew, amongst other non-Jewish Jews. Once I can ignore the solidarity that is being forced on me, then perhaps this anti-Semitism will become less raw and aggressive."[16] In addition, the "desire to belong" influenced his political views, orienting him toward a fervent nationalism at odds with his mother's far more radical and leftist stance. Above all, it seems to have had some influence on his views as a scholar and teacher of art history.

The greatest influence on Pevsner, most scholars agree, was that of Wilhelm Pinder, with whom he studied at Leipzig. Pinder was interested in the relationship between art and the general "spirit of the age" and between art and national character. Art history to him was thus a form of *Geistesgeschichte* [History of the human and national spirit].[17] Pevsner took this view over and combined it with a strong commitment to the ideas and ideals of Bauhaus modernism. Modern art and architecture should reflect the essential character of twentieth-century society and twentieth-century society (in contrast to that of the nineteenth century) was characterized—in Pevsner's view—not by individualism, consumerism, free trade, and free enterprise ("*Manchestertum*"), but by anonymity, collectivism, planning, and functionality. "The Modern Movement is a genuine and independent style," he wrote in the last paragraph of his now classic *Outline of European Architecture,* and "this fact is full of promise." "For over a hundred years," he explained, "no style in that sense had existed. As Western civilization

---

15 Pevsner quoted in Harries, *Nikolaus Pevsner: The Life*, p. 47; Arendt quoted ibid., p. 39.
16 Susie Harries, *Nikolaus Pevsner: The Life*, pp. 39–40. For these brief biographical details about the young Nikolaus Pevsner and his family I am completely indebted to Harries, who kindly made an early typescript of the first chapters of her richly informed biography of Pevsner available to me over a decade ago when she began work on her book and asked me for my recollections of Pevsner's visit to Baltimore. I consulted this typescript while awaiting delivery of her book. Most of the material derived here from the typescript is to be found in Chapters 1 and 2 (pp. 1–41) of the printed book.
17 Even in 1940, when Britain and Germany were at war, Pevsner was a refugee in Britain, and Pinder's allegiance to the National Socialist regime had been made unequivocally clear, Pevsner dedicated his *Academies of Art, Past and Present* (Cambridge: Cambridge University Press, 1940), which, by his own account in the Preface, was largely written in Germany in the early 1930s, to "W.P. in grateful and faithful remembrance of the past." Pinder, we are also informed, is "the greatest of living German art historians" (p. 13).

had become more and more subdivided it had lost its faculty to create a language of its own. An atomised society cannot have an architectural style. Can we not take it then that the recovery of a true style in the visual arts, one in which once again building rules, and painting and sculpture serve, [...] indicates the return of unity in society too?"[18]

That statement, in a book published by Penguin in England in 1943, at the height of the war against Nazi Germany, defines Pevsner's lifelong vision of the relation of part and whole, individual and society, the individual work of art and the total culture of which it is taken to be (and, in his opinion, should be) a part. An "atomised" society—that is, a *Gesellschaft*, a constructed union, in contrast to an organic *Gemeinschaft*, in the terms made famous by the great turn-of-the-century German sociologist Ferdinand Tönnies—is a society, in which the function of the state is simply to facilitate and to regulate (to the minimum degree necessary) the competing drives and demands of the original, autonomous, individual units constituting it. Such a society cannot have a unified "style," according to Pevsner. Its artists, enjoying the freedom guaranteed by liberal constitutions, will conceive of their work not in its relation to a social whole of which they and their art are part, but as a free, independent activity ("l'art pour l'art"), the products of which are informed exclusively by individual feelings and perceptions, address only other individuals as individuals, and generally aim to provide sensuous pleasure or stimulation rather than meaning. French Impressionism is often held up (and denounced) by Pevsner as the leading example of this kind of art.[19] In such circumstances, the arts themselves become independent of each other. Pevsner would go so far as to assert that "as long as there was a genuine style in art, the representational arts were in the service of architecture. [...] In Germany, the *Gesamtkunstwerk*—which for Wagner, from within an all-encompassing liberalism, was later an object of longing and striving—was a reality until the end of the Baroque, that is to say until the bourgeois revolution. In Wagner's time, however, and more crassly still, in the Wilhelminian age, painting attracted all the

---

18   *An Outline of European Architecture*, 5th edn (Harmondsworth, Middlesex: Penguin Books, 1957), p. 285.
19   "Um die Kunst des endenden 19. Jahrhunderts in ihrer ganzen Entartung zu erkennen, muss man vom Soziologischen und nicht vom Ästhetischen her an sie herantreten" ["To assess the art of the end of the nineteenth century in all its decadence, it has to be approached from the angle of sociology, not esthetics"]. ("Kunst der Gegenwart und Kunst der Zukunft," p. 2; see note 20 below). The term "Entartung" was to acquire a particularly unfortunate resonance as a result of the notorious 1937 exhibition of "Entartete Kunst" organized by the Nazis in Munich.

greatest talents." To Pevsner, in contrast, "all healthy art is [grounded] in architecture" and the autonomization of painting was "a symptom of life-threatening disease."[20] Painting, in short, is related to architecture as part to whole. It follows that paintings belong in buildings, as part of a total design, not in art galleries and museums.[21] A true "style" in art develops only in the context of an integrated community, which its members, including architects and artists, naturally and instinctively feel themselves called upon to serve.

---

20 Quoted, with the permission of Dieter Pevsner, from the typescript of an unpublished paper, *Kunst der Gegenwart, Kunst der Zukunft* (circa 1934; copy communicated to me by Susie Harries circa 1999), p. 4. Pevsner never abandoned the core views expressed in this paper. A decade later, in the Introduction to *An Outline of European Architecture* (Harmondsworth: Penguin Books, 1943; 2nd revised edn, 1951), he wrote: "An age without painting is conceivable, though no believer in the life-enhancing function of art would want it. An age without easel-painting can be conceived without any difficulty, and, thinking of the predominance of easel-pictures in the 19th century, might be regarded as a consummation devoutly to be wished" (p. 20); and in the Introduction to the 5th edition (1957): "The very fact that in the 19th century easel-painting flourished at the expense of wall-painting and ultimately of architecture, proves into what a diseased state the arts (and Western civilization) had fallen. The very fact that the Fine Arts today seem to be recovering their architectural character makes one look into the future with some hope" (p. 24).

21 "To assess the art of the end of the nineteenth century in all its decadence, it has to be approached from the angle of sociology, not esthetics. What the painter painted arose for his personal amusement and not in relation to the public, that is, to a totality [*Gesamtheit*] he wanted to serve because he felt himself to be an integral part of it. Pictures were conceived and produced in the studio or in nature. They were then displayed in their hundreds at art exhibitions, which by their very nature were visited by extremely small numbers of persons. Thus the people came into contact with the products of art only when these came into the possession of public collections. There they were met with understandable horror by all who saw things quite differently and who wanted quite different things to be represented in pictures from what the artists in their isolated circles had produced. [...] The task to which the Impressionist painters devoted their energies engaged and pleased only the most sensitive, delicate, and high-strung viewers, for the sole object worthy of painting was held to be the representation of any thing in the environment, however insignificant, as it appeared to the eye of a particular painter at a particular, fleeting moment and in a particular, rapidly changing light. Sublimated materialism, extreme individualism, pure nineteenth century. All higher purposes of representational art are rejected with unforgivable frivolity and criminal superficiality" (*Kunst der Gegenwart, Kunst der Zukunft*, p. 2). Pevsner's position was not as eccentric as it might at first seem. One is reminded of Quatremère de Quincy's celebrated critique of Napoleon's pillaging of the art works of Italy in order to fill his museum of world art in Paris. The paintings were integral parts of the buildings—mostly churches—for which they had been made, Quatremère objected; removing them in order to display them in a museum was an act of vandalism. The revival of mural painting in the 1920s and 1930s (the Mexican Mural movement, the Public Works of Art project under the New Deal, and the experiments of Heinrich Vogeler at Worpswede in Germany) indicates that Pevsner's ideas were far from idiosyncratic in his own time. As he himself declared, "Longing for the mural, for monumentality of format and content, has now seized hold of artists too," even if it is still "rarely satisfied" (*Kunst der Gegenwart, Kunst der Zukunft*, p. 18).

Pevsner's position, as an art historian and judge of art, was thus anti-individualistic and anti-liberal. "Whoever feels with joy that he is part of a *Gemeinschaft*, in which he is ready to lose his particularity, must give up belief in English liberalism and individualism along with the idea that every man's home is his 'castle,'" he declared. "To such a person, the uniform is a garment of honour."[22] The community Pevsner envisaged was defined, as it was for Pinder, not in the universal humanitarian terms of the political Left, but in terms of national or ethnic groups—French, German, Italian, Spanish, English. Whence the celebrated, and to many English people themselves, somewhat mystifying title of his 1955 B.B.C. Reith lectures: "The Englishness of English Art." These were, in fact, an extensive development of lectures which he had given during his brief stint in the early 1930s as a *Privatdozent* at the University of Göttingen and of which he had presented a summary in the form of a talk at the University of London in January 1934. The summary was also published a month later in Germany as a short article, entitled "Das Englische in der englischen Kunst," in the weekly magazine *Deutsche Zukunft*.[23]

Since art, in Pevsner's view, is the expression of an age, a social structure, a people, and a culture, its regeneration—its return to "health"—will be achieved only through the regeneration of the people and the social structure whose life and values it expresses. No purely artistic movement can cure the "extravagant individualism" which continues to plague even the German Expressionists, despite their angry revolt against "l'art pour l'art." "Only the regeneration of man in the new spirit of the new state can" ["allein die menschliche Wiedergeburt im neuen Geiste des neuen Staates"].[24] Pevsner was thus brought face to face with the politics of Germany in 1933 and with the claim of the National Socialists that they were about to bring about the transformation he desired. For a time he appears to have believed that the new order they were introducing was a significant step toward the modern century, "cold as steel and glass," of which the modern style in art and architecture—collectivist, anonymous, and "totalitarian," in his own words—was the full and

---

22 *Kunst der Gegenwart, Kunst der Zukunft*, p. 20.
23 *Deutsche Zukunft*, 2 (4 February 1934): 15. The editor of this weekly was Fritz Klein, a journalist known for his nationalist and conservative political stance. Pevsner's article took the form of a review of a current exhibition of "British Art" at the Royal Academy in London. In addition, the Reith lectures drew on a number of short articles on different aspects of English art that Pevsner published in English in 1941.
24 *Kunst der Gegenwart, Kunst der Zukunft*, p. 19.

appropriate expression.²⁵ After all, with Peter Behrens and (above all) Walter Gropius, German architects had taken over the lead in defining the modern style from pioneering, but still hesitant and in some respects backward-looking, English figures like William Morris, Norman Shaw, and Charles Voysey.²⁶ As architecture and society were intimately related, might not the bold, young National Socialist German state be the truly modern state that was destined to replace the tired, ageing, fractious, and disintegrating liberal societies of the West, and especially of England, the "spirit" of which was resistant to radical change and new beginnings? To be sure, it was necessary to defend Gropius and the modern movement from the attacks of some Party leaders, including Hitler himself, but the modern movement that Pevsner fearlessly defended stood for a unified, functional, standardized style appropriate to a mass society. Toward the products of the broader, highly differentiated movement we today mostly think of as "modern," he often expressed feelings of impatience and disdain, albeit he demonstrated greater understanding than the Nazis for the predicament of the alienated artists who created such products.

It is not altogether surprising therefore that, as a young teacher of art history at Göttingen,²⁷ Pevsner was not at first ill-disposed to the new National Socialist Germany. For there was nothing democratic (in our usual Western sense of the word) about his ideal of a totally planned, healthy, environment, every part of which has been designed with an eye to an orderly, well functioning whole; there was nothing democratic about his conception of a whole in which everything and everyone has a proper place, contributes to the whole and is in turn sustained and protected by the whole. There was no suggestion in his writing of input

---

25 The terms "cold as steel and glass" and "totalitarian" come from the final section, on Gropius, in Pevsner's *Pioneers of the Modern Movement* (London: Faber and Faber, 1936, p. 206). "The artist who is representative of this century of ours must needs be cold, as he stands for a century cold as steel and glass, a century the precision of which leaves less space for self-expression than did any period before. However the great creative brain will find its own way, even in times of overpowering collective energy, even with the medium of this new style of the twentieth century which, because it is a genuine style as opposed to a passing fashion, is totalitarian" (p. 206). In postwar editions of this work, such as *Pioneers of Modern Design from William Morris to Walter Gropius* (New York: Museum of Modern Art, 1949), "totalitarian" was prudently softened to "universalist" (p. 135).
26 *Pioneers of Modern Design*, pp. 7–19.
27 Pevsner completed a doctorate on baroque architecture in 1924; after a stint as an assistant curator at the celebrated Dresden Gallery, he obtained a position as *Privatdozent* at Göttingen, where he worked in close association with the Institute for English Studies and taught courses on English art and architecture.

from democratically elected bodies in the making of planning decisions. Pevsner was not a social democrat and he was certainly not a Communist. Had he not complained that his mother's circle was "too democratic and unpatriotic"? Like a fair number of better-off, educated, and assimilated Jews, he was a nationalist and a conservative. But he agreed with the otherwise much-feared extreme Left that the liberal era belonged to the past and he may well have hoped that Germany, which he claimed had taken the lead in overcoming the individualism, historicism, and eclecticism of the liberal era in architecture, would also take the lead in designing a new, modern social order, free from the chaotic irregularity and discord of liberalism. The corporate state—"cold as steel and glass" and "totalitarian"—could have been seen by Pevsner as the political equivalent of the modern movement in architecture and design to which he was so completely committed.

"During the 1920s and 1930s," according to Stephen Games, "Pevsner was as excited by the Nazis as his fellow countrymen, and for the same reasons"[28]—the most important of which, it needs to be emphasized, was seeing his country finally emerge from the humiliation and chaos imposed on it, in the eyes of the vast majority of Germans, by the Versailles treaty. One of the young scholar's colleagues from his time as *Privatdozent* at the University of Göttingen—his first teaching position, obtained in 1929—is reported by Games to have said that "Pevsner felt sympathy for Hitler's national feelings. He felt like a German, agreed that Hitler represented a turning point in Germany's history and felt grateful for him after the humiliation of Versailles. Hitler traded on national sentiment and that's what Pevsner was in contact with too when talking about art and national characteristics."[29] Pevsner seems not to have been unduly perturbed by the anti-Semitic element in Hitler's speeches and writings, dismissing it, as others did at the time, as "propaganda" primarily intended to win popular support. The daughter of an Englishman in the English department at Göttingen University with whom Pevsner was friendly tells of a rather "heated argument" her father and Pevsner had "about Hitler's intentions toward the Jews":

> My father said to Pevsner "What do you think about the Nazis?" and Pevsner said "They're a good thing: we need a bit of self-confidence." And my

---

28 *Pevsner on Art and Architecture: The Radio Talks*, ed. Stephen Games (London: Methuen, 2002) Introduction, p. xxiv.
29 Edeltrud König in an interview with Games, reported in Stephen Games, *Pevsner—The Early Life*, p. 178.

father said "Have you actually read *Mein Kampf?"* and Pevsner said "It's just propaganda: it's not to be taken seriously." He couldn't believe there could be any terrible repercussions. He was very typical of Jewish intellectuals who thought themselves completely German. My father was amazed at his obstinacy and refusal to take the threat seriously."[30]

Perhaps, in addition, as Games suggests, "Pevsner felt safe because he was no longer Jewish." His older son Tom, who had been brought up in ignorance of his Jewish background, told Games: "I never felt threatened by the Nazis. I remember on one occasion, that there were police sirens and asking what they were and being told that they were going to a *Lokal* [bar] to beat up Jews. I was never aware that any of this affected us. It was never an issue."[31]

Even the suspension of the Göttingen University mathematician Richard Courant, along with several other Jewish faculty members in April 1933, appears not to have been seen by Pevnser as a danger signal. "We knew lots of people in Göttingen who lost their jobs," the English lecturer's daughter recalled. "Professor Courant was my father's greatest friend. He lost his job on the first day of the new law [the Civil Service Law of 7 April]. It should have been a warning to Pevsner."[32] Pevsner decided, however, to stay put if possible and support the changes.

This reaction was noted with surprise by the English lecturer's sister-in-law, Francesca Wilson, a Quaker, who in April and May 1933 was travelling in Germany to find out what help the Society of Friends could give to Germans whose life had been made difficult by the new regime. At a garden party given by her lecturer brother-in-law, Wilson met Pevsner and immediately took to him. A brief account of their encounter was included in an article she wrote about her visit to Germany for the *Birmingham Post*:

> One of the most interesting conversations I have had [...] was with a *Privatdozent*, who the day before had been asked not to lecture. He was tall and blonde — only a German with a sixth sense for a Jew would have known that he wasn't Aryan — dignified and refined, not only in appearance, but in cast of mind. He told us of his bewilderment. He had no Jewish affinities. He had been brought up as a German in German culture. [...] "I love Germany," he said. "It is my country. I am a Nationalist, and in spite of the way I am treated, I want this movement to succeed. There is no alternative but chaos. [...] There are worse things than Hitlerism; I think your Press in England does not realise that. [...] And there is much idealism in the movement. There are many things in it which I greet with enthusiasm and which I myself have preached in my writings. I

---

30 Games, *Pevsner — The Early Life*, p. 180.
31 Ibid., p. 184.
32 Ibid., p. 186.

consider compulsory labour which is to start next January an excellent thing. All young men will have six months' service for the state, and no matter what their rank in life they will all work together. Hitler is planning public works on a vast scale to cure the unemployment problem. [...] Then there is much that is puritan and moral in the movement—a great drive is to be made against luxury, vice and corruption. For fifteen years we have been humiliated by the outside Powers. No wonder that Hitler appeals to our youth when he tells them to believe in themselves again, that the future is theirs to mould, that if they are united Germany will no longer be the pariah of the world. [...][33]

Francesca Wilson also apparently accepted the explanation Pevsner gave her of the Nazi movement's anti-Semitism:

The anti-Semitic propaganda of the last twelve years was largely directed against Polish Jews. [...] There were many of them—poor, uneducated, half-civilized people, who, with their inborn skill as moneychangers, made their fortunes during the inflationary period and earned their unpopularity by their noisy *nouveau riche* airs and still more by being mixed up in all sorts of corruption scandals and swindles. [...] Many of them vanished when the mark was stabilized and went off to reap the harvest of the falling franc or to America. Men of this kind are now confused with Jews long established in this country with the highest traditions of loyalty and good citizenship. A large percentage of people recognize this mistake, though they can only say so in private.[34]

Like so many others, including perhaps Oppenheim, Pevsner could well have thought or hoped that violent, rowdy, and indiscriminate anti-Semitism would subside as the regime became established and more self-confident, and that it would cease to affect assimilated German Jews, especially those who had renounced their Judaism and converted in order to become fully German. Or, alternatively, he might not unreasonably have wondered, given the instability of the Weimar years, how long the new regime would last.

Lola Pevsner's younger sister may have hit the nail on the head when she reported to one of Pevsner's recent biographers that the political views of her brother-in-law, about which there was seemingly no secret, were a reflection of his personality: he was a man who liked order.[35]

---

33 Extracts from Francesca Wilson's *Birmingham Post* article cited in Games, *Pevsner—The Early Life*, pp. 187–88, and in *Pevsner on Art and Architecture: The Radio Talks*, Introduction, p. xxiv. See also Susie Harries, *Nikolaus Pevsner: The Life*, pp. 125–26.
34 Cit. Games, *Pevsner—The Early Life*, pp. 187–88.
35 "I know he saw all the positive sides of National Socialism, which were probably the economic ones," Games quotes her as saying, "but that was because of the sort of person he was. He got annoyed when students walked out of the room during his lectures. That annoyed him and he always said 'What I'd really like is to lock them in. Once they're inside, that's where they should stay'" (Games, *Pevsner—The Early Life*, pp. 188–89).

However much Pevsner may have sympathized with the new regime, he too was informed at the end of April 1933 that the courses he had planned to give in the summer semester had been suspended. In September of the same year, he was officially dismissed from his position as *Privatdozent* at Göttingen and encouraged to resign from all professional bodies and associations in Germany.[36] The regime's anti-Jewish legislation had now affected him directly and as he depended on his teaching for his livelihood, the prospect of no longer being able to teach in Germany forced him to consider emigration. In addition, there was no sign of any abatement of Nazi anti-Semitic propaganda. On the contrary, even the schooling of the Pevsner children was becoming a problem. At first Pevsner tried to find a position in Italy. At least that was not too far from Germany. Clearly, Italian fascism did not bother him, and — like Paul Oskar Kristeller, the well-known German Jewish Renaissance scholar — he approached Giovanni Gentile, the philosopher and the author in 1925 of the *Manifesto of Fascist Intellectuals*, for help. It was only somewhat grudgingly, when an Italian position did not work out, that he agreed to go along with Lola's preference and look for a position in England. In October he went to England to see what could be done and managed to obtain an eighteen-month research fellowship for 1934–1935 in the Commerce Department at the University of Birmingham, funded in part by the Academic Assistance Council. This led to his meeting the enlightened furniture designer and manufacturer Gordon Russell, and to his securing an appointment as design adviser to the firm — the only source of regular income he had for several years, even though he soon made a mark as a writer of articles in the *Architectural Review*. Finally, he brought his family over (March 1936) and in October 1942 he was appointed to a part-time lectureship at Birkbeck College in the University of London (at the princely salary of £100 per annum), thus beginning his long association with the college and a brilliant career in the land in which he had so unenthusiastically sought refuge. Until the outbreak of war in 1939, however, the ties with Germany were not completely broken. The Pevsner children went back on holiday to visit members of their parents' families who were still there. In fact Uta, Nikolaus and Lola's daughter, was stranded in Germany without a proper exit visa when war broke out and spent the war years there in semi-hiding.

While waiting for the results of his job search in England, moreover, Pevsner intervened in a widely publicized debate that had flared up

---

36 Susie Harries, *Nikolaus Pevsner: The Life*, p. 129.

between Goebbels and Wilhelm Furtwängler, the conductor of the Berlin Philharmonic. The position he took in that debate—essentially a defence of Goebbels' view that art is not autonomous but should spring from the experience of a people and be in the service of the state in which that people is organized as a polity—may seem surprising, even somewhat shocking. It needs to be emphasized, however, that it was not inconsistent with the aesthetics Pevsner championed throughout his life and that it represents an entirely coherent view of art and its relation to society. It should not be imagined that Goebbels had a monopoly on this view—it was widely held on the Left, including the moderate Left, as well as on the extreme Right— and it is not discredited by the fact that Goebbels expounded an ugly, racist version of it. In the circumstances it was undoubtedly poor moral and political judgment on Pevsner's part to engage in the debate, and it is hard to imagine that there was not a streak of opportunism in his decision to do so, a hope of convincing the new rulers of Germany that he was in no way a critic or enemy of the regime. But there is no intellectual duplicity in the argument itself that he presented. And its coincidence, superficially at least, with important aspects of the position expounded in the debate by Goebbels can help to explain the positive attitude Pevsner exhibited, for a time, toward the new regime.

As conductor of the Berlin Philharmonic, Furtwängler, who, on the whole, accepted the new order in his native land, had to intervene repeatedly to defend, as best he could, the Jewish musicians in his orchestra threatened with dismissal—among them, his extraordinarily gifted 24-year old Polish-born concertmaster, Szymon Goldberg. In a letter to Goebbels, Furtwängler criticized the Civil Service Law of 7 April barring non-Aryans from employment in theatres and other arts institutions in receipt of national, state or municipal funding. "I feel that I am first and foremost an artist," he wrote, "and that I am therefore apolitical in the sense of party politics."

> Art and artists exist to create love, not hate; to unite, not to divide. Ultimately, there is only one dividing line I recognise: that between good and bad art. However, while the dividing line between Jews and non-Jews is being drawn with merciless theoretical precision, that other dividing line, the one that in the long run is so important for our music life, yes, the dividing line between good and bad, seems to have far too little significance attributed to it. […]
>
> Music cannot be made contingent in the same way as other essentials such as potatoes and bread. If concerts offer nothing, then people will not attend. That is why the question of quality is not just a nice idea; it is of vital importance. If the fight against Jewry concentrates on those artists

who are rootless and destructive and who seek to succeed through kitsch, sterile virtuosity and the like, then that is quite acceptable; the fight against those people and the attitude they embody (which unfortunately many non-Jews also do) cannot be pursued thoroughly or systematically enough. If, however, this campaign is also directed at truly great artists, then it ceases to be in the interest of Germany's cultural life. [...]

It must therefore be stated clearly that men such as [Bruno] Walter, [Otto] Klemperer, [Max] Reinhardt [the theatre director] and others must be allowed to exercise their talents in Germany in the future as well, in exactly the same way as Kreisler, Huberman, Schnabel and other great instrumentalists of the Jewish race. It is only just that we Germans should bear in mind that in the past we had in Joseph Joachim one of the greatest violinists and teachers in the German classical tradition, and in Mendelssohn even a great German composer.

Therefore I repeat, our fight should be against the rootless, subversive and destructive spirits, but not against the real artist, who in his art [...] is always a creative figure [...] and as such helps build up our culture. That is what I mean when I make my appeal to you, in the name of German art, in the hope that perhaps irreversible damage [...] can be prevented from taking place.[37]

As *Reichsminister für Volksaufklärung und Propaganda*, Goebbels responded:

I, as a German political man, cannot recognise only the one line of demarcation that you would establish: that between good and bad art. Art must not only be good; it must be conditioned by the needs of the people—or, to put it better, only an art which springs from the integral soul of the people can in the end be good and have meaning for the people for whom it was created. Art in an absolute sense, as liberal democracy knows it, has no right to exist. Any attempt to further such an art would in the end cause the people to lose its inner relationship to art, and the artist to isolate

---

37 Quoted by Fred Prieberg, *Trial of Strength: Wilhelm Furtwängler and the Third Reich* (London: Quartet Books, 1991; orig. German 1986), Ch. 2, p. 340, note 27; also, more briefly, by Roger Sessions, "Music and Nationalism," in the American League of Composers' quarterly *Modern Music*, 11 (November-December, 1933): 3–13 (pp. 5–6); and Harvey Sachs, "The Furtwängler Case," http://orelfoundation.org/index.php/journal/journalArticle/the_furtw228ngler_case/. Furtwängler maintained his position in a 1934 exchange with Goebbels over the official banning of Hindemith's *Mathis der Maler* and in his own private notebooks, where in 1933 he wrote: "The nationalisation of music [...] leads everywhere to its ruin," and in 1939: "People imagine it is possible to eliminate liberalism, intellectualism, individualism, and lack of connection in art by an act of violence. That may well work in politics, but in art, as in love, there are no acts of violence" (*Wilhelm Furtwänglers Aufzeichnungen 1924–1954*, ed. Elisabeth Furtwängler and Günter Birkner [Wiesbaden: F. A. Brockhaus, 1980], pp. 95, 190). On the Furtwängler-Goebbels exchanges, see also Sam H. Shirakawa, *The Devil's Music Master: The Controversial Life and Career of Wilhelm Furtwängler* (New York and Oxford: Oxford University Press, 1992), pp. 150–57.

himself from the moving forces of his time, shut away in the airless chambers of "art for art's sake." Art must be good, but beyond that must be conscious of its responsibility, competent, close to the people, and combative in spirit.[38]

The exchange of letters was published in several Berlin newspapers on 11 April 1933, no doubt with the intention of creating the impression, especially in the outside world beyond Germany, that the regime was willing to engage in open discussion of its principles and policies. Comment was thus in a way invited, and did immediately fill the news media.[39] As an art historian with strong views on the issue under discussion, Pevsner was naturally moved to intervene. He did so twice, first in a four-page article, "Zum Briefwechsel Furtwängler-Goebbels" ["On the exchange of letters between Furtwängler and Goebbels"], which appeared under the rubric "Randbemerkungen" ["Marginal Comments"] in the theological journal *Zeitwende* for July 1933, and then in the March 1934 number of the strongly nationalist *Der Türmer*. (This was a magazine that devoted many pages to the arts and architecture, inclined in general toward conservative artistic practices, such as "Heimatkunst," and had veered still further to the Right under its newly appointed [1933] editor Friedrich Castelle, a prolific writer, journalist, and early member of the NSDAP.) In addition, the Furtwängler-Goebbels exchange was referred to directly in an unpublished paper by Pevsner entitled "Kunst der Gegenwart und Kunst der Zukunft" ["Art of the Present and Art of the Future"] and indirectly in the article on "Das Englische in der englischen Kunst," referred to earlier.

In the *Zeitwende* article, Pevsner first states what the controversy is about. It is, he writes, exclusively about the fundamental question of the mission of art, its capacities, its aims, and its goals. The radically opposed views expressed by the musician and the politician, it is emphasized, reflect not an opposition of two individuals or even of two social groups, but rather a

---

38 Quoted by Roger Sessions, "Music and Nationalism," pp. 5–6.
39 The *Deutsche Allgemeine Zeitung,* for instance, (which, despite its far-Right conservative slant, occasionally ran foul of the Nazis and had several issues banned) commented: "It is a welcome surprise to find that in the new Germany men of such dignity and standing can debate issues of cultural and political importance in public. Wilhelm Furtwängler showed admirable indifference to public unpopularity by courageously and openly defending his Jewish colleagues and fellow-artists. [...] and Propaganda Minister Goebbels was equally admirable both in his forthright statement of his own position and the way in which, where he felt able to do so, he was ready to acknowledge points of agreement. Above all, one must laud the way in which neither man made use of political or artistic jargon or claptrap, preferring instead to use those intellectual weapons of thesis and antithesis in what was truly an intellectual duel" (DAZ, 12 April 1933, cit. Prieberg, *Trial of Strength*, p. 52).

fundamental historical shift from the era of nineteenth-century liberalism to that of a new conception of the state and its relation to the people and the national will. Furtwängler "nobly" defends the liberal position, according to which art is its own highest ideal (hence the primary and exclusive discrimination among works of art between "good" and "bad"), and which culminates at the turn of the century in the doctrine of "l'art pour l'art" elaborated and defended by writers such as Paul Verlaine and Oscar Wilde, and by artists such as Max Liebermann and James McNeill Whistler. Wilde is quoted as having declared that there are neither moral nor immoral books, only books that are well written and books that are badly written. Likewise, Liebermann, the follower of the French Impressionists, is cited, here and in several other Pevsner essays, for his remark that "What is represented in a work of visual art has absolutely no bearing on its merit." Goebbels is adroitly, if somewhat crassly, complimented: "Knowledgeable as he is in art history, he recognized the deeper significance of Furtwängler's argument. For his reply was not an anti-Semitic pamphlet [kein antisemitisches Thesenblatt], but a little essay in art theory." The crux of Goebbels's argument is then summarized: "Art should not only be good, but should be seen to have a relation to the people; in other words, only an art that is created out of a deep connection with the people can, in the end, be good, and have meaning for the people for which it was created. There is no place for art in the absolute sense in which it is understood by liberal democratism. Attempts to promote such an art would result only in the people's having no inner relation to art and in the artists' themselves being shut up in the airless domain of 'l'art pour l'art.' Art has to be good, but it also has to be conscious of its responsibilities, technically skilful, close to the people, and combative."

As an art historian, Pevsner points out that Furtwängler's view of art as the highest human ideal, as autonomous, and indeed as standing above the state, "arose around 1800." From the perspective of the fourth decade of the twentieth century, however, it "belongs to the past. In today's thinking, the state—or, rather, the people whose will is organized in the form of the state—has become the higher ideal, art the subordinate one; it follows that the artist who personally has no connection with the state will receive no support from the state, no matter what the artistic merit of his work. Artistic ability can never serve as an excuse for a defective outlook." Prudently, Pevsner adds that "equally the artist's outlook cannot be an excuse for lack of artistic talent" and points out that Goebbels acknowledges this. The lesson Goebbels wants to communicate is that "works of art should no longer be approached in a spirit of aesthetic ataraxy; that what is presented to our eyes or ears should no longer be disregarded as of no significance; that the only relevant question should no longer be whether the work is 'good' or 'bad'; and finally that art too should be seen as serving an end beyond itself." According to Pevsner, these views are supported by a long, indeed by "the best" tradition:

> All the great art of the Middle Ages served an end beyond itself; the Catholic art of the Baroque and French art of the Classical Age served. Turning passionately around 1810 against the easy-going 'liberal' painting of the Rococo, the German Nazarene painters longed to serve. It was only in the 19th century that portrait, landscape, and still life came to occupy centre stage in the visual arts. But the new spirit of the present time will assuredly bring forth a new history painting. Even if that involves at first some sacrifice of artistic quality, at least a healthy relation will have been re-established between those who produce and those who consume art. And this remembrance of the past had to happen now. Goebbels's position is related not only to past centuries of art, but to the living momentum of the art of the last few decades. For in the opposition to Impressionism around 1890 and then again in the art that has been produced since 1905–1910 there was a re-evaluation of content and of meaning in the work of art. In the visual arts, one has only to think of van Gogh's longing for a new religious art, of Klinger and Hodler, Munch and Ensor. And are not the improperly named "Neue Sachlichkeit" [a movement in art and literature], political poetry, the *Reportageroman* [the documentary novel], the political film, the musical organizations among today's youth, highly varied expressions of a common longing to reunite with the driving forces of the age and with the struggle on their behalf?[40]

The article "Kunst und Staat" ["Art and State"] in *Der Türmer* opens on a programmatic statement: "In an authoritarian state the relation to art has to be different from what it is in a liberal state. Accordingly, compared with the 19th and early 20th centuries, there is bound to be fundamental change in this domain too at the present historical moment." The aim of the essay, the reader is told, is to investigate "what art may expect from the state today and what the state may expect from art." A brief history of the relation between art and the state follows. In the Middle Ages it is not possible to speak of the state. The masters of iron or glass works and of the guilds received commissions from the local Cathedral chapter or monastery, from the Kaiser, the king, noblemen, cities, and guilds. Neither

---

40 "Randbemerkungen: Zum BriefwechselFurtwängler-Goebbels," *Zeitwende*, 9 (July-December 1933): 67–71 (p. 71).

Raphael nor Dürer ever received a commission from the state. This situation changed only with the absolutist regimes of the Baroque Age. Regulation of economic activity by the state in mercantilism had its inevitable counterpart in state organization and regulation of art. At the Court of Louis XIV of France it was deemed necessary to employ every possible means in order to exhibit and represent the power of the monarch. Hence it was essential that the monarch have at his disposal an art capable of satisfying this need. That was the underlying reason for Colbert's establishing the *Académie de peinture et de sculpture* in 1648. The Academy's task, in line with the policy of mercantilism, was to promote high-quality home-produced art and thus halt the import of foreign products. At the same time, it was expected to propagate a particular style, "le grand goût," and by training the young in it, ensure its spread. Artists who refused to conform to the new court and state-sponsored style were marginalized. "By strictly applying this policy the French state and the Paris Academy certainly blocked the free development of individual genius, but they also ensured a generally high level of quality and a unified style and, above all, set up a healthy relationship between artistic demand and artistic production."

The seventeenth-century citizens' republic of Holland stood in stark political contrast to France, Pevsner goes on. "Correspondingly, the relation of art and the state in Holland was completely different from that which obtained in France. The Court and the city governments were only to a very limited extent a source of commissions. The market for art consisted of a mass of citizens with little structural unity or unity of taste. The Dutch artists' community was likewise a swarm of the most heterogeneous individual personalities. Each individual painted whatever caught his fancy. It was thus not to be expected that the supply of pictures produced in the artists' studio would correspond in any reliable way to demand. Thus a proletariat of artists arose, for the first time, in the Holland of that period, but so too did the figure of the genius who is not understood by his society. Rembrandt created what his inner voice prescribed. The works of his mature and late periods are not directed toward any public. He was demonstrably not interested in taking account of the public's wishes. In this way the natural balance between art and the public domain, which had been so much a matter of course in the Middle Ages, was destroyed."

With this uprooting of the artist, seventeenth-century Holland "anticipated a situation that became unavoidable throughout the entire Western world [...] in the 19th century." Though ecclesiastical art still flourished in eighteenth-century Germany in conditions similar to the Middle Ages, it was around

1800, in German Classicism and Romanticism, that the theoretical basis of a new view of the relation of art to the state was developed, above all in the work of Friedrich Schiller. The artist was seen as divinely inspired, the equal of kings and princes, and the great educator of mankind. Art, therefore, should not serve, it should rule. Indeed, art allows us to imagine an ethical state in the future, but it should on no account submit to any existing state. "The sacred autonomy of art was thus established and its superiority to state and society proclaimed." As an example of the new outlook, Pevsner cites the defiant rejection of the authority of the Prussian state and the Berlin Academy of Art by Asmus Carstens, the neo-classical artist, who in 1796 told the Chief Minister of Prussia Friedrich Anton von Heinitz that he belonged not to the Academy (from which he received a pension) but to Humanity and that he alone was responsible for seeing that the talent God had entrusted to him was put to proper use. Again the Nazarene artists are invoked as exceptions to the artists' new view of themselves, inasmuch as they looked back for inspiration to an earlier time when the artist still served "Truth" in the form of Biblical history and the teachings of the Church.

"But as of the 1830s, the triumph of democracy and individualism [...] became unstoppable. The Impressionist art of the last third of the century is its monstrous product. Art was now no longer, as the educator of humanity, the highest ideal, but existed only for its own sake. That was the Gospel taught by Gautier, Verlaine, and Wilde. As far as painting is concerned, the only point of it was to reproduce the impressions nature made on an individual painter at a particular moment in time. Hence – extreme individualism and extreme relativism. Such an art could not be relevant to the state and could not be affected by a big idea. 'Painters with big ideas are always bad painters,' Max Liebermann was not ashamed to declare. Conversely a strong, self-confident state would naturally not know where to begin with this kind of artistic practice." Thus Bismarck's Empire, faced with the demand that it employ artists in the national enterprise, had to fall back on painters of the caliber of Anton von Werner and on sculptors like Reinhold Begas and his students. More talented artists, which also meant artists more sensitive to the spirit of their time, would not have let themselves be employed on grand prestige projects like the Siegesallee; as prisoners of the age of liberalism in which they had come into the world and achieved greatness, they were inevitably individualists. There was no way in which they could be induced to submit to the will of the state. So if anybody or anything is to be reproached, it is not the state, but the age itself, along with the artists who, proud of their exceptional status, stood fully behind it.

The Impressionists looked down with contempt on history painters [*peintres d'histoire, Historienmaler*]: "German history, but bad pictures," they would say. Anyone would have been taken for a fool who, pointing to one of their productions, dared to retort, in the spirit of the Middle Ages, "A good picture, but *only a bunch of asparagus.*" Even today, Pevsner complained, all too few artists are willing to embrace such a revaluation of values, despite having had the experience of Expressionism—which paved the way for such a revaluation through its re-engagement with the moral and political issues of public life and a return to firmness of line and strong, pure colours (even though the Expressionists themselves could not escape the individualism of their atomized society). Likewise, the emergence of a new unified architectural style determined by the needs of a building's inhabitants and a revival of respect for craft and applied art—as opposed to the dominant historicism in architecture and the nineteenth-century disdain for all forms of applied art—are signs of the rejection of an individualism that has outlived its day.

To these symptoms of rejuvenation must be added the growing role of "militant art," political painting and poetry, propaganda posters, and the like. As in the *Zeitwende* essay, Pevsner acknowledges here the danger of kitsch; he even suggests that it will be necessary for contemporary art to go through a stage of kitsch before it is restored to health. After all, he argues, the ideologically motivated painter of today's kitsch has at least an important advantage over the artistically gifted and esoteric Cubist in that his production corresponds to a clear demand.

Art, in short, must once again become a users' art [*Gebrauchskunst*] as it was in the Middle Ages and in the Age of the Baroque. For a use is served not only by knives and forks, cushions and houses, but by the national and social novel, the altarpiece, and the political painting, the only difference being that in one case the end being served is material and in the other it is mental or spiritual. In the earlier periods, the leading ideas were religious; in the present time they are political. The implication of this for art, Pevsner insists, cannot be disregarded. At this point in the article, he naturally enough evokes the Furtwängler-Goebbels exchange: "The new men in the German Reich require that art be political, just as they require that science be political. That position was clearly articulated for the first time from the side of the authorities by Dr. Goebbels on April 11th of last year in his reply to Furtwängler. It was not decreed thereby that in the future all art is to have a political slant [...] but rather that the future development should be seen, after the total dominance of pure painting in Impressionism, as tending decisively in favor of a return to painting with a purpose, hence to history painting. [...] This 'militant' art will therefore certainly enjoy the fullest encouragement of the state. And by encouraging what serves it, the state will be in a position to form an authentic style encompassing all forms of artistic creation as in the Middle Ages and the France of Louis XIV."

In return, art is entitled to expect assistance from the state in carrying out its own internal reforms, such as basing art education on craft and thus reuniting so-called "free" and "applied" art. In addition, Pevsner adds in an important concluding paragraph, an art that is joyfully dedicated to the service of the state is entitled to expect that the artist's creativity will be given as much freedom as it needs for its full development. In so arguing, Pevsner emphasizes, he is not trying to smuggle the idea of "free" or "pure" art back into the picture: "There can be no question of that. The demands of the state take precedence over those of art." But the inflexible application of a policy can result in so restricting the creativity of the artist that it fades and withers away: "Here it is one of the duties of the state to act generously and with understanding." It has to win the co-operation of art and artists, all too many of the best of whom, in recent years, have chosen to stand aside: "Winning them over is a task worthy of statesmen."[41]

From our present perspective, as suggested earlier, Pevsner's intervention in the Furtwängler-Goebbels debate and the sympathetic understanding he showed in both the 1933 and the 1934 articles for Goebbels' position can only be considered, at best, moral and political misjudgements, even if the case he made for re-establishing a strong relation between art and the people was in itself entirely defensible. In addition, in 1933–1934, Pevsner might still have hoped that his positive appreciation of Goebbel's position—together with the fact that he was a convert to Lutheranism and did not in any way identify as a Jew—might convince the authorities to reconsider his dismissal from his position at Göttingen and permit him to start teaching again and so support his family in Germany. Moreover, he was not the only non-Aryan in the art world to see some good in the new regime and want to give it a chance. When a rumour was spread (probably at Göring's instigation) that Furtwängler, who was about to succeed Toscanini in 1936 as conductor of the New York Philharmonic, had agreed to resume the podium at the Berlin State Opera, there was an outcry in the U.S. against the appointment of a man who had apparently made

---

41 Nikolaus Pevsner, "Kunst und Staat," *Der Türmer*, 36 (March, 1934): 514–17.

his peace with the Nazis. Several musicians also tried to get Toscanini to cancel a scheduled appearance as conductor at Bayreuth and threatened to cease performing with him if he did not. At that point Fritz Kreisler, the celebrated Austrian violinist (who, though he never identified himself as a Jew and was in fact raised as a Catholic, was generally regarded as at least half-Jewish) protested publicly: "The musicians concerned do not understand the meaning and the dynamic strength of the national movement which the current German government has brought to life. The nationalist sentiments which now hold sway over the German people have overcome the lethargy and blank despair into which the vast majority of the people had sunk in the post-war period."[42] Kreisler, who had made his home in Berlin, did finally leave Germany himself in 1938 — not, however, it appears, because of harassment by the Nazis but, after the *Anschluss* of that year, in order to avoid being drafted, as an Austrian citizen, into the German army.[43]

* * *

Two further cases, both from the circle of disciples of the poet Stefan George, will round out this admittedly "unscientific" [*unwissenschaftlich*] sampling of relatively favourable responses by Jews and part-Jews to the new National Socialist regime, in its early stages at least.[44] Jews, as is well known, were prominent in the narrow circle of George's "chosen" and counted among those closest to him.[45] In fact, some non-Jewish members complained about this to the Master, who reassured them that he would be careful not to allow Jews to outnumber others among his intimates. On

---

42 Cit. in Prieberg, *Trial of Strength*, p. 50. On Kreisler's Jewishness — his father was apparently Jewish, his mother may have been a Christian, he himself was raised as a Catholic, not a Jew — see Amy Biancolli, *Fritz Kreisler: Love's Sorrow, Love's Joy* (Portland, OR: Amadeus Press, 1998), Ch. 8 ("Kreisler the Catholic, Kreisler the Jew"), pp. 183–208.
43 Biancolli, *Fritz Kreisler*, pp. 199–201. He also renounced his Austrian citizenship at this time and accepted a longstanding offer from the French government to become a French citizen.
44 Though such cases, as need hardly be emphasized, were not common, they are revealing; see Daniel Azuélos, *L'entrée en bourgeoisie des Juifs allemands et le paradigme libéral (1800–1933)* (Paris: Presses de l'université Paris-Sorbonne, 2005), p. 79.
45 According to Rainer Kolk, one quarter of the forty to forty-five individuals admitted to the George circles in Heidelberg, Marburg, and Berlin were Jewish ("'Verkannte Brüder', Entjudete Juden," in Gert Mattenklot, Michael Philipp, Julius Schoeps, eds., *Stefan George und das deutsch-jüdische Bürgertum zwischen Jahrhundertwende und Emigration* [Hildesheim, Zurich and New York: G. Olms, 2001], p. 56. For material on Ernst Kantorowicz and Edith Landmann, I am indebted to Robert E. Norton, *Secret Germany: Stefan George and his Circle* (Ithaca and London: Cornell University Press, 2002) and especially Ulrich Raulff, *Kreis ohne Meister: Stefan Georges Nachleben* (Munich: C. H. Beck, 2009).

his own attitude toward Jews, toward the anti-Semitism of the National Socialists, and—in spite of many pleas from Jewish members of his circle that he announce his position publicly—toward the anti-Jewish legislation passed in Germany in the last year of his life, the poet-prophet was characteristically reticent or equivocal. He died in Switzerland in 1933 without ever having taken a clear stand on any of the burning issues of his time, not least among them the Nazi regime and its anti-Semitic policies.[46] Maintaining the integrity of his own circle, as Ulrich Raulff has demonstrated, was always his top priority. His realm, he would emphasize, in the face of repeated attempts to identify the Third Reich with his "New Reich" and Hitler with the prophesied "Führer," was of the spirit and no material, historical reality could ever correspond directly to it—though some might well come closer than others. For that reason he also discouraged those admitted into his circle from taking a stand in the ideological and political controversies of the time. This did not prevent him from defending his younger disciples, many of whom supported the National Socialist "revolution," against criticism from the older disciples, or from observing that "it was the first time that the views he had held had had an external resonance," or from responding to Edith Landmann, when she pointed to the brutal form this "resonance" had taken, that "in the realm of politics, things were different."[47]

---

46   For excellent short summaries of George's ambivalent attitude to the National Socialist regime, see Yakov Malkiel's essay on Kantorowicz in Arthur R. Evans, Jr., ed., *On Four Modern Humanists: Hofmannsthal, Gundolf, Curtius, Kantorowicz* (Princeton: Princeton University Press, 1970), pp. 197–99; Michael Landmann, *Erinnerungen an Stefan George. Seine Freundschaft mit Julius and Edith Landmann* (Amsterdam: Castrum Peregrini, 1980), pp. 47–52; for a more extensive treatment, see Martin Ruehl, "'In this Time without Emperors': The Politics of Ernst Kantorowicz's *Kaiser Friedrich der Zweite* reconsidered," *Journal of the Warburg and Courtauld Institutes*, 63 (2002): 187–242. See also on his elusiveness in the matter of the Jews, the last page of Edith Landsmann's *Gespräche mit Stefan George* (Düsseldorf and Munich: Helmut Küper, vormals Georg Bondi, 1963), p. 209.

47   Landmann, *Gespräche mit Stefan George*, p. 209. Landmann herself had noted in an appreciation of the recently published (1928) vol. 9 of George's Collected Works, that George's "New Reich" appeared at an historically opportune moment. Announced by an angel of destruction that warns: "Ich bin gesandt mit Fackel und mit Stahl,/ Dass ich Euch härte, nicht dass Ihr mich weichet" ["I have been sent with blazing torch and steel,/ So I should harden you, not so you should soften me"], the New Reich of the poet's vision, according to Landmann, was not an abstraction but appropriate to the times: "However deeply rooted the New Reich was in the inner being of the poet, perhaps its hour had at last come from the outside. This mind that had taken such care to set itself apart from the world was acutely sensitive to the particular historical moment in which it was placed and to the demands and possibilities of the time. A clear, unblemished space for the new was created only after the War had removed all traces of the old" ("Stefan George. Das Neue Reich," *Logos: Internationale Zeitschrift für Philosophie der Kultur*,

The anti-Jewish policies of the Nazi regime, however, did not allow his Jewish devotees the luxury of distance and non-commitment enjoyed by the Master himself. Among those still living (Friedrich Gundolf had died in 1931 and Berthold Vallentin a month after Hitler came to power) the poet Karl Wolfskehl left Germany for Switzerland in 1933 and later emigrated to New Zealand; Ernst Morwitz moved to the United States in 1936; Edith Landmann (one of a small number of women close to George) joined her son in Basel, Switzerland, where her late husband, another George admirer, had occupied the chair of economics (1910–1927); Erich von Kahler left for his native Prague in 1933, moved from there to Zurich, and finally emigrated to America in 1938; and Ernst Kantorowicz fled to England via Holland in 1938, after *Kristallnacht*, and from there also emigrated the following year to the United States.

Kantorowicz's immensely successful *Kaiser Friedrich II*, first published in 1927, has been described as "meant both to endorse George's vision of absolute power as embodied in a single, heroic figure and to instil in its readers an active enthusiasm for its forms and expressions"; as "overtly and intentionally political"; and as "a prescription in historical guise, an instruction manual on the language, character, and style [...] of heroic, messianic leadership";[48] in short, as an elegantly written, scholarly anticipation of what was to transpire, albeit in crass and vulgar form, in 1933. The author himself was at first exempted from the provisions of the 7 April Civil Service Law banning non-Aryans from public service positions. In his own words, "as a volunteer in the war from August 1914, as a soldier at the front for the entire duration of the war, as a fighter after the war against Poland, the Spartacists, and the Soviet Republics in Posen, Berlin, and Munich, I do not have to face removal from service because of my Jewish descent." He nevertheless felt morally obliged to ask for a leave

---

20 [1931]: 88–104 [pp. 96, 104]). Landmann's son, Georg Peter Landmann, likewise noted, referring to George's poem "Der Täter" [The Doer, Activist, Perpetrator, identified by George himself in another poem, "Jahrhundertspruch," as follows: "Vielleicht wer jahrlang unter euern mördern sass/ In euren zellen schlief: steht auf und tut die tat" — "Perhaps he who for years sat among your murderers,/ Slept in your prison cells, will stand up and do the deed"] that "George trug die Elemente des Täters stark in sich, und die Versuchung, aus dem Kreis der Kunst in handelnde, etwa gar ins politische Leben hinauszutreten, war ihm nicht fremd, aber er beschränkte sich und blieb der Dichter" ["George had strong elements of the Täter in himself, and the temptation to step out of the circle of art into active, even into political life, was not unknown to him. But he restrained himself and remained the poet"] (G. P. Landmann, *Vorträge über Stefan George* [Düsseldorf and Munich: Helmut Küpper, formerly Georg Bondi, 1974], p. 205).

48 Norton, *Secret Germany*, pp. 667, 670.

of absence from Frankfurt University, where he was then teaching, and to protest against the law and the racist ideology that inspired it in a letter dated 20 April (not, probably, by accident Hitler's birthday) to the Prussian Minister of Science, Art, and Education [*Wissenschaft, Kunst und Volksbildung*], in the name of "every German and truly nationally minded Jew."

> ...Although, in view of my publications about the Hohenstaufen Emperor Frederick II, I need no papers bearing a specific date, be it the day before yesterday or yesterday or today, to guarantee my attitude toward a Germany that has recovered its national orientation; although there has been no wavering, even in the face of recent events, in my fundamentally positive position, which is not grounded in or influenced by any tendencies of the times or events of the day, toward a nationally ruled Reich, [...] I nevertheless feel obligated, as a Jew, to draw my conclusions from what has happened and to request a leave of absence beginning with the upcoming summer semester. For as long as every German Jew—as in the present period of revolution—can be considered a "traitor" solely on the basis of his Jewish descent; as long as every Jew, because he is a Jew, is judged racially inferior; as long as the mere fact of having any Jewish blood in one's veins implies a defective attitude; as long as every German Jew sees himself exposed to daily violations of his honour without the possibility of obtaining personal or legal satisfaction; [...] and as long as every Jew, precisely when he declares his full support of a national Germany, comes inescapably under suspicion of acting out of fear or of only seeking personal advantage in announcing his convictions, or [...] of wishing to secure his economic existence; as long, therefore, as every German and truly nationally minded Jew, in order to avoid that kind of suspicion, has to hide his national convictions in shame instead of being able to make them known freely and spontaneously, it seems to me incompatible with the dignity of a university professor to carry out in a responsible manner the duties of his office, based as they are solely on inner truth, and it also seems that to resume teaching in silence, as if nothing had happened, would be a violation of the students' sense of shame.[49]

This was certainly a courageous gesture on Kantorowicz's part. Aside from the rejection of anti-Semitism, however, the values his statement expresses and the terms ("honour," affirming a "national Germany," "national convictions") in which it is couched demonstrate considerable proximity to the values and terms trumpeted by National Socialism. Moreover, the writer explicitly asserts his "positive position" toward a "nationally ruled

---

49   Cit. in Eckhart Grünewald, *Ernst Kantorowicz und Stefan George: Beiträge zur Biographie des Historikers bis zum Jahre 1938 und zu seinem Jugendwerk, "Kaiser Friedrich der Zweite"* (Wiesbaden: Franz Steiner, 1982), pp. 114–15.

Reich." In a second gesture that must have taken considerable courage, Kantorowicz gave a provocative lecture in Frankfurt six months later, on 14 November, in which he in effect denounced the Third Reich—not, indeed, for being authoritarian or undemocratic or repressive or for its persecution of non-Aryans, but for being a false and deceptive version, a betrayal of George's dream of a "New Reich" to be inspired and led by Germany, as once before a great Reich had been led by Frederick II.

Some of the older and many of the younger members of the George Circle were inclined not to highlight the differences between Hitler's Third Reich and George's "New Reich" but, on the contrary, to soften the boundary line between the two and to present the Master reverentially as the visionary who had foreseen the great future that was in fact presently beginning to be realised.[50] "Eka" (as Ernst Kantorowicz was called in the Circle), however, went to great pains in what Manfred Riedel describes as "eine fulminante Abschiedsrede" [an explosive farewell address] to emphasize precisely that difference. George's "Secret Germany," Kantorowicz proclaimed, was "like a Last Judgment and Resurrection of the Dead, always immediately close, indeed present," for it is "the secret community of the poets and wise men, of the heroes and holy men, of the sacrificers and the sacrificed, whom Germany has brought forth for itself and who in turn have brought forth Germany. [...] As a community, it is a realm of Gods like Olympus, a realm of the spirit, like the medieval state of saints and angels, a realm of mortal men like Dante's [...] 'humana civilitas,' [...] a realm both of this world and not of this world... at once here and not here... a realm at once of the Living and of the Dead, a realm that changes and yet is eternal and immortal."[51] As Ulrich Raulff notes, before an audience that was certainly familiar with his book on Frederick II, "Kantorowicz dared to speak of a Germany that had nothing in common with the empirical reality of the Third Reich. His Germany is in fact a polemical construct directed *against* that current Reich," Raulff argues, for, in Kantorowicz's words, "it is a realm of the soul in which at all times and for all time the same deeply German Emperors rule and reign, unique in rank and kind. To be sure, the entire nation has never yet bowed enraptured under their sceptre. Nevertheless, their reign is eternal and perpetual and goes on in deepest concealment *in opposition to* the external

---

50 Raulff, *Kreis ohne Meister*, p. 157.
51 Cit. ibid., p. 161. See also Manfred Riedel, *Geheimes Deutschland: Sefan George und die Brüder Stauffenberg* (Cologne, Weimar and Vienna: Böhlau, 2006), p. 14.

reality of the day and thus *for the sake of* eternal Germany." It is not possible "to take possession of these monarchs of 'secret Germany' by dragging their image through the streets, making them over so that they will please the marketplace and then celebrating them as one's own flesh and blood."[52]

As in the letter to the Prussian Minister of Science, Art, and Education, however, Kantorowicz's opposition is, as Raulff puts it, "contaminated by the poison it rejects"[53]—i.e. the Messianic, soteriological enthusiasm of both George's élitist vision and the cheap, mass-produced counterfeit visible on the contemporary German street and marketplace. Moreover, between the letter to the Prussian Minister of Science, Art, and Education and the lecture in Frankfurt on 10 July 1933, Kantorowicz had written a birthday greeting to the Master himself in which he at least entertained the possibility that the Third Reich might, after all, be the path to the fulfilment of the Master's prophecy. If that were the case, he conceded, then all "German and truly nationally minded Jews" would have to welcome it and stoically accept their fate, which, he suggested, might well be suicide.

> "May Germany become as the Master has dreamed!" And if current events are not merely the grimace of that desired ideal but really are the true path to its fulfilment, then may everything turn out for the best. And then it is of no consequence whether the individual can—or more accurately, may—join in the march, or steps aside instead of cheering. "Imperium transcendat hominem," Frederick II declared, and I would be the last person to contradict him. If the fates block one's entrance to the "Reich"—and as the "Jew or Coloured," as the new linguistic coupling has it, is necessarily excluded from the state founded on race alone—then it will be necessary to summon *amor fati* and make decisions accordingly.[54]

It is only fair to add that Kantorowicz's last letter to George, dated

---

52 Cit. in Raulff, *Kreis ohne Meister*, p. 163. It is hard to convey Kantorowicz's highly inventive, poetic, and prophetic language in translation. Only someone with a literary talent equal to his could translate it adequately.

53 Ibid., p. 168. Likewise, Manfred Riedel, *Geheimes Deutschland*: "Kantorowicz's lecture still retained Georgian visions of a past and future Reich originally of European genesis and stamp. But it was borne along by an eschatological faith and delivered in the emotional tones of a prophetic conviction that was not too far removed from the emotional rhetoric of the speaker's political opponents" (p. 14).

54 Letter from Kantorowicz to George, 10 July 1933, cit. Grünewald, *Ernst Kantorowicz und Stefan George*, pp. 122–23; note that Kantorowicz appears to particularly resent the "new linguistic coupling" of "Jew and coloured," rather as other German Jews resented being "coupled" with "*Ostjuden*." On Kantorowicz's ambivalent response to National Socialism, see especially Martin Ruehl, "'In this Time without Emperors': The Politics of Ernst Kantorowicz's *Kaiser Friedrich der Zweite* reconsidered," pp. 225–36.

26 November 1933, testifies to a less fatalistic determination to defend "secret Germany" against the "new" Germany using the weapons available to him, i.e. works of scholarship and public lectures. "After disgust, shock, and pain," he writes "hatred is beginning to prove productive."[55] On 22 February 1935, Kantorowicz did in fact deliver one of the midnight lectures broadcast on Wolfgang Frommel's cautiously independent program on Frankfurt Radio. At once "erudite" and "bursting with timely innuendoes," it has been said, this radio lecture, entitled "Deutsches Papsttum" [German Papacy], was delivered by "a daredevil Kantorowicz under dramatic circumstances, outwitting the Third Reich's monitoring officers."[56]

It is surprising that Frommel dared to invite a Jewish scholar to broadcast on his programs (Jews were prohibited from publishing and all forms of public address); it is no less noteworthy that Kantorowicz did not leave Germany definitively until the *Kristallnacht* pogrom in 1938 forced him to flee. His property (a comfortable apartment in Berlin's West End and a small estate in the lake-studded Mecklenburgische Schweiz) had not been confiscated; he was still able to carry on his research thanks to the politeness of gentlemanly archivists and palaeographers; he may have thought it his duty as a loyal member of the *George Kreis* to stand firm in Germany, doing what he could to counter the current distortion of the Master's teaching; and "finally," as a young colleague from his later years at Berkeley pointed out, "there may have been a glimmer of hope" — which significant numbers of patriotic, conservative German non-Aryans as well as Gentiles appear to have entertained for varying periods of time — "that the nightmare would soon come to a harmless end."[57]

Another Jewish devotee of George, the philosopher Edith Landmann, came to the same conclusion Kantorowicz had reached in his fatalistic letter to George of 10 July. In the face of the Master's silence on the question of the Jews, she thought seriously of suicide. She rejected this solution, however, as a "betrayal" of the Master, to whom unconditional loyalty and devotion were due.[58] Even if he did not raise his voice in the vulgar marketplace, had he not made his position clear over many years by selecting a large number of Jews as well as Christians to be the "bearers of his Reich," the repositories of "secret Germany"?

---

55 Ibid., p. 126.
56 Yakov Malkiel in Arthur R. Evans Jr., ed., *On Four Modern Humanists*, p. 195, note 30.
57 Ibid., pp. 193–94.
58 Raulff, *Kreis ohne Meister*, pp. 149–50.

In her determination that she should not be separated from George by the slightest crack, Landmann even expressed some understanding of anti-Semitism, inasmuch at least as it was directed toward *"Ostjuden,"* Zionists, and Communists—rather as Naumann and his followers, in their determination not to let the slightest distance separate them from the German *Volk,* sought to distance themselves instead from those same social groups. In an address to other troubled Jewish servants of "secret Germany" (*Omaruru. An die deutschen Juden, die zum geheimen Deutschland hielten*), composed in the summer of 1933, Landmann stated:

> You all know that, with regard to the kind of Jews who spread across Germany after the War and indeed long before it, I was, like you, an anti-Semite out of love for the German *Volk.* Do you seriously believe that it was possible for me to feel any kind of community with that kind of Jews or, for that matter, with today's Jewish youth which, having grown up with nothing but Zionism and Communism, has as little sense of the German spirit as the Germans themselves.[59]

Moreover,

> so many of the ideas of the Third Reich, however distorted the form in which they now come to us, were long the ideas that filled our hearts. [...] Anyone who has been carried away by this shattering of the entire world-structure of liberalism, by this enraged and resolute turning away from the 19th century, by this frenzy of unity and purity, anyone who believes that, out of shared hostility [to the world of liberalism] or for whatever other reason, and with whatever inner reservations, he may not stand aside from the great German breakthrough, cannot deny the necessity of a policy with regard to the Jews.[60]

Should one then give up one's Jewishness? That is not really an option, Landmann acknowledges: "With all our immersion in the German spirit, we cannot drive the Jewish blood from our veins. Should we then drive out the German spirit in us, transform ourselves back into pious old Jews or make ourselves over into modern nationalist or internationalist Jews?" Suicide would be preferable to that: "It would be better for us to do ourselves in."[61] Landmann's desperate clinging to the German spirit, as communicated to her through George, is demonstrated in the wildly Utopian solution she proposed in her tract to those Jews who "remained faithful to 'secret

---

59 Quoted ibid., p. 150, footnote 102.
60 Quoted ibid., p. 151, footnote 103.
61 Quoted ibid., p. 152.

Germany'": the founding of a settlement of German Jews in the former German colony of South-West Africa (present-day Namibia), where, as in a cloister, the Master's dream would be preserved from contamination by the "karikatur und pöbelhaftigkeit" ["caricature and loutish demagogy"] that had overwhelmed Germany itself. Jews, who had always been faithful to the Law and carried it with them into all the lands where they settled, might well be especially suited to be the guardians of the Master's vision in drastically unfavourable times.

From the outset, however, Landmann knew her scheme was impractical. George's death in December 1933 seemed to her to mark the death of Germany: "Germania fuit." She moved to Basel and, after much soul-searching, in due course became a Zionist.[62]

---

62 See Michael Landmann's text and the extracts from his mother's letters in Michael Landmann, *Erinnerungen an Stefan George. Seine Freundschaft mit Julius und Edith Landmann* (Amsterdam: Castrum Peregrini Press, 1980).

17. By Way of Conclusion

Because of their "hyperacculturation," in Ritchie Robertson's phrase, their love of and faith in Germany, their identification with German culture, their desire to belong and to be seen as belonging *in toto* to the German *Volk*, their joy at the emergence of their country from the discord, disorder, and shame of the Versailles settlement, their eagerness to have Germany restored to national greatness and international respect, and—not least—their lack of commitment to liberal democracy, which many of them, like their Aryan compatriots, associated with their country's enemies and held responsible both for the humiliating defeat of the *Kaiserreich* and for the social and economic chaos of the despised Republic that followed, the leaders of the Jewish veterans' association (*Reichsbund jüdischer Frontsoldaten*) and of the *Verband nationaldeutscher Juden*, as well as highly educated and cultured professionals of Jewish origin (like Schoeps and Pevsner) and idealist Jewish members of the exclusive George-Kreis were able to discern some good, for a time at least, in the new National Socialist regime. Such reservations as they had were chiefly due to the regime's racially defined anti-Semitism, because of which they were effectively barred from participating in the national revival they welcomed. It is not as surprising as it might at first have appeared, therefore, that Max von Oppenheim—who, after all, as the son of a Christian mother and a Jewish convert father was only half Jewish, even by the standards of the Nuremberg Laws—could greet the new regime in a seemingly positive spirit, decide to stay in Germany and work for his country's victory over its enemies in World War II as he had done in World War I, even though, like many national conservatives, including some of the military top brass, he appears to have been sceptical of Hitler's aggressive military schemes.[1] Moreover, he belonged to an exceptionally

---

1 Emerging from his study in the Savignyplatz, after a two-hour conversation with his old boyhood friend, the diplomat Prince Hermann Hatzfeld, on 2 September 1939

wealthy, old-established, and thoroughly assimilated family, whose services to Imperial Germany had been recognized by the conferring of titles and even the benevolent personal interest of the Kaiser; he also had friends and colleagues, from his time of service with the *Auswärtiges Amt* and from his membership in elite social clubs and circles, in high places. His behaviour was no different from that of many in all ranks, from upper to lower, of the military, the various state bureaucracies, and the *Auswärtiges Amt*, even when they harboured reservations about the new regime.

Above all, the identity, the very being of the Oppenheims, was tied up with institutions in Germany: in the case of Waldemar and Friedrich Carl (and even, to some extent, Max von Oppenheim) with the Oppenheim Bank; in Max's case, with his Museum, with the treasures he had uncovered at Tell Halaf, with his *Stiftung*. These were his legacy to Germany and to posterity. Different political regimes might come and go, these institutions and treasures, which were now part of Germany's heritage, had to be defended at all costs. For Max, ensuring the survival of his life's work probably justified all his efforts to ingratiate himself with the regime. After its fall, he did not hesitate—for the same reasons—to try to get on the right side of the new powers that be. His letter of 21 June to Ernst Herzfeld, for example, is marked at one and the same time by expressions of what seem like genuine friendship and interest and by an unpleasantly ingratiating tone.

The tables had certainly been turned. Herzfeld—who had lost his university position in the mid-1930s because of the racial laws and had had to emigrate—was now a respected member of the élite Institute for Advanced Study in Princeton, and Oppenheim—who had lived under the National Socialist regime in relative comfort—was down and out. In his letter Oppenheim recalls their friendship and the happy times of their collaboration, inquires with apparent (and possibly genuine) interest about Herzfeld's family (a sister and a nephew) and about his work, and explains apologetically that he had been trying to obtain Herzfeld's current address for some time but had only recently been able to get hold of it. There is no mention anywhere in the letter of the racial discrimination from which Herzfeld had suffered and Oppenheim, after all, had not.

(the day after the invasion of Poland and the day of the British and French ultimatums), he is reported to have greeted Werner Caskel with the words "Mein lieber Caskel! Diesen Krieg verlieren wir" ["My dear Caskel! We shall lose this war"] ("Aus den Erinnerungen eines Orientalisten," in *Festschrift Werner Caskel*, ed. Erwin Gräf [Leiden: E.J. Brill, 1968], pp. 5–30 [p. 30]).

The words "Jew" and "race" are entirely absent from the letter. With complete aplomb, Oppenheim even describes Herzfeld's emigration as "Ihre Abreise" ["your departure"], as though it were the most ordinary, everyday departure in the world and implies, rather startlingly, that it was Herzfeld who broke off relations with him, "causing him thereby much pain." He refers in his letter to "den Abbruch der Beziehungen, […] den Sie vorgenommen haben" ["Your breaking-off of relations"].

It does not seem, however, that Oppenheim made any attempt to contact Herzfeld in the late 1930s, during the first years of the latter's emigration, or that he ever expressed sympathy, or offered help. Perhaps that would have been too compromising and might have endangered the Tell Halaf Museum and the Max von Oppenheim Stiftung. Now, however, in 1946, the old scholar disclaims any close connection with the "scheussliche Nazizeit" ["horrible Nazi period"], during which he had had to struggle, he complains, with "allen möglichen Schwierigkeiten und Widrigkeiten" ["every possible difficulty and adversity"]. He, in short, he seems to imply, was also a victim of the "scheussliche Nazizeit," even perhaps the greater victim, since Herzfeld had managed, after all, to forge a highly successful career for himself in America, whereas he, Oppenheim, had succeeded only "mit der grössten Mühe, mich durchzulavieren" ["with the greatest difficulty in manoeuvring through it"] in order to be able to do what matters most (as Herzfeld was undoubtedly expected to agree) to all scholars—"meine Arbeit fortzusetzen" ["continue my work"] and, above all, "die Stiftung weiterbestehen zu lassen " ["ensure the survival of the Foundation"].

Toward the end of the four-page, single-spaced typewritten letter Oppenheim gets to what one suspects might have been one of the main reasons for his writing it. He is eager, he says, to defend the original controversial dating of the sculptures (which, as we know, had been proposed by Herzfeld) against the views of A. Moortgat, the editor of the forthcoming third volume of the great scholarly study of Tell Halaf being put out by de Gruyter. But with his library gone, "Was kann ich wohl tun, um mir Bücher zu verschaffen? Von der Stiftung-Bibliothek sind, wie gesagt, nur 8–900 Bücher gerettet, nicht mehr. Die Stiftung muss aber wie ein Phönix aus der Asche erstehen. Ich will nichts unversucht lassen, um die Bibliothek wieder aufzurichten" ["What can I do to get hold of books? As I said, only 800–900 books from the Foundation Library were saved. No more. The Foundation has to arise like a phoenix from the ashes. I will spare no effort to build the Library up again"]. In addition to ensuring the survival of the Foundation and the reconstitution of its library, the eighty-odd year old scholar wants to ensure a continued role for his Foundation in the excavation of Tell Halaf. Though he had fought tooth and nail in 1939—unsuccessfully, as we saw—to stop the French from conceding excavation rights at Tell Halaf and Fakhariya to Calvin McEwan and his team from the Chicago Oriental Institute, he now declares that he would welcome the assistance of a well-endowed American partner (which, by implication, Herzfeld with his American connections, could doubtless help him to find): "Glücklich wäre ich, wenn ich mit irgend-einem amerikanischen Institut, einem Museum z.B., in Verbindung setzen könnte, damit dieses gemeinsam mit der Stiftung den Tell Halaf und Fecherija Wassukani ausgraben würde" ["I would be very happy if I could establish contact with some American institution or other, a museum, for instance, that would undertake excavations, in collaboration with the Foundation, at Tell Halaf and Fakhariyah Wassukani"].[2]

For the vast majority of those Germans—Aryans, non-Aryans and *Mischlinge* alike—who could not wholeheartedly support the National Socialist terror state, even for those who were consciously opposed to it, open resistance was hardly an option. Emigration was a drastic and by no means easy step, and few took it who were not under immediate threat. What else were those who did not like everything about the new regime to do, except hang on and hope that it, or at least the worst of it, would pass? For the Oppenheims—Waldemar and Friedrich with their immense personal and psychological, as well as financial investment in the 150-year old family bank; Max with his no less profound investment in the Tell Halaf Museum and the Max von Oppenheim Foundation, the achievements of the labours of a lifetime—emigration, if it was considered, must have been quickly ruled out. The only course was to swim with the tide, so as to ensure as best they could the survival of what was most important to them. And that was not democratic freedoms or individual rights, however they may (or may not) have valued these things. What seems to have counted for them most was their place in German history and in German society, the Bank, the Museum, the Foundation.

---

2 Letter dated Landshut, 21 June 1946, Ernst Herzfeld Papers, the Freer Gallery of Art and Arthur M. Sackler Gallery Archives, B-16. For the complete original text of the letter, see Appendix.

As has been suggested earlier, it is extremely likely that Oppenheim, with real ties to the conservative and traditionalist personnel of the *Auswärtiges Amt*, but apparently none whatsoever to any Jewish organization or community, did not think of himself—whether because he could not or because he would not—as in any respect anything less than one hundred percent German. Characteristically, after he became homeless as a result of the bombing of Dresden and had to be taken in by his sister Wanda von Pocci in 1945, he immediately set about reconnecting with his old friends. Thus on 11 December 1945, he got in touch with von Hentig, informing him about common acquaintances, inquiring about others, telling of his own most recent wartime experiences, and expressing his concern for the future of the Oppenheim Foundation.[3] The historian Sean McMeekin expresses astonishment, indeed outrage at Oppenheim's apparent indifference to the disaster that had befallen the Jews of Europe: "In the section of his memoirs touching on the war, composed in 1946, the Baron blamed Hitler for having unleashed a war in which 'millions of Germans had fallen on the battlefield, and nearly all of Germany's cities, along with her immense and irreplaceable cultural possessions, have been destroyed by enemy bombs.'" "There is not a single word in Oppenheim's voluminous memoirs," McMeekin continues, "about the mass murder of the Jews during the war in Germany, Europe, or the Near East. […] Although it was understandable that he would keep his distance from his Jewish kinsmen in the interest of self-preservation during the Nazi period, one might think the Baron would have spared a thought for Jewish suffering once the world had learned about the Holocaust."[4] From a general moral and humanitarian point of view, Oppenheim's silence on the topic of Jewish suffering certainly does him no credit. But he may well not have felt any special obligation to refer to the Holocaust. In fact he may have chosen not to refer to it in order

---

3 Institut für Zeitgeschichte, Hentig papers, folder 46 www.ifz-muenchen.de/archiv/ed_0113.pdf, p. 17.

4 Sean McMeekin, *The Berlin-Baghdad Express* (Cambridge: Harvard University Press, 2010) p. 364. In his *Die deutsche Katastrophe* (1946), the eminent German historian Friedrich Meinecke expressed his thoughts about the War into which the National Socialists led Germany in similar terms. The book "displays virtually no awareness of the untold suffering inflicted on the victims of the Third Reich and it is disappointingly silent on the persecution of the Jews and the Holocaust. Meinecke's few expressions of regret or pain are evoked by the plight of the German people under attack and in defeat" (Gossman, *Basel in the Age of Burckhardt* [Chicago: University of Chicago Press, 2000], p. 450).

to sustain his own image of himself and the image he wanted others to have of him as fully and completely German. The fact appears to be that Oppenheim did not—and would not—think of Jews as in any way "his kinsmen." He might have been perturbed, as his young friend and Nazi Party member Prüfer was, by the stories circulating about death camps and he must have heard by 1942 about the fate of other individuals classified as "half-Jews," but we have no way of knowing whether or to what extent he felt personally threatened.[5]

It is all the more ironic that he was consistently seen, on the outside, as Jewish. Herbert von Bismarck's dismissal of him, in 1887, as unsuitable for a career in the *Auswärtiges Amt* because of his Jewish family background has already been mentioned, and Ritchie Robertson reminds us that in the early twentieth century a second generation convert like Georg Simmel, both of whose parents had converted, found it difficult to avoid being perceived by ill-disposed colleagues as "Israelite through and through."[6] T.E. Lawrence ("Lawrence of Arabia") who, while excavating with his teachers D. G. Hogarth and Leonard Woolley at Carchemish in July 1912, received an overnight visit from Oppenheim identified him as "the little Jew-German-Millionaire who is making excavations at Tell Halaf."[7] Hogarth himself, as Director of the Arab Bureau of the Cairo Intelligence Department in 1916 referred to him as "that chattering, egotistical Jew."[8] In a report from its special correspondent in Cairo, under the heading "German Intrigues in Egypt—Attempts to Weaken British Power—The

---

5   For information on policy decisions concerning "half-Jews" taken at the Wannsee Conference (January, 1942), see http://half-jewish.net/holocaust/ and http://en.wikipedia.org/wiki/Wannsee_Conference.
6   *The 'Jewish Question' in German Literature 1749–1939*, pp. 243–44.
7   *The Home Letters of T.E. Lawrence and his Brothers* (Oxford: Basil Blackwell, 1954), p. 225, letter to his "small brother," dated from Jerablus (another name for Carchemish) 21 July 1912. These words had been deliberately omitted from David Garnett's 1938 edition of *The Letters of T.E. Lawrence* (London: Jonathan Cape). According to Lawrence, Oppenheim "came about 5 p.m. [...], stayed till 11 p.m. then went off to eat & sleep: came back at 4:30 and stopped till 10 a.m. [...] Invited me over to his place by his relay of post-horses." However, Lawrence found him "such a horrible person" that he never took him up on the invitation. A Year later when Oppenheim apparently tried to spirit some of his finds out of Ottoman Syria, only to have his efforts discovered by the authorities, Lawrence considered him "an ass to have his things taken so and not very virtuous to take all those things from his excavations" (*The Home Letters of T.E. Lawrence and his Brothers*, p. 264, letter dated 21 September 1913, from Carchemish). Not surprisingly, Lawrence kept track of "the Kaiser's spy" during the War, reporting from Military Intelligence Cairo on 3 July 1915 that "Oppenheim went to Jerablus on the 15th. I fancy not with good intentions" (p. 306).
8   Cit. Tilman Lüdke, *Jihad Made in Germany* (Münster: LIT, 2005), p. 71.

Activities of Baron von Oppenheim," the *Times* of London for 6 January 1915 informed its readers of "intrigues which from 1905 onwards were carried on by members of the staff of the German Agency," foremost among them "the Jewish Baron Max von Oppenheim." Also in 1915, Sir Mark Sykes, a key official of Kitchener's in the British War Office, reported from the Middle East that Oppenheim, "a Jew of great wealth," would not hesitate to "incite massacres of Armenians in Turkey and do his best to get our isolated people murdered in Persia." Another memo informing Foreign Minister Grey on 24 October 1915 of alleged German propaganda efforts to create the impression among Muslims that the Kaiser and his Government had embraced Islam, asserted that "the notorious Baron Max von Oppenheim, a Jew, is known to have made speeches in mosques approving of the massacre of Armenians."[9] Recalling his dealings with Oppenheim in the late 1930s, when he had been French High Commissioner in Syria, Gabriel Puaux, a strong French nationalist who had obstructed the activities of the Italian Armistice Commission in Syria after the fall of France, been dismissed by Vichy, and thrown in his lot with de Gaulle, described Oppenheim in an interview after the war with the French-Jewish scholar Isaac Lipschits as a "vieux juif intrigant"[10] ["a scheming old Jew"].

The insistent identification of Oppenheim as a Jew by Germany's enemies clearly reflects their own anti-Semitism or at least their exploitation of anti-Semitic prejudice in order to present an even blacker picture of a fairly formidable foe. Oppenheim was doubly dangerous and evil: as a German and, worse yet, a wily Jew. It is true that there is no reference to anything Jewish about Oppenheim in the many entries about visits to "Onkel Max" in the diaries of Curt Prüfer, even though, as already noted, Prüfer appears to have been himself strongly anti-Semitic[11] and — as personnel director from 1936 until his appointment as ambassador to Brazil in 1939 — is generally held to have done his best to "Nazify" the traditional and conservative

---

9 Memos cited in Donald McKale, "The Kaiser's Spy," *Annales-Histoire, Sciences Sociales*, 51 (November-December 1996): 199–219 (pp. 208–09 and 217, note 40). These reports seem not to be wildly exaggerated; on Oppenheim's disturbing support of Turkish persecution of the Armenians, out of "zealousness to please the German emperor" and "impress the powers that be with displays of demonstrative patriotism," see Vahakn N. Dadrian, *German Responsibility in the Armenian Genocide*, pp. 65–81.
10 *La Politique de la France au Levant 1939–1941*, Ch. 5, p. 85, note 16.
11 In addition to previously mentioned studies of Prüfer by Donald McKale, see Richard Evans, "The German Foreign Office and the Nazi Past," *Neue Politische Literatur*, 56 (2011): 165–83.

Auswärtiges Amt. Perhaps decades of association with the old scholar-diplomat as well as Oppenheim's many services to Germany allowed his former colleagues in the *Auswärtiges Amt* to think of him chiefly as one of their own, with only a negligible defect which they were permitted or perhaps even required to overlook.

From the point of view of the leadership itself, two considerations may have militated in Oppenheim's favour in addition to his past services. First, he had an international reputation; mistreating him would have seriously aggravated the regime's already tarnished reputation in the world outside Germany and, more important, might also have offended many Arabs who thought of him, rightly, as their friend and advocate. Second, he had an expertise in Arab and Middle Eastern affairs as well as valuable contacts in the countries of the Middle East that were not easily replicable and could be useful (as his recommendations to Hentig on the occasion of the latter's mission to Syria testify). The fact that Oppenheim's part-Jewish assistant Werner Caskel also survived the Nazi regime is further evidence of a certain inconsistently applied pragmatism on the part of the authorities. As we saw, Caskel was consulted, as an Arabic scholar, on a planned authoritative translation of *Mein Kampf* into Arabic, took his task seriously and offered pertinent suggestions. The Nazi leadership was not incapable of overlooking racial deficiencies in exceptional cases, as the careers of Field Marshal Milch and Admiral Rogge demonstrate. Perhaps the reasons Oppenheim himself gave for his surviving, unmolested, right through to the end of the War, are close enough, after all, to the truth. (See above, beginning of Part III.)

Though the case of Max von Oppenheim may well be, almost certainly is, *sui generis*, it throws an unusual light on the situation and the mentality of a section (well-to-do and politically conservative) of Germany's long-established and strongly patriotic Jewish and part-Jewish population. Not many in that group were as wealthy and well-connected as he, not many had the resources he could call upon to sustain his cultural and scholarly interests, few pursued such interests more seriously or successfully, and few had the opportunities he had of putting his unreserved patriotism to work in Germany's national interest. To a considerable degree he appears to have succeeded in pushing aside, if never quite eradicating, his own and others' awareness of his Jewish background. Nonetheless, even though he managed to survive his government's racial policies, the moral cost to him of pursuing what turned out to be an impossible complete identification was high. His super-patriotism earned him the dubious distinction of being one of the most eager advocates of the dangerous and morally indefensible policy of exciting and exploiting Muslim religious zealotry as a political and military tool in the imperial war-games of non-Islamic nations, to the extent that he has been accused of providing excuses and justifications for the atrocities perpetrated by Germany's ally Turkey on its Christian Armenian citizens in World War I;[12] and in his World War II activities he

---

12   Vahakn N. Dadrian, *German Responsibility in the Armenian Genocide*, pp. 65–81. Dadrian's work in general and his judgment of Oppenheim's role in the Armenian massacres in particular have been severely criticized: Oppenheim, according to one critic, has been the "object of unsubstantiated innuendo about his complicity in the genocide" and Dadrian "fails to provide any solid evidence that Oppenheim was in any way implicated in the massacres—as opposed to vilifying the Armenians" (Donald Bloxham, "Power Politics, Prejudice, Protest and Propaganda: a Reassessment of the German Role in the Armenian Genocide of WWI," in Hans-Lukas Kieser and Dominik J. Schaller, eds., *Der Völkermord an den Armeniern und die Shoah/ The Armenian Genocide and the Shoah* [Zurich: Chronos, 2002], pp. 213–44 [pp. 221, 240, note 54]). Bloxham concedes that Oppenheim's negative view of the Armenians "may have served […] to rationalize a policy of non-intervention," but insists that that "is qualitatively a different level of responsibility to outright 'stimulation'" (p. 235). While this is true (it could also be said of the behaviour of many Germans in relation to persecution of the Jews in 1933–1945), there was no mistaking that the policy that was being "rationalized" was one of extermination of the Armenians. In a report to Chancellor Bethmann-Hollweg, dated 17 July 1915, even Ambassador von Wangenheim, notorious for his support of the policy of non-intervention, conceded: "It is obvious that the banishment of the Armenians is due not solely to military considerations. Talaat Bey, the Minister of the Interior, has quite frankly said to Dr. Mordtmann of the Embassy, that the Turkish government intended to make use of the World-War and deal thoroughly with its internal enemies, the Christians in Turkey, and that it meant not to be disturbed in this by diplomatic intervention from abroad. The Armenian Patriarch told the same gentleman a few days later that the Turkish government did not intend merely to make the Armenians temporarily innocuous but to expel them from Turkey or rather to exterminate them" (cit. in J. Ellis Barker, "Germany, Turkey and the Armenians," [review of Johannes Lepsius, *Deutschland und Armenien 1914–1918. Sammlung diplomatischer Aktenstücke* [1919]], *Quarterly Review* [London], 463 [April, 1920]: 385–400 [p. 389]). As for Oppenheim's view of the Armenians, it recalls the standard clichés of anti-Semites about Jews: in a four-page memo to Bethmann-Hollweg, dated Damascus, 29 August 1915, Oppenheim refers to the Armenians' "proverbial cunning in commerce, their scheming, their self-promotion and revolutionary spirit, above all their unceasing usurious exploitation of their environment and, most recently, their open hostility to the Turks" (Wolfgang Gust, ed., *Der Völkermord an den Armeniern 1915/16. Dokumente aus dem Politischen Archiv des deutschen Auswärtigen Amts* [Springe: Klampen, 2005], p. 272; see also http://www.armenocide.de/armenocide/armgende. nsf/$$Alldocs/1915-08--DE-001). Oppenheim claims emphatically that Djemal Pasha, who "has repeatedly instigated discussions with me on the Armenian question and ordered his officers to give me more written and verbal details from the files concerning this matter," has done his best to make the removal of the Armenian population from

demonstrated as callous an indifference as any dyed-in-the-wool Nazi to the fate of over 300,000 Jews, a fair number of them refugees from racial persecution in Germany, who had immigrated to Palestine after 1914 and who, he recommended, should be removed in the Middle East settlement that would follow Germany's victory in the war. On the other hand, it is impossible not to admire the talent and dedication that, vain though he undoubtedly was, he brought to his scholarly interest in the Orient; the care, elegance, generosity, and sometimes wit with which he communicated his findings and his enthusiasms; and even his untiring (and undiscriminating) efforts to promote Germany on the world stage, politically, economically, and culturally—despite the fact that he was never permitted to be anything other than a familiar outsider, a wealthy amateur among the academic archaeologists and the professional diplomats alike. Though excessive, there is a grain of truth in the harsh judgment of one of his detractors, the Armenian scholar Vahakn N. Dadrian; Oppenheim's "inveterate urge to impress the powers [that] be with displays of demonstrative patriotism," Dadrian writes, reduced him to a "caricature of an actual patriot. [His] zealousness to please the German emperor and to be of service to the German state was such that he ended up losing a sense of balance and proportion [and] became an opportunist, a careerist and an exceedingly pushy operator."[13] Exceptional as he was in terms of his wealth, his talent, and his personal character, and not even a full Jew, Oppenheim may well have been at the same time exemplary in many respects of a certain class of patriotic, cultivated German Jews of the second half of the nineteenth century and the first decades of the twentieth, to whom complete assimilation into

---

strategically critical areas as orderly as possible. Documentary evidence of this claim is supposedly provided by a number of annexed exchanges between Djemal and Turkish civil and military officers. Oppenheim concedes that "hardships, unavoidable cruelties and terrible family disasters will still take place during the Armenian people's expulsion from their homes and during the transports and resettlements," but insists that "in these difficult times the Turks are attempting to protect themselves against the Armenian danger with all the means available to them." For the Armenians, who, according to Oppenheim, "at the beginning of the present World War [...] basically took sides everywhere with the enemies of Turkey and Germany," are a dangerous and seditious element and there have been many signs of their revolutionary intent. The Turks understandably wish to avoid a repetition of the "bloody, repulsive atrocities that the Armenians carried out against the Mohammedans in Van and the surrounding area" in the spring of 1915 (ibid., pp. 271, 272, 274). Oppenheim thus repeats the official Ottoman account of the events in Van and says nothing in his report about the persecutions that led the Armenians to resort to violence.

13 Vahakn N. Dadrian, *German Responsibility in the Armenian Genocide*, p. 65.

the German nation was the number one priority—the goal relentlessly pursued and never attained. In the words of the French writer Georges-Arthur Goldschmidt, describing the middle-class professional family of converted Jews into which he was born in Germany in 1928, "Il n'y eut pas de meilleurs Allemands que ceux-là."[14]

---

14 "There were no better Germans than these" (Georges-Arthur Goldschmidt, *La traversée des fleuves—autobiographie*, p. 63).

Appendix

Originals of passages translated in the text and translations of passages given in the original.

p. xxvi *et passim*

Oppenheim's letter to Herzfeld:

Bayern, Landshut, den 21. Juni 1946, Altstadt

Mein lieber Prof. Herzfeld!

Soeben habe ich von Frau Prof. Sarre in Ascona Ihre Adresse erhalten. Schon seit langer, langer Zeit wollte ich Ihnen schreiben und den Versuch machen, mich mit Ihnen in Verbindung zu setzen, doch hatte ich mit allen anderen Adressen von Freunden auch die Ihrige in Dresden verloren, wo Ich zum zweiten Male total ausgebombt wurde. Zu meiner Freude hörte, ich von Frau Sarre, dass es Ihnen, Ihrer Schwester und Ihrem Neffen gut ginge, und dass Sie daran dächten, nächstens wieder einmal nach dem Orient zu fahren.

Mir ist es inzwischen schlecht gegangen. Während dieser scheusslichen Nazizeit hatte ich sehr viel mit allen möglichen Schwierigkeiten und Widrigkeiten zu kämpfen. Mit der grössten Mühe ist es mir möglich geworden, mich durchzulavieren und meine Arbeiten fortzusetzen, sowie die Stiftung weiter bestehen zu lassen. Zu den grössten Unannehmlichkeiten gehörte, dass Ich den Kontakt, mit Ihnen, mein lieber Prof. Herzfeld, verloren habe. Ich habe wirklich sehr darunter gelitten. Gehörte doch der Gedankenaustausch mit Ihnen zu dem Schönsten, was ich in den letzten Jahrzehnten hatte. Sie wissen gar nicht, wie oft ich an Sie gedacht habe und wie aufrichtig und herzlich ich Ihnen dankbar geblieben bin für die viele Hilfe und die vielen Anregungen, die Sie mir haben zuteil werden lassen. Ich habe Sie stets als einen meiner Lehrmeister betrachtet. Sie haben mich immer wieder ermutigt, und Sie haben meinen Tell Halaf stets unterstützt. Das Beste, was über diesen geschrieben worden ist, stammt aus Ihrer Feder und ist in Ihren Archäologischen Mitteilungen aus Iran niedergelegt. Es ist tragisch, dass wir, die wir so gute Freunde waren und so lange gemeinsam miteinander gearbeitet haben, dieser Art plötzlich auseinander gekommen sind. Auch hieran ist dieses Scheusal von Hitler und dieser scheussliche Nazismus Schuld gewesen. Diesem Obermistvieh verdanken wir ja auch den schrecklichen Krieg, der Deutschland ruinieren musste.

Seien Sie nun bitte so gut, mein lieber Herzfeld, und schreiben Sie mir gleich ein paar Zeilen. Ich wäre glücklich, von Ihnen wieder eine persönliche Nachricht zu erhalten und zu wissen, dass der Kontakt zwischen uns wieder hergestellt ist. Sie können versichert sein, dass ich durch den Abbruch der Beziehungen, wie man diplomatisch sagen würde, den Sie vorgenommen haben, unendlich gelitten habe und dauernd tief traurig hierüber war.

Ich hoffe, von Ihnen zu hören, dass es Ihnen während der ganzen Zeit, seitdem wir uns nicht mehr gesehen haben, persönlich gut gegangen ist. Es sind das ja ungezählte Jahre.

Ferner, schreiben Sie mir bitte, wie es Ihrer Frau Schwester geht und was Ihr Neffe tut. Ist er auch Gelehrter geworden und Archäologe, für den Orient interessiert, wie Sie? Ich hörte einmal, dass Sie auch in New York doziert hätten, aber weiter in Princeton geblieben wären; stimmt dieses?

Mit Dankbarkeit denke ich an sehr nette Tage, die ich in Princeton verbrachte, als ich, von der Universität eingeladen, dort einen Vortag über den Tell Halaf hielt. Ich erinnere mich leider des Namens des liebenswürdigen Professors nicht mehr, bei dem ich damals dort zu Gast war. Die Herren der Princeton-Universität waren deshalb noch besonders interessant für mich, weil diese ebenfalls in der ALAH, der Städtewüste im Osten der Strasse von Hamah nach Aleppo, Forschungsreisen gemacht haben.

Schreiben Sie mir bitte, was Sie seitdem publiziert haben. Frau Sarre teilte mir nur mit, dass ein neuer Band von Ihnen über Samarra erschienen sei. Handelt dieser auch über die prähistorischen Funde oder was? Dann aber schrieb sie mir, dass Sie auch noch Weiteres publiziert hätten.

Aus Berlin haben Sie ja wohl alle Ihre Sachen nach Amerika gebracht, Ihre schöne Sammlungen und Ihre Bücher? Ich nehme an, auch die amusanten Regale aus meinen Muscherabijen von Cairo. Ihren Gedanken, wieder einmal nach dem Orient zu gehen, finde ich grossartig. Ich hoffe aber, dass Sie dann auch über Deutschland fahren werden und mich hier in Landshut besuchen—wenn ich dann noch am Leben bin. Denn am 15. Juli werde ich 86 Jahre alt. Wie gerne würde ich nach Damaskus übersiedeln, um dort weiterzuarbeiten und meine Tage zu beschliessen, nicht weit von meinen Beduinen und vom Tell Halaf. Die Weissagung, dass meine Knochen in der Wüste bleichen würden, wird aber sicher nicht erfüllt werden.

Was mich angeht, habe ich durch den letzten scheusslichen Krieg alles verloren. Zunächst wurde im August 1943 die Stiftungswohnung am Savigny-Platz 6 ausgebombt. Es war ein Glück, dass ich mit dem Leben davon kam. Unmittelbar daraufging das Tell Halaf-Museum, durch eine Bombe getroffen, in Flammen auf. Ich war inzwischen mit meinem alten treuen Diener-Pfleger Sommer, den Sie ja kennen, nach Dresden, Hotel Bellevue, übergesiedelt. Meine ganze Bibliothek von etwa 42.000 Bänden ist verbrannt. Einen Teil hatte ich mit vielen anderen schönen Sachen der Stiftung nach einem Schloss in der Mark verlegt. Dieses wurde verbrannt und ausgeplündert. Von den orientalischen Realiensammlungen der Stiftung hatte ich weitere wertvolle Gegenstände in die Kellerräume der Museen und in ein anderes Schloss in Mecklenburg geborgen. Dem letzteren ist es ebenso gegangen wie dem erstgenannten. Auch den Sachen im Museum ist vieles widerfahren. Im ganzen sind etwa 8–900 Bände gerettet und einiges wenige von der Sammlung. Das schöne arabische Zimmer aus Damaskus ist natürlich auch verbrannt. Die Tell-Halaf-Original-Steinbilder sind geplatzt aber nicht ganz zerstört. Die Stücke wurden sorgfältig gesammelt und in sich geordnet in die tiefen Keller unter dem Pergamon-Museum verstaut, um, so Gott will, später wieder einmal zusammengesetzt zu werden. Im Grunde haben wir dies ja mit vielen Tell Halaf-Skulpturen, die von dem bösen Tiglatpilesar I, durch die Anzündung des Tempelpalastes des Tell Halaf zum platzen gebracht worden waren, bereits schon einmal ca. 3000 Jahre später, 1930, getan.

Die meisten kleinen Orthostaten wurden vorher schon nach den staatlichen Museen gebracht und bleiben, wie ich hoffe, dort in Sicherheit.

In Dresden wurde ich dan in der Schreckensnacht vom 13./14. Februar 1945 ein zweites Mal ausgebombt und habe dabei alles verloren, was ich dort an Büchern usw. wieder zusammenbringen konnte. Aber auch dieses Mal kam ich mit Sommer lebendig davon. Ich zog zunächst nach einem Vorort von Dresden und von dort, als die Russen näher kamen, zu meiner Schwester, Gräfin Pocci, nach Ammerland in Oberbayern. Dort verblieb ich 5/4 Jahre. Als dann dem zu schön am Starnbergersee gelegenen

Pocci-Schloss die Beschlagnahme und damit notgedrungen auch mir die Ausweisung aus dem Hause drohte, siedelte ich hierher nach Landshut über, wo ich durch Zufall ein sehr nettes Quartier gefunden habe und wo ich wohl meine Tage beenden werde. Trotz aller Schwierigkeiten habe ich meinem Grundsatz treu stets "Kopf hoch, Mut hoch und Humor hoch" gehalten und immer weiter gearbeitet. Es ist mir, allerdings mit grossen Schwierigkeiten gelungen, bereits zwei Bände des Beduinen-Buches und den ersten dicken Band des grossen wissenschaftlichen Tell Halaf-Werkes zur Publikation zu bringen, die ersten beiden bei Harrassowitz, das letzere bei de Gruyter erschienen. Der 3. Band des Beduinen-Buches steht vor der Vollendung. Zu dem 1. Band des Tell Halaf-Werkes ist ein Ergänzungsband über die prähistorischen Funde bereits fertiggestellt. Er lagert seit langem bei Prof. Ernst Weidner in Graz. Das Werk war von der deutschen Forschungs-Gemeinschaft finanziert worden, da ich ja mein ganzes Vermögen eingebüsst hatte. Leider habe ich seit 1 ½ Jahren jedoch nichts mehr von Weidner gehört. Hoffentlich ist dem ausgezeichneten Mann und meinem Manuskript nicht Böses widerfahren. Der Durchschlag desselben und alle weiteren Unterlagen sind verbrannt. In dem 1. Band des Tell Halaf-Werkes wurde mit längeren einleitenden Bemerkungen zu dem Gesamtwerke auch das Manuskript mit der systematischen Behandlung der prähistorischen Funde von Hubert Schmidt abgedruckt.

Der 2. Band mit den architektonischen Ergebnissen durch Langenegger liegt bereits in Fahnen vor, ist aber noch nicht ausgedruckt. An dem dritten, wichtigsten Band über die Skulpturen des Tell Halaf und des Djebelet el Beda und über die Kunst der Subaräer wird jetzt von mir gearbeitet. Ich bin fast am Ende und hoffe ich, diesen Band bald abschliessen zu können. Ich habe mich weiter ganz hierbei auf den von Ihnen in den AMI VI vertretenen Standpunkt gestellt.

Ferner ist von mir ein grösseres Buch über die Geschichte der Mitannier geschrieben worden, deren Hauptstadt Wassukani, wie ich glaube, in Fecherija neben dem Tell Halaf im Chabur-Quellgebiet begraben liegt. Die Fahnen sind bereits gedruckt, aber das Werk ist noch nicht publiziert. Die Drucklagen existieren nicht mehr, gottlob aber noch die Fahnen.

Schliesslich ist eine grosse Karte lediglich auf Grund meiner eigenen Forschungsreisen in Obermesopotamien im Massstabe von 1:500,000 bereits gestochen und Begleitworte dafür sind schon gedruckt, wir wissen aber noch nicht, ob dieses Material gerettet ist.

Sie sehen, mein lieber Prof. Herzfeld, dass ich wohl sehr fleissig gearbeitet habe, dass ich aber sehr grosse Sorgen hatte und noch habe. Ich leide jetzt besonders durch den Mangel an Büchern. Meine Arbeit an dem Skulpturen-Band ist sehr interessant, macht mir aber deshalb grosse Schwierigkeiten, weil ich eben ohne andere Bücher bin. Ich jammere geradezu nach einzelnen Sachen, so insbesondere nach A. Moortgat "Die Kunst des Alten Orients und die Bergvölker", dessen Standpunkt ich in erster Linie bekämpfen muss. Was kann ich wohl tun, um mir Bücher zu verschaffen? Von der Stiftungs-Bibliothek sind, wie gesagt, nur 8–900 Bücher gerettet, nicht mehr. Die Stiftung muss aber wie ein Phönix aus der Asche erstehen. Ich will nichts unversucht lassen, um die Bibliothek wieder aufzurichten. Glücklich wäre ich, wenn ich mich mit irgend einem amerkanischen Institut, einem Museum z.B., in Verbindung setzen könnte, damit dieses gemeinsam mit der Stiftung den Tell Halaf und Fecherija Wassukani ausgraben würde.

Seien Sie bitte so gut, mir zu schreiben, was Sie inzwischen, abgesehen von Ihrem neuen Band über Samarra, publiziert haben. Bitte schreiben Sie mir auch, was etwa von anderen über Angelegenheiten publiziert worden ist, die mit den mich so interessierenden Problemen der Tell Halaf-Steinbilder und ihres Alters zusammenhängen. Ich möchte mir dieses so furchtbar gern beschaffen.

Dann möchte ich noch fragen, ob etwas über die Ausgrabungen des Dr. Mc Ewan, der während des Krieges in Fecherija beim Tell Halaf eine Zeitlang gegraben hat, publiziert worden ist und wie ich mir dieses verschaffen könnte. Ich hörte einmal, dass er vor einiger Zeit in Cairo gestorben sei. Stimmt dieses?

Lebt und wirkt eigentlich Prof. Pöbel noch am Oriental Institute und Henry Field am Field-Museum, beide in Chicago, sowie Götze in Yale und Albright und Levy in Baltimore?

Doch lassen Sie mich diesen schon viel zu langen Brief beenden. Erfreuen Sie mich bitte recht, recht bald durch gute Nachrichten hierher nach Landshut. Wie glücklich wäre ich, von Ihnen zu hören, dass Sie mir wieder gut sind und dass Sie bald hierher kommen werden, um mit mir ehedem Gedanken austauschen zu können.

Mit den herzlichsten Grüssen und innigen Wünschen für Sie, Ihre Frau Schwester und Ihren Neffen

Ihr alter treuer

Signature (Max Oppenheim)

P.S. Sobald die Möglichkeit vorhanden ist, würde ich Ihnen gerne alles, was ich seit Ihrer Abreise veröffentlicht habe, zusenden. Ich habe noch eine Frage: Von welchem Ruinenhügel stammt die vorhistorische Kalkstein-Skulptur, die, wie mir seinerzeit Direktor Breasted mitteilte, von einem Ruinenhügel aus dem Norden des Sindjar mitgebracht wurde. Sie ist im Museum des Oriental Institute ausgestellt und Breasted hatte mir davon Fotos mit der Erlaubnis zur Publikation übergeben. Haben Sie über diese bereits irgendwo etwas geschrieben und was?

p. 9, ch. 1, note 6

Philipp von Eulenburg: "From the Union Club's point of view, anyone who owns racehorses is a 'perfect gentleman.' In addition, very wealthy Jews (like the Oppenheims) are in a position to supply cash on tick. That constitutes more or less the moral foundation of the Club, which sets the tone in 'social' matters and matters of 'honour' and in all questions concerning what is proper and what is 'not done.'"

p. 16, ch. 2, note 5

Teichmann: "Hat Max von Oppenheim im Orient auch–sicher nicht ausschliesslich—eine helle Welt voll Harmonie und Schönheit gesucht? Die Gesellschaft in der Heimat jedenfalls befand sich in einem geschichtlich beispiellosen Umbruch hervorgerufen durch die industrielle Revolution: Massenwanderung von Arbeitskräften, Traditionsverlust, technischer Fortschritt, der zugleich Bewunderung und Angst auslöste, zerbröckelnde religiöse Bindungen, Herausforderung der alten Eliten durch politische Parteien und Gewerkschaften—kurzum ein Zeitgeist der Aufbruchsstimmung und Unruhe. Im Orient konnte sich Oppenheim dagegen [...] in einer Welt wähnen, die archaischen Mustern folgte, in der die Geschichte quasi stehen geblieben zu sein schien..."

p. 18, ch. 2, note 7

Hartmann: "Erschütternd naiv ist der Anfang: 'In older time (wie alt denn? 1000 oder 3000 Jahre?), the Arabian desert (ist mir unbekannt, abgesehen von der Nufud...!) was the roaming-ground of independent (?wirklich? mit der 'Unabhängigkeit' sah es meist faul aus) Beduin tribes with free and healthy minds, etc.!!!' Diese dreckigen, verseuchten Schufte hatten freien und gesunden Sinn!! d.h. verkauften sich Jedem um ein paar Pfennige und waren so 'gesund', dass sie sich gegenseitig auf Jeden, der ihnen vorkam, auffrassen, wenn sie konnten! Diese Naivität, die von unseren weltfremden Stuben-Arabisten gezüchtet wurde, sollte man doch bei einem ernsthaften Mann heute nicht mehr finden."

p. 21

Oppenheim: "Dabei wird keineswegs nur auf die Abstammung von Vaters Seite Wert gelegt, sondern auch auf die von Seiten der Mutter, und zwar kommt es nicht nur auf die rassische Reinheit an, sondern es wird auch auf die Herkunft aus einem Edelgeschlecht gesehen. Unter der Herkunft der Mutter aus einem ungeachteten Stamm, oder gar von einer Schwarzen, haben selbst die grössten Recken der altarabischen Zeit [...] zu leiden gehabt. Auch heute noch hat der Beduine reinen Blutes *aṣīl* kein Konnubium mit Angehörigen von Stammen, die als nicht reinblütig oder unedlen Blutes gelten."

p. 21, ch. 2, note 14

Renan: "From the point of view of physiology, no essential difference between the Semitic race and the Indo-European race is discernible. The sovereign characteristic of beauty is theirs in common, and theirs alone. [...] There is thus no reason, from a physiological perspective, to posit a distinction between Semites and Indo-Europeans of the same order as that which separates Caucasians, Mongols, and Negroes. [...] It was only the study of languages, literatures, and religions, that was to lead here to setting up a distinction that could not be derived from the study of physical features. In the matter of intellectual tendencies and moral instincts, the difference between the two races is no doubt far sharper than it is in the matter of physical traits. Even in that respect, however, it is impossible not to place Semites and Aryans in the same category. Once the Semitic peoples had constituted themselves as a regulated society, they drew closer to the Indo-Europeans. Jews, Syrians, and Arabs participated in turn in the work of general human civilization, [...] something that cannot be said of the Negro race, or of the Tartars, or even of the Chinese race [...]; thus, regarded from the point of view of the intellect, they [Semites and Indo-Europeans] constituted a single family."

p. 22

Ungnad: "Die rassereinen Semiten, wie wir sie noch unter den heutigen Beduinen der arabischen Wüste antreffen, unterscheiden sich körperlich nur wenig von den Indogermanen, denen auch wir angehören und die man heutzutage vielfach mit dem irreführenden Namen *Arier* kennzeichnet. Man stecke einmal einen solchen Wüstensohn in den Ölmantel eines hageren, wettergebräunten nordischen Seefischers und lege diesem die malerische Tracht des Beduinen an! Der Unkundige wird dann nur schwer erkennen, welches der Semit und welches der Europäer ist. Ebenso finden sich [...] sprachlich auffallende Beziehungen zwischen der semitischen und indogermanischen Rasse: alles weist darauf hin, dass die Hypothesen, die Arabien oder gar Afrika als die Urheimat der Semiten betrachten wollen, haltlos sind. Vielmehr durften beide Völker in Zeiten, die weit von unseren ersten geschichtlichen Daten liegen, etwa in Südost- oder Zentral-Europa *ein* Volk mit *einer* Sprache gebildet haben."

p. 23

Oppenheim: "Oft war ich monatenlang in Nordarabien, Syrien und Mesopotamien mit den Beduinen, den freien Söhnen der Wüste, in ihren Zelten zusammen. Ich kannte ihre Seele, ihre Sprache und ihre Sitten genau. Die Leute waren mir lieb geworden, und man empfing mich überall mit offenen Armen."

pp. 29–31

Oppenheim: "1892 wurde es mir möglich, meine Forschungstätigkeit im Orient in grösserem Massstab zu beginnen. Mit dem Ethnographen Wilhelm Joest, einem Kölner Landsmann, reiste ich von Marokko quer durch Nordafrika. Darauf hielt ich mich sieben Monate in Kairo auf, wo ich im Eingeborenenviertel in einem arabischen Hause wohnte. Hier lebte ich ganz wie die einheimischen Mohammedaner, um mich in der arabischen Sprache weiterzubilden und den Geist des Islams sowie Sitten und Gebräuche der Eingeborenen eingehend zu studieren. Ich wollte mich dadurch zu weiteren Expeditionen vorbereiten, die mich in den Osten der arabischen Welt bringen sollten.

"Im Früjahr 1893 führte mich mein Weg nach Damaskus. Von hier trat ich meine erste grosse Forschungsreise in Vorderasien an, die in dem zweibändigen Buche 'Vom Mittelmeer zum Persischen Golf durch den Hauran und die Syrische Wüste' behandelt ist.

"Für die Beduinenangelegenheiten stand mir während der Expedition ein guter Berater zur Seite, nämlich Manṣūr Naṣr, ein Neffe des Schech Midjwel el Meşrab [...], des Gatten der schönen englischen Lady Digby, die durch ihre seltsamen Geschicke bekannt geworden ist. Sie hatte sich nach einem abenteuerlichen Leben an verschiedenen Höfen Europas schliesslich auf einer Reise von Damaskus nach Palmyra im Jahre 1853 in Schech Midjwel, den Führer ihrer beduinischen Eskorte, verliebt und ihn geehelicht. Diesem blieb sie im Gegensatz zu ihren früheren europäischen Gatten und Freunden treu. Alljährlich teilte sie mit ihm sechs Monate lang das Leben in der Wüste, bis sie in ihrem Hause in Damaskus im August 1881 starb.

"Schon auf dieser Reise des Jahres 1893 konnte ich reiches Material über die Beduinen sammeln. [...] Während dieser Expedition erwachte in mir die Liebe zu dem wilden, ungebundenen Leben der Wüstensöhne. [...]

"Schon in Kairo hatte ich mich daran gewöhnt, wie es noch zu jener Zeit bei der dortigen besseren Mittelklasse üblich war, nicht mit Messer und Gabel, sondern mit den Fingern zu essen—wobei nur die rechte Hand gebraucht werden durfte. Auf der Expedition 1892 ass ich selbstverständlich mit den Beduinen ebenso, ganz gleich, ob ich deren Gast oder Gastgeber war. Im ständigen Zusammenleben mit ihnen im Sattel und im Zelt lernte ich immer besser ihre Gewohnheiten kennen. Sie fühlten, dass ich ihnen wohlwollte, dass ich Verständnis für ihre Eigentümlichkeiten und Sitten hatte. So waren auch sie mir wohlgesinnt und gaben mir bereitwillig auf meine Fragen Antwort. [...]

"Meine Rückreise aus Mesopotamien führte mich über den Persischen Golf und Indien nach unserer damals jungen, schönen Kolonie Ostafrika, wo ich anlässlich einer Expedition in das Innere ein umfangreiches Landgebiet in Usambara erwarb, auf dem später durch einen Freundeskreis Plantagen angelegt wurden.*

"Von dort kehrte ich nach Kairo zurück. Hier traf ich Anfang 1894 mit Zuber Pascha zusammen, der sich im ägyptischen Sudan durch Sklavenjagden ein grosses Fürstentum gegründet hatte. Da er aber zu stark zu werden begann, hatte ihn der Khedive Ismail nach Kairo gelockt, wo er in einem schönen Palast wie in einem goldenen Gefängnis zurückgehalten wurde. Von Zuber Pascha erhielt ich ausserordentlich interessante

---

* Das von dem Häuptling Kipanga von Handei gekaufte, mehrere Quadratmeilen grosse Urwaldgebiet wurde von mir der zuletzt von dem früheren Bezirksamtmann von Tanga, Freiherrn von St. Paul Hillaire, geleiteten "Rheinischen Handel-Plantagen-Gesellschaft" überwiesen, die hier mit grossem Erfolg zunächst Kaffee und dann, als der Kaffeewurm auftrat, Sisal baute, bis durch den Weltkrieg auch diese in bester Entwicklung befindliche Plantage für Deutschland verloren ging."

Mitteilungen über einen seiner ehemaligen Unterfeldherren, Rabeh. Dieser hatte vor den Ägyptern nicht kapitulieren wollen und war mit einer grossen Anzahl seiner früheren Soldaten und deren Familien vom Nil aus westwärts gewandert.

"In Deutschland berichtete ich hierüber, ebenso über weitere Erkundigungen, die ich in Kairo über das Tschadseegebiet sowie über den nicht nur religiös, sondern auch politisch bedeutungsvollen mohammedanischen Orden der Senussi usw. eingezogen hatte. Dies wurde der Anlass, dass das Auswärtige Amt mir anbot, im Wettbewerb mit Frankreich und England, an der Spitze einer deutschen Expedition nach dem Hinterlande von Kamerun aufzubrechen, um die Gebiete bis zum Tschadsee für Deutschland zu erwerben. [...]

"Aber unsere Expedition konnte nicht ausgeführt werden. In dem Wettkampf zwischen Frankreich, England und Deutschland war jener Rabeh den europäischen Mächten zuvorgekommen. Wie ein schwarzer Napoleon hatte er im Siegesmarsch vom ägyptischen Sudan aus alle Länder südlich von Wadai und dann die grossen Reiche von Baghirmi und Bornu erobert. Seine Herrschaft war jedoch nur von kurzer Dauer. Er fiel in einer Schlacht gegen die Franzosen. Das von ihm gegründete Reich ging in Trümmer. Bei der Aufteilung seiner Gebiete durch die europäischen Kolonialmächte wurde meine schon marschbereite Expedition mit in die Wagschale geworfen. Damals erhielt Deutschland den sog. "Caprivi-Zipfel" unserer Kamerun-Kolonie, nämlich grosse Teile von Baghirmi und Bornu und damit den Zugang zum Tschadsee.

"Von nun an blieb ich im Dienste des Auswärtigen Amtes. Ich wurde unserer diplomatischen Vertretung in Kairo zugeteilt, von wo aus ich alle Angelegenheiten der islamischen Welt zu beobachten hatte.

"Kein Platz konnte sich hierfür besser eignen. Die ägyptische Presse, arabisch in der Sprache des Koran geschrieben, war für die ganze islamische Welt vom Atlantischen Ozean bis China von ausschlaggebender Bedeutung. In der Türkei duldete der unumschränkt herrschende Sultan `Abd ul Hamid keine freie Meinungsäusserung der Zeitungen. Kairo dagegen war der Sitz aller mohammedanischen politischen Flüchtlinge, besonders auch der aus dem Osmanischen Reiche.

"Auch zum Sultan `Abd ul Hamid gewann ich die besten Beziehungen. [...]

"Sultan `Abd ul Hamid hatte mich aufgefordert, stets bei ihm vorzusprechen, wenn ich Konstantinopel besuchte, was ich auch regelmässig tat.

p. 33

Herbert von Bismarck: "Ich bin einmal dagegen, weil Juden, selbst wenn sie Begabung haben, doch immer taktlos und aufdringlich werden, sobald sie in bevorzugte Stellungen kommen. Ferner ist der Name als gar zu semitisch bekannt und fordert Spott und Gelächter heraus. Ausserdem würden die übrigen Mitglieder unseres diplomatischen Korps, auf dessen ausgesuchte Beschaffenheit ich stets grosse Mühe verwende, es peinlich empfinden, wenn man ihnen einen Judenbengel bloss deshalb zugesellt, weil sein Vater Geld zusammengejobbert hat."

pp. 33-34

Holstein: "Oppenheim hat zwei Eigenschaften, die bisher als disqualifying gelten. Vollblut-Semit (Halbbluts haben wir die Menge) und Mitglied einer Bankiersfamilie. Von Leuten dieser Kategorie liegen zahlreiche Anträge vor; man kann sie nur ablehnen wenn man sich auf ein Prinzip stützt. Macht man eine Ausnahme, so hat man Ärger."

p. 34, ch. 3, note 2

Holstein: "Ich bin fest übezeugt, dass es sich hier nicht bloss um einen Semiten handelt, sondern dass durch die von ihm gemachte Bresche alsbald mehere von seinesgleichen nachdrängen werden. Jetzt ist die Gesellschaft resigniert, da sie weisst, dass keine Semiten überhaupt genomen werden—ich meine keine Vollblut-Juden. Ist aber einer mal reingekommen, so wird ein Zetergeschrei entstehen, wenn man andere ablehnt."

p. 35, ch. 3, note 5

Hatzfeld: "Ich kenne den Baron Oppenheim schon seit einer Reihe von Jahren und habe seine Thätigket und Erfolge in der Erforschung des Islams—ein Fach, für welches er eine besondere Begabung zu besitzen scheint—stets mit Interesse verfolgt. Leider scheinen sich aber jetzt, wie ich höre, bezüglich der Art seiner Verwendung im auswärtigen Dienste gewisse Bedenken geltend gemacht zu haben… Soweit ich die Sachlage übersehe, knüpfen dieselben sich an die Abstammung des Barons Oppenheim, gegen welche gewisse Vorurtheile in einigen Kreisen bei uns gehegt werden, und es wird deshalb als wünschenswert bezeichnet, ihm nicht eine Anstellung im eigentlichen diplomatischen Dienst, sondern nur eine temporäre Attachierung bei einer orientalischen Mission anzubieten."

p. 35, ch. 3, note 6

Döscher: "Die Mehrheit der deutschen Diplomaten war aristokratischer Herkunft, evangelischer Konfession, vermögend, militärisch aus- und juristisch vorgebildet. Gegen Ende der Wilhelminischen Ära gewannen auch—meist nobilitierte—Vertreter des vermögenden Grossbürgertums Zugang zum diplomatischen Dienst, während er jüdischen und sozialdemokratischen Bewerbern bis zum November 1918 verschlossen blieb. Konservatismus mit antiliberalen, antiparlamentarischen und antisemitischen Akzenten bestimmte die Grundeinstellung der meisten Diplomaten."

p. 38

Oppenheim: "Meine Berichterstattung an das Auswärtige Amt [...] war ausserordentlich vielseitig. Meine Aufgabe war von Cairo aus die Bewegungen der ganzen islamischen Welt zu beobachten. In erster Linie musste ich mich natürlich mit den eingeborenen Verhältnissen des Nillandes selbst beschäftigen und dann mich bemühen, Nachrichten über alle Strömungen und die Muhammedaner betreffenden Ereignisse der ganzen Welt zu erhalten."

pp. 37-38, ch. 3, note 11

Holstein: "Wissen Sie etwas von einem Freiherrn von Oppenheim, Mitglied des Union-Klubs, welcher vor etwa zwei Jahren dem Generalkonsulat Kairo 'als Orientalist' ohne näher definierte amtliche Stellung beigegeben wurde? Er sollte die in der Welt des Islam angeblich herrschende Gährung beobachten, um Europa rechtzeitig zu warnen, wenn etwa ein Ausbruch bevorstände. Zu dem Behufe solle er Fühlung mit eingeborenen nehmen auch wohl Karawanen-Reisen mitmachen, um sich auf den grossen Märkten im Inneren über die in der Welt des Islam herrschende Stimmung zu orientieren. So war die Sache gedacht. Karawanenreisen hatder p. Oppenheim ungefähr soviele gemacht wie ich: dagegen hat er gelegentlich einen Bericht geschrieben über Unterhaltungen mit Eingeborenen, hat aber namentlich sich der Führung vornehmer deutscher Reisender gewidmet, ausserdem ein gastfreies Haus gemacht, kurz alles getan, was geeignet war, seine Übernahme in die diplomatische Karriere zu ermöglichen. Halbblut Juden haben wir schon manche gehabt, bzw. haben sie noch, aber Vollblut-Semiten, wie Mendelssohn, Warschauer, Bleichröder, Oppenheim haben wir bisher noch nicht." [Now, however, he has learned that

Oppenheim] "nach Berlin kommen werde, um zu betreiben, einesteils, dass er jetzt endlich in die Diplomatie übernommen werde, anderenteils, dass man seine Lokalkenntnisse bei der ägytpischen Reise seiner Majestät verwertet, kurz Oppenheim möchte mitreisen."

p. 39

Oppenheim: "sahen in mir einen Mann, der trotz seiner gehobenen Stellung in der europäischen Gesellschaft und seines Ansehens unter den europäischen Diplomaten mit ihnen gerne zusammen war, der nicht auf sie herabschaute, wie die Engländer oder meisten anderen Europäer dies taten, die sich nicht direkt mit ihnen verständigen konnten, der vielmehr Freude an dem Leben, das sie damals noch führten, hatte und gerne an diesem teilnahm. Es hat dies naturgemäss zur Folge, dass sie mir mehr und mehr ihr Herz ausschütteten, wenn wieder einmal die Wogen der Cromer'schen Eingebohrenenpolitik höher schlugen, auf Grund dieses oder jenes Ereignisses verschärfte Massnahmen durch die Okkupationsmacht eintraten oder aber auch, wenn die Rede auf die Stimmung der eingeborenen Welt dem Khediven, den Türken oder irgend einem anderen Faktor gegenüber kam. Sie wussten, dass ich sie nicht verraten würde."

p. 43

Von Schoen: "Eine gewisse Animosität gegen ihn ist in Frankreich und England entstanden, als er in der Zeit, wo wir in schärferem Gegensastz zu Frankreich wegen Marokko standen, durch Reisen und fachmännische Auskunft über Marokko die deutsche Politik zu informieren suchte. Das wird ihm nicht verdacht werden können. Dass es den Franzosen und Engländern missfiel ist begreiflich."

p. 53

Abdul Hamid II: "Les liens de la religion qui nous unissent tous doivent être resserrés davantage d'année en année; c'est là qu'est notre espoir pour l'avenir! L'Angleterre, la France, la Russie et la Hollande ne sont-elles pas toutes en ma puissance? Un mot du Calife suffirait pour déchaîner le Djihâd! Et alors, malheur aux puissances chrétiennes! Le moment n'est pas venu encore, mais il viendra, auquel tous les fidèles musulmans se lèveront comme un seul homme pour briser le joug du Giaour—les 85 millions de musulmans des possessions anglaises, les 30 millions des colonies hollandaises, les 10 millions de la Russie, etc."

p. 53

Abdul Hamid II: "Tous les ennemis de l'Angleterre—et de fait toutes les puissances du monde devraient être de ce nombre, mais plus spécialement la Russie, la France et l'Allemagne—tous les ennemis de l'Angleterre devraient attacher une valeur particulière à notre amitié. Point n'est besoin d'être très intelligent pour comprendre que moi, le Calife, le Commandeur des Croyants, je pourrais d'un seul mot faire courir un grand danger à la domination anglaise dans l'Inde. Les ennemis de l'Angleterre ont laissé échapper le moment propice. La Russie et l'Allemagne auraient pu facilement renverser avec mon aide le château de cartes de l'Angleterre dans l'Inde. L'empereur allemand fut trop chevaleresque et sans doute a-t-il au fond du coeur un faible pour ses blonds cousins; puis aussi il se croyait tenu à des ménagements à cause des liens de parenté. C'est dommage que l'on n'ait pas su profiter de l'occasion favorable, c'est alors qu'on aurait dû régler ses comptes à l'Angleterre, pour toutes les brutalités qu'elle s'était permises à l'égard des autres nations, pour les violences dont ont été victimes les pauvres Hindous. Le jour de la vengeance viendra quand même! Les Hindous se lèveront et briseront le joug de l'Angleterre."

p. 61

Snouck Hurgronje: "toutes les intrigues, toutes les calomnies ou autre armes venimeuses pour se nuire réciproquement dans l'esprit du Sultan et se porter des coups mortels"

p. 64

Hartmann: "Der Sturm, den das Vorgehen der Italiener in der islamischen Welt erregt hat, treibt seltsame Blüten. Es ist verständlich, dass die Empörung über den 'Banditenstreich' selbst die ergriff, die die Nachkommen der Landräuber all die Jahrhunderte seit dem Aufkommen des Islam sind, oder gar der Hordenleute, deren Rasse den Boden Ungarns zerstampften, und die sich vor Wien legten. Das Gedächtnis versagt ja, ach! in solcher Lage so leicht. Sehen wir nun aber, wie die Entrüstung sich äussert. Die harmlosere Form ist die Androhung des Boykotts aller Italiener durch all Muslime. Die scharfe Form ist die Androhung des Heiligen Krieges, d.h. des Kampfes gegen *alle* Ungläubigen, ausgenommen die vom Leiter der Gemeinde ausdrücklich als Freunde des Islam bezeichneten. Dieser Gedanke ist Wahnwitz. Er wurde aber kürzlich von angesehenen Muslimen sorgfältig formuliert, und diese

Formulierung ist überall versandt worden und kann Unheil anrichten, wenn nicht rechtzeitig gewarnt wird."

pp. 65-66

Hartmann: "Europa lacht über die blutrünstigen Reden, mit denen man die zu neunzig Prozent verständnislosen armen Teufel zur Siedehitze zu bringen hofft, die aus den entferntesten Enden der Islamwelt zur heiligen Übung sich eingefunden haben. Europa lacht über die Drohung mit dem Heiligen Kriege. Es hat in den letzten Jahren recht oft damit drohen hören, ohne dass das Geringste erfolgt ist. Es kam nicht einmal ein unheiliger Krieg bei dem Geschrei heraus. Der 'Heilige Krieg'! Wissen diese Leute noch nicht, dass Kriegführen Geld kostet, schrecklich viel Geld? Wer soll die grosse Kriegskasse füllen? Wer soll sie verwalten? Wer soll die panislamischen Heere führen? Sind die Intellektuellen in Berlin so einfältig, zu glauben, dass ein Krieg der gesamten Islamwelt gegen die Ungläubigen sich heute noch ins Werk setzen lässt? Es ist seltsam, dass gerade sie für den Heiligen Krieg eintreten. Diese Pose steht ihnen gar nicht. Ja, sie könnte ihnen verhängnisvoll werden. Träger *des* Islam, der den Heiligen Krieg im Ranzen führt, sind die starren Dogmatiker, die an den unsinnigsten Bestimmungen des Heiligen Rechts, des Schariat, festhalten (Steinigung wegen unerlaubten Geschlechtsverkehrs, achtzig Peitschenhiebe für einen Weinrausch, Handabhauen für einen Diebstahl). *Das* ist der Geist des Panislamismus. Wenn die dünne Schicht der islamischen Intellektuellen in den europäischen Hauptstädten mit diesem Geiste liebäugelt, wenn sie bei keiner Gelegenheit unterlässt, auf die angebliche grosse Gefahr des Panislamismus hinzuweisen, so ist da eine Komödie, die zu politischen Zwecken gespielt wird. Zugleich liegt darin ein Doppelspiel, sofern eben jene Leute sonst immer das Nationale auf ihre Fahne schreiben und als Jungtürke, Jungägypter, Jungperser ihren Völkern Erneuerung predigen und dabei gerade den religiösen Gedanken hintanstellen. Sie sollen sich hüten: erregen sie den Fanatismus der islamischen Massen, so werden diese sie sich genau ansehen und ihnen übel mitspielen, wenn man sie als Ungläubige, als Schweinefleischesser, als Weintrinker erkannt hat."

p. 67

Tavilet: "... die ganz inkohärent zu einer nur äusserlichen Einheit zusammengepressten iranischen-arischen, semitischen und türkischen Stämme ein gemeinsames Band [...], das die anscheinend ziellose Willkür der geschichtlichen Vereinheitlichung so heterogener Elemente durch ein inneres lebendiges Band ersetzen könnte."

p. 68

Tavilet: "Immerhin wird mit der stärkeren Einsetzung eines national-kulturellen Volksempfindens im Osten auch die dominierende Stellung der religiösen Doktrin sich abschwächen und mit der Entwicklung moderner Wirschaftsbedürfnisse und Lebensformung auch die Starrheit überkommener Anschauungen sich lockern. [...] So können wir schliessen: Unter den gegebenen Verhältnissen ist der panislamische Gedanke nur mit dem Osmanentum als führender Kraft überhaupt denkbar, als eine Reaktion auf den Panslawismus nicht unmöglich, ebensowenig aber als rein religiöse Bewegung durchführbar, da das türkische Reich, solange es noch europäische Macht, militärtechnisch, finanziell und diplomatisch sich nicht vom 'Konzert' der Mächte bis zur Isolation ablösen kann, um, schimärischen Ideen anhangend, darüber seine wirklichen Interessen zu versäumen. Deshalb wird auch der panislamische Gedanke, mag er immerhin türkischen Politikern und Patrioten ein mehr oder weniger stiller Wunsch sein, sich für die absehbare Zukunft kaum auf eine so feste Basis stellen lassen, um ihm zuliebe das Risiko eines möglichen Verlustes des bereits Errungenen gerechtfertigt erscheinen zu lassen."

pp. 77-78

Louis Mercier: "Nevertheless, I am convinced that all of us who have lived for long years in close contact with a Muslim population, whether Eastern or Western, have had many occasions to feel that the idea of *jihad* has persisted through time, to the point of dominating, perhaps unconsciously, the whole life of this population, imprinting itself on its deepest aspirations, and influencing its attitudes in its relations with 'infidels.'"

p. 100, ch. 5, note 42

Wolff-Metternich: "Le gouvernement turc ne s'est laissé détourner de l'exécution de son programme—*liquidation de la question arménienne par l'extermination de la race arménienne*—ni par nos admonestations ni par celles de l'Ambassade américaine et du Nonce apostolique, ni par les menaces des puissances de l'Entente, et encore moins par la crainte de l'opinion publique dans les pays occidentaux. [...] Il ne faut pas voir dans l'islamisation par force des Arméniens une mesure inspirée par le fanatisme religieux, du moins pas en premier lieu. Ce genre de sentiment était probablement étranger aux potentats Jeune Turcs. Mais il n'en demeure pas moins vrai que tout bon patriote ottoman doit avant tout faire profession d'appartenir à l'islam. En Orient, religion et nationalité ne font qu'un; l'histoire de l'Empire turc, du début à nos jours, est là pour nous le prouver et tout Ottoman en porte la conviction au plus profond de lui-même. Les déclarations officielles et officieuses qui affirment le contraire, ainsi que tout l'attirail de citations du coran et de la tradition, font partie des belles phrase que l'on sert aux Européens depuis l'époque des firmans de la réforme pour les convaincre de la tolérance de l'islam et des Ottomans. De même, si les ministres démentent les informations qui circulent sur les persécutions religieuses, c'est avant tout pour des questions de bon ton; mais leurs protestations comportent quand même une part de vérité dans la mesure où le motif directeur n'est pas le fanatisme religieux, mais la volonté d'amalgamer les Arméniens avec l'élément musulman de l'Empire."

pp. 102-103

Seidt: "Wer im Politischen Archiv des Auswärtigen Amts in Berlin in der Aktenserie 'Unternehmungen und Aufwiegelungen gegen unsere Feinde' einen kühl kalkulierten, sorgfältig geplanten 'Griff nach der Weltmacht' sucht, der wird enttäuscht. Sicher dachte Max von Oppenheim kühn in den Kategorien deutscher Weltmachtpolitik und entwarf ein Gesamtkonzept, das der Reichsregierung ein in sich schlüssiges Revolutionierungsprogramm für den Orient vorlegte. Aber sein Plan entbehrte der sorgfältigen Vorbereitung und der materiellen Grundlage. Zur Umsetzung fehlte es an Personal und Material. Sachkunde und Ausrüstung waren nicht vorhanden. Die Schüsse von Sarajewo und der Kriegsausbruch hatten das Deutsche Reich, sieht man von den Aufmarschplänen des Grossen Generalstabs ab, unvorbereitet getroffen. Max von Oppenheims Traum vom 'Heiligen Krieg' musste zu einem schmerzhaften Erwachen führen.

"Berlin begann zu improvisieren. Nachdem Anfang November 1914 der Unterstaatssekretär im Auswärtigen Amt, Arthur Zimmermann, Oppenheims Denkschrift in das Grosse Hauptquartier gesandt hatte, wurde zur Koordinierung die Nachrichtenstelle fur den Orient, kurz: NO, gegründet. Zunächst in Berlin-Mitte, im Reichskolonialamt in der Mauerstrasse 45/46 untergebracht, ubersiedelte die NO später in eigene Räume in der Tauentzienstrasse 19a. Von dort aus arbeiteten Oppenheim und seine Mitarbeiter, vor allem sein Stellvertreter Schabinger von

Schowingen, eng mit dem Auswärtigen Amt zusammen, wo der junge Diplomat Otto von Wesendonck für die Aufwiegelungsaktionen zuständig war. Ein anderer Angehöriger des Auswärtigen Amts, Rudolf Nadolny, übernahm als Hauptmann der Reserve und Chef der Sektion Politik im Stellvertretenden Generalstab die Verbindung zu den militärischen Stellen.

"Während in Berlin erst schrittweise die organisatorischen Grundlagen geschaffen wurden, bestätigten sich vor Ort in Konstantinopel die skeptischen Erwartungen Niedermayers. Der deutsche Orientalist Ernst Jäckh, der vom 12. bis 22. Dezember 1914 in Konstantinopel die Chancen einer Revolutionierung des Ostens sondierte, fasste nach seiner Rückkehr am 3. Januar 1915 seine Erfahrungen ernüchtert zusammen. In seinem 'Bericht über die Organisation in Konstantinopel zur Revolutionierung feindlicher Gebiete' zeichnete Jäckh ein düsteres Bild: 'Der allgemeine Eindruck lässt sich dahin zusammenfassen, dass alle diese Arbeiten verspätet und improvisiert eingesetzt haben, da im Frieden nichts vorbereitet worden ist.' Jäckhs Bericht und die Akten des Auswärtigen Amts belegen eine erschütternde Diskrepanz zwischen politischem Wollen und operativen Fähigkeiten, zwischen hochgespannten Zielen und nicht vorhandenen Instrumenten. Improvisation und Wunschdenken ersetzten sorgfältige Planung und umsichtige Aufklärung."

p. 121, ch. 7, note 3

Oppenheim: "Land und Leute in ihrer geschichtlichen Entwickelung und in ihrer ethnographischen und religiösen Eigenart zu schildern. Dabei habe ich es für meine Pflicht gehalten, die reichhaltige Literatur, welche Geschichte und Geographie von Syrien und Mesopotamien behandelt und welche neben Werken klassischer griechisch-römischer und arabischer Autoren sowie moderner arabischen Chronisten eine ganze Reihe älterer europäischer Reisewerke und sehr zahlreiche neuere wissenschaftliche Arbeiten umfasst–die zum Teil in schwer zugänglichen Zeitschriften verstreut sind–von Fall zu Fall anzuziehen."

p. 121, ch. 7, note 4

Oppenheim: "Nur eines kann meines Erachtens den Beduinen gegenüber fruchten: das ist Machtentfaltung, starke Garnisonen mit guten auf Maultieren, Kamelen oder Pferde berittenen Regimentern, welche die Beduinen im Schach halten und sie nachhaltig verfolgen und energisch strafen, wenn sie die Bauern besteuern oder ausplündern, und, wenn nicht anders möglich, das ganze Volk aus Mesopotamien hinaus in die Wüste Arabiens werfen."

p. 133, ch. 7, note 29

Oppenheim: "Die subaräische Kultur hat sicherlich dieselbe Bedeutung wie die altbabylonische und altägyptische. Durch die Entdeckung des Tell Halaf und der Steinbilder des Djebelet el Beda ist auch für Obermesopotamien der Nachweis des Bestehens dieser dritten selbständigen Kultur Vorderasiens, und zwar bis in die allerälteste prähistorische Zeit, erbracht." (1931 German text, pp. 52–53)

p. 137

Oppenheim: "... die Frage, die so viele Künstler heute beschäftigt, eine auf einem Sockel befindliche Büste herzustellen, erschien hier in eigenartiger einfacher Weise gelöst. Vom Menschen hatte der Stein nur den Kopf, selbst die Schultern und Armansätze der griechischen Hermen fehlten. Statt dessen liefen zwei viereckig gearbeitete Steinstreifen vorn an der Säule herab, und auf einer derselben waren Keilschriftzeichen angebracht. An den beiden Seitenflächen aber waren flügelartige Ansätze erkennbar, als ob die Figur mit herabfallenden Flügeln dargestellt wäre. Der untere Teil der Steinsäule wurde nicht gefunden. Die Lippen des Kopfes waren schmal, die Nase, von der nur ein Teil erhalten war, muss allem Anschein nach stark gewesen sein; die Augen—eines wurde gefunden—waren aus glatt poliertem schwarzen Basalt, sie ruhten in einer weissen Gipsumrahmung. Im übrigen war die Statue wie die übrigen Bildwerke des Tell Halaf aus dunklem, vulkanischem Gestein hergestellt. Die Haare zeigten keine herabfallenden Locken, wie bei den anderen im Tell Halaf gefundenen Figuren, doch waren sie sorgfältig geordnet, und über die Stirn schlang sich eine Spange, von der ein merkwürdiger Kopfputz herabfiel. Derselbe bestand an den Seiten und am Hinterkopf aus Bändern, die in aufwärts gedrehten Kringeln ausliefen, rechts und links von den Schläfen hingen zwei besonders starke Bänder herab, und zwischen diesen, unter dem Kinn, zeigten sich wieder ähnlich kleinere Bänder am Hals. Die ganze Art dieses Kopfputzes, sowie das Mystische im Gesichtsausdruck der Frau lässt den Gedanken unabweisbar erscheinen, dass der Bildhauer das Gesicht zwischen den beiden grossen Bändern an den Schläfen mit einem Schleier bedeckt darstellen wollte, von dessen unterem Teil die kleinen Bändchen am Halse herabfielen. Ganz ähnliche Schleier finden sich heute noch bei gewissen mehr oder weniger sesshaft gewordenen Beduinenstämmen Unter-Ägyptens und vor allem bei den Araberinnen des Persischen Golfes. In der verschleierten Frau des Tell Halaf dürften wir das älteste Beispiel eines verschleierten Bildes von Stein vor uns haben. Vielleicht haben wir es hier mit der schon im alten Testament genannten babylonischen Pfahlgöttin zu thun, der Ischtar, aus welcher die syrische Astarte und die Venus wurde."

pp. 138–140

Oppenheim: "Das letzte Schürfloch D lage einige Schritte nordwestlich von dem hervorgehenden. Hier machten wir den merkwürdigsten unserer Funde, Stein 14. Es war der Torso einer menschlichen Gestalt, von der ich auf den ersten Blick den Eindruck gewann, dass der Künstler damit ein verschleiertes Frauenbild, ein Göttin darstellen wollte. Der Kopf wuchs unmittelbar aus einem viereckigen Steinstück hervor, das nur wenig breiter war als der Hals. Schultern und Arme fehlten. Von der Brustgegend an abwärts war der Stein nach innen zu abgeflacht, derart, dass nur an den Rändern zwei breite, erhabene, eckige Streifen senkrecht verliefen. Auf dem linken Streifen waren zwei Zeilen Keilschrift eingemeisselt, über denen oben eine kleine Querschrift angebracht war. Unten war die Steinsäule schräg abgebrochen, was leider auch eine Verstümmelung der Inschrift zur Folge hatte. An der Seite des Steines waren schuppenartige Motive vorhanden, die vielleicht Ansätze von Flügeln sein sollten.

"Die Behandlung des Gesichts hatte im Gegensatz zu den groben männlichen Zügen auf den anderen Orthostaten etwas durchaus weichliches und verschwommenes. Das Antlitz war ganz flach dargestellt, die Backenknochen und das Oval der Wangen nur angedeutet. Die Lippen waren sehr fein behandelt, eine Eigentümlichkeit, welche übrigens dieses Bild mit den anderen des Tell Halaf teilte. Nur die Nase, von der nur ein Teil erhalten war, ragte kräftig hervor. Das Kinn war bartlos und glatt, die Konturen kaum erkennbar. Das Gesicht trat nur in sehr geringem Masse aus dem Hals hervor, der eine kaum merkliche Verengung darstellte. Die Augenhöhlen waren sehr gross. Der obere Teil des Kopfes war geborsten, und beim Graben vielen die beiden Teile auseinander. Der Riss ging gerade über die Augen. Das eine Auge war unversehrt vorhanden: ein schwarzer, blank polierter eiförmiger Kern aus Basalt, 5 cm lang, 3 cm breit und 3 cm hoch, umgeben von einer weissen gipsartigen Masse. Dies steinerne Auge fiel zu Boden und wurde vonmir nach Hause gebracht. Die andere Augenhöhle war leer.

"Auf dem Haupte befand sich eine käppchenartige, der Kopfform sich anschmiegende Bedeckung, welche über den Stirn in einem breiten Bande abschloss. Das Käppchen hatte flache ringelartige Verzierungen. (Vielleicht wollte der Künstler auch nur ein Stirnband auf dem Kopfe und die Haare in ringelartiger flach aufliegender Form darstellen.) Von dem Stirnbande fielen vor den Ohren bis zu den Schultern zwei kräftige Bänder herab, deren Ende nach aussen und aufwärts schneckenförmig geringelt waren. Zwischen diesen, unterhalb des Kinnes, fand der eigenartige Kopfputz in einer wagerechten Linie seinen Abschluss, von der wiederum kleinere Bändchen bis zur Brustgegend herabfielen. Auch diese endigten meist (von dreien immer je zwei) in nach aussen aufgedrehten Kringeln. Abwechselnd war immer ein längeres und kürzeres geringeltes und dann ein noch kürzeres ungeringeltes Bändchen gruppiert. [...]

"Die ganze Art dieses Kopfputzes sowie das Mystische in dem Gesichtsausdruck lässt den Gedanken unabweisbar erscheinen, dass wir es mit einem Frauenkopf zu tun haben, und dass der Bildhauer das Gesicht zwischen den beiden von den Schläfen herabhängenden grossen Bändern mit einem Schleier bedeckt darstellen wollte, von dessen unterem Teile die kleinen Bändchen am Halse herabfielen. Ganz ähniche Schleier werden heute noch von den arabischen Frauen des persischen Golfes und von den Frauen ägyptischer Beduinen in der Nähe des Suezkanales getragen. [...]

"Haben wir es bei der verschleierten Göttin des Tell Halaf mit einer hermenartigen Büste zu tun, oder ist das von mir freigelegte säulenartige Steinstück nur der Teil einer gewaltigen Steinplatte gewesen, eines Orthostaten mit der Leibe eines Sphinx? Für die erstere Auffassung spricht namentlich die gerade Haltung des Kopfes und die Behandlung der Brustgegend. Dagegen legt der Verlauf der Linien des Hinterhauptes und des Nackenansatzes auf dem Steinfragment 15 die Vermutung näher, dass der Kopf auch unserer Göttin unmittelbar in den Rücken einer vierfüssigen Tiergestalt überging. Auch die Steinstreifen vorne könnten zu einer Figur ähnlich wie auf Stein 1 gehören. Spätere Ausgrabungen werden dieses Problem lösen."

p. 151, ch. 8, note 7

Führer durch das Tell Halaf-Museum: "Das Tell Halaf-Museum wird von der von Baron von Oppenheim begründeten 'Max von Oppenheim Stiftung (Orient-Forschungs-Institut),' Berlin, Savigny Platz 6, verwaltet. Das Forschungsgebiet der Stiftung ist der alte und neue Vordere Orient. Freiherr von Oppenheim hat die ihm von der französisch-syrischen

Mandatregierung erteilte Konzession zur Ausgrabung der Ruinenstätten von Tell Halaf, Fescherija-Waschukani und Djebelet el Beda auf den Namen seiner Stiftung eintragen lassen. Auf diese Weise ist dafür gesorgt, dass die Ausgrabungsarbeiten, die noch viele Jahre beanspruchen werden, auch nach seinem Ableben, fortgeführt werden können."

p. 164, ch. 10, note 7

Schacht: "Man stempele die Juden in jedem gewünschten Masse zu Einwohnern minderen Rechts durch entsprechende Gesetze, aber für die Rechte, die man ihnen lassen will, gewähre man ihnen staatlichen Schutz gegen Fanatiker und Ungebildete."

p. 165

Köhler: "Der Entzug des gesellschaftlichen Ansehens und des sozialen Status schränkte zudem den Aktionsradius der Bankiers ein und bereitete damit letzlich den Ausschluss aus dem Wirtschaftsleben vor. Eine Untersuchung der repressiven Vor- und Rahmenbedingungen der 'Arisierung' von Privatbanken kann damit nicht auf die Veränderungen der Geschäftsbilanzen als Ergebnis von Boykott und ökonomischer Ausgrenzung begrenzt bleiben, sondern muss ausserökonomische Verdrängungsmechanismen einbeziehen."

p. 206, ch. 12, note 3

Festschrift: "To mark his 70th birthday, these essays are dedicated, in deepest admiration and friendship, to Max Freiherr von Oppenheim, generous benefactor and promoter of scholarship, justly esteemed investigator of the cultures of the ancient Middle East, who, with a felicitous hand, brought to light the treasures of Tell Halaf and awakened them to new life, outstanding authority on the land and peoples, arts and sciences of the Islamic world, munificent founder of the Institute for Middle East Research, by...."

p. 215

Renan: "Je me représente l'apparition des langues sémitiques et celle des langues ariennes comme deux apparitions distinctes, quoique parallèles, en ce sens que deux fractions d'une même race, séparées immédiatement après leur naissance, les auraient produites sous l'empire de causes analogues, suivant des données psychologiques presque semblables..."

p. 216, ch. 12, note 19

Günther: "Über das erste Auftreten der dinarischen Rasse lässt sich heute noch wenig sagen. Sie muss wohl mit der vorderasiatischen Rasse zusammen urpsrünglich eine einheitliche Menschengruppe gebildet haben, deren Urheimat im Gebiet des Kaukasus zu vermuten ist. Dann muss nach der Abwanderung eines Teils dieser Menschengruppe eine Änderung der Auslese in anderer Umwelt aus der urpsrünglich einheitlichen Menschengruppe zwei gebildet haben, die sich durch mehrere Merkmale unterscheiden, doch nicht so, dass ihre Zusammengehörigkeit nicht noch immer erkennbar bliebe."

p. 218

Ungnad: "Die uns so wenig sympathischen Eigenschaften der vorderasiatischen Steilköpfe treten je weiter in den Hintergrund, je mehr wir uns von den Gebieten entfernen, in denen Mischungen mit anderen Rassen stattgefunden haben, und auch die durchschnittliche Körperhöhe scheint nach derselben Richtung hin zuzunehmen, sodass zum Beispiel die Tscherkessen in Ziskaukasien, die ebenfalls eine Kaukasussprache sprechen, sich körperlich und seelisch schon stark der dinarischen Rasse zuneigen. Ihr Stolz, ihre Verwegenheit, ihre gastfreundliche Gesinnung einerseits, ihr in der Blutrache zum Ausdruck kommender Jähzorn andererseits, sind Eigenschaften, die wir auch unter europäischen Volksstämmen antreffen, bei denen dinarische Rasse vorwiegt. Auch den im Kaukasus selbst auf russischem Gebiet sesshaften Völkerschaften derselben Rasse wird in Beschreibungen durchaus kein uns abstossender Charakter zuerkannt, wenn man etwa von der bei ihnen meist üblichen gewaltsamen Selbsthilfe absieht, die unserm heutigen Rechtsempfinden zuwiderlauft, die sich aber auch bei Dinariern allgemein vorfindet. Da sich Völker immer dort auch seelisch am reinsten erhalten, wo sie Artfremdes sich fernhalten und namentlich die ihnen arteigene Sprache bewahren konnten, so wäre es m. E. voreilig, die vorderasiatischen Steilköpfe in Bausch und Bogen als minderwertig zu verdammen. Die Sache liegt vielmehr so, dass sich die schlechten Charakterzüge erst in den Gebieten entwickelt haben, die Jahrtausende lang unter dem Joche anderer Rassen geschmachtet haben. Hier konnten sich die Unterworfenen um so besser erhalten, je mehr sie sich den Herren anzupassen versuchten, und da eine solche Anpassung der seelischen Eigenschaften nur bis zu einem allgemeinmenschlichen Grade möglich ist, mussten Verstellung, Heuchelei,

Geldgier und Unehrlichkeit im allgemeinen das ersetzen, was ihnen an sich rassefremd war: diese Volksteile der unterworfenen Rasse setzten sich im Laufe der Zeit durch Auslese immer mehr durch, während die, die sich weniger anzupassen vermochten, ausgemerzt wurden. Es zeigt sich auch hier wieder die Gefährlichkeit der Unterdrückung arteigenen Volkstums nicht nur für die Unterworfenen, sondern in letzter Linie auch für die Herrscherschicht, die in rassefremdem Gebiet schliesslich auch degeneriert und zugrunde geht. Andrerseits hat Russland, das den Kaukasusvölkern seine indogermanische Sprache nicht aufzwang, nur gute Erfahrungen damit gemacht."

p. 222

Teichmann: "Während das neue Regime mit Fackelzug und Jubelgesängen dessen Triumph am Brandenburgr Tor feierte, sass Max von Oppenheim mit zwei Gästen, Cornelius Vanderbilt jr. aus New York und seinem Neffe Harold von Oppenheim, unweit davon in einem Tanzlokal, als 'einige halb-betrunkene Männer in das Lokal stürzten und brüllten: 'Die Juden heraus!' Der Wirt und die Kellner beruhigten Sie mit der Versicherung, es wären keine Juden im Saale. Nach einiger Zeit kamen sie wieder, worauf einer der Gäste in energischer Weise gegen sie auftrat, wobei es beinahe zu einem Hangemenge gekommen wäre. Daraufhin verzogen sich diese Leute, um nicht mehr wiederzukommen.'"

p. 227, ch. 12, note 40

Prüfer: "aus deutschem Munde, allerdings jenem eines SS-Mannes, hörte ich hier auf der Fahrt durch Spanien zum ersten Male von der Massenverschickung der Juden mit kalter Selbstverständlichkeit sprechen. Zwar waren über diese Verschickungen Gerüchte aus Deutschland und Berichte aus feindlicher Quelle zu uns gedrungen, sie schienen uns jedoch so ungeheuerlich zu sein, dass wir sie, wie so viele andere Nachrichten der gegnerischen Propaganda, die sich als unrichtig erwiesen hatten, für 'Greuelmärchen' und zum mindesten für Übertreibungen gehalten hatten. Im weiteren Verlauf der Reise verstärkte sich der ungünstige Eindruck. Die uns entgegengesandten Herren aus dem Auswärtigen Amt und der NSDAP sprachen untereinander mit völliger Gelassenheit über Dinge, die so unwahrscheinlich klangen, dass wir sie nicht geglaubt hätten, wenn irgend welche Reisende sie uns erzählt hätten."

pp. 235-236

Seidt: "Hitler wollte keine Zusammenarbeit mit den von den Briten unterworfenenen und ausgebeuteten Kolonialvölkern. Er erinnerte sich noch genau an die Jahre 1920/1921, als seine Partei begann, in München Fuss zu fassen. Damals wurde in nationalistischen Zirkeln der bayerischen Hauptstadt erörtert, die NSDAP als 'Freiheitsbewegung der deutschen Nation' einem 'Bund der unterdrückten Nationen' anzuschliessen. Hitler wurden damals Ägypter und Inder vorgestellt, die auf ihn 'den Eindruck schwatzhafter Wichtigtuer, bar jedes realen Hintergrunds machten.' Er war aufgebracht, dass es sogar und gerade im nationalen Lager Deutsche gab, 'die sich von solchen aufgeblasenen Orientalen blenden lassen.' Deshalb trat er schon sehr früh in München politischen Beziehungen seiner Partei zu Vertretern unterdrückter Kolonialvölke konsequent entgegen: 'Ich habe mich gegen solche Versuche immer gewehrt. Nicht nur, dass ich Besseres zu tun hatte, als in so unfruchtbaren "Besprechungen" Wochen zu vertrödeln, hielt ich auch, selbst wenn es sich dabei um autorisierte Vertreter solcher Nationen gehandelt hätte, das ganze für untauglich, ja schädlich.'"

pp. 240-241

Exchange of views between Hitler and Husseini, the Grand Mufti (including the Mufti's opening statement to Hitler, which was omitted from the main text):

F 1/0 018–24

Auszeichnung des Gesandten Schmidt (Büro RAM)

Geheime Reichssache   BERLIN, den 30. November 1941
Füh. 57a g. Rs.
AUFZEICHNUNG ÜBER DIE UNTERREDUNG ZWISCHEN DEM FÜHRER UND DEM GROSSMUFTI VON JERUSALEM, IN ANWESENHEIT DES REICHSAUSSENMINISTERS UND DES GESANDTEN GROBBA IN BERLIN AM 28. NOVEMBER 1941

Der Grossmufti bedankte sich zunächst beim Führer für die grosse Ehre, die ihm dieser erwiese, indem er ihn empfinge. Er benutze die Gelegenheit, um dem von der gesamten arabischen Welt bewunderten Führer des Grossdeutschen Reiches seinen Dank für die Sympathie auszusprechen, die er stets für die arabische und besonders die palästinensische Sache gezeigt habe und der er in seinen öffentlichen Reden deutlichen Ausdruck verliehen habe. Die arabischen Länder seien der festen Überzeugung, dass Deutschland den Krieg gewinnen würde und dass es dann um die arabische Sache gut stehen würde. Die Araber seien die natürlichen Freunde Deutschlands, da sie die gleichen Feinde wie Deutschland, nämlich die Engländer, die Juden und die Kommunisten, hatten. Sie seien daher auch bereit, von ganzem Herzen mit Deutschland zusammenzuarbeiten und stünden zur Teilnahme am Kriege zur Verfügung, und zwar nicht nur negativ durch Verübung von Sabotageakten und Anstiftung von Revolutionen, sondern auch positiv durch Bildung einer arabischen Legion. Die Araber konnten für Deutschland als Verbündete nützlicher sein, als es vielleicht auf den ersten Blick den Anschein habe, sowohl aus geographischen Gründen als auch wegen der Leiden, die ihnen von den Engländern und Juden zugefügt worden seien. Zudem besassen sie zu allen muselmannischen Nationen enge Beziehungen, die sie für die gemeinsame Sache benutzen könnten. Die arabische Legion würde mit Leichtigkeit aufzustellen sein. Ein Appell des Mufti an die arabischen Länder sowie an die Gefangenen arabischer, algerischer, tunesischer und marokkanischer Nationalität in Deutschland würde eine grosse Anzahl von kampfeswilligen Freiwilligen ergeben. Vom Siege Deutschlands sei die arabische Welt fest überzeugt, nicht nur weil das Reich eine grosse Armee, tapfere Soldaten und geniale militärische Führer besässe, sondern weil der Allmächtige niemals einer ungerechten Sache den Sieg verleihen könne.

Die Araber erstrebten in diesem Kampf die Unabhängigkeit und Einheit Palästinas, Syriens und des Irak. Sie hatten das vollste Vertrauen zum Führer und erwarteten von seiner Hand den Balsam für die Wunden, die ihnen die Feinde Deutschlands geschlagen hatten.

Der Mufti erwähnte sodann das Schreiben, das er von Deutschland erhalten habe, in dem ausgeführt sei, dass Deutschland keine arabischen Länder besetzt halte und die Unabhängigkeits- und Freiheitsbestrebungen der Araber verstünde und anerkenne, ebenso wie es für die Beseitigung der national-jüdischen Heimat eintrete.

Im jetzigen Augenblick würde für die propagandistische Einwirkung auf die arabischen Völker eine öffentliche Erklärung in diesem Sinne von grösstem Nutzen sein. Sie würde die Araber aus ihrem augenblicklichen Lahmungszustand aufrütteln und ihnen neuen Mut geben. Sie würde ausserdem dem Mufti die Arbeit der geheimen Organisierung des Arabertums für den Augenblick des Losschlagens erleichtern. Gleichzeitig könne er zusagen, dass die Araber voller Disziplin den richtigen Augenblick geduldig erwarten und erst auf einen Befehl von Berlin losschlagen würden.

Zu den Vorgängen im Irak bemerkte der Mufti, dass die Araber dort keineswegs etwa von Deutschland zum Angriff auf England aufgefordert worden seien, sondern lediglich auf einen direkten Angriff Englands auf ihre Ehre gehandelt hätten.

Die Türken würden seiner Ansicht nach die Errichtung einer arabischen Regierung in den Nachbargebieten begrüssen, da sie lieber eine schwächere arabische Regierung als starke europäische Regierungen in den Nachbarländern sähen und im übrigen von den 1,7 Millionen Arabern, die in Syrien, Transjordanien, Irak und Palästina wohnten, nichts zu befürchten hatten, da sie selbst ein Volk von 17 Millionen seien.

Auch Frankreich würde gegen die Vereinigung nichts einzuwenden haben, da es bereits im Jahre 1936 Syrien die Unabhängigkeit gewährt habe und bereits im Jahre 1933 der Vereinigung von Irak und Syrien unter König Feisal zugestimmt hatte.

Unter diesen Umständen erneuere er die Bitte, der Führer möge eine öffentliche Erklärung abgeben; damit die Araber nicht die Hoffnung, die eine so grosse Kraft im Leben der Völker darstelle, verlören. Mit dieser Hoffnung im Herzen seien die Araber, wie gesagt, bereit zu warten. Sie hatten es mit der sofortigen Durchführung ihrer Bestrebungen nicht eilig; ein halbes oder ein ganzes Jahr konnten sie leicht zuwarten. Wenn ihnen jedoch durch eine derartige Erklärung eine solche Hoffnung nicht gegeben würde, sei zu erwarten, dass die Engländer den Nutzen daraus ziehen würden.

Der Führer erwiderte, dass die grundsätzliche Einstellung Deutschlands zu diesen Fragen, wie das vom Mufti bereits selbst ausgesprochen sei, klar wäre. Deutschland trete für einen kompromisslosen Kampf gegen die Juden ein. Dazu gehöre selbstverständlich auch der Kampf gegen die jüdische Heimstätte in Palästina, die nichts anderes sei als ein staatlicher Mittelpunkt für den destruktiven Einfluss der jüdischen Interessen. Deutschland wisse auch, dass die Behauptung, das Judentum übe die Rolle eines Wirtschaftspioniers in Palästina aus, eine Lüge sei. Dort arbeiteten nur die Araber, nicht aber die Juden. Deutschland sei entschlossen, Zug um Zug eine europäische Nation nach der anderen zur Lösung des Judenproblems aufzufordern und sich im gegebenen Augenblick mit einem gleichen Appell auch an aussereuropäische Völker zu wenden.

Gegenwärtig stehe Deutschland in einem Kampf auf Leben und Tod gegen zwei Machtpositionen des Judentums: Grossbritannien und Sowjetrussland. Theoretisch sei der Kapitalismus Englands und der Kommunismus Sowjetrusslands voneinander verschieden, in Wirklichkeit jedoch verfolge das Judentum in beiden Ländern ein gemeinsames Ziel. Dieser Kampf sei das Entscheidende; auf der politischen Ebene stelle er sich im Grunde als eine Auseinandersetzung zwischen Deutschland und England dar, weltanschaulich sei es ein Kampf zwischen dem Nationalsozialismus und dem Judentum. Selbstverständlich würde Deutschland dem im gleichen Ringen stehenden Arabertum positive und praktische Hilfe zukommen lassen, denn platonische Zusicherungen seien in einem Kampf um Sein oder Nichtsein, wo das Judentum die britischen Machtmittel fur seine Zwecke einsetzen könne, zwecklos.

Die Unterstützung der Araber müsste materieller Art sein. Wie wenig in einem solchen Kampf Sympathien allein hülfen, sei an der Unternehmung im Irak klar geworden, wo die Umstände eine wirklich durchschlagende praktische Hilfe nicht zugelassen hätten. Trotz aller Sympathien habe die deutsche Hilfe nicht genügt und der Irak sei von den britischen Machtmitteln, das heisst von dem Vormunde der Juden, besiegt worden.

Der Mufti müsse jedoch einsehen, dass in dem gegenwärtigen Kampf auch das Schicksal der arabischen Welt mit entschieden werde. Der Führer müsse daher nüchtern und kühl abwagend als Verstandesmensch und primär als Soldat, als Führer der deutschen und alliierten Armeen denken und sprechen. Alles, was geeignet sei, in diesem riesigen Kampf der gemeinsamen Sache und daher auch dem Arabertum zu helfen, müsse geschehen. Alles jedoch, was zu einer Schwächung der militärischen Lage beitragen könne, müsse trotz evtl. Unpopularität zurückgestellt werden.

Deutschland stehe in sehr schweren Kämpfen, um sich den Zugang zum nord-kaukasischen Gebiet zu eröffnen. Die Schwierigkeiten lagen vor allem im Nachschub, der infolge der Zerstörung der Eisenbahnen und Strassen sowie des einsetzenden Winters ausserordentlich erschwert sei. Wenn in diesem Augenblick der Führer in einer Erklärung das Problem Syrien vorwegnähme, so würde dies diejenigen Elemente in Frankreich stärken, die unter dem Einfluss de Gaulles stehen. Sie würden die Erklärung des Führers als eine Absicht der Auflösung des französischen Kolonialreiches auslegen und ihre Landsleute auffordern, lieber gemeinsame Sache mit den Engländern zu machen und zu retten zu versuchen, was noch zu retten wäre. Man würde in Frankreich die deutsche Erklärung bezüglich Syriens auf die französischen Kolonien im allgemeinen beziehen, und daher würden im jetzigen Augenblick daraus neue Schwierigkeiten in Westeuropa entstehen, das heisst ein Teil der deutschen Wehrmacht würde im Westen gebunden werden und nicht mehr für den Ostfeldzug zur Verfügung stehen.

Der Führer gab sodann dem Mufti folgende Erklärung ab, indem er ihn bat, sie in seinem tiefsten Herzen zu verschliessen:

1) Er (der Führer) werde den Kampf bis zur völligen Zerstörung des jüdisch-kommunistischen europäischen Reiches fortführen.

2) Im Zuge dieses Kampfes würde zu einem heute noch nicht genau nennbaren, aber jedenfalls nicht fernen Zeitpunkt von den deutschen Armeen der Südausgang Kaukasiens erreicht werden.

3) Sobald dieser Fall eingetreten sei, würde der Führer von sich aus der arabischen Welt die Versicherung abgeben, dass die Stunde der Befreiung für sie gekommen sei. Das deutsche Ziel würde dann lediglich die Vernichtung des im arabischen Raum unter der Protektion der britischen Macht lebenden Judentums sein. In dieser Stunde würde dann auch der Mufti der berufenste Sprecher der arabischen Welt sein. Es würde ihm obliegen, die von ihm insgeheim vorbereitete arabische Aktion auszulösen. Dann würde auch Deutschland die Reaktion Frank-reichs auf eine derartige Erklärung gleichgültig sein können.

Wenn Deutschland sich den Weg über Rostow zum Iran und nach Irak erzwinge, würde dies gleichzeitig den Beginn des Zusammenbruchs des britischen Weltreichs bedeuten. Er (der Führer) hoffe, dass sich für Deutschland im nächsten Jahre die Möglichkeit ergeben werde, das Kaukasische Tor nach dem Mittleren Orient aufzustossen. Es sei besser, im Dienst der gemeinsamen Sache mit der arabischen Proklamation noch einige Monate zu warten, als dass sich Deutschland selbst Schwierigkeiten schüfe, ohne den Arabern dadurch helfen zu können.

Er (der Führer) verstehe durchaus die Sehnsucht der Araber nach einer öffentlichen Erklärung, wie sie der Grossmufti verlange. Er gäbe diesem jedoch zu bedenken, dass er (der Führer) selbst fünf Jahre lang Staatsoberhaupt des Deutschen Reichs gewesen sei, ohne seiner eigenen Heimat gegenüber die Erklärung der Befreiung abgeben zu können. Er habe damit bis zu dem Augenblickwarten müssen, in dem auf Grund der durch die Waffen geschaffenen Tatsache die Erklärung erfolgen konnte, dass der Anschluss vollzogen sei.

In dem Augenblick, in dem Deutschlands Tankdivisionen und Luftgeschwader südlich des Kaukasus erschienen, könne auch der vom Grossmufti erwartete öffentliche Appell an die arabische Welt erfolgen.

Der Grossmufti erwiderte, dass sich seiner Ansicht nach alles so verwirklichen werde, wie es der Führer angedeutet habe. Er sei absolut beruhigt und zufrieden gestellt durch die Worte, die er vom deutschen Staatsoberhaupt vernommen hatte. Er frage jedoch, ob es nicht möglich sei, wenigstens insgeheim eine Abmachung mit Deutschland zu treffen, so wie er sie dem Führer vorher skizziert habe.

Der Führer antwortete, dass er ja bereits soeben diese vertrauliche Erklärung dem Grossmufti gegenüber abgegeben habe.

Der Grossmufti bedankte sich dafür und bemerkte abschliessend, dass er voller Vertrauen mit nochmaligem Dank für die Interessenahme an der arabischen Sache vom Führer, scheide.

SCHMIDT

pp. 245-248

Oppenheim Memorandum:

Dokument 2:
Denkschrift zur Revolutionierung des Vorderen Orients Mitte 1940.

Als Leiter des Nachrichtenwesens für den Orient im Auswärtigen Amt, später bei der Botschaft in Konstantinopel während des Weltkrieges, erlaube ich mir, in dem Augenblick, wo der Krieg gegen England in seine entscheidende Phase eintritt, das Folgende vorzutragen:

Es ist jetzt für uns der Moment gekommen, energisch im Vorderen Orient gegen England zu arbeiten. Zwei Aufgaben sind dringlich:

1) Berlin mit direkten, zuverlässigen Nachrichten aus dem Vorderen Orient zu versorgen.
2) Die Revolutionierung, zunächst Syriens gegen die englischen Besetzungs-Pläne, dann der angrenzenden arabischen Gebiete, des Irak, Transjordaniens, Palästinas und Saudi-Arabiens. Das Ziel wäre, britische Streitkräfte zu binden, die Ölausfuhr und damit die Versorgung der britischen Kriegs- und Handelsflotte zu verhindern, den Verkehr durch den Sueskanal für die Engländer lahm zulegen und letzlich die britische Vorherrschaft

im Vorderen Orient zu vernichten.

Zur Durchführung dieser Aufgabe sollte so rasch wie möglich der frühere Gesandte in Bagdad, Dr. Grobba, nach Syrien entsandt werden. Syrien ist das einzige Land, von dem aus der Kampf gegen England zur Zeit geführt werden kann. Dr. Grobba müsste seinen Sitz in Damaskus haben. Für die laufenden Geschäfte, so die Angelegenheiten der Reichsdeutschen in Syrien usw., könnte ein konsularischer Beamter, vielleicht mit Sitz in Beirut, unter ihm arbeiten. Dr. Grobba dagegen würde seine ganze Kraft der Revolutionierung des Vorderen Orients gegen England zu widmen haben. Dr. Grobba ist dort als der gefährlichste Gegner Englands bekannt; sein Name würde wie ein Programm wirken, sein Erscheinen und seine Arbeit in Damaskus wie ein Aufruf zum Kampf, nicht nur für Syrien, sondern für alle arabischen Länder. Diese warten zum Teil–insbesondere der Irak–nur auf einen Wink Deutschlands, um gegen England vorzugehen. Dr. Grobba ist noch bei Ibn Saud als Gesandter akkreditiert, er ist mit dem Mufti von Jerusalem, der sich jetzt in Bagdad befindet, befreundet. Selbstredend müsste er geeignete Helfer und die entsprechenden Geld–und sonstigen Mittel, Rundfunk–und Sendegeräte etc. zur Hand haben. Auch müsste ihm die Mitverfügung über die Waffen der zu demobilisierenden französischen Armee eingeräumt werden; diese Waffen sollten den Arabern zum Kampf gegen England überlassen werden. Nicht nur für diesen Punkt, sondern auch für seine anderen Aufgaben muss natürlich vorher eine Verständigung mit Italien erzielt werden.

In Syrien ist der bisherige französische Oberkommissar Botschafter Puaux, der seit seinem vergeblichen Kampf in Wien gegen den Nationalsozialismus unser grosser Feind ist, zu entfernen und das jetzige französenfreundliche syrische Direktorium durch eine uns genehme syrische Regierung zu ersetzen.

Im Irak ist der pro-englische Aussenminister Nuri as-Sa'id, eventuell gewaltsam, zu beseitigen. Die irakische Armee hätte den englischen Flughafen von al-Habbaniya zu zerstören und mit Hilfe der Stämme den Kampf mit den britischen Truppen aufzunehmen, die Ölleitung nach Haifa zu sperren und die Engländer aus dem ganzen Irak, insbesondere aus Basra, hinauszuwerfen.

In Transjordanien ist der Emir Abdallah, der sich vollkommen den Engländern verschrieben hat, zu entfernen.

In Palästina ist der Kampf gegen die Engländer und Juden mit voller Kraft wieder aufzunehmen. Hierzu müsste Ibn Saud die Hand bieten.

Er wird dies aber nur tun, wenn man ihm al-Aqaba und Ma'an, Orte im südlichen Transjordanien, auf die er einen wohlbegründeten Anspruch hat, zusagt. Möglicherweise wird er darüber hinaus ganz Transjordanien verlangen. In Palästina sollte eine Regierung unter dem Mufti eingerichtet werden. In Jerusalem könnte eine Ausnahmeregie eingeführt werden, in dem Vertreter der verschiedenen Konfessionen (Katholiken, Protestanten, Orthodoxen) und der Juden unter dem Mufti mitzuwirken hätten. Von den Juden sollten in Palästina nur diejenigen, die vor dem Weltkrieg dort waren, belassen werden.

Was Syrien angeht, so ist die Entscheidung über seine Zukunft nicht leicht. Der Irak wünscht die Einverleibung dieses Landes, die muslimischen Syrier und auch ein Teil der christlichen, nämlich die Griechisch-Orthodoxen, würde es zweifellos begrüssen, wenn ihre Heimat mit dem Irak vereinigt werden würde. Dagegen wird Ibn Saud diese Vereinigung mit allen Mitteln zu hintertreiben suchen, weil er ein persönlicher Gegner der im Irak herrschenden Dynastie (der früheren Grossscherifen von Mekka) ist, und weil er die Entstehung eines grösseren Reiches an seiner Nordgrenze fürchten würde. Der einfachste Ausweg wäre es, einen der Söhne Ibn Sauds auf den zu errichtenden syrischen Thron zu setzen (eine direkte Einverleibung Syriens in Saudi-Arabien kommt schon aus religiösen Gründen nicht in Betracht, weil das in Saudi-Arabien herrschende fanatische Wahhabitentum in Syrien unannehmbar wäre). Der saudische Prinz müsste auf die Einführung seiner Glaubenslehre in Syrien verzichten. Der Libanon wäre wieder wie vor dem Weltkrieg als ein Bezirk mit eigener Verwaltung innerhalb des syrischen Staates zu konstituieren. Selbstverständlich müssten die Gebiete, die von den Franzosen dem Libanon zugeschlagen worden sind, Tripolis, Saida, Sur, die Bekaa mit Baalbek und der Hermon von dem neuen Verwaltungsbezirk wieder abgetrennt werden.

Nach dem Friedensschluss, nach siegreich beendigtem Kampf gegen England, wäre ein Staatenbund der genannten arabischen Länder von Vorderasien zu schaffen, in dem auch Jemen und die kleineren Staaten der arabischen Halbinsel wie Oman, Bahrein, Kuweit usw. vertreten sein müssten.

Ägypten ist bisher ausserhalb der vorliegenden Betrachtung geblieben. Es sei diesbezüglich nur kurz erwähnt, dass die Einbeziehung Ägyptens in den genannten Staatenbund sicherlich von grosser Bedeutung wäre. Im Augenblick würde ich eine möglichst gute Behandlung der noch in Deutschland befindlichen Ägypter für nützlich halten, die man die

Unfreundlichkeiten nicht entgelten lassen sollte, welche die ägyptische Regierung unter englischem Druck den in Ägypten lebenden Deutschen zugefügt hat. Wir machen in unserer Presse auf alle Anzeichen des Gegensatzes zwischen der ägyptischen Regierung, dem ägyptischen Volk und seiner Armee und den Engländern aufmerksam und lassen dadurch erkennen, dass wir die Ägypter als heimlichen Bundesgenossen ansehen. Auf der anderen Seite dürfen wir jedoch nicht die in Deutschland befindlichen Ägypter als feindliche Ausländer behandeln.

Zum Schluss möchte ich darauf hinweisen, dass eine besondere, freundliche Behandlung der gefangenen Marokkaner, Algerier und Tunesier gute Früchte tragen würde. Während des Weltkrieges waren alle muslimischen Kriegesgefangenen, auch alle indischen, in einem eigenen Lager bei Wünsdorf in der Nähe von Berlin untergebracht. Man hatte ihnen dort eine Moschee errichtet, Gefangenenzeitungen wurden in den einschlägigen Sprachen für sie hergestellt usw.

Die Hauptsache ist, dass der Gesandte Dr. Grobba möglichst rasch nach dem Vorderen Orient geht. Es wäre wohl gut, wenn er vor seiner Ausreise mit dem Emir Shakib Arslan in Genf Fühlung nähme, um mit ihm die Fragen der staatlichen Neuordnung im arabischen Raum, insbesondere in Syrien, zu besprechen. Shakib Arslan, der durchaus und wie ich genau weiss, seit Jahrzehnten auf deutschem Boden steht, verfügt über eine ungeheure Personen- und Sachkenntnis und seine Ratschläge würden daher, wenn wir uns mit diesen Problemen ernsthaft beschäftigen, sehr nützlich sein.

Solange die Entsendung des Gesandten Grobba nach Syrien undurchführbar ist, weil Deutschland noch die französische Stellung in Syrien anerkennt, möchte die Einleitung der geplanten Aktionen von Ankara aus vorgenommen werden, vielleicht durch Vermittlung der dortigen irakischen Gesandtschaft. Sollten diese Verhandlungen dann das Resultat haben, dass der Irak sich auf unsere Seite stellt, so müsste eine neue syrische Nationalregierung ausgerufen und provisorisch irgendwo an der syrisch-irakischen Grenze eingerichtet werden. Diese Regierung müsste dann sofort von Deutschland und Italien anerkannt werden. Die Tatsache der Anerkennung müssten wir dann der französischen Regierung mitteilen, indem wir sie zugleich davon verständigen, dass der Gesandte Grobba zur Wahrung der deutschen Interessen in Syrien und als Beobachter unserer Regierung nach Damaskus geschickt wird.

Ich verkenne keineswegs die Schwierigkeiten der arabischen

Aufständischen, der noch intakten englischen Armee im Irak und in Palästina entgegenzutreten. Die Widerstandskraft der englischen Truppen wird aber bei weiteren deutschen Erfolgen gegen England erheblich abnehmen, zumal es sich zum grossen Teil um Kolonialtruppen handelt.

Ferner würden schon durch den Aufstand die Engländer in ihrer Position in Ägypten und in Indien geschwächt werden. Das Erdöl würde jedenfalls für die Engländer in Haifa gesperrt werden, und was besonders wichtig ist, die Besetzung Syriens durch die Engländer würde verhindert und die Verbindung zwischen den Engländern im Irak und den Türken würde unter-brochen werden.

Das nächste Ziel der etwa mit irakischen Vertretern zu führenden Verhandlungen müsste sein, zu erreichen, dass der Irak den Wunsch nach Wiederaufnahme der Beziehungen mit Deutschland äussert. Durch Eingehen auf diesen Wunsch würde die Rückkehr des Gesandten Dr. Grobba nach dem Irak ermöglicht werden. Von dort aus könnte er mit syrischen Nationalisten in Verbindung treten, um nach Aufruf einer syrischen unabhängigen Regierung nach Damaskus überzusiedeln.

(From Wolfgang G. Schwanitz, "Max von Oppenheim und der 'Heilige Krieg'," *Sozial.Geschichte*, 3 [2004], pp. 55–59)

pp. 265–266

De Gaulle: "L'infiltration allemande dans l'Empire continue. En Syrie une mission allemande dirigée par von Hentig et Roser est arrivée Damas 26 janvier et a visité Alep via Homs. Ostensiblement cette mission est économique mais son but est l'espionnage, la propaganda anti-britannique et le contact avec les nationalistes. Ils ont rencontré les leaders nationalistes les plus hostiles à la France ainsi que tous les Syriens germanophiles. En particulier Sadi Kailani."

"Von Hentig était en 1916 le principal collaborateur de von Niedermayer chargé de provoquer l'entrée en guerre de l'Afghanistan aux côtés de l'Allemagne." [He had been] "nommé par le gouvernement nazi directeur de la section d'Asie à la Wilhelmstrasse. Sa présence en Syrie autorisée par Vichy met en relief visées allemandes non seulement sur Syrie mais également sur pays situés entre Syrie et Indes."

pp. 266-267

Les Allemands en Syrie sous le gouvernement de Vichy: "M. von Hentig commença de travailler l'opinion, en s'adressant de préférence aux milieux hostiles à la France. Sa propagande prit d'abord une forme insidieuse. Dans une réunion à l'hôtel Métropole, à laquelle il invita, le 25 janvier, les principaux chefs politiques et religieux, il les séduisit par une grande affabilité et affecta de glisser—par courtoisie—sur les problèmes épineux que posait forcément l'administration française. Mais cette discrétion fut de courte durée. Bientôt, dans la même maison, on projetait entre autres le film *"Sieg im Westen"* (Victoire à l'Ouest), où la défaite de la France était rendue sensible sous les formes les plus frappantes. En même temps, M. von Hentig demandait aux Musulmans leurs vues sur la constitution d'un empire arabe, il envisageait la réunion d'un congrès de l'Islam à Damas, il incitait à la formation de groupements de jeunesse sur le modèle allemand, il encourageait les extrémistes contre les Anglais et leur conseillait de s'entendre avec le mouvement irakien des Fatoui. Le tout à la barbe des représentants de Vichy. Puis la propagande clandestine de la maison transmettait les mots d'ordre, qui n'allaient pas tarder à réapparaître dans le pays sous forme de revendications, de cris et d'émeutes. [...] Bientôt la supériorité du Français est mise en question, et son droit à rester titulaire d'un mandat. Enfin le parallèle s'établissait avec la race élue, la race allemande, seule digne de régner. Et la populace d'Alep, de Hama, de Damas se mettait à chanter:

> Bala Missiou, bala Mister,
> Kelloh barra, haïdé sikter,
> Bissama Allah, oua alard Hitler.
> (*"Plus de Monsieur, plus de Mister: tous dehors, fichez le camp. Au ciel Allah, sur terre Hitler!"*)

"Toute cette activité fut encore multipliée par un voyage que MM. von Hentig et Roser firent à travers la Syrie pour présenter leurs films et pour prêcher ouvertement l'avènement de l'ère allemande. A Damas, à Tripoli, à Lattaquieh, à Alep, et jusqu'au-delà de l'Euphrate, ils entreprirent, avec un apparat officiel, toute une tournée de visites aux notables, aux chefs religieux, aux écoles. [...] Partout enfin, où les gens croyaient avoir à se plaindre, on leur expliquait qu'il n'était plus utile de tenir compte des Français, qui n'avaient plus que l'ombre de l'autorité: qu'un avenir tout autre se préparait; et que c'était avec ceux qui tenaient cet avenir dans leurs mains qu'il fallait s'entendre. Aussi un tailleur du souk el-hodja, à Damas, se mit-il, au mois de mars, à confectionner des drapeaux à croix gammée pour quelques particuliers qui s'attendaient à en faire un prochain usage."

p. 288

Verband nationaldeutscher Juden: "Der Verband nationaldeutscher Juden bezweckt den Zusammenschluss aller derjenigen Deutschen jüdischen Stammes, die bei offenem Bekennen ihrer Abstammung sich mit deutschem Wesen und deutscher Kultur so unauflöslich verwachsen fühlen, dass sie nicht anders als deutsch empfinden und denken können. Er bekämpft alle Äusserungen und Betätigungen undeutschen Geistes, mögen sie von Juden oder Nichtjuden ausgehen, die das Wiedererstarken deutscher Volkskraft, deutscher Rechtlichkeit und deutschen Selbstgefühls beeinträchtigen und damit den Wiederaufstieg Deutschlands zu einer geachteten Stellung in der Welt gefährden."

p. 291

Reichsbund jüdischer Frontsoldaten: "Wir haben es schon öfter ausgedrückt, dass die nazionalsozialistische Weltanschauung schon in ihren Anfangsgründen viele Juden angezogen haben würde, ähnlich wie der Faschismus in Italien, wenn sie nicht, darin unähnlich ihrem italienischen Bruder, den Kampf gegen die Juden in eigenem Lande zum Programm erhoben hätte. Wir stellen heute die Frage, wie lange die führenden und klardenkenden nationalsozialistischen Männer der heutigen Regierung diesen Programmpunkt aufrecht zu erhalten gedenken."

p. 294

Schoeps: "Man mag zu Adolf Hitler stehen, wie man will, seine politische Leistung wird man nicht schmälern können, dass eben er es fertig gebracht hat, die Menschen aus ihrer privaten Isolierung herauszureissen und die Massen [...] über seine Person wieder an die Nation zu binden."

p. 294, ch. 16, note 5

Schoeps: "Galt der Staat im liberalen Zeitalter einerseits als Funktionär der Gesellschaft und andererseits der Kultur, so sind heute in den entpolitisierten Bildungs- und Gesellschaftsraum Kräfte eingebrochen, deren Positiva sehr problematisch sein mögen, die aber den liberalen Ideologien gegenüber einig sind, dass der Sinn des Staates auf jeden Fall nicht der ist, Konsumentenansprüche zu garantieren." [The liberal credo]"dass nur durch Besitz und Bildung wirkliche politische Verantwortung erwachsen könne, dass politische Bindung und Verantwortung aus Bildungs- and Besitzgütern erwachse, ist mit dem Bankrott des liberalen Gesellschaftsdenkens einfach erledigt worden. Die heutige Situation hat eine neue Wirklichkeit erschlossen, dass nämlich das 'bündische' Prinzip als der konträre Gegensatz zum sozialistischen Kollektiv allmählich politisch wird."

p. 299

Pevsner: "Ihr [der Architektur] haben die darstellenden Künste gedient, solange es einen echten Stil gegeben hat. [...] Bis zum Ende der deutschen Barok, d.h. bis zur bürgerlichen Revolution, ist das Gesamtkunstwerk Wirklichkeit gewesen, das Wagner nachher mitten aus dem Liberalismus heraus so sehnsüchtig suchen musste. Denn in seiner Zeit, und noch krasser in der folgenden 'wilhelminischen' hat ja — ein Symptom lebensgefährlicher Erkrankung — die Malerei alle grössten Begabungen der bildenden Kunst an sich gezogen."

p. 311

Pevsner: "Um die Kunst des endenden 19. Jhdts. in ihrer ganzen Entartung zu erkennen, muss man vom Soziologischen und nicht vom Ästhetischen her an sie herantreten. Was der Maler malte, entstand zu seinem persönlichen Spasse und nicht in Hinblick auf das Publikum, d.h. eine Gesamtheit, der er hätte dienen wollen, da er sich als ihren Teil empfand. Die Bilder wurden in der Natur und im Atelier konzipiert und fertiggestellt. Dann kamen sie zu Hunderten in Kunstausstellungen, die von vorn herein nur von ganz wenigen besucht wurden. So kam das Volk mit den künstlerischen Hervorbringungen nur in Berührung, wenn sie in den Besitz öffentlicher Sammlungen übergingen. Da begegnete ihnen dann das begreiflich Entsetzen aller derer, die so anders sahen und so anderes auf den Bildern sehen wollten, als die Künstler in ihrem abgeschlossenem Zirkel geschaffen hatten."

p. 301

Pevsner: "Wer sich froh als Teil einer grossen Gemeinschaft fühlt, in der er bereit ist aufzugehen, der muss den Glauben an den englischen Liberalismus und Individualismus von dem Hause jedes Einzelnen, das sein 'castle' sei, herzhaft ablehnen. Für ihn ist der Uniform ein Ehrenkleid."

p. 311

Pevsner: "Die ganze grosse Kunst des Mittelalters hat gedient, die katholische Kunst der Barokzeit, die französische Kunst der Klassik hat gedient. Dienen wollten die deutschen Nazarener, als sie sich um 1810 leidenschaftlich gegen die lockere 'liberale' Malerei des Rokoko wandten. Erst im 19. Jahrhundert haben dann in der bildenden Kunst Bildnis, Landschaft und Stilleben dei zentrale Stellung innegehabt. Der neue Geist wird wohl eine neue 'Historienmalerei' emportragen. Mag das zunächst eine Einbusse an ästhetischen Werten bedeuten, eine Wiederaufnahme der gesunden Verbindung von Kunstproduzenten und– Konsumenten wird es auf jeden Fall sein. Und diese Rückbesinnung musste jetzt kommen. Goebbels knüpft mit dem, was er lehrt, nicht nur an vergangene Jahrhunderte an, sondern auch an die lebendigsten Kräfte in der Kunst der letzten Jahrzehnte. Denn schon der Opposition gegen den Impressionismus um 1890 und dann wieder seit 1905/10 ging es um eine Neubewertung des Inhalts, der Thesen im Kunstwerk. Aus dem Gebiete der bildenden Kunst genügt es an van Goghs Sehnsucht nach einer neuen religiösen Kunst, an Klinger und Hodler, an Munch und Enssor zu erinnern. Und bedeutet denn die zu Unrecht sogenannte Neue Sachlichkeit mit der Tendenzdichtung, dem Reportageroman, dem politischen Film, die musikalische Jugendbewegung, die evangelisch-liturgische Musikbewegung, dis sozialkritische Malerei etwas anderes als den verschiedenartigen Ausdruck einer gemeinsamen Sehnsucht nach der Einheit mit den treibenden Kräften der Zeit und dem Kampfe für sie?"

p. 312

Pevsner: "In vollem politischen Gegensatz zu Frankreich steht im 17. Jahrhundert die Bürgerrepublik Holland. Dementsprechend ist auch das Verhältnis der Kunst zum Staate ein gänzlich anderes. Als Auftraggeber kamen der Hof und die städtischen Behörden nur in beschränktem Masse in Betracht. Eine in ihrer Struktur und in ihrem Geschmack wenig einheitliche Menge von Bürgern bildete die Schicht der Käufer. Ein Gewimmel verschiedenartiger Individualitäten ist auch die holländische Künstlerschaft. Ein jeder malte, was ihn reizte. Sicherheit über die Uebereinstimmung der so in der Werkstatt geschaffenen Bilder mit dem Bedarf liess sich kaum erwerben. So gibt es im Holland jener Zeit zum ersten Male ein Künstler-Proletariat, aber auch zum ersten Male das von der Mitwelt nicht vestandene Genie. Rembrandt schuf, was seine innere Stimme ihm vorschrieb. An ein Publikum wenden sich seine reifen und seine späten Werke nicht. Denn er zeigt sich nicht bereit, auf deren Wünsche Rücksicht zu nehmen.Der natürliche Ausgleich zwischen Kunst und Oeffentlichkeit, so selbstverständlich, als die Meisterwerke der mittelalterlichen Malerei und Plastik entstanden, ist zerstört.

"Holland nimmt mit dieser Entwurzelung des Künstler einen Zustand vorweg, der für das ganze Abendland erst mit dem 19. Jahrhundert verbindlich wurde. [...] So ist die heilige Autonomie der Kunst begründet, ihre Ueberlegenheit über Staat und Gesellschaft proklamiert."

p. 313

Pevsner: "Dann aber, seit den dreissiger Jahren war der Siegeszug der Demokratie und des Individualismus (der ja seinerseits auch auf die Romantik zurückführt) unaufhaltsam geworden. Der Impressionismus des letzten Jahrhundertdrittels ist seine Ausgeburt. Nun war die Kunst nicht mehr höchstes Ideal, weil sie die Erziehung des Menschengeschlechts zur Aufgabe hatte [as in Schiller's *Letters on the Aesthetic Education of Humanity*], sondern einzig um ihrer selbst willen. Gautier, Verlaine, Wilde lehren dieses Evangelium. Was die Malerei betrifft, so wurde es nun ihr alleiniger Sinn, diejenigen Eindrücke wiederzugeben, welche der einzelne Künstler in einem bestimmten Augenblick vor der Natur empfing—extremer Individualismus also und extremer Relativismus.

"Eine solche Kunst konnte dem Staat nichts angehen, konnte überhaupt keine grosse Idee etwas angehen. 'Die Maler mit den grossartigen Ideen sind dumme, schlechte Maler,' so hat sich Max Liebermann nicht geschämt es auszudrücken. Umgekehrt hätte natürlich auch ein starker und seiner selbst bewusster Staat nichts mit dieser Art Kunstübung anfangen können."

p. 314

Pevsner: "Voll Verachtung sah der Impressionist auf den Historienmaler hinab und sagte: Deutsche Geschichte, aber schlechte Bilder—also wertlos. Und Jahrzehnte lang hätte der bei Allen an der Kunst Teilnehmenden für einen Narren gegolten, der es gewagt hätte, gemäss der selbstverständlichen Ueberzeugung des Mittelalters zu sagen: Ein gutes Bild, aber nur Spargel—also wertlos."

pp. 314-315

Pevsner: Die neuen Männer im deutschen Reiche verlangen eine politische Kunst, so wie sie eine politische Wissenschaft verlangen. Das wurde von autoritativer Seite zum ersten Male am 11. April vorigen Jahres von Dr. Goebbels in seiner Antwort an Furtwängler ausgesprochen. Damit ist nicht dekretiert, dass es künftig nur noch Tendenzkunst geben solle, obwohl in der Tat z.B. die zweckfreien Gattungen der Malerei—also Landschaft, Stilleben, Sittenbild—erst Schöpfungen der Renaissance und des Barok gewesen sind. Vielmehr wird man sich die Entwicklung so vorzustellen haben, dass nach der Alleinherrschaft der zweckfreien Malerei im Impressionismus nun das Schwergewicht mit aller Entschiedenheit wieder auf die zweckgebundene, also die 'Historien'-Malerei gelegt werden wird. [...] Diese 'militante' Kunst wird also gewiss die teilnahmsvollste Förderung beim Staate finden. Und wenn er hier fördert, was ihm dient, wird er imstande sein, einen echten, alle Kunstäusserungen umfassenden Stil zu formen, so wie ihn das Mittelalter und das Frankreich Ludwig XIV besessen hat."

p. 317, ch. 16, note 47

Edith Landmann: "Wie immer auch im Innersten des Dichters angelegt, dennoch war vielleicht von aussen her die Stunde für das Neue Reich erst jetzt gekommen. Dieser von der Welt so streng sich sondernde Geist besass von je das feinste Ohr für die Weltstunde, in der er stand, für die Förderungen und Möglichkeiten des Tages. Erst als der Krieg die letzten Reste des alten weggefegt war reiner Boden da für neuen Anfang."

p. 319

Kantorowicz: "Obwohl ich als Kriegsfreiwilliger vom August 1914, als Frontsoldat während der Dauer des Krieges, als Nachkriegskämpfer gegen Polen, Spartakus und Räterepublik in Posen, Berlin und München eine Dienstentlassung wegen meiner jüdischen Abstammung nicht zu gewärtigen habe; obwohl ich auf Grund meiner Veröffentlichungen über den Stauferkaiser Friedrich den Zweiten für meine Gesinnung gegenüber einem wieder national gerichteten Deutschland keines Ausweises von vorgestern, gestern oder heute bedarf; obwohl meiner jenseits aller Zeitströmungen und Tagesereignisse begründete, grundsätzlich positive Einstellung gegenüber einem national regierten Reich auch durch die jüngste Geschehnisse nicht hat ins Wanken kommen können, [...] so sehe ich mich als Jude noch gezwungen aus dem Geschehen die Folgerungen zu ziehen und im kommenden Sommersemester meine Lehrtätigkeit ruhen zu lassen. Denn solange jeder deutsche Jude—wie in der gegenwärtigen Zeit der Umwalzung—schon durch seine Herkunft für einen 'Landesverräter' gelten kann; solange jeder Jude als solcher rassenmässig für minderwertig erachtet wird; solange die Tatsache, überhaupt jüdisches Blut in den Adern zu haben, zugleich einen Gesinnungsdefekt involviert; solange jeder deutsche

Jude sich einer täglichen Antastung seiner Ehre ausgesetzt sieht ohne die Möglichkeit, persönliche oder gerichtliche Genugtuung zu erzwingen, solange ihm als Studenten das akademische Bürgerrecht versagt, der Gebrauch der deutschen Sprache nur als 'Fremdsprache' gestattet wird; […] und solange jeder Jude, gerade wenn er ein nationales Deutschland voll bejaht, unfehlbar in den Verdacht gerät, durch das Bekunden seiner Gesinnung nur aus Furcht zu handeln oder bloss seinen persönlichen Vorteil zu suchen, nach Pfründen jagen und seine wirtschaftliche Existenz sichern zu wollen; solange daher jeder deutsche und wahrhaft national gesinnte Jude, um einen derartigen Verdacht zu entgehen, seine nationale Gesinnung eher schamhaft verbergen muss, als dass er sie unbefangen kundtun dürfte: solange erscheint es mir als unvereinbar mit der Würde eines Hochschullehrers, sein nur auf innerer Wahrheit begründetes Amt verantwortlich zu versehen, und solange auch als eine Verletzung des Schamgefühls der Studenten, seine Lehrtätigkeit, als wäre nichts geschehen, stillschweigend wieder aufzunehmen."

p. 320

Kantorowicz: "… ist gleich einem Jüngsten Gericht und Aufstand der Toten stets unmittelbar nahe, ja gegenwärtig. […] Es ist die geheime Gemeinschaft der Dichter und Weisen, der Helden und Heligen, der Opfrer und Opfer, welche Deutschland hervorgebracht hat und die Deutschland sich dargebracht haben … Es ist als Gemeinschaft ein Götterreich wie der Olymp, ist ein Geisterreich wie der mittelalterliche Heiligen- und Engelsstaat, ist ein Menschenreich wie Dantes […] 'Humana civilitas' […ein Reich] 'zugleich von dieser und nicht von dieser Welt…ein Reich zugleich da und nicht da.'"

p. 321, ch. 16, note 53

Riedel: "Die Rede bewahrte Georgesche Visionen eines gewesenen und künftigen Reiches ursprünglich europäischer Herkunft und Prägung. Aber sie war getragen von einem eschatologischen Glauben und gesprochen im Pathos prophetischer Überzeugung, das formal der pathetischen Rhetorik des politischen Gegners nicht allzufern stand."

pp. 320-321

Kantorowicz: "Es ist ein Seelenreich, in welchem immerdar die gleichen deutschesten Kaiser eigensten Ranges und eigenster Artung herrschen und tronen, unter deren Zepter sich zwar noch niemals die ganze Nation aus innerster Inbrunst gebeugt hat, deren Herrentum aber dennoch immerwährend und ewig ist und in tiefster Verborgenheit *gegen* das jeweilige Aussen lebt und dadurch *für* das ewige Deutschland."

"Mit Gewalt ist dieser Himmel niemals zu stürmen."

p. 321

Kantorowicz: "'Es möge Deutschland so werden, wie es sich der Meister erträumt hat!' Und wenn das heutige Geschehen nicht bloss die Grimasse jenes Wunchbildes ist, sondern tatsächlich der wahre Weg zu dessen Erfüllung, so möge das alles zum Guten ausschlagen–und dann ist es gleichgültig, ob der einzelne auf diesem Weg mitschreiten kann–vielmehr: darf–oder statt zu jubeln beiseite tritt. 'Imperium transcendat hominem,' erklärte Friedrich II und ich wäre der letzte, der hier widerspräche."

p. 323

Edith Landmann: "Ihr wisst, dass ich angesichts der Art von Juden, die sich nach und lange schon vor dem Kriege in Deutschland breitgemacht, Antisemit war genau wie Ihr, aus Liebe zum deutschen Volk. Glaubt Ihr im Ernst, es wäre mir noch eine Gemeinschaft mit dieser Art von Juden möglich, und gar mit der heutigen Jugend der Juden, die, nur noch mit Zionismus und Kommunismus aufgewachsen, von deutschem Geiste ebensowenig ahnt wie die Deutschen selbst?"

"[…] weil so viele Gedanken des Dritten Reichs, in welcher Verzerrung immer sie verwirklicht werden, die Gedanken längst auch unseres Herzens waren. […] Und wer einmal von dieser Erschütterung des ganzen liberalen Gefüges der Welt, von dieser rasenden, entschlossenen Abkehr vom 19. Jahrhundert, von diesem Taumel barbarischer Absolutheit mit ergriffen ist, wer aus gleicher Gegnerschaft, aus sonst irgend einem Grunde, in welchem inneren Abstande auch immer, dem grossen deutschen Aufbruch nicht glaubt fernbleiben zu dürfen, der wird die Notwendigkeit einer Judenpolitik nicht leugnen können."

p. 323

Edith Landmann: "Das jüdische Blut können wir bei allem deutschen Geist nicht aus uns heraus tun. Sollen wir nun etwa den deutschen Geist aus uns herausreissen, uns zurückverwandeln in alt fromme oder moderne nationale oder auch internationale Juden? Lieber bringen wir uns um."

Index of Proper Names

Abbas Hilmi II. Khedive of Egypt, 38, 40, 45
Abdulhamid II. Ottoman Sultan, 28, 29, 31, 38, 39, 44, 52, 53, 54, 55, 65, 69, 70, 349, 350
Abdul Huda. Adviser of Abdulhamid II, 31, 59
Abetz, Otto. German ambassador to France, 274
Adenauer, Konrad. German Chancellor, 168
Adivar, Halid Edib. Turkish writer, 82
al-Afghānī, Jamal al Din. Panislamist leader, 54, 55
al-Gailani, Rashid. Iraqi politican, 232, 233, 234, 236, 239, 240, 242, 248, 249, 255, 261, 266
al-Husseini, Amin. Grand Mufti of Jerusalem, 221, 234, 236, 237, 239, 248, 249, 251, 254, 257, 265, 268, 270, 275
Ali Yusuf, Shaykh. Egyptian nationalist, 38
Almazan, Andreu. Mexican general and politician, 182
Almazan, Elizabeth Pitt de. Mistress of Harold von Oppenheim, 181
al-Mifdai, Jamil. Iraqi politician, 234
al-Mukhtar, Omar. Senussi rebel leader, 235
al-Quwatli, Shukri. Head of anti-colonialist *Bloc national* in Syria, 275
al-Said, Nuri. Iraqi politician, 234, 246, 249, 251, 256
al-Senussi, Sidi Mohammed bin Ali. Muslim holy man, leader of Senussi brotherhood, 69, 70
al-Senussi, Sidi Mohammed el Mahdi. Son and successor of above, 70-71
al-Senussi, Sayyyid Ahmed Sharif. Successor of el Mahdi as leader of Senoussi, 72, 79-80
al-Suhrawardy, Sir Abdullah al-Ma'mūn. Barrister and Islamic scholar, 48
Amanullah. King of Afghanistan, 250
Arco auf Valley, Anton von. Son of Emmy von Oppenheim, assassin of Kurt Eisner, 201, 202, 203
Arco auf Valley, Ferdinand von. Brother-in-law of Jacob and Marcus Wallenberg, 189, 201
Arendt, Hannah. German-Jewish philosopher, 297
Arslan, Adel. Brother of Shakib Arslan, 268
Arslan, Shakib. Pan-Islamist leader, 209, 231, 232, 233, 247, 248, 268, 275, 369
Artbauer, Otto C. German travel writer, 77
Astor, John Jacob. American businessman, 32
Augusta. Wife of Wilhelm I, Empress of Germany, 4, 7

Bachofen, Johann Jacob. Swiss scholar, 17
Badia y Leblich, Domingo (Ali Bey al-Abbasi). Spanish traveller in Middle East, 14, 26
Badoglio, Field Marshal Pietro. Italian soldier and statesman, 229
Baeck, Leo. Leader of German Jewish Community, 293
Becker, Carl. German oriental scholar, 47, 49, 55, 63, 98, 101, 103, 108, 123

Behrens. Jewish banking family, 179
Belzoni, Giovanni Battista. Explorer of Egyptian antiquities, 18
Bernstorff, Johann Heinrich von. German diplomat, 16, 40, 96
Bessam, Mohammed Ibn. Middle Eastern businessman, 31, 108
Bethmann Hollweg, Theobald von. Chancellor of Germany, 84, 97, 333
Bismarck, Herbert von. German Foreign Secretary, son of Otto von Bismarck,7, 33, 34, 36, 168, 313, 330, 347
Bismarck, Otto von. German Chancellor, 80
Bleichröder. Jewish Banking family, 38, 348
Blomberg, Generaloberst Werner von. German Minister of War and Commander-in-Chief of Wehrmacht, 186
Blunt, Lady Jane. British traveller in Middle East, 19
Bopp, Franz. German scholar of historical linguistics, 213
Börries, Freiherr von Münchausen. German poet, 26
Bosch, Robert. German industrialist, 189, 190
Bräunlich, Erich. German oriental scholar, 16, 20, 120, 206, 208, 278, 280
Buchan, John. Novelist. xv, 16, 17
Buckingham, James Silk, Traveller and writer, 14
Bülow, Bernhard-Heinrich von. German Foreign Secretary, 41
Bulwer-Lytton, Edward. British novelist, 15
Bulwer-Lytton, Edward Robert. Viceroy of India, 51
Burckhardt, Jacob. Swiss historian, 216
Burckhardt, Jean-Louis (Johann Ludwig). Swiss traveller and explorer, 14, 18, 19
Bürkner, Gottlieb, Admiral. Nazi naval officer, 188
Burton, Richard. British traveller in Middle East, 14, 19, 27

Byron, Lord. Poet, 26
Camecho, Manuel Avila. President of Mexico, 181
Camp, Raymond R. American writer, 150
Campbell Thompson, Reginald. British archaeologist, 109, 129
Canaris, Admiral Wilhelm. Head of the Abwehr (German Counter-Intelligence), 186, 187, 188, 194, 195, 197, 198, 232, 260, 277, 286
Carstens, Asmus. German neo-classical artist, 313
Caskel, Werner. German oriental scholar, 16, 20, 120, 162, 208, 209, 277, 278,280, 281, 332
Castelle, Friedrich. German journalist and editor, 309
Chan, Wilhelm. Director of Oppenheim Bank, 167
Chassériau, Théodore. Painter, 14
Cholidis, Nadja. Contemporary German archaeologist, 126, 153, 161
Christie, Agatha. British writer, 144
Churchill, Winston. Prime Minister of Great Britain, 188, 194
Clare (Klaar), George. Viennese writer, 173
Clarke, Carter W. Deputy Chief of allied military intelligence, 193
Clauss, Ferdinand. German scholar of race, 211
Colbert, Jean-Bapiste. Seventeenth-century French statesman, 312
Columbani. Chief of Police in French mandate of Syria, 268
Courant, Richard. German-Jewish mathematician, 304
Cromer, Evelyn Baring, Lord. British Consul-General in Egypt, 39, 40, 45, 60, 96, 349
Cudahy, John C. American ambassador to Belgium, 236
Dalton, Sir Hugh. British Labour M.P., 35
Daudet, Alphonse. French writer, 216
de Boer, Tjitze. Dutch oriental scholar, 18

de Gaulle, Charles. Leader of Free French, 240, 261, 263, 264, 265, 272, 273, 331
Delacroix, Eugène. Painter, 14, 17
Delitzsch, Friedrich. German oriental scholar, 22, 214, 215
Deniker, Joseph. Russian-born French naturalist and anthropologist, 213
Dentz, Henri. Vichy-appointed High Commisssioner in Syria, 262, 267
Dicey, Edward. British journalist, 57
Diercks, Gustav. Author of *Hie Allah!*, 98
Digby, Lady Jane. British adventuress, 19, 29, 344
Disraeli, Benjamin. British Prime Minister, 19, 25, 26, 45, 51, 220
Djemal Pasha. Ottoman Navy Minister, 82, 83, 91, 100, 102, 333
Dodd, William. American ambassador to Germany, 180
Dostoievsky, Feodor. Novelist, 298
Duesterberg, Theodor. Leader of Stahlhelm veterans' association, 183
Dumas, Alexandre. Writer, 15
Dürer, Albrecht. Artist, 312

Eisner, Kurt. First President of Bavarian Socialist Republic, 201, 202, 203
el-Khalidi, Saleb. Contributor to The Spectator, 69
Engels, Pauline. Mother of Max von Oppenheim, 11
Ensor, James. Painter, 311
Enver Pasha. Ottoman War Minister, 58, 82, 83, 86, 87, 100, 102
Eulenburg, Philipp, Fürst von. German politician and diplomat, 9, 34, 37, 342

Faisal. Son of Hussein, sharif of Mecca, future King of Iraq, 38, 101
Faris Pasha. Sheikh of the Shammar Bedouins, 23
Favray, Antoine de. Painter, 13
Ferguson, Adam. British social and political theorist, 15
Field, Louise Maunsell. American novelist, 150
Fischer, Eugen. Director of Kaiser Wilhelm Institute of Anthropology, 216
Fischer, Fritz. Modern German historian, 42, 102
Fould, Benedict. Jewish banker, 4
Frank, Theodor. Jewish Director of Deutsche Bank, 166
Frankfort, Henri. Director of Warburg Institute, London, 150
Franz Josef. Emperor of Austria, 7
Frederick II. Holy Roman Emperor, 319, 320
Frick, Wilhelm. German Interior Minister, 175, 211
Friedrich Wilhelm III. Emperor of Germany, 7
Fritsch, Generaloberst Werner von. Commander-in-Chief of German army, 186
Frommel, Wolfgang. Writer, 295, 322
Funk, Walter. German Minister for Economic Affairs, replacing Schacht, 166
Furtwängler, Wilhelm. Orchestra conductor, 307, 308, 309, 310, 314, 315, 375

Galli, Gottfried, author of *Dschihad. Der Heilige Krieg Islams* (1915), 99
Games, Stephen. Biographer of Sir Nicholas Pevsner, 303, 304
Gauguin, Paul. Painter, 217
Gautier, Theophile. Writer, 313
Geibel, Emanuel. Poet, 101
Gentile, Giovanni. Philosopher, theorist of fascism, 306
George, Stefan. Poet, 174, 289, 295, 316, 317, 318, 320-24, 325, 377
Gérôme, Jean-Léon. Painter, 14, 17
Gersdorff, Rudolf Christian von. German military officer, 197
Gobineau, Count Arthur de. Author of *De l'Inégalité des races humaines*, 213
Goebbels, Joseph. German Minister of Propaganda, 208, 307, 308, 309, 310, 311, 315, 374, 375
Goerdeler, Carl. Mayor of Leipzig, leading figure in German Resistance, 174, 187, 189, 190, 194, 195, 197, 286, 289

Goldberg, Szymon. First violinist of Berlin Philharmonic, 307
Goldschmidt-Hergenhahn, Gabriele. Wife of Waldemar von Oppenheim, 179
Goldziher, Ignaz. Hungarian-Jewish scholar of Islam 18, 25, 123
Gordon Childe, V. British Archaeologist, 129, 148
Gordon, Major-General Charles George. Governor of the Sudan, 49
Göring, Hermann. Commander-in-chief of Luftwaffe, 166, 178, 212, 224, 270, 315
Gorst, Sir Eldon. British Consul-General in Egypt, replaced Cromer, 40, 45
Gottheil, Richard. American Semitic scholar, 42
Grant, Madison. American anthropologist, and eugenicist, 213
Granville, George Leveson Gower, Earl. British Foreign Secretary, 52
Grey, Sir Edward. British ambassador to the Porte, later Foreign Secretary, 57, 59, 60, 331
Griessmann family, 198, 199
Grobba, Fritz. German diplomat, 231, 232, 233, 234, 244, 245, 247, 248, 250, 254-260, 263, 264, 273, 275, 361, 367, 369, 370
Gropius, Walter. Modern German architect, 302
Gundolf, Friedrich. Jewish disciple of Stefan George, 318
Günther, Hans F.K. German race theorist, 27, 211, 216, 217, 219, 220, 221
Gwinner, Arthur von. Director of Deutsche Bank, 114

Habicht, Theodor. German Foreign Under-Secretary, 243, 250, 253, 254, 257, 270
Haddad, Osman Kemal. Private secretary of al-Husseini, 254, 260
Haffner, Sebastian. German journalist and author, 202
Halim Pasha, Said. Ottoman Grand Vizier, 83

Hambro, Charles Jocelyn. British banker, 194
Harden, Maximilian. German Journalist, 288
Hardinge, Sir Charles. Viceroy of India, 59
Harries, Susie. Writer, author of biography of Sir Nicholas Pevsner, 297, 298, 300
Hartmann, Martin. German oriental scholar, 18, 64-67, 71, 342, 350, 351
Hatzfeld, Paul, Graf von. German diplomat, 33, 34, 156, 347
Hauser, Otto. Popular German writer, 221
Hebat. Hurrian mother goddess, 127
Heinitz, Friedrich Anton von. Head of the Prussian Academy, 313
Hentig, Werner Otto von. German diplomat, 226, 232, 233, 237, 250, 259, 260, 263-70, 271, 272, 273, 274, 275, 295, 329, 332, 370, 371
Herwarth, Hans von. German diplomat, 174
Herzfeld, Ernst. German-Jewish oriental scholar and archaeologist, xi, xiii, xxvi, 103, 127, 128, 129, 130, 132, 153, 207, 209, 278, 279, 280, 281, 282, 326-28, 337-42
Herzl, Theodor. Founder of modern Zionism, 26
Hess, Rudolf. Hitler's Deputy-Führer, 236
Hewins, Ralph. British journalist and author, 191
Heydt, Eduard von der. German banker, 156, 205, 206
Himmler, Heinrich. Reichsführer of the SS, head of the Gestapo, 186, 187, 188, 192, 195, 196
Hindemith, Paul. Composer, 308
Hitler, Adolf. German Chancellor, xviii, 96, 164, 172, 173, 174, 175, 177, 178, 179, 181, 183, 184, 185, 186, 187, 190, 191, 192, 193, 194, 195, 197, 199, 202, 208, 209, 216, 222, 224, 225, 226, 235, 236, 237, 238, 239, 240, 242, 242, 249, 257, 259, 263, 264, 265, 266, 267, 268, 270, 277, 278, 286, 287, 289, 290, 294,

302, 303, 305, 317, 318, 319, 320, 329, 338, 345, 357, 361, 362, 363, 364, 365, 366, 371, 372
Hodler, Ferdinand. Painter, 311
Hogarth, David George. British archaeologist, 119, 330
Holbein, Hans. Painter, 10
Holstein, Friedrich von. Head of political department of German Foreign office, 9, 33, 34, 37, 347, 348-49
Hourani, Albert. British historian of Middle East, 54
Huberman, Bronislaw. Polish-Jewish violinist, 308
Hugenberg, Alfred. German media magnate and rightwing politician, 184, 205
Humann, Carl. German engineer, discoverer of Pergamon, xix
Hussein ibn Ali. Sharif of Mecca, 38, 93, 101

Ibn Saud (Abdul-Aziz). King of Saudi Arabia, 245, 246, 263, 367, 368
Ingres, Jean-Auguste-Dominique. Painter, 14, 17
Ismail Pasha. Ottoman Khedive of Egypt, 30, 345

Jäckh, Ernst. German scholar and politician, xvii, xviii, 83, 98, 101, 102, 103, 354
Jensen, Peter. German oriental scholar, 130
Jeremias, Alfred. German oriental scholar, 142
Joachim, Joseph. Violinist and teacher, 308
Jordan, Julius. German archaeologist, 210

Kahler, Erich von. Literary scholar, 318
Kantorowicz, Ernst. Scholar, member of *George-Kreis* (disciples of poet Stefan George), 220, 295, 316, 317, 318-22, 376-78
Kapara, ruler of small Aramaean kingdom in 9th or 10th century B.C., 127, 128, 129, 130, 131, 132, 141
Kaufmann, Otto. Director of Oppenheim Bank, 167
Kessler, Harry Graf. German soldier, diplomat, patron of the arts, 150
Khairi, Sheikh ul-Islam, Grand Mufti of Constantinople, 87, 89, 93
Klemperer, Otto. Conductor, 308
Klinger, Max. Artist, 311
Koldewey, Robert. German architect and archaeologist, famous for his work at Babylon, 124, 126
König, Edeltrud. Colleague of Sir Nicholas Pevsner at Göttingen University, 303
Kreisler, Fritz. Violinist, 308, 316
Kress von Kressenstein, Friedrich Freiherr. German General in WWI, 91
Kristeller, Paul Oskar. German Renaissance scholar, 306
Kümmel, Otto. Director-General of German State Museums, 210
Kurlbaum, Alfred. Father-in-law of Sir Nicholas Pevsner, 297
Kurlbaum, Karola ("Lola"). Wife of Sir Nicholas Pevsner, 297, 305, 306
Kusserow, Heinrich von. German diplomat and politician, grandson of Salomon Oppenheim, 10, 29

Laborde, Léon de. French archaeologist and explorer of Middle East, 14
Landau, Jacob. Historian of Middle East, 55, 58, 103
Landmann, Edith. Philosopher, Jewish disciple of Stefan George, 293, 318, 322-324
Landmann, Julius. Economist, admirer of Stefan George, 318
Langenegger, Felix. German architect, 130, 340
Lapouge, Georges Vacher de. French eugenicist and race scholar, 213
Lawrence, T.E. ("Lawrence of Arabia"). British army officer and archaeologist, xix, 19, 101, 119, 129, 265, 330
Layard, Austen Henry. British excavator of Nineveh, 135
Lepsius, Johannes. German Orientalist and missionary, 100-01, 103

Lepsius, Karl Richard. German explorer, 14
Levetzov, Magnus von. German naval officer, Berlin chief of police, 224
Liebermann, Max. Painter, 310, 313, 375
Linant de Bellefonds, Louis. French engineer, explorer of Egypt, 14
Lissauer family, 198, 199
Loesener, Bernhard. In charge of racial affairs, German Ministry of the Interior, 175-77
Loewenstein, Leo. Officer of *Reichsbund jüdischer Frontsoldaten*, 290
Louis Ferdinand. Second son of Crown Prince Wilhelm of Germany, 223
Louis XIV. King of France, 312
Lowther, Sir Gerard. British ambassador to the Porte, 57, 59
Lubenchik, Naftali. Revisionist Zionist, 269
Lueger, Karl. Austrian politician, mayor of Vienna, 173

"Mahdi" of Sudan (Muhammad Ahmed bin Abdallah), 71
Mallowan, Max. British archaeologist, 129, 144
Maluf, Tannus and Elias. Max Oppenheim's Lebanese servants, 122
Martin, Lutz. Contemporary German archaeologist, 161
Mayer, Paul Yogi. Founder of Jewish youth group *Schwarzes Fähnlein*, 290
McEwan, C.W. American archaeologist, 212, 328
McMeekin, Sean. Contemporary historian, 329
Méchin, Jacques-Benoist. French writer and diplomat, 274
Meissner, Bruno. German scholar of early languages, 130
Meissner, Heinrich August. German engineer, 44
Melchers, Wilhelm. Head of Middle East section of German Foreign Office, 260-63, 264
Melka, Robert. American historian, 268, 273-74
Memling, Hans. Painter, 10
Mendelssohn, Jewish banking family, 38, 165, 348
Mendelssohn, Felix. German composer, 308
Menemencioglu, Numan. Secretary-General, Turkish Ministry of Foreign Affairs, 271
Mercier, Louis. French oriental scholar, 77
Metternich. See Wolff-Metternich
Metzger, Chantal. French historian, 232, 268
Michelet, Jules. French historian, 17
Midjwel el Meṣrab, Sheikh. Last husband of Lady Jane Digby, 29
Milch, Erhard. State Secretary of German Aviation Ministry, 178, 286, 332
Mittwoch, Eugen. German-Jewish Oriental scholar, 92, 209
Moltke, Helmuth, "the Elder." German military chief, hero of Franco-Prussian war, 80
Moltke, Helmuth, "the Younger." Chief of General Staff at outbreak of WWI, 80, 94
Moortgat, Anton. Belgian-born German archaeologist, 207, 341
Moortgat-Correns, Ursula. German archaeologist, 162
Morgenthau, Henry. American Ambassador to the Porte, 89-91, 95
Moritz, Bernhard. German oriental scholar, 93, 110, 208, 237, 238
Morris, William. British artist and social critic, 302
Morwitz, Ernst. Jewish friend and disciple of Stefan George, 174, 318
Moscheles, Ignaz. Czech-Jewish composer, 97
Mosley, Sir Oswald. Leader of British Union of Fascists, 225
Müller, Karl. German architect, 130
Müller, Max. German orientalist and philosopher, Fellow of All Souls, Oxford, 213
Mukhtar Pasha, Gazi Ahmed. Ottoman High Commissioner in Egypt, 40, 41
Munch, Edvard. Painter, 311
Munir Pasha, Salih. Ottoman ambassador to France, 57

Musil, Alois. Explorer and scholar of the Middle East, cousin of the celebrated writer, 15
Mussolini, Benito. Italian Head of State, 192, 229, 235, 259
Mustafa Pasha, Kamil. Egyptian nationalist, 38, 44

Nadolny, Rudolf. German ambassador to Soviet Union, 174, 354
Napoleon I. Emperor of France, 31, 80, 300, 346
Napoleon III, 80
Naumann, Friedrich. German journalist, 41
Naumann, Max. Founder of *Verband deutsch-nationaler Juden*, 287-89, 323
Neurath, Freiherr Konstantin von. German Foreign Minister, 208, 210
Nicolson, Sir Arthur. British diplomat, 57, 59
Nicolson, Sir Harold. British politician, 35
Nicosia, Francis. American historian, 237-38, 270
Niebuhr, Carsten. Danish explorer of Middle East, 14, 18
Niedermayer, Oskar von. German soldier and adventurer, 92, 233, 266, 370

Oppenheim. German Jewish banking family, 3-10, 107-108, 151, 163-64, 167-70, 171, 198, 203, 205, 326, 328
Oppenheim, Abraham, 3, 4, 5, 6, 7, 10, 168, 169
Oppenheim, Albert von. Father of Max, 7, 9, 10, 11, 13, 29, 168
Oppenheim, Alfred von, 129
Oppenheim, Charlotte, 4, 6, 7, 10, 168, 169
Oppenheim, Dagobert (David), 5, 10, 168, 169
Oppenheim, Eberhard von, 179, 180, 201
Oppenheim, Eduard von, 7, 8, 10, 11, 13, 29, 156, 205
Oppenheim, Emmy von, 189, 201
Oppenheim, Eva von, 10
Oppenheim, Florence (Flossy) von, 6, 9, 196

Oppenheim, Friedrich Carl von, 167, 168, 169, 171, 172, 179-80, 182, 184, 197-201, 277, 280-81, 326, 328
Oppenheim, Gabriele von, 179
Oppenheim, Harold von, 181, 222
Oppenheim, Max von. *Passim*
Oppenheim, Ruth von, 179-80, 200
Oppenheim, Salomon, 3, 4, 9, 10
Oppenheim, Simon, 3, 4, 5, 6, 7, 8, 10, 11
Oppenheim, Simon Alfred von, 8, 9, 30, 156, 168, 179, 180, 181, 201, 203, 222, 277, 280
Oppenheim, Therese, 3, 6, 11
Oppenheim, Waldemar von, 167, 168, 172, 179, 181, 187-97, 201, 203, 205, 222, 226, 228, 277, 280, 291, 326, 328
Oppenheim, Wanda von, 280
Oster, Major-General Hans. Deputy-Head of Abwehr (German Counter-Intelligence), 187, 195
Özcan, Azmi. Modern Turkish historian 49

Palgrave, William Gifford. Arabist and traveller in Middle East, 14, 18, 19
Pavlov, Aleksander A. TASS correspondent in Stockholm, 193
Peel, William Robert Wellesley, 1st Earl. Chairman of the Peel Commission, 249
Perlmann, Annie. Mother of Sir Nicholas Pevsner, 296
Pétain, Marshal Philippe. Chief of State of Vichy France, 262, 263
Peters, Karl. Reichsminister for the Kilimanjaro region of German East Africa, 57
Peters, Rudolf. Contemporary Dutch scholar of Islam, 76-78
Petersen, Rudolf. Hamburg businessman, 178-79
Pevsner, Dieter and Florence. Son and daughter-in-law of Sir Nicholas Pevsner, 296
Pevsner, Sir Nicholas. German-born British art historian, 296-316, 373-76
Pevsner, Tom. Son of Sir Nicholas Pevsner, 304
Pewsner, Hugo (Gilel). Father of Sir Nicholas Pevsner, 296

Pferdmenges, Robert. German banker, partner of Sal. Oppenheim jr. Bank, 168, 169, 170, 180, 199
Pinder, Wilhelm. German art historian, teacher of Sir Nicholas Pevsner, 298, 301.
Playfair, General I.S.O. British historian of war in Middle East, 261, 265
Pocci, Franz, Graf von. Popular nineteenth-century Bavarian artist and composer, 280
Pocci, Franz-Karl, Graf von. Son of Franz von Pocci; husband of Wanda von Oppenheim, 280
Pococke, Richard. British traveller in Middle East, 14
Prüfer, Curt. German diplomat, 42, 206, 227-29, 231, 232, 233, 234, 243, 258, 259, 275, 330, 331, 360
Puaux. Gabriel. French High Commissioner in Syria, 246, 262, 331, 367

Quaatz, Reinhold. Adviser and confidant of Alfred von Hugenberg, 184
Quatremère de Quincy, Antoine-Chrysostome. French archaeologist and theorist of architecture, 300
Quinet, Edgar. French historian, 17

Rabeh. Leader of private army in Africa, 30, 31, 346
Rahn, Rudolf. Official at German embassy in Paris, 274
Raphael. Painter, 312
Rathenau, Walter. German statesman, 288, 297
Reinerth, Hans. Scholar of pre-history, 211
Reinhardt, Max. Theater director, 308
Rembrandt van Rijn. Painter, 10, 312
Renan, Ernest. French scholar and writer, 21, 213-15, 343, 358
Reuter, Gabriele. German novelist, 150
Ribbentrop, Joachim von. German Foreign Minister, 191, 195, 210, 236, 243, 244, 250, 254, 259, 260, 262, 263, 270, 314
Richthofen, Herbert von. German diplomat, 228, 232
Rigg, Bryan. American historian, 177, 286
Ritterbusch, Paul. German legal scholar and academic, 209
Robertson, Ritchie. British literary scholar, 325
Rogge, Bernhard. German naval commander, 286, 332
Rohlfs, Friedrich Gerhard. German geographer and explorer, 20, 80
Roosevelt, Franklin D. President of U.S.A., 188, 222
Rosen, Friedrich. German oriental scholar and diplomat, 93, 97
Rosenberg, Alfred. National Socialist ideologist and racial theorist, 178, 211, 250
Roser, Alfred. German Intelligence agent, 260, 265, 267, 370, 371
Rubens, Peter Paul. Painter, 10
Rügemer, Werner. German journalist and writer, 170
Ruisdael, Jacob. Painter, 10
Rumbold, Sir Horace. Vice-Chairman of Peel Commission, 249, 250
Russell, Gordon. British furniture designer, 306

Said, Edward. Modern American scholar, 14
Saladin. First Sultan of Egypt and Syria, founder of Ayyubid dynasty, 28, 42, 98, 99
Sarre, Frau Professor. Wife of German oriental scholar Friedrich Sarre, 337
Sarruma. Hurrian god of the mountains, 127
Saxe Coburg Gotha, Carl-Eduard, Graf von, 32
Schabinger von Schowingen, Karl-Emil. German diplomat, successor of Max von Oppenheim as director of Nachrichtenstelle für den Orient, xxiv, 87, 89, 92, 353
Schacht, Hjalmar. President of Reichsbank and German Minister of Economics, 164, 166, 198, 358
Scheel, Helmuth. German Oriental scholar, Director of Berlin

Akademie der Wissenschaften, 209, 281

Schellenberg, Walther. Head of German foreign intellligence after dissolution of Abwehr (1944), 196

Schiller, Friedrich. German poet, 313

Schliemann, Heinrich. German amateur archaeologist, excavator of Troy, xix

Schmidt, Hubert. German scholar of pre-history, 130

Schnabel, Arthur. Pianist, 308

Schoen, Freiherr Wilhelm von. German diplomat and Foreign Secretary, 38, 43

Schoeps, Hans-Joachim. Prussian-Jewish historian and philosopher of religion, 185-86, 287, 293-96, 316, 325, 372

Schröder, Kurt von. Cologne banker, 192

Schubert, Franz. Composer, 181

Schurman, Jacob Gould. U.S. Ambassador to Germany, 153

Schwanitz, Wolfgang G. Contemporary scholar of Middle East, xix-xx, xxiv, 248, 258, 370

Sebottendorf, Rudolf von. Founder of the *Thule Gesellschaft*, 202

Seidt, Hans Ulrich. Contemporary German historian, 102-03, 235-36, 353-54, 361

Seldte, Franz. Founder and leader of Stahlhelm veterans' association, 183

Senoussi. See al-Senoussi

Seton-Williams, Marjorie. Australian archaeologist, 226

Shaw, Richard Norman. Late ninetenth-century British architect, 302

Shawkat, Muhammad Naji. Iraqi politician, 251-52, 254, 256, 258, 267

Siemens, Georg von. Director of Deutsche Bank, 109, 110, 114

Smith, Adam. Moral philosopher and economist, 15

Smith, Myron Bement. American archaeologist, art historian and Oriental scholar, 153

Snouck Hurgronje, Christiaan. Dutch scholar of Islam, 55, 61, 62, 63, 64, 87, 98, 100, 101, 350

Sobernheim, Moritz. German oriental scholar, 237, 238

Sommer, Adolf. Max von Oppenheim's manservant, 279, 280, 339

Souchon, Rear-Admiral Wilhelm. German naval officer, 82

Speer, Albert. Architect, German Minister of Armaments and War Poduction, 178

Speiser, Ephraim A. American Assyriologist, 132, 133, 134

Stalin, Joseph. General Secretary of the Communist Party and Preident of the Soviet Union, 193, 216

Stauffenberg, Claus, Graf von. German army officer, leading member of plot to assasinate Hitler, July 20 1944, 200

Steen, Jan. Dutch painter, 10

Stern, Avraham. Revisionist Zionist leader, 269

Stinnes, Hugo. German industrialist, 156, 188

Storrs, Sir Ronald. Official of British Colonial Office, Oriental Secretary in Cairo, Military Governor of Jerusalem, 44

Streicher, Julius. Nazi propagandist, publisher of *Der Stürmer*, 176

Stuermer, Harry. German anti-war writer, 82, 103, 104, 105

Sumner Welles, Benjamin. American Foreign Under-Secretary, 191

Sykes, Sir Mark. Conservative British M.P., adviser to British government on Middle East, 60, 331

Teniers, David. Painter, 10

Teshub. Hurrian weather god, 127

Thyssen, August. German industrialist, 156

Tolstoy, Lev. Writer, 48

Tönnies, Ferdinand. German sociologist, 299

Toynbee, Arnold J. British historian, 82

Ungnad, Arthur. German oriental

scholar, 21, 22, 27, 133, 213, 214, 215-19, 220, 221, 343-44, 359-60
Vallentin, Berthold. German writer, member of, George-Kreis, 318
van Gogh, Vincent. Painter, 234
Vanderbilt Jr., Cornelius. Grandson of the American railroad magnate, journalist and newspaper publisher, 222, 223-25
Vanderbilt, Mrs. Grace Cornelius. Wife of Cornelius Vanderbilt III, 32
Velasquez, Diego. Painter, 10
Verlaine, Paul. Poet, 310, 313
Victoria. Queen of Great Britain, Empress of India, 51
Victoria. Wife of Friedrich Wilhelm III, Emperor of Germany, daughter of Queen Victoria, 7
Vogeler, Heinrich. German artist, 300
Von Papen, Franz. German statesman and diplomat, 95, 184, 192, 209, 248, 251, 252, 254, 256, 258-60, 262, 271
Vorontsov, Captain Mikhail Aleksandrovich. Soviet officer, 193
Voysey, Charles. British architect, 302

Wallach, Jeduda L. Israeli scholar, 103
Wallenberg. Swedish banking family, 189, 190, 193
Wallenberg, Gertrud, 189
Wallenberg, Jacob, 143, 144, 145, 146, 148
Wallenberg, Marcus, 143, 146, 147, 148
Wallott, Paul. German architect, 216
Walter, Bruno. German musician, 308
Wangenheim, Hans Freiherr von. German Ambassador to the Porte, 40, 86, 87, 96, 99, 100, 333
Warburg. German Jewish banking family, 164, 166, 167, 169, 171, 289
Warburg, Aby. German art and cultural historian, 25
Warschauer. German Jewish banking family, 38, 348
Wassermann, Oscar. Jewish Director of Deutsche Bank, 166, 172
Wassmuss, Wilhelm. German diplomat, 92, 265
Wavell, Sir Archibald. British commander-in-chief in the Middle East, 262

Weidner, Ernst. Austrian oriental scholar, 210
Weizmann, Chaim. Chemist and Zionist leader, 10
Weizsäcker, Ernst von. German Foreign Secretary, 187, 226, 233, 237, 244, 254, 257, 258, 260, 262, 263, 271
Werner, Anton von. German artist, 313
Whistler, James McNeill. American artist, 310
Wilde, Oscar. Writer, 310, 313
Wilhelm I. Emperor of Germany, 7
Wilhelm II. Emperor of Germany, 9, 18, 28, 37, 40, 41, 43, 47, 86, 89, 93, 96, 97, 98, 99, 109, 121, 178, 223, 275, 297, 326, 331
Wilhelm, son of Wilhelm II. Crown Prince of Germany, 223
Wilson, Francesca. British Quaker, friend of colleague of N. Pevsner at Göttingen, 304, 305
Woermann, Ernst. German Foreign Under-Secretary, 239, 242, 244, 252, 253-54, 257, 270-71, 274
Wohlthat, Helmut. Official in charge of foreign currency questions at German Ministry of Economics, 198
Wolff-Metternich, Count Paul. German diplomat, 36, 39, 40, 100, 352-53
Woolf, Virginia and Leonard. British writers, 35
Woolley, Sir Charles Leonard. British archaeologist, excavated at Ur, 129, 130, 132, 330

Zimmermann, Arthur, German diplomat and Foreign Secretary, 95, 353
Zuber Pasha. Leader of a private army that conquered Darfur for Egyptian Khedive, 30
Zur Mühlen, Hermynia. Austrian writer, xvii, xix, 15, 174

This book does not end here…

At Open Book Publishers, we are changing the nature of the traditional academic book. The title you have just read will not be left on a library shelf, but will be accessed online by hundreds of readers each month across the globe. We make all our books free to read online so that students, researchers and members of the public who can't afford a printed edition can still have access to the same ideas as you.

Our digital publishing model also allows us to produce online supplementary material, including extra chapters, reviews, links and other digital resources. Find *The Passion of Max von Oppenheim* on our website to access its online extras. Please check this page regularly for ongoing updates, and join the conversation by leaving your own comments:

http://www.openbookpublishers.com/9781909254206

If you enjoyed the book you have just read, and feel that research like this should be available to all readers, regardless of their income, please think about donating to us. Our company is run entirely by academics, and our publishing decisions are based on intellectual merit and public value rather than on commercial viability. We do not operate for profit and all donations, as with all other revenue we generate, will be used to finance new Open Access publications.

For further information about what we do, how to donate to OBP, additional digital material related to our titles or to order our books, please visit our website, http://www.openbookpublishers.com.

www.ingramcontent.com/pod-product-compliance
Lightning Source LLC
Chambersburg PA
CBHW051623230426
43669CB00013B/2164